# Lecture Notes in Computer Science    2397

Edited by G. Goos, J. Hartmanis, and J. van Leeuwen

**Springer**
*Berlin*
*Heidelberg*
*New York*
*Barcelona*
*Hong Kong*
*London*
*Milan*
*Paris*
*Tokyo*

Giorgio Ghelli   Gösta Grahne (Eds.)

# Database Programming Languages

8th International Workshop, DBPL 2001
Frascati, Italy, September 8-10, 2001
Revised Papers

 Springer

Series Editors

Gerhard Goos, Karlsruhe University, Germany
Juris Hartmanis, Cornell University, NY, USA
Jan van Leeuwen, Utrecht University, The Netherlands

Volume Editors

Giorgio Ghelli
Univesità di Pisa, Dipartimento di Informatica
Corso Italia 40, 56125 Pisa, Italy
E-mail: ghelli@di.unipi.it

Gösta Grahne
Concordia University, Department of Computer Science
1455 De Maisonneuve Blvd. West
Montréal, Québec, Canada H3G 1M8
E-mail: grahne@cs.concordia.ca

Cataloging-in-Publication Data applied for

Die Deutsche Bibliothek - CIP-Einheitsaufnahme

Database programming languages : 8th international workshop ; revised
papers / DBPL 2001, Frascati, Italy, September 8 - 10, 2001. Gösta Grahne ;
Giorgio Ghelli (ed.). - Berlin ; Heidelberg ; New York ; Barcelona ; Hong Kong ;
London ; Milan ; Paris ; Tokyo : Springer, 2002
    (Lecture notes in computer science ; 2397)
    ISBN 3-540-44080-1


CR Subject Classification (1998): H.2, H.3

ISSN 0302-9743
ISBN 3-540-44080-1 Springer-Verlag Berlin Heidelberg New York

Springer-Verlag Berlin Heidelberg New York,
a member of BertelsmannSpringer Science+Business Media GmbH

http://www.springer.de

© Springer-Verlag Berlin Heidelberg 2002
Printed in Germany

Typesetting: Camera-ready by author, data conversion by Olgun Computergrafik
Printed on acid-free paper     SPIN: 10873560     06/3142     5 4 3 2 1 0

# Preface

The papers in this volume represent the technical program of the 8th Biennial Workshop on Data Bases and Programming Languages (DBPL 2001), that was held during September 8–10, 2001, in Frascati, located on the beautiful hills surrounding Rome, in an area favored by the ancient Roman patricians who built their summer residences there. DBPL 2001 continued the tradition of excellence initiated by its predecessors in Roscoff, Finistère (1987), Salishan, Oregon (1989), Nafplion, Argolida (1991), Manhattan, New York (1993), Gubbio, Umbria (1995), Estes Park, Colorado (1997), and Kinloch Rannoch, Scotland (1999).

Databases grew out of a separation between physical and logical data, thus enabling high-level query languages. Database query languages have evolved in expressive power and structural capabilities. Programming languages have seen a development from assembly languages to high-level declarative paradigms. Thus the two areas approach each other as they mature. Earlier successful cross-fertilizations between the fields include the combination of relational theory, type theory and object-oriented languages, resulting in object-oriented databases, object-relational databases and persistent programming languages. The combination of database logic programming and constraint programming produced deductive and constraint databases. Recently, with the emergence of semi-structured data models, there is a renewed synergy between databases and programming languages, in particular in the design of languages to manipulate XML data.

The DBPL 2001 Program Co-Chairs were Giorgio Ghelli (Pisa) and Gösta Grahne (Montréal). The Program Committee Members were Catriel Beeri (Jerusalem), Diego Calvanese (Rome), Richard Connor (Glasgow), Alon Halevy (Seattle), Leonid Libkin (Toronto), Gianni Mecca (Potenza), Frank Neven (Limburg), Benjamin Pierce (Philadelphia), Chris Ramming (Menlo Park), Jérôme Siméon (Murray Hill), Victor Vianu (San Diego), and Philip Wadler (Basking Ridge). We warmly thank the Program Committee members for devoting their time and effort generously to DBPL 2001.

In response to the call for papers, the Program Committee received 36 submissions. The submission process and the Committee's extensive deliberations were carried out using the Confman Software (http://confman.unik.no /˜confman). Technical support during this process was generously provided by Jianfei Zhu from Concordia University. The Program Committee accepted 18 papers for presentation at the workshop. The papers were grouped into technical sessions on Semistructured Data, OLAP and Datamining, XML, Spatial Databases, Systems, Schema Integration, Index Concurrency, User Languages, and Rules. Here we find both traditional DBPL topics, as well as the new thrust of Semistructured Data and XML, a theme that made its first appearance in the DBPL series in 1997.

DBPL 2001 also featured an invited talk by Tony Bonner (Toronto) on "Languages for workflows and e-commerce," and an invited tutorial by Dan Suciu (Seattle) on "Type-checking in semi-structured databases," in addition to the technical program. Dr. Bonner's talk gave a survey of the development of declarative languages for the transaction-oriented applications of workflows and e-commerce. These applications represent new functionalities required for high-level database languages. Dr. Suciu's invited tutorial gave a background in type checking in programming languages, and it explained very recent advances in type-checking XML and semi-structured databases.

The main raison d'être for DBPL has always been to overcome the so-called impedance mismatch between databases and programming languages. Although the term impedance mismatch was coined it's already some time since, as we heard Bill Gates emphasize during his keynote talk at ACM SIGMOD/PODS in 1998, it still remains a major challenge for the Database and Programming Language communities. We believe that the research carried out by these communities has created a body of knowledge that can be tapped in facing the challenge of providing the technology for high-level expressive and yet optimizable database programming languages in the context of XML and semi-structured data.

DBPL 2001 was partially hosted and sponsored by the local establishment of the European Space Agency ESA (http://www.esa.int), the European Space Research Institute ESRIN (http://www.esa.int/esrin), and by the Esprit Working Group AppSem (Applied Semantics, http://www.md.chalmers.se/Cs/Research/Semantics/APPSEM/). On behalf of the DBPL community we gratefully acknowledge their valuable support. Many thanks are also due to Ettore Ricciardi of the National Research Council of Pisa, for the impeccable local arrangements.

During the workshop, only mimeographed informal proceedings were distributed. The papers in this volume were revised by the authors based on the comments from the refereeing stage and ensuing discussions during the workshop, and were subjected to a final acceptance by the Program Committee. We are very grateful to Paolo Manghi, from the University of Pisa, who functioned as Production Editor for the final compilation of the material.

The 9th Biennial Workshop on Data Bases and Programming Languages (DBPL 2003) will be held in Berlin in September 2003, and will be Co-Chaired by Georg Lausen (Freiburg) and Dan Suciu (Seattle).


Pisa, Italy, and Montréal, Québec
May 2002                                          Giorgio Ghelli, Gösta Grahne

# Organization

DBPL 2001 was organized by the Dipartimento di Informatica, University of Pisa (Italy), and the Department of Computer Science, Concordia University (Canada).

## Conference Chairs

Giorgio Ghelli (University of Pisa, Italy)
Gösta Grahne (Concordia University, Canada)

## Program Commitee

Catriel Beeri (Jerusalem)
Diego Calvanese (Rome)
Richard Connor (Glasgow)
Alon Halevy (Seattle)
Leonid Libkin (Toronto)
Gianni Mecca (Potenza)

Frank Neven (Limburg)
Benjamin Pierce (Philadelphia)
Chris Ramming (Menlo Park)
Jérôme Siméon (Murray Hill)
Victor Vianu (San Diego)
Philip Wadler (Basking Ridge)

## External Referees

Marcelo Arenas
Enrico Franconi
Tony Bonner
Zack Ives
Alfons Kemper
Paolo Atzeni
Alin Deutsch
Renzo Orsini
Gottfried Vossen
Riccardo Rosati
Riccardo Torlone
Luca Cabibbo
Rick Snodgrass
Mary Fernandez

Giuseppe De Giacomo
Lee Chin Soon
Val Tannen
Dan Suciu
Peter Buneman
Arnaud Sahuguet
Peter Fankhauser
Wang-Chiew Tan
Daniele Nardi
Paolo Merialdo
Nils Klarlund
Dana Florescu
Keishi Tajima
Danilo Montesi

Alberto Mendelzon
Pratik Mukhopadhyay
Luigi Dragone
Matthew Fuchs
Sanjeev Khanna
Haruo Hasoya
Vladimir Gapeyev
Francesco Donini
Francesco Scarcello
Giovanbattista Ianni
Peter Sewell
Giuseppe Santucci

## Proceedings Production Editor

Paolo Manghi (University of Pisa, Italy)

## Confman Webmaster

Jianfei Zhu (Concordia University, Canada)

## Local Arrangements

Ettore Ricciardi (National Research Council of Pisa, Italy)

## Sponsoring Institutions

European Space Agency (ESA)
European Space Research Institute (ESRIN)
Esprit Working Group AppSem

# Table of Contents

# Typechecking for Semistructured Data

Dan Suciu

University of Washington

## 1 The Problem

Semistructured data is used in data exchange applications, like B2B and EAI, and represents data in a flexible format. Every data item has a unique tag (also called *label*), and data items can be *nested*. Formally, a semistructured data instance is a tree whose nodes are labeled with tags and leaves are labeled with data values. XML [Con98] is a standard syntax for describing such trees; Fig. 1 shows a tree representing a semistructured data instance and its XML syntax. We will refer interchangeably to semistructured data instances as trees or XML trees.

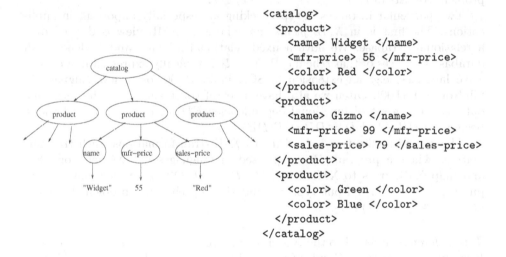

```
<catalog>
    <product>
        <name> Widget </name>
        <mfr-price> 55 </mfr-price>
        <color> Red </color>
    </product>
    <product>
        <name> Gizmo </name>
        <mfr-price> 99 </mfr-price>
        <sales-price> 79 </sales-price>
    </product>
    <product>
        <color> Green </color>
        <color> Blue </color>
    </product>
</catalog>
```

**Fig. 1.** An XML Example and its Tree Representation

In a data exchange application some agreement is necessary on the data's structure in order to allow one program to understand the data produced by another. At minimum one should agree on the *taxonomy*, i.e. the meaning of the different tags. For example, an application must be able to understand the difference between tags like **sales-price**, **mfr-price**, and **suggested-price**. Little or no formalism is needed for such an agreement, and the common wisdom is that applications will look for the tags they need, and ignore all the other tags in the data. At a more detailed level, an agreement should also constrain

G. Grahne and G. Ghelli (Eds.): DBPL 2001, LNCS 2397, pp. 1–20, 2002.

the *structure*. For example a data item with a `price` tag must contain an integer value, while a data item with a `product` tag must contain nested items labeled `name`, `price`, and `description`. An agreement on the structure enables applications to navigate the data in a meaningful way. We call a collection of constraints on the structure a *type*. Several type formalism have been proposed for semistructured data [BDFS97,GW97,BM99], and several are considered for XML [Con98,BLM+99,BFRW84].

A type in semistructured data, $\tau$, is simply a set of trees, $\tau \subseteq \mathcal{U}$, where $\mathcal{U}$ denotes all (unranked) trees. Such a set is also called a tree language. While type formalisms differ in what sets of trees they can define as types, it is always easy to check if a *data instance* (i.e. a tree) is of a given type[1]. In the case of XML, this is done at parse time, and is called *validation*. Most XML parsers today are validating parsers. A much harder problem arises when the semistructured data instance is generated automatically by a program, since then one needs to *typecheck* the program.

*Typechecking.* Formally, given a program $P : \mathcal{V} \to \mathcal{U}$ that takes an input $x$ from a set $\mathcal{V}$ and returns a tree $P(x)$, and given a type $\tau \subseteq \mathcal{U}$, the typechecking problem consists of checking: $\forall x \in \mathcal{V}, P(x) \in \tau$.

Two particular instances of typechecking are especially important in applications. The first is in *XML publishing*, where an XML view is defined over a relational database. We have a fixed relational schema, and $\mathcal{V}$ denotes all database instances of that schema; $P : \mathcal{V} \to \mathcal{U}$ is typically expressed in a declarative language, e.g. an extension of SQL in [SSB+00] or a new language in SilkRoute [FST00]. Often we also have a set of constraints over the relational database, e.g. a set of functional dependencies $FD$. In this case typechecking becomes: $\forall DB \in \mathcal{V}, FD \models DB \Rightarrow P(DB) \in \tau$.

The second application is in XML to XML transformations; such transformations where a program $P$ is expressed in languages like XQuery, or XSL, and map XML trees to XML trees, $P : \mathcal{U} \to \mathcal{U}$. Often we have both an input type $\tau_1$ and an output type $\tau_2$, and the typechecking problem becomes: $\forall t \in \mathcal{U}, t \in \tau_1 \Rightarrow P(t) \in \tau_2$.

*Type Inference.* Related to the typechecking problem is the *type inference problem*: given the program $P$, infer the type $\{P(x) \mid x \in \mathcal{V}\}$. If this is a valid type, and we can infer it, then typechecking can be done by checking containment between two types: $\{P(x) \mid x \in \mathcal{V}\} \subseteq \mathcal{U}$, which is in general decidable for types in semistructured data. As we shall see however, such a strategy fails, even in the simplest cases, and we need to address typechecking with different methods.

*Connection to Programming Languages.* Typechecking and type inference have been intensively studied in functional programming languages [Mit96]. There are three significant differences in semistructured data, however. First, types in semistructured data are *global* constraints on the data, while in programming

---

[1] In some powerful type systems [BM99] this problem is hard.

languages they are *local* constraints. For example, a type for semistructured data may define a type of lists by a regular expression, say $(a^*.b^*.c.b^*) \mid (a^*.c.a^*.b^*)$, which says in which all a elements come before all the b elements, and that there be exactly one c element, anywhere in the list. Types in programming languages define only local properties, e.g. they cannot define the list type above, but only the approximation $(a \mid b \mid c)^*$, in which all elements of the list are either a or a b or a c. Second, the typechecking and type inference problems are defined differently. For example, in the *typed lambda calculus* we are given an expression in which each variable is annotated with a type, and are asked to check whether all operations in that program are of correct type. In type inference, the types of the variables have been erased, and we are asked to re-discover them. Both are problems are decidable are are formulated on the syntactic representation of the program. They differ from their counterparts in semistructured data, which require us to check a property of the semantics of a program: this is in general undecidable, if we don't impose any restrictions on the programming language. Third, the goals of typechecking and type inference differ from semistructured data to programming languages [Tan01]. In the former the goal is to validate documents; in the latter it is to ensure that there will be no runtime type error.

Clearly, the bar for typechecking is set higher in semistructured data than in programming languages, and one may wonder if the bar is too high [Wad01], making the problem undecidable and, thus, impractical. We argue that it is not, for several reasons. First, typechecking *is* decidable for certain restricted languages. There is precedence in query languages, for example one can check if a view defined by a conjunctive query satisfies certain integrity constraints (e.g. a functional dependency). Second, alternative (syntactic) approaches to typechecking in semistructured data have limitations that may be annoying in practice. As we show here, correct programs cannot be typechecked by a system relying on type inference, and have to be rejected, leaving the user wondering what to do. And, finally, the best way to find out if the bar is too high is to set it there and try ! This is precisely what has been done in [MSV00,AMN+01b,AMN+01a], leading to a characterization of the boundary of the decidable and undecidable cases.

# 2  Background

## 2.1  The Data

We consider an alphabet $\Sigma$, whose elements we call tags, or labels and assume $\Sigma$ is finite. We denote with $\mathcal{U}_\Sigma$ the set of ordered, finite trees whose nodes are labeled with elements from $\Sigma$. Sometimes we allow the semistructured data to also carry some *data values* on the leaves. For this, we assume an infinite set $D$ of data values to be given, and denote with $\mathcal{U}_\Sigma(D)$ the set of trees in which every internal node is labeled with a value in $\Sigma$, and every leaf is labeled either with some value in $\Sigma$ or some value in $D$. A *semistructured data instance* is a tree in $\mathcal{U}_\Sigma(D)$.

To denote trees, we use a simple syntax:

$$T ::= \sigma(F) \mid \sigma' \quad F ::= T \mid T, F$$

where $\sigma \in \Sigma$ and $\sigma' \in \Sigma \cup D$.

*Example 1.* The following is an example of a semistructured data instance, whose tree representation is shown in Fig. 1:

```
catalog(product(name("Widget"),
                mfr-price(55),
                color("Red")),
        product(name("Gizmo"),
                mfr-price(99),
                sales-price(79)),
        product(name("Super-Widget"),
                color("Green"),
                color("Blue")))
```

## 2.2   The Types

One may be tempted to define a type as a regular tree language, but here we run into a technical problem. Tree automata (and regular tree languages) are defined in terms of ranked alphabets, while our $\Sigma$ is unranked. Several approaches have been proposed to extend regular tree languages to unranked trees. They all turn out to be equivalent, but each may be useful in a different situation. We present them here, and begin by revising regular tree languages.

*Ranked Trees and Tree Automata.* A ranked alphabet, $\Omega$, is a set partitioned into $k$ subsets, $\Omega = \Omega_0 \cup \ldots \cup \Omega_k$. A ranked tree over $\Omega$ is a finite, ordered tree where every node with $i$ children is labeled with a symbol from $\Omega_i$. We denote $T_\Omega$ the set of ranked $\Omega$-trees.

A tree automaton is a device that accepts or rejects ranked trees. The definition below is adapted from [Tho90], and slightly modified.

**Definition 1.** *A non-deterministic top-down tree automaton is* $A = (\Omega, Q, q_0, P)$ *where $Q$ is a finite set of states, $q_0 \in Q$ is the initial state and $P \subseteq \bigcup_{i=0,k} \Omega_i \times Q \times Q^i$.*

We write $(a, q) \to q_1 q_2 \ldots q_i$ whenever $(a, q, q_1, \ldots, q_i) \in P$.

Given $t \in T_\Omega$, the automaton computes by assigning states to nodes in $t$. First it assigns $q_0$ to the root node. Whenever some node $u$ with symbol $a$ has been assigned a state $q$, and there exists a transition $(a, q) \to q_1 \ldots q_i$ in $P$, then the state $q$ is removed from $u$, and the states $q_1, \ldots, q_i$ are assigned to its children. In particular, if $u$ is a leaf ($i = 0$) then we only remove the state from $u$. The tree is accepted if we can remove all states from the tree. $L(A)$ denotes the set of trees accepted by $A$, and is called *regular tree language*. Notice that we can equally well describe the computation in reverse, from the leaves to the root; this defines a *bottom-up tree automaton*.

What is known about tree automata? Bottom-up and top-down tree automata define the same set of regular tree languages, regular tree languages are closed under boolean operations (union, intersection, difference), and it is decidable whether one regular language is contained in another.

*Regular Unranked Tree Languages.* Brüggemann-Klein et al. [BKMW98] extend tree automata to unranked trees. The problem here is that a symbol $a \in \Sigma$ has no rank, hence we need to specify potentially infinitely many transitions $(a, q) \rightarrow q_1 \dots q_n$, for all $n \geq 0$. An unranked tree automaton is defined as before, but now $P$ is a subset of $\Sigma \times Q \times Q^*$, and may be infinite, but is such that for every $a \in \Sigma$ and $q \in Q$, the set $\{w \mid (a, q, w) \in P\} \subseteq Q^*$ is a regular set. This allows us to give a finite description of $P$, as a set of triples $(a, q, E)$, where $E$ is a regular expression over the alphabet $Q$. Moreover, for each $a \in \Sigma, q \in Q$, we need exactly one pair $(a, q, E)$ in $P$ (we can collapse multiple pairs by taking the union of the regular expressions, and, for missing pairs, we introduce one with an empty regular expression). Computations on unranked trees are now straightforward extensions of computations on ranked trees. A *unranked regular tree language* is a set $\tau \subseteq \mathcal{U}_\Sigma$ accepted by some unranked tree automaton.

*XDuce Types.* XDuce [HP00] is a functional programming language for XML. It defines XML types in a practical syntax, which has also been adopted by the XQuery working group [FFM+01]. We give here a slightly simplified definition, and start with an example. Assuming Integer and String to be predefined types, the following defines three new types, CatalogType, ProductsType, and ProductType:

```
CatalogType  = catalog(ProductsType)
ProductsType = (product(ProductType))*
ProductType  = (name(String), mfr-price(Integer),
                (sales-price(Integer))?, (color(String))*)
```

CatalogType defines a set of trees; each tree in this set has the root labeled catalog, and its children form a forest which belongs to the type ProductsType. This defines a set of forests, in which each forest has the root nodes labeled product, and the children of type ProductType, etc. As syntactic sugar, we allow a more concise syntax, where the type identifier ProductType has been substituted with its definition:

```
CatalogType = catalog(ProductsType)
ProductsType = product(name(String), mfr-price(Integer),
                       sales-price(Integer)?, color(String)*)*
```

Formally, we are given a set $Q$ type identifiers. A *unit type* is a pair $(\sigma, q)$ with $\sigma \in \Sigma$ and $q \in Q$. We denote $\sigma(q)$ such a unit type. Next, we consider regular expressions over unit types:

$$E ::= \sigma(q) \mid \epsilon \mid E, E \mid (E|E) \mid E* \mid E?$$

where $\sigma(q)$ is a unit type. A *type definition*, $TD$, is a set of pairs $(q, E)$, where $q \in Q$ and $E$ is a regular expression, such that for every $q \in Q$, there exists exactly one pair $(q, E) \in TD$. The semantics of a type definition is given by a straightforward fixpoint construction, see [HP00]. Under this semantics each type identifier in $Q$ denotes a set of *forests*, not of trees. For our purposes, we will assume a distinguished type identifier $q_0$ (the "root") in $Q$ and a pair $(q_0, \sigma(q))$ in $TD$, where $\sigma(q)$ is a unit type. This guarantees that the meaning of $q_0$ is a set of trees. In the example above, $q_0$ is `CatalogType`.

In our definition we have ignored the base types; they can be added easily.

There has been considerable effort at the W3C to define schemas for XML. The XML standard itself [Con98] defines DTDs, *Document Type Definitions*. Several attempts have been made to extend DTDs, and the current official recommendation is XML-Schema [BLM$^+$99,BFRW84]. While both DTDs and XML-Schema types can be expressed as XDuce types, neither DTDs nor XML-Schema can express *all* XDuce types. In DTDs the restriction is that, if two unit types with the same tag, $\sigma(q)$ and $\sigma(q')$, occur in a type definition $TD$, then their types identifiers must be the same, i.e. $q = q'$. In other words there is a 1-1 correspondence from tags to type identifier, and therefore we can drop the latter and use tags instead. A DTD is then a set of pairs $(\sigma, E)$, where $\sigma \in \Sigma$ and $E$ is a regular expression over $\Sigma$. In XML-Schema the restriction is relaxed to the following: for every pair $(q_1, E_1) \in TD$, if two unit types with the same tag, $\sigma(q)$ and $\sigma(q')$ occur in $E_1$, their types have to be identical, i.e. $q = q'$. Here the same tag may still have different types, but only when occurring in different contexts, one in $(q_1, E_1)$, the other in $(q_2, E_2)$, with $q_1 \neq q_2$.

*Specialized DTDs.* Papakonstantinou and Vianu [PV00] generalize DTD's to *specialized DTDs*. A specialized DTD consists of two alphabets, $Q$ and $\Sigma$, a DTD over $Q$, and a function $f$ from $Q$ to $\Sigma$. The set it defines consists of homeomorphic images of the first DTD under the function $f$.

*They are All Equivalent.* It turns out that these three distinct type definitions are equivalent; they define the same class of unraked, regular tree languages. More interestingly, they correspond precisely to regular (ranked) tree languages, in two different ways. In a very naive sense, one is to view any ranked alphabet $\Omega$ as an unranked alphabet, and define a function, $u : \mathcal{T}_\Omega \to \mathcal{U}_\Omega$ that just forgets the ranks. Then for every regular tree language $\tau$, $u(\tau)$ is a unranked regular trees language. More interestingly, we can encode unranked trees as ranked trees. Several such encodings are possible. We present here a particular encoding, which will be useful later, in Sec. 4.

Given the unranked alphabet $\Sigma$, associate to it the ranked alphabet $\Omega$: $\Omega_0 = \{|\}, \Omega_2 = \Sigma \cup \{-\}$. Define the following "encoding" function on trees, $e : \mathcal{U}_\Sigma \to \mathcal{T}_\Omega$, and the associated encoding function on forests, $f : \mathcal{U}_\Sigma^* \to \mathcal{T}_\Omega$:

$$e(\sigma) \stackrel{\text{def}}{=} \sigma(|,|) \qquad\qquad e(\sigma(F)) \stackrel{\text{def}}{=} \sigma(f(F),|)$$
$$f(T, F) \stackrel{\text{def}}{=} -(e(T), f(F)) \qquad f(T) \stackrel{\text{def}}{=} e(T)$$

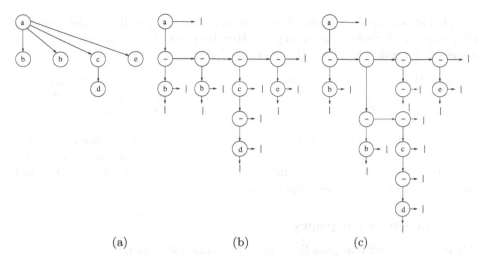

(a)                          (b)                          (c)

**Fig. 2.** Encoding of an unranked tree (a) into a binary tree (b); another binary tree (c)

Fig. 2 (a) and (b) illustrates the effect of the encoding function. In the other direction, we define a decoding function, $d : \mathcal{T}_\Omega \to \mathcal{U}_\Sigma^*$:

$$d(-(T_1, T_2)) \overset{\text{def}}{=} d(T_1), d(T_2)$$
$$d(\sigma(T_1, T_2)) \overset{\text{def}}{=} \sigma(d(T_1), d(T_2)) \quad \sigma \in \Sigma$$
$$d(|) \overset{\text{def}}{=} \varepsilon$$

Here $F_1, F_2$ denotes the concatenation of the forests $F_1$ and $F_2$. It is easy to check that $\forall t \in \mathcal{U}_\Sigma$, $d(e(t)) = t$, and that some trees in $\mathcal{T}_\Omega$ are not correct encodings, for example if they have too many occurrences of $-$, like the tree illustrated in Fig. 2 (c). The decoding function works on all trees in $\mathcal{T}_\Omega$; for example it maps the tree in Fig. 2 (c) to that in (a); we will need this in Sec. 4. For now, we summarize below the common knowledge on the relationship between unranked and ranked tree regular languages. The theorem below is straightforward to prove, and similar statements can be found in [BKMW98,MSV00,HP01].

**Theorem 1.**

1. Let $\Sigma$ be an unranked alphabet, and $\tau \subseteq \mathcal{U}_\Sigma$. The following are equivalent: (a) $\tau$ is accepted by an automaton on unranked trees, (b) $\tau$ is definable by an XDuce type, (c) $\tau$ is definable by a specialized DTD.
2. Given an unranked alphabet $\Sigma$, let $\Omega$ be its associated alphabet of rank 2 and let $\tau \subseteq \mathcal{U}_\Sigma$. Then the following are equivalent: (a) $\tau$ is an unranked regular tree language (b) $e(\tau)$ is a regular tree language.
3. Given a ranked alphabet $\Omega$, a set $\tau \subseteq \mathcal{T}_\Omega$ is regular iff $u(\tau)$ is a regular set of unranked trees.

It is interesting to see what happens to the ranked trees that are not valid encodings. If we take some arbitrary regular language $\tau \subseteq \mathcal{T}_\Sigma$ and decode it,

$d(\tau)$ is *not* necessarily regular. To see why this happens, recall that the sequence of leaves on all trees in some regular tree language form a context free, not necessarily regular language. However, the following two properties hold:

**Proposition 1.** *(1) Let $\tau$ be an unranked, regular tree language in $\mathcal{U}_\Sigma$. Then $d^{-1}(\tau)$ is a regular tree language in $\mathcal{T}_\Omega$. (2) Let $\tau$ be a (ranked) regular tree language in $\mathcal{T}_\Omega$. Then $e^{-1}(\tau)$ is an unranked regular tree language.*

*Containment is Decidable.* The important property we take from the connection to regular tree languages is that, for any two types of semistructured data $\tau_1, \tau_2$, it is decidable whether $\tau_1 \subseteq \tau_2$. Indeed, this is equivalent to $e(\tau_1) \subseteq e(\tau_2)$, and containment of regular tree languages is decidable.

## 2.3   The Query Languages

There are two different paradigms for processing XML data.

**Declarative** XML-QL and XQuery are declarative languages for mapping XML to XML; systems like Xperanto [SSB+00] and SilkRoute [FST00] have declarative languages for mapping relational databases to XML. It is debatable what exactly makes a query language "declarative", but it is agreed that evaluation in a declarative language proceeds in two steps: first find all bindings of the variables, then compute some result fragment for each binding. This process results in a flat collection; to build nested collections, queries have to be nested. An important consequence for typechecking is that the nesting structure in the query defines precisely the nesting structure in the output XML document. Hence we can statically determine how deep the resulting XML document will be.

**Functional languages** In XSL and XDuce, an XML to XML transformation is expressed by traversing the input document with recursive functions. In XSL for example we start from the root and normally proceed downwards; at any point however we may continue with the current node's parent, or even start again at the root. Along the way we can bind "parameters" to certain nodes, and access them later during the recursion.

We describe two small language formalisms capturing the two paradigms.

**TreeQL.** TreeQL is a language for mapping relational databases to trees. It was introduced in [AMN+01a] as an abstraction of RXL [FST00]. TreeQL uses *conjunctive queries* to construct trees. We denote with $CQ$ the set of conjunctive queries. Given $q \in CQ$, $headVar(q)$ denotes its free variables; if $\bar{X} \subseteq headVar(q)$, then $\Pi_{\bar{X}}(q)$ denotes the projection of $q$ on the variables $\bar{X}$: this is still a conjunctive query. For some database instance $DB = (D, R_1, \ldots, R_k)$, $q(DB)$ denotes the result of $q$ on $DB$. We assume here that the databases are ordered, hence $q(DB)$ is an ordered set of tuples. Finally, we denote $q \subseteq q'$ if[2] $q(DB) \subseteq q'(DB)$ for all database instances $DB$, and say that $q$ is contained in $q'$.

---

[2] Recall that containment of conjunctive queries is decidable.

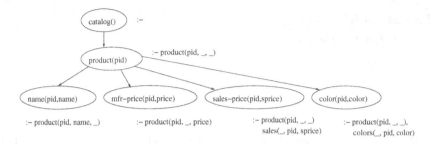

**Fig. 3.** TreeQL query for Example 2

A program $P$ in TreeQL is a tree in $\mathcal{U}_{\Sigma \times CQ}$. Hence, each node $u$ in $P$ is labeled both with a tag, and with a conjunctive query, denoted $q_u$. Formally:

**Definition 2.** *A TreeQL program is a tree $P \in \mathcal{U}_{\Sigma \times CQ}$ such that, whenever $u$ is the parent node of $v$ then the following hold: (1) headVar($q_u$) $\subseteq$ headVar($q_v$) and (2) $\Pi_{headVar(q_u)}(q_v) \subseteq q_u$.*

Given an ordered database $DB$ $P(DB) \in \mathcal{U}_\Sigma$ is defined as follows. Its nodes are pairs $(u, \bar{x})$, such that $u \in nodes(P)$ and $\bar{x} \in q_u(DB)$. The tag of $(u, \bar{x})$ is the same as that of $u$. A node $(u, \bar{x})$ is the parent of $(v, \bar{y})$ if $u$ is the parent of $v$ and $\bar{x} = \Pi_{headVar(q_u)}(\bar{y})$. The containment condition (2) above guarantees that every node has a parent (except the root). The nodes are ordered lexicographically, using the order in $P$ and in $DB$.

*Example 2.* Consider the following relational database schema:

product(<u>pid</u>, name, mfrprice), colors(<u>cid</u>, pid, color), sales(<u>sid</u>, pid, price)

The following is a TreeQL program:

```
catalog() :-
  product(pid) :- product(pid, _, _)
    name(pid, name) :- product(pid, name, _)
    mfr-price(pid, price) :- product(pid, _, price)
    sales-price(pid, sprice) :-
            product(pid, _, _), sales(_, pid, sprice)
    color(pid, color) :-
            product(pid, _, _), colors(_, pid, color)
```

We wrote the conjunctive query in Datalog notation, used the XML output tag as head predicate, and indentation to define the tree structure. Fig. 3 illustrates the same program graphically. On some database instance, the program computes an XML tree as follows. First, it computes the query for catalog(), returning a single value (the empty tuple): this corresponds to the root node. Next it computes the query for product(pid). For each tuple in the answer it constructs a node labeled product. Next, it computes name(pid, name), and for each answer it constructs a node labeled name: its parent is the product node with the same id, etc.

$$E ::= \text{let fun } f_1(x) = E_1$$
$$\quad \text{fun } f_2(x) = E_2$$
$$\quad \ldots$$
$$\quad \text{fun } f_n(x) = E_n$$
$$\quad \text{in } F$$
$$\quad | \; F$$
$$F ::= x \;\; | \;\; \sigma(F) \;\; | \;\; \text{tag } (x)(F) \;\; | \;\; F_1, F_2 \;\; | \;\; () \;\; | \qquad\qquad (*)$$
$$\quad \text{if } P \text{ then } F_1 \text{ else } F_2 \; |$$
$$\quad f(x) \;\; | \;\; f(\text{down } (x)) \;\; | \;\; f(\text{up } (x)) \;\; | \;\; f(\text{left } (x)) \;\; | \;\; f(\text{right } (x))$$
$$P ::= (\text{tag } (x) = \sigma) \;\; | \; x = y \;\; |$$
$$\quad \text{hasDown } (x) \;\; | \;\; \text{hasUp } (x) \;\; | \;\; \text{hasLeft } (x) \;\; | \;\; \text{hasRight } (x)$$

**Fig. 4.** The Language RecQL

**RecQL.** We introduce here RecQL, a functional language mapping an input tree to an output tree. RecQL is designed to express precisely the tree transformations expressible in $k$-pebble tree transducers [MSV00]. Fig. 4 defines RecQL. A program consists of an expression, $E$, in which has several mutually recursive functions. Functions take a single node as input parameter, and can construct result forests, test predicates, or call other functions recursively. The forest constructors are: the tree denoted by a variable $x$; singletons $\sigma(F)$, where $\sigma \in \Sigma$, and tag $(x)(F)$, where tag $(x)$ denotes the tag associated to the node $x$; forest concatenation $F_1, F_2$; and the empty forest (). Recursive calls can be applied either to a node $(f(x))$, or to one of its neighbors: left-most child (down $(x)$), parent (up $(x)$), left sibling (left $(x)$), or right sibling (right $(x)$). Finally, the predicate tag $(x) = \sigma$ checks whether the label of node $x$ is $\sigma$, $x = y$ checks whether $x$ and $y$ are the same node, while hasDown $(x)$, hasUp $(x)$, hasLeft $(x)$, hasRight $(x)$ test whether the node $x$ has the corresponding neighbor. Function definitions may be nested, and usual scoping rules apply.

We impose the following restriction on function calls: the variable $x$ must be defined in the same block as $f$ or a surrounding block For example, considering the definition fun $f(x) = $ let fun $g(y) = $ let fun $h(z) = F_h$ in $F_g g'(y') = F_{g'}$ in $F_f$, then $F_g$ (the body of $g$) may contain the function calls $g(Up(y))$, $g'(Down(x))$, $h(y)$, and $f(Up(x))$, but not the function call $f(y)$, because $y$ is defined in an inner block from $f$. This restriction is imposed in order to make the proof of the typechecking theorem (Theorem 4) possible[3].

A program is an expression with a unique free variable, $t$.

The fact that we construct *forests* as opposed to *trees* gives us extra expressive power, as we shall see in a moment. Since the function definitions may be nested, we can refer to variables in their outer scope variables; this also gives us extra power. Notice that programs do not necessarily terminate.

---

[3] We leave open the question whether this restriction is necessary.

*Example 3.* The following program takes a tree $t$ as input and returns a list of all leaves:

```
result(let fun f(x) = if hasDown(x) then aux(down(x)) else x
           fun aux(x) = f(x), (if hasRight(x) then aux(right(x))
                                          else ())
       in f(t))
```

On input `a(b(c,d(e)),f(g))` the program returns `result(c,e,g)`. The function `aux` helps us applying `f` on all children of the current node. This is a common idiom, and we will use the abbreviation `apply[f]` for such a construction. That is, the function above can be rewritten as:

```
result(let fun f(x) = if hasDown(x) then apply[f](x)
                      else x in f(t))
```

As a second example, we illustrate a program which copies the entire tree, renaming all a's to b's:

```
result(let fun f(x) = if tag(x) = a then b(apply[f](x))
                      else tag(x)(apply[f](x))
       in f(t))
```

Finally, the last program takes a list, `root(a1(..), ..., an(..))` and returns the cartesian product of the list with itself, `result(pair(a1,a1), pair(a1, a2), ..., pair(an,an))`:

```
result(let fun f(x) = let g(y) = pair(tag(x)(), tag(y)())
                      in apply[g](t)
       in apply[f](t))
```

Notice that this function satisfies the restriction on recursive calls: $g$ is called recursively on on $t$, a variable which is visible within its scope.

*Relationship to Practical Languages.* TreeQL is defined almost identical to RXL, a language for publishing XML from relational databases used in SilkRoute [FST00]. Xperanto [SSB+00] uses a much richer language which is an extension of SQL. RecQL corresponds to a subset of XSL and, more closely, to the formal XSLT0 fragment described in [BMN00a,BMN00b]. Like XSL it can express recursive calls on children, parents, siblings, and can simulate recursive calls on descendants and ancestors that are allowed in XSL. It can simulate to some extent parameters in XSL, through the use of global variables. XSL however allows a new tree to be constructed and bound to a parameter: this cannot be simulated in RecQL. Another limitation in RecQL is that we cannot compare two data values, i.e. cannot express joins.

## 3   Type Inference and Its Limitations

Consider the program in Fig. 3. Reading it carefully, we can actually infer its output type, written in XDuce syntax (and ignoring the base types):

```
T   = catalog(T1*)
T1  = product(name, mfr-price, sales-price*, color*)
```

The result has a `catalog` tag on the root, and multiple `product` subelements. Each product has exactly one `name` and one `mfr-price`, because `pid` is a key in `product`, but may have arbitrary many `sales-prices` and `colors`.

This approach is very simple, and very powerful. For example if we are given an output type:

```
T'   = catalog(T1'*)
T1'  = product(name, description?, mfr-price*,
               (sales-price,sales-date?)*, color*)
```

then we are able to deduce that $P$ typechecks w.r.t. $T'$. For that, we use the fact that containment of unranked regular tree languages is decidable (Sec. 2).

What makes this even more appealing is that we can use constraints on the input database to refine the inferred input type. For example, assume that in the table `sales(pid, price)` the following Functional Dependency holds: `pid → sid` (i.e. `pid` is also a key). Then every product has at most one sales prices, and we can refine the inferred type to:

```
T   = catalog(T1*)
T1  = product(name, mfr-price, sales-price?, color*)
```

XDuce [HP00] describes type inference rules for a more complex language, and XQuery algebra, which is currently discussed at the W3C, follows a similar approach.

Unfortunately, type inference is not complete, not even for the simplest language and the simplest restrictions on types. Consider the following example. The relational schema has a single table, `R(x,y)`. The TreeQL query is:

```
result() :-
  a(x, y) :- R(x, y)
  b(x, y) :- R(x, y)
```

The inferred output type would be:

$$T = \text{result}(a*, b*)$$

But in fact, the "real" inferred type is:

$$T_r = \{\text{result}(a^n, b^n) \mid n \geq 0\}$$

since we have the same number of a's and b's. Obviously, this is not a regular tree language, hence we cannot "infer" it. Is perhaps $T$ the best type one can infer? Unfortunately not; consider the following type:

$$T1 = \text{result}() \mid \text{result}(a, a*, b, b*)$$

It rules out the cases when there are no a's but there are b's, and vice versa. For the same reason T2 below is better than T1:

$$T2 = \texttt{result}() \mid \texttt{result}(a, b) \mid \texttt{result}(a, a, a*, b, b, b*)$$

Obviously, we will not be able to obtain a "best" type.

As a result, a system using type inference to do typechecking may reject correct programs. Assume that we want to check if our program outputs XML trees of type T1. The answer is "yes", but the system would first infer the output type T, observe that $T \not\subseteq T1$, and answer "no".

RecQL programs have the same problem. Consider the following program P:

```
result(let fun f(x) = apply[g](x), apply[h](x)
            fun g(x) = a
            fun h(x) = b
       in f(t))
```

On some input tree `root(t1, ..., tn)` it returns the tree $\texttt{result}(a^n, b^n)$, and the same arguments apply as above.

## 4    Type Checking and Its Limitations

In practice, however, we need to solve the typechecking, not the type inference problem. Are there any methods that allow us to do typechecking without type inference? The answer is yes, in some cases, but not in general. We illustrate below with both TreeQL and RecQL.

### 4.1    Typechecking TreeQL

We illustrate on an example. Consider the following TreeQL program P:

```
result() :-
    a(x,y) :- q1(x,y)
    b(x,y) :- q2(x,y)
```

where q1 and q2 are some conjunctive queries. Assume that we want to check whether its output belongs to the type T2 in Sec. 3. We can proceed as follows. First compute the complement of T2:

```
T2' =   result(a,a*) | result(b,b*) |
        result(a,b,b,b*) | result(a,a,a*,b)
```

If P does not typecheck w.r.t. T2, then there exists some database instance DB s.t. P(DB) is of type T2'. We have to consider four cases, we illustrate here the case when P(DB) is in `result(a,b,b,b*)`. Hence q1(DB) has exactly one tuple in the answer, $\bar{x}1$, and q2(DB) has at least two tuples, let $\bar{x}2, \bar{x}2'$ be two such tuples. Since q1, q2 are conjunctive, we can find a subset database $DB_0$ s.t. $\bar{x}1 \in q1(DB_0)$ and $\bar{x}2, \bar{x}2' \in q2(DB_0)$, and the size of $DB_0$ is bound by the sizes of q1 and q2 only. In other words, if there exists an counterexample database, then there exists a "small" one, and we can typecheck by simply computing P on all "small" databases.

This generalizes, provided that we restrict the output type $\tau$ as follows:

– $\tau$ is a DTD.
– every regular expression occurring in $\tau$ is "star-free".

**Theorem 2.** *[MSV00] Typechecking is decidable for TreeQL over databases with functional dependencies, and for star-free output DTDs.*

Star-free regular expressions [Tho90] are much more expressive than their name suggests. We are not allowed to use the Kleene closure, however we can use the complement, denoted *compl*, and the empty set $\emptyset$. For example, if $\Sigma = \{a, b, c\}$, then $compl(\emptyset)$ denotes $\Sigma^*$, $compl(\Sigma^*.b.\Sigma^* \mid \Sigma^*.c.\Sigma^*)$ denotes $a^*$. Thus, regular expressions like $a^*.b^*.(c \mid a.b^*)$ and even $(a.b)^*$ are star-free. In fact, *all* examples of regular expressions used in this paper are star-free. An example which is not star-free is $(a.a)^*$.

The algorithm that results from the proof of Theorem 2, unfortunately, is not practical, since it enumerates all databases up to a certain size.

What happens if we drop the restrictions on the output type? In that case typechecking becomes undecidable [AMN+01a].

## 4.2   Typechecking for RecQL

RecQL seems much more powerful than TreeQL but, surprisingly, we can decide typechecking for RecQL, and without any restrictions to the output type. The catch, as we will see, is that there are no joins in RecQL.

We start with an example. Consider the program P at the end of Sec.3. On some input tree $\texttt{root}(\texttt{t}_1, \ldots, \texttt{t}_n)$ it returns the tree $\texttt{result}(\texttt{a}^n, \texttt{b}^n)$. Suppose that we are given some input type $\tau_1$ and some output type $\tau_2$, and we want to typecheck: $\forall t \in \mathcal{U}_\Sigma.t \in \tau_1 \Rightarrow P(t) \in \tau_2$. The test $P(\tau_1) \subseteq \tau_2$ would suffice, but we cannot "infer" the type $P(\tau_1)$. It turns out, however, that we can always do inverse type inference, i.e. compute $P^{-1}(\tau_2)$. In other words, this is always an unraked regular tree language. Then typechecking reduces to: $\tau_1 \subseteq P^{-1}(\tau_2)$. To see an example, consider $\tau_2$ to be: $\texttt{result}((\texttt{a},\texttt{a})\texttt{*},(\texttt{b},\texttt{b})\texttt{*})$, i.e. we must have an even number of a's, and an even number of b's. Then $P^{-1}(\tau_2)$ consists of all trees in which the root has an even number of children, $\texttt{root}(\texttt{t}_1, \ldots, \texttt{t}_{2n})$, which is indeed a unranked regular tree language.

Proving typechecking for the general case relies on a theorem in [MSV00], where typechecking is done for $k$-pebble tree transducers. Without revising these devices here, we restate that result in terms of RecQL. Let $\Omega$ be a ranked alphabet, $\Omega = \Omega_0 \cup \Omega_2$. Trees in $\mathcal{T}_\Omega$ are complete binary trees, i.e. every node is either a leaf or has two children identified as the left and the right child. Notice that our encoding of unranked trees into ranked trees are special cases of such trees, see Fig. 2. Define $\text{RecQL}_\Omega$ to be the following adaptation of RecQL to trees in $\mathcal{T}_\Omega$. RecQL$_\Omega$ has the same definition as RecQL in Fig. 4, except for the forest constructors (the line marked $(*)$ in Fig. 4), which now becomes:

$$F ::= x \mid \sigma \mid \sigma(F, F) \mid \mathsf{tag}\ (x) \mid \mathsf{tag}\ (x)(F, F)$$

We show here the following:

**Proposition 2.** *RecQL$_\Omega$ expresses precisely the transformations expressed by deterministic $k$-pebble tree transducers.*

*Proof.* (Sketch) Recall that a $k$-pebble transducer has its set of states partitioned into $k$ subsets, $Q = Q_1 \cup \ldots \cup Q_k$, with all states from $Q_i$ describing transitions for pebble $i$. First we show how to translate a $k$-pebble transducer into a RecQL$_\Omega$ program. The program will have one function $f_{q_1 q_2 \ldots q_i}(x_i)$ for each $i$-tuple of states $q_1 \in Q_1, \ldots, q_i \in Q_i$, for $i = 1, \ldots, k$: thus there will be exponentially more functions than states. All functions of the form $f_{q_1 \ldots q_i q_{i+1}}$ are defined within the scope of the function $f_{q_1 \ldots q_i}$, and they can access all pebbles $x_1, x_2, \ldots, x_i$ (the variables of the functions $f_{q_1}, f_{q_1 q_2}, \ldots, f_{q_1 q_2 \ldots q_i}$). Each function $f_{q_1 q_2 \ldots q_i}(x_i)$ simulates the transitions of state $q_i$: it test the current tag ( iftag $(x_i) = \sigma$ then $\ldots$) and the presence/absence of the other pebbles (if $x_i = x_j$ then $\ldots$), then simulates the corresponding transition in the transducer. For example we simulate an *up* move, to some state $q_i'$, with the expression $f_{q_1 q_2 \ldots q_i'}(\mathsf{up}\ (x_i))$. To simulate a *place* move, which places the next pebble, $i + 1$, on the root and continue in some state $q_{i+1} \in Q_{i+1}$ we call the function $f_{q_1 \ldots q_i q_{i+1}}(t)$, where $t$ is the variable bound to the root of the tree. To simulate a *pick* move, in which we pick the pebble $i$ and continue with pebble $i - 1$ in some state $q_{i-1}' \in Q_{i-1}$, we call the function $f_{q_1 q_2 \ldots q_{i-1}'}(x_{i-1})$. Notice that this function satisfies the restriction since $x_{i-1}$ is defined in the same block as $f_{q_1 q_2 \ldots q_{i-1}'}(x_{i-1})$. Finally, for an output transition, in which some symbol $\sigma$ is output and the computation proceeds in states $q_i'$ and $q_i''$, we write the expression $\sigma(f_{q_1 \ldots q_i'}(x_i), f_{q_1 \ldots q_i''}(x_i))$.

For the reversed direction, we are given a RecQL$_\Omega$ program and need to construct an equivalent $k$-pebble transducer. We do this by a number of transformations that essentially transform it into a $k$-pebble transducer, with each function corresponding to a state. In the first transformation we pull the conditionals up, e.g. rewrite $\sigma(\text{if } P \text{ then } F_1 \text{ else } F_2, F)$ into if $P$ then $\sigma(F_1, F)$ else $\sigma(F_2, F)$. In the second transformation we ensure that all expressions on the leaves of the conditionals are function calls, like $f(x)$ or $f(\mathsf{up}\ (x))$, or an output symbol followed by two calls, e.g. $\sigma(f(\mathsf{up}\ (x)), g(\mathsf{down}\ (y)))$. For that we break more complicated expressions by introducing additional functions. The third transformation is to ensure that each call to an inner function is the root as argument: for that we replace a call $f(x_i)$ with a call $f'(t)$ where $f'$ is a new inner function, i.e. defined in the same block as $f_i$, which performs a depth-first search of the tree until it finds the node $x_i$, and there it calls $f$ (it is allowed to call $f$ with some other argument than the root because it is at the same level). The fourth transformation does something similarly for calls to function in outer blocks. That is, if $f_i(x_j)$ is a function call inside some block $> i$ to some function $f_i$ define in block $i$ and the argument $x_j$ is a variable defined by the block $j < i$, then we do the following. We replace the expression $f_i(x_j)$ with $f_i'(x_i)$ where $f_i'$ is a new function added to block $i$, which does a traversal of the tree until it places $x_i$ on the same node as $x_j$, then calls $f_i(x_i)$. Finally, the last transformation is one in which we remove predicates on global variables. For example, if a function at nesting depth $i$, $f_i(x_i)$, contains a predicate of the form if $x_j = \sigma \ldots$ where $x_j$ is defined in some lower block $j < i$, then we replace $f_i$ with two copies, $f_i', f_i''$, one which corresponds to the case $x_j = \sigma$ the other to the case $x_j \neq \sigma$, and let the functions that call $f_i$ perform the test $x_j = \sigma$ and call either $f_i'$ or $f_i''$. This results in an exponential growth of the number of functions. We treat similarly predicates of the form $x_i = x_j$. After all these transformations are completed the resulting program corresponds directly to a $k$-pebble transducer.

We can now formally restate the main result in [MSV00].

**Theorem 3.** *[MSV00] For any program $P$ in $RecQL_\Omega$ and any regular tree language $\tau$, $P^{-1}(\tau)$ is also a regular tree language. In consequence typechecking for $RecQL_\Omega$ is decidable.*

This result is for ranked trees. We now transfer this result to RecQL and unranked trees, using the encoding in Sec. 2, and its properties in Prop. 1. In the following we fix an unranked alphabet $\Sigma$, and denote $\Omega$ is associated, ranked alphabet of rank 2.

**Proposition 3.** *For every RecQL program $P$, there exists some $RecQL_\Omega$ program $P_\Omega$ s.t. $\forall t \in \mathcal{U}_\Sigma$, $d(P_\Omega(e(t))) = P(t)$.*

*Proof.* (Sketch) $P_\Omega$ differs from $P$ in the way it traverses the input tree and the way it constructs the output tree.

- On the input tree, $e(t)$, $P_\Omega$ simulates $P$ by traversing on the nodes labeled with $-$. The moves down $(x)$, up $(x)$, left $(x)$, and right $(x)$ now become down (down $(x)$), up (up $(x)$), up $(x)$ and right (down $(x)$) (technically these expressions are illegal; we need to introduce a new function, for every occurrence of such a move). Whenever we need tag $(x)$ (in a forest constructor or a conditional) we need to move one step down and get it (this, again, requires us to introduce a new function).
- On the output tree, we add extra nodes labeled $-$. We change the forest constructors, $F$ to $F_\Omega$, as follows:

$$(\sigma(F))_\Omega \stackrel{\text{def}}{=} \sigma(-(F_\Omega, |), |) \quad \text{same for tag } (x)(F)$$
$$(F_1, F_2)_\Omega \stackrel{\text{def}}{=} -((F_1)_\Omega, (F_2)_\Omega)$$
$$()_\Omega \stackrel{\text{def}}{=} |$$

Notice that the new program $P_\Omega$ will not return a correct encoding, because it adds too many nodes labeled $-$. That is, its result will look more like Fig. 2 (c) rather than (b). Hence, $P_\Omega(e(t))$ is in general not equal to $e(P(t))$; only the weaker statement in Prop. 3 holds. However, here we can use Prop. 1 and obtain the following result:

**Theorem 4.** *For any program P in RecQL and any unranked regular tree language $\tau$, $P^{-1}(\tau)$ is also an unraked regular tree language. In consequence type-checking for RecQL is decidable.*

*Proof.* From Proposition 3 it follows:

$$P^{-1}(\tau) = e^{-1}(P_\Omega^{-1}(d^{-1}(\tau)))$$

By Prop. 1 $d^{-1}(\tau)$ is a regular tree language, hence, by Theorem 3 $P_\Omega^{-1}(d^{-1}(\tau))$ is a regular tree language, hence $e^{-1}(P_\Omega^{-1}(d^{-1}(\tau)))$ is an unranked regular tree language.

Despite its appeal, this positive result has little practical consequences in its current form. The complexity of the decision procedure that follows from the proof in [MSV00] is hyper-exponential. While no lower bound has been shown so far, typechecking is at least as complex as containment of regular tree languages, which is DEXPTIME complete [Sei90].

Moreover, the result in Theorem 4 is brittle: typechecking becomes undecidable if we add data value joins. More precisely, assume that we add the data values to our input trees, i.e. consider trees in $\mathcal{U}_\Sigma(D)$. Now leaf nodes in the input tree may be labeled with elements from $D$. Assume that we extend the definition of RecQL in Fig. 4 with a predicate that checks the equality of two data values:

$$P ::= \mathsf{tag}\ (x) =\mathsf{tag}\ (y) \tag{1}$$

where $x, y$ are two node variables. We did not need such a predicate before, when $\Sigma$ was finite and known in advance (we could have simply compared each $x$ and $y$ which each symbol in $\Sigma$). Denoting RecQL$^=$ the extended language, it turns out that typechecking for RecQL$^=$ is undecidable. This is easily seen by reduction from the finite satisfiability problem for First Order Logic. Namely, given a vocabulary with one binary relation $R(x, y)$, one can encode finite structures over $R$ as trees in $\mathcal{U}_\Sigma(D)$, with a small alphabet $\Sigma$. For example, we could take $\Sigma = \{a, b\}$ and encode the finite structure $\{(3, 5), (5, 1), (3, 2)\}$ as $a(b(3, 5), b(5, 1), b(3, 2))$. Given a formula in first order logic, $\varphi$, one can write a program $P$ in RecQL$^=$ which checks whether the formula is true on the (structure encoded by the) input tree. If yes, then it returns a $c$; otherwise it returns a $d$. Assume the output type to be $\tau = \{d\}$. Then $P$ typechecks if and only if $\varphi$ is not satisfiable. Notice that we need the equality operator (1) because $\varphi$ may contain the equality predicate.

## 5    Related Work

An extensive treatment of semistructured data, with additional references can be found in [ABS99]. Various types for semistructured data have been proposed in [BDFS97,GW97,BM99]; for XML, DTDs are described in the XML recommendation [Con98], while XML-Schema is now a separate recommendation [BLM+99]. Automata for unranked trees are described in [BKMW98], and specialized DTD's in [PV00]. Murata [Mur96] describes type inference for certain transformations, expressed with tree automata. The XDuce programming language and it's associated XML type inference problem are discussed in [HP00,HP01]; the XQuery Semantics document describes type inference for a much richer language [FFM+01], which is used to define formally the semantics of XQuery. $k$-Pebble tree transducers are introduced in [MSV00] and shown to have a decidable typechecking problem. A connection between $k$-pebble tree transducers and a fragment of XSL is discussed in [BMN00a,BMN00b]. The typechecking problem for other languages, with joins, is studied in [AMN+01b,AMN+01a].

# 6   Discussion

XML typechecking is clearly an important problem, because we need to validate dynamically generated XML documents. We have seen two approaches to typechecking: an incomplete method, based on heuristic type inference, and two complete methods, using specialized algorithms. None is completely satisfactory in practice. The first results in systems that reject correct programs without warnings. The second may work in some cases, but the decidable cases seem to be more the exception than the rule. Moreover, even where typechecking is decidable, the complexity is high.

   Today, the front-runner in practice is the type inference method, because it is easy to extend, even if incompletely, to a variety of language constructs. What is intriguing about type inference is that, despite its theoretical incompleteness, it seems to be "complete" for practical applications. In our example in Sec. 3, the types T1 an T2 that caused typechecking to fail are artificial, and one can argue that such types do not occur in practice. One could make the argument that with the inferred type T the system can correctly typecheck the program for all "practical" output types (since the output types on which it fails, like T1, are "artificial"). But so far no formal statements of this kind have been proven. This raises several questions:

- Is there a notion of "practical" types for which type inference is complete? This notion should exclude the types T1, T2 in Sec. 3, while allow interesting types with Kleene closures (perhaps with the limitations of star-free languages), alternations, and optional elements.
- Is it possible to issue a warning when type inference fails? We would like the typechecking algorithm to return yes, no, or unknown rather than return false negatives.
- As alternative techniques to type inference one might consider approximation, or randomized typechecking algorithm. Of course, type inference offers an approximation algorithm already, but it is not clear yet that is is the best in practice.

# Acknowledgments

The author is supported by the NSF CAREER Award 0092955, a Sloan Fellowship and a gift from Microsoft Research.

# References

ABS99.      S. Abiteboul, P. Buneman, and D. Suciu. *Data on the Web : From Relations to Semistructured Data and XML.* Morgan Kaufmann, 1999.

AMN⁺01a.   N. Alon, T. Milo, F. Neven, D. Suciu, and V. Vianu. Typechecking XML views of relational databases. In *LICS*, pages 421–430, 2001.

AMN⁺01b.   N. Alon, T. Milo, F. Neven, D. Suciu, and V. Vianu. XML with data values: Typechecking revisited. In *PODS*, pages 138–149, 2001.

BDFS97.    Peter Buneman, Susan Davidson, Mary Fernandez, and Dan Suciu. Adding structure to unstructured data. In *Proceedings of the International Conference on Database Theory*, pages 336–350, Deplhi, Greece, 1997. Springer Verlag.

BFRW84.    A. Brown, M. Fuchs, J. Robie, and P. Wadler. MSL: a model for W3C XML Schema. In *Proceedings of WWW10*, Hong Kong, May 1984.

BKMW98.    A. Bruggemann-Klein, M. Murata, and D. Wood. Regular tree languages over non-ranked alphabets, 1998. Available at
           `ftp://ftp11.informatik.tu-muenchen.de/pub/misc/caterpillars/`.

BLM⁺99.    D. Beech, S. Lawrence, M. Maloney, N. Mendelsohn, and H. Thompson. Xml schema part 1: Structures, May 1999.
           `http://www.w3.org/TR/xmlschema-1/`.

BM99.      Catriel Beeri and Tova Milo. Schemas for integration and translation of structured and semi-structured data. In *Proceedings of the International Conference on Database Theory*, pages 296–313, 1999.

BMN00a.    G. J. Bex, S. Maneth, and F. Neven. A formal model for an expressive fragment of XSLT. In Lloyd et al., editor, *Computational Logic – CL 2000*, volume 1861 of *Lecture Notes in Artificial Intelligence*, pages 1137–1151. Springer, 2000.

BMN00b.    G. J. Bex, S. Maneth, and F. Neven. A formal model for an expressive fragment of XSLT, 2000. To appear in Information Systems.

Con98.     World Wide Web Consortium. Extensible markup language (xml) 1.0, 1998. `http://www.w3.org/TR/REC-xml`.

FFM⁺01.    P. Fankhauser, M. Fernandez, A. Malhotra, M. Rys, J. Simeon, and P. Wadler. XQuery 1.0 formal semantics, 2001. available from the W3C, `http://www.w3.org/TR/query-semantics`.

FST00.     M. Fernandez, D. Suciu, and W. Tan. SilkRoute: trading between relations and XML. In *Proceedings of the WWW9*, pages 723–746, Amsterdam, 2000.

GW97.      Roy Goldman and Jennifer Widom. DataGuides: enabling query formulation and optimization in semistructured databases. In *Proceedings of Very Large Data Bases*, pages 436–445, September 1997.

HP00.      Haruo Hosoya and Benjamin C. Pierce. XDuce: An XML processing language (preliminary report). In *WebDB'2000*, pages 226–244, 2000. `http://www.research.att.com/conf/webdb2000/`.

HP01.       Haruo Hosoya and Benjamin C. Pierce. Regular expression pattern match-
            ing for xml. In *ACM SIGPLAN, SIGACT Symposium on Principles of
            Programming Languages (POPL)*, pages 67–80, January 2001.
Mit96.      John C. Mitchell. *Foundations for Programmng Languages*. MIT Press,
            1996.
MSV00.      T. Milo, D. Suciu, and V. Vianu. Typechecking for XML transformers. In
            *Proceedings of the ACM Symposium on Principles of Database Systems*,
            pages 11–22, Dallas, TX, 2000.
Mur96.      Makoto Murata. Transformation of documents and schemas by patterns
            and contextual conditions. In C. Nicholas and D. Wood, editors, *Proceed-
            ings of Third International Workshop on Principles of Document Process-
            ing (PODP)*, pages 153–169, Palo Alto, CA, September 1996.
PV00.       Y. Papakonstantinou and V. Vianu. DTD inference for views of XML
            data. In *Proceedings of PODS*, pages 35–46, Dallas, TX, 2000.
Sei90.      Helmut Seidl. Deciding equivalence of finite tree automata. *SIAM J.
            Comput*, 19(3):424–437, 1990.
SSB⁺ 00.    J. Shanmugasundaram, E. Shekita, R. Barr, M. Carey, B. Lindsay, H. Pi-
            rahesh, and B. Reinwald. Efficiently publishing relational data as xml
            documents. In *Proceedings of VLDB*, pages 65–76, Cairo, Egipt, Septem-
            ber 2000.
Tan01.      Val Tannen. Personal communication, 2001.
Tho90.      W. Thomas. Automata on infinite objects. In *Formal Models and Seman-
            tics*, volume B of *Handbook of Theoretical Computer Science*, chapter 4,
            pages 133–192. Elsevier, Amsterdam, 1990.
Wad01.      Phil Wadler. Personal communication, 2001.

# Optimization Properties for Classes
# of Conjunctive Regular Path Queries

Alin Deutsch and Val Tannen

University of Pennsylvania,
200 South 33rd Str. 19104 Philadelphia, PA, USA
{adeutsch,val}@saul.cis.upenn.edu

**Abstract.** We are interested in the theoretical foundations of the optimization of conjunctive regular path queries (CRPQs). The basic problem here is deciding query containment both in the absence and presence of constraints. Containment without constraints for CRPQs is EXPSPACE-complete, as opposed to only NP-complete for relational conjunctive queries. Our past experience with implementing similar algorithms suggests that staying in PSPACE might still be useful. Therefore we investigate the complexity of containment for a hierarchy of fragments of the CRPQ language. The classifying principle of the fragments is the expressivity of the regular path expressions allowed in the query atoms. For most of these fragments, we give matching lower and upper bounds for containment in the absence of constraints. We also introduce for every fragment a naturally corresponding class of constraints in whose presence we show both decidability and undecidability results for containment in various fragments. Finally, we apply our results to give a complete algorithm for rewriting with views in the presence of constraints for a fragment that contains Kleene-star and disjunction.

## 1   Introduction

Semistructured data models and query languages [1] have become a very active area of interesting research in databases. In this paper we are interested in semistructured query languages, more precisely in theoretical foundations of query optimization for such languages. We concentrate on two computational problems:

- The problem of query equivalence (more generally, query containment), with or without integrity constraints.
- The problem of rewriting queries to make (some) use of views, again with or without integrity constraints.

For queries on relational, complex values, dictionary and OO data, these problems can be solved nicely and uniformly with a strengthening of the classical ideas on tableaux and chase. (See the chase extension in [23] and the chase & backchase technique for rewriting with views in [9].) Although the problems have theoretically intractable lower bounds, these bounds are in terms of query

G. Grahne and G. Ghelli (Eds.): DBPL 2001, LNCS 2397, pp. 21–39, 2002.
© Springer-Verlag Berlin Heidelberg 2002

and constraint size. It turns out that these techniques are in fact practical for practical-size queries and constraints [22]. Our experience with implementing them suggests that a necessary condition for practicality is the ability to decide containment in polynomial space. Can this be done for semistructured languages?

At the theoretical core of such languages lie the *conjunctive regular path queries (CRPQs)* of [13,6]. Here is an example:

$$Q(Y, Z) \leftarrow \text{start } (a^*|b).c \ X \ , \ X \ a.b^* \ Y \ , \ X \ c^* \ Z$$

This is interpreted in a graph whose edge labels are taken from a set containing $a, b, c$ while **start** is a constant node. The query returns the set of pairs $(Y, Z)$ of nodes such that for some node $X$ there are paths $\text{start} \rightarrow X$, $X \rightarrow Y$, $X \rightarrow Z$ whose labels belong to the regular languages $(a^*|b).c$ , $a.b^*$ , $c^*$ respectively.

However, containment of general CRPQs is EXPSPACE-complete [6,13]! Therefore, in this paper we pay attention to restricted fragments of CRPQs. This is an approach validated by practice: typical users exploit only a fraction of the expressive power of regular expressions. This is based on the experiences of users of the semistructured query language StruQL [12], but also of the XML query language XML-QL [8], and it is supported by the restrictions on path expressions imposed by the XPath standard [27]. Here is a very simple example of query optimization in such a fragment. Consider the query

$$A(N) \leftarrow \text{start } * \ X \ , \ X \ name.John \ Y, \ X \ *.tells.name \ N$$

which returns the names of persons who find out a secret from somebody connected directly or indirectly to John. Assume that the following view is materialized

$$Divulge(V, W) \leftarrow \ \text{start } * \ U, \ U \ name \ V \ , \ U \ tells \ W$$

and the following integrity constraint holds

$$(\text{tellAll}) \ \forall X, Y \ [ \ X \ *.tells.* \ Y \rightarrow \ X \ tells \ Y \ ]$$

saying that our database models a society in which whenever two of its members share a secret, eventually everybody connected to them shares that secret. *Under this constraint*, the query $A$ can be equivalently rewritten to use *Divulge*:

$$A'(N) \leftarrow Divulge(X, Y) \ , \ X \ John \ Z, \ Y \ name \ N.$$

Depending on the storage schema, $A'$ may be cheaper to evaluate. In the extended version [11] we show a detailed example of how the methods we develop in this paper succeed in finding this rewriting.

To study various fragments of CRPQs we develop a novel technique. [6,13] use automata-theoretic techniques but here we will try something different: reductions to problems formulated in the relational setting. The fragments for which we prove upper bounds and decidability results are such that we can translate queries and dependencies into relational versions, over a special relational schema. For example, the query $Q$ shown above translates to the following union of relational conjunctive queries:

$$Q'(y, z) = C_1(y, z) \ \cup \ C_2(y, z)$$
$$C_1(y, z) \leftarrow a^*(\text{start}, w_1) \ , \ c(w_1, X) \ , \ a(x, w_2), \ b^*(w_2, y) \ , \ c^*(x, z)$$
$$C_2(y, z) \leftarrow b(\text{start}, w_1) \ , \ c(w_1, X) \ , \ a(X, w_2) \ , \ b^*(w_2, y) \ , \ c^*(x, Z)$$

We think of $C_1, C_2$ as ordinary relational conjunctive queries over a schema containing $a, a^*, b^*, c, c^*$. A priori $a$ and $a^*$ etc., are independent binary relation symbols, but we interpret them only in relational instances in which certain relational constraints hold. The constraints are first-order and they say, for example, that $a^*$ is transitive, reflexive, and includes $a$. Of course, transitive closure itself cannot be expressed in first-order logic. It is therefore remarkable that first-order reasoning suffices for some of the semistructured language fragments we consider in this paper. However, we also provide undecidability results that together with the aforementioned EXPSPACE lower bound [6] show some of the theoretical limits of what can be done about optimization in semistructured languages.

**Organization of the Remainder of This Paper.** In section 2 we define the classes (language fragments) of queries and dependencies under study here, as well as their translation into relational correspondents. In section 3 we summarize our results and discuss some related work. Section 4 contains our results on upper bounds for pure query containment while section 5 contains the corresponding lower bound results. Section 6 presents our results on deciding (or not!) containment of queries in the presence of dependencies. Section 7 extends the chase & backchase technique [9] to two of the fragments we study. We conclude in section 8.

Due to space limitations, we have relegated some proofs and a worked example to the full paper [11], which also contains the extension to unions and disjunction of the chase. Although this extension, in the form that we need, has not—apparently—been published previously, it will not surprise anyone with an understanding of the classical chase.

## 2    Queries and Constraints

**Databases.** Let $\mathcal{L}$ be a set of *labels*. For technical reasons we assume that $\mathcal{L}$ is infinite, but of course only a finite number of labels will occur in a given database, query, or constraint. A *semistructured database* is a finite directed graph whose edges are $\mathcal{L}$-labeled. Equivalently, we can be given a set $N$ (the nodes of the graph) and a finite set of labels from $\mathcal{L}$, each interpreted as a non-empty binary relation on $N$.

A word about **constants** denoting nodes. The upper bound and decidability results do *not*, as stated, assume the presence of such constants. Equalities between distinct constants cause the usual problem [2] and our results can be extended straightforwardly to deal with this. For clarity of exposition we have omitted this extension. On the other hand, some of our examples and even some of the constructions used in lower bounds and undecidability results do use constants denoting nodes. Such use is in fact inessential and is made for the same reasons of clarity.

**Queries: CRPQs.** A *conjunctive regular path query (CRPQ)* [13,6] has the general form

$$Q(x_1, \ldots, x_n) \leftarrow A_1, \ldots, A_m \qquad (1)$$

Here the *atoms* (*conjuncts*) $A_i$ are either equalities $y = z$ or *regular path atoms* of the form $y \ R \ z$ where $R$ is a regular expressions defined by [1]

$$R ::= l \mid \_ \mid R^* \mid R_1.R_2 \mid (R_1|R_2) \tag{2}$$
$$* \stackrel{\text{def}}{=} \_^*$$

where $l$ ranges over labels in $\mathcal{L}$ and $\_$ means *any* (single) label. Of course, each *distinguished* variables $x_j$ must also occur in the right hand side. As indicated, we follow [13] in using the *shorthand* $*$ for $\_^*$.

If $B$ is a semistructured database, an atom $x \ R \ y$ is *satisfied* by a valuation that maps $x, y$ to nodes $s, t$ in $B$ if there is a path from $s$ to $t$ in $B$ which spells out a word in the language denoted by the regular expression $R$. We extend this definition of atom satisfaction to give semantics to whole CRPQs in the way that is usual for conjunctive queries. Query containment is also defined as usual.

**Unions of CRPQs.** In spite of being called "conjunctive", CRPQs contain implicit forms of disjunction, most glaringly because of the $|$ operator in regular expressions. In fact, we are naturally led to consider *unions of CRPQs* as the class of queries of interest. It is easy to see that the EXPSPACE upper bound on containment [13,6] still holds for unions of CRPQs.

**Containment and Dependencies.** Much of the early relational database theory dealt with conjunctive (tableau) queries and *embedded dependencies* [2] which are logical assertions of the special form

$$\forall \boldsymbol{x} \ [C_1(\boldsymbol{x}) \rightarrow \exists \boldsymbol{y} \ C_2(\boldsymbol{x}, \boldsymbol{y})] \tag{3}$$

where $C_1, C_2$ are conjunctions of relational atoms or (in $C_2$) equalities [2]. Such dependencies are tightly related to containment assertions [28]. Given two (type-compatible) conjunctive queries $Q_1, Q_2$ it is easy to construct an embedded dependency that is equivalent (in each database instance) to the containment $Q_1 \subseteq Q_2$. It is equally easy to construct an equivalent containment assertion from any given embedded dependency.

In this paper we will consider several classes of queries, and for each of them we will identify a class of dependencies (constraints) that has this kind of tight correspondence with the containment of queries from the associated class.

**Add Disjunction: DEDs.** Generalizing from conjunctive queries to *unions of conjunctive queries*, we consider the associated class of *disjunctive embedded dependencies (DEDs)* which are logical assertions of the form

$$\forall \boldsymbol{x} \ [C_1(\boldsymbol{x}) \rightarrow \bigvee_{i=1}^{m} \exists \boldsymbol{y}_i \ C_{2,i}(\boldsymbol{x}, \boldsymbol{y}_i)] \tag{4}$$

where $C_1, C_{2,i}$ are as in (3). We don't need disjunction in the premise of the implication because it is equivalent to conjunctions of DEDs. We have the following

---

[1] We ask the reader to distinguish between the $|$ in regular expressions and the *meta* use of $|$ as part of the BNF for the syntax.

[2] The notation $\boldsymbol{x}$ abbreviates $x_1, \ldots, x_n$.

tight correspondence: the containment of two unions of conjunctive queries is equivalent to a finite number of DEDs, and a single DED is equivalent to the containment of a conjunctive query into a union of conjunctive queries.

A DED is *full* if it does not have existentially quantified variables. The *chase* [3] can be extended to DEDs, giving a decision procedure for containment of unions of conjunctive queries under a set of full DEDs (see [15] for a partial treatment and the extended version of this paper [11] for a sketch of the results we use.)

**Semistructured Constraints: DERPDs.** As with DEDs, we define the class of dependencies that corresponds to unions of conjunctive regular path queries (CRPQs). We call such dependencies *disjunctive embedded regular path dependencies (DERPDs)* and they are defined as assertions that have the same logical form as DEDs, see (4), but in which $C_1, C_{2,i}$ are conjunctions of regular path atoms $x\ R\ y$ or equalities. The definition for satisfaction of a given DERPD in a given semistructured database follows from the usual meaning of logical connectives and quantifiers and from the satisfaction for regular path atoms given earlier.

When the regular expressions are restricted to single labels in $\mathcal{L}$, CRPQs are equivalent to the usual conjunctive queries and DERPDs to just DEDs seen over a relational schema consisting of binary symbols from $\mathcal{L}$.

**Examples.** DERPDs can express a large variety of constraints on semistructured data. As we saw, they generalize most relational dependencies of interest. In addition we can express constraints similar to the ones DTDs [26] specify for XML. The first two below say that "any person has exactly one social security number". The third says that "telephone numbers can only be of two (if any) kinds, voice or fax" while the fourth is a kind of generalized join-like dependency.

$$\forall x\ [\textbf{start} * . person\ x\ \rightarrow\ \exists y\ x\ ssn\ y]$$

$$\forall x \forall y_1 \forall y_2\ [\textbf{start} * . person\ x\ \wedge\ x\ ssn\ y_1\ \wedge\ x\ ssn\ y_2\ \rightarrow\ y_1 = y_2]$$

$$\forall x \forall y \forall z\ [x\ telNo\ y\ \wedge\ y\ _ \ z\ \rightarrow\ y\ voice\ z\ \vee\ y\ fax\ z]$$

$$\forall x \forall y \forall z\ [x\ child\ y\ \wedge\ y\ child\ z\ \rightarrow\ z\ grandparent\ x]$$

**Fragments: $F$-Queries and $F$-Dependencies.** Since containment of CRPQs is EXPSPACE-complete [6] we study *fragments* of the language defined by restricting the regular expressions allowed in atoms (conjuncts). The simplest fragment, allowing just labels and concatenation, is equivalent to conjunctive queries over binary relations. Between these and general CRPQs we consider the fragments described by the table below. For any fragment $F$, we call the corresponding queries $F$-*queries*. Applying the same restriction to the atoms that appear in dependencies, we define corresponding classes of DERPDs, calling the respective constraints $F$-*dependencies*. The correspondence discussed above, between containment assertions and dependencies, continues to hold for each fragment $F$. The fragments called W and Z have technical importance but their definitions did not suggest anything better than choosing these arbitrary names.

| Fragment name | Regular expressions syntax |
|---|---|
| conj. queries | $R \rightarrow l \mid R_1.R_2$ |
| $(*)$ | $R \rightarrow l \mid * \mid R_1.R_2$ |
| $(*,\mid)$ | $R \rightarrow l \mid * \mid R_1.R_2 \mid (R_1\mid R_2)$ |
| $(*,\_)$ | $R \rightarrow l \mid \_ \mid * \mid R_1.R_2$ |
| $(l^*)$ | $R \rightarrow l \mid l^* \mid R_1.R_2$ |
| $(*,\_,l^*,\mid)$ | $R \rightarrow l \mid * \mid \_ \mid l^* \mid R_1.R_2 \mid (R_1\mid R_2)$ |
| $W$ | $R \rightarrow l \mid \_ \mid S^* \mid R_1.R_2 \mid (R_1\mid R_2)$ |
| | $S \rightarrow l \mid \_ \mid S_1.S_2$ |
| $Z$ | $R \rightarrow S \mid S^*$ |
| | $S \rightarrow l \mid S_1.S_2 \mid (S_1\mid S_2)$ |
| CRPQs | $R \rightarrow l \mid \_ \mid R^* \mid R_1.R_2 \mid (R_1\mid R_2)$ |

| Containment of | Upper bound | Containment of | Lower bound |
|---|---|---|---|
| conjunctive queries | NP  [7] | conjunctive queries | NP  [7] |
| $(*)$-queries | NP  [13] or corollary 1 | $(*)$-queries | $\downarrow$ |
| unions of conj. queries | $\Pi_2^p$  [24] | unions of conj. queries | $\Pi_2^p$  [24] |
| unions of $(*,\mid)$-queries | $\uparrow$ | $(*,\mid)$-queries | $\Pi_2^p$  remark 2 |
| unions of $(*,\_)$-queries | $\uparrow$ | $(*,\_)$-queries | $\Pi_2^p$  theorem 3 |
| unions of $(l^*)$-queries | $\uparrow$ | $(l^*)$-queries | $\Pi_2^p$  theorem 3 |
| unions of $(*,\_,l^*,\mid)$-queries | $\Pi_2^p$  theorem 2 | $(*,\_,l^*,\mid)$-queries | $\downarrow$ |
| unions of $W$ queries | ? | $W$ queries | PSPACE theorem 4 |
| unions of $Z$ queries | $\uparrow$ | $Z$ queries | EXPSPACE |
| unions of CRPQs | EXPSPACE [13,6] | CRPQs | [6] and remark 3 $\downarrow$ |

**Fig. 1.** Upper and lower bounds for containment

**First-Order Relational Translation.** At the core of our technique is a translation of semistructured queries and dependencies into first-order logic, namely into (unions of) conjunctive queries and DEDs *over a special relational schema* that includes $l$ and $l^*$ as well as $\_$ and $*$ as separate binary relation symbols. A priori these symbols are independent, but we will try to capture *some* of the Kleene star semantics through relational dependencies.

Our translation is designed for the $(*, \_, l^*, |)$-fragment only. It relies essentially on the fact that in this fragment concatenation and $|$ are *not* nested inside Kleene stars.

The first thing we do is **translate away** $|$. Using the equivalence $(a|b).c = (a.c)|(b.c)$ we move $|$ in the outermost position in the $(*, \_, l^*, |)$-regular expressions. Then, we note that $Q \leftarrow \ldots, x \; R_1|R_2 \; y, \ldots$ is equivalent to $Q_1 \cup Q_2$ where $Q_i \leftarrow \ldots, x \; R_i \; y, \ldots$. For dependencies, we note that $x \; R_1|R_2 \; y$ is equivalent to $x \; R_1 \; y \vee x \; R_2 \; y$ after which logical equivalences bring the disjunctions out. A disjunction in the premise of the implication in a dependency is equivalent to a conjunction (a set) of dependencies. To summarize:

*Remark 1.* By translating away the $|$, any $(*, \_, l^*, |)$-query becomes an equivalent union of $(*, \_, l^*)$-queries. Similarly, any $(*, \_, l^*, |)$-dependency becomes an equivalent set of $(*, \_, l^*)$-dependencies.

Next, we translate any $(*, \_, l^*)$-queries and dependencies into (relational) conjunctive queries and DEDs over the special schema

$$\mathcal{L}\text{-}Rel \stackrel{\text{def}}{=} \{l \mid l \in \mathcal{L}\} \cup \{l^* \mid l \in \mathcal{L}\} \cup \{\_, *\} \cup \{N\}$$

in which all symbols are binary relations with the exception of $N$ which is unary (the need for $N$ is explained below).

The **translation** $\mathcal{T}(Q)$ of a $(*, \_, l^*)$-query $Q$ is defined by translating its conjuncts according to the rules (for each binary $r$ in $\mathcal{L}$-$Rel$)

$$\mathcal{T}(x \; r \; y) = r(x, y)$$
$$\mathcal{T}(x \; R_1.R_2 \; y) = \mathcal{T}(x \; R_1 \; v), \mathcal{T}(v \; R_2 \; y)$$

The variable $v$ is (implicitly) existentially quantified and so it must be fresh each time its rule is applied. For example, $Q(x, y) \leftarrow x \; a.*.b \; y$, translates to $Q'(x, y) \leftarrow a(x, z), *(z, u), b(u, y)$.

The **translation** $\mathcal{T}(d)$ of a $(*, \_, l^*)$-dependency $d$ is defined similarly. The presence of concatenation in the conclusion of the implication in $d$ will add existentially quantified variables, while the presence of concatenation in the premise of the implication in $d$ will add universally quantified variables.

**Example of Translation.** Let $d$ be the dependency

$$\forall x \forall y \; [x \; (a|b).* \; y \; \rightarrow \; \exists z \; y \; *.(a|b) \; z]$$

It translates to the following set of two DEDs

$$\forall x \forall y \forall u \; [x \; a \; u \wedge u \; * \; y \rightarrow [\exists z_1 \exists v_1 \; y \; * \; v_1 \wedge v_1 \; a \; z_1] \vee [\exists z_2 \exists v_2 \; y \; * \; v_2 \wedge v_2 \; b \; z_2]]$$
$$\forall x \forall y \forall u \; [x \; b \; u \wedge u \; * \; y \rightarrow [\exists z_1 \exists v_1 \; y \; * \; v_1 \wedge v_1 \; a \; z_1] \vee [\exists z_2 \exists v_2 \; y \; * \; v_2 \wedge v_2 \; b \; z_2]]$$

Now, $\mathcal{T}(Q)$ is a relational query and $\mathcal{T}(d)$ is a relational dependency, both over the schema $\mathcal{L}$-$Rel$. However, we will use them not over arbitrary instances of $\mathcal{L}$-$Rel$ but only over instances that satisfy specific sets of relational dependencies. To deal with the various fragments, we consider two such sets

**The $\Sigma_*$ Dependencies:**

(node$_l$)    $\forall x \forall y \; [l(x,y) \rightarrow N(x) \wedge N(y)]$        (node$_*$)    $\forall x \forall y \; [*(x,y) \rightarrow N(x) \wedge N(y)]$

(base)    $\forall x \forall y \; [l(x,y) \rightarrow *(x,y)]$                        (refl$_*$)    $\forall x \; [N(x) \rightarrow *(x,x)]$

(trans$_*$)    $\forall x \forall y \forall z \; [*(x,y) \wedge *(y,z) \rightarrow *(x,z)]$

where $l$ ranges over $\mathcal{L}$. (This is an infinite set of dependencies but of course only finitely many matter for a given database, query, or dependency.) Here we see how we use $N$: we want the chase with (refl$_*$) to apply only to variables $x$ that are already present.

**The $\Sigma_{l*}$ Dependencies:** are obtained by replacing $*$ with $l^*$ in $\Sigma_*$ above.

The intention behind these dependencies is to narrow the gap between the semistructured meaning of the Kleene star and the arbitrary interpretation that could be given to the relational schema $\mathcal{L}$-$Rel$. We can associate directly to each semistructured database a relational $\mathcal{L}$-$Rel$-instance that satisfies $\Sigma_* \cup \Sigma_{l*}$ (call it a $\Sigma_* \cup \Sigma_{l*}$-instance). But this will not cover $\Sigma_* \cup \Sigma_{l*}$-instances containing pairs of distinct nodes which are not connected by any path with labels from $\mathcal{L}$. Of course, it is not possible to close the gap this way, since transitive closure is not first-order definable. It is therefore remarkable that first-order reasoning suffices for some of the semistructured language fragments we consider in this paper.

**Full Dependencies.** Relational dependencies (3) and DEDs (4) are called *full* when they do not have existentially quantified variables. In the case of DERPDs fullness must be more complicated because concatenation in regular expressions introduces an implicit existential. Here we take a very simple approach.

Let $d$ be an $(*, \_, l^*, |)$-dependency and let $\mathcal{T}(d)$ be the set of DEDs into which $d$ translates. We say that $d$ is a *full dependency* if each DED in $\mathcal{T}(d)$ is full.

## 3    Summary of Results

**Containment for $F$-Queries.** We summarize in figure 1 our new results on the complexity of deciding containment for queries in the various fragments, putting them in the context of known results.

The upper bounds are for containment of unions of $F$-queries, with the remarkable exception of the $(*)$-fragment for which containment of $(*)$-queries is in NP, just like containment of conjunctive queries. This was already shown in [13]. Motivated by the study of containment *under dependencies*, the new technique introduced here reproves, along the way, this NP bound, see corollary 1 [3].

Our new upper bound result is that containment of unions of $(*, \_, l^*, |)$-queries is in $\Pi_2^p$ (theorem 2). It can be seen from the lower bounds table that this is a tight bound.

---

[3] Although we do not consider it explicitly here, the fragment obtained by adding just $\_$ to labels and concatenation is easily seen to yield no surprises: containment is still in NP.

We have tried to state our lower bound results in their strongest form, for $F$-queries rather than unions of $F$-queries. It is not surprising to see a $\Pi_2^p$ lower bound in the presence of $|$. This does not follow directly from [24] but we have

*Remark 2.* The $\Pi_2^p$-hardness proof in [24] for the lower bound on containment of unions of conjunctive queries can be adapted to containment of $F$-queries provided that $F$ includes $|$.

It is surprising however what happens in the absence of $|$. While containment of $(*)$-queries is in NP, we show in theorem 3 that containment of $(l^*)$-queries is $\Pi_2^p$-hard. Moreover a simple variation of the same proof applies to the $(*, \_)$-fragment. Therefore, we find that the increase in complexity does not stem from the mere presence of the Kleene star in the query, but from the *interaction* between $l$ and $l^*$ or between $\_$ and $\_^*$.

A more liberal nesting of regular expressions within the Kleene star increases complexity. If we allow concatenation inside the Kleene star, we get the W-fragment, for which we show in theorem 4 a PSPACE lower bound on containment. We don't know (mainly because of difficulties with a relational translation) if this bound is tight, which is why we put a question mark in the corresponding upper bound entry. If in addition we allow disjunction within the Kleene star, we obtain the Z-fragment which is as bad as general CRPQs:

*Remark 3.* The EXPSPACE-hardness proof in [6] applies to containment of Z-queries.

| Containment of | Under what constraints | Decidable? |
|---|---|---|
| conjunctive queries | full relational dependencies | YES ([3]) |
| unions of conjunctive queries | full DEDs | YES ([11]) |
| unions of $(*, |)$-queries | full $(*, |)$-deps. | YES (theorem 5) |
| unions of $(*, \_)$- queries | full V-deps. | YES (theorem 6) |
| $(*, \_)$-query in union of $(*, \_)$-queries | full DEDs over special models | NO (theorem 7) |
| $(l^*)$-query in union of $(l^*)$-queries | full DEDs | NO (theorem 8) |

**Fig. 2.** Results for containment under dependencies

**Containment under Dependencies.** The chase technique in classical relational theory gives us the decidability of containment of conjunctive queries under full dependencies [2]. Decidability extends straightforwardly to containment of unions of conjunctive queries under full DEDs (see the full paper [11]).

This nice situation for relational languages contrasts with the situation for semistructured languages, as summarized in figure 2. The general problem studied is containment of unions of $F$-queries under full $F$-dependencies. It turns out that even containment of $(l^*)$-queries under just full DEDs is undecidable (theorem 8).

There is some good news, as our technique carries through in theorem 5 to prove decidability for the $(*, |)$-fragment.

We leave open the general problem corresponding to the $(*, \_)$, but we have two partial results that suggest that the problem might be complicated. We show decidability in the case of a restricted class of $(*, \_)$-dependencies, that we call V-*dependencies* (definition in section 6). And we show *undecidability* with just DEDs in the case of a class of *special models* (also defined in section 6).

In our two undecidability proofs, just like in the proof of theorem 3, we make essential use of of the *interaction* between $l$ and $l^*$ or between $\_$ and $\_^*$.

**Rewriting with Views under Dependencies.** Given a set $V$ of views, a set $D$ of dependencies expressing integrity constraints, and a query $Q$, we are interested in finding "rewritings" $Q'$ which mention some of the views (but may still contain labels from $Q$) and are *exactly* equivalent to $Q$.

We do not study this problem in its full generality, but rather we look at extending to some of the $F$-fragments the *chase&backchase (C&B)* algorithm that we introduced in [9]. This algorithm relies on the chase with dependencies. In view of the undecidability results we have obtained for other $F$-fragments, we have looked at rewriting with views only for the $(*)$- and $(*, |)$-fragments.

In theorem 9 we show that (essentially) the C&B algorithm is complete for the $(*)$-fragment, in the sense that it finds all rewritings that are *minimal* in a precise sense.

For the $(*, |)$-fragment we extend the original C&B algorithm to account for disjunction, and we prove that this extended version is also complete.

**Related Work.** Perhaps the closest in spirit is [4], which gives an EXPTIME-complete decision procedure for containment of queries and constraints expressed in a different fragment of CRPQs, which corresponds to description logics. This fragment allows unrestricted regular expressions in the conjuncts, but restricts the shape of the query graph (thus being incompatible with our classification principle for query fragments). The corresponding dependencies allow unrestricted regular path expressions and even cardinality constraints, but have restricted shape and in particular cannot express functional dependencies. As a matter of fact, [14] shows that, when adding functional dependencies to a generalization of description logics called the Guarded Fragment of first order logic, satisfiability (and hence containment) becomes undecidable. None of our query fragments is contained in description logics.

The class of $(*)$-queries was introduced in [13] (under the name of "simple StruQL$_0$ queries") as a class of semistructured queries using transitive closure and whose containment problem is in NP. The decision procedure was based on an automata-theoretic argument which was applicable to CRPQs with arbitrary regular path expressions.

[19,20] study the expressivity and satisfiability of queries over tree structures, in formalisms that are equivalent to MSO. Classes of tree structures are given as grammars, which can be viewed as constraints on their structure in a broader sense.

[5] gives a complete algorithm for finding rewritings of regular path queries (i.e. single-conjunct CRPQs) with views defined by regular path queries. The path expressions allowed in the conjunct are unrestricted, but no constraints are taken into account, and only complete rewritings are obtained (that is, rewritings mentioning only views). [17] addresses the problem of finding arbitrary rewritings of regular path queries, and [16] gives an algorithm for the related problem of *answering* regular path queries using incomplete views.

# 4  Upper Bounds

(∗)-**Queries.** Recall that a (∗)-query is a CRPQ whose atoms allow only regular expressions built from labels, ∗, and their concatenation. For example, $Q(x,y) \leftarrow x\, a. * .b\, y$, $y\, c\, x$ is a (∗)-query, as opposed to $Q'(y) \leftarrow x\, a.b^*.c\, y$ (because of $b^*$) and $Q''(y) \leftarrow x\, a|b\, y$ (because of |).

We have shown in section 2 how to translate any (∗)-query into a conjunctive query $\mathcal{T}(Q)$ over the schema $\mathcal{L}\text{-}Rel$. While not obvious, it turns out that reasoning about $\mathcal{T}(Q)$ under the set of dependencies $\Sigma_*$ introduced in section 2 suffices (see [11] for proof):

**Proposition 1.** *Let $Q_1$, $Q_2$ be two (∗)-queries. The containment $Q_1 \subseteq Q_2$ is valid if and only if $\Sigma_* \models \mathcal{T}(Q_1) \subseteq \mathcal{T}(Q_2)$.*

Next, we observe that the dependencies in $\Sigma_*$ are full hence the chase with them terminates, giving a decision procedure for $\Sigma_* \models \mathcal{T}(Q_1) \subseteq \mathcal{T}(Q_2)$ [3,2] We denote with $chase_{\Sigma_*}(Q)$ the result of chasing the query $Q$ with the dependencies in $\Sigma_*$.

**Theorem 1.** *The (∗)-query $Q_1$ is contained in the (∗)-query $Q_2$ if and only if there exists a containment mapping (see [2]) from $\mathcal{T}(Q_2)$ into $chase_{\Sigma_*}(\mathcal{T}(Q_1))$.*

**Corollary 1. (see also [13])** *(∗)-query containment is NP-complete.*

*Proof:* First notice that the size of $\mathcal{T}(Q)$ is linear in that of $Q$. The time to chase is polynomial in the size of the queries, but exponential in the maximum size of a dependency and the maximum arity of the relations in the schema [3]. However, the dependencies in $\Sigma_*$ have fixed size and the maximum arity of a relation in the schema is 2. The upper bound follows noting that the containment mapping can be found in NP. For the lower bound, note that the proof of NP-hardness for containment of conjunctive queries in [7] holds even if all relations are binary. •

**Example.** Consider $Q_1(x_1, x_3) \leftarrow x_1\, a\, x_2$, $x_2\, b.c\, x_3$ and $Q_2(y_1, y_2) \leftarrow y_1\, *$ $.a. * \, y_2$. It is easy to see that $Q_1$ is contained in $Q_2$. We show how we infer this using theorem 1. The translation to conjunctive queries yields $TQ_1 = \mathcal{T}(Q_1)$ and $TQ_2 = \mathcal{T}(Q_2)$, with $TQ_1(x_1, x_3) \leftarrow a(x_1, x_2), b(x_2, u_1), c(u_1, x_3)$ and $TQ_2(y_1, y_2) \leftarrow *(y_1, v_1), a(v_1, v_2), *(v_2, y_2)$. Note that there is no containment mapping from $TQ_2$ to $TQ_1$ as the latter contains no ∗-atoms to serve as image for the former's ∗-atoms. But by chasing $TQ_1$ with ($node_a$) and then with ($refl_*$), we

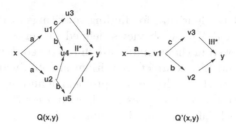

Fig. 3. Counterexample queries for proposition 2

obtain $Q'(x_1, x_3) \leftarrow N(x_1), N(x_2), *(x_1, x_1), a(x_1, x_2), b(x_2, u_1), c(u_1, x_3)$, thus creating an image for $TQ_2$'s conjunct $*(y_1, v_1)$. We continue chasing with (base$^b_*$), then (base$^c_*$) and (trans$_*$), obtaining $Q''(x_1, x_3) \leftarrow N(x_1), N(x_2), *(x_1, x_1), a(x_1, x_2), b(x_2, u_1), c(u_1, x_3), *(x_2, u_1), *(u_1, x_3), *(x_2, x_3)$. Now $\{y_1 \mapsto x_1, y_2 \mapsto x_3, v_1 \mapsto x_1, v_2 \mapsto x_2\}$ is a containment mapping from $T(Q_2)$ into $Q''$. There are further applicable chase steps, omitted here as they only add new atoms and hence do not affect the existence of the containment mapping. •

**Unions of $(*, \_, l^*, |)$-Queries.** The idea we have just used to handle $(*)$-queries is easily extended to $(*, |)$-queries (giving a $\Pi^p_2$ procedure), but how about other fragments? Can we deal with $(l^*)$-queries using their relational translation and the set $\Sigma_{l^*}$ of dependencies defined in section 2? The answer is negative, which is surprising given the syntactic similarity of the $(*)$- with the $(l^*)$-fragment.

**Proposition 2.** *There exist $(l^*)$-queries $Q, Q'$ such that $Q \subseteq Q'$ but $\Sigma_{l^*} \not\models T(Q) \subseteq T(Q')$.*

*Proof:* Here are the queries (see figure 3 for possibly helpful graph representations of $Q, Q'$):

$Q(x, y) \leftarrow x\ a\ u_1,\ x\ a\ u_2,\ u_1\ c\ u_3,\ u_1\ b\ u_4,\ u_2\ b\ u_5, u_2\ c\ u_4,\ u_3\ l.l\ y,\ u_4\ l.l^*\ y,\ u_5\ l\ y$
$Q'(x, y) \leftarrow x\ a\ v_1,\ v_1\ b\ v_2,\ v_1\ c\ v_3,\ v_2\ l\ y,\ v_3\ l.l.l^*\ y$

To see that $Q$ is contained in $Q'$, observe that $ll^* = l \cup lll^*$ and $Q$ is equivalent to the union of queries $Q_1 \cup Q_2$ where $Q_1, Q_2$ are obtained by replacing the conjunct $u_4\ ll^*\ y$ with $u_4\ l\ y$, respectively $u_4\ lll^*\ y$ in $Q$. But both $Q_1, Q_2$ are contained in $Q'$, as witnessed by the containment mappings $\{v_1 \mapsto u_1, v_2 \mapsto u_4, v_3 \mapsto u_3\}$ and $\{v_1 \mapsto u_2, v_2 \mapsto u_5, v_3 \mapsto u_4\}$. Intuitively, for any instance $I$, and any mapping from $Q$ to $I$, depending on whether $u_4\ l.l^*\ y$ in $Q$ is satisfied by a path of length 1 or at least 2, $v_1\ c\ v_3$ in $Q'$ is satisfied by the same path which satisfies either $u_1\ c\ u_3$ or $u_2\ c\ u_4$, respectively.

On the other hand, according to the chase theorem [2], $T(Q)$ is not contained in $T(Q')$ under $\Sigma_{l^*}$ because there is no containment mapping from $T(Q')$ into $chase_{\Sigma_{l^*}}(T(Q))$. (Intuitively, what $\Sigma_{l^*}$ does not capture is the *minimality* of $l^*$: it only states that $l^*$ contains the reflexive transitive closure of $l$, but it doesn't rule out pairs of nodes that aren't reachable via a path of $l$-edges. Instances containing such a pair $(s, t)$ are counterexamples for the containment: conjunct

$u_4$ $ll^*$ $y$ in $Q$ is satisfied by the endpoints of the path $r \xrightarrow{l} s \xrightarrow{l^*} t \xrightarrow{l} q$ even if $s$ has no outgoing $l$-edge, while $v_3$ $lll^*$ $y$ in $Q'$ is not.) •

A simple variation of the counterexample above applies to $(*, \_)$-queries. In any case, if the same idea would have applied it would have given us NP algorithms, and we show in theorem 3 that containment for both the $(l^*)$- and the $(*, \_)$-fragment is $\Pi_2^p$-hard! Therefore, we will take another route towards a containment test.

We start from the observation that $\Sigma_* \cup \Sigma_{l^*}$ is sufficient in deciding containment of $Q_1$ in $Q_2$ in the restricted case in which $Q_1$ contains no Kleene star (no $*$ or $l^*$), and $Q_2$ is a $(*, \_, l^*)$-query. We call $Q_1$ *star-free*.

**Proposition 3.** *The star-free query $Q_1$ is contained in the $(*, \_, l^*)$-query $Q_2$ if and only if there is a containment mapping from $\mathcal{T}(Q_2)$ to chase$_{\Sigma_* \cup \Sigma_{l^*}}(\mathcal{T}(Q_1))$.*

A proof sketch is given in the full paper [11]. Next we show how to use proposition 3 to decide containment even if $Q_1$ is a proper $(*, \_, l^*)$-query.

In the rest of this section $l$ will denote either a label in $\mathcal{L}$ or the symbol $\_$. Observe that for any $l \in \mathcal{L} \cup \{\_\}$, $l^* = \bigcup_{0 \leq p} l^p$, where $l^p$ is short for the concatenation of $p$ successive $l$'s. More generally, let $Q(l_1^*, \ldots, l_n^*)$ be a $(*, \_, l^*)$-query in which $(l_1^*, \ldots, l_n^*)$ are all the *occurrences* of starred symbols (the $l_i$'s are not necessarily distinct). Such a query is equivalent to an infinite union of star-free queries:

$$Q(l_1^*, \ldots, l_n^*) = \bigcup_{0 \leq p_1, \ldots, 0 \leq p_n} Q(l_1^{p_1}, \ldots, l_n^{p_n})$$

The key to our containment test is that this infinite union can be replaced with a finite one. For any $(*, \_, l^*)$-query $Q$ let $sfs(Q)$ be the *star-free size* of $Q$, defined as the count of all occurrences of non-Kleene-starred labels in $Q$. For example, for $Q(x, y) \leftarrow x\ a.b^*\ y$ , $y\ *.c\ z$ we have $sfs(Q) = 2$.

**Proposition 4.** *Let $Q_1, Q_2$ be two $(*, \_, l^*)$-queries and let $k \overset{def}{=} sfs(Q_2) + 1$. Then, $Q_1 \subseteq Q_2$ if and only if*

$$\bigcup_{0 \leq p_1 \leq k, \ldots, 0 \leq p_n \leq k} Q_1(l_1^{p_1}, \ldots, l_n^{p_n}) \subseteq Q_2$$

The proof is given in the full paper [11]. We can now give our decision procedure for containment of unions of $(*, \_, l^*, |)$-queries, which has four steps:

**Step 1:** We first translate away the $|$, obtaining finite unions $U_1, U_2$ of $(*, \_, l^*)$-queries.

**Step 2:** Next we use proposition 4 to obtain from $U_1$ a finite union of star-free queries $SF_1$, which must be checked for containment in $U_2$ [4].

**Step 3:** Containment of $SF_1$ in $U_2$ is decided using the following easy result:

---

[4] An alternative way of obtaining $SF_1$ is by chasing the queries in $U_1$ with $\forall x \forall y\ [l^*(x, y) \rightarrow x = y \vee \exists z\ l(x, z) \wedge l^*(z, y)]$ (and similarly for $*$). This would result in a non-terminating chase, which we however could stop after sufficiently many steps.

**Proposition 5.** *The union of star-free queries $\bigcup_{i=1}^{n} Q_i$ is contained in the union of $(*, \_, l^*)$-queries $\bigcup_{j=1}^{m} Q'_j$ if and only if for every $1 \le i \le n$ there is a $1 \le j \le m$ such that $Q_i \subseteq Q'_j$.*

**Step 4:** Finally, checking each star-free $Q_i$ for containment in $Q'_j$ is done using proposition 3.

The upper bound for this algorithm is straightforward, proven in [11]:

**Theorem 2.** *Containment of unions of $(*, \_, l^*, |)$-queries is in $\Pi_2^p$.*

# 5   Lower Bounds

$(l^*)$-**Queries**, $(*, \_)$-**Queries.** The $|$ operator corresponds to the union and containment for unions of conjunctive queries is $\Pi_2^p$-complete [24]. But it turns out that even in the absence of $|$ we have $\Pi_2^p$-hardness results, with completely different proofs:

**Theorem 3.** *Containment of $(l^*)$-queries is $\Pi_2^p$-hard. Containment of $(*, \_)$-queries is $\Pi_2^p$-hard.*

As we pointed out in figure 1, the $\Pi_2^p$ lower bound for containment of $(*, \_, l^*, |)$-queries follows (independently) from three sources: the two lower bounds in the previous theorem and the one in remark 2.

**W-Queries.** The following result shows that a more liberal nesting of regular path expressions within the Kleene star is problematic in terms of complexity of containment. If we allow concatenations of labels within the Kleene star, we obtain the W-fragment, whose lower bound for containment is PSPACE (a proof is in the full paper [11]):

**Theorem 4.** *Containment of W-queries is PSPACE-hard.*

As pointed out in remark 3, a bit more nesting yields EXPSPACE-hardness!

# 6   Containment under Dependencies

**The $(*, |)$-Fragment.** This is where our technique of relational translation is most effective. First recall that by translating $|$ away, any union of $(*, |)$-queries is equivalent to a union of $(*)$-queries. Recall also that any set $C$ of $(*, |)$-dependencies is translated into a set $T(C)$ of DEDs. By definition, "the dependencies in $C$ are full" means that the DEDs in $T(C)$ are full.

Since the DEDs in $\Sigma_*$ are all full, the fact that containment of unions of $(*, |)$-queries under full $(*, |)$-dependencies is decidable follows from our extension of the chase to DEDs [11] and the following result:

**Theorem 5.** *Let $C$ be a set of full $(*, |)$-dependencies, and $U_1, U_2$ two unions of $(*, |)$-queries. Let the equivalent unions of $(*)$-queries be $\bigcup_{i=1}^{n} Q_i$, respectively $\bigcup_{j=1}^{m} Q'_j$. Then $U_1$ is contained in $U_2$ under $C$ if and only if for every $1 \le i \le n$ there exists $1 \le j \le m$ such that $T(Q_i)$ is contained in $T(Q'_j)$ under $\Sigma_* \cup T(C)$.*

The proof exploits the work we already did in section 4 and is omitted.

**The $(*, \_)$-Fragment.** As stated, this problem is open. However, we have two variations of it, one decidable, the other one, surprisingly, not.

**Variation 1: V-Dependencies.** Consider a subclass of full $(*, \_)$-dependencies, called V-dependencies, which disallow

- occurrences of the wildcard $\_$ in the premise of the implication, and
- occurrences of $*$ in the conclusion of the implication (see formula (4)).

**Theorem 6.** *Containment of unions of $(*, \_)$-queries under full V-dependencies is decidable.*

The proof is omitted. The decision procedure is basically the same as the one for deciding containment of unions of $(*, \_, l^*)$-queries without dependencies: consider only a finite union of star-free queries, and check containment chasing with $\Sigma_*$ and (as only difference from that case) with the translation of the V-dependencies.

**Variation 2: Attributed Models.** Suppose now that we restrict the full $(*, \_)$-dependencies even more, forcing their atoms to be star-free. We obtain precisely the full DEDs. But assume that we allow a special class of semistructured databases, in which the data graph can be "adorned" by attaching attributes to its nodes. More precisely, attributed models have schema $\mathcal{L}\text{-}Rel \cup \mathcal{A})$, where $\mathcal{A}$ is a set of binary relations names, called *attributes*, who are disjoint from $\mathcal{L}$. The only difference between an attribute and a label is that the former is not included in the interpretation of $\_$, while the latter is [5].

**Theorem 7.** *Containment of a $(*, \_)$-query in a union of $(*, \_)$-queries under full DEDs, but over attributed models, is undecidable.*

The proof is omitted, but very similar to that of theorem 8.

**The $(l^*)$-Fragment.** Surprisingly, this problem is undecidable, despite the syntactic similarity of the $(l^*)$ and $(*)$-fragments. We show a stronger undecidability result, which holds even if the dependencies are star-free, thus corresponding to purely relational full DEDs.

**Theorem 8.** *The containment of an $l^*$-query in a union of $l^*$-queries in the presence of full DEDs is undecidable.*

*Proof:* By reduction from the following problem: Given context-free grammar $G = (\Sigma, N, S, P)$ where $\Sigma$ is the set of terminals (containing at least two symbols), $N$ the nonterminals, $S \in N$ the start symbol, $P \subseteq N \times (\Sigma \cup N)^*$ the productions, and $L(G)$ the language generated by $G$, it is undecidable if $L(G) = \Sigma^*$ [18].

---

[5]  This model is similar in spirit to the XML data model and XPath specification [27], where attribute nodes are not reachable by navigation along the `child` axis.

**The Reduction.** Given context-free grammar $G = (\Sigma, N, S, P)$, we construct an instance of containment as follows:

$$Q \subseteq_D Q_S \cup Q_{cyc} \cup \bigcup_{\sigma_1 \neq \sigma_2 \in \Sigma} Q_{\sigma_1, \sigma_2}$$

$Q() \leftarrow b\ H^*\ e \quad (b, e\ constants, H \notin \Sigma \cup N),$

$Q_{\sigma_1, \sigma_2}() \leftarrow x\ \sigma_1\ y,\ x\ \sigma_2\ y \quad (\sigma_1, \sigma_2 \in \Sigma),$

$Q_S() \leftarrow b\ S\ e,$

$Q_{cyc}() \leftarrow x\ H.H^*\ x$

$D$ consists of the following full, star-free DERPDs (DEDs):

(fn) $\quad \forall x, y, z\ [x\ H\ y \wedge x\ H\ z\ \to y = z],$

(inj) $\quad \forall x, y, z\ [y\ H\ x \wedge z\ H\ x\ \to y = z]$

(symb) $\quad \forall x, y\ [x\ H\ y \to \bigvee_{\sigma \in \Sigma} x\ \sigma\ y],$

$(d_p)\quad \forall x_0, \ldots, x_k\ [\bigwedge_{i=1}^{k} x_{i-1}\ M_i\ x_i \to x_0\ N\ x_k]$

$\quad$ (for every $p = N \to M_1 \ldots M_k \in P$)

Now observe that (5) below holds for any binary queries. In addition, we claim that (6) holds as well, by construction, implying that it is a reduction.

$$Q \not\subseteq_D Q_S \cup Q_{cyc} \cup \bigcup_{\sigma_1 \neq \sigma_2 \in \Sigma} Q_{\sigma_1, \sigma_2}$$

$$\Leftrightarrow \tag{5}$$

$$\exists I\ [I \models D \wedge Q(I) \neq \emptyset \wedge Q_S(I) = \emptyset \wedge Q_{cyc}(I) = \emptyset \wedge \bigwedge_{\sigma_1 \neq \sigma_2 \in \Sigma} Q_{\sigma_1, \sigma_2}(I) = \emptyset]$$

$$\Leftrightarrow \tag{6}$$

$$\exists (w \in \Sigma^*)\ w \notin L(G)$$

The intuition behind the claim is that the instance $I$ which is a counterexample for containment encodes a word $w$ from $\Sigma^* \setminus L(G)$.

**Proof of Claim (6):** $\Rightarrow$: Assuming the standard interpretation of $H^*$, $Q(I) \neq \emptyset$ implies that there exists a path of $H$-edges from b to e in $I$. $Q_{cyc}(I) = \emptyset$ implies that all paths of $H$-edges are simple (no cycles). $I \models (fn) \wedge (inj)$ implies that there is a unique (simple) path of $H$-edges from b to e which we call *the $H$-chain*. $I \models (symb)$ says that every $H$-edge has in parallel with it a $\sigma$-edge for some symbol $\sigma \in \Sigma$, and it follows from $\bigwedge Q_{\sigma_1, \sigma_2}(I) = \emptyset$ that this edge is unique. The $H$-chain thus corresponds to a string $w$ in $\Sigma^*$, of length equal to that of the $H$-chain. Each $H$-edge along the chain corresponds to a position in $w$. We make the following *subclaim*: let $x, y$ be the source, respectively target nodes of a subchain of the $H$-chain, and let $u$ be the corresponding substring of $w$. Let $N$ be any nonterminal such that there exists a derivation of $u$ in $G$ starting from $N$. Then there is an $N$-edge from $x$ to $y$ in $I$. The subclaim is shown by induction on the length of the derivation, and it uses the fact that $I \models \bigwedge_{p \in P}(d_p)$. Together with $Q_S(I) = \emptyset$, the subclaim implies that there is no derivation of $w$ in $G$ starting from the start symbol $S$, in other words $w \notin L(G)$.

$\Leftarrow$: Starting from $w$, build the minimal model $I$ consisting of (i) an $H$-chain of length $|w|$, (ii) the corresponding parallel edges spelling $w$, and (iii) for every subchain from node $x$ to node $y$ corresponding to the substring $u$ of $w$, and every nonterminal $N$ from which there is a derivation of $u$ in $G$, add an $N$-edge from $x$ to $y$. (i) implies $(I \models (fn) \wedge (inj)) \wedge Q_{cyc}(I) = \emptyset \wedge Q(I) \neq \emptyset$, (ii) ensures

$(I \models (symb)) \land \bigwedge Q_{\sigma_1,\sigma_2}(I) = \emptyset$ and (iii) guarantees $I \models \bigwedge_{p \in P}(d_p)$. $w \notin L(G)$ and the minimality of the model enforce $Q_S(I) = \emptyset$. •

## 7    Rewriting with Views under Dependencies

[9] introduces the *chase&backchase (C&B)* algorithm for rewriting queries with views under dependencies [6]. Due to space constraints we can only sketch here the idea and we omit proofs. The strategy of the C&B algorithm is to reduce the problem of rewriting with views to the problem of rewriting under dependencies. If $V_i$ is a view name and $QV_i$ the query that defines it, we capture $V_i$ by writing a pair of inclusion dependencies that essentially say $V_i \subseteq QV_i$ and $QV_i \subseteq V_i$. Denote the set of all such pairs of dependencies with $D_V$ and let us also assume that we rewrite under an additional set $D$ of dependencies.

The C&B algorithm on a query $Q$ has two phases. First the **chase** of $Q$ with $D \cup D_V$. The dependencies in $D_V$ that apply are full, so if those in $D$ are full too, the chase will terminate, with a query we call the **universal plan** $UP$ because it explicitly mentions all views that can be used to answer $Q$. The second phase is the **backchase** which considers all *subqueries* of the universal plan $UP$ (subsets of its conjuncts, mentioning all distinguished variables). The output of the algorithm is the set of those subqueries equivalent to $Q$ for whom the removal of any conjunct compromises this equivalence. We call such queries *minimal* rewritings of $Q$ [7]. The subqueries of the universal plan are tested for equivalence to $Q$ again by chasing (see [11] for an illustration on our motivating example).

**The (∗)-Fragment.** The C&B algorithm applies almost directly here. We should point out that the views may not be binary relations and therefore the rewritings we obtain will not correspond to pure (∗)-queries, but rather may contain relational atoms with the view names. We have the following *completeness* result for the algorithm:

**Theorem 9.** *Let $Q$ be a (∗)-query, $V$ be a set of (∗)-views and $D$ be a set of full (∗)-dependencies. Let $E = \Sigma_* \cup T(D) \cup T(D_V)$ and let $UP = chase_E(T(Q))$ (the chase terminates).*

*Then, for any minimal rewriting $Q'$ of $Q$ with $V$, $T(Q')$ is a subquery of $UP$.*

**The (∗, |)-Fragment.** In this case the query and views translate to unions of conjunctive queries and the (∗, |)-dependencies translate to DEDs. If we plug into the C&B method the extended chase with DEDs (see [11]), we obtain a *union of universal plans* $U_1, \ldots, U_n$ after the chase phase. Each $U_i$ plan is backchased yielding a set of minimal subqueries $S_i$. Every entry in the cartesian product

---

[6] This is done in [9] for *path-conjunctive* queries and dependencies, which generalize the relational setting to a data model with dictionaries and complex values that also captures the OO setting.

[7] Under a *monotonic cost assumption* minimal queries are cheaper.

$S_1 \times \ldots \times S_n$ corresponds to a set of queries whose union is a rewriting of $\mathcal{T}(Q)$. We call this extension of the C&B algorithm the *disjunctive C&B* algorithm. We say that a union of queries is *reduced* if all members are minimal and none of them is contained in another member. The following result implies that the disjunctive C&B algorithm is *complete* for the $(*, |)$-fragment.

**Theorem 10.** *Given a* $(*, |)$*-query $Q$, and one of its reduced rewritings $Q' = Q'_1 \cup \ldots \cup Q'_m$, for every $1 \leq j \leq m$, there is some $1 \leq i \leq n$ such that $\mathcal{T}(Q'_j)$ is a subquery of $U_i$.*

## 8   Conclusions

In this work, we propose a classification of conjunctive regular queries (CRPQ) and the associated constraint languages by the expressivity of the regular path expressions allowed in the conjuncts. We have studied the complexity of containment, with or without integrity constraints for the various fragments proposed. For certain fragments we have also studied the completeness of a specific kind of algorithm (chase & backchase) for rewriting with views under constraints.

A subtle observation that can be made based on the results we have obtained is that _ is "more" than the union (the | actually) of the labels that occur in a given context. Indeed, one might attempt to contradict the decidability for the $(*, |)$-fragment by reducing $(*, \_)$-queries and -dependencies to $(*, |)$-queries and -dependencies, using a translation like $\_ = l_1 | \ldots | l_n | f$ where $l_1, \ldots, l_n$ are all the labels mentioned in the queries and dependencies and $f$ is a fresh label. This attempt fails because it does not capture the equivalence $* = \bigcup_{n \geq 0} \_^n$, which in turn is essential for the undecidability result. Of course, the correct translation an infinite disjunction of labels takes us out of the languages considered here.

We conclude that as a query language feature regular expressions are surprisingly "naughty", in the sense that adding supposedly innocuous operators to some fragments causes surprising increases in complexity. (For example, adding either $*$ or $\_$ to the fragment of conjunctive queries does not affect complexity of containment –still NP–, but adding *both* raises the complexity to $\Pi_2^p$.)

We are leaving some interesting problems open. One is the upper bound on containment in the W fragment. Another open problem is the decidability of containment under constraints in the $(*, \_)$-fragment. The reader can see that several open questions can be formulated about rewriting with views in certain fragments.

Since the submission of this work, we have applied our results to conjunctive queries over XML documents with XPath [27] expressions in their conjuncts [10].

## References

1. S. Abiteboul, P. Buneman, and D. Suciu. *Data on the Web: From Relations to Semistructured Data and XML*. Morgan Kaufman, 1999.
2. S. Abiteboul, R. Hull, and V. Vianu. *Foundations of Databases*. Addison-Wesley, 1995.

3. C. Beeri and M. Vardi. A proof procedure for data dependencies. *JACM*, 31(4), 1984.
4. D. Calvanese, G. De Giacomo, and M. Lenzerini. On the Decidability of Query Containment under Constraints In *PODS*, 1998.
5. D. Calvanese, G. De Giacomo, M. Lenzerini, and M. Vardi. Rewriting of Regular Expressions and Regular Path Queries. In *PODS*, 1999.
6. D. Calvanese, G. De Giacomo, M. Lenzerini, and M. Vardi. Containment of conjunctive regular path queries with inverse. In *KR*, 2000.
7. Ashok Chandra and Philip Merlin. Optimal implementation of conjunctive queries in relational data bases. In *STOC*, 1977.
8. A. Deutsch, M. Fernandez, D. Florescu, A. Levy, and D. Suciu. A Query Language for XML. In *WWW8*, 1999.
9. Alin Deutsch, Lucian Popa, and Val Tannen. Physical Data Independence, Constraints and Optimization with Universal Plans. In *VLDB*,1999.
10. A. Deutsch and V. Tannen. Containment and Integrity Constraints for XPath Fragments. In *KRDB 2001*.
11. A. Deutsch and V. Tannen. Optimization Properties for Classes of Conjunctive Regular Path Queries. Technical Report MS-CIS-01-20, University of Pennsylvania, 2001. Available from `http://db.cis.upenn.edu/cgi-bin/Person.perl?adeutsch`
12. M. Fernandez, D. Florescu, J. Kang, A. Levy, and D. Suciu. Strudel: A web-site management system. In *SIGMOD*, 1997.
13. Daniela Florescu, Alon Y. Levy, and Dan Suciu. Query containment for conjunctive queries with regular expressions. In *PODS*, 1998.
14. E. Grädel. On the restraining power of guards. *J. of Symbolic Logic*, 64, 1999.
15. Gösta Grahne and Alberto O. Mendelzon. Tableau techniques for querying information sources through global schemas. In *ICDT*, 1999.
16. G. Grahne and A. Thomo. An optimization technique for answering regular path queries. In *WebDB*, 2000.
17. G. Grahne and A. Thomo. Algebraic rewritings for regular path queries. *ICDT'01*.
18. J. Hopcroft and J. Ullman. *Introduction to automata theory, languages, and computation*. Addison-Wesley, 1979.
19. Frank Neven and Thomas Schwentick. Query automata. In *PODS*, 1999.
20. Frank Neven and Thomas Schwentick. Expressive and efficient pattern languages for tree-structured data. In *PODS*, 2000.
21. C. Papadimitriou. *Computational Complexity*. Addison-Wesley, 1994.
22. L. Popa, A. Deutsch, A. Sahuguet, and V. Tannen. A Chase Too Far? *SIGMOD* 2000.
23. Lucian Popa and Val Tannen. An equational chase for path-conjunctive queries, constraints, and views. In *ICDT*, 1999.
24. Yehoushua Sagiv and Mihalis Yannakakis. Equivalences among relational expressions with the union and difference operators. *Journal of the ACM*, 27, 1980.
25. P. van Emde Boas. The convenience of tilings. In A. Sorbi(Ed.) *Complexity, Logic, and Recursion Theory*, pp. 331–363, 2000.
26. W3C. Extensible Markup Language (XML) 1.0. W3C Recommendation 10-February-1998. Available from `http://www.w3.org/TR/1998/REC-xml-19980210`.
27. W3C. XML Path Language (XPath) 1.0. W3C Recommendation 16 November 1999. Available from `http://www.w3.org/TR/xpath`.
28. M. Yannakakis and C. Papadimitriou. Algebraic dependencies. *JCSS*, 25, 1982.

# View-Based Query Answering
# and Query Containment
# over Semistructured Data

Diego Calvanese[1], Giuseppe De Giacomo[1],
Maurizio Lenzerini[1], and Moshe Y. Vardi[2]

[1] Dipartimento di Informatica e Sistemistica, Università di Roma "La Sapienza"
Via Salaria 113, I-00198 Roma, Italy
lastname@dis.uniroma1.it
[2] Department of Computer Science, Rice University, P.O. Box 1892
Houston, TX 77251-1892, USA
vardi@cs.rice.edu

**Abstract.** The basic querying mechanism over semistructured data, namely regular path queries, asks for all pairs of objects that are connected by a path conforming to a regular expression. We consider conjunctive two-way regular path queries ($C2RPQ_c$'s), which extend regular path queries with two features. First, they add the inverse operator, which allows for expressing navigations in the database that traverse the edges both backward and forward. Second, they allow for using conjunctions of atoms, where each atom specifies that a regular path query with inverse holds between two terms, where each term is either a variable or a constant. For such queries we address the problem of view-based query answering, which amounts to computing the result of a query only on the basis of a set of views. More specifically, we present the following results: (1) We exhibit a mutual reduction between query containment and the recognition problem for view-based query answering for $C2RPQ_c$'s, i.e., checking whether a given tuple is in the certain answer to a query. Based on such a result, we can show that the problem of view-based query answering for $C2RPQ_c$'s is EXPSPACE-complete. (2) By exploiting techniques based on alternating two-way automata we show that for the restricted class of tree two-way regular path queries (in which the links between variables form a tree), query containment and view-based query answering are, rather surprisingly, in PSPACE (and hence, PSPACE-complete). (3) We present a technique to obtain view-based query answering algorithms that compute the whole set of tuples in the certain answer, instead of requiring to check each tuple separately. The technique is parametric wrt the query language, and can be applied both to $C2RPQ_c$'s and to tree-queries.

## 1 Introduction

Semistructured data are usually modeled as labeled graphs, and methods for extracting information from semistructured data incorporate special querying mechanisms that are not common in traditional database systems [1]. One such

G. Grahne and G. Ghelli (Eds.): DBPL 2001, LNCS 2397, pp. 40–61, 2002.

basic mechanism is the one of regular path queries (RPQs), which retrieve all pairs of nodes in the graph connected by a path conforming to a regular expression [11,3]. Regular expressions provide a (limited) form of recursion, which is used in regular path queries to flexibly navigate the database graph.

In order to increase the expressiveness of RPQs, in this paper we consider two basic additions. First, we add to RPQs the inverse operator, which allows for expressing navigations in the database that traverse the edges both backward and forward. Second, we extend RPQs with the possibility of using conjunctions of atoms, where each atom specifies that one regular path query with inverse holds between two terms, where each term is either a variable or a constant. Notably, several authors argue that these kinds of extensions are essential for making RPQs useful in real settings (see for example [10,11,44]). The resulting queries will be called *conjunctive two-way regular path queries* (C2RPQ$_c$'s), and capture the core of virtually all query languages for semistructured data [11,3,32], including the ones for XML [29,19]. In this paper, we consider also a restricted form of C2RPQ$_c$'s, called *tree two-way regular path queries* (T2RPQ$_c$'s), in which the body of the query has the structure of a tree, if we view each variable as a node and each atom in the query as an edge. T2RPQ$_c$'s are a generalization of several subclasses of queries, including generalized path expressions [11,3] and branching path queries [43,45], which have been studied extensively both in semistructured and XML data. Notably, XPath expressions [26] can be captured by T2RPQ$_c$'s in which the transitive closure operator is used in a limited way.

Semistructured data pose challenging problems to the research on databases [57]. Among them, reasoning on queries and views is expected to be particularly difficult, due to the presence of recursion in RPQs. For example, containment of Datalog queries with no limitations on recursion, is undecidable [49]. Here, we concentrate on two reasoning services involving queries that are relevant in database management. The first one is checking *containment*, i.e., verifying whether, for every database, one query yields a subset of the result of another one. The second one is *view-based query answering*, which amounts to computing the answer to a query having information only on the extension of a set of views. Both problems are crucial in several contexts, such as information integration [52], data warehousing [56], query optimization [23], mobile computing [6], and maintaining physical data independence [51]. Indeed, they have been investigated and largely solved for relational databases. Instead, for the case of semistructured data and XML, the above problems are largely unexplored and fundamental results are still missing [55].

Most of the results on query containment concern relational conjunctive queries and their extensions [22,37,53,47,24,53]. In particular, [22] shows that containment of conjunctive queries is NP-complete. One interesting special case for which containment is tractable is when the right-hand side query has bounded treewidth [25], and, in particular, when it is acyclic. Other papers consider the case of conjunctive query containment in the presence of various types of constraints [5,28,20,41,42,12]. Conjunctive RPQs without inverse have been studied in [33], where an EXPSPACE algorithm for query containment in this class is presented. In [16], it is shown that containment for conjunctive two-way regular path queries without constants is EXPSPACE-complete. The complexity of query containment for conjunctive RPQs has been studied in [30] under various restrictions on the allowed classes of regular expressions.

View-based query answering has been investigated in [40,46] for the case of conjunctive queries (with or without arithmetic comparisons), in [4] for disjunctive views, in [50,27,35] for queries with aggregates, in [31] for recursive queries and nonrecursive views, and in [13,7] for queries expressed in Description Logics. Comprehensive frameworks for view-based query answering, as well as several interesting results for various query languages, are presented in [34,2].

Recently view-based query processing has been studied for the case of RPQs. It has been shown that computing the RPQ which is the maximal rewriting of an RPQ wrt a set of RPQ views can be done in 2EXPTIME, and verifying the existence of a nonempty rewriting is EXPSPACE-complete [14]. View-based query answering for RPQs is PSPACE-complete in combined complexity and coNP-complete in data complexity [15]. In [17] the above results on view-based query rewriting and query answering have been extended to 2RPQs, i.e., RPQs extended with the inverse operator. The relationship between view-based query answering and query rewriting has been studied in [18].

None of the above results apply to C2RPQ$_c$'s or T2RPQ$_c$'s. Thus, decidability and complexity of query containment and view-based query answering is still an open problem for such queries.

Our goal is to devise techniques and characterize the computational complexity of the two problems for the two classes of queries. In particular, we present the following main contributions:

1. We exhibit a mutual reduction between query containment and view-based query answering for the case of C2RPQ$_c$'s (see Section 3). The reduction applies also to the case where the query in the right-hand side of the containment, and, respectively, the query to be answered using the views, is a T2RPQ$_c$.

2. Based on the technique presented in [16], we devise in Section 4 an EXPSPACE algorithm for view-based query answering for C2RPQ$_c$'s, thus showing that the problem is EXPSPACE-complete. By virtue of the reduction illustrated in Section 3, the same complexity result holds for query containment. This is the first result showing that view-based query answering is decidable in the case where both the query and the views are expressed in a query language for semistructured data with at least the power of conjunctive queries with constants.

3. By exploiting techniques based on alternating two-way automata we show in Section 5 that, in the case where the views are C2RPQ$_c$'s and the query to be answered is a T2RPQ$_c$, view-based query answering is PSPACE-complete. This represents a provable exponential improvement wrt the case of C2RPQ$_c$'s. The same bound holds for query containment when the right-hand side query is a T2RPQ$_c$. These results are rather surprising in view of the fact that, while tree automata seem the natural formal tool for tree-queries, containment of such automata is EXPTIME-complete [48].

4. View-based query answering has been generally tackled in the form of the so-called *recognition problem*: the input includes a tuple and the goal is to check whether such a tuple is a certain answer to the query, i.e., whether the tuple satisfies the query in every database coherent with the views. However, traditional query answering consists of retrieving *all* tuples satisfying the query. A further question addressed in this paper is whether we can devise a method to characterize the whole set of certain answers to a query, rather than just solving the recognition problem tuple by tuple. We present a solution to this problem, both for the case of C2RPQ$_c$'s (Section 4.4) and for T2RPQ$_c$'s (Section 5.4), by illustrating how to compute a representation of the whole set of certain answers. The method computes such a representation with the same computational complexity as the corresponding methods for checking whether a tuple is a certain answer. To the best of our knowledge, this is the first technique that deals with view-based query answering rather than checking if a tuple is a certain answer.

The result on T2RPQ$_c$'s shows that C2RPQ$_c$'s exhibit a behavior analogous to the case of ordinary conjunctive queries: cycles in the right-hand side query constitute a source of complexity for containment checking [58]. Observe that it is the query structure and not the database structure that determines the complexity, since, containment (and hence query answering) of conjunctions of RPQs is already EXPSPACE-hard over linear databases [16].

In the next section we introduce all concepts and definitions used in the subsequent sections. Section 6 concludes the paper, by pointing out several possible extensions of our work.

## 2  Databases and Queries

We consider a *semistructured database* (DB) $\mathcal{B}$ as an edge-labeled graph $(\mathcal{D}, \mathcal{E})$, where $\mathcal{D}$ is the set of nodes (representing objects) and $\mathcal{E}$ is the set of edges (representing binary relations) labeled with elements of an alphabet $\Delta$ [1]. We denote an edge from $x$ to $y$ labeled by $p$ with $x \xrightarrow{p} y$. We use constants as names for nodes, and we impose the *unique name assumption*, i.e., we disallow two constants to denote the same node. In the following, we do not distinguish between a node and the constant naming it.

The basic querying mechanism on a DB is that of *regular path queries* (RPQs). An RPQ $R$ is expressed as a regular expression or a finite automaton, and computes the set of pairs of nodes of the DB connected by a path that conforms to the regular language $L(R)$ defined by $R$. We consider queries that extend regular path queries with both the inverse operator, and the possibility of using conjunctions, variables, and constants.

Formally, let $\Sigma = \Delta \cup \{p^- \mid p \in \Delta\}$ be the alphabet including a new symbol $p^-$ for each $p$ in $\Delta$. Intuitively, $p^-$ denotes the inverse of the binary relation

---

[1] All the techniques presented in this paper can be adapted to the case of *rooted DBs*, i.e., to the case where the DB is an edge-labeled rooted graph (see Section 6), and to the case where nodes are labeled.

*p*. If $r \in \Sigma$, then we use $r^-$ to denote the *inverse* of $r$, i.e., if $r$ is $p$, then $r^-$ is $p^-$, and if $r$ is $p^-$, then $r^-$ is $p$. *Two-way regular path queries* (2RPQs) are expressed by means of regular expressions or finite automata over $\Sigma$ [16,17]. Thus, in contrast with RPQs, 2RPQs may use also the inverse $p^-$ of $p$, for each $p \in \Delta$. When evaluated over a DB $\mathcal{B}$, a 2RPQ $R$ computes the set $ans(R, \mathcal{B})$ of pairs of nodes connected by a semipath that conforms to the regular language $L(R)$ defined by $R$. A *semipath* in $\mathcal{B}$ from $x$ to $y$ is a sequence of the form $(y_1, r_1, y_2, r_2, y_3, \ldots, y_q, r_q, y_{q+1})$, where $q \geq 0$, $y_1 = x$, $y_{q+1} = y$, and for each $i \in \{1, \ldots, q\}$, either $y_i \xrightarrow{r_i} y_{i+1}$ or $y_{i+1} \xrightarrow{r_i^-} y_i$ is in $\mathcal{B}$. The semipath *conforms to* $R$ if $r_1 \cdots r_q \in L(R)$. The semipath is *simple* if each $y_i$, for $i \in \{2, \ldots, q\}$, is a node that does not occur elsewhere in the semipath.

Finally, we add to 2RPQs the possibility of using conjunctions of atoms, where each atom specifies that a regular path query with inverse holds between two terms, where a term is either a variable or a constant. More precisely, a *conjunctive two-way regular path query with constants* (C2RPQ$_c$) $Q$ is a formula of the form

$$Q(x_1, \ldots, x_n) \leftarrow y_1 \, E_1 \, y_2 \wedge \cdots \wedge y_{2m-1} \, E_m \, y_{2m}$$

where $x_1, \ldots, x_n$ are variables, called *distinguished variables*, $y_1, \ldots, y_{2m}$ are either variables or constants, and $E_1, \ldots, E_m$ are 2RPQs.

We consider also a restricted form of C2RPQ$_c$'s, called *tree two-way regular path queries* (T2RPQ$_c$'s). In a T2RPQ$_c$, the body of the query has the structure of a tree, if we view each variable and each constant as a node and each atom $y \, E \, y'$ as an edge from $y$ to $y'$, and consider different occurrences of constants as different nodes of the tree.

In the following we assume that the variables in the head of a query are pairwise distinct. This assumption can be made without loss of generality, since, if a variable $x$ occurs twice in the head, we can replace one of the occurrences by a fresh variable $y$ and introduce the (equality) atom $x \, \varepsilon \, y$ in the body. Also, we assume that each distinguished variable occurs among $y_1, \ldots, y_{2m}$, since we can always add to the body an atom $x_i \, \varepsilon \, x_i$. For the same reason we can avoid constants in the head of a query. Notice that adding such atoms to the body does not destroy the tree structure of a T2RPQ$_c$.

The *answer set* $ans(Q, \mathcal{B})$ to a C2RPQ$_c$ $Q$ over a DB $\mathcal{B} = (\mathcal{D}, \mathcal{E})$ is the set of tuples $(d_1, \ldots, d_n)$ of nodes of $\mathcal{B}$ such that there is a mapping $\sigma$ from the variables and the constants of $Q$ to $\mathcal{D}$ with

- $\sigma(x_i) = d_i$ for every distinguished variable $x_i$,
- $\sigma(c) = c$ for every constant $c$, and
- $(\sigma(y), \sigma(y')) \in ans(E, \mathcal{B})$ for every conjunct $y \, E \, y'$ in $Q$.

Given two C2RPQ$_c$'s $Q_1$ and $Q_2$, we say that $Q_1$ is *contained* in $Q_2$, written $Q_1 \subseteq Q_2$, if for every DB $\mathcal{B}$, $ans(Q_1, \mathcal{B}) \subseteq ans(Q_2, \mathcal{B})$. The problem of *query containment* (QC) is checking whether one query is contained in another one. Obviously, $Q_1 \not\subseteq Q_2$ iff there is a *counterexample* DB to $Q_1 \subseteq Q_2$, i.e., a DB $\mathcal{B}$ with a tuple in $ans(Q_1, \mathcal{B})$ and not in $ans(Q_2, \mathcal{B})$.

In view-based query answering, we consider a DB that is accessible only through a set of C2RPQ$_c$ views $\mathcal{V} = \{V_1, \ldots, V_k\}$. Each view $V_i$ is characterized by its definition $def(V_i)$ in terms of a C2RPQ$_c$, and by its extension $ext(V_i)$ in terms of a set of constant tuples. We denote the set of constants appearing either in $ext(V_1) \cup \cdots \cup ext(V_k)$ or in $def(V_1) \cup \cdots \cup def(V_k)$ by $\mathcal{D}_V$. We say that a DB $\mathcal{B}$ is *consistent with a view* $V_i$ if all tuples in its extension satisfy the definition of the view in $\mathcal{B}$, i.e., if $ext(V_i) \subseteq ans(def(V_i), \mathcal{B})$ [2]. We say that $\mathcal{B}$ is *consistent with* $\mathcal{V}$ if it is consistent with each view $V_i \in \mathcal{V}$.

Given a set $\mathcal{V} = \{V_1, \ldots, V_k\}$ of C2RPQ$_c$ views, a C2RPQ$_c$ $Q$ of arity $n$ whose constants are in $\mathcal{D}_V$, and an $n$-tuple $\vec{t}$ of constants[3] in $\mathcal{D}_V$, the problem of *view-based query answering* (QA) consists in deciding whether $\vec{t}$ is a *certain answer* to $Q$ wrt $\mathcal{V}$, written $\vec{t} \in cert(Q, \mathcal{V})$, i.e., whether $\vec{t} \in ans(Q, \mathcal{B})$, for every DB $\mathcal{B}$ that is consistent with $\mathcal{V}$. Given a set $\mathcal{V} = \{V_1, \ldots, V_k\}$ of C2RPQ$_c$ views, and a C2RPQ$_c$ $Q$ of arity $n$, the problem of *computing the set of certain answers* consists in characterizing all $n$-tuples of constants in $\mathcal{D}_V$ that are certain answers to $Q$ wrt $\mathcal{V}$. As for the computational complexity of view-based query answering, we concentrate on *combined complexity*, i.e., we measure the complexity with respect to the size of the query, the view expressions, and the data in the view extensions.

## 3  Relationship between QA and QC

There is a strong connection between QA and QC. In particular, [2] discusses mutual reductions between the two problems (Theorem 4.1 in [2]). Next we show that such reductions can be adapted to our case.

For the reduction from QA to QC, consider an instance of QA with C2RPQ$_c$ views $\mathcal{V} = \{V_1, \ldots, V_k\}$, definitions $def(V_i)$ and extensions $ext(V_i)$, for $i \in [1..k]$, where we ask whether the tuple $(c_1, \ldots, c_n)$ is in the certain answer to the C2RPQ$_c$ $Q$ of arity $n$. From such an instance, we construct a C2RPQ$_c$ $Q_\mathcal{V}$ such that $Q_\mathcal{V} \subseteq Q$ iff $(c_1, \ldots, c_n) \in cert(Q, \mathcal{V})$. We define $Q_\mathcal{V}$ as follows:

$$Q_\mathcal{V}(x_1, \ldots, x_n) \leftarrow x_1 \varepsilon c_1 \wedge \cdots \wedge x_n \varepsilon c_n \wedge \bigwedge_h \alpha_h$$

where $x_i \varepsilon c_i$ denotes an equality between the distinguished variable $x_i$ and the constant $c_i$, and we have one $\alpha_h$ for each view $V_i$ (of arity $n_i$) and each tuple $(d_1, \ldots, d_{n_i})$ in $ext(V_i)$. Such an $\alpha_h$ is obtained from the body of $def(V_i)$ by replacing the distinguished variables $x_1, \ldots, x_{n_i}$ respectively by $(d_1, \ldots, d_{n_i})$ and by replacing the non-distinguished variables with fresh ones. Note that, if the query $Q$ in QA is a T2RPQ$_c$, then we obtain an instance of QC in which the right-hand side query is a T2RPQ$_c$.

By using the same line of reasoning as in the proof of Theorem 4.1 in [2] we get:

---

[2] As often done, we assume views to be *sound*, but not necessarily *complete* [2,15].

[3] We use $\vec{t}$ to denote tuples of constants of the appropriate arity, and $\vec{t}[i]$ to denote the $i$-th component of tuple $\vec{t}$.

**Theorem 1.** *Let $Q_{\mathcal{V}}$ be defined as above. Then $(c_1, \ldots, c_n) \in cert(Q, \mathcal{V})$ iff $Q_{\mathcal{V}} \subseteq Q$.*

The size of the QC instance obtained as specified above is polynomial with respect to the size of the QA instance. Therefore, we can conclude that QA is polynomially reducible to QC.

For the reduction from QC to QA, consider an instance of QC asking whether $Q_1 \subseteq Q_2$, where $Q_1(\vec{z}) \leftarrow \beta_1(\vec{z}, \vec{y}_1)$ and $Q_2(\vec{z}) \leftarrow \beta_2(\vec{z}, \vec{y}_2)$. From such an instance of QC, we construct an instance of QA as follows. We have only one view $V_{Q_1}$, whose extension is constituted by a single tuple $(c_1, \ldots, c_n)$ with the constants $c_1, \ldots, c_n$ not occurring in $Q_1$ and $Q_2$, and whose definition is:

$$V_{Q_1}(x_1, \ldots, x_n) \leftarrow x_1 \varepsilon c_1 \wedge \cdots \wedge x_n \varepsilon c_n \wedge \beta_1(\vec{z}, \vec{y}) \wedge \bigwedge_{z_i \in \vec{z}} z_i \, p_i^{new} \, c_1$$

where $x_1, \ldots, x_n$ are fresh variables, $\beta_1(\vec{z}, \vec{y})$ is the body of $Q_1$, and $p_i^{new}$ are new symbols that do not appear in the alphabet of $Q_1$ and $Q_2$. The query we want to answer with the view is:

$$Q_{Q_2}(x_1, \ldots, x_n) \leftarrow x_1 \varepsilon c_1 \wedge \cdots \wedge x_n \varepsilon c_n \wedge \beta_2(\vec{z}, \vec{y}) \wedge \bigwedge_{z_i \in \vec{z}} z_i \, p_i^{new} \, c_1$$

where $x_1, \ldots, x_n$ are fresh variables, and $\beta_2(\vec{z}, \vec{y})$ is the body of $Q_2$. Finally, we ask whether $(c_1, \ldots, c_n) \in cert(Q_{Q_2}, \{V_{Q_1}\})$. Note that, if $Q_2$ is a T2RPQ$_c$, then we obtain an instance of QA in which the query to answer using the views is a T2RPQ$_c$.

Again, by using the same line of reasoning as in the proof of Theorem 4.1 in [2] we get:

**Theorem 2.** *Let $V_{Q_1}$ and $Q_{Q_2}$ be defined as above. Then $Q_1 \subseteq Q_2$ iff $(c_1, \ldots, c_n) \in cert(Q_{Q_2}, \{V_{Q_1}\})$.*

It is easy to see that the above construction provides a polynomial reduction from QC to QA.

## 4   QA and QC for C2RPQ$_c$'s

The technique for QA for C2RPQ$_c$'s we present is based on searching for a "counterexample DB" to the QA problem, i.e., a DB consistent with the views in which the given tuple does not satisfy the query. For our purposes, it is crucial to show that we can limit our search to counterexample DBs of a special form, called canonical DBs. Such DBs can be represented as finite words and we exploit finite word automata. In particular, we make use of standard one-way automata (1NFA) and two-way automata (2NFA) [36].

## 4.1   Canonical Databases

Let $\mathcal{D}_V$ be the set of constants appearing in the extensions of the views. We introduce a set $\mathcal{D}_E$ of new constants, called *skolem constants*, one constant $y_{V,\vec{t}}$ for each view $V \in \mathcal{V}$, each non-distinguished variable $y$ appearing in $def(V)$, and each tuple $\vec{t}$ in $ext(V)$. On such constants we do not enforce the unique name assumption, i.e., we may have two skolem constants denoting the same node. Let $\mathcal{D}_N = \mathcal{D}_V \cup \mathcal{D}_E$. In the following, to distinguish actual constants from skolem constants, we refer to the former as *proper constants*. We use the term *constants* for both proper and skolem constants.

**Definition 1.** *Given a set $\mathcal{V}$ of C2RPQ$_c$ views, a DB is called $\mathcal{V}$-canonical if it is composed of a set of simple semipaths $(\alpha, r_1, x_1, \dots, x_{n-1}, r_n, \beta)$, one for each view $V \in \mathcal{V}$, each tuple $\vec{t} \in ext(V)$, and each atom of the form $y E y'$ in $def(V)$, where*

- *$\alpha$ is $\vec{t}[i]$ if $y$ is the $i$-th distinguished variable in $def(V)$, $\alpha$ is $y$ if $y$ is a proper constant, and $\alpha$ is $y_{\vec{t},V}$ if $y$ is a non-distinguished variable (similarly for $\beta$),*
- *$r_1 \cdots r_n \in L(E)$, and*
- *$x_1, \dots, x_{n-1}$ are not in $\mathcal{D}_N$ and do not occur in any other semipath in the set.*

The following theorem, which can be shown similarly to an analogous theorem in [16], provides an important characterization of QA in terms of $\mathcal{V}$-canonical DBs.

**Theorem 3.** *Let $Q$ be a C2RPQ$_c$ of arity $n$, $\mathcal{V}$ a set of views, and $\vec{t}$ a tuple of proper constants. If there exists a DB $\mathcal{B}$ that is consistent with $\mathcal{V}$ such that $\vec{t} \notin ans(Q, \mathcal{B})$, then there exists a $\mathcal{V}$-canonical DB $\mathcal{B}'$ that is consistent with $\mathcal{V}$ and such that $\vec{t} \notin ans(Q, \mathcal{B}')$.*

By Theorem 3, we can restrict the search for a counterexample DB to $\mathcal{V}$-canonical DBs only. The basic idea that allows us to exploit automata is that we can represent such DBs in a linearized form as special words, and use two-way automata to check that candidate counterexample DBs satisfy all required conditions [16,17].

More precisely, each $\mathcal{V}$-canonical DB $\mathcal{B}$ can be represented as a word $w_{\mathcal{B}}$ over the alphabet $\Sigma \cup \mathcal{D}_N \cup \{\$\}$ of the form

$$\$d_1 w_1 d_2 \$ d_3 w_2 d_4 \$ \cdots \$ d_{2m-1} w_m d_{2m} \$$$

where $m$ is some positive integer, $d_1, \dots, d_{2m}$ are in $\mathcal{D}_N$, $w_i \in \Sigma^*$, and the $\$$ acts as a separator. In particular, each symbol $d_i$ represents a node of $\mathcal{B}$, and $w_{\mathcal{B}}$ consists of one subword $d_{2i-1} w_i d_{2i}$, for each simple semipath conforming to $w_i$ in $\mathcal{B}$, from the constant $d_{2i-1}$ to the constant $d_{2i}$. Observe that we may have that $w_i = \varepsilon$, and in such a case $d_{2i-1}$ and $d_{2i}$ represent the same node, which is denoted by two different constants. Obviously, this can be the case only if at least one of $d_{2i-1}$ and $d_{2i}$ is a skolem constant, otherwise the unique name assumption is violated.

## 4.2   Automaton Accepting Canonical DBs

To verify whether $w_\mathcal{B}$ represents a DB $\mathcal{B}$ that is consistent with the views $\mathcal{V}$, we construct for each view $V \in \mathcal{V}$, each tuple $\vec{t} \in ext(V)$, and each atom $R$ of the form $y\,E\,y'$ in $def(V)$, an 1NFA $A_{V,\vec{t},R}$ that accepts the language $\$\cdot\alpha\cdot E\cdot\beta$, where $\alpha$ is $\vec{t}[i]$ if $y$ is the $i$-th distinguished variable in $def(V)$, $\alpha$ is $y$ if $y$ is a proper constant, and $\alpha$ is $y_{V,\vec{t}}$ if $y$ is a non-distinguished variable (similarly for $\beta$).

We now construct a 1NFA $A_\mathcal{V}^-$ that accepts the concatenation of the languages accepted by all 1NFAs $A_{V,\vec{t},R}$, in some fixed order (chosen arbitrarily), and of the language $(\$\cdot \sum_{y\in\mathcal{D}_E,y'\in\mathcal{D}_N}(y\cdot y'))^*\cdot\$$, representing additional equalities between skolem constants in $\mathcal{D}_E$ and (skolem or proper) constants in $\mathcal{D}_N = \mathcal{D}_V \cup \mathcal{D}_E$. The 1NFA $A_\mathcal{V}^-$ accepts words representing candidate counterexample DBs, in which however the unique name assumption for proper constants is not enforced.

We then construct a 2NFA $A_{\neg UNA}$ that accepts words of the form above in which the unique name assumption is violated by equating two distinct proper constants (taking into account also transitivity and symmetry of equality). To do so we exploit the ability of 2NFAs to: (i) move on the word both forward and backward; (ii) "jump" from one position in the word with a certain symbol to any other position (either preceding or succeeding) with the same symbol [17].

$A_{\neg UNA}$ is the disjoint union of one 2NFA $A_{c,c'} = (\Sigma, S, s_0, \delta, \{c'\})$ for each pair of distinct proper constants $c$ and $c'$ in $\mathcal{D}_V$, where $S = \mathcal{D}_N \cup \{s_0, s^\hookrightarrow, s^\hookleftarrow\}$, and $\delta$ is defined as follows:

1. Starting from the initial state, the automaton searches for the symbol $c$, and when it finds it, it switches to the corresponding state. When it is in the final state $c'$, it moves to the end of the word and accepts.

$$(c,0) \in \delta(s_0, c)$$
$$(s_0, 1) \in \delta(s_0, \ell) \quad \text{for each } \ell \in \Sigma$$
$$(c', 1) \in \delta(c', \ell) \quad \text{for each } \ell \in \Sigma$$

2. When in a state corresponding to a constant, the automaton moves either forward or backward. For each $d \in \mathcal{D}_N$, and for each $\ell \in \Sigma$

$$(d, 1) \in \delta(d, \ell)$$
$$(d, -1) \in \delta(d, \ell)$$

3. When the automaton reaches a constant $d_1$ while it is in the state corresponding to $d_1$, and $d_2$ appears immediately to the right of $d_1$, the automaton may switch to the state corresponding to $d_2$. Similarly, if $d_2$ appears immediately to the left of $d_1$. For each $d_1, d_2 \in \mathcal{D}_N$

$$(s^\hookrightarrow, 1) \in \delta(d_1, d_1)$$
$$(d_2, 0) \in \delta(s^\hookrightarrow, d_2)$$
$$(s^\hookleftarrow, -1) \in \delta(d_1, d_1)$$
$$(d_2, 0) \in \delta(s^\hookleftarrow, d_2)$$

Let $A_\mathcal{V}$ be the 1NFA obtained as the intersection of $A_\mathcal{V}^-$ and of the complement of $A_{\neg UNA}$. $A_\mathcal{V}$ accepts words representing $\mathcal{V}$-canonical DBs consistent with the views in which the unique name assumption is satisfied. We call a word $w$ accepted by $A_\mathcal{V}$ a $\mathcal{V}$-*word*.

## 4.3   Automaton for a Single Tuple

Let $Q(\vec{x})$ be a C2RPQ$_c$ of arity $n$ with distinguished variables $\vec{x}$. Adapting the construction in [16], we construct a 1NFA $A_{Q(\vec{t})}$ that, given a tuple $\vec{t}$ of proper constants, accepts the words representing DBs $\mathcal{B}$ such that $\vec{t} \in ans(Q(\vec{x}), \mathcal{B})$. To define $A_{Q(\vec{t})}$, we have to check for each 2RPQ in $Q(\vec{t})$, i.e., the query obtained by substituting the distinguished variables $\vec{x}$ with $\vec{t}$, whether the corresponding atom is satisfied. To check whether a pair of constants $(d_1, d_2)$ explicitly appearing in a word representing a DB $\mathcal{B}$, is in the answer to a 2RPQ $E$, one can again exploit the ability of 2NFAs to move back and forth on a word and to jump from one position in the word representing a constant to any other position in the word representing the same constant.

Now, observe that, to check whether a certain tuple $\vec{t}$ of proper constants is in $ans(Q(\vec{x}), \mathcal{B})$, the distinguished variables $\vec{x}$ of $Q(\vec{x})$ are mapped to the constants of $\vec{t}$, which explicitly appear in the word representing the linearized DB, while the non-distinguished variables may be mapped to any node of the DB, i.e., to any symbol in the corresponding word. Hence, for each atom $d\, E\, d'$ of $Q(\vec{t})$ involving only proper constants assigned to the distinguished variables, we can directly construct a 2NFA that checks whether the atom is satisfied. On the other hand, for an atom involving a non-distinguished variable $y$, we need to explicitly represent where $y$ is mapped to in the word, since we have to guarantee that all occurrences of $y$ in distinct atoms are mapped to the same node. We represent such mappings of non-distinguished variables of $Q(\vec{t})$ as *annotations* of $\mathcal{V}$-words. More precisely, the $\mathcal{V}$-word $\$\ell_1 \cdots \ell_r\$$, with each symbol $\ell_i \neq \$$ annotated with a set $\gamma_i$ of non-distinguished variables, is represented by the word $\$(\ell_1, \gamma_1) \cdots (\ell_r, \gamma_r)\$$ over the alphabet $((\Sigma \cup \mathcal{D}_N) \times 2^\mathcal{Y}) \cup \{\$\}$, where $\mathcal{Y}$ is the set of non-distinguished variables of $Q(\vec{x})$. The intended meaning is that the variables in $\gamma_i$ are mapped in $\mathcal{B}_w$ to the node $\ell_i$, if $\ell_i \in \mathcal{D}_N$, and are mapped to the target node of the edge corresponding to the occurrence of $\ell_i$, if $\ell_i \in \Sigma$.

Given a word $w'$ representing an annotated $\mathcal{V}$-word $w$, a 1NFA $A_{Q(\vec{t})}^{an}$ can check if each atom in $Q(\vec{t})$ is satisfied in the DB represented by $w$, given the annotation in $w'$. We first define the following automata:

- A 1NFA $A_s$ that checks that for every non-distinguished variable $y$,
  - either $y$ appears in the annotation of a single occurrence of a symbol in $\Sigma$, and it does not appear in the annotation of any other position in the word;
  - or $y$ appears in the annotation of every occurrence of a symbol $d \in \mathcal{D}_N$, and it does not appear in the annotation of any other symbol different from $d$.

- A 1NFA $A_\$$ that checks that every occurrence in $w$ of a symbol preceding a \$ is annotated in $w'$ with the same set of variables as the symbol preceding it. This takes into account equalities introduced by subwords of the form $\$d_1 d_2\$$, as well as that the symbol $a$ in a subword of the form $\cdots ad\$$ actually represents the target node of the $a$-edge, i.e., $d$ itself.
- A 2NFA $A_q$ that checks that each atom in $Q(\vec{t})$ is satisfied in $\mathcal{B}_w$, given the assignment to the non-distinguished variables represented by the annotation in $w'$. Such an automaton can be constructed by exploiting the ability of 2NFAs to move in both directions and jump on the word, as discussed above.

The 1NFA $A^{an}_{Q(\vec{t})}$ is constructed as the product of $A_s$, $A_\$$, and of the 1NFA equivalent to $A_q$. Next we define a 1NFA $A_{Q(\vec{t})}$ that simulates the guess of an annotation of a $\mathcal{V}$-word, and emulates the behaviour of $A^{an}_{Q(\vec{t})}$ on the resulting annotated word. The simulation of the guess and the emulation of $A^{an}_{Q(\vec{t})}$ can be obtained simply by constructing $A^{an}_{Q(\vec{t})}$ and then projecting out the annotation from the transitions. Observe that $A_{Q(\vec{t})}$ has the same number of states as $A^{an}_{Q(\vec{t})}$. Complementing $A_{Q(\vec{t})}$ and intersecting it with $A_\mathcal{V}$, we obtain a 1NFA $A_{\neg Q(\vec{t}),\mathcal{V}}$ having the following property.

**Theorem 4.** *Let $\mathcal{V}$ be a set of C2RPQ$_c$ views, $Q$ a C2RPQ$_c$ of arity $n$, $\vec{t}$ an $n$-tuple of proper constants, and $A_{\neg Q(\vec{t}),\mathcal{V}}$ the 1NFA constructed above. Then, $\vec{t} \in cert(Q, \mathcal{V})$ if and only if $A_{\neg Q(\vec{t}),\mathcal{V}}$ is empty.*

**Theorem 5.** *QA and QC for C2RPQ$_c$'s are EXPSPACE-complete.*

*Proof.* The lower bound for QC follows from EXPSPACE-hardness of QC for C2RPQ$_c$'s without constants and inverse, shown in [16]. By Theorem 2 we obtain the same lower bound for QA.

For the upper bound for QA, we appeal to the construction above.

The 1NFA $A_\mathcal{V}$ is the intersection of a 1NFA $A_\mathcal{V}^-$, which is polynomial in the size of $\mathcal{V}$ (i.e., the view definitions and view extensions), and of a 1NFA that complements the 2NFA $A_{\neg UNA}$, which is exponential in the number of proper constants in the view extension and view definitions.

As for $A_{Q(\vec{t})}$, we observe that the number of states of the 2NFA $A_q$, is polynomial in the size of $Q$ and the number of constants in the view extensions, while the number of states of the 1NFAs $A_s$ and $A_\$$ is exponential in the number of variables of $Q$ and the number of constants in the view extensions. $A_{Q(\vec{t})}$ is obtained by projecting out the annotation from the intersection of $A_s$, $A_\$$, and of the 1NFA equivalent to $A_q$. Hence $A_{Q(\vec{t})}$ is a 1NFA exponential in the size of $Q$ and the number of proper constants in the view extensions.

$A_{\neg Q(\vec{t}),\mathcal{V}}$ is obtained from the intersection of $A_\mathcal{V}$ and of the 1NFA that complements $A_{Q(\vec{t})}$. Hence, $A_{\neg Q(\vec{t}),\mathcal{V}}$ is a 1NFA of size double exponential in the size of $Q$ and the number of proper constants. Considering that nonemptiness is NLOGSPACE and that we can build $A_{\neg Q(\vec{t}),\mathcal{V}}$ "on the fly" while checking for emptiness [16], we get an EXPSPACE upper bound for QA. By Theorem 2 we get also an EXPSPACE upper bound for QC.

## 4.4   Automaton for Whole Answer Set

We show now how to modify the construction in the previous subsection to obtain *all* tuples that are not in $cert(Q(\vec{x}), \mathcal{V})$.

We represent each answer to $Q(\vec{x})$, with arity $n$, as a word in the language $\mathcal{L}_t = 1 \cdot \mathcal{D}_V \cdot 2 \cdot \mathcal{D}_V \cdots n \cdot \mathcal{D}_V$, and we first construct an automaton accepting the set of words in $\mathcal{L}_t$ representing tuples that are *not* certain answers to $Q(\vec{x})$.

To do so, we construct a 1NFA $A_{Q(\vec{x})}$ that accepts all words of the form $w_{\vec{t}} \diamond w_{\mathcal{B}}$, where

- $w_{\mathcal{B}}$ represents a $\mathcal{V}$-canonical DB $\mathcal{B}$,
- $w_{\vec{t}}$ is a word in $\mathcal{L}_t$ representing a tuple $\vec{t}$ that is *not* in $ans(Q(\vec{x}), \mathcal{B})$, and
- "$\diamond$" acts as a separator.

The 1NFA $A_{Q(\vec{x})}$ is obtained from $A_{Q(\vec{t})}$ by changing the construction of $A_q$ as explained below. Let $\vec{x} = (x_1, \ldots, x_n)$. The automaton uses the prefix $w_{\vec{t}}$, representing a tuple $\vec{t} = (c_1, \ldots, c_n)$, to obtain the mapping from $x_i$ to $c_i$, for $i \in \{1, \ldots, n\}$, and once it has performed such a mapping, it proceeds essentially as $A_q$.

Let us first consider an atom in $Q(\vec{x})$ of the form $x_i E x_j$, where $x_i$ and $x_j$ are respectively the $i$-th and $j$-th distinguished variable, and assume that $E$ is represented as a 1NFA $E = (\Sigma, S, \{s_0\}, \delta, \{s_f\})$ over the alphabet $\Sigma$. As shown in [16,17], one can construct from $E$ a 2NFA that checks whether a specified pair of constants $(d, d')$ is in $ans(E, \mathcal{B})$. Such an automaton has the form $A' = (\Sigma', S', \{s_0'\}, \delta', \{s_f'\})$, where $\Sigma' = ((\Sigma \cup \mathcal{D}_N) \times 2^{\mathcal{Y}}) \cup \{\$\}$, $S' = S \cup \{s_0', s_f'\} \cup \{s^{\leftarrow} \mid s \in S\} \cup S \times \mathcal{D}_N$, and $\delta_A$ is defined as in [16]. The states $s^{\leftarrow}$ are used to evaluate $E$ moving backward on the word, while states $(s, d)$ are used to search for occurrences of $d$ while in state $s$ of $E$. We define the 2NFA $A'' = (\Sigma'', S'', \{s_0''\}, \delta'', \{s_f''\})$, where $\Sigma'' = \Sigma' \cup \{\diamond, 1, \ldots, n\}$, $S'' = S' \cup \{s_0'', s_0^i, s_f''\} \cup \{s_0^d, s_f^d, s_f^{d\diamond}, s_f^{dd} \mid d \in \mathcal{D}_N\}$ and $\delta''$ is obtained by adding to $\delta'$ the following transitions:

$$
\begin{aligned}
(s_0'', 1) &\in \delta''(s_0'', \ell) && \text{for each } \ell \neq i \\
(s_0^i, 1) &\in \delta''(s_0'', i) && \\
(s_0^d, 1) &\in \delta''(s_0^i, d) && \text{for each } d \in \mathcal{D}_N \\
(s_0^d, 1) &\in \delta''(s_0^d, \ell) && \text{for each } \ell \neq \diamond \\
((s_0, d), 1) &\in \delta''(s_0^d, \diamond) && \\
(s_f^d, 1) &\in \delta''(s_f, d) && \text{for each } d \in \mathcal{D}_N \\
(s_f^d, -1) &\in \delta''(s_f^d, \ell) && \text{for each } d \in \mathcal{D}_N \text{ and } \ell \neq \diamond \\
(s_f^{d\diamond}, -1) &\in \delta''(s_f^d, \diamond) && \text{for each } d \in \mathcal{D}_N \\
(s_f^{d\diamond}, -1) &\in \delta''(s_f^{d\diamond}, \ell) && \text{for each } d \in \mathcal{D}_N \text{ and } \ell \neq d \\
(s_f^{dd}, -1) &\in \delta''(s_f^{d\diamond}, d) && \text{for each } d \in \mathcal{D}_N \\
(s_f'', -1) &\in \delta''(s_f^{dd}, j) && \text{for each } d \in \mathcal{D}_N
\end{aligned}
$$

Intuitively, $A''$ finds the constant $d$ associated to $x_i$ in the prefix, then runs $E$ starting from an occurrence of $d$ in the postfix, and finally, when $E$ finishes, checks that it has finished on the constant $d'$ associated to $x_j$ in the prefix.

We can proceed in a similar way for the atoms in $Q(\vec{x})$ where only one of the involved variables is a distinguished one. In this case we have to add only the transitions at the beginning, when the distinguished variable is the first one, and those at the end, when the distinguished variable is the second one. If both variables are non-distinguished, we use exactly the same 2NFA as in $A_q$.

Finally, we complement $A_{Q(\vec{x})}$ and intersect it with the 1NFA accepting the concatenation of $\mathcal{L}_t\cdot\diamond$ and of the language accepted by $A_\mathcal{V}$. Then we project away from the resulting automaton the part following "$\diamond$" (including the symbol "$\diamond$"), and obtain the 1NFA $A_{\neg Q(\vec{x}),\mathcal{V}}$ that accepts the set of tuples not in $cert(Q(\vec{x}),\mathcal{V})$. Observe that the latter projection can be obtained by simply removing all transitions labeled by "$\diamond$".

**Theorem 6.** *Let $\mathcal{V}$ be a set of C2RPQ$_c$ views, $\mathcal{D}_\mathcal{V}$ the set of constants appearing in the view extensions and view definitions, $Q$ a C2RPQ$_c$ of arity $n$, and $A_{\neg Q(\vec{x}),\mathcal{V}}$ the 1NFA constructed above. Then, $\mathcal{L}(A_{\neg Q(\vec{x}),\mathcal{V}}) = \{1c_1\cdots nc_n \mid (c_1,\ldots,c_n) \notin cert(Q,\mathcal{V})\}$.*

Observe that all changes in the construction of $A_{\neg Q(\vec{x}),\mathcal{V}}$ wrt the construction of $A_{\neg Q(\vec{t}),\mathcal{V}}$ are polynomial. We get that, given a tuple $\vec{t}$, $A_{\neg Q(\vec{x}),\mathcal{V}}$ can be used to decide QA for $\vec{t}$ in a computationally optimal way.

**Theorem 7.** *Checking whether a word $1c_1\cdots nc_n$, representing a tuple $(c_1,\ldots,c_n)$, is not accepted by $A_{\neg Q(\vec{x}),\mathcal{V}}$ is EXPSPACE-complete.*

Observe that one could compute the whole answer set for QA by constructing for each single tuple $\vec{t}$ of constants in $\mathcal{D}_\mathcal{V}$ the automaton $A_{\neg Q(\vec{t}),\mathcal{V}}$, and then checking it for emptiness. The advantage of constructing $A_{\neg Q(\vec{x}),\mathcal{V}}$ instead, lies in the fact that such a construction factors out the common parts of the various $A_{\neg Q(\vec{t}),\mathcal{V}}$ leaving only a small part of the automaton specialized for each tuple.

# 5    QA and QC for T2RPQ$_c$'s

We study now QA and QC in the case where the query to answer using the views (resp., the right-hand side query for QC) is a T2RPQ$_c$. To do so we exploit two-way alternating word automata (2AFAs).

## 5.1    Two-Way Alternating Automata

Given a set $X$, we define the set $B^+(X)$ as the set of all positive Boolean formulas over $X$, including 'true' and 'false' (i.e., for all $x \in X$, $x$ is a formula, and if $\varphi_1$ and $\varphi_2$ are formulas, so are $\varphi_1 \wedge \varphi_2$ and $\varphi_1 \vee \varphi_2$). We say that a subset $X' \subseteq X$ *satisfies* a formula $\varphi \in B^+(X)$ (denoted $X' \models \varphi$) if, by assigning 'true' to all members of $X'$ and 'false' to all members of $X \setminus X'$, the formula $\varphi$ evaluates to 'true'. Clearly 'true' is satisfied by every subset of $X$ (including the empty set) and 'false' cannot be satisfied.

In the following we denote the concatenation of $I$ and $J$, where $I, J \in \mathbb{N}^*$, with $IJ$. A *tree* is a finite set $T \subseteq \mathbb{N}^*$ such that, if $Ii \in T$, where $I \in \mathbb{N}^*$ and $i \in \mathbb{N}$, then also $I \in T$. $T$ is *complete* if, whenever $Ii \in T$, then also $Ij \in T$ for every $j \in [1..i]$. The elements of $T$ are called *nodes*. When referring to trees, we make also use of the standard notions of *root, successor, descendant, predecessor,* and *leaf.* Given an alphabet $\Sigma$, a $\Sigma$-*labeled tree* is a pair $(T, V)$, where $T$ is a tree and $V : T \to \Sigma$ maps each node of $T$ to an element of $\Sigma$. A $k$-*ary tree*, where $k$ is a positive integer, is a tree $T \subseteq [1..k]^*$.

Two-way alternating automata generalize 1NFAs with the ability to move on the input string in both directions, and with the possibility to perform universal or existential moves (actually a combination of both). Formally, a *two-way alternating automaton* (2AFA) [21,39,9] $A = (\Gamma, S, S_0, \delta, S_f)$ consists of an alphabet $\Gamma$, a finite set of states $S$, a set $S_0 \subseteq S$ of initial states, a transition function $\delta : S \times \Sigma \to B^+(S \times \{-1, 0, 1\})$, and a set $S_f \subseteq S$ of accepting states. Intuitively, a transition $\delta(s, a)$ spawns several copies of $A$, each one starting in a certain state and with the head on the symbol to the left of $a$ ($-1$), to the right of $a$ ($1$), or on $a$ itself ($0$), and specifies by means of a positive Boolean formula how to combine acceptance or non-acceptance of the spawned copies. A *run* of $A$ on a finite word $w = a_0 \cdots a_\ell$ is a labeled tree $(T, r)$, where $r : T \to S \times [0..\ell + 1]$. A node in $T$ labeled by $(s, i)$ describes a copy of $A$ that is in state $s$ and reads the letter $a_i$ of $w$. The labels of adjacent nodes of $T$ have to satisfy the transition function $\delta$. Formally, $r(\varepsilon) = (s_0, 0)$ where $s_0 \in S_0$, and for all nodes $I$ with $r(I) = (s, i)$ and $\delta(s, a_i) = \varphi$, there is a (possibly empty) set $Z = \{(s_1, c_1), \ldots, (s_h, c_h)\} \subseteq S \times \{-1, 0, 1\}$ such that $Z \models \varphi$ and for all $j \in [1..h]$, there is a successor of $I$ in $T$ labeled $(s_j, i + c_j)$. The run is *accepting* if all leaves of the run are labeled by $(s, \ell + 1)$ for some $s \in S_f$. $A$ accepts $w$ if it has an accepting run on $w$. The set of words accepted by $A$ is denoted $L(A)$.

It is known that 2AFAs define regular languages [39], and that, given a 2AFA with $n$ states accepting a regular language $L$, one can construct a 1NFA with $2^{O(n^2)}$ states, accepting $L$ (see [8,38]). In addition, by exploiting the same idea used in the reduction in [54] from 2NFAs to 1NFAs, we can show the following result.

**Theorem 8.** *Given a 2AFA with $n$ states accepting a language $L$, one can construct a 1NFA with $2^{O(n)}$ states, accepting the complement of $L$.*

### 5.2    T2RPQ$_c$'s

Obviously, QA for the case where the query to be answered is a T2RPQ$_c$ is a special case of QA for C2RPQ$_c$'s. However, the special tree-structure of the query $Q$ to be answered allows us to avoid the construction of the doubly exponential automaton for $Q$. Instead, to build $A_{Q(\vec{t})}$ we make use of 2AFAs, which can directly simulate the evaluation of a T2RPQ$_c$ on words representing canonical DBs, without the need to introduce annotations for the non-distinguished variables of $Q$. In particular, we exploit the ability of 2AFAs to: (i) move on the word both forward and backward, which corresponds to traversing edges of the

DB in both directions; (ii) "jump" between positions in the word representing the same node; (iii) check a "conjunction" of conditions.

To denote a T2RPQ$_c$ we use variables indexed with nodes of a tree, each of which is represented as usual by a (possibly empty) sequence of integers, denoting the path leading from the root to the node. Let the set $\mathcal{I}$ of indices of the variables in the query be a finite $k$-ary tree (for some $k$) and let $Q$ be the T2RPQ$_c$ of arity $n$

$$Q(x_1, \ldots, x_n) \leftarrow \bigwedge_{y_I, y_{Ij} \in \mathcal{I}} y_I \, E_{Ij} \, y_{Ij}$$

where $I$ is the sequence of integers denoting a node in the tree, $Ij$ is the sequence denoting the $j$-th successor of node $I$, and $E_{Ij}$ denotes the regular expression in the (unique) atom involving variables or proper constants $y_I$ and $y_{Ij}$. Notice that the body of the query has the structure of a tree, i.e., each variable appears at most once as right variable in an atom, and, except for $y_\varepsilon$, if a variable appears as left variable in an atom, then it must also appear as right variable in some other atom.

### 5.3  Automaton for a Single Tuple

We first address the problem of checking whether a tuple $\vec{t}$ is in the certain answer to a T2RPQ$_c$ $Q$ wrt a set of C2RPQ$_c$ views $\mathcal{V}$.

We can build the automaton $A_\mathcal{V}$ accepting $\mathcal{V}$-words representing $\mathcal{V}$-canonical DBs exactly as in Section 4.2. Let $w$ be a $\mathcal{V}$-word over the alphabet $\Sigma \cup \mathcal{D}_N \cup \{\$\}$, representing a $\mathcal{V}$-canonical DB $\mathcal{B}_w$. We construct a 2AFA $A_{Q(\vec{t})}$, that accepts $w$ if and only if $\vec{t} \in ans(Q, \mathcal{B}_w)$.

To construct $A_{Q(\vec{t})}$, we assume that each $E_I$ is represented as a 1NFA $E_I = (\Sigma, S_I, s_I^0, \delta_I, s_I^f)$ over the alphabet $\Sigma$, and that the automata for different $E_I$'s have disjoint sets of states. Then $A_{Q(\vec{t})} = (\Sigma^Q, S^Q, \{s_\varepsilon^f\}, \delta^Q, F^Q)$, where $\Sigma^Q = \Sigma \cup \mathcal{D}_N \cup \{\$\}$, and $S^Q$, $F^Q$, and $\delta^Q$ are defined below.

For simplicity, we use the following notation for transitions of 2AFAs: we write $(s', \ell') \in \delta^Q(s, \ell)$ meaning that $\delta^Q(s, \ell)$ is a disjunction of transitions, and that $(s', \ell')$ is one of the disjuncts.

We first construct for each atom $y_I \, E_J \, y_J$ (with $J = Ij$ for some $j$) in the query a part of $A_{Q(\vec{t})}$ that checks that such atom is satisfied in the $\mathcal{V}$-canonical DB represented by the current word. To do so, we introduce in $S^Q$ a set of states $S_J^Q = S_J \cup \{s^\leftarrow \mid s \in S_J\} \cup \{s^\rightarrow \mid s \in S_J\} \cup S_J \times \mathcal{D}_N$ and add the following transitions to $\delta^Q$ (this construction is a variation of the one in [16]):

1. $(s^\leftarrow, -1) \in \delta^Q(s, \ell)$, for each $s \in S_J$ and $\ell \in \Sigma \cup \mathcal{D}_N$. At any point such transitions make the automaton ready to scan one step backward by placing it in "backward-mode".
2. $(s_2, 1) \in \delta^Q(s_1, r)$ and $(s_2, 0) \in \delta^Q(s_1^\leftarrow, r^-)$, for each transition $s_2 \in \delta_J(s_1, r)$ of $E_J$. These transitions correspond to the transitions of $E_J$ that are performed forward or backward according to the current "scanning mode".

3. For each $s \in S_J$ and each $d \in \mathcal{D}_N$

$$((s,d),0) \in \delta^Q(s,d)$$
$$((s,d),0) \in \delta^Q(s^\leftarrow,d)$$
$$((s,d),1) \in \delta^Q((s,d),\ell), \quad \text{for each } \ell \in \Sigma^Q$$
$$((s,d),-1) \in \delta^Q((s,d),\ell), \quad \text{for each } \ell \in \Sigma^Q$$
$$(s,0) \in \delta^Q((s,d),d)$$
$$(s,1) \in \delta^Q(s,d)$$

On a symbol representing a node $d$ while in a state $s$, the automaton may enter into "search-for-$d$-mode", reflected in a state $(s,d)$ (first and second clause) and move to any other occurrence of $d$ in the word. When it finds such an occurrence, the automaton exits search-mode (second last clause) and continues its computation either forward (last clause) or backward (see item 2).

4. For each $s \in S_J$ and each $d_1, d_2 \in \mathcal{D}_N$

$$(s^\leftrightarrow,1) \in \delta^Q((s,d_1),d_1) \qquad\qquad ((s,d_2),0) \in \delta^Q(s^\leftrightarrow,d_2)$$

Whenever the automaton reaches a symbol representing a node $d_1$ while it is in search-for-$d_1$-mode, and $d_2$ appears immediately to the right of $d_1$, the automaton may switch to search-for-$d_2$-mode. This takes into account that two adjacent symbols $d_1 d_2$ actually represent the same node of the DB. Notice that switching from search-for-$d_2$-mode to search-for-$d_1$-mode is already taken into account by exiting search-for-$d_1$-mode (transition 5 in 3), switching to backward-mode (point 1), and switching to search-for-$d_2$-mode while exiting from backward-mode (second transition in item 3).

Observe that the separator symbol $\$$ does not allow transitions except in search-mode. Its role is to force the automaton to move in the correct direction when exiting search-mode.

We then "connect" the different parts of $A_{Q(\vec{t})}$ corresponding to the different atoms in the query by taking into account the tree structure of the query.

1. $(s^f_\varepsilon, 1) \in \delta^Q(s^f_\varepsilon, \ell)$ for each $\ell \in \Sigma^Q$. These transitions place the head of the automaton in some randomly chosen position of the input string.

2. Consider now a variable or proper constant $y_I$, and all atoms in which $y_I$ appears on the left of the regular expression. Let such atoms be $y_I E_{Ij} y_{Ij}$, for $j \in [1..m_I]$:

   - if $y_I$ is a distinguished variable $x_i$, then we add the transition $(s^0_{I1}, 0) \wedge \cdots \wedge (s^0_{Im_I}, 0) \in \delta^Q(s^f_I, \vec{t}[i])$, where $\vec{t}[i]$ is the $i$-th component of $\vec{t}$, and $s^0_{Ij}$ is the starting state of the part of the automaton for $y_I E_{Ij} y_{Ij}$;
   - If $y_I$ is a proper constant $c$, then we add the transition $(s^0_{I1}, 0) \wedge \cdots \wedge (s^0_{Im_I}, 0) \in \delta^Q(s^f_I, c)$;
   - if $y_I$ is a non-distinguished variable of $Q$, then we add the transitions $(s^0_{I1}, 0) \wedge \cdots \wedge (s^0_{Im_I}, 0) \in \delta^Q(s^f_I, \ell)$, for each $\ell \in \Sigma \cup \mathcal{D}_N$.

These transitions connect in the appropriate way $s_I^f$ (which is either the final state of $A_I$ or the initial state $s_\varepsilon^f$ of $A^{Q_2}$) with the starting states $s_{Ij}^0$ of the parts of the automaton corresponding to the atoms $y_I\, E_{Ij}\, y_{Ij}$, without moving on the input string. They also check that distinguished variables or constants are mapped to the appropriate nodes in the word. Note that the one above are the only "and"-transitions used in the automaton.

3. $(s,1) \in \delta^Q(s,\ell)$, for each $s \in F^Q$ and each $\ell \in \Sigma^Q$. These transitions move the head of the automaton to the end of the input string, when the automaton enters a final state.

We still have to specify the set $F^Q$ of final states of $A_{Q(\vec{t})}$. For each variable or constant $y_J$ which is a leaf of the tree representing $Q$ (and which appears only in an atom $y_I\, E_J\, y_J$):

- If $y_J$ is a distinguished variable $x_i$, then we introduce in $S^Q$ a new state $s_J^F$, add the transition $s_J^F \in \delta^Q(s_J^f, \vec{t}[i])$, and add $s_J^F$ to the set $F^Q$ of final states of $A_{Q(\vec{t})}$. This corresponds to checking that the distinguished variable $x_i$ is actually mapped to $\vec{t}[i]$.
- If $y_J$ is a proper constant $c$, then we introduce in $S^Q$ a new state $s_J^F$, add the transition $s_J^F \in \delta^Q(s_J^f, c)$, and add $s_J^F$ to the set $F^Q$ of final states of $A_{Q(\vec{t})}$. This corresponds to checking that the constant $c$ is actually mapped to itself.
- If $y_J$ is a non-distinguished variable of $Q$, then we simply add $s_J^f$ to the set $F^Q$ of final states of $A_{Q(\vec{t})}$.

Observe that the mapping of non-distinguished variables of $Q$ to nodes of a $\mathcal{V}$-canonical DB represented by a $\mathcal{V}$-word $w$ accepted by $A_{Q(\vec{t})}$ is not explicited as an annotation of $w$. However, the existence of an accepting run of $A_{Q(\vec{t})}$ over $w$ guarantees the existence of such a mapping, since each branching in the query is handled by an "and"-transition in the automaton. In this way the different occurrences of a non-distinguished variable in the body of $Q$ are all mapped to the same node, which is represented by the symbol in $w$ at which the "and"-transition in the run occurs.

Finally, we define $A_{\neg Q(\vec{t}),\mathcal{V}}$ as the intersection of the 1NFA $A_\mathcal{V}$ and of the 1NFA corresponding to the complement of $A_{Q(\vec{t})}$ (see Theorem 8).

**Theorem 9.** *Let $\mathcal{V}$ be a set of C2RPQ$_c$ views, $Q$ a T2RPQ$_c$ of arity $n$, $\vec{t}$ an $n$-tuple of proper constants, and $A_{\neg Q(\vec{t}),\mathcal{V}}$ the 1NFA constructed above. Then, $\vec{t} \in cert(Q,\mathcal{V})$ if and only if $A_{\neg Q(\vec{t}),\mathcal{V}}$ is empty.*

Considering the construction above we get the following complexity characterization.

**Theorem 10.** *QA for C2RPQ$_c$ views and a T2RPQ$_c$ query, and QC between a C2RPQ$_c$ and a T2RPQ$_c$ are PSPACE-complete.*

*Proof.* QC is clearly PSPACE-hard, since already containment of regular expressions (and hence RPQs) is PSPACE-hard [36]. By Theorem 2 we obtain the same lower bound for QA.

For the upper bound for QA, by Theorem 9, it suffices to check the emptiness of $A_{\neg Q(\vec{t}),\mathcal{V}}$, which is the intersection of the 1NFA $A_{\mathcal{V}}$ and of the 1NFA corresponding to the complement of $A_{Q(\vec{t})}$. The 1NFA $A_{\mathcal{V}}$ is the intersection of a 1NFA $A_{\mathcal{V}}^-$ which is polynomial in the size of $\mathcal{V}$ (i.e., the view definitions and view extensions) and of a 1NFA, called $A_{UNA}$ in the following, that complements the 2NFA $A_{\neg UNA}$, which is exponential in the number of proper constants in the view extension and view definitions.

The 2AFA $A_{Q(\vec{t})}$ is polynomial in $Q$. By Theorem 8, the 1NFA corresponding to the complement of $A_{Q(\vec{t})}$, called $A_{\neg Q(\vec{t})}$ in the following, is exponential in $Q$. However, we can check "on-the-fly" whether $A_{\mathcal{V}}^- \cap A_{UNA} \cap A_{\neg Q(\vec{t})}$ is empty, and we do not need to construct $A_{UNA}$ and $A_{\neg Q(\vec{t})}$ explicitly: Whenever the emptiness algorithm wants to move from a state $s_1$ of the intersection of $A_{\mathcal{V}}^-$, $A_{UNA}$, and $A_{\neg Q(\vec{t})}$ to a state $s_2$, it guesses $s_2$ and checks that it is directly connected to $s_1$. Such a check can be done in time polynomial in the sizes of $A_{\mathcal{V}}^-$, $A_{UNA}$, and $A_{\neg Q(\vec{t})}$ [54]. Once this has been verified, the algorithm can discard $s_1$. Thus, at each step the algorithm needs to keep in memory at most two states and there is no need to generate all of $A_{UNA}$ and $A_{\neg Q(\vec{t})}$ at any single step of the algorithm.

Considering Theorem 2, we also get that QC for the case where the query on the left-hand side is a C2RPQ$_c$ and the one on the right-hand side is a T2RPQ$_c$ can be decided in PSPACE.

### 5.4   Automaton for Whole Answer Set

The technique developed in Section 4.4 to compute the whole set of certain answers can be adapted also to the case where the query to be answered is a T2RPQ$_c$. Observe that we cannot deal with each RPQ separately, as done in Section 4.4. Instead, at those points where the automaton for a single tuple checks the presence of a proper constant assigned to a distinguished variable, the automaton for the whole answer set has to check that the proper constant encountered in the word is mapped in the prefix to the index of the distinguished variable that the automaton expects. This can be done by adding a suitable conjunct in the transition of the automaton that switches to a state from which the check is done.

As for the case of C2RPQ$_c$'s, this construction maintains the same computational complexity as the one for a single tuple. Hence, using the automaton for the whole answer set, one can decide in PSPACE whether a certain tuple is in the certain answer to a T2RPQ$_c$ wrt a set of C2RPQ$_c$ views.

## 6   Conclusions

We have studied query containment and view-based query answering for the class of C2RPQ$_c$'s. We have presented a mutual reduction between the two problems, and we have shown that both are EXPSPACE-complete in the general case, and PSPACE-complete in the special case of T2RPQ$_c$'s. Observe that PSPACE and EXPSPACE algorithms currently can be implemented in time that is respectively exponential and doubly exponential in the size of the input. Hence, the results for T2RPQ$_c$'s imply that query containment for not too large queries is indeed feasible, since it can be done in time that is exponential in a small number. This has to be contrasted with the general case where even containment for moderately sized queries appears to be infeasible, since it requires time that is doubly exponential, which is a large amount of time even for small queries.

For the sake of simplicity, we did not consider union in this paper. However, all the results presented here can be directly extended to unions of C2RPQ$_c$'s (respectively, unions of T2RPQ$_c$'s). Also, as already mentioned, they can be easily extended to the case of rooted DBs, i.e., to the case where the DB is an edge-labeled rooted graph. In particular, the notion of root can be simulated both in query containment and in query answering. For query containment, it is sufficient to add one variable to the left-hand side query and suitable atoms to enforce that it is connected to all other variables (and hence to all nodes of the counterexample database). For view-based query answering, the root can be modeled by means of a distinguished constant that is forced to be connected to all other constants appearing in the view extensions by means of an additional view with definition $V(x, y) \leftarrow x \, \Sigma^* \, y$.

In the future, we aim at extending our work in order to take into account the following aspects. (i) While we have assumed in this paper that views are sound (they return a subset of the answers to the associated query), in data integration views can also be used to model data sources that are either complete (they return a superset of the answers to the associated query) or exact (they are both sound and complete). We conjecture that our techniques for view-based query answering can be adapted in order to take into account both complete and exact views. (ii) It would be interesting to study the complexity of view-based query answering with respect to the size of the view extensions only (data complexity), as done in [15,17] for RPQs and 2RPQs.

# References

1. S. Abiteboul, P. Buneman, and D. Suciu. *Data on the Web: from Relations to Semistructured Data and XML*. Morgan Kaufmann, Los Altos, 2000.
2. S. Abiteboul and O. Duschka. Complexity of answering queries using materialized views. In *Proc. of PODS'98*, pages 254–265, 1998.
3. S. Abiteboul, D. Quass, J. McHugh, J. Widom, and J. L. Wiener. The Lorel query language for semistructured data. *Int. J. on Digital Libraries*, 1(1):68–88, 1997.
4. F. N. Afrati, M. Gergatsoulis, and T. Kavalieros. Answering queries using materialized views with disjunction. In *Proc. of ICDT'99*, volume 1540 of *LNCS*, pages 435–452. Springer, 1999.
5. A. V. Aho, Y. Sagiv, and J. D. Ullman. Equivalence among relational expressions. *SIAM J. on Computing*, 8:218–246, 1979.
6. D. Barbará and T. Imieliński. Sleepers and workaholics: Caching strategies in mobile environments. In *Proc. of ACM SIGMOD*, pages 1–12, 1994.

7. C. Beeri, A. Y. Levy, and M.-C. Rousset. Rewriting queries using views in description logics. In *Proc. of PODS'97*, pages 99–108, 1997.
8. J.-C. Birget. State-complexity of finite-state devices, state compressibility and incompressibility. *Mathematical Systems Theory*, 26(3):237–269, 1993.
9. J. A. Brzozowski and E. Leiss. Finite automata and sequential networks. *Theor. Comp. Sci.*, 10:19–35, 1980.
10. P. Buneman. Semistructured data. In *Proc. of PODS'97*, pages 117–121, 1997.
11. P. Buneman, S. Davidson, G. Hillebrand, and D. Suciu. A query language and optimization technique for unstructured data. In *Proc. of ACM SIGMOD*, pages 505–516, 1996.
12. D. Calvanese, G. De Giacomo, and M. Lenzerini. On the decidability of query containment under constraints. In *Proc. of PODS'98*, pages 149–158, 1998.
13. D. Calvanese, G. De Giacomo, and M. Lenzerini. Answering queries using views over description logics knowledge bases. In *Proc. of AAAI 2000*, pages 386–391, 2000.
14. D. Calvanese, G. De Giacomo, M. Lenzerini, and M. Y. Vardi. Rewriting of regular expressions and regular path queries. In *Proc. of PODS'99*, pages 194–204, 1999.
15. D. Calvanese, G. De Giacomo, M. Lenzerini, and M. Y. Vardi. Answering regular path queries using views. In *Proc. of ICDE 2000*, pages 389–398, 2000.
16. D. Calvanese, G. De Giacomo, M. Lenzerini, and M. Y. Vardi. Containment of conjunctive regular path queries with inverse. In *Proc. of KR 2000*, pages 176–185, 2000.
17. D. Calvanese, G. De Giacomo, M. Lenzerini, and M. Y. Vardi. Query processing using views for regular path queries with inverse. In *Proc. of PODS 2000*, pages 58–66, 2000.
18. D. Calvanese, G. De Giacomo, M. Lenzerini, and M. Y. Vardi. View-based query processing and constraint satisfaction. In *Proc. of LICS 2000*, pages 361–371, 2000.
19. D. Chamberlin, D. Florescu, J. Robie, J. Simeon, and M. Stefanescu. XQuery: A query language for XML. W3C Working Draft, Feb. 2001. Available at `http://www.w3.org/TR/xquery`.
20. E. P. F. Chan. Containment and minimization of positive conjunctive queries in oodb's. In *Proc. of PODS'92*, pages 202–211, 1992.
21. A. K. Chandra, D. C. Kozen, and L. J. Stockmeyer. Alternation. *J. of the ACM*, 28(1):114–133, 1981.
22. A. K. Chandra and P. M. Merlin. Optimal implementation of conjunctive queries in relational data bases. In *Proc. of STOC'77*, pages 77–90, 1977.
23. S. Chaudhuri, S. Krishnamurthy, S. Potarnianos, and K. Shim. Optimizing queries with materialized views. In *Proc. of ICDE'95*, Taipei (Taiwan), 1995.
24. S. Chaudhuri and M. Y. Vardi. On the equivalence of recursive and nonrecursive Datalog programs. In *Proc. of PODS'92*, pages 55–66, 1992.
25. C. Chekuri and A. Rajaraman. Conjunctive query containment revisited. In *Proc. of ICDT'97*, pages 56–70, 1997.
26. J. Clark and S. DeRose. XML Path Language (XPath) version 1.0 – W3C recommendation 16 november 1999. Technical report, World Wide Web Consortium, 1999. Available at `http://www.w3.org/TR/1999/REC-xpath-19991116`.
27. S. Cohen, W. Nutt, and A. Serebrenik. Rewriting aggregate queries using views. In *Proc. of PODS'99*, pages 155–166, 1999.
28. A. C. K. David S. Johnson. Testing containment of conjunctive queries under functional and inclusion dependencies. *J. of Computer and System Sciences*, 28(1):167–189, 1984.

29. A. Deutsch, M. F. Fernandez, D. Florescu, A. Levy, and D. Suciu. XML-QL: A query language for XML. Submission to the World Wide Web Consortium, Aug. 1998. Available at http://www.w3.org/TR/NOTE-xml-ql.
30. A. Deutsch and V. Tannen. Optimization properties for classes of conjunctive regular path queries. In *Proc. of DBPL 2001*, 2001.
31. O. M. Duschka and M. R. Genesereth. Answering recursive queries using views. In *Proc. of PODS'97*, pages 109–116, 1997.
32. M. F. Fernandez, D. Florescu, J. Kang, A. Y. Levy, and D. Suciu. Catching the boat with strudel: Experiences with a web-site management system. In *Proc. of ACM SIGMOD*, pages 414–425, 1998.
33. D. Florescu, A. Levy, and D. Suciu. Query containment for conjunctive queries with regular expressions. In *Proc. of PODS'98*, pages 139–148, 1998.
34. G. Grahne and A. O. Mendelzon. Tableau techniques for querying information sources through global schemas. In *Proc. of ICDT'99*, volume 1540 of *LNCS*, pages 332–347. Springer, 1999.
35. S. Grumbach, M. Rafanelli, and L. Tininini. Querying aggregate data. In *Proc. of PODS'99*, pages 174–184, 1999.
36. J. E. Hopcroft and J. D. Ullman. *Introduction to Automata Theory, Languages, and Computation*. Addison Wesley Publ. Co., Reading, Massachussetts, 1979.
37. A. C. Klug. On conjunctive queries containing inequalities. *J. of the ACM*, 35(1):146–160, 1988.
38. O. Kupferman, N. Piterman, and M. Y. Vardi. Extended temporal logic revisited. In *Proc. of CONCUR 2001*, volume 2154 of *LNCS*, pages 519–535. Springer, 2001.
39. R. E. Ladner, R. J. Lipton, and L. J. Stockmeyer. Alternating pushdown and stack automata. *SIAM J. on Computing*, 13(1):135–155, 1984.
40. A. Y. Levy, A. O. Mendelzon, Y. Sagiv, and D. Srivastava. Answering queries using views. In *Proc. of PODS'95*, pages 95–104, 1995.
41. A. Y. Levy and M.-C. Rousset. Combining Horn rules and description logics in CARIN. *Artificial Intelligence*, 104(1–2):165–209, 1998.
42. A. Y. Levy and D. Suciu. Deciding containment for queries with complex objects. In *Proc. of PODS'97*, pages 20–31, 1997.
43. J. McHugh and J. Widom. Optimizing branching path expressions. Technical report, Stanford University, 1999. Available at http://www-db.stanford.edu\penalty-\@M/pub/papers/mp.ps.
44. T. Milo and D. Suciu. Index structures for path expressions. In *Proc. of ICDT'99*, volume 1540 of *LNCS*, pages 277–295. Springer, 1999.
45. Y. Papakonstantinou and V. Vianu. DTD inference for views of XML data. In *Proc. of PODS 2000*, pages 35–46, 2000.
46. A. Rajaraman, Y. Sagiv, and J. D. Ullman. Answering queries using templates with binding patterns. In *Proc. of PODS'95*, 1995.
47. Y. Sagiv and M. Yannakakis. Equivalences among relational expressions with the union and difference operators. *J. of the ACM*, 27(4):633–655, 1980.
48. H. Seidl. Deciding equivalence of finite tree automata. *SIAM J. on Computing*, 19(3):424–437, 1990.
49. O. Shmueli. Equivalence of Datalog queries is undecidable. *J. of Logic Programming*, 15(3):231–241, 1993.
50. D. Srivastava, S. Dar, H. V. Jagadish, and A. Levy. Answering queries with aggregation using views. In *Proc. of VLDB'96*, pages 318–329, 1996.
51. O. G. Tsatalos, M. H. Solomon, and Y. E. Ioannidis. The GMAP: A versatile tool for phyisical data independence. *VLDB Journal*, 5(2):101–118, 1996.

52. J. D. Ullman. Information integration using logical views. In *Proc. of ICDT'97*, volume 1186 of *LNCS*, pages 19–40. Springer, 1997.
53. R. van der Meyden. *The Complexity of Querying Indefinite Information*. PhD thesis, Rutgers University, 1992.
54. M. Y. Vardi. A note on the reduction of two-way automata to one-way automata. *Information Processing Letters*, 30(5):261–264, 1989.
55. V. Vianu. A web odyssey: From Codd to XML. In *Proc. of PODS 2001*, 2001. Invited talk.
56. J. Widom (ed.). Special issue on materialized views and data warehousing. *IEEE Bull. on Data Engineering*, 18(2), 1995.
57. J. Widom (ed.). Special issue on materialized views and data warehousing. *IEEE Bull. on Data Engineering*, 22(3), 1999.
58. M. Yannakakis. Algorithms for acyclic database schemes. In *Proc. of VLDB'81*, pages 82–94, 1981.

# Model-Checking Based Data Retrieval

Agostino Dovier[1] and Elisa Quintarelli[2]

[1] Dip. di Matematica e Informatica, Università di Udine
Via delle Scienze 206, 33100 Udine, Italy
`dovier@dimi.uniud.it`
[2] Dip. di Elettronica e Informazione, Politecnico di Milano
Piazza Leonardo da Vinci 32, 20133 Milano, Italy
`quintare@elet.polimi.it`

**Abstract.** In this paper we develop a new method for solving queries on semistructured data. The main idea is to see a database as a Kripke Transition System (a model) and a query as a formula of the temporal logic *CTL*. In this way, the retrieval of data fulfilling a query is reduced to the problem of finding out the states of the model which satisfy the formula (the model-checking problem) that can be done in linear time.

**Keywords.** Semistructured DBs, Temporal Logic, Model-Checking.

## 1 Introduction

Most of the information accessible through the Web are typically *semistructured*, i.e. neither raw data nor strictly typed data [1]. It is a common approach to represent semistructured data by using directed labeled graphs [4,28,7]. A lot of work has been done to face the problem of accessing in a uniform way this kind of data with graph-based queries. In some approaches queries are really graphs [19,12,27] while, in others, queries can be written in extended SQL languages [3,2,6]. In both cases, the data retrieval activity requires the development of graph algorithms. In fact, queries (graphical or not) are expected to extract information stored in labeled graphs. In order to do that, it is required to perform a kind of *matching* of the "query" graph with the "database instance" graph. More in detail, we need to find subgraphs of the instance of the database that match (e.g., they are isomorphic or somehow similar to) the query graph. In [13,4] the concept of similarity used is bisimulation [21]. Even if the problem of establishing whether two graphs are bisimilar or not is polynomial time [20,25], the task of finding subgraphs isomorphic or bisimilar is NP-complete [16] and hence, not applicable to real-life size problems.

Graphical queries can be easily translated into logic formulae. Techniques for translating graphs in formulae have been exploited in literature [5]. The novel ideas of this work are to associate a *modal* logic formula $\Psi$ to a graphical query, and to interpret database instance graphs as *Kripke Transition Systems (KTS)*. We use a modal logic with the same syntax as the temporal logic *CTL*; the notion of different instants of *time* represents the number of links the user needs to follow to reach the information of interest. This way, finding subgraphs of

G. Grahne and G. Ghelli (Eds.): DBPL 2001, LNCS 2397, pp. 62–77, 2002.

the database instance graph that match the query can be performed by finding nodes of the $KTS$ derived from the database instance graph that satisfy the formula $\Psi$. This is an instance of the *model-checking* problem, and it is well-known that if the formula $\Psi$ belongs to the class $CTL$ of formulae, then the problem is decidable and algorithms running in linear time on both the sizes of the $KTS$ and the formula can be employed [11].

We identify a family of graph-based queries that are correctly represented by $CTL$ formulae. As immediate consequence, an effective procedure for efficiently querying semistructured databases can be directly implemented on a model checker. We use a "toy" query language called $\mathbb{W}$. It can be considered as a representative of several approaches in which queries are graphical or can easily be seen as graphical (cf., e.g., Lorel [2], G-Log [27], GraphLog [12], and UnQL [19]). We will relate $\mathbb{W}$ to UnQL, GraphLog, and G-Log and show the applicability of the method for implementing (parts of) these languages. We have also effectively tested the approach using the model-checker NuSMV.

## 2 Transition Systems and $CTL$

In this section we recall the main definitions and results of the model-checking problem for the branching time temporal logic $CTL$ [18].

**Definition 1.** *A Kripke Transition System (KTS) over a set $\Pi$ of atomic propositions is a structure $\mathcal{K} = \langle \Sigma, \mathcal{A}ct, \mathcal{R}, I \rangle$, where $\Sigma$ is a set of states, $\mathcal{A}ct$ is a set of actions, $\mathcal{R} \subseteq \Sigma \times \mathcal{A}ct \times \Sigma$ is a total transition relation, and $I : \Sigma \to \wp(\Pi)$ is an interpretation (we assume, w.l.o.g., that $\Pi \cap \mathcal{A}ct = \emptyset$).*

**Definition 2.** *Given the sets $\Pi$ and $\mathcal{A}ct$ of atomic propositions and actions, CTL formulae are recursively defined as follows:*

1. *each $p \in \Pi$ is a CTL formula;*
2. *if $\varphi_1$ and $\varphi_2$ are CTL formulae, $a \subseteq \mathcal{A}ct$, then $\neg\varphi_1$, $\varphi_1 \wedge \varphi_2$, $\mathsf{AX}_a(\varphi_1)$, $\mathsf{EX}_a(\varphi_1)$, $\mathsf{AU}_a(\varphi_1, \varphi_2)$, and $\mathsf{EU}_a(\varphi_1, \varphi_2)$ are CTL formulae[1].*

$\mathsf{A}$ and $\mathsf{E}$ are the universal and existential path quantifiers, while $\mathsf{X}$ (neXt) and $\mathsf{U}$ (Until) are the linear-time modalities. Composition of formulae of the form $\varphi_1 \vee \varphi_2$, $\varphi_1 \to \varphi_2$, and the modalities $\mathsf{F}$ (Finally) and $\mathsf{G}$ (Generally) can be defined in terms of the $CTL$ formulae: $\mathsf{F}(\varphi) = \mathsf{U}(\text{true}, \varphi)$, $\mathsf{G}(\varphi) = \neg\mathsf{F}(\neg\varphi)$ (cf. [18]).

A *path* (fullpath in [18]) in a KTS $\mathcal{K} = \langle \Sigma, \mathcal{A}ct, \mathcal{R}, I \rangle$ is an infinite sequence $\pi = \langle \pi_0, a_0, \pi_1, a_1, \pi_2, a_2, \dots \rangle$ of states and actions ($\pi_i$ denotes the $i$-th state in the path $\pi$) s.t. for all $i \in \mathbb{N}$ it holds that $\pi_i \in \Sigma$ and either $\langle \pi_i, a_i, \pi_{i+1} \rangle \in \mathcal{R}$, with $a_i \in \mathcal{A}ct$, or there are not outgoing transitions from $\pi_i$ and for all $j \geq i$ it holds that $a_j$ is the special action $\circlearrowright$ (which is not in $\mathcal{A}ct$) and $\pi_j = \pi_i$.

**Definition 3.** *Satisfaction of a CTL formula by a state $s$ of a KTS $\mathcal{K} = \langle \Sigma, \mathcal{A}ct, \mathcal{R}, I \rangle$ is defined recursively as follows:*

- *If $p \in \Pi$, then $s \models p$ iff $p \in I(s)$. Moreover, $s \models$ true and $s \not\models$ false;*
- *$s \models \neg\phi$ iff $s \not\models \phi$;*

---

[1] When $a$ is of the form $\{m\}$ for a single action $m$, we simply write $\mathsf{A(E)X(U)}_m$.

- $s \models \phi_1 \wedge \phi_2$ iff $s \models \phi_1$ and $s \models \phi_2$;
- $s \models \mathsf{EX}_a(\phi)$ iff there is a path $\pi = \langle s, x, \pi_1, \ldots \rangle$ s.t. $x \in a$ and $\pi_1 \models \phi$;
- $s \models \mathsf{AX}_a(\phi)$ iff for all paths $\pi = \langle s, x, \pi_1, \ldots \rangle$, $x \in a$ implies $\pi_1 \models \phi$;
- $s \models \mathsf{EU}_a(\phi_1, \phi_2)$ iff there is a path $\pi = \langle \pi_0, \ell_0, \pi_1, \ell_1 \ldots \rangle$, and $\exists j \in \mathbb{N}$ s.t. $\pi_0 = s$, $\pi_j \models \phi_2$, and $(\forall i < j)\, (\pi_i \models \phi_1$ and $\ell_i \in a)$;
- $s \models \mathsf{AU}_a(\phi_1, \phi_2)$ iff for all paths $\pi = \langle \pi_0, \ell_0, \pi_1, \ell_1 \ldots \rangle$ such that $\pi_0 = s$, $\exists j \in \mathbb{N}$ s.t. $\pi_j \models \phi_2$ and $(\forall i < j)(\pi_i \models \phi_1$ and $\ell_i \in a)$.

**Definition 4.** *The* model-checking problem *can be stated in two instances. The* local *model-checking: given a KTS $\mathcal{K}$, a formula $\varphi$, and a state $s$ of $\mathcal{K}$, verifying whether $s \models \varphi$. The* global *model-checking: given a KTS $\mathcal{K}$, and a formula $\varphi$, finding all states $s$ of $\mathcal{K}$ s.t. $s \models \varphi$.*

If $\Sigma$ is finite, the global model-checking problem for a *CTL* formula $\varphi$ can be solved in linear running time on $|\varphi| \cdot (|\Sigma| + |\mathcal{R}|)$ [11].

# 3   Syntax of the Query Language $\mathbb{W}$

In this section we describe the syntax of the language $\mathbb{W}$, a very simple graph-based language that we will use to characterize Database queries that have a temporal-logic interpretation.

**Definition 5.** *A $\mathbb{W}$-graph is a directed labeled graph $\langle N, E, \ell \rangle$, where $N$ is a (finite) set of nodes, $E \subseteq N \times (\mathcal{C} \times \mathcal{L}) \times N$ is a set of labeled edges of the form $\langle m, label, n \rangle$, $\ell$ is a function $\ell : N \longrightarrow \mathcal{C} \times (\mathcal{L} \cup \{\bot\})$. $\bot$ means 'undefined', and*

- $\mathcal{C} = \{$ solid, dashed $\}$ *denotes how the lines of nodes and edges are drawn.*
- $\mathcal{L}$ *is a set of labels.*

$\ell$ can be seen as the composition of the two single-valued functions $\ell_\mathcal{C}$ and $\ell_\mathcal{L}$. With abuse of notation, when the context is clear, we will use $\ell$ also for edges: if $e = \langle m, \langle c, k \rangle, n \rangle$, then $\ell_\mathcal{C}(e) = c$ and $\ell_\mathcal{L}(e) = k$. Two nodes may be connected by more than one edge, provided that edge labels be different.

**Definition 6.** *If $G = \langle N, E, \ell \rangle$ is a $\mathbb{W}$-graph, then the size of $G$ is $|G| = |N| + |E|$; $G_s = \langle N_s, E_s, \ell|_{N_s} \rangle$ is the solid subgraph of $G$, i.e. $N_s = \{n \in N : \ell_\mathcal{C}(n) = solid\}$ and $E_s = \{\langle m, \langle solid, \ell \rangle, n \rangle \in E : m, n \in N_s\}$; given two sets of nodes $S, T \subseteq N$, $T$ is accessible from $S$ if for each $n \in T$ there is a node $m \in S$ such that there is a path in $G$ from $m$ to $n$.*

**Definition 7.** *A $\mathbb{W}$-instance is a $\mathbb{W}$-graph $G$ such that $\ell_\mathcal{C}(e) = solid$ for each edge $e$ of $G$ and $\ell_\mathcal{C}(n) = solid$ and $\ell_\mathcal{L}(n) \neq \bot$ for each node $n$ of $G$.*

**Definition 8.** *A $\mathbb{W}$-query is a pointed $\mathbb{W}$-graph, namely a pair $\langle G, \nu \rangle$ with $\nu$ a node of $G$ (the point). A $\mathbb{W}$-query $\langle G, \nu \rangle$ is accessible if the set $N$ of nodes of $G$ is accessible from $\{\nu\}$.*

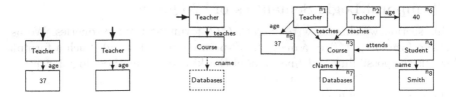

**Fig. 1.** Three W-queries and a W-instance

See Fig. 1 for some examples of W-graphs. Dashed nodes and lines are introduced to allow a form of negation. The meaning of the first query is: collect all the teachers aged 37. The second query asks for all the teachers that have declared some age (observe the use of an undefined node). The third query, instead, requires to collect all the teachers that teach some course, but not Databases.

## 4    W-Instances as Kripke Transition System

In this section we show how to build the *KTS* associated with a W-instance.

**Definition 9.** *Let $G = \langle N, E, \ell \rangle$ be a W-instance; we define the KTS $\mathcal{K}_G = \langle \Sigma_G, Act_G, \mathcal{R}_G, \mathcal{I}_G \rangle$ over the set of atomic propositions $\Pi_G$ as follows:*

- *$\Pi_G$ is the set of all the node labels of $G$: $\Pi_G = \{p : (\exists n \in N)(p = \ell_{\mathcal{L}}(n)\}$.*
- *The set of states is $\Sigma_G = N$.*
- *The set of actions $Act_G$ includes all the edge labels. In order to capture the notion of* before *we also add in $Act_G$ actions for the inverse relations and for the negation of all the relations introduced[2]. Thus, if $m \xrightarrow{p} n$ belongs to $E$ we add the actions $p, p^{-1}, \bar{p}, \bar{p}^{-1}$. We define two sets: $Act_G^+ = \{p, p^{-1} : (\exists m \in N)(\exists n \in N)(\langle m, p, n \rangle \in E)\}$ and $Act_G = \{q, \bar{q} : q \in Act_G^+\}$.*
- *The ternary transition relation $\mathcal{R}_G$ is defined as follows: let $\tilde{E}_G = E \cup \{\langle n, p^{-1}, m \rangle : \langle m, p, n \rangle \in E\}$. Then $\mathcal{R}_G = \tilde{E}_G \cup \{\langle m, \bar{p}, n \rangle : m, n \in N, p \in Act_G^+, \langle m, p, n \rangle \notin \tilde{E}\}$. Moreover, we can assume, for each state $s$ with no outgoing edge in $E$ (a leaf in $G$) to add a self-loop edge labeled by the special action $\circlearrowleft$ that is not in $Act_G$.*
- *The interpretation function $\mathcal{I}_G$ can be defined as follows. In each state $n$ the only formulae that hold are the unary atom $\ell_{\mathcal{L}}(n)$ and* true: $\mathcal{I}_G(n) = \{$true$, \ell_{\mathcal{L}}(n)\}$ [3].

Observe that: $|\mathcal{R}_G| = |Act_G^+| \cdot |N|^2 \le |E| \cdot |N|^2$ since for each pair of nodes, exactly one between $q$ or $\bar{q}$ holds, for $q = p$ or $q = p^{-1}$, $q \in \Pi_G$. For instance, consider the graph $G = \langle \Sigma_G = \{n_1, \ldots, n_8\}, E, \ell \rangle$ of Fig. 1. It holds that:

- $\Pi_G = \{$ Teacher, Course, Student, 37, 40, Databases, Smith$\}$,
- $\mathcal{I}(n_1) = \{$true, Teacher$\}, \mathcal{I}(n_2) = \{$true, Teacher$\}, \ldots, \mathcal{I}(n_8) = \{$true, Smith$\}$.

---
[2] Actually, negated edges are not always needed to be effectively stored—cf. Sect. 6.
[3] The two unary atoms represent the basic local properties of a system state. Other properties can be added, if needed.

# 5     Temporal Logic Semantics of W-Queries

In this section we show how to extract *CTL* formulae from W-queries. We associate a formula $\Psi_\nu(G)$ to a query (a W-pointed graph) $\langle G, \nu \rangle$. Such a formula allows us the possibility to define a model-checking based methodology for querying a W-instance. We anticipate this definition in order to make the meaning of formula encoding more clear.

**Definition 10 (Querying).** *Given a* W-*instance* $I$ *and a* W-*query* $\langle G, \nu \rangle$, *let* $\mathcal{K}_I$ *be the KTS associated with* $I$ *and* $\Psi_\nu(G)$ *the CTL formula associated with* $\langle G, \nu \rangle$. *Querying* $I$ *with* $G$ *amounts to solve the global model-checking problem for* $\mathcal{K}_I$ *and* $\Psi_\nu(G)$, *namely find all the states* $s$ *of* $\mathcal{K}_I$ *such that* $s \models \Psi_\nu(G)$.

## 5.1     Technique Overview

In order to explain the technique, we start our analysis by considering simple queries in which the pointed graph consists of two nodes (Fig. 2).

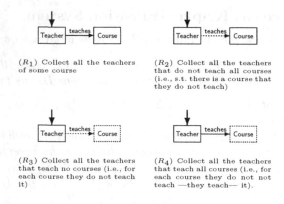

$(R_1)$ Collect all the teachers of some course

$(R_2)$ Collect all the teachers that do not teach all courses (i.e., s.t. there is a course that they do not teach)

$(R_3)$ Collect all the teachers that teach no courses (i.e., for each course they do not teach it)

$(R_4)$ Collect all the teachers that teach all courses (i.e., for each course they do not not teach —they teach— it).

**Fig. 2.** Simple queries

Query $R_1$ has no dashed part: only positive information is required. Its meaning is to look for nodes labeled Teacher that are connected with nodes labeled Course by an edge labeled teaches. The *CTL* formula must express the statement "In this state Teacher formula is true and there is one next state reachable by an edge labeled teaches, where the Course formula is true", i.e.

$$\text{Teacher} \wedge \text{EX}_{\text{teaches}}(\text{Course})$$

The *CTL* operator *neXt* (used either as EX or AX) captures the notion of following an edge in the graph. Thanks to this operator, we can easily define a path on the graph, nesting formulae that must be satisfied by one (or every) next state.

Query $R_2$ contains a dashed edge teaches that introduces a negative information. $R_2$ requires the existence of two nodes, and the *non*-existence of one edge labeled teaches between them. We can express this statement by

$$\text{Teacher} \wedge \text{EX}_{\overline{\text{teaches}}}(\text{Course})$$

The availability of the negation of the predicate symbol teaches, allows us to say that the relation teaches does not hold between two nodes is the same as requiring that, between the same pair of nodes, the relation $\overline{\text{teaches}}$ holds.

The meaning of query $R_3$, where there are dashed edges and nodes, is rather different. This formula is true if "there is a node labeled Teacher s.t., for all the nodes labeled Course, the relation teaches is not fulfilled". A *CTL* formula that states this property is the following:

$$\text{Teacher} \wedge \text{AX}_{\text{teaches}}(\neg\text{Course})$$

To give a semantics to query $R_4$, first replace the solid edge labeled teaches with the dashed edge labeled $\overline{\text{teaches}}$. Then use the same interpretation as for query $R_3$:

$$\text{Teacher} \wedge \text{AX}_{\overline{\text{teaches}}}(\neg\text{Course})$$

Its meaning is: "it is true if Teacher is linked by edges labeled teaches to all the Course nodes of the graph". Note the extremely compact way for expressing universal quantification.

## 5.2  Admitted Queries

We will show how to encode W-queries in *CTL* formulae. The equivalence result with G-log (Sect. 7) and the NP-completeness of the subgraph bisimulation problem ([16]) prevents us to encode all possible queries in a framework that can be solved in polynomial time. We will encode four families of queries $Q = \langle G, \mu \rangle$:

- $Q$ is an acyclic *accessible* query (Sect. 5.4).
- $G$ is an acyclic *solid* graph (Sect. 5.4).
- $G$ is an acyclic graph and after the application of a rewriting procedure, it becomes acyclic and accessible from $\{\mu\}$ (Sect. 5.4).
- $G$ is in one of the forms above with some leaf nodes replaced by simple solid cycles (Sect. 5.5).

## 5.3  Query Translation

As initial step, we associate a formula $\varphi$ to each node and edge of a graph $G$. Then we will use this notion for the definition of the formula.

**Definition 11.** *Let* $G = \langle N, E, \ell \rangle$ *be a* W-*graph. For all nodes* $n \in N$ *and for all edges* $e = \langle n_1, \langle c, p \rangle, n_2 \rangle \in E$, *we define:*

$$\varphi(n) = \begin{cases} \ell_{\mathcal{L}}(n) & \text{if } \ell_{\mathcal{L}}(n) \neq \bot \\ \text{true} & \text{otherwise} \end{cases} \qquad \varphi(e) = \begin{cases} p & \text{if } \ell_{\mathcal{C}}(e) = \ell_{\mathcal{C}}(n_2) \\ \overline{p} & \text{otherwise} \end{cases}$$

## 5.4  Acyclic Graphs

**Definition 12.** *Let* $G = \langle N, E, \ell \rangle$ *be an acyclic* W-*graph, and* $\nu \in N$. *The formula* $\Psi_\nu(G)$ *is defined recursively as follows (cf. Fig. 3):*

- let $b_1, \ldots, b_h$ $(h \geq 0)$ be the successors of $\nu$ s.t. $\ell_{\mathcal{C}}(b_i) = solid$,
- let $c_1, \ldots, c_k$ $(k \geq 0)$ those s.t. $\ell_{\mathcal{C}}(c_i) = dashed$,

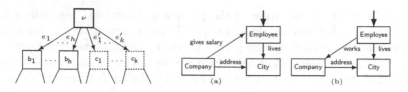

**Fig. 3.** Graph for computing $\Psi_\nu(G)$ and two equivalent acyclic queries

- for $i = 1, \ldots, h$ and $j = 1, \ldots, k$ let $e_i$ be the edge which links $\nu$ to $b_i$ and $e'_j$ the one which links $\nu$ to $c_j$. If $\ell_C(\nu) = solid$, then:

$$\Psi_\nu(G) = \varphi(\nu) \wedge \bigwedge_{i=1\ldots h} EX_{\varphi(e_i)}(\Psi_{b_i}(G)) \wedge \bigwedge_{j=1\ldots k} AX_{\varphi(e'_j)}(\Psi_{c_j}(G))$$

else ($\ell_C(\nu) = dashed$):

$$\Psi_\nu(G) = \neg\varphi(\nu) \vee \bigvee_{i=1\ldots h} AX_{\varphi(e_i)}(\Psi_{b_i}(G)) \vee \bigvee_{j=1\ldots k} EX_{\varphi(e'_j)}(\Psi_{c_j}(G))$$

Given a graph $G$, let $\bar{G}$ be the graph obtained from $G$ by complementation of the colors of edges and nodes (solid becomes dashed and vice versa). It is immediate to prove, by induction on the depth of the subgraph of $G$ that can be reached from a node $\nu$, that $\Psi_\nu(G) = \neg\Psi_\nu(\bar{G})$. Moreover, by the recursive definition of the formula, and by the acyclicity of $G$, $\Psi_\nu(G)$ is a *CTL* formula.

**Definition 13.** *Let $G = \langle N, E, \ell \rangle$ be an acyclic $\mathbb{W}$-graph, $\nu \in N$, and $Q = \langle G, \nu \rangle$ be an accessible query. The formula associated to $Q$ is $\Psi_\nu(G)$.*

Observe that each node and edge of $G$ is used to build the formula.

*Remark 1.* The size of the formula $\Psi_\nu(G)$ can grow exponentially w.r.t. $|G|$, since the construction of the formula involves the unfolding of a DAG. However, it is only a representation problem: It is easy to compute the formula avoiding repetitions of subformulae and keeping the memory allocation linear w.r.t. $|G|$.

The condition on the accessibility of all nodes of $G$ for $\nu$ can be weakened. Consider, for instance, the two goals of Fig. 3. If works is the inverse relation of gives salary (i.e. gives salary$^{-1}$), then one expects the same results from queries (a) and (b). Thus, the idea is to swap the direction of some edges, replacing the labeling relation with its inverse[4].

**Algorithm 1** *Let $G = \langle N, E, \ell \rangle$ be an acyclic solid $\mathbb{W}$-graph and $\nu \in N$.*

1. *Let $\hat{G} = \langle N, \hat{E} \rangle$ be the non-directed graph obtained from $G$ defining $\hat{E} = \{\{m, n\} : \langle m, \ell, n \rangle \in E\}$.*

---

[4] Recall that in the KTS associated to a $\mathbb{W}$-instance, inverse relations for all the relations involved occur explicitly: the framework is tuned to deal also with this case.

2. *Identify each connected component of $\hat{G}$ by one of its nodes. Use $\nu$ for its connected component. Let $\mu_1, \ldots, \mu_h$ be the other chosen nodes.*
3. *Execute a breadth-first visit of $\hat{G}$ starting from $\nu, \mu_1, \ldots, \mu_h$.*
4. *Consider the list of nodes $\nu = n_0 < n_1 < \cdots < n_k$ ordered by the above visit.*
5. *Build the $\mathbb{W}$-graph $\boldsymbol{G} = \langle N, \boldsymbol{E}, \ell \rangle$ from $G$ as follows:*

$$\boldsymbol{E} = (E \setminus \{\langle n_a, \langle c, p \rangle, n_b \rangle \in E : b < a\}) \cup$$
$$\{\langle n_b, \langle c, p^{-1} \rangle, n_a \rangle : \langle n_a, \langle c, p \rangle, n_b \rangle \in E \wedge b < a\}$$

The above algorithm always produces an acyclic graph, since the edges follow a strict order of the nodes. All the nodes of each connected component of $\hat{G}$ are accessible from the corresponding selected node $(\nu, \mu_1, \ldots, \mu_h)$ by construction (they have been reached by a visit). Algorithm 1 can be implemented so as to run in time $O(|N| + |E|)$ and, for each node $\nu, \mu_1, \ldots, \mu_h$, we can compute:

$$\Psi_\nu(\boldsymbol{G}), \Psi_{\mu_1}(\boldsymbol{G}), \ldots, \Psi_{\mu_h}(\boldsymbol{G})$$

We recall here the semantics of $\mathsf{EF}_a(\phi)$ (see Sect. 2): $s \models \mathsf{EF}_a(\phi)$ iff there is a path $\langle \pi_0, \ell_0, \pi_1, \ell_1 \cdots \rangle$ s.t. $\pi_0 = s$ and $\exists j \in \mathbb{N}$ s.t. $\pi_j \models \phi$ and $(\forall i < j) \, \ell_i \in a$.

**Definition 14.** *Let $G = \langle N, E, \ell \rangle$ be an acyclic solid $\mathbb{W}$-graph and $\nu \in N$. Let $Q = \langle G, \nu \rangle$ a $\mathbb{W}$-query. The formula associated with $Q$ is ($Act_G$ is as in Def. 9):*

$$\Psi_\nu(\boldsymbol{G}) \wedge \mathsf{EF}_{Act_G}(\Psi_{\mu_1}(\boldsymbol{G})) \wedge \cdots \wedge \mathsf{EF}_{Act_G}(\Psi_{\mu_h}(\boldsymbol{G}))$$

Observe that Algorithm 1 terminates even if $G$ admits cycles (save self-loops). However, in these cases, the semantics of the query is lost. Cyclic queries require different modal operators (see Sect. 5.5).

Let us study one more family of acyclic queries that can be handled, via reduction to the accessible query case.

**Definition 15.** *Let $G = \langle N, E, \ell \rangle$ be an acyclic $\mathbb{W}$-graph, let $\nu \in N$, $\ell_C(\nu) = $ solid, and $Q = \langle G, \nu \rangle$ be a $\mathbb{W}$-query.*

1. *Let $G_s = \langle N_s, E_s, \ell|_{N_s} \rangle$ its solid subgraph (cf. Def. 6).*
2. *Apply the Algorithm 1 to $G_s$. Let $\nu, \mu_1, \ldots, \mu_h$ be the root nodes.*
3. *Swap in $G$ the same edges that have been swapped by Algorithm 1 in $G_s$ obtaining the graph $\boldsymbol{G}$.*
4. *If $\boldsymbol{G}$ is acyclic, then compute the formulae $\Psi_\nu(\boldsymbol{G}), \Psi_{\mu_1}(\boldsymbol{G}), \ldots, \Psi_{\mu_h}(\boldsymbol{G})$*
5. *If all the nodes of $G$ have been visited during the last phase, then the formula associated with $Q$ is: $\Psi_\nu(\boldsymbol{G}) \wedge \mathsf{EF}_{Act_G}(\Psi_{\mu_1}(\boldsymbol{G})) \wedge \cdots \wedge \mathsf{EF}_{Act_G}(\Psi_{\mu_h}(\boldsymbol{G}))$*

Let us explain why we applicate the algorithm only to $G_s$. Consider, for example, the query $(a)$ in Fig. 4. According to Def. 15, its formula is:

$$\mathsf{Teacher} \wedge \mathsf{AX}_{\neg\mathsf{teaches}}(\neg\mathsf{Course}) \wedge \mathsf{EF}_{Act_G}(\mathsf{Student} \wedge \mathsf{AX}_{\neg\mathsf{attends}}(\neg\mathsf{Course})) \quad (1)$$

which requires to find those Teachers who teach all the Courses, if there is somewhere a Student who attends all the Courses.

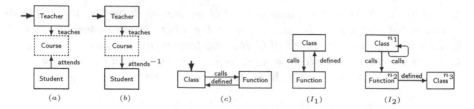

**Fig. 4.** W-queries and W-instances

The Algorithm 1 should replace the edge labeled attends in the query $(a)$ with an edge labeled attends$^{-1}$, as depicted in the query $(b)$ of Fig. 4, leading to:

$$\text{Teacher} \wedge \text{AX}_{\neg\text{teaches}}(\neg\text{Course} \vee \text{AX}_{\text{attends}^{-1}}\text{Student}) \tag{2}$$

The two formulae have different models. (1) is closer than (2) to the interpretation of graph-based formulae in other frameworks (e.g. G-Log).

### 5.5 Cyclic Queries

In this section we extend the technique assigning a temporal formula to queries admitting cycles. We make use of the Generally operator, used as $\text{EG}_a(\phi)$, whose semantics is (see Sect. 2): $s \models \text{EG}_a(\phi)$ iff there is a path $\pi = \langle \pi_0, \ell_0, \pi_1, \ell_1 \ldots \rangle$, s.t. $\pi_0 = s$ and $\forall j \in \mathbb{N} \; \pi_j \models \phi$ and $\ell_j \in a$.

Consider the query $(c)$ in Fig. 4. It requires to collect *all the classes which call a function defined inside theirselves*. This property could be expressed by:

$$\Psi_{(c)} = \text{Class} \wedge \text{EX}_{\text{calls}}(\text{Function} \wedge \text{EX}_{\text{defined}}(\text{Class})) \wedge$$
$$\text{EG}_{\{\text{calls,defined}\}}((\text{Class} \vee \text{Function}) \wedge \text{Class} \rightarrow \text{X}_{\text{calls}}(\text{Function}) \wedge$$
$$\text{Function} \rightarrow \text{X}_{\text{defined}}(\text{Class}))$$

The modal operator X is used without any path quantifier. This is allowed in $CTL^*$ but not in $CTL$ [18]. The first part of the formula $\Psi_{(c)}$ is aimed at identifying cycles of length greater than or equal to two, and the Generally operator imposes to retrieve only cyclic paths where nodes labeled Class alternate with nodes labeled Function.

With the $CTL$ logic it is only possible to approximate the translation of this kind of cyclic queries:

$$\Psi'_{(c)} = \text{Class} \wedge \text{EX}_{\text{calls}}(\text{Function} \wedge \text{EX}_{\text{defined}}(\text{Class})) \wedge$$
$$\text{EG}_{\{\text{calls,defined}\}}(\text{Class} \rightarrow \text{EX}_{\text{calls}}(\text{Function} \wedge \text{EX}_{\text{defined}}(\text{Class})))$$

The node Class of instance $(I_1)$ in Fig. 4 satisfies both the formulas $\Psi_{(c)}$ and $\Psi'_{(c)}$, while the node $n_1$ of instance $(I_2)$ in Fig. 4 satisfies $\Psi'_{(c)}$ but not $\Psi_{(c)}$. Thus, the $CTL$ translation gives only an approximation of the $CTL^*$ one.

Since the model-checking problem for $CTL^*$ is PSPACE complete, we accept this loss of precision, and we assign a formula to a (pointed) cycle.

**Definition 16.** *The formula* $\Psi_{\nu_1}(G)$ *associated to a red cyclic graph* $G = \langle\{\nu_1,$ $\ldots, \nu_n\}, \{\langle\nu_1, \ell_1, \nu_2\rangle, \langle\nu_2, \ell_2, \nu_3\rangle, \ldots, \langle\nu_{n-1}, \ell_{n-1}, \nu_n, \rangle, \langle\nu_n, \ell_n, \nu_1\rangle\}, \ell, \nu_1\rangle$   *is defined as:*

$$\Psi_{\nu_1}(G) = \Psi_{\nu_1}(C) \wedge \mathsf{EG}_{\{\ell_1,\ldots,\ell_n\}}(\varphi(\nu_1) \to \Psi_{\nu_1}(C))$$

*where* $\varphi(\nu_1)$ *is as in Def. 11,* $\Psi_{\nu_1}(C)$ *is the formula associated to the DAG* $C = \langle\{\nu_1, \ldots, \nu_{n+1}\}, \{\langle\nu_1, \ell_1, \nu_2\rangle, \langle\nu_2, \ell_2, \nu_3\rangle, \ldots, \langle\nu_{n-1}, \ell_{n-1}, \nu_n, \rangle, \langle\nu_n, \ell_n, \nu_{n+1}\rangle\}\rangle,$ *rooted at* $\nu_1$, *and* $\nu_{n+1}$ *is a "copy" of* $\nu_1$, *i.e. a new node s.t.* $\ell(\nu_{n+1}) = \ell(\nu_1)$.

If a graph $G$ is in one of the forms of the previous sections and, moreover, instead of some leaf nodes it contains cycles of the form above (this test can be easily performed using the graph of the strongly connected components), we can use the formula in Def. 16 as subroutine to compute the global formula.

# 6   Complexity Issues and Implementation of the Method

Let us state the main computational results of our approach:

**Theorem 2.** *Let* $\langle G, \nu\rangle$ *be a* W*-query in one of the forms described in Sect. 5.2. Querying a* W*-instance* $I$ *with* $G$ *can be done in linear time on* $|\mathcal{K}_I|$ *and* $|\Psi_\nu(G)|$.

The proof of the theorem follows from [11]. When computing $\mathcal{K}_I$, a quadratic time and space complexity is introduced as negative relations are computed and stored. We will discuss later on in this section when this extra complexity can be avoided.

As far as the size of the formula is concerned, as discussed in Remark 1, even if $|\Psi_\nu(G)|$ can grow exponentially with $|G|$, it is natural to represent it using a linear amount of memory. This compact representation is allowed by the model-checker NuSMV.

**Corollary 1.** *Querying a* W*-instance* $I$ *with a* W*-query* $G$ *can be done in time linear on* $|I|^2$ *and* $|G|$.

As shown in Sect. 5.5 for cyclic queries, it seems to be impossible to map all the queries in *CTL* formulae. This fact can be formally justified. The semantics of acyclic W-queries without negation can be proved to be equivalent to that of G-Log queries without negation (Sect. 7). If we extended this equivalence result to cyclic queries (even without negation), we would provide a polynomial time implementation for a subset of G-Log in which data retrieval is equivalent to the subgraph bisimulation problem, proved to be NP complete in [16].

We have effectively tested the data retrieval technique presented in the previous sections by using the model checker NuSMV [10]. Due to lack of space, we do not enter here into the details of the implementation (see [17]). We only stress here on the fact that negated edges (relations) are not always needed to be explicitly stored in the model. If the query expresses negation only by means of dashed edges entering dashing nodes, we can avoid to store explicitly negated edges (we translate the formula with an universal quantification on paths, cf. Fig. 2), obtaining linear time complexity instead of quadratic complexity. This fact can be

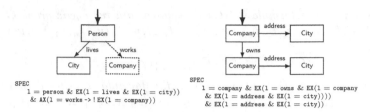

**Fig. 5.** Translation of Queries in NuSMV

proved using the fact that model-checkers use 'paths' to traverse a KTS and thus to find pairs (or tuples) of nodes connected with a certain edge.

As already said, a formula can be stored as a DAG, without the unnecessary loss of space due to the repetition of subformulae. This allows linear time dependency on the size of the query. Two examples are reported in Fig. 5.

## 7   Comparison and Applicability of the Method

We have studied the applicability of the method to three existing query languages for semistructured data: UnQL, GraphLog, and G-Log. Due to lack of space, we give only a brief overview here. For further details, see [17]. Then we discuss in detail the problems related to the implementation of the *join* operation in our framework.

**UnQL** is a language for querying data organized as a rooted directed graph with labeled edges [3]. A rooted graph is a pointed graph such that all the nodes are accessible from the root node (the point). UnQL database instances can be immediately and completely mapped to $\mathbb{W}$-instances. Basically, it is sufficient to encode labeled edges into labeled nodes. We replace every labeled edge $m \xrightarrow{label} n$ by the two edges $m \longrightarrow \mu, \mu \longrightarrow n$, where $\mu$ is a new node labeled *label*.

In order to encode UnQL queries into modal formulae we have used the modal operator B (Before), whose meaning is the following (we have omitted edge names since all labels have been moved to nodes): $s \models \mathsf{AB}\phi$ iff for all paths $\pi = \langle \ldots, x, _-, s, _-, \pi_1, \ldots \rangle$, it holds that $x \models \psi$, whereas $s \models \mathsf{EB}\psi$ iff there is a path $\pi = \langle \ldots, x, _-, s, _-, \pi_1, \ldots \rangle$ such that $x \models \psi$ [5].

The expression (1): **select** $t$ **where** $R1 \Rightarrow \backslash t \leftarrow DB$ computes *the union of all trees $t$ such that $DB$ contains an edge $R1 \Rightarrow t$ emanating from the root*. This concept can be expressed by the temporal formula $\varphi_{(1)} = \bot \wedge \mathsf{EB}(R1)$.

The UnQL expression (2): **select** $t$ **where** $\backslash \ell \Rightarrow \backslash t \leftarrow DB$ retrieves *any edge emanating from the root* and is translated by the formula $\varphi_{(2)} = \bot \wedge \mathsf{EB}(\neg \bot \wedge \mathsf{EB}(DB))$.

An UnQL query that looks at arbitrarily depth into the database to find *all edges with a numeric label* is (3): **select** $\{\ell\}$ **where** $_-* \Rightarrow \backslash \ell \Rightarrow _- \leftarrow DB, isnumber(\ell)$. It can be easily translated into the *CTL* formula $\psi_{(3)} = \neg \bot \wedge number$. Note that *number* is an atomic proposition that holds in numeric states of the original database.

---
[5] The B operator can be removed (by using X) since inverse relations can be stored.

The UnQL query: **select**  $\{Tup \Rightarrow \{A \Rightarrow x, D \Rightarrow z\}\}$
$\qquad\qquad$ **where**  $R1 \Rightarrow Tup \Rightarrow \{A \Rightarrow \backslash x, C \Rightarrow \backslash y\} \leftarrow DB,$
$\qquad\qquad\qquad\quad R2 \Rightarrow Tup \Rightarrow \{C \Rightarrow \backslash y, D \Rightarrow \backslash z\} \leftarrow DB$

computes *the join of R1 and R2 on their common attribute C and the project onto A and D*. UnQL queries expressing a join condition on a graph do not have a corresponding temporal formula, as we discuss at the end of the section.

Although we have not developed an algorithm to translate UnQL queries into CTL formulae, we can conclude that our approach allows to correctly deal with join-free queries of UnQL.

**GraphLog** is a query language based on a graph representation of both data and queries [12]. Queries represent graph patterns corresponding to paths in databases. For example, the graph $I$ in Fig. 6 is a representation of a flights schedule database. Each flight number is related to the cities it connects (by the predicates *from* and *to*, respectively) and to the departure and arrival time (by the predicates *departure* and *arrival*).

GraphLog represents databases by means of *directed labeled multigraphs* which precisely correspond to W-instances; these databases are not required to be rooted and therefore the corresponding W-graphs are not necessarily rooted. Queries ask for patterns that must be present or absent in the database graph. A graphical query is a set of query graphs, each of them defining (constructive part) a set of new edges (relations) that are added to the graph whenever the path (non-constructive part) specified in the query itself is found (or not found for negative requests). More in detail, a query graph is a directed labeled multigraph with a distinguished edge (it defines a new relation that will hold, after the query application, between two objects in a chosen database whenever they fulfill the requirements of the query graph) and without isolated nodes. Moreover, each edge is labeled by a literal (i.e. positive or negative occurrence of a predicate applied to a sequence of variables and constants) or by a *closure literal*, which is simply a literal followed by the positive closure operator; each distinguished edge can only be labeled by a positive non-closure literal.

For example, graph $(G)$ in Fig. 6 requires to find in a database two flights $F1$ and $F2$ departing from and arriving to the same city $C$, respectively. The edge 'result' will connect $F1$ and $F2$. The *CTL* formula associated with the non-costructive part of this query is:

$$\Psi(G) = \mathsf{Flight} \wedge \mathsf{EX_{to}}(\mathsf{City} \wedge \mathsf{EX_{from-1}}\mathsf{Flight})$$

(which describes the node $F1$). $\Psi(G)$ is satisfied by the state labeled 109.

The possibility to express closure literals causes some difficulties in the translation of query graphs into *CTL* formulae. Consider for example, the two query graphs in Fig. 7 representing relationships between people. Their natural translation into *CTL* should be:

$\Psi(Q_1) = \mathsf{Person} \wedge (\mathsf{EX_{parent}}\mathsf{Person}) \rightarrow (\mathsf{Person} \wedge \mathsf{EX_{parent}}(\mathsf{Person}\wedge$
$\qquad\qquad \mathsf{EX_{relative-1}}\mathsf{Person}))$
$\Psi(Q_2) = \mathsf{Person} \wedge (\mathsf{EX_{relative}}(\mathsf{Person} \wedge \mathsf{EX_{relative}}\mathsf{Person})) \rightarrow$
$\qquad\qquad (\mathsf{Person} \wedge \mathsf{EX_{relative}}(\mathsf{Person} \wedge \mathsf{EX_{relative}}(\mathsf{Person} \wedge \mathsf{EX_{relative-1}}\mathsf{Person})))$

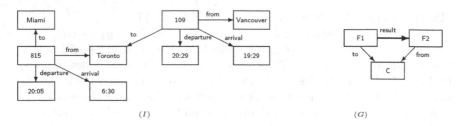

**Fig. 6.** GraphLog representation of a database and a query

It is easy to see that the node $n$ of the instance graph $\mathcal{I}$ in Fig. 7 satisfies the formula $\Psi(Q_1)$ but does not fulfill the natural interpretation of relationship between people. The problem is that in $CTL$ it is not possible to constrain that the last unary predicate Person in $\Psi(Q_1)$ has to be satisfied by the same state of the first unary predicate Person.

In order to overcome this limitation one should firstly compute the closure of labeled graphs representing databases. Intuitively, computing graph-theoretical closure entails inserting a new edge labeled $a$ between two nodes, if they are connected via a path of any length composed of edges that are all labeled $a$ in the original graph (see [14] for an application of graph closure to XML documents). Computing the closure is well-known to be polynomial time w.r.t. the size of nodes of the graph.

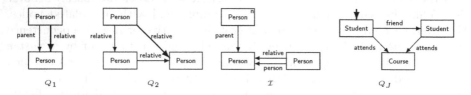

**Fig. 7.** Two query graphs, an instance, an a 'join' query

We can conclude that our approach based on model-checking techniques allows to correctly deal with join-free queries of GraphLog without closure operators.

**G-Log** [27], as GraphLog, is a query language in which data, queries, and generic rules are expressed by graphs. As far as instances are concerned, syntax of G-Log instances is the same as that of W. G-Log queries allow more flexibility then W-ones. Nevertheless, often G-Log queries has only one "green" node with an edge pointing to a "red" node $\nu$. These queries are the same as W-queries, in which $\nu$ is the node pointed by the query. In G-Log two kinds of nodes are allowed, complex and atomic nodes, but this feauture can be simulated by modifying the co-domain of the *label* function. Instead, solid edges are forbidden to enter into dashed nodes in G-Log. This feauture of W is one of the main points for programming nesting quantification and for expressing in a compact way the universal quantification. Only existential requirements are instead allowed in G-Log queries. If a $W$ query fulfills this further requirement, is a G-Log query.

Semantics of query application is given in [27] via the notion of *graph embedding* and in [13] (cf. [17]) using the notion of *subgraph bisimulation* (both NP complete). We have formally proved that for acyclic queries that are allowed both in $W$ and in G-log (with the semantics of [13]) the results of query application is the same in the two languages. We have already discussed (Sect. 6) that for complexity limits we cannot extend the method to all cyclic queries.

The problem of expressing *join* conditions by means of *CTL* formulae remains open, because in the propositional modal logics framework there is no way to distinguish different states having the same set of local properties. A possibility to overcome this problem is to add to the set of local properties of each state an identificator of the state (of course, we assume that the set of all states is finite). For example, the $W$-query $Q_J$ in Fig. 7 requires to find all the Students that attend a Course together with (at least) one friend. If we know that the identificators of Course nodes are $c_1$ and $c_2$, we could translate the query with the *CTL* formula

$$(\mathsf{Student} \wedge \mathsf{EX}_{\mathsf{attends}}(\mathsf{Course} \wedge c_1) \wedge \mathsf{EX}_{\mathsf{friend}}(\mathsf{Student} \wedge \mathsf{EX}_{\mathsf{attends}}(\mathsf{Course} \wedge c_1)))\vee$$
$$(\mathsf{Student} \wedge \mathsf{EX}_{\mathsf{attends}}(\mathsf{Course} \wedge c_2) \wedge \mathsf{EX}_{\mathsf{friend}}(\mathsf{Student} \wedge \mathsf{EX}_{\mathsf{attends}}(\mathsf{Course} \wedge c_2)))$$

This translation causes an explosion of the formula size and it requires also to know in advance the set of identificators of a certain state (in the example the Course state).

## 8   Conclusions and Future Work

In this work we have shown how it is possible to effectively solve the data retrieval problem for semistructured data using techniques and algorithms coming from the model-checking community. Note that this approach could also be applied to XML-based languages such as Quilt [8] and XPath [29]. The input and output of these languages are documents usually modeled as trees. Once again, in this setting model-checking algorithms can correctly deal with properties expressing conditions to be satisfied on paths but without joins, grouping, or aggregation functions of SQL.

Some other works on this direction are [9,23,24]. In [9] the author proposes an approach for inferring properties of models by using a model checker. He extends the syntax of *CTL* by allowing the special symbol '?', and characterizes a subset of this new language that allows linear-time decidability. In [23] the authors suggest to query data using 'query automata', that are particular cases of two-ways deterministic tree automata. They show the equivalence with formula expressible in second-order monadic logic. In [24] they identifies subclasses of formulae/automata that allow efficient algorithms. A future work is to determine the exact relationships with our approach.

The *graph-formula* translation could be extended to a wider family of graphs including join conditions, and it might be interesting to find the exact subset of $CTL^*$ (whose model-checking problem is PSPACE complete) needed to translate queries of interest. Moreover, similar techniques are shown to be possible for extracting formulae from SQL-like queries. The modal logic semantics forces a bisimulation equivalence between subgraphs fulfilling the same formula. This allows us to say that two nodes with the same properties are equivalent but not to require that they are the same node. This prevents us to model correctly the *join* operation. We have implemented the method on the model-checker NuSMV. However, for an effective implementation on Web-databases some form of heuristic (e.g. check part of the domain name) must be applied in order to cut the search space for accessible data (that can be all the web). This issue is studied in [15] in a slight different context. Another future direction is to mix this technique with constraint-based data retrieval (where temporal formulae can be used directly).

## Acknowledgements

Nico Lavarini has contributed with his Master's Thesis to the earlier stages of the research presented in this work. We thank also A. Cimatti, R. Giacobazzi, C. Piazza, M. Roveri, and L. Tanca for useful discussions.

## References

1. S. Abiteboul. Querying semi-structured data. In *Proc. of ICDT*. Vol. 1186 of *LNCS*, pp. 1–18, 1997.
2. S. Abiteboul, D. Quass, J. McHugh, J. Widom, and J. L. Wiener. The Lorel query language for semistructured data. *Int'l J. on Digital Libraries*, 1(1):68–88, 1997.
3. P. Buneman, S. B. Davidson, G. G. Hillebrand, and D. Suciu. A Query Language and Optimization Techniques for Unstructured Data. In *Proc. of the 1996 ACM SIGMOD*, pp. 505–516, 1996.
4. P. Buneman, S. B. Davidson, G. G. Hillebrand, and D. Suciu. Adding structure to unstructured data. In Proc. of *Database Theory; 6th Int'l Conf.*, pp. 336–350, 1997.
5. P. J. Cameron. First-Order Logic. In L. W. Beineke and R. J. Wilson (Eds.): *Graph Connections. Relationships Between Graph Theory and other Areas of Mathematics*. Clarendon Press, 1997.
6. L. Cardelli and G. Ghelli. A query language for semistructured data based on the Ambient logic. In Proc. of *ESOP 2001*, Vol. 2028 of LNCS, pp. 1–22, 2001.
7. S. Ceri, S. Comai, E. Damiani, P. Fraternali, S. Paraboschi, and L. Tanca. XML-GL: a graphical language for querying and restructuring XML documents. *Proc. of WWW8*, Canada, 1999.
8. D. Chamberlin, J. Rubie, and D. Florescu. Quilt: An XML Query Language for Heterogeneous Data Sources. In *Proc. of the World Wide Web and Databases, Third International Workshop WebDB 2000*, Vol. 1997 of LNCS, pp. 1–25, 2001.
9. W. Chan. Temporal-logic Queries. In *Proc. of 12th CAV*. Vol. 1855 of LNCS, pp. 450–463. Chicago, USA, 2000.

10. A. Cimatti, E. M. Clarke, F. Giunchiglia, and M. Roveri. NuSMV: a new Symbolic Model Verifier. *Proc. of 11th CAV*. Vol. 1633 of LNCS, pp. 495–499, 1999.
11. E. M. Clarke, E. A. Emerson, and A. P. Sistla. Automatic verification of finite-state concurrent system using temporal logic specification. *ACM TOPLAS*, 8(2):244–263, 1986.
12. M. P. Consens and A. O. Mendelzon. GraphLog: a Visual Formalism for Real Life Recursion. In Proc. of the 9th *ACM PODS'90*, pp. 404–416, 1990.
13. A. Cortesi, A. Dovier, E. Quintarelli, and L. Tanca. Operational and Abstract Semantics of a Query Language for Semi-Structured Information. In *Proc. of DDLP'98*, pp. 127–139. GMD Report 22, 1998. Extended Version to appear in *Theoretical Computer Science*.
14. E. Damiani and L. Tanca. Blind Queries to XML Data. In *Proc. of 11th International Conference, DEXA 2000*, Vol. 1873 of LNCS, pp. 345–356, 2000.
15. L. de Alfaro. Model Checking the World Wide Web. In *Proc. of 13th Conference on Computer Aided Verification*, Vol. 2102 of LNCS, pp. 337–349, 2001.
16. A. Dovier and C. Piazza. The Subgraph Bisimulation Problem and its Complexity. Univ. di Udine, Dip. di Matematica e Informatica, RR 27/00, Nov. 2000.
17. A. Dovier and E. Quintarelli. Model-Checking Based Data Retrieval. Technical Report, Politecnico di Milano, May 2000 (www.elet.polimi.it/~quintare).
18. E. A. Emerson. Temporal and modal logic. In J. van Leeuwen, editor, *Handbook of Theoretical Computer Science*, vol. B: Formal Models and Semantics. Elsevier, and MIT Press, 1990.
19. M. Fernandez, D. Florescu, A. Levy, and D. Suciu. A query language for a web-site management system. *SIGMOD Record*, 26(3):4–11, 1997.
20. P. C. Kannellakis and S. A. Smolka. CCS Expressions, Finite State Processes, and Three Problems of Equivalence. *Information and Computation*, 86(1):43–68, 1990.
21. R. Milner. A Calculus of Communicating Systems. Vol. 92 of LNCS, 1980.
22. M. Müller-Olm, D. Schmidt, and B. Steffen. Model-checking. A tutorial introduction. In *Proc. of SAS'99*. Vol. 1694 of LNCS, pp. 330–354, 1999.
23. F. Neven and T. Schwentick. Query Automata. In *Proc. of the 18th ACM SIGACT-SIGMOD-SIGART Symp. on Princ. of DB Systems*, ACM Press, pp. 205–214, 1999.
24. F. Neven and T. Schwentick. Expressive and Efficient Pattern Languages for Tree-Structured Data. In *Proc. of the 19th ACM SIGACT-SIGMOD-SIGART Symp. on Princ. of DB Systems*, ACM Press, pp. 145–156, 2000.
25. R. Paige and R. E. Tarjan. Three Partition refinements algorithms. *SIAM J. on Computing*, 16(6):973–989, 1987.
26. Y. Papakonstantinou, H. Garcia-Molina, and J. Widom. Object exchange across heterogeneous information sources. In *Proc. of the 11th ICDE*, pp. 251–260, 1995.
27. J. Paredaens, P. Peelman, and L. Tanca. G–Log: A Declarative Graphical Query Language. *IEEE TKDE*, 7(3):436–453, 1995.
28. D. Quass, A. Rajaraman, Y. Sagiv, J. Ullman, and J. Widom. Querying Semistructured Heterogeneus Information. In *Proc. of DOOD'95*, pp. 319–344, 1995.
29. World Wide Web Consortium. *XML Path Language (XPath) version 1.0*. www.w3.org/TR/xpath.html, W3C Reccomendation, November 1999.

# A Temporal Query Language for OLAP: Implementation and a Case Study

Alejandro A. Vaisman[1] and Alberto O. Mendelzon[2]

[1] Universidad de Buenos Aires
avaisman@dc.uba.ar
[2] University of Toronto
mendel@db.toronto.edu

**Abstract.** Commercial OLAP systems usually treat OLAP dimensions as static entities. In practice, dimension updates are often necessary in order to adapt the multidimensional database to changing requirements. In earlier work we proposed a temporal multidimensional model and *TOLAP*, a query language supporting it, accounting for dimension updates and schema evolution at a high level of abstraction. In this paper we present our implementation of the model and the query language. We show how to translate a *TOLAP* program to SQL, and present a real-life case study, a medical center in Buenos Aires. We apply our implementation to this case study in order to show how our approach can address problems that occur in real situations and that current non-temporal commercial systems cannot deal with. We present results on query and dimension update performance, and briefly describe a visualization tool that allows editing and running *TOLAP* queries, performing dimension updates, and browsing dimensions across time.

## 1 Introduction

In models for OLAP (On Line Analytical Processing) [7,2,9], data is represented as a set of *dimensions* and *fact tables*. Dimensions are usually organized as hierarchies, supporting different levels of data aggregation. We argued in earlier work [5,6,10] that, although commercial OLAP tools largely do not support updates to dimension tables, these updates are likely to occur in many real-life situations. For instance, in Figure 1, a dimension *Geography* is represented as a hierarchy with levels *city, province, region, country,* and a distinguished level *All*. A business decision may allow regions to be spread across different countries(which is not allowed in the dimension of Figure 1). This change may be incorporated by deleting the edge joining the *region* and *country* levels, and adding a new edge from *region* to *All*.

Furthermore, thinking of a data warehouse as a materialized view of data located in multiple sources [14], it may happen that the structure of these sources changes, a new source is added, or an old one dropped. Any of these changes may require updates to the structure of some dimensions.

In earlier work [10] we showed that in an evolving OLAP scenario like the above, systems need temporal features to keep track of the different states of

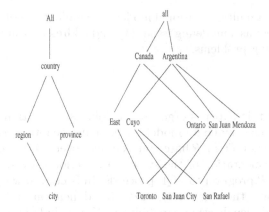

**Fig. 1.** A *Geography* dimension

a data warehouse throughout its lifespan. We introduced the *temporal multidi-mensional data model,* and a temporal OLAP query language called *TOLAP.* We showed that *TOLAP* expresses typical OLAP queries in a concise and ele-gant fashion. Moreover, *TOLAP* fully supports schema evolution and versioning, unlike the best-known temporal query languages such as TSQL2, which only supports schema versioning in a limited way ([12], p.29).

In this paper we present our implementation of the model and the query language. We show how to translate a *TOLAP* program to SQL and present a real-life case study, using data from a medical center in Buenos Aires, Ar-gentina. We apply our implementation to this case study in order to show how our approach can address problems that occur in real situations and that current non-temporal commercial systems cannot deal with. We present results on query and dimension update performance, and briefly describe a visualization tool that allows editing and running *TOLAP* queries, performing dimension updates, and browsing dimensions across time.

### Related Work

As mentioned above, in previous work we argued that in practice one encoun-ters a wide range of possible dimension updates which the existing models fail to capture. Kimball analyzes this problem to some degree [7], introducing the con-cept of *slowly changing dimensions*, which partially covers updates to dimension instances. Kimball suggests some partial solutions, like timestamping dimension tuples with their validity intervals. This proposal neither takes schema versioning into account, nor considers complex dimension updates.

Work carried out at the *Time Center* at the University of Arizona [1] analyzes the performance of several SQL queries on three different implementations of an OLAP schema: "time series" fact tables, an "event" fact table, and dimensions timestamped in the way proposed by Kimball. This work was, to our knowledge, the first to suggest an approach to temporal OLAP. Our work went further by proposing a model and a query language to address temporal issues at a higher level of abstraction.

More recently, a multidimensional model for handling complex data considers the temporal aspect as a modeling issue [11], and addresses it in conjunction with other data modeling problems.

## Paper Outline

The remainder of this paper is organized as follows: in Section 2 we review the temporal multidimensional data model. In Section 3 we introduce the case study, along with a review of *TOLAP* based on examples over this case. In Section 4 we describe the implementation of the system. In Section 5 we show how a translation of a *TOLAP* program to SQL proceeds. In Section 6 we present different tests performed over the case study, discussing dimension update performance, expressiveness and visualization capabilities. We conclude in Section 7.

## 2   The Temporal Multidimensional Model

Due to space limitations we will introduce the *Temporal Multidimensional Model* informally and by an example. We refer to our previous work for full details [10].

### 2.1   Temporal Dimensions

In what follows, we will consider time as discrete; that is, a point in the time-line, called a *time point*, will correspond to an integer.

A temporal dimension schema is a directed acyclic graph where each node represents a *level*, and each edge is labeled with the time interval within which the edge was/is valid. At any instant $t$, the graph is a partial order with a unique bottom level $l_{inf}$ and a unique top level *All*.

Each dimension, at any time instant $t$, has an associated *instance* obtained by mapping each level to a set of *elements*. For each pair of levels connected by an edge, an instance defines a function $\rho$ called *rollup,* that maps the elements of the source level to the elements of the destination level. The rollup function from level $l_1$ to level $l_2$ at instant $t$ is denoted by $\rho[t]_{l_1}^{l_2}$. Moreover, dimension instances must satisfy the *consistency condition* : at every instant $t$ in the dimension's lifespan, for every pair of paths from one level to another, composing the rollup functions along the two paths yields identical functions.

**Notation:** In the figures of this section, a label $t_i$ associated to an edge in a graph, will mean that the edge is valid for all $t \geq t_i$, and a label $t_i^*$, that the edge was valid for all $t < t_i$. If an edge has no label, it is valid for all the dimension's lifespan.

*Example 1.* Consider the dimension *Store* in Figure 2, with levels *storeId*, *storeType*, *city*, *region*, and *All*. The figure depicts the history of this dimension as follows: the initial levels were *storeId*, *city*, *region* and *All*. At time $t_1$, level *storeType* was added above *storeId*. As there is only one possible top level, an edge is also added between *storeType* and *All*. This is called a *Generalization* [5].

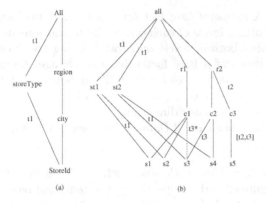

**Fig. 2.** (a) Temporal dimension schema (b) Temporal dimension instance

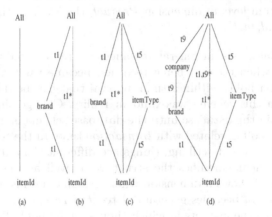

**Fig. 3.** A series of updates to dimension *Product*

Figure 2(b) shows a possible instance for the dimension *Store*. Here, store $s_5$ was valid between $t_2$ and $t_3$, and store $s_3$ was moved from city $c_1$ to city $c_2$ at time $t_3$ ($\rho^{city}_{storeId} [t_3] = c_2$).

Figure 3 shows a sequence of updates to a temporal dimension *Product*. Initially, *Product* consisted only of level *itemId*, and the distinguished level *All*. After that, level *brand* is added to the dimension, although the initial state is not lost (Figure 3(b)). Later, the type of the item is inserted, with level name *itemType*. Finally, the *company* an item belongs to is also added above level *brand* (Figure 3(d)).

## 2.2  Temporal Fact Tables

Factual data is stored in temporal fact tables. We will assume that given a set of dimensions $D$, a temporal fact table has a column for each dimension in $D$, a column for a distinguished dimension *Measure*, and a column for the

*Time* dimension. A *temporal base fact table* is a temporal fact table such that its levels are the bottom levels of each one of the dimensions in $D$ (plus *Measure* and *Time*). As these bottom levels may vary during the lifespan of the data warehouse, the schema of a base fact table can change. Keeping track of the different versions of the fact tables is called, like in temporal database literature, *schema versioning.* Note, however, that the attributes in any column of a fact table always belong to the same dimension.

A *Temporal Multidimensional Database* is a set of temporal dimensions and temporal fact tables.

*Example 2.* Given $D = \{Store, Product\}$ where dimensions *Store* and *Product* are the ones of Figures 2 and 3 respectively, the temporal base fact table associated to $D$ would have levels $\{storeId, itemId, m, t\}$, where $m$ is the measure and $t$ is the time associated to a fact. If updates occur such that at time $t_{12}$, *brand* becomes the bottom level of dimension *Product,* the levels in the fact table will be $\{storeId, brand, m, t\}$.

In temporal databases, in general, instances are represented using *valid* time, this is, the time when the fact being recorded became valid. On the contrary, a database schema holds within a time interval that can be different from the one within which this schema was valid in reality. Changes in the real world are not reflected in the database until the database schema is updated. Schema versioning, thus, is often related with *transaction* time. In the temporal multidimensional model we are describing, things are different than above. An update to a dimension schema modifies the structure as well as the instance of the dimension. Figure 2 shows a dimension where schema and instance updates occurred. When *storeId* becomes generalized to *storeType*, the associated rollups must correspond to the instants in which they actually hold. Thus, we consider that temporal dimensions are represented by *valid* time. It is straightforward to extend the model for supporting temporal dimensions with valid and transaction times. However, at the moment, our implementation supports valid time for dimensions.

Fact table instances can be represented using valid and transaction times, because the model supports user-defined time dimensions. In our implementation, valid and transaction times for fact tables are supported through system-maintained and user-defined time attributes. In Subsection 2.3 we give an example of these kinds of time attributes. When a bottom level of a dimension is deleted or a level is added below it, the schema of the associated fact tables are modified, and new versions are created for them automatically. Thus, in our implementation, fact table versioning is represented using transaction time.

## 2.3   The Case Study: A Medical Data Warehouse

Throughout this paper we will refer to a real-life case study, a medical center in Argentina. We will use this example to illustrate the need for temporal management in OLAP. We used six months of data from medical procedures performed on inpatients at the center. Each patient receives different services, including radiographies, electrocardiograms, medicine, disposable material, and so on. These services are denoted "Procedures". Data was taken from different tables in the clinic's operational database. Figure 4 shows the final state of the dimensions. We will explain in Section 6 how we simulated a temporal environment in which these dimensions were created at different times.

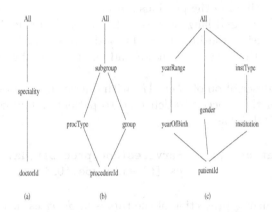

**Fig. 4.** Dimensions in the case study

Dimension *Procedure,* with bottom level *procedureId,* and levels *procedureType, subgroup* and *group,* describes the different procedures available to patients. Dimension *Patient,* with bottom level *patientId,* and levels *yearOfBirth* and *gender,* represents information about the person under treatment. Age intervals are represented by a dimension level called *yearRange*. Patients are also grouped according to their health insurance institution. Moreover, these institutions are further grouped into types (level *institutionType*), such as private institutions, labor unions, etc. Dimension *Doctor* gives information about the available doctors (identified by *doctorId*) and their *specialities* (a level above *doctorId*). There is also a user-defined dimension *Time,* with levels *day, week* and *month.*

A fact table holds data about procedures delivered to patients by a certain doctor on a certain date. We call this fact table *Services,* and its schema contains the bottom levels of the dimensions above, plus the measure. The fact table schema is : *Services(doctorID,procedureId, patientID,day,quantity,t),* where $t$ represents the system-maintained time dimension, and *quantity* is the measure. For instance, a tuple <doc1,10.01.01,pat120,10,2, "10/10/2000"> means that doctor "doc1" prescribed two special radiographies to patient "pat120" on day "10" which corresponds to October 10th, 2001. In this case study, the system-maintained and user-defined times are synchronized, meaning that there is a correspondence between the values of attributes "day" and "t"(e.g., day "11" corresponds to October 11st, 2000). This synchronization, however, is not mandatory in the model. Thus, both times can take independent values.

## 3  TOLAP

In this section we describe the temporal OLAP language *TOLAP* (*Temporal OLAP*) [10]. *TOLAP* combines some of the features of temporal query languages like TSQL2 or SQL/TP [12,13] with some of the high-order features of languages like HiLog or SchemaLog [4,8], in an OLAP setting. We highlight *TOLAP*'s main characteristics by means of examples, using the schema of the medical center described in the previous section .

*TOLAP* is a rule-based language; as in Datalog, each rule defines the predicate in the head using the literals in the body. It would be easy to give an SQL-like syntax to the language, but we find the rule-based syntax clearer and more concise.

We begin our description of *TOLAP* with queries not involving aggregates. A query returning the procedures delivered to patients affiliated to unions will be expressed in *TOLAP* as:

```
SrvU(proc,pat,qty,t) ←— Services(doc,proc,pat,day,qty,t),
                        pat[t]→insType:'Union';
```

This query returns a projection of the tuples in *Services* such that pat rolled up to *'Union'* when the service was delivered. Variable pat represents an element in the lowest level of the dimension *Patient*. A tuple in *Services* will contribute to the result if a patient pat was served by doctor doc on day day at time t, and pat was affiliated to an institution of type 'Union' at the time of being treated. The expression pat[t]→insType:'Union' is called a *rollup atom*, and Services(doc,proc,pat,day,qty,t) is a *fact atom*.

Queries with aggregates can readily be expressed in *TOLAP*. For example, consider the query: "total number of services per procedure type and week."

```
SP(ty,w,SUM(qty)) ←— Services(doc,proc,pat,day,qty,t),
                     proc[t]→procType:ty, day→week:w;
```

Descriptive attributes of dimension levels can be used in *TOLAP* queries. Suppose we want the total number of services delivered by Dr. Roberts each week. In *TOLAP*:

```
SB(w,SUM(qty)) ←— Services(doc,proc,pat,day,qty,t),day→week:w,
                  doc[t]→doctorId:dr, dr.name='Roberts';
```

The rollup function represented by the rollup atom doc[t]→doctorId:dr will be the identity during the intervals in which doctorId is the dimension's bottom level. Thus, the atom doc[t]→doctorId:dr allows defining the attribute name as an attribute of the level doctorId, no matter the location of this level within the dimension's hierarchy. The expression dr.name='Roberts' is called a *descriptive atom*.

*TOLAP* also allows querying the metadata, supporting queries with no fact table in the body of the rules, which we call *metaqueries*. For example: "List the periods during which no heart surgery was available."

```
NoHeart(t) ←── !Procedure:procId:proc[t]→group:g,
               g.desc='Heart Surgery'.
```

The term !Procedure:procId:proc[t] is a *negated rollup atom*. Note that we must specify the name of the dimension and level for variable proc in the atom Procedure:procId:proc[t]→group:g, because there is no fact table in the body of the rule to which proc could be bound.

As in Datalog, rules can be composed into programs. For example: "patients who were administered procedures belonging to types delivered more than one hundred times." We first compute the total number of procedures by type, and use the result in the final query.

```
PT(ty,COUNT(qty)) ←── Services(doc,proc,pat,day,qty,t),
                      proc[t]→procType:ty;
         Q(pat) ←── Services(doc,proc,pat,day,qty,t), q ≥ 100,
                      Ty100(ty,q), proc[t]→procType[t]:ty;
```

The expression $q \geq 100$ is called a *constraint atom*.

## 4   Implementation

The system was implemented on an ORACLE 8.04 database. The parser and visual interfaces were written in Java using Borland's Java Builder. Dimension updates were implemented as ORACLE's PL-SQL stored procedures and functions.

Two different data structures were considered for representing dimensions: a "fixed schema" versus a "non-fixed schema" approach. In both of them, a relation with schema of the form (*dimensionId, loLevel, toLevel, From, To*) represents the structure of the dimensions in the data warehouse across time. A tuple in this relation means that in the dimension identified by *dimensionId*, level *loLevel* rolled up to level *toLevel* between instants *From* and *to*. For example, the schema of the data warehouse introduced in Section 2 will be represented by a relation with tuples $< D1, procedureId, procedureType, t_1, Now >$, $< D1, procedureId, group, t_2, Now >$, $< D1, group, subgroup, t_5, Now >$, and so on.

We briefly discuss how instances of the dimensions are stored under each kind of representations.

**Fixed Schema.** Each dimension instance is represented by a relation with schema (*loLevel, upLevel, loVal, upVal, From, To*). Each tuple in this relation represents a rollup $\rho_{loLevel}^{upLevel}[(From, To)](loVal) = upVal$. As an example, the instances of dimension *Procedure* of Section 3, would be represented by a relation with tuples of the form $< procedureId, procedureType, pr_1, ty_1, t_1, t_3 >$,

$< procedureId, subgroup, pr_1, sg_1, t_2, t_3 >$, and so on. Thus, as new levels are added to the dimension, new tuples are inserted,but the relation's schema does not change. For instance, adding a new level *priceRange* above *procedureId* implies adding tuples like $< procedureId, priceRange, pr_1, 200to300, t_6, Now >$.

In this representation, dimension updates can be easily implemented, except updates that add or delete edges between levels, called *Relate* and *Unrelate* respectively [5,6]. These updates require self-joining the relation, in order to check consistency. Moreover, translation to SQL would be awkward, and the resulting SQL queries would require, again, self-joining temporal relations, as seen in the first SQL example below. In fact, self-joining temporal relations will be necessary each time the transitive closure of the rollup functions must be computed.

**Non-fixed Schema.** In this case there is also one relation for each dimension, but each dimension level is mapped to an attribute in this relation. A single tuple captures all the possible paths from an element in the bottom level, to the distinguished element "all". Two attributes, *From* and *To*, indicate, as usual in the temporal database field, the interval within which a tuple is valid. For example, a relation representing dimension *Procedure* will have schema: {*procedureId, procedureType, group, subgroup, From, To*}.

This structure requires more complicated algorithms for supporting dimension updates. For instance, adding a dimension level above a given one (generalization), or below the bottom level(specialization), induces a schema update of the relation representing the dimension instance: a new column will be added to this relation. If a level is deleted, no schema update occurs (i.e., the corresponding column is not dropped), in order to preserve the dimension's history. In the example above, a column *priceRange* would be added. However, the translation process is simpler, and the subsequent query performance better, because computing the transitive closure of the rollup functions reduces to a single relation scan.

To make these ideas more concrete, let us show how a *TOLAP* query is translated to SQL in each approach. (In Section 5 we give more details of this translation process.) Consider the query *"total procedures by group."* This query reads in *TOLAP* :

```
GTot(g,SUM(qty)) ←— Services(doc,proc,pat,day,qty,t), proc[t] → group:g;
```

Assuming that no schema update affected the fact table *Services*, the SQL equivalent of the *TOLAP* query above in the fixed schema approach will look like (for the sake of clarity we do not show here how time granularity is handled in the translation):

```
SELECT P1.upLevel,SUM(quantity)
FROM Services S, Procedure P, Procedure P1, Time T
WHERE
```

```
S.procedureId = P.loVal AND P.loLevel = 'procedureId' AND
P.upLevel = P1.loLevel AND    P.upLevel = 'subgroup' AND
P1.upLevel = 'group' AND
S.time BETWEEN P.From AND P.To AND
S.time BETWEEN P1.From AND P1.To
GROUP BY P1.upLevel
```

In the non-fixed schema representation, the SQL equivalent for the query is:

```
SELECT P.group,SUM(quantity)
FROM Services S, Procedure P
WHERE
   S.procedureId = P.procedureId AND S.time BETWEEN P.From AND P.To
GROUP BY P.subgroup
```

Notice that computing the rollup from *procedureId* and *group* is straightforward, while in the first approach the self-join of the table *Procedure* is required.

These arguments led us to choose the non-fixed schema approach for our *TOLAP* implementation.

## 5   Translating *TOLAP* into SQL

The user interacts with the system through a visual interface. A dimension update module, a *TOLAP* parser and a *TOLAP* translator access the database through a JDBC driver. The *TOLAP* translator translates each atom into an SQL statement and builds the equivalent SQL query. We will show how a *TOLAP* rule of the form

$$Q(x,y,Ag(m)) \longleftarrow F(x_i,y_j,m,t), \; x_i[t] \rightarrow l_i{:}x, \; y_j[Now] \rightarrow l_j{:}y, \; Dim{:}l{:}r[t] \rightarrow p{:}z;$$

is translated to SQL. We assume that $x_i$ is bound to a dimension $D_i$ and $y_j$ to dimension $D_j$. Also, $m$ represents the measure of the fact table $F$.

### 5.1   Translating *TOLAP* Atoms

- For each *rollup atom* like $x_i[t] \rightarrow l_i{:}x$, a selection clause is built as follows:
  $F.i = Dim_i.\text{bottom}$ AND $F.\text{time}$ BETWEEN $Dim_i.\text{From}$ AND $Dim_i.\text{To}$
  Dimension $Dim_i$ is the table representing the dimension $D_i$. The first conjunct joins this dimension to the fact table on the attribute representing the bottom level. The actual name of the column $F.i$ is taken from the fact table's metadata. The second conjunct corresponds to the join between the fact table and the "Time" dimension.
- Each *time constant* is translated to a selection clause. The second rollup atom in the rule above will be translated as[1]:
  $F.j = Dim_j.\text{bottom}$ AND $Dim_j.\text{To} = Now$

---

[1] In an actual implementation, *Now* can be replaced by *Sysdate()* or any function returning the current time.

- A rollup atom $Dim:l:r[t] \rightarrow p:z$, not bound to any fact table, is translated as an EXISTS clause.

```
EXISTS
  (SELECT *
  FROM Dim
  WHERE
  F.Time BETWEEN Dim.From AND Dim.To)
```

The WHERE clause is omitted if the join with the time dimension is not required.
- If the rollup atom $x \rightarrow Y:x$ corresponds to a user-defined time dimension, the atom is translated as
    $F.j = Dim_j.bottom$
- A *constraint atom* of the form $x \{<, =\}$ C, where C is a constant term, is translated as a selection condition in the WHERE clause. If the constraint atom is *negated* this condition is treated in the usual way (a NOT predicate is added).
- A *negated rollup atom* is translated as a NOT EXISTS clause. Suppose that in the query above we add the negated atom
  $!(y_j[Now] \rightarrow l_1:\text{'a'})$, where 'a' represents a constant. This atom is converted into an SQL expression of the form:

```
NOT EXISTS(
  SELECT *
  FROM Dim_j
  WHERE
  Dim_j.To=Now AND Dim_j.l_1 ='a' AND F.j = Dim_j.bottom)
```

where $l_1$ is the attribute representing level $l_1$. A *negated descriptive atom* is translated analogously.
- A *predicate atom* is translated as a table in the FROM clause, with the conditions which arise from the variables or constants in it.

## 5.2  *TOLAP* Rules

So far we tackled the problem of translating each atom in a *TOLAP* rule separately. Now we will explain the translation of the whole rule. We put all the pieces of the WHERE clause together and use aggregation and projection for the rollup from the bottom levels of the dimensions $D_i$ and $D_j$ to the levels $l_i$ and $l_j$ in the head of the clause. Thus, the SQL query generated by the *TOLAP* query above will look like this:

```
SELECT Dim_i.l_i, Dim_j.l_j, Ag(measure)
FROM F_1, Dim_i, Dim_j
WHERE
```

```
F_1.i = Dim_i.bottom AND F_1.j = Dim_j.bottom AND
F_1.time BETWEEN Dim_i.From AND Dim_i.To AND Dim_j.To = Now AND
  EXISTS
  (SELECT *
  FROM Dim
  WHERE
  F_1.Time BETWEEN Dim.From AND Dim.To )
GROUP BY Dim_i.l_i, Dim_j.l_j
```

The term **measure** is the measure in the fact table, bound to variable m. The fact table subindex represents the version of the fact table. So far there is only one version, as no schema update has occurred yet. However, we claimed that one of the main *TOLAP* features is the ability to deal with schema updates triggered by an specialization or a deletion of a bottom level. In the system's catalog, in a table describing fact table data, a new tuple is stored each time a dimension update affects a fact table in the data warehouse. Thus, given a fact table $F$, this fact table may have versions F_1, F_2 and so on, with different schemas. Given a *TOLAP* rule $\Gamma$ with a fact table $F$ in the body, the SQL query $Q$ equivalent to $\Gamma$ will be such that $Q = Q_1 \cup Q_2 \cup \ldots \cup Q_n$, where $Q_i$ are the queries involving facts occurred in the intervals $I_i$ in which each F_i holds. If the query includes an aggregate function, call it $f_{AGG}$, one more aggregation must be performed, in order to consider duplicates in each subquery. Thus, $Q_{AGG} = f_{AGG}(Q)$

Finally, *TOLAP* programs are compiled by translating each rule, creating temporary tables for each predicate in the head of a rule.

## 5.3  Join Elimination

There are cases in which the join between dimensions and fact tables is not needed. This situation arises when a variable in the head of the rule is bound to the bottom level of a fact table in the body, or to a level that was the bottom level at least during some interval $I_i$. Our implementation takes advantage of this fact, and does not generate the join.

*Example 3.* Let us consider the query "total procedures by procedureId and doctor speciality". Assume that the fact table *Services* was split into *Services_1* and *Services_2*, holding before and after a time instant $t_5$ respectively. In *Services_1*, the levels *procedureId* and *speciality* were the bottom levels corresponding to the dimensions *Procedure* and *Doctor*. In *Services_2*, these bottom levels were *procedureId* and *doctorId*. The query in *TOLAP*, and its SQL equivalent are:

```
PS(pro,sp,SUM(qty)) ⟵ Services(doc,prac,pat,day,qty,t),
                      doc[t]→speciality:sp,
                      prac[t]→procedureId:pro;
SELECT procedureId,speciality,SUM(quantity)
FROM (
  SELECT procedureId,speciality, SUM(quantity)
```

```
FROM Services_1
GROUP BY procedureId,speciality
UNION ALL
SELECT procedureId,speciality, SUM(quantity)
FROM Services_2, Doctor
WHERE
Services_2.Time BETWEEN Doctor.From AND Doctor.To AND
Services_2.doctorId=Doctor.doctorId
GROUP BY procedureId,speciality )
GROUP BY procedureId,speciality
```

Notice that, as *speciality* and *procedureId* were the bottom levels of Services_1, no join is needed in the first subquery.

## 5.4 Subquery Pruning

If a *TOLAP* rule contains a constraint atom with a condition over time such that the lifespan of some version of the fact table does not intersect with the interval determined by the constraint, the subquery corresponding to that version of the fact table is not generated by the translator, as it will not yield any tuple in the output. For instance, in Example 3, adding the constraint $t < d_6$ will prevent the first subquery from being generated.

## 5.5 Translating to TSQL2

Although at first sight TSQL2 might appear as the obvious target for translating *TOLAP* queries into an SQL-like query language, a more detailed analysis will show some drawbacks of this approach. In what follows we will assume that the reader is familiar with the design of TSQL2 [12].

TSQL2 has an *implicit* time data model. This feature, although useful for queries involving temporal joins, makes it difficult to express queries like the ones we deal with here. This is related to the problem of *lack of universality* of TQSL2, as studied by Chen and Zaniolo [3].

Although for some queries using TSQL2 would reduce or eliminate the need for complex expressions involving time, most of the time these expressions do not actually affect performance. Moreover, explicit time management makes *TOLAP* semantics easy to capture, whereas implicit time management turns this task difficult. For example, in TSQL2 the join of valid time relations returns another valid time relation. In order to avoid this behavior, different constructions must be used, for example the SNAPSHOT statement, which produces a non-temporal relation. Granularities must be explicitly handled using the CAST construct, often combined with PERIOD and other operators like INTERSECT or CONTAINS. Thus, although aparently simpler, the generated code contains many TSQL2 keywords, reducing portability and delivering no benefit, as *TOLAP* already hides all time management from the user.

For an example, consider the query:"total number of procedures by procedure subgroup and institution type" (we will be using this query for measuring performance later in Section 6):

```
Q(b,c,SUM(qty)) ←— Services(doc,prac,pat,day,qty,t),
                   prac[t]→subgroup:c, pat[t]→institutionType:b;
```

For the sake of simplicity we will assume that there is only one fact table version. In TSQL2, this query would read (in bold we indicate the TSQL2 keywords):

```
SELECT SNAPSHOT COL_0, COL_1, SUM(SUM_2)
FROM (
   SELECT SNAPSHOT DIMENSION_PROCEDURE.subgroup AS COL_0,
   DIMENSION_PATIENT.instType AS COL_1,SUM(QUANTITY) AS SUM_2
   FROM SERVICES_1, DIMENSION_PATIENT, DIMENSION_PROCEDURE
   WHERE VALID(DIMENSION_PATIENT) CONTAINS VALID(SERVICES_1)
   AND SERVICES_1.PATIENTID = DIMENSION_PATIENT.PATIENTID AND
   VALID(DIMENSION_PROCEDURE) CONTAINS VALID(SERVICES_1)
   AND SERVICES_1.PROCID = DIMENSION_PROCEDURE.PROCID
   GROUP BY DIMENSION_PATIENT.INSTTYPE,
   DIMENSION_PROCEDURE.SUBGROUP)
GROUP BY COL_0, COL_1
```

As *TOLAP* allows considering different instants for rollup evaluation, even using TSQL2 as the target language cannot prevent explicit time management. Suppose the query above is replaced by:

```
Q(b,c,SUM(qty)) ←— Services(doc,prac,pat,day,qty,t),
                   proc[Now]→subgroup:c,
                   pat[''10/10/2000'']→institutionType:b;
```

In this case, since the granularities of the arguments of the rollup functions and the dimensions differ, the translator must also generate the TSQL2 statements for casting these differences.

For the translation above, we assumed that the fact table was created as an EVENT relation, and the dimension tables as STATE relations. However, these assumptions carry further problems: as update semantics for TSQL2 is different than the semantics of dimension updates, ad-hoc modifications are needed to make the translation work. This would be much more expensive than generating the SQL expressions for explicit time management. Another problem would be the limited support provided by TSQL2 for schema versioning.

From the above we conclude that the benefits of translating *TOLAP* to TSQL2 are outweighed by the problems involved in adapting TSQL2's semantics to the semantics of *TOLAP*.

# 6   The Medical Clinic Case Study

In this section we apply the temporal approach to the case study introduced in Section 2.3. Our temporal multidimensional data model lets us not only modify the dimensions on-line, but keep track of the history of the medical data warehouse. We will present a simulated scenario based on real data extracted from the system described in Section 2.3.

The objective of the study was to test the ability of the temporal approach and *TOLAP* to address user needs more fully than commercially available non-temporal OLAP tools. Using our implementation, we wanted to study: (a) performance, by measuring response time of dimension updates and *TOLAP* queries; (b) expressive power and abstraction, by posing queries which could not be easily expressed in non-temporal environments and comparing them with their SQL equivalent; and (c) visualization capabilities, through a graphical environment that supports browsing dimensions and fact tables across time, updating dimensions, and temporal querying of the warehouse.

## 6.1   Data Preparation

The testing scenario was prepared applying the following dimension updates. Dimension *Procedure* was created with bottom level *procedureId*. Subsequent operations performed using the graphic interface generalized this level to level *subgroup*. Level *procedureId* was then generalized to *procType*. Finally, *subgroup* was generalized to *group*, and *procType* related to *group*. (See Section 2.3 for explanations of these and all other dimension levels mentioned in this section). In the *Patient* dimension, the initial bottom level *patientId* represents information about the person under treatment. This level was then generalized to *yearOfBirth, gender* and *institution,* in that order. Levels *yearOfBirth* and *institution* were further generalized into *yearRange* and *institutionType* respectively. For dimension *Doctor,* in order to show how schema versioning is handled in *TOLAP*, we assumed that although facts were recorded at the *doctorId* level, this level was temporarily deleted, originating the second version of the fact table, called *Services_2.* Thus, during a short interval, the dimension's bottom level was *speciality,* later specialized into level *doctorId,* which triggered the creation of the third version of the fact table, denoted *Services_3.* Finally, a user-defined *Time* dimension was created, with granularity *day,* allowing expressing aggregates over time. The dimension's hierarchy is the following: *day* rolls up to *week* and *month*; *week* and *month* roll up to *All.* The three resulting fact table versions have the following schemas: (a) *Services_1:{procId, patientId, doctorId, day, quantity, tmp}*, where *tmp* represents the built-in time dimension, and *quantity* is the number of procedures delivered; (b) *Services_2:{procId, patientId, speciality, day, quantity, tmp}*; (c) *Services_3:{procId, patientId, doctorId, day, quantity, tmp}*. The fact tables were populated off-line.

The following table depicts the number of tuples in each table of the relational representation, after all the updates above occurred.

| Table | # of tuples |
|-----------|-------------|
| Patient | 16383 |
| Procedure | 11253 |
| Doctor | 822 |
| Time | 730 |
| Services_1 | 26040 |
| Services_2 | 12464 |
| Services_3 | 17828 |

We also performed several updates at the instance level, simulating situations where new doctors were hired, others left, new procedures were created, or patients moved from one institution to another.

The tests were run on a PC with an Intel Pentium III 600Mhz processor, with 128 Mb of RAM memory and a 9Gb SCSI Hard Disk. The Database Management System was an ORACLE 8.04 database running on top of a Windows NT 4 (Service Pack 5) Operating System.

## 6.2   Discussion of Results

**Performance.** Figure 5 shows one of sets of $TOLAP$ queries we ran. Query Q1 has three rollup atoms in the body, while query Q3 has only one. We also ran the three queries replacing variable $t$ by the constant $Now$ (i.e., the current values of the rollups are considered for aggregation instead of the values holding at the time of the service, see [10] for details).

---

```
Q1: Q(a,b,c,SUM(qty)) ←── Services(doc,proc,pat,day,qty,t),
                          doc[t]→speciality:a, proc[t]→subgroup:c,
                          pat[t]→institutionType:b ;
Q2:   Q(b,c,SUM(qty)) ←── Services(doc,proc,pat,day,qty,t),
                          proc[t]→subgroup:c, pat[t]→institutionType:b;
Q3:     Q(b,SUM(qty)) ←── Services(doc,proc,pat,day,qty,t),
                          pat[t]→institutionType:b;
```

---

**Fig. 5.** Queries

Finally, we included a constraint atom in the three queries, to see the influence of the subquery pruning step. The constraint $t <$ ''02/08/2001'' leaves out fact tables $Services\_2$ and $Services\_3$, while the constraint $t <$ ''02/13/2001'' leaves out fact table $Services\_3$. For instance, query Q3 was modified as follows:

```
Q(b,SUM(qty)) ←── Services(doc,proc,pat,day,qty,t),
                  pat[t]→institutionType:b, t <''02/13/2001'' ;
```

The table below shows the query execution times for the three sets of queries described above. Each query was ran three times, and the average response time is displayed in the table, expressed in seconds. The numbers between parentheses represent the number of tuples in the query result. We see that subquery pruning reduces execution times by a factor between two and four in this example. Of course, this will depend on the size of the pruned fact table.

| | Query type | Q1 | Q2 | Q3 |
|---|---|---|---|---|
| 1 | $t$ | 290 (977) | 130 (361) | 40 (4) |
| 2 | $t = Now$ | 250 (977) | 110 (361) | 30 (4) |
| 3 | $t <$ "02/08/2001" | 60 (289) | 50 (95) | 15 (4) |
| 4 | $t <$ "02/13/2001" | 140 (620) | 125 (230) | 20 (4) |

We measured execution times for dimension updates in different ways. For instance, the table below shows the results of performing a sequence of dimension updates over dimension *Patient*. We include execution times for dimension updates over an equivalent non-temporal dimension *Patient* (created in *initial* mode, which does not account for the dimension's history). These results are indicated in the rightmost two columns of the following table.

| # tuples in dim. | Update | Time (s) | # tuples (nt) | Time (s)(nt) |
|---|---|---|---|---|
| 2727 | create dimension | 2 | 2727 | 2 |
| 2727 | Gen. *patientId* to *gender* | 20 | 2727 | 20 |
| 5452 | Gen. *patientId* to *age* | 30 | 2727 | 18 |
| 8179 | Gen. *patientId* to *institution* | 230 | 2727 | 20 |
| 10906 | Gen. *age* to *ageRange* | 30 | 2727 | 10 |
| 13633 | Delete *gender* | 15 | 2727 | 3 |
| 16356 | Delete *institution* | 20 | 2727 | 3 |
| 21808 | Delete *age* | 25 | 2727 | 3 |

**Expressiveness.** The queries below exemplify *TOLAP*'s expressive power applied to this case study. These queries cannot be expressed in a non-temporal model without ad-hoc design.

For example, suppose a user wants to analyze the doctors' workloads, in order to estimate future needs. The following query measures how the arrival of a new doctor influences the number of patients served by a doctor named *Roberts*: "list the total number of services delivered weekly by Dr. Roberts while Dr. Richards was not working for the clinic."

```
patRob(w,SUM(qty)) ←── Services(doc,proc,pat,day,qty,t), day→week:w,
                       doc[t]→doctorId:d, d.name='Roberts',
                       !Doctor:doctorId:dd[t]→All:all, dd.name='Richards'.
```

Notice that the negated atom is not bound to the fact table. Also notice the use of the user-defined *Time* dimension.

The following query returns the number of services delivered by Dr. Roberts while both doctors were employed at the clinic.

```
patRob(w,SUM(qty)) ←── Services(doc,proc,pat,day,qty,t),day→week:w,
                       doc[t]→doctorId:d, d.name='Roberts',
                       Doctor:doctorId:dd[t]→All:all, dd.name='Richards'.
```

The next query illustrates how to check patients who were served when they were affiliated to 'MEDICUS' and are currently affiliated to 'OSDE'.

```
changePlan(pat) ←— Services(doc,proc,pat,day,m,t),
                    pat[t]→institution:'MEDICUS',
                    pat[Now]→institution:'OSDE'.
```

**Visualization Capabilities.** The third goal of our experiments consisted in exercising on this case study the graphical environment we developed to support the temporal multidimensional model. We used this environment to perform the dimension updates reported above and to browse the structures and instances of the dimensions across time, in order to test usefulness and performance of the tool. The graphic interface supports: (a) Browsing dimensions and instances across time, and seeing how they were hierarchically organized throughout their lifespan. (b) Performing dimension updates (c) Importing rollup functions from text files. (d) Browsing different versions of a fact table. (e) Sending *TOLAP* programs to the query engine, and displaying they results without leaving the environment, including the possibility to see the generated SQL query.

## 7   Conclusion and Future Work

We have described the implementation of *TOLAP*, a temporal OLAP query language introduced in a previous work [10]. We discussed two different relational representation alternatives, and gave details of the translation from *TOLAP* to SQL, or program, showing that a query that is concisely expressed in *TOLAP* takes many lines of complex SQL code. Finally, we tested our implementation on a real-life case study. Our preliminary results on query and dimension update performance suggest that *TOLAP* can be useful for overriding the limitations of non-temporal OLAP commercial tools.

Many research directions remain open. Query optimization in *TOLAP* is an obvious one. Also, *TOLAP* can be extended to allow the definition of integrity constraints, which could be easily introduced within our visualization tool. Another issue deserving attention is adding update support to *TOLAP*, allowing bulk updates like "delete all customers who have not completed any transaction since 1998." Transactions in update expressions in *TOLAP* could be also addressed. For example, the expression above may be followed by: "classify all customers who did not perform any transaction since 1999 as 'low priority customers' ".

## Acknowledgements

The authors wish to thank Daniel Grippo and Claudio Tirelli, at the University of Buenos Aires for their help with the implementation of *TOLAP*.

This work was partially supported by the Natural Sciences and Engineering Research Council of Canada, and by the FOMEC program for the University of Buenos Aires.

# References

1. R. Bliujute, S. Saltenis, G. Slivinskas, and G. Jensen. Systematic change management in dimensional data warehousing. *Time Center Technical Report TR-23*, 1998.
2. L. Cabibbo and R. Torlone. A logical approach to multidimensional databases. In *EDBT'98: 6th International Conference on Exteding Database Technology*, pages 253–269, Valencia, Spain, 1998.
3. C.X. Chen and C. Zaniolo. Universal temporal extesions for database languages. In *Proceedings of IEEE/ICDE'99*, Sydney, Australia, 1999.
4. W. Chen, M. Kifer, and D.S. Warren. Hilog as a platform for database language. In *Proceedings of the 2nd. International Workshop on Database Programming Languages*, pages 315–329, Oregon Coast, Oregon, USA, 1989.
5. C. Hurtado, A.O. Mendelzon, and A. Vaisman. Maintaining data cubes under dimension updates. *Proceedings of IEEE/ICDE'99*, 1999.
6. C. Hurtado, A.O. Mendelzon, and A. Vaisman. Updating OLAP dimensions. *Proceedings of ACM DOLAP'99*, 1999.
7. R. Kimball. *The Data Warehouse Toolkit*. J.Wiley and Sons, Inc, 1996.
8. L.V.S Lakshmanan, F. Sadri, and I.N. Subramanian. Logic and algebraic languages for interoperability in multidatabase systems. *Journal of Logic Programming 33(2), pp.101–149*, 1997.
9. W. Lehner. Modeling large OLAP scenarios. In *EDBT'98: 6th International Conference on Exteding Database Technology*, Valencia, Spain, 1998.
10. A.O. Mendelzon and A. Vaisman. Temporal queries in OLAP. In *Proceedings of the 26th VLDB Conference*, Cairo, Egypt, 2000.
11. T.B Pedersen and C. Jensen. Multidimensional data modeling for complex data. *Proceedings of IEEE/ICDE'99*, 1999.
12. Richard Snodgrass. *The TSQL2 Temporal Query Language*. Kluwer Academic Publishers, 1995.
13. D. Toman. A point-based temporal extension to sql. In *Proceedings of DOOD'97*, Montreaux, Switzerland, 1997.
14. J. Widom. Research problems in data warehousing. In *Proceedings of the 4th International Conference on Information and Knowledge Management*, 1995.

# Attribute Metadata for Relational OLAP and Data Mining

T.H. Merrett

McGill University, Montréal, Canada

**Abstract.** To build the $d$-dimensional *datacube*, for on-line analytical processing, in the relational algebra, the database programming language must support a loop of $d$ steps. Each step of the loop involves a different attribute of the data relation being cubed, so the language must support attribute metadata. A set of attribute names is a relation on the new data type, **attribute**. It can be used in projection lists and in other syntactical postions requiring sets of attributes. It can also be used in nested relations, and the **transpose** operator is a handy way to create such nested metadata. Nested relations of attribute names enable us to build decision trees for classification data mining. This paper uses OLAP and data mining to illustrate the advantages for the relational algebra of adding the metadata type **attribute** and the **transpose** operator.

**Keywords.** relational algebra, datacube, data mining, association, classification, decision trees, nested relations, metadata

## 1 Introduction

In introducing the term "on-line analytical processing" (OLAP), Codd [2] wrote

..relational DBMS were never intended to provide the very powerful functions for data synthesis, analysis and consolidation that is being defined as multi-dimensional data analysis

and this is certainly true of SQL and current commercial database systems [4]. We will show that a database programming language which thoroughly integrates programming language and relational database concepts can be used to build any specific datacube without arbitrary extensions or operators.

The classical relational algebra shows limitations, as Codd says, when it tries to generalize this implementation to arbitrary datacubes, because it has no facility to loop over the attributes of a relation. A simple adaptation of the relational algebra to permit this—it is hardly an extension—is to allow *metadata* of type **attribute** among the legal attribute types (such as **integer**, **boolean**, **string**, etc.).

Non-first-normal form, or *nested* relations [6], have been discussed almost as long as Codd's original "flat" relations, with considerable emphasis on special algebras and operators to convert between nested and flat relations (e.g., [5, 3], etc.). If the classical relational algebra is complemented by a "domain algebra",

G. Grahne and G. Ghelli (Eds.): DBPL 2001, LNCS 2397, pp. 97–118, 2002.

which is useful in many other ways [7], the only new syntactic construct needed to express and work with nested relations is a mechanism which forms a collection of attributes; the rest is provided by subsuming the relational algebra into the domain algebra.

To build a decision tree, say for classification data mining, we need to choose an attribute using information theory, examine the values for this attribute, and then, for each value, repeat the cycle with other attributes. This requires that we have information about attributes and their values, both available at the same level, and both accessible to the domain and relational algebras. We introduce an operator to create a nested relation which forms the "transpose" of the attribute-value pairs in each tuple. This transpose has two attributes, one of which is, of course, of type **attribute**.

In this paper, we review the domain algebra, mainly via the application of constructing specific datacubes. In section 3, we introduce **attribute** metadata, and go on to apply it to building general datacubes and to start building decision trees. We then review nested relation operations as an extension of the domain algebra, and apply them to association data mining. Section 5 describes the new **transpose** operator of the domain algebra, and uses it to construct decision trees for classification data mining.

## 2    The Domain Algebra

The domain algebra has been around for a couple of decades, but not widely used, which has had unfortunately expensive consequences in terms of programming effort and confusion. It is thus appropriate to review it briefly here, saving illustrative examples for section 2.2, which uses it to build a datacube.

The algebra (which should have been named "attribute algebra") constructs new attributes from existing attributes in two ways. *Scalar* operations work "horizontally" (in terms of the usual table representation of relations) along the tuples. *Aggregation* operators work "vertically" along attributes.

All the normal calculations we might expect to be able to do on *scalar* data have corresponding scalar operators in the domain algebra: arithmetic, logical operations, string operations, the usual mathematical functions, and conditional expressions. Here are some examples, where the variables ($N$, $P$, *Windy*, etc.) are attributes. Each of these examples will be used later in the paper.

> $N + P$
> $sum1/sum2$
> $(N + P) * \lg(N + P) - N \lg(N) - P \lg(P)$
> **if** *Windy*$=$"ANY" **then** 0 **else** $N$

A domain algebra statement is distinguished from a relational algebra statement syntactically, and it is helpful to give that syntax here. The attribute resulting from the first expression, above, can be named *np* using

> **let** *np* **be** $N + P$;

Special uses of the scalar domain algebra are renaming

  **let** $N$ **be** *totN*;

and creating constant attributes

  **let** *seq* **be** 0;

or

  **let** *Windy* **be** "ANY";

We will omit the **let .. be** in the remaining examples of this subsection, showing only domain algebra expressions.

The *aggregation* operations of the domain algebra are of two kinds, *reduction*, and *functional mapping*, and these each break into two subcategories. We consider only reduction here, and its subcategories, *simple reduction* and *equivalence reduction*. These generalize the five aggregation functions of SQL, which are written

| | |
|---|---|
| **red + of** $A$ | // sum values of attribute $A$ |
| **red + of** 1 | // count |
| **red min of** $A$ | // find least value of attribute $A$ |
| **red max of** $A$ | // find greatest value of attribute $A$ |

and the average is a scalar division of two aggregations

  **(red + of** $A$**)/red + of** 1

The same statistics can be calculated for groups of tuples that form equivalence classes determined by having the same value for a specified attribute or set of attributes, say $G, H$.

  **equiv + of** $A$ **by** $G, H$
  **equiv + of** 1 **by** $G, H$
  **equiv min of** $A$ **by** $G, H$
  **equiv max of** $A$ **by** $G, H$

An average we shall make use of in building a decision tree is

  **(equiv + of** *npinp* **by** *Outlook, Humidity)*
  **/ equiv + of** *np* **by** *Outlook, Humidity*

The advantage of this notation is that it can be used to express any aggregate or statistic we can define, such as a standard deviation, without limiting the programmer to a pre-defined set of functions. Not only +, **min** and **max** can be used, but any associative and commutative operator, such as multiplication or, as we shall see later, the natural and outer joins of the relational algebra.

## 2.1 Actualization: Relational Algebra

Apart from the improved flexibility over SQL, the foregoing domain algebra seems pretty trivial. It involves, however, a significant subtlety, which is responsible for the considerable intellectual simplification it permits in tackling complex problems. This is that every domain algebra operation is completely independent of relations; no relation is referred to in any expression of the domain algebra. The attributes produced by the domain algebra are *virtual*. So, of course, to populate them with data, they must be *actualized* in the context of some relation or other. This can be done by the relational algebra, with no syntactic extensions.

It may be helpful to think of a domain algebra atatement as the definition of a parameterless function, whose name is the identifier following **let** and whose body is the expression following **be**: no execution results when the language interpreter encounters the domain algebra statement. Execution is postponed until the newly defined attribute is used somewhere in the relational algebra.

The advantage of the independence of the domain algebra from relations is that we can think separately about the two aspects of any problem which involves both relational operations and calculations on the attributes. It also enables us to implement the domain algebra in any syntax which already contains relational operations, such as SQL, without syntactic modifications.

However, anticipating the need in nested relations for relational operators, such as natural join, to appear explicitly in **red** and **equiv** expressions of the domain algebra, we are going to have to alter the formulation of SQL. We discuss this now, because the relational algebra is, as we said, the context in which virtual attributes are actualized. We need a syntax which makes explicit the unary and binary operators of the relational algebra, and which clearly distinguishes expressions from statements. We call this "programming notation", to distinguish it from SQL which, as a query language, was never intended for programming.

The most straightforward means of actualizing a virtual attribute created by the domain algebra is through *projection*. Here is an example, using first SQL then programming notation.

Suppose we have a relation

$Training(Outlook, Humidity, Windy, N)$

and the domain algebra

**let** *totN* **be equiv** + **of** $N$
**by** *Outlook, Humidity*;

Then the sum can be actualized, together with the other relevant attributes, using

**select** *Outlook, Humidity, totN* **from** *Training*;

The programming notation for the projection is almost the same

[*Outlook, Humidity, totN*] **in** *Training*;

and there is no apparent motivation for the change. But let us go on to the next step we will have to take in the next section, namely to rename *totN* back to $N$.

**let** *totN* **be equiv** + **of** $N$ **by** *Outlook, Humidity*;
**let** $N$ **be** *totN*;

We need two projections, one after the other, because if we try to actualize the virtual $N$ in a relation which already has an actual $N$ there would be ambiguity in the result. In SQL, we would have to write this

> **select** *Outlook, Humidity, Windy, N*
> **from**
> **select** *Outlook, Humidity, totN*
> **from** *Training*;

while programming notation is tidier

> [*Outlook, Humidity, Windy, N*] **in** [*Outlook, Humidity, totN*] **in** *Training*;

So far, the notational differences are not a big deal. Let us go on to *selection*, which SQL writes

> **select** <attribute list>
> **from** <relation>
> **where** <tuple conditional expression>

and programming notation writes

> [<attribute list>] **where** <tuple conditional expression>
>     **in** <relational expression>

This rearrangement of the SQL order puts the <relational expression> last so that compound expressions are more easily further articulated.

We proceed to *binary* operators, the joins, which programming notation writes as infix expressions of explicit operators. This also allows compound expressions to be built up, and several types of join to be defined. We use three in this paper, extensions to relations of the set operations of intersection, union, and difference.

Programming notation is

> <relational expression> <join operator> <relational expression>

or, if the join attributes must be named explicitly because their names are not common to the two operands,

> <relational expression> [<attribute list><join operator><attribute list>]
>     <relational expression>

The natural join generalizes set intersection, and we write the operator as **natjoin**. The similar generalization of set union gives the outer join, which we call **union**. Finally, set difference becomes **diff**, the difference join. Since in the paper we mainly use these latter two as ordinary set operators, we do not explain the extensions, which require null values in the case of **union**.

We can discuss the difference in notation in terms of a natural join between a relation *ShoppingBaskets(xact, item)* and a relation *ShoppingBaskets'(xact, item')*. (This pairs up all items that share the same transaction in an association-mining implementation.) SQL uses an expression which closely resembles its unary operators,

**select** *

**from** *ShoppingBaskets, ShoppingBaskets′*

**where** *ShoppingBaskets.xact= ShoppingBaskets′.xact*

While this makes explicit that equality across relations between the attributes of the names, *xact* and *xact*, is tested, it does not make explicit the higher-level idea that a natural join is being described. The programming notation,

*ShoppingBaskets* **natjoin** *ShoppingBaskets′*

uses the **natjoin** operator so that we can explicitly ascribe all the known properties of the natural join to this expression.

The apparent greater generality of SQL joins is only apparent: programming notation can always use a selection operator to change the join condition from equality to something else. On the other hand, useful operations such as outer and difference joins cannot be expressed using only the above SQL.

We will also use a fourth join, **comp**, the natural composition, which is a natural join followed by projecting only the non-join attributes. For example,

*ShoppingBaskets* **comp** *ShoppingBaskets′*

would be translated into the above SQL, modified only in the first line, which becomes

**select** *item, item′*

**Comp** deserves a special name, rather than being implemented just as a join followed by a projection, because it is frequently used to join a relation with itself on different attributes from the two sides, so that cumbersome attribute renaming would be required by the join-project implementation.

**Comp** actually belongs to a separate family of relational joins from the three others. This family extends the set-*comparison* operators (subset, superset, set equality) to relations, and includes the **division** operator, which we do not use in this paper. **Comp** corresponds to the test for non-empty intersection of two sets.

**Comp** and the other joins in this family exclude the join attributes from the result, and raise the possibility (when they are used as set comparisons) that the result may have *no* attributes. We now assert that a *nullary* relation serves as a Boolean, with the empty state interpreted as `false` and the non-empty state as `true`. We can therefore also use the nullary projection,

[] **in** <relational expression>

which is true if the value of the relational expression contains any tuples, and can be pronounced "something in <relational expression>".

So far, we have looked at *expressions* only of the relational algebra. They may be combined into compound expressions of arbitrary complexity (although it is not usually practical to write more than a join or two, and a couple of selection-projections in a single expression). We must say how relational expressions can be written into statements of the programming language. There are two kinds of statement.

The *assignment* statement creates a new relation, or overwrites an old one, from the value of a relational expression, just as assignment statements in any imperative programming language do. The syntax is

<identifier><– <relational expression>

The domain algebra and all the relational algebra operators described so far, except for the assignment operator, are *functional*, in the technical sense that the same operands always give the same results, and there are no side-effects. Functional programming is very elegant and avoids most of the opportunities a programmer has for error in non-functional languages. Database programmming, however, can be *purely* functional only by copying entirely every relation one wishes to "change", and this is prohibitively expensive. So we need non-functional **update** operations, which have the side-effect of changing a relation in place.

SQL offers three separate commands for this, one for each of insert, change, and delete operations, with the insert command unfortunately differing from the other two by unfortunately working with only one tuple. It is cleaner to make them all relational and to avoid the ambiguity of the word, "update" by using it only to refer to relations, not tuples. It is also cleaner to isolate the update operations from the conditions determining which parts of the relation are affected. The selection-projection and joins already discussed are ample to provide this control.

Here are the three cases of the **update** statement.

> **update** $R$ **add** $S$;
> **update** $R$ **delete** $S$;
> **update** $R$ **using** $S$ **change** <statements>;

$S$ is always a relation, and the **using** $S$ clause (which is optional) in the change command uses the natural join of $S$ with $R$ to select the parts of $R$ that will change. The <statements> in this case are usually assignment statements changing values of attributes. They may contain domain algebra expressions on the right hand side. Of course, $S$ may be any relational expression in all three cases. It may also be preceded by a join operator, if simple **natjoin** is not enough for the task.

We have introduced four binary operators of the relational algebra. We have reviewed the programming notation we will use in the paper for these operators and for the unary selection-projection combination, and we have justified the programming notation as a replacement for the SQL query language for flexibility and generality.

One more unary operator is useful. Because the relational algebra is high-level, and abstracts over looping, it has no concept of an individual tuple. This is good because it requires the programmer to avoid tuple-by-tuple thinking, which can result in exceedingly poor utilization of secondary storage, as well as diminishing the level of abstraction. (SQL uses the "cursor" concept to violate this abstraction.) However, the notion of a singleton relation, i.e., containing only one tuple, is sometimes useful semantics, and we have an operator which guarantees its result to be either singleton or empty. **Pick** followed by a relational expression returns a relation consisting of a single tuple of the operand, selected nondeterministically (and not removed from the operand). (**Pick** is also the mechanism for introducing nondeterminism into the language.)

We need only now return to the actualization of virtual attributes, which we have illustrated in the context of projection. *Anywhere* in the relational algebra that an actual attribute can occur, so can a virtual attribute. It can be actualized in a join as well as in a projection; it can be tested in a selection or in a join. Furthermore, anonymous domain algebra *expressions* can often replace the name of an actual attribute, with the exception being any usage that would place an anonymous attribute in the result relation. (Even this exception is partially lifted when we come to nested relations in section 4.)

## 2.2   Multidimensional Databases

To illustrate the domain algebra and its interaction with the relational algebra, we will build a datacube in three dimensions. We do not have room in this paper for sophisticated algorithms which compute only partial datacubes based on space and speed tradeoffs, so we content ourselves with simply constructing the whole datacube.

We choose data which we use later in the paper to build a decision tree, from the classic paper [9].

*Training* ( *Outlook  Temperature Humidity Windy Class*)

| | Outlook | Temperature | Humidity | Windy | Class |
|---|---|---|---|---|---|
| 1 | sunny | hot | high | f | N |
| 2 | sunny | hot | high | t | N |
| 3 | overcast | hot | high | f | P |
| 4 | rain | mild | high | f | P |
| 5 | rain | cool | normal | f | P |
| 6 | rain | cool | normal | t | N |
| 7 | overcast | cool | normal | t | P |
| 8 | sunny | mild | high | f | N |
| 9 | sunny | cool | normal | f | P |
| 10 | rain | mild | normal | f | P |
| 11 | sunny | mild | normal | t | P |
| 12 | overcast | mild | high | t | P |
| 13 | overcast | hot | normal | f | P |
| 14 | rain | mild | high | t | N |

(The first column is a tuple identifier for later reference, and is not part of the data.) The first four attributes are the data supplied for classification, and *Class* indicates whether the tuple is a positive or a negative instance of the classification sought.

We first take advantage of the fact that *Temperature* will turn out to have no effect on the final decision tree, and use a relational algebra projection to eliminate it. Since we will be building a datacube with counts of the numbers of N and the numbers of P entries, we create these counts with the domain algebra, and we use the projection to actualize the counts. The result is a new form of *Training*, which we shall use from now on.

> **let** $N$ **be equiv** + **of if** *Class*="N" **then** 1
>    **else** 0 **by** *Outlook, Humidity, Windy*;
> **let** $P$ **be equiv** + **of if** *Class*="P" **then** 1
>    **else** 0 **by** *Outlook, Humidity, Windy*;
> *Training* <− [*Outlook, Humidity, Windy, N, P*] **in** *Training*;

| *Training* | (*Outlook* | *Humidity* | *Windy* | *N* | *P*) |
|---|---|---|---|---|---|
| 1,8 | sunny | high | f | 2 | 0 |
| 2 | sunny | high | t | 1 | 0 |
| 9 | sunny | normal | f | 0 | 1 |
| 11 | sunny | normal | t | 0 | 1 |
| 3 | overcast | high | f | 0 | 1 |
| 12 | overcast | high | t | 0 | 1 |
| 13 | overcast | normal | f | 0 | 1 |
| 7 | overcast | normal | t | 0 | 1 |
| 4 | rain | high | f | 0 | 1 |
| 14 | rain | high | t | 1 | 0 |
| 5,10 | rain | normal | f | 0 | 2 |
| 6 | rain | normal | t | 1 | 0 |

(Since tuple order does not matter in relations, but can help the reader, we have rearranged the tuples for clarity.) We see that two tuples have in two cases contributed to a negative or a positive count, and that, since both are negative or both are positive, *Temperature* has no effect on the final classification. This means that the problem is reduced to three dimensions and so is easy to visualize. (The number of dimensions makes no difference to the calculations.) We also see that *Training* contains a Cartesian product of the values for *Outlook, Humidity,* and *Windy*, and so is not sparse: in such a case, the full datacube may be constructed with minimum relative overhead of space.

Now we build the datacube. This requires three steps. The first sums the counts in the *Windy* direction. The second sums the counts, including the sums for *Windy* from the first step, in the *Outlook* direction. The third step sums all counts, including previous sums, in the *Humidity* direction. (The order in which these directions is chosen is irrelevant; any one of 3!=6 loops will give the same result. In $d$ dimensions, there will be $d$ steps, and $d!$ ways of ordering them.) Figure 1 may be helpful in visualizing the process and the result.

The implementation involves equivalence reduction and renaming in the domain algebra, and projection and update in the relational algebra. The first step is

> **let** $N$ **be** *totN*;
> **let** $P$ **be** *totP*;
> **let** *Windy* **be** "ANY";
> **let** *totN* **be equiv** + **of** $N$ **by** *Outlook, Humidity*;
> **let** *totP* **be equiv** + **of** $P$ **by** *Outlook, Humidity*;
> **update** *Training* **add** [*Outlook, Humidity, Windy, N, P*] **in**
>    [*Outlook, Humidity, totN, totP*] **in** *Training*;

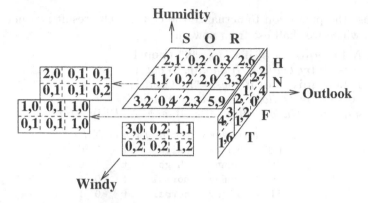

**Fig. 1.** The DataCube for the Weather Classification

Note that summing over *Windy* means grouping by the complementary attributes, *Outlook* and *Humidity*, and that the projection that actualizes these sums also retains *Outlook* and *Humidity*.

The tuples that are added to *Training* by this first step are

| *Training* (*Outlook* | *Humidity* | *Windy* | *N* | *P*) | | |
|---|---|---|---|---|---|---|
| 1,2,8 | sunny | high | ANY | 3 | 0 |
| 9,11 | sunny | normal | ANY | 0 | 2 |
| 3,12 | overcast | high | ANY | 0 | 2 |
| 7,13 | overcast | normal | ANY | 0 | 2 |
| 4,14 | rain | high | ANY | 1 | 1 |
| 5,6,10 | rain | normal | ANY | 1 | 2 |

These form the front face (*Outlook, Humidity*) of figure 1.

The second and third steps are identical to the first, but with the attribute names replaced as follows.

| Step | Sum Attribute | Group Attributes |
|---|---|---|
| 1 | *Windy* | *Outlook, Humidity* |
| 2 | *Outlook* | *Humidity, Windy* |
| 3 | *Humidity* | *Outlook, Windy* |

The second step adds the six tuples corresponding to the (*Humidity, Windy*) face of figure 1; and the third step generates the twelve tuples of the (*Outlook, Windy*) face.

## 3   Attribute Metadata

None of the foregoing discussion is new with this paper, although it may come as a surprise to some readers that the classical relational algebra, minimally extended, and augmented by an independent domain algebra, can get so far with analytical programming and multidimensional database applications. (It can also be used for topological analysis, logic programming, spatial data and G.I.S., temporal data, transitive closure, inference engines, and inheritance and instantiation, among other topics well beyond the scope of this paper.) In this section, we propose a new construct.

We saw in section 2.2 that a loop of $d$ steps was needed to build a $d$-dimensional datacube, and that what changed from step to step was the set of attributes involved. To write that code generally as a loop, and for any number of attributes, we allow a type **attribute** for attributes, and we introduce, temporarily (it will be replaced later by the more general **transpose** operator), an operator, **AttribsOf**, which creates a relation of all the attributes of the operand. Finally, let us introduce syntax that permits relational expressions, whose result is a relation on a single attribute of type **attribute**, to be used anywhere an unordered set of attributes was formerly allowed, i.e., in projection lists and after the **by** clause of an equivalence reduction.

As for any metadata, we need two special operators, **eval** and **quote**. **Eval** applies to any metadata variable (which must be a singleton, unary relation on an attribute of type **attribute**) and replaces the variable by its value. We will see an example below. **Quote** applies to any attribute name, and converts it to **attribute** metadata. Section 3.2 illustrates this.

### 3.1    The General DataCube

Here is the example of section 2.2 implemented as a single loop, using these ideas. Note that we can now use any operator of the relational algebra on sets of attributes.

```
o      let N be totN;
o      let P be totP;
n      domain attr attribute;
n      relation AllAttribs(attr) <- AttribsOf Training;
n      // Outlook, Humidity, Windy, N, P
n      relation ClassAttribs(attr) <- {(N), (P)};
n      relation TotAttribs(attr) <- {(totN), (totP)};
n      PropAttribs <- AllAttribs diff ClassAttribs;
n      LoopAttribs <- PropAttribs;
n      while [] in LoopAttribs
n      { Attrib <- pick LoopAttribs;
n// Pick the next of Outlook, Humidity, Windy
n          update LoopAttribs delete Attrib;
n// and don't use it again
o          let eval Attrib be "ANY";
o          let totN be equiv + of N by (PropAttribs diff Attrib);
o          let totP be equiv + of P by (PropAttribs diff Attrib);
o          update Training add [AllAttribs] in
           [PropAttribs diff Attrib union TotAttribs] in Training;
n      }
```

In the above program, the lines prefixed "o" are the old code from section 2.2, adapted for the general loop. The lines prefixed "n" are new code needed to initialize and use the set of attributes that control the loop. Inspection of the

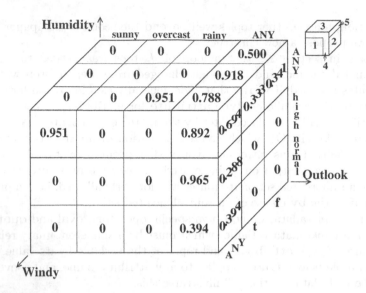

**Fig. 2.** The DataCube for the Weather Decision Tree

differences from section 2.2, and the discussions in sections 2 and 2.1, will make the meaning clear.

## 3.2  The Decision Tree

With attribute metadata, we can take the first step in building a decision tree, both for the specific three-dimensional example of weather classification, and in general. This involves building a datacube in which the aggregates are information values. We will be looking for minimum information values to choose an attribute as a node of the decision tree (because information is a measure of surprise, and, once we have the decision tree it should be able to predict exactly (no surprise) the class of any test tuple). This means that we must connect an attribute to the minimum information value, and that means we need attribute metadata.

The information datacube is built in $2d - 1$ steps in $d$ dimensions (instead of the $d$ steps needed for the ordinary datacube we just built). Figure 2 shows why two extra steps are needed in the three dimensional case: the small cube schematically shows the aggregates generated by the first three steps, and the aggregates remaining to be generated by steps 4 and 5. The generalization to any number of dimensions is easy.

The numbers on the big cube are the information values computed by the code below. If we think of the cube as made up of $4 \times 3 \times 3 = 36$ blocks, the subsequent minimization must find the smallest number on any block with more than one number, and identify the attribute that is normal to this face. (For example, the minimum of 0.892, 0.788, and 0.694, on the corner block, is the latter, and the face it is on is normal to the *Outlook* attribute. This will make *Outlook* the root of the decision tree.)

As for the first datacube, we will approach the implementation in two stages of generalization. In the first stage, we show how to write each step of the loop explicitly for the specific three-dimensional example. In the second stage, we use attribute metadata to write the whole loop generally. Here are five lines of preliminary domain algebra, followed by step 1 explicitly.

> **let** $N$ **be** *totN*;
> **let** $P$ **be** *totP*;
> **let** *np* **be** $N + P$;
> **let** *npinp* **be** $np \times \lg(np) - N \times \lg(N) - P \times \lg(P)$;
> **let** *inf* **be** *totinf*;
> //1. Outlook, Humidity
> **let** *totN* **be equiv** + **of** $N$ **by** *Outlook, Humidity*;
> **let** *totP* **be equiv** + **of** $P$ **by** *Outlook, Humidity*;
> **let** *totinf* **be** (**equiv** + **of** *npinp* **by** *Outlook, Humidity*)/
>    **equiv** + **of** *np* **by** *Outlook, Humidity*;
> **let** *accum* **be quote** *Windy*;
> **let** *Windy* **be** "ANY";
> **update** *Training* **add** [*Outlook, Humidity, Windy, N, P, inf, accum*] **in**
>    [*Outlook, Humidity, totN, totP, totinf*] **in** *Training*;

Steps 2 and 3 look very like this, apart from the same permutation of attributes that we saw for the datacube. These three steps generate 24 of the 33 aggregates shown in figure 2. Step 4 returns to *Outlook–Humidity* to complete the six aggregates indicated in figure 2, and step 5 revisits *Humidity–Windy* to find the remaining three. Here is step 4.

> //4. Outlook, Humidity
> **let** *totN* **be equiv** + **of if** *Windy*="ANY" **then** 0 **else** $N$ **by** *Outlook, Humidity*;
> **let** *totP* **be equiv** + **of if** *Windy*="ANY" **then** 0 **else** $P$ **by** *Outlook, Humidity*;
> **let** *totinf* **be**
>    (**equiv** + **of if** *Windy*="ANY" **then** 0 **else** *npinp* **by** *Outlook, Humidity*)/
>    **equiv** + **of if** *Windy*="ANY" **then** 0 **else** *np* **by** *Outlook, Humidity*;
> **let** *accum* **be quote** *Windy*;
> **let** *Windy* **be** "ANY";
> **update** *Training* **add** [*Outlook, Humidity, Windy, N, P, inf, accum*] **in**
>    [*Outlook, Humidity, totN, totP, totinf*] **in** *Training*;

Note that we avoid accumulating over the already computed aggregates corresponding to "ANY" values. Apart from this, the code is identical to step 1.

The generalization, using metadata, to relations on any set of attributes, is easily achieved along the same lines as above, and we mention only that

> **let** *accum* **be quote** *Windy*;

and its variants can be simply replaced by

> **let** *accum* **be** *Attrib*;

The only significant change is that the sequence of attributes that were randomly **pick**ed in the first $d$ steps must be repeated in the same order in the final $d - 1$ steps. This requires storing them, together with sequence numbers, in a temporary relation *Loop2Attribs*, and rearranging the control statements of the loop so *Loop2Attribs* can be initialized. These changes illustrate new idioms but no new language ideas, so we omit the code.

The next, and last, task in building the decision tree is to find the mimimum information values in the right groupings and then to search through the datacube we have just generated to select the tuples that make up the decision tree. For this, we need the **transpose** operator, which in turn needs nested relations.

## 4    Nested Relations

With the domain algebra and a cleaned-up relational algebra, we get nested relations for free (syntactically, that is: the implementation is more difficult, although everything we are about to say can be built with non-nested relations). The linguistic step is to subsume the relational algebra into the domain algebra.

Nested relations are relations whose attribute values may themselves be relations. Thus, to work with them, we need a formalism to create new relation-valued attributes from existing ones. The domain algebra, with relational operations incorporated into it, gives the needed formalism.

Although nested relations add nothing whatsoever to the *functionality* of the "flat" relational and domain algebras, which is what we have discussed so far, they do at times simplify our *thinking*, and so have a rightful place in secondary storage programming. They also repair an aesthetic inegality of the data types in the programming language: numbers, strings, and other scalar data types have hitherto had privileges that relations have not, namely the ability to be included as values in relational tuples. Nesting gives relations these privileges, too.

To review the ideas, consider the relation *ShoppingBaskets*(*xact, item*) which was mentioned in section 2.1 and which we will be using for association mining in section 4.1. Here is the domain algebra, with a new, relation-making operator, to convert the *item* attributes to a nested relation.

> **let** *xactset* **be relation**(*xact*);

If this were actualized, each of the original tuples would have a singleton *xactset*(*xact*) relation, which is not very interesting. Let us use the relational **union** operator, now legal to be used in the domain algebra, to combine all items for each transaction.

> **let** *xacts* **be equiv union of** *xactset* **by** *item.*

Actualizing this latter by the projection

> *SBsets* <− [*item, xacts*] **in** *ShoppingBaskets* ;

gives one tuple for each item, containing the item, *item*, and the set of associated transactions, *xacts*(*xact*).

We see from this the importance of being able to name the relational operators.

Similarly, relational operators can be used in scalar expressions of the domain algebra, to combine nested relations horizontally within each tuple.

To complement the **relation** construct in the domain algebra, which groups a set of attributes into a nested relation, we need a mechanism to flatten a nested relation by removing a level of nesting. Just as the nesting mechanism, **relation**, creates singleton nested relations, the inverse must start with a singleton nested relation, or else the resulting values will not fit into the tuple. Besides the non-deterministic **pick**, a projection onto the attribute resulting from a **red**uction aggregation is a good means of producing singleton results. This is a good way to unnest, because we can make such a result anonymous. Then, only the name of the nested relation is known, not the name of the attribute in it, and we can make the convention that, in such a case, the level of the attribute is raised one notch to become an attribute in the containing relation. Thus, no new syntax is needed for unnesting.

Here is an example, continuing the above, in which we count the number of items in each *xact* set, and raise the count to be an attribute of the containing relation that results.

> **let** *count* **be** [**red** + **of** 1] **in** *xacts*;

Since *count* is a virtual attribute created by a projection, it would normally be a nested relation, with the attributes named in the projection list. However, the projection list contains a domain algebra expression, not a name, and so *count* has no attribute. Because the domain algebra expression is a reduction aggregate, it has only one value, and so *count* can now be a flattened attribute containing only this value (in the parent tuple). Actualization could take the form

> *SBsetsAgg* <− [*item*, *xacts*, *count*] **in** *SBsets*;

Here is a very small collection of sample data for each of the above relations. In the three nested relations, a line separates each tuple, so we can see the singletons and how they merge into a single tuple.

| *ShoppingBasket* (*item*    *xact*) | | *item xactset*) (*xact*) |
|---|---|---|
| milk | 2 | ⇒ milk    2 |
| bread | 1 | bread    1 |
| bread | 2 | bread    2 |
| bread | 3 | bread    3 |

⇓

| *SBsets* (*item xacts*) (*xact*) | | *SBsetsAgg* (*item    xacts  count*) (*xact*) |
|---|---|---|
| milk | 2 | ⇒ milk    2    1 |
| bread | 1 | bread    1    3 |
| | 2 | 2 |
| | 3 | 3 |

The research literature on nested relations has focussed on algebras at the relational level, and got rather stuck on the unpleasant property of the nest and unnest operators at this level that they are not inverses of each other. But the interesting aspect of nesting is the useful manipulations. Since these, and unnesting, are entirely subsumed in the domain algebra with no new syntax or operators required, we think we have a useful formalism without awkward problems.

The following section illustrates the value of nesting and shows the above constructs, before we return in section 5.1 to the weather classification problem.

## 4.1   Association Data Mining

Association data mining [8, 1] attempts to find rules of the form "if one set of items occurs in a given situation, then a second set of items also occurs", for specific sets of items. The usual motivation offered is to help retail stores to discover associations among sets of products in customers' shopping baskets. *ShoppingBaskets* gives an example which appeared early in the literature.

| ShoppingBaskets | | SingletonRules' | | cover/ |
|---|---|---|---|---|
| (xact | item) | (item' | item) | confden |
| 8 | beans | beans | rice | 1/2 |
| 9 | beans | beer | bread | 1/2 |
| 2 | beer | beer | butter | 1/2 |
| 5 | beer | beer | milk | 1/2 |
| 1 | bread | bread | beer | 1/5 |
| 2 | bread | bread | butter | 4/5 |
| 3 | bread | bread | coffee | 3/5 |
| 4 | bread | bread | milk | 2/5 |
| 7 | bread | butter | beer | 1/5 |
| 1 | butter | butter | bread | 4/5 |
| 2 | butter | butter | coffee | 3/5 |
| 3 | butter | butter | milk | 2/5 |
| 4 | butter | coffee | bread | 3/3 |
| 6 | butter | coffee | butter | 3/3 |
| 1 | coffee | coffee | milk | 1/3 |
| 3 | coffee | milk | beer | 1/2 |
| 4 | coffee | milk | bread | 2/2 |
| 2 | milk | milk | butter | 2/2 |
| 4 | milk | milk | coffee | 1/2 |
| 9 | rice | rice | beans | 1/2 |
| 10 | rice | | | |

The second relation, *SingletonRules'*, lists all possible associations of singleton *antecedent* sets (*item'*) and singleton *consequent* sets (*item*). The virtual attributes, *cover* and *confden*, are counts of the number of transactions associated, respectively, with *item* and *item'*, and with *item'*. These two quantities are subject to user-specified criteria for selecting rules: *confden*, which is the "cover" of the antecedents, must exceed some absolute number, say 3 in this case (or a fraction of the total number of transactions, say 0.3); *cover* is the cover of the rule, i.e., of the intersection of the set of transactions associated with the antecedent and the set of transactions associated with the consequent; the ratio *cover/confden*, called the "confidence" of the rule, must exceed a magnitude specified by the user, say 0.8.

Here is the domain and relational algebra to generate singleton rules under these two criteria.

> **let** *cover* **be equiv** + **of** 1 **by** *item*;
> **let** *confden* **be equiv** + **of** 1 **by** *item*;
> **let** *item*′ **be** *item*;
> *SingletonRules* <− [*item*′, *item*]
> > **where** *item*′ ≠ *item* **and** *cover/confden* ≥ 0.8 **in** *ShoppingBaskets*
> > **natjoin** [*xact, item*′, *confden*] **where** *confden* ≥ 3 **in** *ShoppingBaskets*;

*SingletonRules*′, shown above, would be produced by the last line with both criteria set to 0; *SingletonRules* can be thought of as the selection on *SingletonRules*′ that gives the rules

> *if* {bread} *then* {butter}
> *if* {butter} *then* {bread}
> *if* {coffee} *then* {bread}
> *if* {coffee} *then* {butter}

(Note that, although the code defining *cover* and *confden* is identical, different values result because actualization is done in different contexts.)

So far we have not used nested relations. Nor have we produced more than singleton rules. The interesting problem is to deal with all possible *sets* of items. We do this in two stages. First, we find all possible item sets and their associated transaction sets and covers. Then we use a nested adaptation of the above code to discover the rules. The code we show for this procedure is not optimally efficient; publication space precludes greater sophistication.

Finding all the item sets over the *cover* threshhold, and their associated transaction sets, starts with nesting operations like the one we considered in section 4.

> **let** *items* **be relation**(*item*);
> **let** *xactset* **be relation**(*xact*);
> **let** *xacts* **be equiv union of** *xactset*;
> **let** *cover* **be** [**red** + **of** 1] **in** *xacts*;
> *SBsets* <− [*items, xacts*] **where** *cover* ≥ *mincover* **in** *ShoppingBaskets*;

This gives singleton sets of items, and the associated transaction sets. To extend the result to all sets of items, we use a form of transitive closure. This needs six statements of the domain algebra, which we show as the first six statements in the next paragraph, and a recursive view which we do not have room here to explain. The result is the relation *SBsetsClos*(*items, xacts*), with three tuples from *SBsets*, e.g., ({bread}, {1,2,3,4,7}), and four new tuples, e.g., ({bread,butter,coffee}, {1,3,4}).

Part two of the calculation adapts the SingletonRules code to nested relations.

> **let** *items'* **be** *items*;
> **let** *xacts'* **be** *xacts*;
> **let** *items''* **be** *items* **union** *items'*;
> **let** *xacts''* **be** *xacts* **natjoin** *xacts'*;
> **let** *items* **be** *items''*;
> **let** *xacts* **be** *xacts''*;
> **let** *confden* **be** [**red** + **of** 1] **in** *xacts*;
> **let** *cover* **be** [**red** + **of** 1] **in** *xacts''*;
> *GeneralRules* <− [*items'*, *items*]
>      **where** (**not**(*items* **comp** *items'*) **and** [] **in** *xacts''*
>           **and** *cover*/*confden* ≥ 0.8
>      **in** (*SBsetsClos* **natjoin** [*xacts'*, *items'*, *confden*] **where** *confden* ≥ 3
>      **in** *SBsetsClos*);

What this code does is

1. prepare to rename the nested relations *items* and *xacts*, and to rename the results back again,
2. define unions of *items* sets (nested relations) and intersections of *xacts* sets,
3. count the numbers of transactions for the antecedent set of *items* and for the whole rule (intersecting *xacts* sets for each item), and
4. join *SBsetsClos* with itself, as above for singleton rules, selecting on the two criteria.

The result is seven rules, including the four singleton rules we found earlier, and

> *if* {coffee} *then* {bread, butter}
> *if* {bread, coffee} *then* {butter}
> *if* {butter, coffee} *then* {bread}

This calculation is trivially extended to deal with multiple-attribute properties instead of the unary nested relation, *items*(*item*).

## 5    The Transpose Operator

Now that we have described relational nesting, and given it a good workout by implementing associative data mining, we can return to attribute metadata and classification mining. The **transpose** operator creates a nested relation which includes an attribute of type **attribute**. It effectively converts each tuple of an ordinary relation into a set of attribute-value pairs, which we can use to write code which examines both attributes and values, as needed to build the decision tree.

The result of **transpose** is a binary nested relation, with one attribute of type **attribute** and the other capable of holding any type of data, which we call type **universal**. Consider the statements

**domain** *attr* **attribute**;
**domain** *val* **universal**;
**let** *xpose* **be** [*attr, val*] **transpose** $A, B, C$;

and the relation

$$R(A\ B\quad C)\quad xpose$$
$$(attr\ val)$$

| | | | | |
|---|---|---|---|---|
| "a" | 1 | true | A | "a" |
| | | | B | 1 |
| | | | C | true |
| "b" | 1 | false | A | "b" |
| | | | B | 1 |
| | | | C | false |

We see the (virtual) result of **transpose** on all the attributes of $R$.

We can now show how to find all attributes of a relation (the temporary **AttribsOf** operator in section 3.1).

   *AllAttribs* <−

[**red union of** [*attr*] **transpose** *Outlook, Humidity, Windy, N, P*] **in** *Training*; **Transpose** can be used to transpose not only all the attributes of a relation, but also any subset of them.

## 5.1  Classification Data Mining

With nested relations and the **transpose** operator, we can now take the final step in building the decision tree for the weather classification problem, and in general. Our goal is to construct the decision tree represented as a set of rules, as in the relation $DT$.

| $DT($Outlook | Humidity | Windy | *pivot*<br>(*accum*) | *notANY*<br>(*attr*) | *NP* )<br>(*attr*) |
|---|---|---|---|---|---|
| ANY | ANY | ANY | Outlook | | $N$<br>$P$ |
| sunny | ANY | ANY | Outlook<br>Humidity | Outlook | $N$<br>$P$ |
| overcast | ANY | ANY | Outlook<br>Humidity | Outlook | $P$ |
| rainy | ANY | ANY | Outlook<br>Windy | Outlook | $N$<br>$P$ |
| sunny | high | ANY | Outlook<br>Humidity<br>Windy | Outlook<br>Humidity | $N$ |
| sunny | normal | ANY | Outlook<br>Humidity<br>Windy | Outlook<br>Humidity | $P$ |
| rainy | ANY | f | Outlook<br>Humidity<br>Windy | Outlook<br>Windy | $P$ |
| rainy | ANY | t | Outlook<br>Humidity<br>Windy | Outlook<br>Windy | $N$ |

The new attributes, *pivot*, *notANY*, and *NP*, are defined

> **let** *pivot* **be pick equiv union of relation**(accum)
>    **by** *Outlook, Humidity, Windy*;
> **domain** *attr* **attribute**;
> **domain** *val* **universal**;
> **let** *notANY* **be** [*attr*] **where** *val*≠"ANY" **in**
>    [*attr*, *val*] **transpose** *Outlook, Humidity, Windy*;
> **let** *NP* **be** [*attr*] **where** *val*≠0 **in** [*attr*, *val*] **transpose** *N, P*;

The relation *DT* can be used as a set of rules by selecting singleton *NP* values (either *N* or *P*), as in

> *if Outlook* = {"overcast"} *then* P

or

> *if Outlook* = {"sunny"} *and Humidity* = {"high"} *then* N

etc. Or it can be construed as a tree whose root is the tuple where *notANY* is empty, first-level nodes where |*notANY*| = 1, and so on. Searching this tree closely follows the method for extracting it from the original *Training* set, which we now give.

We first find the minimum information, and the attribute responsible for it, for each block in figure 2.

> **let** *ct* **be** [**red** + **of** 1] **in** *notANY*;
> *Min* <− [*Outlook, Humidity, Windy, ct, notANY, NP, pivot*]
>    **in** [*Outlook, Humidity, Windy, accum*]
>    **where** *inf* = **equiv min of** *inf*
>       **by** *Outlook, Humidity, Windy* **in** *Training*;

We can then write a loop of *d* steps to find each of the *d* levels of the decision tree. Here we give the first and the second steps; the second becomes the general step just by changing the value for *ct* in the selection.

> // Step 0.
> *DT0* <− [*Outlook, Humidity, Windy, notANY, NP, pivot*]
>    **where** *ct* = 0 **in** *Min*;
> // Step 1.
> **let** *pivot'* **be** *pivot*;
> **let** *pivot''* **be** *pivot* **union** *pivot'*;
> **let** *pivot* **be** *pivot''*;
> **let** *ctNP* **be** [**red** + **of** 1] **in** *NP*;
> *DT1* <− [*Outlook, Humidity, Windy, notANY, NP, pivot*]
>    **in** [*Outlook, Humidity, Windy, notANY, NP, pivot''*]
>    **in** ((**where** *ct* = 1 **in** *Min*) [*notANY* **natjoin** *pivot'*]
>    [*pivot'*]**where** *ctNP* > 1 **in** *DT0*)

When *ctNP* = 1, we have a leaf node, or a final rule, as indicated above, and so that branch of the tree-building may stop. The whole loop must stop when all branches have ended in leaves.

Note that the natural join in this code joins two relations on equality of join attributes which are themselves relations.

$DT$ is just the **union** of all the $DT$i's generated by the loop.

*Postscript* Two other classifications, One-rule and Bayesian, use much simpler calculations than the decision tree, and can be built as simple variants of the above, using only the top-level aggregates.

## 6  Conclusion

We have implemented two forms of data mining, classification by decision tree, and association, using only the relational and domain algebras. However, it is not the purpose of this paper to contribute to data mining, which is why we have presented only simple and inefficient algorithms.

The purpose of the paper has been to demonstrate that the relational algebra, with suitable notation, together with the domain algebra (and relational recursion and looping), suffice to do sophisticated programming. We have used nested relations, which come effectively for free with the domain algebra. We have introduced in this paper metadata of type **attribute**, and simple related operators and syntax, to write the general loops needed for datacube and decision tree construction. We expect these new constructs to be generally useful in relational database programming.

The attribute metadata type has recently been implemented. Every other technique used in this paper (domain algebra, nested relations, etc.) is implemented and running in one or more research systems.

## Acknowledgements

We are indebted to the Natural Science and Engineering Research Council of Canada for support under grant OGP0004365. This work was motivated by work on *spatial* OLAP and data mining, supported by the Networks of Centres of Excellence program through the GEOIDE Project, GEODEM. Andrey Rozenberg has built attribute metadata and its operators into the *relix* implementation of the language.

## References

1. R. Agarwal, T. Imielinski, and A. Swami. Mining association rules between sets of items in large databases. In P. Buneman and S. Jajodia, editors, *Proceedings of the 1993 ACM International Conference on Management of Data, May 26-28, 1993*, pages 207–16, Washington, D.C., May 1993. ACM Press.
2. E.F. Codd, S.B. Codd, and C.T. Salley. Providing OLAP to user-analysts: An IT mandate. Technical report, E.F. Codd & Associates, Hyperion Solutions, Sunnyvale, CA, 1993. http://www.arborsoft.com/essbase/wht_ppr/coddps.zip, http://www.arborsoft.com/essbase/wht_ppr/coddTOC.html.
3. P. Fischer and S. Thomas. Operators for non-first-normal-form relations. In *Proc. 7th COMPSAC*, pages 464–75, Chicago, November 1983.

4. J. Gray, S. Chaudhuri, A. Bosworth, A. Layman, D. Reichert, M. Venkatarao, F. Pellow, and H. Pirahesh. Data cube: A relational aggregation operator generalizing group-by, cross-tab, and sub-totals. *Data Mining und Knowledge Discovery*, 1:29–53, 1997.

5. G. Jaeschke and H.-J. Schek. Remarks on the algebra of non first normal form relations. In *Proc. ACM Symposium on Principles of Database Systems*, pages 124–38, March 1982.

6. A. Makinouchi. A consideration on normal form of not-necessarily normalized relations in the relational model. In A.G. Merten, editor, *Proc. 3rd Internat. Conf. on Very Large Data Bases*, pages 447–53, October 1977. examples of nest, recursive nest; discusses normalization, dep.

7. T.H. Merrett. Experience with the domain algebra. In C. Beeri, U. Dayal, and J.W. Schmidt, editors, *Proc. 3rd Internat. Conf. on Data and Knowledge Bases: Improving Usability und Responsiveness*, pages 335–46, San Mateo, California, July 1988. Morgan Kaufmann Publishers Inc.

8. G. Piatetsky-Shapiro. Discovery, analysis, and presentation of strong rules. In G. Piatetsky-Shapiro, editor, *Knowledge Discovery in Databases*, pages 229–48. AAAI/MIT Press, 1991.

9. J.R. Quinlan. Induction of decision trees. *Machine Learning*, 1(1):81–106, 1986.

# On Monotone Data Mining Languages

Toon Calders[1] and Jef Wijsen[2]

[1] Research Assistant of the Fund for Scientific Research – Flanders (Belgium)
(F.W.O. – Vlaanderen), University of Antwerp
calders@uia.ua.ac.be
[2] University of Mons-Hainaut, Belgium
jef.wijsen@umh.ac.be

**Abstract.** We present a simple Data Mining Logic (DML) that can express common data mining tasks, like "Find Boolean association rules" or "Find inclusion dependencies." At the center of the paper is the problem of characterizing DML queries that are amenable to the levelwise search strategy used in the a-priori algorithm. We relate the problem to that of characterizing monotone first-order properties for finite models.

## 1  Introduction

In recent years, the problem of finding frequent itemsets in market-basket data has become a popular research topic. The input of the problem is a database storing baskets of items bought together by customers. The problem is to find sets of items that appear together in at least $s\%$ of the baskets, where $s$ is some fixed threshold; such sets are called *frequent itemsets*. Although the problem of finding frequent itemsets can easily be stated as a graph-theoretical problem, the formulation in marketing terms [1] probably contributed much to the success of the problem.

The *a-priori* algorithm is probably the best-known procedure to solve this problem. It is based on a very simple property: If a set $X$ of items is no frequent itemset, then no superset of $X$ is a frequent itemset either. This property has been given different names; in [4, page 231] it is called *anti-monotone*, and defined as: "If a set cannot pass a test, all of its supersets will fail the same test as well." The *a-priori* algorithm thus first searches for singleton frequent itemsets, and then iteratively evaluates ever larger sets, while ignoring any set that cannot be frequent because a subset of it turned out to be infrequent in earlier iterations. The anti-monotonicity property underlying the *a-priori* algorithm has subsequently been generalized to *levelwise search* [11]. As a matter of fact, the a-priori trick is applicable in many other data mining tasks, such as the discovery of keys, inclusion dependencies, functional dependencies, episodes [10, 11], and other kinds of rules [16]. With the advent of data mining primitives in query languages, it is interesting and important to explore to which extent the a-priori technique can be incorporated into next-generation query optimizers.

During an invited tutorial at ICDT'97, Heikki Mannila raised an interesting and important research problem:

G. Grahne and G. Ghelli (Eds.): DBPL 2001, LNCS 2397, pp. 119–132, 2002.

"What is the relationship between the logical form of sentences to be discovered and the computational complexity of the discovery task?" [10, slide 51]

It is natural to ask a related question about the relationship between the logical form of sentences and the applicability of a given data mining technique, like the a-priori technique:

"What is the relationship between the logical form of sentences to be discovered and the applicability of a given data mining technique?"

This question is of great importance when we move to database systems that support data mining queries. Data mining querying differs from standard querying in several respects [5], and conventional optimizers that were built for standard queries, may not perform well on data mining queries. Next-generation query optimizers must be able to decide which data mining optimization techniques are effective for a given data mining query. In the domain of mining frequent itemsets and association rules, there has been a number of recent papers relating to the second question raised above. Lakshmanan et al. [7, 12] have introduced the paradigm of constrained frequent set queries. They point out that users typically want to impose constraints on the itemsets to be discovered (for example, itemsets must contain *milk*); they then explore the relationships between the properties of constraints on the one hand and the effectiveness of certain pruning optimizations on the other hand. Tsur et al. [15] explore the question of how techniques like the a-priori algorithm can be generalized to parameterized queries with a filter condition, called query flocks. In spite of these works, it seems fair to say that the relationship between the form of sentences to be discovered and the applicability of data mining techniques has not been systematically explored, and that a clean unifying framework is currently missing.

In this paper, we further explore from a logic perspective the relationship between the form of sentences to be discovered and the applicability of the a-priori technique. To this extent, we first have to decide upon which logic to use. The logic should allow expressing some basic rule (or dependency) mining tasks, like mining Boolean association rules, functional dependencies, or inclusion dependencies. As dependencies are mostly stated in terms of attributes, we propose a logic, called Data Mining Logic (DML), that extends relational tuple calculus with variables ranging over attributes and over sets of attributes (i.e., over relational schemas). We do not claim originality for the DML way of querying schemas; in fact, variables ranging over attribute and relation names also appear in other languages [8, 13]. Our main objective was not to design a new language, however, but rather to answer the question of which classes of queries are amenable to levelwise search. DML provides an adequate framework for exploring that question. Moreover, we believe that the generality of the language allows "transplanting" the results in other frameworks. The main contribution of the paper lies in revealing a significant relationship between the applicability of the a-priori technique in DML queries and monotone first-order properties for finite models.

The paper is organized as follows. Section 2 illustrates DML by an example. The syntax and semantics of DML are defined in Section 3. In Section 4, we show how certain common data mining tasks can be expressed in DML. Section 5 introduces subset-closed and superset-closed queries; these are the queries that admit levelwise search. Unfortunately, these query classes are not recursive. Section 6 introduces a recursive subclass of superset-closed queries, called positive queries. Although many "practical" superset-closed queries can be expressed positively, the class of positive queries does not semantically cover the whole class of superset-closed queries. The latter result is proved in Sections 7 through 9. Finally, Section 10 concludes the paper. Detailed proofs of all lemmas and theorems can be found in [3].

## 2   Introductory Example

We extend the relational tuple calculus with *attribute-variables* that range over attributes, and *schema-variables* that range over sets of $n$-ary tuples of attributes. In the following example, $X$ is an attribute-variable and $\mathcal{X}$ a unary schema-variable. The query asks for sets $\mathcal{X}$ of attributes such that at least two distinct tuples $t$ and $s$ agree on each attribute of $\mathcal{X}$. Requiring that $t$ and $s$ be distinct is tantamount to saying that they disagree on at least one attribute $Z$.

$$\{\mathcal{X} \mid \exists t(\exists s(\neg \exists Y(\mathcal{X}(Y) \wedge t.Y \neq s.Y) \wedge \exists Z(t.Z \neq s.Z)))\} \qquad (1)$$

For the relation:

$$\begin{array}{c|cccc} R & A & B & C & D \\ \hline & 0 & 0 & 0 & 1 \\ & 0 & 0 & 1 & 2 \\ & 0 & 1 & 1 & 3 \\ & 1 & 1 & 2 & 2 \end{array}$$

the result is:

$$\begin{array}{c} \mathcal{X}^{(1)} \\ \hline \{A, B\} \\ \{A, C\} \\ \{A\} \\ \{B\} \\ \{C\} \\ \{D\} \\ \{\} \end{array}$$

Note that $\{B, C\}$ is not in the answer set, since $R$ does not contain two distinct tuples that agree on both $B$ and $C$. One can easily verify that whenever a set appears in the above result then all its subsets appear as well. Moreover, this property remains true no matter what is the schema or the content of the input relation $R$. We will say that the query is *subset-closed*.

## 3   DML Syntax and Semantics

### 3.1   Syntax

We define our Data Mining Logic (DML). The idea is to extend relational tuple calculus with *attribute-variables* that range over attributes, and *schema-variables* that range over sets of $n$-ary tuples of attributes. For simplicity, we assume that the database consists of a single relation; therefore there is no need to introduce predicate symbols.

## DML Alphabet

- Denumerably many *attribute-variables* $X, Y, Z, X_1, Y_1, Z_1, \ldots$
- Denumerably many *tuple-variables* $t, s, t_1, s_1, \ldots$
- For every $n \in \mathbb{N}$, at most denumerably many *n-ary schema-variables* $\mathcal{X}, \mathcal{Y}, \mathcal{X}_1, \mathcal{Y}_1, \ldots$
- A set $\mathbf{C}$ of *constants*.

For simplicity, the arity of a schema-variable may be denoted in superscript: $\mathcal{X}^{(n)}$ denotes an $n$-ary schema-variable. Attribute-variables and tuple-variables together are called *simple-variables*.

## Atomic DML Formulas

1. If $X$ and $Y$ are attribute-variables, $t$ and $s$ are tuple-variables, and $a$ is a constant, then $X = Y$, $t.X = s.Y$, and $t.X = a$ are atomic DML formulas.
2. If $\mathcal{X}$ is an $n$-ary schema-variable, and $X_1, \ldots, X_n$ are attribute-variables, then $\mathcal{X}(X_1, \ldots, X_n)$ is an atomic DML formula.

## DML Formulas

1. Every atomic DML formula is a DML formula.
2. If $\delta_1$ and $\delta_2$ are DML formulas, then $\neg \delta_1$ and $(\delta_1 \vee \delta_2)$ are DML formulas.
3. If $\delta$ is a DML formula and $X$ is an attribute-variable, then $\exists X(\delta)$ is a DML formula.
4. If $\delta$ is a DML formula and $t$ is a tuple-variable, then $\exists t(\delta)$ is a DML formula.

Note that the existential quantifier $\exists$ can be followed by an attribute-variable as well as a tuple-variable. These two usages of $\exists$ will have different semantics. Since attribute-variables and tuple-variables are assumed to be distinct, the double use of $\exists$ does not result in any confusion.

A DML formula is called *closed* iff all occurrences of simple-variables (i.e., tuple-variables and attribute-variables) are bound, where boundedness is defined as usual. A closed DML formula is also called a *DML sentence*. The abbreviations $\wedge, \rightarrow, \leftrightarrow, \mathbf{true}, \mathbf{false}, \forall, \neq$, with conventional precedence relationship, are introduced as usual. In addition we introduce the abbreviations:

- $\forall \mathcal{X}(X_1, \ldots, X_n)(\delta)$   for $\forall X_1(\ldots(\forall X_n(\mathcal{X}(X_1, \ldots, X_n) \rightarrow (\delta)))\ldots)$, and
- $t = s$   for $\forall X(t.X = s.X)$.

**DML Queries.** A *DML query* is an expression of the form $\{\mathcal{X}_1, \ldots, \mathcal{X}_m \mid \delta\}$, where $\delta$ is a DML sentence and $\mathcal{X}_1, \ldots, \mathcal{X}_m$ are exactly all distinct schema-variables occurring in $\delta$ ($m \geq 1$).

## 3.2  DML Semantics

We assume the existence of a set **att** of *attributes*. A *schema* is a finite, nonempty set of attributes[1]. A *tuple* over the schema $S$ is a total function from $S$ to the set **C** of constants. A *relation* is a finite set of tuples.

The notion of *DML structure* is defined relative to a schema $S$: It is a pair $\langle R, \Sigma \rangle$ where $R$ is a relation over $S$ and $\Sigma$ is a *schema-variable assignment* assigning some $\Sigma(\mathcal{X}^{(n)}) \subseteq 2^{(S^n)}$ to every $n$-ary schema-variable $\mathcal{X}^{(n)}$. For convenience, the schema of $R$ will be denoted $|R|$.

A *DML interpretation* is a pair $\langle \langle R, \Sigma \rangle, \sigma \rangle$ where $\langle R, \Sigma \rangle$ is a DML structure and $\sigma$ is a *simple-variable assignment* assigning some tuple over $|R|$ (which may or may not belong to $R$) to every tuple-variable $t$, and assigning some $\sigma(X) \in |R|$ to every attribute-variable $X$.

The *satisfaction of DML formulas* is defined relative to a DML interpretation $\langle \langle R, \Sigma \rangle, \sigma \rangle$ [2]:

$$
\begin{array}{ll}
\langle \langle R, \Sigma \rangle, \sigma \rangle \models X = Y & \text{iff } \sigma(X) = \sigma(Y) \\
\langle \langle R, \Sigma \rangle, \sigma \rangle \models t.X = s.Y & \text{iff } \sigma(t)(\sigma(X)) = \sigma(s)(\sigma(Y)) \\
\langle \langle R, \Sigma \rangle, \sigma \rangle \models t.X = a & \text{iff } \sigma(t)(\sigma(X)) = a \\
\langle \langle R, \Sigma \rangle, \sigma \rangle \models \mathcal{X}(X_1, \ldots, X_n) & \text{iff } (\sigma(X_1), \ldots, \sigma(X_n)) \in \Sigma(\mathcal{X}) \\
\langle \langle R, \Sigma \rangle, \sigma \rangle \models \neg \delta & \text{iff } \langle \langle R, \Sigma \rangle, \sigma \rangle \not\models \delta \\
\langle \langle R, \Sigma \rangle, \sigma \rangle \models \delta_1 \vee \delta_2 & \text{iff } \langle \langle R, \Sigma \rangle, \sigma \rangle \models \delta_1 \text{ or } \langle \langle R, \Sigma \rangle, \sigma \rangle \models \delta_2 \\
\langle \langle R, \Sigma \rangle, \sigma \rangle \models \exists X(\delta) & \text{iff } \langle \langle R, \Sigma \rangle, \sigma_{X \to A} \rangle \models \delta \text{ for some } A \in |R| \\
\langle \langle R, \Sigma \rangle, \sigma \rangle \models \exists t(\delta) & \text{iff } \langle \langle R, \Sigma \rangle, \sigma_{t \to r} \rangle \models \delta \text{ for some } r \in R
\end{array}
$$

As mentioned before, we use only a single relation $R$ to simplify the notation. Importantly, the semantics specifies that the quantification $\exists X(\delta)$, where $X$ is an attribute-variable, is over the (finite) schema $|R|$ of $R$. Also, the quantification $\exists t(\delta)$, where $t$ is a tuple-variable, is over the (finite) relation $R$. For example, the statement $\exists t(\exists X(t.X = 1))$ is satisfied relative to a DML interpretation $\langle \langle R, \Sigma \rangle, \sigma \rangle$ if the value 1 occurs somewhere in the relation $R$. The statement $\exists t(\mathbf{true})$ is satisfied if $R$ contains at least one tuple.

The satisfaction of closed DML formulas does not depend on the simple-variable assignment $\sigma$. We write $\langle R, \Sigma \rangle \models \delta$ iff $\langle \langle R, \Sigma \rangle, \sigma \rangle \models \delta$ for every simple-variable assignment $\sigma$.

The answer to a DML query is defined relative to a relation $R$. The answer to the DML query $\{\mathcal{X}_1, \ldots, \mathcal{X}_m \mid \delta\}$ is the set:

$$
\{(\Sigma(\mathcal{X}_1), \ldots, \Sigma(\mathcal{X}_m)) \mid \langle R, \Sigma \rangle \text{ is a DML structure satisfying } \delta\} \ .
$$

---

[1] The extension to schemas without attributes is possible but less pertinent in a data mining context.

[2] If $f$ is a function then $f_{x \to a}$ is the function satisfying $f_{x \to a}(y) = f(y)$ for every $y$ other than $x$, and $f_{x \to a}(x) = a$. $f_{x \to a, y \to b}$ is a shorthand for $(f_{x \to a})_{y \to b}$.

# 4   Additional Examples

## 4.1   Frequent Itemsets and Non-trivial Functional Dependencies

Consider a relation where every attribute represents a product, and every tuple a customer transaction. For a given row $t$ and attribute $A$, the value $t(A) = 1$ if the product $A$ was bought in the transaction $t$, and $t(A) = 0$ otherwise. Next, to be able to store two transactions containing exactly the same products, a special attribute $TID$ is needed that serves as the unique transaction identifier. We assume that the values 0 and 1 are not used to identify transactions, so that $TID$ cannot possibly be interpreted as a product. The data mining problem is to find frequent itemsets [1]: Find sets $\mathcal{X}$ of attributes such that at least $n$ distinct tuples have value $= 1$ for all attributes of $\mathcal{X}$. The value $n > 0$ is an absolute support threshold in this example. The DML query is as follows:

$$\{\mathcal{X} \mid \exists t_1, \ldots, t_n (\bigwedge_{1 \le i < j \le n} t_i \ne t_j \wedge \forall \mathcal{X}(Y)(t_1.Y = 1 \wedge \ldots \wedge t_n.Y = 1))\} \quad (2)$$

The following DML query asks for non-trivial functional dependencies, i.e., functional dependencies whose right-hand side is not a subset of the left-hand side:

$$\{\mathcal{X}, \mathcal{Y} \mid \forall t(\forall s((\forall \mathcal{X}(X)(t.X = s.X)) \to (\forall \mathcal{Y}(Y)(t.Y = s.Y)))) \\ \wedge \exists \mathcal{Y}(Y)(\neg \mathcal{X}(Y))\} \quad (3)$$

For the relation:

$$\begin{array}{c|cc} R & A & B \\ \hline & 0 & 0 \\ & 0 & 1 \\ & 1 & 2 \end{array}$$

the result is:

$$\begin{array}{cc} \mathcal{X} & \mathcal{Y} \\ \hline \{B\} & \{A\} \\ \{B\} & \{A, B\} \end{array}$$

The two lines of the result encode the functional dependencies $\{B\} \to \{A\}$ and $\{B\} \to \{A, B\}$ respectively. The discovery of functional dependencies has been studied for many years now (see for example [6, 9]).

## 4.2   The Use of Binary Schema-Variables: Inclusion Dependencies

In all examples introduced so far, all schema-variables were unary, i.e., had arity 1. We now illustrate the need for binary schema-variables. In the example, sets of attribute pairs are used to encode inclusion dependencies that hold in a single relation. An inclusion dependency $\langle A_1, \ldots, A_n \rangle \subseteq \langle B_1, \ldots, B_n \rangle$ can be encoded by the set $\{(A_1, B_1), \ldots, (A_n, B_n)\}$. The dependency states that for every tuple $t$ in the relation under consideration, there is a tuple $s$ such that $t(A_1) = s(B_1)$ and $\ldots$ and $t(A_n) = s(B_n)$. In the following query, the binary schema-variable $\mathcal{X}^{(2)}$ is used to range over inclusion dependencies.

$$\{\mathcal{X}^{(2)} \mid \forall s(\exists t(\forall \mathcal{X}(Y, Z)(Y \ne Z \wedge s.Y = t.Z)))\} \quad (4)$$

$$\mathcal{X}^{(2)}$$

$$
\begin{aligned}
&\overline{\{(A,B),(A,C)\}}\\
&\{(A,B),(A,D)\}\\
&\{(A,B),(B,C)\}\\
&\{(A,D),(E,C)\}\\
&\{(A,B)\}\\
&\{(A,C)\}\\
&\{(A,D)\}\\
&\{(B,C)\}\\
&\{(E,C)\}\\
&\{\}
\end{aligned}
$$

For the relation:

$$
\begin{array}{c|ccccc}
R & A & B & C & D & E\\
\hline
 & 1 & 2 & 3 & 4 & 5\\
 & 1 & 1 & 2 & 1 & 5\\
 & 1 & 1 & 1 & 4 & 5\\
 & 1 & 2 & 5 & 1 & 5
\end{array}
$$
the result is:

Note that the result is again subset-closed.

## 5  Subset-Closed and Superset-Closed DML Queries

The basic property underlying the a-priori algorithm [1] is that every subset of a frequent itemset is also a frequent itemset. This property is generalized for DML queries and called *subset-closed*:

**Definition 1.** *Let $\delta$ be a DML sentence with schema-variable $\mathcal{X}$. $\delta$ is subset-closed in $\mathcal{X}$ (or, $\mathcal{X}$-subset-closed) iff for every DML structure $\langle R, \Sigma \rangle$, for every $T \subseteq \Sigma(\mathcal{X})$, if $\langle R, \Sigma \rangle \models \delta$ then $\langle R, \Sigma_{\mathcal{X} \to T} \rangle \models \delta$. A DML sentence $\delta$ is subset-closed iff it is subset-closed in every schema-variable. A query $\{\mathcal{X}_1, \ldots, \mathcal{X}_m \mid \delta\}$ is subset-closed (in $\mathcal{X}_i$) iff $\delta$ is subset-closed (in $\mathcal{X}_i$, $i \in [1..m]$).*

*Superset-closed DML formulas and queries are defined in the same way (replace $T \subseteq \Sigma(\mathcal{X})$ by $T \supseteq \Sigma(\mathcal{X})$).*

Note incidentally that the construct of subset-closedness does not rely on a fixed underlying schema; that is, Definition 1 considers any relation $R$ over any schema. Clearly, subset-closedness and superset-closedness are complementary notions, in the sense that the negation of a subset-closed DML sentence is superset-closed and *vice versa*.

Recognizing subset-closed queries is significant from a data mining perspective because these queries are amenable to query optimization by levelwise search, in the same way as the problem of mining frequent itemsets is solved by the a-priori algorithm. The search first examines which singletons are solutions, and then iteratively examines ever larger sets, but without examining any set that cannot be a solution because in earlier iterations, a proper subset of it turned out to be no solution. This is the general idea; it is worth pointing out that also on a more detailed level, techniques of the a-priori algorithm generalize to subset-closed queries, for example, the candidate generation consisting of join and prune steps [4, Chapter 6].

The same technique applies to superset-closed queries, in which case the search starts from the largest set and iteratively examines sets of lower cardinality, but without ever examining any set that cannot be a solution because one of its supersets was no solution.

If future optimizers for data mining queries have to incorporate a-priori optimization, then they should be able to recognize subset/superset-closed queries. Unfortunately, the class of subset-closed DML queries is not recursive.

**Theorem 1.** *Subset-closedness of DML queries is undecidable.*

Theorem 1 raises the problem of finding a recursive subclass of the class of subset-closed queries that semantically covers a large (or the entire) class of subset-closed queries. Positive DML queries are a candidate.

## 6   Positive DML Queries

**Definition 2.** *A DML formula $\delta$ that contains the schema-variable $\mathcal{X}$, is positive in $\mathcal{X}$ (or $\mathcal{X}$-positive) iff every symbol $\mathcal{X}$ lies within the scope of an even number of negations. A DML formula $\delta$ is positive iff it is positive in every schema-variable. A query $\{\mathcal{X}_1, \ldots, \mathcal{X}_m \mid \delta\}$ is positive (in $\mathcal{X}_i$) iff $\delta$ is positive (in $\mathcal{X}_i$, $i \in [1..m]$).*

Note incidentally that positive, unlike subset-closed, is defined for DML formulas that may not be closed.

**Lemma 1.** *Let $\delta$ be a DML sentence. If $\delta$ is $\mathcal{X}$-positive, then $\delta$ is $\mathcal{X}$-superset-closed. If $\neg\delta$ is $\mathcal{X}$-positive, then $\delta$ is $\mathcal{X}$-subset-closed.*

For example, the application of Lemma 1 tells us that the query (1) in Section 2 is subset-closed. By the same lemma , the query (2) for finding frequent sets and the query (4) for finding inclusion dependencies, both introduced in Section 4, are subset-closed. Note that abbreviations have to be spelled out before testing positiveness. In particular, $\forall\mathcal{X}(Y)(\delta)$ becomes $\forall Y(\neg\mathcal{X}(Y) \vee \delta)$. The lemma does not apply to the query (3) for finding functional dependencies. When the query is spelled out

$$\{\mathcal{X}, \mathcal{Y} \mid \forall t(\forall s((\exists X(\mathcal{X}(X) \wedge t.X \neq s.X)) \vee \neg(\exists Y(\mathcal{Y}(Y) \wedge t.Y \neq s.Y))))$$
$$\wedge \exists Y(\mathcal{Y}(Y) \wedge \neg\mathcal{X}(Y))\} , \tag{5}$$

it turns out that both $\mathcal{X}$ and $\mathcal{Y}$ occur within an even and an odd number of negations.

Because subset-closed and superset-closed are complementary notions, it is sufficient to focus on superset-closed in what follows. Unfortunately, the (recursive) class of positive DML queries does not semantically cover the whole class of superset-closed DML queries; this negative result obtains even if only queries with a single schema-variable are considered.

## 7   A Superset-Closed DML Query with a Single Schema-Variable That Cannot Be Expressed Positively

In Sections 8 and 9, we show that not every $\mathcal{X}$-superset-closed DML sentence is equivalent to some $\mathcal{X}$-positive DML sentence. The proof relies on Stolboushkin's refutation [14] of Lyndon's Lemma (that every monotone first-order property is expressible positively) for finite models. Although Lyndon's Lemma was first refuted for finite models in [2], we rely on Stolboushkin's construction of a first order (FO) sentence $\Omega$ in the signature $\langle H, < \rangle$, where $H$ and $<$ are two binary predicate symbols, such that $\Omega$ is finitely $<$-monotone[3], but $\Omega$ is finitely equivalent to no $<$-positive FO sentence.

In general, the failure of Lyndon's Lemma for DML is not surprising, as DML is essentially FO in which one can talk about attributes; $n$-ary schema-variables correspond to $n$-ary predicate symbols, and attribute-variables to FO variables. The new contribution however is that Lyndon's Lemma fails for DML even if only DML queries with a single schema-variable $\mathcal{X}$ are considered. Such queries suffice for expressing several common data mining problems, like finding frequent sets or inclusion dependencies.

We define a mapping $\mathbf{D}(\cdot)$ from FO formulas to DML formulas and we show that $\mathbf{D}(\Omega)$ is (i) $\mathcal{X}$-superset-closed but (ii) equivalent to no $\mathcal{X}$-positive DML sentence. The mapping $\mathbf{D}(\cdot)$ is such that $<$-monotone FO sentences are mapped to $\mathcal{X}$-superset-closed DML sentences (Lemma 4), so that (i) is instantly verified. To establish (ii), we define a "backward" mapping $\mathbf{F}(\cdot)$ from DML formulas to FO formulas such that:

- $\mathcal{X}$-positive DML sentences are mapped through $\mathbf{F}(\cdot)$ on $<$-positive FO sentences (Lemma 2), and
- every DML sentence equivalent to $\mathbf{D}(\Omega)$ is mapped through $\mathbf{F}(\cdot)$ onto a FO sentence equivalent to $\Omega$ (Lemma 7).

In Sections 8 we define the mappings between DML and FO. Section 9 introduces the properties introduced above, which finally allow concluding the existence of an $\mathcal{X}$-superset-closed DML sentence that is equivalent to no $\mathcal{X}$-positive DML sentence (Theorem 2).

## 8    Mappings

### 8.1    Structure Encodings

The mapping $\mathcal{D}(\cdot)$ maps FO structures of signature $\langle H, < \rangle$ to DML structures. If $I$ is a FO structure of signature $\langle H, < \rangle$, then $\mathcal{D}(I) = \langle R, \Sigma \rangle$ will "encode" the information in $I$ using the following encoding scheme:

- The schema $|R|$ is the domain of $I$.
- Every tuple $t$ of $R$ encodes an element of $I(H)$ as follows. A tuple $t$ with $t(A) = 1$, $t(B) = 2$, and $t(X) = 0$ otherwise, encodes that $(A, B) \in I(H)$. A tuple $t$ with $t(A) = 3$ and $t(X) = 0$ otherwise, encodes that $(A, A) \in I(H)$. Every element in $I(H)$ is encoded in this way by a tuple in $R$; moreover, $R$ contains no other tuples.

---

[3] $\Omega$ being finitely $<$-monotone means that for any (finite) structure $I$ of signature $\langle H, < \rangle$, if $I \models \Omega$ and $I(<) \subseteq T$ than $I_{<\rightarrow T} \models \Omega$.

– A binary schema-variable $\mathcal{X}$ is used for encoding $<$, i.e., $\Sigma(\mathcal{X}) = I(<)$. No other schema-variables will occur in the mappings.

*Example 1.* Let $I$ be a FO structure of signature $\langle H, < \rangle$ and universe $\{A, B, C, D, E\}$. Let $I(H) = \{(A, B), (A, D), (A, E), (C, E), (C, C)\}$. Then $\mathcal{D}(I)$ is a DML structure $\langle R, \Sigma \rangle$ with $R$ as follows:

| $R$ | $A$ | $B$ | $C$ | $D$ | $E$ |
|---|---|---|---|---|---|
| | 1 | 2 | 0 | 0 | 0 |
| | 1 | 0 | 0 | 2 | 0 |
| | 1 | 0 | 0 | 0 | 2 |
| | 0 | 0 | 1 | 0 | 2 |
| | 0 | 0 | 3 | 0 | 0 |

## 8.2    Interpretation Encodings

The mapping $\mathcal{D}(\cdot)$ is extended from structures to interpretations. The DML formulas $\delta$ considered will contain attribute-variables, tuple-variables, and a single binary schema-variable $\mathcal{X}$. As explained before, the binary FO predicate symbol $<$ is tied to the schema-variable $\mathcal{X}$. In addition, FO variables are *tied* to simple-variables as follows:

– a FO variable $x$ is tied to each attribute-variable $X$, and
– two FO variables $t_1, t_2$ are tied to each tuple-variable $t$.

Let $I$ be a FO structure of signature $\langle H, < \rangle$, and $\nu$ a variable assignment to the variables tied to the simple-variables of the DML formula $\delta$. The mapping $\mathcal{D}(\cdot)$ is extended to the *FO interpretation* $\langle I, \nu \rangle$ as follows; $\mathcal{D}(\langle I, \nu \rangle)$ is the DML interpretation $\langle \langle R, \Sigma \rangle, \sigma \rangle$ with the following characteristics:

– $\langle R, \Sigma \rangle = \mathcal{D}(I)$, as previously defined,
– $\sigma(X) = \nu(x)$ for every attribute-variable $X$, and
– for every tuple-variable $t$, if $(\nu(t_1), \nu(t_2)) \in I(H)$, then $\sigma(t)$ is the tuple in $R$ encoding $(\nu(t_1), \nu(t_2))$ in $I(H)$; otherwise $\sigma(t)(X) = 4$ for all $X \in |R|$. Note that if $(\nu(t_1), \nu(t_2))$ does not belong to $I(H)$, then $R$ contains no tuple encoding $(\nu(t_1), \nu(t_2))$. In that case $\sigma(t)$ is chosen to be a tuple that takes the value 4 in all attributes. Such tuple does not belong to $R$, as only the values 0, 1, 2, and 3 can occur in $R$ under the given encoding.

## 8.3    Formula Mappings

The formula mappings are coined with the mapping $\mathcal{D}(\cdot)$ from FO interpretations to DML interpretations in mind. The formula mappings $\mathbf{D}(\cdot)$ and $\mathbf{F}(\cdot)$ are established such that $I \models \phi$ if and only if $\mathcal{D}(I) \models \mathbf{D}(\phi)$ (Lemma 3), and $\mathcal{D}(I) \models \delta$ if and only if $I \models \mathbf{F}(\delta)$ (Lemma 5). The mapping $\mathbf{D}(\cdot)$ maps FO formulas of signature $\langle H, < \rangle$ to DML formulas and is defined next:

$$C_1 = \forall t (\forall X (t.X = 0 \lor t.X = 1 \lor t.X = 2 \lor t.X = 3))$$
$$C_2 = \forall t (\exists X (t.X = 1 \lor t.X = 2 \lor t.X = 3))$$
$$C_3 = \forall t (\forall X (\forall Y ((X \neq Y \land t.X = t.Y) \rightarrow t.X = 0)))$$
$$C_4 = \forall t ((\exists X (t.X = 1)) \leftrightarrow (\exists Y (t.Y = 2)))$$
$$C_5 = \forall t ((\exists X (t.X = 3)) \rightarrow \neg \exists Y (t.Y = 1 \lor t.Y = 2)))$$
$$C = (C_1 \land \ldots \land C_5)$$

The DML formula $C$ is such that every DML structure satisfying $C$ can be thought of as the "encoding" by $\mathcal{D}(\cdot)$ of some FO structure $I$ of signature $\langle H, < \rangle$.

$$\mathbf{D}(\phi) = \mathbf{D}'(\phi) \land C$$
$$\mathbf{D}'(\neg \phi) = \neg \mathbf{D}'(\phi)$$
$$\mathbf{D}'(\phi_1 \lor \phi_2) = \mathbf{D}'(\phi_1) \lor \mathbf{D}'(\phi_2)$$
$$\mathbf{D}'(\exists x(\phi)) = \exists X (\mathbf{D}'(\phi))$$
$$\mathbf{D}'(H(x,y)) = \exists t ((t.X = 1 \land t.Y = 2) \lor (t.X = 3 \land t.Y = 3))$$
$$\mathbf{D}'(x < y) = \mathcal{X}(X, Y)$$

The mapping $\mathbf{F}(\cdot)$ maps DML formulas to FO formulas.

$$\mathbf{F}(X = Y) = x = y$$
$$\mathbf{F}(t.X = s.Y) = \mathbf{F}((t.X = 0 \land s.Y = 0) \lor \ldots \lor (t.X = 4 \land s.Y = 4))$$
$$\mathbf{F}(t.X = 0) = x \neq t_1 \land x \neq t_2 \land H(t_1, t_2)$$
$$\mathbf{F}(t.X = 1) = x = t_1 \land x \neq t_2 \land H(t_1, t_2)$$
$$\mathbf{F}(t.X = 2) = x \neq t_1 \land x = t_2 \land H(t_1, t_2)$$
$$\mathbf{F}(t.X = 3) = x = t_1 \land x = t_2 \land H(t_1, t_2)$$
$$\mathbf{F}(t.X = 4) = \neg H(t_1, t_2)$$
$$\mathbf{F}(t.X = a) = \mathbf{false} \text{ if } a \notin \{0, 1, 2, 3, 4\}$$
$$\mathbf{F}(\mathcal{X}(X, Y)) = x < y$$
$$\mathbf{F}(\neg \delta) = \neg \mathbf{F}(\delta)$$
$$\mathbf{F}(\delta_1 \lor \delta_2) = \mathbf{F}(\delta_1) \lor \mathbf{F}(\delta_2)$$
$$\mathbf{F}(\exists X(\delta)) = \exists x (\mathbf{F}(\delta))$$
$$\mathbf{F}(\exists t(\delta)) = \exists t_1 (\exists t_2 (H(t_1, t_2) \land \mathbf{F}(\delta)))$$

In what follows, $\delta$ denotes a DML formula, and $\phi$ a FO formula of signature $\langle H, < \rangle$. $I$ denotes a FO structure of signature $\langle H, < \rangle$. $\langle R, \Sigma \rangle$ denotes a DML structure; since $\mathcal{X}$ is the only schema-variable involved, it suffices to specify $\Sigma(\mathcal{X})$.

## 9    A-priori and Finitely Monotone Properties

The mappings defined in the previous section satisfy certain properties which eventually allow concluding that the class of positive queries does not semantically cover the whole class of superset-closed queries.

**Lemma 2.** *Let $\delta$ be a DML formula. If $\delta$ is $\mathcal{X}$-positive, then $\mathbf{F}(\delta)$ is $<$-positive.*

We recall that detailed proofs of all lemmas and theorems can be found in [3].

**Lemma 3.** *Let $\phi$ be a FO sentence of signature $\langle H, < \rangle$. $I \models \phi$ iff $\mathcal{D}(I) \models \mathbf{D}(\phi)$.*

**Corollary 1.** *Let $\phi_1$ and $\phi_2$ be two FO sentences of signature $\langle H, < \rangle$. If $\mathbf{D}(\phi_1) \equiv \mathbf{D}(\phi_2)$, then $\phi_1 \equiv \phi_2$.*

**Lemma 4.** *Let $\phi$ be a FO sentence of signature $\langle H, < \rangle$. If $\phi$ is $<$-monotone, then $\mathbf{D}(\phi)$ is $\mathcal{X}$-superset-closed.*

**Lemma 5.** *Let $\delta$ be a DML sentence. $I \models \mathbf{F}(\delta)$ iff $\mathcal{D}(I) \models \delta$.*

**Lemma 6.** *Let $\delta$ be a DML sentence. If $\delta \models C$, then $\delta \equiv \mathbf{D}(\mathbf{F}(\delta))$.*

**Lemma 7.** *Let $\delta$ be a DML sentence and $\phi$ a FO sentence of signature $\langle H, < \rangle$. If $\mathbf{D}(\phi) \equiv \delta$, then $\phi \equiv \mathbf{F}(\delta)$.*

**Theorem 2.** *There exists an $\mathcal{X}$-superset-closed DML sentence with a single schema-variable $\mathcal{X}$ that is equivalent to no $\mathcal{X}$-positive DML sentence.*

*Proof.* By [14], we can assume the existence of a FO sentence $\Omega$ of signature $\langle H, < \rangle$ that is finitely $<$-monotone but that is finitely equivalent to no $<$-positive FO sentence. By Lemma 4, $\mathbf{D}(\Omega)$ is $\mathcal{X}$-superset-closed. It suffices to show that $\mathbf{D}(\Omega)$ is equivalent to no $\mathcal{X}$-positive DML sentence. Assume on the contrary the existence of an $\mathcal{X}$-positive DML sentence $\delta$ that is equivalent to $\mathbf{D}(\Omega)$. By Lemma 7, $\Omega \equiv \mathbf{F}(\delta)$. Since $\delta$ is $\mathcal{X}$-positive, $\mathbf{F}(\delta)$ is $<$-positive (Lemma 2). This contradicts our assumption about $\Omega$. □

## 10    Discussion and Future Work

DML allows expressing data mining queries that ask for rules involving sets of attributes, like "Find frequent itemsets" and "Find functional dependencies." The a-priori technique directly applies to all subset-closed and superset-closed DML queries. Since a DML query is subset-closed if and only if its negation is superset-closed, it suffices to focus on superset-closedness. Superset-closedness of DML queries is undecidable. It is an open problem whether there exists a recursive subclass of superset-closed DML queries such that every superset-closed DML query is equivalent to some query in this subclass. We revealed a significant relationship between superset-closedness in DML and finitely monotone first order properties. Each positive DML query is superset-closed, but there exist superset-closed queries with a single schema-variable that cannot be expressed positively. One may hope that the class of all positive DML queries and their negations semantically covers all "practical" DML queries that are amenable to a-priori optimization. Anyway, as long as we do not know a recursive subclass of the class of superset-closed DML queries that semantically covers the whole class of superset-closed DML queries, query optimizers can use positiveness of a query as a criterion for determining the applicability of a-priori pruning.

We list two interesting problems for future work. The first problem concerns the extension of DML with aggregate functions, which are obviously needed in many data mining tasks. The query (2) for finding frequent sets, introduced in Section 4, can probably be expressed more naturally by using some *count* function. An interesting problem is to find recursive subclasses of subset/superset-closed queries in the presence of aggregate functions.

Secondly, certain subqueries of a DML query can be subset/superset-closed, even though the query itself is not. In this case, a-priori optimization could still be applied on these subqueries. Recall, for example, that the DML query for finding non-trivial functional dependencies (queries (3) and (5) in Sections 4 and 6 respectively) is neither subset-closed nor superset-closed. However, if we omit the requirement that the functional dependencies be non-trivial, the query (5) reduces to:

$$\{\mathcal{X}, \mathcal{Y} \mid \forall t (\forall s ((\exists X(\mathcal{X}(X) \wedge t.X \neq s.X)) \vee \neg (\exists Y(\mathcal{Y}(Y) \wedge t.Y \neq s.Y)))) \} \ . \ (6)$$

By Lemma 1, the query (6) is $\mathcal{X}$-superset-closed and $\mathcal{Y}$-subset-closed, which is tantamount to saying that if the functional dependency $X \to Y$ is satisfied, and $X \subseteq X'$ and $Y' \subseteq Y$, then $X' \to Y'$ must necessarily be satisfied as well. This property again allows a-priori pruning in the following way: In order to find all non-trivial functional dependencies satisfied by a given relation (query (5)), one could use the a-priori trick on the query that finds all functional dependencies that are satisfied (query (6)), and filter away those that are trivial. The filter corresponds to the following subquery of query (5) that was left out in query (6):

$$\{\mathcal{X}, \mathcal{Y} \mid \exists Y(\mathcal{Y}(Y) \wedge \neg \mathcal{X}(Y)) \} \ . \tag{7}$$

That the latter query is $\mathcal{X}$-subset-closed and $\mathcal{Y}$-superset-closed, is of second importance. This way of optimizing queries by exploiting the a-priori technique on subset/superset-closed subqueries, resembles the idea underlying query flocks [15]; we believe that further research is needed to assess its feasibility and usefulness.

# References

1. R. Agrawal, T. Imielinski, and A. Swami. Mining association rules between sets of items in large databases. In *Proc. ACM SIGMOD Int. Conf. Management of Data*, pages 207–216, Washington, D.C., 1993.
2. M. Ajtai and Y. Gurevich. Monotone versus positive. *Journal of the ACM*, 34(4):1004–1015, 1987.
3. T. Calders and J. Wijsen. On monotone data mining languages. Technical Report 2001-08, Universitaire Instelling Antwerpen, Department of Mathematics & Computer Science, 2001.
4. J. Han and M. Kamber. *Data Mining: Concepts and Techniques*. Morgan Kaufmann, 2000.

5. T. Imielinski and H. Mannila. A database perspective on knowledge discovery. *Comm. of the ACM*, 39(11):58–64, 1996.
6. M. Kantola, H. Mannila, K.-J. Räihä, and H. Siirtola. Discovering functional and inclusion dependencies in relational databases. *Internat. Journal of Intelligent Systems*, 7:591–607, 1992.
7. L. V. S. Lakshmanan, R. Ng, J. Han, and A. Pang. Optimization of constrained frequent set queries with 2-variable constraints. In *Proc. ACM SIGMOD Int. Conf. Management of Data*, pages 157–168, 1999.
8. L. V. S. Lakshmanan, F. Sadri, and S. N. Subramanian. SchemaSQL—An extension to SQL for multi-database interoperability. *To appear in ACM Trans. on Database Systems*.
9. S. Lopes, J.-M. Petit, and L. Lakhal. Efficient discovery of functional dependencies and Armstrong relations. In *Proc. 7th Int. Conf. on Extending Database Technology (EDBT 2000)*, LNCS 1777, pages 350–364. Springer, 2000.
10. H. Mannila. Methods and problems in data mining. In *Proc. Int. Conf. on Database Theory*, Delphi, Greece, 1997.
11. H. Mannila and H. Toivonen. Levelwise search and borders of theories in knowledge discovery. *Data Mining and Knowledge Discovery*, 1(3):241–258, 1997.
12. R. T. Ng, L. V. S. Lakshmanan, J. Han, and A. Pang. Exploratory mining and pruning optimizations of constrained associations rules. In *Proc. ACM SIGMOD Int. Conf. Management of Data*, pages 13–24. ACM Press, 1998.
13. K. A. Ross. Relations with relation names as arguments: Algebra and calculus. In *Proc. ACM SIGACT-SIGMOD-SIGART Symposium on Principles of Database Systems*, pages 346–353. ACM Press, 1992.
14. A. Stolboushkin. Finitely monotone properties. In *Proc. 10th IEEE Symp. on Logic in Comp. Sci.*, pages 324–330, 1995.
15. D. Tsur, J. D. Ullman, S. Abiteboul, C. Clifton, R. Motwani, S. Nestorov, and A. Rosenthal. Query flocks: a generalization of association-rule mining. In *Proc. ACM SIGMOD Int. Conf. Management of Data*, pages 1–12, 1998.
16. J. Wijsen, R. Ng, and T. Calders. Discovering roll-up dependencies. In *Proc. ACM SIGKDD Int. Conf. Knowledge Discovery and Data Mining*, pages 213–222, San Diego, CA, 1999.

# Reasoning about Keys for XML

Peter Buneman[1,*], Susan Davidson[1,**], Wenfei Fan[2,***],
Carmem Hara[3], and Wang-Chiew Tan[1,*]

[1] University of Pennsylvania, Philadelphia, PA 19104-6389, USA
[2] Bell Laboratories, Murray Hill, NJ 07974-0636, USA
[3] Universidade Federal do Parana, Curitiba, PR 81531-990, Brazil

**Abstract.** We study absolute and relative keys for XML, and investigate their associated decision problems. We argue that these keys are important to many forms of hierarchically structured data including XML documents. In contrast to other proposals of keys for XML, these keys can be reasoned about efficiently. We show that the (finite) satisfiability problem for these keys is trivial, and their (finite) implication problem is finitely axiomatizable and decidable in PTIME in the size of keys.

## 1 Introduction

Keys are of fundamental importance in databases. They provide a means of locating a specific object within the database and of referencing an object from another object (e.g. relationships); they are also an important class of constraints on the validity of data. In particular, value-based keys (as used in relational databases) provide an invariant connection from an object in the real world to its representation in the database. This connection is crucial for modifying the database as the world that it models changes.

As XML is increasingly used to model real world data, it is natural to require a value-based method of locating an element in an XML document. Key specifications for XML have been proposed in the XML standard [22], XML Data [23], and XML Schema [26]. The authors have recently [4] proposed a key structure for XML which has the following benefits:

1. Keys are defined with path expressions and may involve attributes, subelements or more general structures. Equality is defined on tree structures instead of on simple text, referred to as *value equality*.
2. Keys, in their general form, are defined relative to a set of context nodes, referred to as *relative keys*. Such keys can be concatenated to form a hierarchical key structure, common in scientific data sets. An *absolute key* is a special case of a relative key, which has a unique context node: the root.
3. The specification of keys does not depend on any typing specification of the document (e.g. DTD or XML Schema).

* Supported by NSF IIS 99-77408 and NSF DL-2 IIS 98-17444
** Supported by NSF DBI99-75206
*** Currently on leave from Temple University. Supported in part by NSF IIS 00-93168.

G. Grahne and G. Ghelli (Eds.): DBPL 2001, LNCS 2397, pp. 133–148, 2002.

```
                                              ⟨book  isbn=234⟩
                                                ⟨title⟩ XML ⟨/title⟩
      ⟨db⟩                                      ⟨author⟩
        ⟨book  isbn=123⟩                          ⟨name⟩
          ⟨title⟩ HTML ⟨/title⟩                     ⟨first-name⟩ Tim ⟨/first-name⟩
          ⟨author⟩                                   ⟨last-name⟩ Bray ⟨/last-name⟩
            ⟨name⟩                                 ⟨/name⟩
              ⟨first-name⟩ Tim ⟨/first-name⟩     ⟨/author⟩
              ⟨last-name⟩ Bray ⟨/last-name⟩      ⟨author⟩
            ⟨/name⟩                                ⟨name⟩
          ⟨/author⟩                                  ⟨first-name⟩ Jean ⟨/first-name⟩
          ⟨chapter  number=1⟩ text ⟨/chapter⟩        ⟨last-name⟩ Paoli ⟨/last-name⟩
          ⟨chapter  number=10⟩ text ⟨/chapter⟩     ⟨/name⟩
        ⟨/book⟩                                   ⟨/author⟩
                                                ⟨chapter  number=1⟩ text ⟨/chapter⟩
                                                ⟨chapter  number=12⟩ text ⟨/chapter⟩
                                              ⟨/book⟩
                                            ⟨/db⟩
```

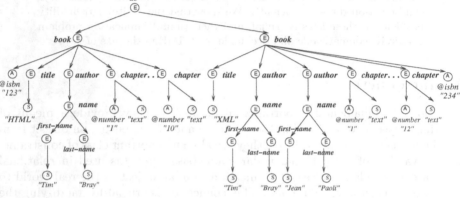

**Fig. 1.** Example of some XML data and its representation as a tree

In developing our notion of keys for XML, we start with a tree model of data as used in DOM [21], XSL [25,27], XQL [19] and XML Schema [26]. An example of this representation for some XML data is shown in Fig. 1 in which nodes are annotated by their type: $E$ for element, $A$ for attribute, and $S$ for string (or PCDATA). Some value-based keys for this data might include: 1) A book node is identified by @isbn; 2) An author node is identified by name, no matter where the author node appears; and 3) Within any subtree rooted at book, a chapter node is identified by @number. These keys are defined independently of any type specification. The first two are examples of absolute keys since they must hold globally throughout the tree. Observe that name has a complex structure. As a consequence, to test whether two authors violate this constraint involves testing value-equality on the subtrees rooted at their name nodes. The last one is an example of a relative key since it holds locally within each subtree rooted at a book. It should be noted that a chapter @number is not a key for the set of all chapter nodes in the document since two different books have chapters with @number= 1. It is worth remarking that proposals prior to [4] are not capable of expressing the second and third constraints.

One of the most interesting questions involving keys is that of logical implication, i.e., deciding if a new key holds given a set of existing keys. This is important for minimizing the expense of checking that a document satisfies a set of key constraints, and may also provide the basis for reasoning about how constraints can be propagated through view definitions. Thus a central task for the study of XML keys is to develop an algorithm for determining logical implication. It is also desirable to develop a sound and complete set of inference rules for generating symbolic proofs of logical implication. The existence of such inference rules, referred to as *axiomatizability*, is a stronger property than the existence of an algorithm, because the former implies the latter but not the other way around [2]. Another interesting question is whether a set of keys is "reasonable" in the sense that there exists some (finite) document that satisfies the key specification (*finite satisfiability*).

In relational databases, these decision problems for keys (and more generally, functional dependencies) have been well studied (cf. [2,18]). The finite satisfiability problem is trivial: given any finite set of keys over a relational schema, one can always find a finite instance of the schema that satisfies the keys. Implication of relational keys is also easy, and is decidable in linear time.

For XML the story is more complicated since the hierarchical structure of data is far more complex than the 1NF structure of relational data. In some proposals keys are not even finitely satisfiable. For example, consider a key of XML Schema (in a simplified syntax): $(//*, [id])$, where "$//*$" (in XPath [24] syntax) traverses to any descendant of the root of an XML document tree. This key asserts that any node in an XML tree must have a unique id subelement (of text value) and its id uniquely identifies the node in the entire document. However, it is clear that no finite XML tree satisfies this key because any id node must have an id itself, and this yields an infinite chain of id nodes. For implication of XML keys, the analysis is even more intriguing. Keys of XML Schema are defined in terms of XPath [24], which is a powerful yet complicated language. A number of technical questions in connection with XPath are still open, including the containment of XPath expressions which is important in the interpretation of XML keys. To the best of our knowledge, the implication problem for keys defined in XML Schema is still open, as is its axiomatizability.

In contrast, we show in this paper that the keys of [4] can be reasoned about efficiently. More specifically, we show that they are finitely satisfiable and their implication is decidable in PTIME. Better still, their (finite) implication is *finitely axiomatizable*, i.e., there is a finite set of inference rules that is sound and complete for implication of these keys. In developing these results, we also investigate value-equality on XML subtrees and containment of path expressions, which are not only interesting in their own right but also important in the study of decision problems for XML keys.

Despite the importance of key analyses for XML, little previous work has studied this issue. The only closely related work is [10,11]. For a class of keys and foreign keys, the decision problems were studied in the absence [11] and presence [10] of DTDs. The keys considered there are defined in terms of XML attributes and are not as expressive as keys studied in this paper. Integrity constraints defined in terms of navigation paths have been studied for semistructured data [1] and XML in [3,7,8,9]. These constraints are generalizations of inclusion dependencies and are not capable of expressing keys. Generalizations of functional dependencies have also been studied [13,16]. However these generalizations were investigated in database settings, which are quite different from the tree model for XML data. Surveys on XML constraints can be found in [6,20].

The remainder of the paper is organized as follows. Section 2 defines value equality and (absolute and relative) keys for XML. Section 3 establishes the finite axiomatizability and complexity results: First, we give a quadratic time algorithm for determining inclusion of path expressions. The ability to determine inclusion of path expressions is then used in developing inference rules for keys, for which a PTIME algorithm is given. Finally, Sec. 4 identifies directions for further research. All the proofs are given in the full version of the paper [5].

## 2   Keys

As illustrated in Fig. 1, our notion of keys is based on a tree model of XML data. Although the model is quite simple, we need to do two things prior to defining keys: the first is to give a precise definition of value equality for XML keys; the second is to describe a path language that will be used to locate sets of nodes in an XML document. We therefore introduce a class of regular path expressions, and define keys in terms of this path language.

### 2.1   A Tree Model and Value Equality

An XML document is typically modeled as a node-labeled tree. We assume three pairwise disjoint sets of labels: $\mathbf{E}$ of element tags, $\mathbf{A}$ of attribute names, and a singleton set $\{\mathbf{S}\}$ denoting text (PCDATA).

**Definition 1.** *An XML tree is defined to be $T = (V, lab, ele, att, val, r)$, where (1) $V$ is a set of nodes; (2) lab is a mapping $V \rightarrow \mathbf{E} \cup \mathbf{A} \cup \{\mathbf{S}\}$ which assigns a label to each node in $V$; a node $v$ in $V$ is called an* element *(E node) if $lab(v) \in \mathbf{E}$, an* attribute *(A node) if $lab(v) \in \mathbf{A}$, and a text node (S node) if $lab(v) = \mathbf{S}$; (3) ele and att are partial mappings that define the edge relation of $T$: for any node $v$ in $V$,*

- *if $v$ is an element then $ele(v)$ is a sequence of elements and text nodes in $V$ and $att(v)$ is a set of attributes in $V$; for each $v'$ in $ele(v)$ or $att(v)$, $v'$ is called a* child *of $v$ and we say that there is a (directed) edge from $v$ to $v'$;*
- *if $v$ is an attribute or a text node then $ele(v)$ and $att(v)$ are undefined;*

*(4) val is a partial mapping that assigns a string to each attribute and text node: for any node $v$ in $V$, if $v$ is an A or S node then $val(v)$ is a string, and $val(v)$ is undefined otherwise; (5) $r$ is the unique and distinguished root node. An XML tree has a tree structure, i.e., for each $v \in V$, there is a unique path of edges from root $r$ to $v$. An XML tree is said to be finite if $V$ is finite.*

---

We do not consider foreign keys and DTDs in the current paper.

For example, Fig. 1 depicts an XML tree that represents an XML document.

With this, we are ready to define value equality on XML trees. Let $T = (V, lab, ele, att, val, r)$ be an XML tree, and $n_1, n_2$ be two nodes in $V$. Informally, $n_1, n_2$ are value equal if they have the same tag (label) and in addition, either they have the same (string) value (when they are S or A nodes) or their children are pairwise value equal (when they are E nodes). More formally:

**Definition 2.** *Two nodes $n_1$ and $n_2$ are* value equal, *denoted by $n_1 =_v n_2$, iff (1) $lab(n_1) = lab(n_2)$; (2) if $n_1, n_2$ are A or S nodes then $val(n_1) = val(n_2)$; and (3) if $n_1, n_2$ are E nodes, then (a) for any $a_1 \in att(n_1)$, there exists $a_2 \in att(n_2)$ such that $a_1 =_v a_2$, and vice versa; and (b) if $ele(n_1) = [v_1, \ldots, v_k]$, then $ele(n_2) = [v'_1, \ldots, v'_k]$ and for all $i \in [1, k]$, $v_i =_v v'_i$. That is, $n_1 =_v n_2$ iff their subtrees are isomorphic by an isomorphism that is the identity on string values.*

As an example, in Fig. 1, the `author` subelement of the first `book` and the first `author` subelement of the second `book` are value equal.

## 2.2   Path Languages

There are many options for a path language, ranging from very simple ones involving just labels to more expressive ones such as regular languages or even XPath. However, to develop inference rules for keys we need to be able to reason about inclusion of path expressions (the *containment* problem). It is well known that for regular languages, the containment problem is not finitely axiomatizable; and for XPath, although nothing is known at this point we strongly suspect that it is not much easier. We therefore restrict our attention to the path language $PL$, which is expressive enough to be interesting yet simple enough to be reasoned about efficiently. We will also use a simpler language ($PL_s$) in defining keys, and therefore show both languages in the table below.

| Path Language | Syntax |
|---|---|
| $PL_s$ | $\rho ::= \epsilon \mid l.\rho$ |
| $PL$ | $q ::= \epsilon \mid l \mid q.q \mid \_*$ |

In $PL_s$, a path is a (possibly empty) sequence of node labels. Here $\epsilon$ denotes the empty path, node label $l \in \mathbf{E} \cup \mathbf{A} \cup \{\mathbf{S}\}$, and "." is a binary operator that concatenates two path expressions. The language $PL$ is a generalization of $PL_s$ that allows "$\_*$", a combination of wildcard and Kleene closure. This symbol represents any (possibly empty) finite sequence of node labels. These languages are fragments of regular expressions [14], with $PL_s$ contained in $PL$.

A path in $PL_s$ is used to describe a path in an XML tree $T$, and a path expression in $PL$ describes a set of such paths. Recall that an attribute node or a text node is a leaf in $T$ and it does not have any child. Thus a path $\rho$ in $PL_s$ is said to be *valid* if for any label $l$ in $\rho$, if $l \in \mathbf{A}$ or $l = \mathbf{S}$, then $l$ is the last symbol in $\rho$. Similarly, we define *valid* path expressions of $PL$. In what follows we assume that the regular language defined by a path expression of $PL$ contains only valid paths. For example, *book.author.name* is a valid path in $PL_s$ and $PL$, while $\_*.author$ is a valid path expression in $PL$ but it is not in $PL_s$.

We now give some notation that will be used throughout the rest of the paper. Let $\rho$ be a path in $PL_s$, $P$ a path expression in $PL$ and $T$ an XML tree.

**Length.** The *length* of path $\rho$, denoted by $|\rho|$, is the number of labels in $\rho$ (the empty path has length 0). By treating "$\_*$" as a special label, we also define the length of $PL$ expression $P$, denoted by $|P|$, to be the number of labels in $P$.

**Membership.** We use $\rho \in P$ to denote that path $\rho$ is in the regular language defined by path expression $P$. For example, *book.author.name* $\in$ *book.author.name* and *book.author.name* $\in$ $\_*.name$.

**Reachability.** Let $n_1, n_2$ be nodes in $T$. We say that $n_2$ is *reachable* from $n_1$ by following path $\rho$, denoted by $T \models \rho(n_1, n_2)$, iff $n_1 = n_2$ if $\rho = \epsilon$, and if $\rho = \rho'.l$, then there exists $n$ in $T$ such that $T \models \rho'(n_1, n)$ and $n_2$ is a child of $n$ with label $l$. We say that node $n_2$ is *reachable* from $n_1$ by following path expression $P$, denoted by $T \models P(n_1, n_2)$, iff there is a path $\rho \in P$ such that $T \models \rho(n_1, n_2)$. For example, if $T$ is the XML tree in Fig. 1, then all the **name** nodes are reachable from the root by following *book.author.name* and also by following $\_*$.

**Node set.** Let $n$ be a node in $T$. We use $n[\![P]\!]$ to denote the set of nodes in $T$ that can be reached by following the path expression $P$ from node $n$. That is, $n[\![P]\!] = \{n' \mid T \models P(n, n')\}$. We shall use $[\![P]\!]$ as abbreviation for $r[\![P]\!]$, when $r$ is the root node of $T$. For example, referring to Fig. 1 and let $n$ be the first **book** element, then $n[\![chapter]\!]$ is the set of all **chapter** elements of the first book and $[\![\_*.chapter]\!]$ is the set of all **chapter** elements in the entire document.

**Definition 3.** *The* value intersection *of node sets* $n_1[\![P]\!]$ *and* $n_2[\![P]\!]$, *denoted by* $n_1[\![P]\!] \cap_v n_2[\![P]\!]$, *is defined by:*

$$n_1[\![P]\!] \cap_v n_2[\![P]\!] = \{(z, z') \mid \exists \rho \in P, \; z \in n_1[\![\rho]\!], \; z' \in n_2[\![\rho]\!], \; z =_v z'\}$$

That is, $n_1[\![P]\!] \cap_v n_2[\![P]\!]$ consists of node pairs that are value equal and are reachable by following the same simple path in the language defined by $P$ starting from $n_1$ and $n_2$, respectively. For example, let $n_1$ and $n_2$ be the first and second **book** elements in Fig. 1, respectively. Then $n_1[\![author]\!] \cap_v n_2[\![author]\!]$ is the set consisting of a single pair $(x, y)$, where $x$ is the **author** subelement of the first book and $y$ is the first **author** subelement of the second book.

## 2.3   A Key Constraint Language for XML

We are now in a position to define keys for XML and what it means for an XML document to satisfy a key constraint.

**Definition 4.** *A* key constraint $\varphi$ *for XML is an expression of the form*

$$(Q, (Q', \{P_1, \ldots, P_k\})),$$

*where $Q$, $Q'$ and $P_i$ are PL expressions such that for all $i \in [1, k]$, $Q.Q'.P_i$ is a valid path expression. The path $Q$ is called the* context path, *$Q'$ is called the* target path, *and $P_1$, ..., $P_k$ are called the* key paths *of $\varphi$.*

*When $Q = \epsilon$, we call $\varphi$ an* absolute key, *abbreviated to $(Q', \{P_1, \ldots, P_k\})$; otherwise $\varphi$ is called a* relative key. *We use $\mathcal{K}$ to denote the language of keys, and $\mathcal{K}_{abs}$ to denote the set of absolute keys in $\mathcal{K}$.*

A key $\varphi = (Q, (Q', \{P_1, \ldots, P_k\}))$ specifies the following: (1) the context path $Q$, starting from the root of an XML tree $T$, identifies a set of nodes $[\![Q]\!]$; (2) for each node $n \in [\![Q]\!]$, $\varphi$ defines an absolute key $(Q', \{P_1, \ldots, P_k\})$ that is to hold on the subtree rooted at $n$; specifically,

- the target path $Q'$ identifies a set of nodes $n[\![Q']\!]$ in the subtree, referred to as the *target set*,
- the key paths $P_1, \ldots, P_k$ identify nodes in the target set. That is, for each $n' \in n[\![Q']\!]$ the values of the nodes reached by following the key paths from $n'$ uniquely identify $n'$ in the target set.

For example, the keys on Fig. 1 mentioned in Sec. 1 can be written as follows:
(1) @isbn is a key of book nodes: $(book, \{@isbn\})$;
(2) name is a key of author nodes no matter where they are: $(\_*.author, \{name\})$;
(3) within each subtree rooted at a book, @number is a key of chapter relative to book: $(book, (chapter, \{@number\}))$.
The first two are absolute keys of $\mathcal{K}_{abs}$ and the last one is a relative key of $\mathcal{K}$.

**Definition 5.** *Let* $\varphi = (Q, (Q', \{P_1, \ldots, P_k\}))$ *be a key of* $\mathcal{K}$. *An XML tree* $T$ *satisfies* $\varphi$, *denoted by* $T \models \varphi$, *iff for any* $n$ *in* $[\![Q]\!]$ *and any* $n_1, n_2$ *in* $n[\![Q']\!]$, *if for all* $i \in [1, k]$ *there exist a path* $\rho \in P_i$ *and nodes* $x \in n_1[\![\rho]\!]$, $y \in n_2[\![\rho]\!]$ *such that* $x =_v y$, *then* $n_1 = n_2$. *That is,*

$$\forall n \in [\![Q]\!] \ \ \forall n_1 \, n_2 \in n[\![Q']\!] \ ((\bigwedge_{1 \leq i \leq k} n_1[\![P_i]\!] \cap_v n_2[\![P_i]\!] \neq \emptyset) \rightarrow n_1 = n_2).$$

As an example, let us consider $\mathcal{K}$ constraints on the XML tree $T$ in Fig. 1. (1) $T \models (book, \{@isbn\})$ because the @isbn attributes of the two book nodes in $T$ have different string values. However, $T \not\models (book, \{author\})$ because the two books agree on the values of their first author.
(2) $T \not\models (\_*.author, \{name\})$ because the author of the first book and the first author of the second book agree on their names but they are distinct nodes.
(3) $T \models (book, (chapter, \{@number\}))$ because in the subtree rooted at each book node, the @number attribute of each chapter has a distinct value.

Several subtleties are worth pointing out. First, observe that each key path can specify a *set* of values. For example, consider $\psi = (book, \{@isbn, author\})$ on the XML tree $T$ in Fig. 1, and note that the key path author reaches two author subelements from the second book node. In contrast, this is not allowed in most proposals for XML keys, e.g., XML Schema. The reason that we allow a key path to reach multiple nodes is to cope with the semistructured nature of XML data. Second, the key has no impact on those nodes at which some key path is *missing*. Observe that for any $n \in [\![Q]\!]$ and $n_1, n_2$ in $n[\![Q']\!]$, if $P_i$ is missing at either $n_1$ or $n_2$ then $n_1[\![P_i]\!]$ and $n_2[\![P_i]\!]$ are by definition disjoint. This is similar to *unique constraints* introduced in XML Schema. In contrast to unique constraints, however, our notion of keys is capable of comparing nodes at which a key path may have multiple values. Third, it should be noted that two notions of equality are used to define keys: value equality $(=_v)$ when comparing nodes reached by following key paths, and node identity $(=)$ when comparing two nodes in the target set. This is a departure from keys in relational databases, in which only value equality is considered.

Our definition of a key allows key values to be "scoped" by their paths. As an example, the XML data in Fig. 2.a satisfies the key $\langle$part, $\{\_*.@id\}\rangle$, and the XML data in Fig. 2.b satisfies the key $\langle$book, $\{\_*.isbn\}\rangle$. Although in the first example our definition of keys captures the intended meaning, we would probably want the second example to violate the key. That is, one might want isbn to be a key for book no matter where it occurs in a book. It is possible to reformulate our constraint language to be able to express both examples by modifying the definition of value intersection (Def. 3), but we do not yet know whether the proofs in this paper can be extended to a more general definition.

```
⟨part⟩
    ⟨widget id=1⟩⟨/widget⟩          ⟨book isbn=123⟩
⟨/part⟩                             ⟨/book⟩
⟨part⟩                              ⟨book⟩
    ⟨gadget id=1⟩⟨/gadget⟩              ⟨identifier isbn=123/⟩
⟨/part⟩                             ⟨/book⟩

        (a)                                (b)
```

**Fig. 2.** XML data and scope of key paths

## 2.4   Decision Problems

As mentioned in Sec. 1, the satisfiability and implication analyses of XML keys are far more intriguing than their relational databases counterpart.

We first consider satisfiability of keys of our constraint language $\mathcal{K}$. Let $\Sigma$ be a finite set of keys in $\mathcal{K}$ and $T$ be an XML tree. We use $T \models \Sigma$ to denote that $T$ satisfies $\Sigma$. That is: for any $\psi \in \Sigma$, $T \models \psi$.

The (finite) satisfiability problem for $\mathcal{K}$ is to determine, given any finite set $\Sigma$ of keys in $\mathcal{K}$, whether there exists a (finite) XML tree satisfying $\Sigma$.

As observed in Sec. 1, keys defined in some proposals (e.g., XML Schema) may not be finitely satisfiable at all. In contrast, any key constraints of $\mathcal{K}$ can always be satisfied by a finite XML tree, including the single node tree. That is,

**Observation.** Any finite set $\Sigma$ of keys in $\mathcal{K}$ is finitely satisfiable.

Next, we consider implication of $\mathcal{K}$ constraints. Let $\Sigma \cup \{\varphi\}$ be a finite set of keys of $\mathcal{K}$. We use $\Sigma \models \varphi$ to denote $\Sigma$ implies $\varphi$; that is, for any XML tree $T$, if $T \models \Sigma$, then $T \models \varphi$.

There are two implication problems associated with keys: The implication problem is to determine, given any finite set of keys $\Sigma \cup \{\varphi\}$, whether $\Sigma \models \varphi$. The finite implication problem is to determine whether $\Sigma$ finitely implies $\varphi$, that is, whether it is the case that for any finite XML tree $T$, if $T \models \Sigma$, then $T \models \varphi$.

Given any finite set $\Sigma \cup \{\varphi\}$ of keys in $\mathcal{K}$, if there is an XML tree $T$ such that $T \models \bigwedge \Sigma \wedge \neg\varphi$, then there must be a finite XML tree $T'$ such that $T' \models \bigwedge \Sigma \wedge \neg\varphi$.

We are grateful to one of the referees for pointing this out and for providing the example.

Thus key implication has the finite model property (see [5] for a proof) and as a result:

**Proposition 1.** *The implication and finite implication problems for keys coincide.*

In light of this we can also use $\Sigma \models \varphi$ to denote that $\Sigma$ finitely implies $\varphi$.

# 3   Key Implication

We now study the finite implication problem for keys. Our main result is:

**Theorem 1.** *The finite implication problem for $\mathcal{K}$ is finitely axiomatizable and decidable in PTIME in the size of keys.*

We provide a finite axiomatization and a PTIME algorithm for determining finite implication of $\mathcal{K}$ constraints. In contrast to their relational database counterparts, the axiomatization and algorithm are nontrivial. A road map for the proof of the theorem is as follows. We first study containment of path expressions in the language *PL* defined in the last section, since the axioms rely on path inclusion. We then provide a finite set of inference rules and show that it is sound and complete for finite implication of $\mathcal{K}$ constraints. Finally, taking advantage of the inference rules, we develop a PTIME algorithm for determining finite implication. We shall also present complexity results in connection with finite implication of absolute keys in $\mathcal{K}_{abs}$.

## 3.1   Inclusion of *PL* Expressions

A *PL* expression $P$ is said to be *included* (or *contained*) in *PL* expression $Q$, denoted by $P \subseteq Q$, if for any XML tree $T$ and any node $n$ in $T$, $n[\![P]\!] \subseteq n[\![Q]\!]$. That is, the nodes reached from $n$ by following $P$ are contained in the set of the nodes reached by following $Q$ from $n$. We write $P = Q$ if $P \subseteq Q$ and $Q \subseteq P$.

In the absence of DTDs, $P \subseteq Q$ is equivalent to the containment of the regular language defined by $P$ in the regular language defined by $Q$. Indeed, if there exists a path $\rho \in P$ but $\rho \notin Q$, then one can construct an XML tree $T$ with a path $\rho$ from the root. It is obvious that in $T$, $[\![P]\!] \not\subseteq [\![Q]\!]$. The other direction is immediate. Therefore, $P \subseteq Q$ iff for any path $\rho \in P$, $\rho \in Q$.

We investigate inclusion (containment) of path expressions in *PL*: given any *PL* expressions $P$ and $Q$, is it the case that $P \subseteq Q$? As will become clear shortly, this is important to the proof of Theorem 1. It is decidable with a low complexity:

**Theorem 2.** *There are a sound and complete finite set of inference rules and a quadratic time algorithm for determining inclusion of PL expressions.*

It is worth mentioning that *PL* is a star-free regular language (cf. [28] for a definition). The inclusion problem for general star-free languages is co-NP complete [15]. For inclusion of *PL* expression, we are able to provide a set of inference rules in Table 1, denoted by $\mathcal{I}^p$, and to develop a quadratic time algorithm.

**Table 1.** $\mathcal{I}^p$: rules for $PL$ expression inclusion

$$\frac{P \in PL}{\epsilon.P \subseteq P \quad P \subseteq \epsilon.P \quad P.\epsilon \subseteq P \quad P \subseteq P.\epsilon} \quad \text{(empty-path)}$$

$$\frac{P \in PL}{P \subseteq P} \quad \text{(reflexivity)} \qquad \frac{P \in PL}{P \subseteq \_^*} \quad \text{(star)}$$

$$\frac{P \subseteq P' \quad Q \subseteq Q'}{P.Q \subseteq P'.Q'} \quad \text{(composition)} \qquad \frac{P \subseteq Q \quad Q \subseteq R}{P \subseteq R} \quad \text{(transitivity)}$$

*Proof sketch:* The soundness of $\mathcal{I}^p$ can be verified by induction on the lengths of $\mathcal{I}^p$-proofs. The proof of completeness is based on a simulation relation defined on the nondeterministic finite automata (NFA [14]) that characterize $PL$ expressions. More specifically, let the NFA for $PL$ expressions $P$ and $Q$ be $M(P) = (N_1, C \cup \{\_\}, \delta_1, S_1, F_1)$ and $M(Q) = (N_2, C \cup \{\_\}, \delta_2, S_2, F_2)$ respectively. Observe that the alphabets of the NFA have been extended with the special character "$\_$" which can match any letter in $C$. We define a *simulation relation*, $\lhd$, on $N_1 \times N_2$. For any $n_1 \in N_1$ and $n_2 \in N_2$, $n_1 \lhd n_2$ iff the following conditions are satisfied: (1) If $n_1 = F_1$ then $n_2 = F_2$. (2) If $\delta_1(n_1, \_) = n_1$ then $\delta_2(n_2, \_) = n_2$. (3) For any $l \in C$, if $\delta_1(n_1, l) = n_1'$ for some $n_1' \in N_1$, then either (a) there exists a state $n_2' \in N_2$ such that $\delta_2(n_2, l) = n_2'$ and $n_1' \lhd n_2'$, or (b) $\delta_2(n_2, \_) = n_2$ and $n_1' \lhd n_2$. The simulation is defined in such a way that $P \subseteq Q$ is equivalent to $S_1 \lhd S_2$. Intuitively, this means that starting with the start states of $M(P)$ and $M(Q)$ and given an input string, every step taken by $M(P)$ in accepting this string has a corresponding step in $M(Q)$ according to the simulation relation. In light of $\mathcal{I}^p$ and the claims, we provide in Algorithm 1 a recursive function $Incl(n_1, n_2)$ for testing inclusion of $PL$ expressions. We use $visited(n_1, n_2)$ to keep track of whether $Incl(n_1, n_2)$ has been evaluated before, which ensures that each pair $(n_1, n_2)$ is checked at most once. The function $Incl(n_1, n_2)$ returns true iff $n_1 \lhd n_2$. Since $P \subseteq Q$ iff $S_1 \lhd S_2$, $P \subseteq Q$ iff $Incl(S_1, S_2)$. Its complexity is kept low by the use of the boolean $visited$. See [5] for details.     ∎

### 3.2   Axiomatization for Absolute Key Implication

Recall that an absolute key $(Q', S)$ is a special case of a $\mathcal{K}$ constraint $(Q, (Q', S))$, i.e., when $Q = \epsilon$. As opposed to relative keys, absolute keys are defined on the entire XML tree $T$ rather than on certain subtrees of $T$. The problem of determining implication of absolute keys is simpler than that for relative keys. Since most of the rules for relative key implication are an obvious generalization of those for absolute keys, we start by giving a discussion on the rules for absolute key implication. The set of rules, denoted by $\mathcal{I}_{abs}$, is shown in Table 2.

**Algorithm 1.** $Incl(n_1, n_2)$

1. if $visited(n_1, n_2)$ then return false else mark $visited(n_1, n_2)$ as true;
2. process $n_1, n_2$ as follows:
   Case 1: if $n_1 = F_1$ then
               if $n_2 = F_2$ and $(\delta_1(F_1, \_) = \emptyset$ or $\delta_2(F_2, \_) = F_2)$
               then return true;
               else return false;
   Case 2: if $\delta_1(n_1, a) = n_1'$ and $\delta_2(n_2, a) = n_2'$ for letter $a$
               and $\delta_1(n_1, \_) = \emptyset$ and $\delta_2(n_2, \_) = \emptyset$
               then return $Incl(n_1', n_2')$;
   Case 3: if $\delta_1(n_1, a) = n_1'$ and $\delta_2(n_2, \_) = n_2$ and $\delta_2(n_2, a) = n_2'$ for letter $a$
               then return $(Incl(n_1', n_2)$ or $Incl(n_1', n_2'))$
               else if $\delta_1(n_1, a) = n_1'$ and $\delta_2(n_2, \_) = n_2$ and $\delta_2(n_2, a) = \emptyset$
               then return $Incl(n_1', n_2)$;
3. return false

**Table 2.** $\mathcal{I}_{abs}$: Rules for absolute key implication

$$\frac{(Q, S) \quad P \in PL}{(Q, S \cup \{P\})} \text{ (superkey)} \qquad \frac{(Q, S \cup \{P_i, P_j\}) \quad P_i \subseteq P_j}{(Q, S \cup \{P_i\})} \text{ (containment-reduce)}$$

$$\frac{(Q.Q', \{P\})}{(Q, \{Q'.P\})} \text{ (subnodes)} \qquad \frac{(Q, S) \quad Q' \subseteq Q}{(Q', S)} \text{ (target-path-containment)}$$

$$\frac{(Q, S \cup \{\epsilon, P\}) \quad P' \in PL}{(Q, S \cup \{\epsilon, P.P'\})} \text{ (prefix-epsilon)} \qquad \frac{S \text{ is a set of } PL \text{ expressions}}{(\epsilon, S)} \text{ (epsilon)}$$

- *superkey*. If $S$ is a key for the nodes in $[\![Q]\!]$ then so is any superset of $S$. This is the only rule of $\mathcal{I}_{abs}$ that has a counterpart in relational key inference.
- *subnodes*. Since we have a tree model, any node $v \in [\![Q.Q']\!]$ must be in the subtree rooted at a unique node $v'$ in $[\![Q]\!]$. Therefore, if a key path $P$ identifies a node in $[\![Q.Q']\!]$ then $Q'.P$ uniquely identifies nodes in $[\![Q]\!]$.
- *prefix-epsilon*. Note that $n_1 =_v n_2$ if $n_1[\![\epsilon]\!] \cap_v n_2[\![\epsilon]\!] \neq \emptyset$. In addition, for any $n_1, n_2 \in [\![Q]\!]$, if $n_1[\![P.P']\!] \cap_v n_2[\![P.P']\!] \neq \emptyset$ and $n_1 =_v n_2$, then $n_1[\![P]\!] \cap_v n_2[\![P]\!] \neq \emptyset$. Thus by the definition of keys, $S \cup \{\epsilon, P.P'\}$ is also a key for $[\![Q]\!]$.
- *containment-reduce*. For any nodes $n_1, n_2$ in $[\![Q]\!]$, if $n_1[\![P_i]\!] \cap_v n_2[\![P_i]\!] \neq \emptyset$, then we must have $n_1[\![P_j]\!] \cap_v n_2[\![P_j]\!] \neq \emptyset$ given $P_i \subseteq P_j$. Thus by the definition of keys $S \cup \{P_i\}$ is also a key for $[\![Q]\!]$.
- *target-path-containment*. A key for the set $[\![Q]\!]$ is also a key for any subset of $[\![Q]\!]$. Observe that $[\![Q']\!] \subseteq [\![Q]\!]$ if $Q' \subseteq Q$.
- *epsilon*. There is only one root, and thus any set of $PL$ expressions forms a key for the root.

**Table 3.** $\mathcal{I}$: Inference rules for key implication

$$\frac{(Q, (Q', S)) \quad P \in PL}{(Q, (Q', S \cup \{P\}))} \qquad \text{(superkey)}$$

$$\frac{(Q, (Q'.Q'', \{P\}))}{(Q, (Q', \{Q''.P\}))} \qquad \text{(subnodes)}$$

$$\frac{(Q, (Q', S \cup \{P_i, P_j\})) \quad P_i \subseteq P_j}{(Q, (Q', S \cup \{P_i\}))} \qquad \text{(containment-reduce)}$$

$$\frac{(Q, (Q', S)) \quad Q_1 \subseteq Q}{(Q_1, (Q', S))} \qquad \text{(context-path-containment)}$$

$$\frac{(Q, (Q', S)) \quad Q_2 \subseteq Q'}{(Q, (Q_2, S))} \qquad \text{(target-path-containment)}$$

$$\frac{(Q, (Q_1.Q_2, S))}{(Q.Q_1, (Q_2, S))} \qquad \text{(context-target)}$$

$$\frac{(Q, (Q', S \cup \{\epsilon, P\})) \quad P' \in PL}{(Q, (Q', S \cup \{\epsilon, P.P'\}))} \qquad \text{(prefix-epsilon)}$$

$$\frac{(Q_1, (Q_2, \{Q'.P_1, \ldots, Q'.P_k\}))}{(Q_1.Q_2, (Q', \{P_1, \ldots, P_k\}))} \qquad \text{(interaction)}$$
$$\frac{}{(Q_1, (Q_2.Q', \{P_1, \ldots, P_k\}))}$$

$$\frac{Q \in PL, \; S \text{ is a set of } PL \text{ expressions}}{(Q, (\epsilon, S))} \qquad \text{(epsilon)}$$

We omit the proof of the following theorem. Details can be found in [5].

**Theorem 3.** *The set* $\mathcal{I}_{abs}$ *is sound and complete for (finite) implication of absolute keys of* $\mathcal{K}_{abs}$*. In addition, the problem can be determined in* $O(n^4)$ *time.*

## 3.3   Axiomatization for Key Implication

We now turn to the finite implication problem for $\mathcal{K}$, and start by giving in Table 3 a set of inference rules, denoted by $\mathcal{I}$. Most rules are simply generalizations of rules shown in Table 2. The only exceptions are rules that deal with the context path in relative keys. We briefly illustrate these rules below.

- *context-path-containment.* If $(Q', S)$ holds on all subtrees rooted at nodes in $[\![Q]\!]$, then it also holds on subtrees rooted at nodes in subset $[\![Q_1]\!]$ of $[\![Q]\!]$.

– *context-target*. If in a tree $T$ rooted at a node $n$ in $[\![Q]\!]$, $S$ is a key for $n[\![Q_1.Q_2]\!]$, then in any subtree of $T$ rooted at $n'$ in $n[\![Q_1]\!]$, $S$ is a key for $n'[\![Q_2]\!]$. In particular, when $Q = \epsilon$ this rules says that if the (absolute) key holds on the entire document, then it must also hold on any sub-document.

– *interaction*. By the first key in the precondition, in each subtree rooted at a node $n$ in $[\![Q_1]\!]$, $Q'.P_1, \ldots, Q'.P_k$ uniquely identify a node in $n[\![Q_2]\!]$. The second key in the precondition prevents the existence of more than one $Q'$ node under $Q_2$ that coincide in their $P_1, \ldots, P_k$ nodes. Therefore, $P_1, \ldots, P_k$ uniquely identify a node in $n[\![Q_2.Q']\!]$ in each subtree rooted at $n$ in $[\![Q_1]\!]$.

Note that key inference in the XML setting relies heavily on path inclusion. That is why we need to develop inference rules for $PL$ expression inclusion.

Given a finite set $\Sigma \cup \{\varphi\}$ of $\mathcal{K}$ constraints, we use $\Sigma \vdash_{\mathcal{I}} \varphi$ to denote that $\varphi$ is provable from $\Sigma$ using $\mathcal{I}$ (and $\mathcal{I}_p$ for path inclusion).

We next show that $\mathcal{I}$ is indeed an axiomatization for $\mathcal{K}$ constraint implication.

**Lemma 1.** *The set $\mathcal{I}$ is sound and complete for finite implication of $\mathcal{K}$ constraints. That is, for any finite set $\Sigma \cup \{\varphi\}$ of $\mathcal{K}$ constraints, $\Sigma \models \varphi$ iff $\Sigma \vdash_{\mathcal{I}} \varphi$.*

*Proof sketch:* Soundness of $\mathcal{I}$ can be verified by induction on the lengths of $\mathcal{I}$-proofs. For the proof of completeness, we show that if $\Sigma \nvdash_{\mathcal{I}} \varphi$, then there exists a finite XML tree $G$ such that $G \models \Sigma$ and $G \models \neg\varphi$, i.e., $\Sigma \nvDash \varphi$. In other words, if $\Sigma \models \varphi$ then $\Sigma \vdash_{\mathcal{I}} \varphi$. See [5] for the details of the proof.    ∎

Finally, we show that $\mathcal{K}$ constraint implication is decidable in PTIME.

**Lemma 2.** *There is an algorithm that, given any finite set $\Sigma \cup \{\varphi\}$ of $\mathcal{K}$ constraints, determines whether $\Sigma \models \varphi$ in PTIME.*

*Proof sketch:* In Algorithm 2 we provide a function for determining finite implication of $\mathcal{K}$ constraints. The correctness of the algorithm follows from Lemma 1 and its proof. It applies $\mathcal{I}$ rules to derive $\varphi$ if $\Sigma \models \varphi$. The overall cost of the algorithm is $O(n^8)$, where $n$ is the size of keys involved, and therefore we have a PTIME algorithm. The details of the proof can be found in [5].    ∎

Theorem 1 follows from Lemmas 1 and 2.

## 4    Discussion

We have investigated the (finite) satisfiability and (finite) implication problems associated with the XML key constraint language introduced in [4]. These keys are capable of expressing many important properties of XML data; moreover, in contrast to other proposals, this language can be reasoned about efficiently. More specifically, keys defined in this language are always finitely satisfiable, and their (finite) implication is finitely axiomatizable and decidable in PTIME in the size of keys. We believe that these key constraints are simple yet expressive enough to be adopted by XML designers and users.

For further research, a number of issues deserve investigation. First, our results are established in the absence of DTDs. Despite their simple syntax, there

## Algorithm 2. Finite implication of $\mathcal{K}$ constraints

Input: a finite set $\Sigma \cup \{\varphi\}$ of $\mathcal{K}$ constraints, where $\varphi = (Q, (Q', \{P_1, ..., P_k\}))$
Output: true iff $\Sigma \models \varphi$

// Epsilon rule.
1. if $Q' = \epsilon$ then output true and terminate

// Containment-reduce rule.
2. for each $(Q_i, (Q_i', S_i)) \in \Sigma \cup \{\varphi\}$ do
　　　repeat until no further change
　　　　　if $S_i = S \cup \{P', P''\}$ such that $P' \subseteq P''$ then $S_i := S_i \setminus \{P''\}$
3. $X := \emptyset$;

// Use the containment rules, context-target, superkey, subnodes, prefix-epsilon,
　and interaction.
4. repeat until no keys in $\Sigma$ can be applied in cases (a)-(d).
　for each $\phi = (Q_\phi, (Q_\phi', \{P_1', ..., P_m'\})) \in \Sigma$ do
　　// Prove $\varphi$ when $Q_\phi$ contains a prefix of $Q$.
　　(a) if there is $Q_t, R_p$ in $PL$ such that $Q \subseteq Q_\phi.Q_t$, $Q_t.Q'.R_p \subseteq Q_\phi'$, $R_p = \epsilon$ if $m > 1$ and
　　　　for all $j \in [1, m]$ there is $s \in [1, k]$ such that either
　　　　(i) $P_s \subseteq R_p.P_j'$ or
　　　　(ii) there exists $l \in [1, k]$ and $R_j$ in $PL$ such that $P_l = \epsilon$ and $P_s \subseteq R_p.P_j'.R_j$
　　　then output true and terminate

　　// Prove $\varphi$ when $Q$ is contained in a prefix of $Q_\phi$.
　　(b) if there are $Q_c, Q_t, R_p$ in $PL$ such that
　　　　$Q.Q_c \subseteq Q_\phi$, $Q'.R_p \subseteq Q_c.Q_\phi'$, $R_p = \epsilon$ if $m > 1$, $Q' = Q_c.Q_t$ and
　　　　for all $j \in [1, m]$ there is there is $s \in [1, k]$ such that either
　　　　(i) $P_s \subseteq R_p.P_j'$ or
　　　　(ii) there exists $l \in [1, k]$ and $R_j$ in $PL$ such that $P_l = \epsilon$ and $P_s \subseteq R_p.P_j'.R_j$;
　　　　and moreover, there is $(Q, (Q_c, \{Q_t.P_1, ..., Q_t.P_k\}))$ in $X$
　　　then output true and terminate

　　// Produce intermediate results in $X$ when $Q_\phi$ contains a prefix of $Q$.
　　(c) if there are $Q_c, Q_t, R_p$ in $PL$ such that $Q \subseteq Q_\phi.Q_c$, $Q_c.Q' \subseteq Q_\phi'.R_p$, $Q' = Q_t.R_p$ and
　　　　for all $j \in [1, m]$ there is $s \in [1, k]$ such that either
　　　　(i) $R_p.P_s \subseteq P_j'$ or
　　　　(ii) there exists $l \in [1, k]$ and $R_j$ in $PL$ such that $P_l = \epsilon$ and $R_p.P_s \subseteq P_j'.R_j$
　　　then
　　　　(1) if $m = 1$ then $X := X \cup \{(Q, (Q_1, \{Q_2.R_p.P_1, ..., Q_2.R_p.P_k\}))\}$
　　　　　　where $Q_t = Q_1.Q_2$ for some $Q_1, Q_2 \in PL$;
　　　　(2) if $m > 1$ then $X := X \cup \{(Q, (Q_t, \{R_p.P_1, ..., R_p.P_k\}))\}$;
　　　　(3) $\Sigma := \Sigma \setminus \{\phi\}$;

　　// Produce intermediate results in $X$ when $Q$ is contained in a prefix of $Q_\phi$.
　　(d) if there are $Q_c, Q_t, R_p$ in $PL$ such that $Q.Q_c \subseteq Q_\phi$, $Q' \subseteq Q_c.Q_\phi'.R_p$, $Q' = Q_c.Q_t.R_p$ and
　　　　for all $j \in [1, m]$ there is $s \in [1, k]$ such that either
　　　　(i) $R_p.P_s \subseteq P_j'$ or
　　　　(ii) there exists $l \in [1, k]$ and $R_j$ in $PL$ such that $P_l = \epsilon$ and $R_p.P_s \subseteq P_j'.R_j$;
　　　　and moreover, there is $(Q, (Q_c, \{Q_t.R_p.P_1, ..., Q_t.R_p.P_k\}))$ in $X$
　　　then
　　　　(1) if $m = 1$ then $X := X \cup \{(Q, (Q_1, \{Q_2.R_p.P_1, ..., Q_2.R_p.P_k\}))\}$
　　　　　　where $Q_c.Q_t = Q_1.Q_2$ for some $Q_1, Q_2 \in PL$;
　　　　(2) if $m > 1$ then $X := X \cup \{(Q, (Q_c.Q_t, \{R_p.P_1, ..., R_p.P_k\}))\}$;
　　　　(3) $\Sigma := \Sigma \setminus \{\phi\}$;
5. output false

is an interaction between DTDs and our key constraints. To illustrate this, let
us consider a simple DTD $D$:

```
<!ELEMENT  foo  (X, X)>
<!ELEMENT  X    (empty)>
```

and a simple (absolute) key $\varphi = (X, \emptyset)$. Obviously, there exists a finite XML tree that conforms to the DTD $D$ and there exists another finite XML tree that satisfies the key $\varphi$. However, there is no XML tree that both conforms to $D$ and satisfies $\varphi$, because $D$ requires an XML tree to have two distinct $X$ elements, whereas $\varphi$ requires that the path $X$, if it exists, must be unique at the root. This shows that in the presence of DTDs, the analysis of key satisfiability and implication can be wildly different. It should be mentioned that keys defined in other proposals for XML, such as XML Schema [26], also interact with DTDs or other type systems for XML. This issue was recently investigated in [10].

Second, one might be interested in using a different path language to express keys. The containment problem for the full regular language is PSPACE-complete [12], and it is not finitely axiomatizable. Another alternative is the language of [17], which simply adds a single wildcard to $PL$. Despite the seemingly trivial addition, containment of expressions in their language is only known to be in PTIME. It is possible to develop an inclusion checking algorithm with a complexity comparable to the related result in this paper. For XPath [24] expressions, questions in connection with their containment and equivalence, as well as (finite) satisfiability and (finite) implication of keys defined in terms of these complex path expressions are, to the best of our knowledge, still open.

Third, along the same lines as our XML key language, a language of foreign keys needs to be developed for XML.

A final question is about key constraint checking. An efficient incremental checking algorithm for our keys is currently under development.

## Acknowledgments

The authors thank Michael Benedikt, Chris Brew, Dave Maier, Keishi Tajima and Henry Thompson for helpful discussions. They would also like to thank one of the referees for pointing out the possible need for a more general definition of a key constraint (Sec. 2.)

## References

1. S. Abiteboul, P. Buneman, and D. Suciu. *Data on the Web. From Relations to Semistructured Data and XML*. Morgan Kaufman, 2000.
2. S. Abiteboul, R. Hull, and V. Vianu. *Foundations of Databases*. Addison-Wesley, 1995.
3. S. Abiteboul and V. Vianu. Regular path queries with constraints. *Journal of Computer and System Sciences (JCSS)*, 58(4):428–452, 1999.
4. P. Buneman, S. Davidson, W. Fan, C. Hara, and W. Tan. Keys for XML. In *WWW'10*, 2001.
5. P. Buneman, S. Davidson, W. Fan, C. Hara, and W. Tan. Reasoning about absolute and relative keys for XML. Technical Report TUCIS-TR-2001-002, Temple University, 2001.
6. P. Buneman, W. Fan, J. Siméon, and S. Weinstein. Constraints for semistructured data and XML. *SIGMOD Record*, 30(1), 2001.

7. P. Buneman, W. Fan, and S. Weinstein. Path constraints on semistructured and structured data. In *PODS*, 1998.
8. P. Buneman, W. Fan, and S. Weinstein. Interaction between path and type constraints. In *PODS*, 1999.
9. P. Buneman, W. Fan, and S. Weinstein. Path constraints in semistructured databases. *Journal of Computer and System Sciences (JCSS)*, 61(2):146–193, 2000.
10. W. Fan and L. Libkin. On XML integrity constraints in the presence of DTDs. In *PODS*, 2001.
11. W. Fan and J. Siméon. Integrity constraints for XML. In *PODS*, 2000.
12. M. R. Garey and D. S. Johnson. *Computers and Intractability: A Guide to the Theory of NP-Completeness*. W.H. Freeman and Company, 1979.
13. C. S. Hara and S. B. Davidson. Reasoning about nested functional dependencies. In *PODS*, 1999.
14. J. E. Hopcroft and J. D. Ullman. *Introduction to Automata Theory, Languages and Computation*. Addision Wesley, 1979.
15. H. Hunt, D. Resenkrantz, and T. Szymanski. On the equivalence, containment, and covering problems for the regular and context-free languages. *Journal of Computer and System Sciences (JCSS)*, 12:222–268, 1976.
16. M. Ito and G. E. Weddell. Implication problems for functional constraints on databases supporting complex objects. *Journal of Computer and System Sciences (JCSS)*, 50(1):165–187, 1995.
17. T. Milo and D. Suciu. Index structures for path expressions. In *ICDT*, 1999.
18. R. Ramakrishnan and J. Gehrke. *Database Management Systems*. McGraw-Hill Higher Education, 2000.
19. J. Robie, J. Lapp, and D. Schach. *XML Query Language (XQL)*. Workshop on XML Query Languages, Dec. 1998.
20. V. Vianu. A Web odyssey: From Codd to XML. In *PODS*, 2001.
21. W3C. *Document Object Model (DOM) Level 1 Specification*. Recommendation, Oct. 1998. `http://www.w3.org/TR/REC-DOM-Level-1/`.
22. W3C. *Extensible Markup Language (XML) 1.0*, Feb 1998. `http://www.w3.org/TR/REC-xml`.
23. W3C. XML-Data. Note, Jan. 1998. `http://www.w3.org/TR/1998/NOTE-XML-data`.
24. W3C. *XML Path Language (XPath)*. Working Draft, Nov. 1999. `http://www.w3.org/TR/xpath`.
25. W3C. *XSL Transformations (XSLT)*. Recommendation, Nov. 1999. `http://www.w3.org/TR/xslt`.
26. W3C. *XML Schema*. Working Draft, May 2001. `http://www.w3.org/XML/Schema`.
27. P. Wadler. A Formal Semantics for Patterns in XSL. Technical report, Computing Sciences Research Center, Bell Labs, Lucent Technologies, 2000.
28. S. Yu. Regular languages. In G. Rosenberg and A. Salomaa, editors, *Handbook of Formal Languages*, volume 1, pages 41–110. Springer, 1996.

# TAX: A Tree Algebra for XML

H.V. Jagadish[1], Laks V.S. Lakshmanan[2],
Divesh Srivastava[3], and Keith Thompson[1]

[1] University of Michigan, Ann Arbor, MI 48109, USA
{jag,kdthomps}@eecs.umich.edu
[2] University of British Columbia, Vancouver, BC V6T 1Z4, Canada
laks@cs.ubc.ca
[3] AT&T Labs–Research, Florham Park, NJ 07932, USA
divesh@research.att.com

**Abstract.** Querying XML has been the subject of much recent investigation. A formal bulk algebra is essential for applying database-style optimization to XML queries. We develop such an algebra, called TAX (Tree Algebra for XML), for manipulating XML data, modeled as forests of labeled ordered trees. Motivated both by aesthetic considerations of intuitiveness, and by efficient computability and amenability to optimization, we develop TAX as a natural extension of relational algebra, with a small set of operators. TAX is complete for relational algebra extended with aggregation, and can express most queries expressible in popular XML query languages. It forms the basis for the TIMBER XML database system currently under development by us.

## 1 Introduction

XML has emerged as the *lingua franca* for data exchange, and even possibly for heterogeneous data representation. There is considerable interest in querying data represented in XML. Several query languages, such as XQuery [7], Quilt [6], and XML-QL [11] have recently been proposed for this purpose.

This leads us to the question of implementation. If we expect to have large XML data sets, then we must be able to evaluate efficiently queries written in these XML query languages against these data sets. Experience with the successful relational technology tells us that a formal bulk algebra is absolutely essential for applying standard database style query optimization to XML queries.

An XML document is often viewed as a labeled ordered rooted tree. The DOM [22] application interface standard certainly treats XML documents in this way. There often are, in addition, cross-tree "hyperlinks." In our model, we distinguish between these two types of edges. A similar approach has been adopted in [17]. With this model in mind, in this paper we develop a simple algebra, called *Tree Algebra for XML* (TAX), for manipulating XML data modeled as forests of labeled, ordered, rooted trees. The primary challenges we address are: (i) how to permit the rich variety of tree manipulations possible within a

G. Grahne and G. Ghelli (Eds.): DBPL 2001, LNCS 2397, pp. 149–164, 2002.

simple declarative algebra, and (ii) how to handle the considerable heterogeneity possible in a collection of trees of similar objects (e.g., books). If we look at popular XML query languages, most (including XQuery, which is likely to become the standard) follow an approach of binding variables to tree nodes, and then manipulating the use of these variables with free use of looping constructs where needed. A direct implementation of a query as written in these languages will result in a "nested-loops" execution plan. More efficient implementations are frequently possible — our goal is to devise a bulk manipulation algebra that enables this sort of access method selection in an automated fashion.

We begin in Section 2 by discussing the issues in designing a bulk manipulation algebra for XML. This leads up to our data model in Section 3. A key abstraction in TAX for specifying nodes and attributes is that of the *pattern tree*, presented in Section 4. We describe the TAX operators in Section 5. In Section 6, we summarize the expressive power of TAX. We discuss related work in Section 7 and conclude in Section 8.

## 2    Design Considerations

A central feature of the relational data model is the declarative expression of queries in terms of algebraic expressions over *collections of tuples*. Alternative access methods can then be devised for these bulk operations. This facility is at the heart of efficient implementation in relational databases.

If one is to perform bulk manipulations on collections of trees, relational algebra provides a good starting point — after all most relational operations (such as selection, set operations, product) are fairly obvious operations one would want to perform on XML databases. The key issue here is what should be the individual members of these collections in the case of XML. In other words, what is the correct counterpart in XML for a relational tuple?

*Tree Nodes:* One natural possibility is to think of each DOM node (or a tagged XML element, along with its attributes, but not its subelements) as the XML equivalent of a tuple. Each element has some named attributes, each with a unique value, and this structure looks very similar to that of a relational tuple. However, this approach has some difficulties. For instance, XML manipulation often uses structural constructs, and element inclusion (i.e., the determination of ancestor-descendant relationship between a pair of nodes in the DOM) is a frequently required core operation. If each node is a separate tuple, then determining ancestor-descendant relationships requires computing the transitive closure over parent-child links, each of which is stated as a join operation between two tuples. This is computationally prohibitive. Clever encodings, such as in [23], can ameliorate this difficulty, but we are still left with a very low level of query expression if these encodings are reflected in the language and data model. Indeed, such encodings should be viewed as implementation techniques for efficient determination of ancestor-descendant relationships, that can be used independent of which data model and algebra we choose.

An alternative data model is to treat an entire XML tree (representing a document or a document fragment) as a fundamental unit, similar to a tuple. This solves the problem of maintaining structural relationships, including ancestor-descendant relationships. However, trees are far more complex than tuples: they have richer structure, and the problem of heterogeneity is exacerbated. There are two routes to managing this structural richness.

*Tuples of Subtrees:* One route, inspired by the semantics of XML-QL [11], is to transform a collection of trees into a collection of tuples in a first step of query processing; a sensible way is to use tuples of bindings for variables with specified conditions. Much of the manipulation can then be applied in purely relational terms to the resulting collection of tuples. Trees in the answer can be generated in one final step. However, repeated relational construction and deconstruction steps may be required between semantically meaningful operations, adding considerable overhead. Furthermore, such an approach would lead to limited opportunities for optimization.

*Pure Trees:* The remaining route is to manage collections of trees directly. This route sidesteps many of the problems mentioned above, but exacerbates the issue of heterogeneity. It also presents a major challenge for defining algebraic operators, in view of the relative complexity of trees compared to tuples. Our central contribution in this paper is a decisive response to this challenge.

We introduce the notion of a *pattern tree*, which identifies the subset of nodes of interest in any tree in a collection of trees. The pattern tree is fixed for a given operation, and hence provides the needed standardization over a heterogeneous set. All algebraic operators manipulate nodes and attributes identified by means of a pattern tree, and hence they can apply to any heterogeneous collection of trees! With this innovation, we show most operators in relational algebra carry over to the tree domain, with appropriate modifications. We only need to introduce a few additional operators to deal with manipulation of tree structure.

## 3   Data Model

The basic unit of information in the relational model is a tuple. The counterpart in our data model is an ordered, labeled, rooted tree, the *data tree*, such that each node carries data (its label) in the form of a set of attribute-value pairs.

For XML data, each node corresponds to an element, the information content in the node represents the attributes of the element, while its children nodes represent its subelements. For XML, we assume each node has a special attribute called **tag** whose value indicates the type of the element. A node may have a **content** attribute representing its atomic value, whose type can be any one of several atomic types of interest: **int**, **real**, **string**, etc. The notion of node content generalizes the notion of PCDATA in XML documents. For pure PCDATA nodes, this tagname could be just PCDATA, or it could be a more descriptive tagname if one exists. The notions of ID and IDREFS in XML are treated just like any other attributes in our model. See Figure 1(a) for a sample data tree. Node contents are indicated in parentheses.

We assume each node has a virtual attribute called `pedigree` drawn from an ordered domain[1]. Operators of the algebra can access node pedigrees much like other attributes for purposes of manipulation and comparison. Intuitively, the pedigree of a node carries the history of "where it came from" as trees are manipulated by operators. Since algebra operators do not update attribute values, the pedigree of an existing node is not updated either. When a node is copied, all its attributes are copied, including pedigree. When a new node is created, it has a *null* pedigree. As we shall show later, appropriate use of the pedigree attribute can be valuable for duplicate elimination and grouping, and for inducing/maintaining tree order in query answers. It is useful to regard the pedigree as "document-id + offset-in-document." Indeed, this is how we have implemented pedigree in TIMBER, our implementation of TAX. While pedigree is in some respects akin to a lightweight element identifier, it is *not* a true identifier. For instance, if a node is copied, then both the original and the copy have the same pedigree — something not possible with a true identifier.

A relation in a relational database is a collection of tuples with the same structure. The equivalent notion in TAX is a collection of trees, with similar, not necessarily identical, structure. Since subelements are frequently optional, and quite frequently repeated, two trees following the same "schema" in TAX can have considerable difference in their structure.

A relational database is a set of relations. Correspondingly, an XML database should be a set of collections. In both cases, the database is a set of collections. While this is rarely confusing in the relational context, one frequently has the tendency in an XML context to treat the database as a single set, "flattening out" the nested structure. To fight this tendency, we consistently use the term *collection* to refer to a set of tree objects, corresponding to a relation in a relational database. The whole database, then, is a set of collections. Relational implementations have found it useful to support relations as multi-sets rather than sets. Similarly, we expect TAX implementations to implement collections as multi-sets, and perform explicit duplicate elimination, where required.

Each relational algebra operator takes one or more relations as input and produces a relation as output. Correspondingly, each TAX operator takes one or more collections (of data trees) as input and produces a collection as output.

## 4 Predicates and Patterns

### 4.1 Allowable Predicates

Predicates are central to much of querying. While the choice of the specific set of allowable predicates is orthogonal to TAX, any given implementation will have to make a choice in this matter, and this can have a significant effect on the complexity of expression evaluation. For concreteness, we use a representative set, listed below, with a clear understanding that this set is extensible.

---

[1] Pedigrees are not shown in our example data trees to minimize clutter.

For a node (element) $i, any attribute `attr` and value `val` from its domain, the atom $i.`attr` $\theta$ `val` is allowed, where $\theta$ is one of $=, \neq, >$, etc.[2] As a special case, when `attr` is of type string, a wildcard comparison such as $i.`attr` = "*val*", where `val` is a string, is allowed. Similarly, for two nodes $i and $j, and attributes `attr` and `attr'`, the atom $i.`attr` $\theta$ $j.`attr'` is allowed. Specifically, the attribute could be the pedigree: predicates of the form $i.`pedigree` $\theta$ $j.`pedigree`, where $\theta$ is $=$ or $\neq$, are also allowed. In addition, atoms involving aggregate operators, arithmetic (e.g., $i.`attr` + $j.`attr'` = 0), and string operations (e.g., $i.`attr` = $j.`attr'`·"terrorism"), are allowed. Finally, we have predicates based on the position of a node in its tree. For instance, $i.`index` = 1 means that node $i is the first child of its parent. More generally, `index`($i, $j) = n means that node $i is the $n^{th}$ node among the descendants of node $j. Similarly, $i $\theta$ $j, where $\theta$ is one of $=, \neq, $`BEFORE`, means that node $i is the same as, is different from, or occurs before node $j. These positional predicates are based on the preorder enumeration of the data tree.

## 4.2   Pattern Tree

A basic syntactic requirement of any algebra is the ability to specify attributes of interest. In relational algebra, this is accomplished straightforwardly. Doing so for a collection of trees is non-trivial for several reasons. First, merely specifying attributes is ambiguous: attributes of which nodes? Second, specifying nodes by means of id is impossible, since by design, we have kept the model simple with no explicit notion of object id. Third, identifying nodes by means of their position within the tree is cumbersome and can easily become tricky.

If the collections (of trees) we have to deal with are always homogeneous, then we could draw a tree identical to those in the collection being manipulated, label its nodes, and use these labels to unambiguously specify nodes (elements). In a sense, these labels play a role similar to that of column numbers in relational algebra. However, collections of XML data trees are typically heterogeneous. Besides, frequently we do not even know (or care about) the complete structure of each tree in a collection: we wish only to reference some portion of the tree that we care about. Thus, we need a simple, but powerful means of identifying nodes in a collection of trees.

We solve this problem using the notion of a *pattern tree*, which provides a simple, intuitive specification of nodes and hence attributes of interest. It also is particularly well-suited to graphical representation.

**Definition 1 (Pattern Tree)**   Formally, a *pattern tree* is a pair $\mathcal{P} = (T, F)$, where $T = (V, E)$ is a node-labeled and edge-labeled tree such that:

- each node in $V$ has a distinct integer (denoted $i) as its label;
- each edge is labeled `pc` (for parent-child) or `ad` (for ancestor-descendant).
- $F$ is a formula, i.e. a boolean combination of node predicates. ∎

---

[2]   We also allow the variants $i.\_ = `val` (meaning `val` appears as a value of some attribute) and $i.`attr` = \_ (meaning attribute `attr` is defined for node $i).

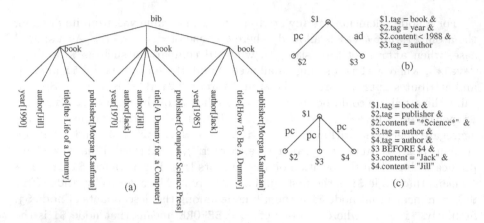

**Fig. 1.** (a) A one-tree XML database, and (b),(c) Two pattern trees

While the formal semantics of patterns are given in the next subsection, here we give some examples. Figure 1(b) shows a pattern that matches books published before 1988 and having at least one author. The edge label **pc** indicates that **year** must be a direct subelement of **book**, while the edge label **ad** indicates that **author** could be any nested descendant subelement. As another example, the pattern in Figure 1(c) matches books published by a publisher whose name contains the string "Science" and authored by Jack and Jill in that order. In both examples, see how the tree and the formula $F$ interact.

We have chosen to allow ancestor-descendant (**ad**) edges, in addition to the basic parent-child (**pc**) edges, in a pattern tree because we believe that one may often wish to specify just such a relationship without involving any intervening nodes, a feature commonly found in XML query languages.

Pattern trees in TAX also permit attributes of nodes to be compared with other node attributes, analogously to selection predicates in relational algebra permitting different attributes to be compared. See, for instance, Figure 1(c), where the positions of two nodes are compared using the **BEFORE** predicate.

## 4.3    Witness Tree

A pattern tree $\mathcal{P} = (T, F)$ constrains each node in two ways. First, the formula $F$ may impose value-based predicates on any node. Second, the pattern requires each node to have structural relatives (parent, descendants, etc.) satisfying other value-based predicates specified in $F$. Of these, the value-based predicates are in turn based on the allowable atomic predicates applicable to pattern tree nodes.

Formally, let $\mathcal{C}$ be a collection of data trees, and $\mathcal{P} = (T, F)$ a pattern tree. An *embedding* of a pattern $\mathcal{P}$ into a collection $\mathcal{C}$ is a total mapping $h : \mathcal{P} \rightarrow \mathcal{C}$ from the nodes of $T$ to those of $\mathcal{C}$ such that:

- $h$ preserves the structure of $T$, i.e. whenever $(u, v)$ is a **pc** (resp., **ad**) edge in $T$, $h(v)$ is a child (resp., descendant) of $h(u)$ in $\mathcal{C}$.
- The image under the mapping $h$ satisfies the formula $F$.

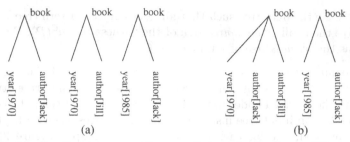

(a)                                     (b)

**Fig. 2.** Results of various operations applied to the database of Figure 1(a)

Let $h : \mathcal{P} \rightarrow \mathcal{C}$ be an embedding and let $u$ be a node in $T$ and $n$ a node in $\mathcal{C}$ such that $n = h(u)$. Then we say the data tree node $n$ *matches* the pattern node $u$ (under the embedding $h$). Note that an embedding need *not* be 1-1, so the same data tree node could match more than one pattern node.

Note also that we have ignored order among siblings in the pattern tree as we seek to embed it in a data tree. Siblings in a pattern tree may in general be permuted to obtain the needed embedding. We have chosen to permit this because such queries seemed to us to be more frequent than queries in which the order of nodes in the pattern tree is material. Moreover, if maintaining order among siblings is desired, this is easily accomplished through the use of ordering predicates (such as **BEFORE**), and can even be applied selectively. For example, Figure 1(c) specifies a pattern that seeks books with authors **Jack** and **Jill**, with **Jack** appearing before **Jill**, and having a publisher ''**\*Science\***'', though we do not care whether the publisher subelement of book appears before or after the author subelements. Thus, TAX permits the graceful melding, even within a single query, of places where order is important and places where it is not.

We next formalize the semantics of pattern trees using a notion of *witness trees* induced by embeddings of a pattern tree into a database:

**Definition 2 (Witness Tree)**   Let $\mathcal{C}$ be a collection of data trees, $\mathcal{P} = (T, F)$ a pattern tree, and $h : \mathcal{P} \rightarrow \mathcal{C}$ an embedding. Then the *witness tree* associated with this is the data tree, denoted $h^{\mathcal{C}}(\mathcal{P})$ defined as follows:

- a node $n$ of $\mathcal{C}$ is present in the witness tree if $n = h(u)$ for some node $u$ in the pattern $\mathcal{P}$, i,e. $n$ matches some pattern node under the mapping $h$.
- for any pair of nodes $n, m$ in the witness tree, whenever $m$ is the closest ancestor of $n$ in $\mathcal{C}$ among those present in the witness tree, the witness tree contains the edge $(m, n)$. Intuitively, each edge in the witness tree corresponds to a sequence of one or more edges in the input data tree that has been collapsed because only the end-point nodes of the sequence are retained in the witness tree.
- the witness tree preserves the order on the nodes it retains from $\mathcal{C}$, i.e. for any two nodes in $h^{\mathcal{C}}(\mathcal{P})$, whenever $m$ precedes $n$ in the preorder node enumeration of $\mathcal{C}$, $m$ precedes $n$ in the preorder node enumeration of $h^{\mathcal{C}}(\mathcal{P})$.

Let $I \in \mathcal{C}$ be the data tree such that all nodes of the pattern tree $T$ map to $I$ under $h$. We then call $I$ the *source tree* of the witness tree $h^{\mathcal{C}}(\mathcal{P})$. We also refer to $h^{\mathcal{C}}(\mathcal{P})$ as the *witness tree* of $I$ under $h$. ∎

The meaning of a witness tree should be straightforward. The nodes in an instance that satisfy the pattern are retained and the original tree structure is restricted to the retained nodes to yield a witness tree. If a given pattern tree can be embedded in an input tree instance in multiple places, then multiple witness trees are obtained, one for each embedding. For example, Figure 2(a) shows three witness trees resulting from embedding the pattern of Figure 1(b) into the database of Figure 1(a) in three different places. The structure of all three witness trees is the same three-node structure, by definition, but the database nodes bound are different. It is permissible for the same database node to appear in multiple witness trees. For instance, the same book appears in the first and second witness trees, once for each possible author node binding.

### 4.4   Tree Value Function

Given a collection of trees, we would like to perform ordering and grouping operations along the lines of ORDERBY and GROUPBY in SQL. In fact, ordering is required if (ordered) trees are to be constructed from (unordered) collections.

However, we once again have to take into account the possible heterogeneity of structure in a collection of trees, making it hard to specify the nodes at which to find the attributes of interest. We solve this problem in a rather general way, by proposing the notion of a *tree value function* (TVF) that maps a data tree (typically, source trees of witness trees) to an ordered domain (such as real numbers). While the exact nature of TVFs may be orthogonal to the algebra, we assume below they are primitive recursive functions on the structure of their argument trees. We typically assume the codomain of a TVF is (partially) ordered. When used for sorting purposes, it must be totally ordered. A simple example tree value function might map a tree to the value of an attribute at a node (or a function of the tuple of attribute values associated with one or more nodes) in the tree (identified by means of a pattern tree); an example using TVFs is presented in Section 5.4. Just like pattern trees, TVFs are used in conjunction with a variety of operators in our algebra.

## 5   The Operators

All operators in TAX take collections of data trees as input, and produce a collection of data trees as output. TAX is thus a "proper" algebra, with composability and closure. The notions of pattern tree and tree value function introduced in the preceding section play a pivotal role in many of the operators.

### 5.1   Selection

The obvious analog in TAX for relational selection is for selection applied to a collection of trees to return the input trees that satisfy a specified selection predicate (specified via a pattern). However, this in itself may not preserve all the information of interest. Since individual trees can be large, we may be interested not just in knowing that some tree satisfied a given selection predicate, but also the manner of such satisfaction: the "how" in addition to the "what". In other words, we may wish to return the relevant witness tree(s) rather than just a single bit with each data tree in the input to the selection operator.

To appreciate this point, consider selecting books that were published before 1988 from a book collection. Let it generate a subset of the input collection, as in relational algebra. But if the input collection comprises a single bibliography data tree with book subtrees, as in Figure 1(a), the selection would return the original data tree, leaving no clue about *which* book was published before 1988.

Selection in TAX takes a collection $C$ as input, and a pattern $P$ and adornment SL as parameters, and returns an output collection. Each data tree in the output is the witness tree induced by some embedding of $P$ into $C$, modified as possibly prescribed in SL. The adornment list, SL, lists nodes from $P$ for which not just the nodes themselves, but specified structural "*relatives*" (e.g., siblings, parent, ancestors, descendants, etc.) of it, need to be returned. A frequently used important special case is the set of descendants of a node. (An element is expected to include all nested subelements in typical XML and XQuery semantics, for instance.) To keep the exposition as simple as possible, we restrict adornments in the foregoing to all descendants: if a node is mentioned in the adornment list, all its descendants are returned in addition to the witness tree. If the adornment list is empty, then just the witness trees are returned. Formally, the output $\sigma_{P,\text{SL}}(C)$ of the selection operator is a collection of trees, one per embedding of $P$ into $C$. The output tree associated with an embedding $h : P \rightarrow C$ is defined as follows.

- A node $n$ in the input collection $C$ belongs to the output iff $n$ matches some pattern node in $P$ under $h$, or $n$ is a descendant of a node $m$ in $C$ which matches some pattern node $w$ under $h$ and $w$'s label appears in the adornment list SL.
- Whenever nodes $n, m$ belong to the output such that among the nodes retained in the output, $n$ is the closest ancestor of $m$ in the input, the output contains the edge $(n, m)$. Intuitively, the output tree preserves the structure of the input, restricted to the retained nodes.
- The relative order among nodes in the input is preserved in the output, i.e. for any two nodes $n, m$ in the output, whenever $n$ precedes $m$ in the preorder enumeration of $C$, $n$ precedes $m$ in the preorder enumeration of the output.

Contents of all nodes, including pedigrees, are preserved from the input. As an example, let $C$ be a collection of book elements in Figure 1(a), and let $P$ be the pattern tree in Fig 1(b). Then $\sigma_{P,\text{SL}}(C)$ produces the collection of trees in Fig 2(a) if the adornment list SL is empty. On the other hand, if SL includes \$1, then the entire subtree is retained for each book (node \$1) in the result.

Because a specified pattern can match many times in a single tree, selection in TAX is a one-many operation. This notion of selection is strictly more general than relational selection.

## 5.2  Projection

For trees, projection may be regarded as eliminating nodes other than those specified. In the substructure resulting from node elimination, we would expect the (partial) hierarchical relationships between surviving nodes that existed in the input collection to be preserved.

Projection in TAX takes a collection $\mathcal{C}$ as input and a pattern tree $\mathcal{P}$ and a projection list PL as parameters. A projection list is a list of node labels appearing in the pattern $\mathcal{P}$, possibly adorned with $*$. The output $\pi_{\mathcal{P},PL}(\mathcal{C})$ of the projection operator is defined as follows.

- A node $n$ in the input collection $\mathcal{C}$ belongs to the output iff there is an embedding $h : \mathcal{P} \rightarrow \mathcal{C}$ such that $n$ matches some pattern node in $\mathcal{P}$ whose label appears in the projection list PL, or $n$ is a descendant[3] of a node $m$ in $\mathcal{C}$ which matches some pattern node $w$, and $w$'s label appears in the projection list PL with a "$*$".
- Whenever nodes $n, m$ belong to the output such that among the nodes retained in the output, $n$ is the closest ancestor of $m$ in the input, the output contains the edge $(n, m)$. Intuitively, the output tree preserves the structure of the input data tree, with every edge in the output tree corresponding to an ancestor-descendant path in the input data tree.
- The relative order among nodes is preserved in the output, i.e., for any two nodes $n, m$ in the output, whenever $n$ precedes $m$ in the preorder enumeration of $\mathcal{C}$, $n$ precedes $m$ in the preorder enumeration of the output tree.

Contents of all nodes, including pedigrees, are preserved from the input. As an example, suppose we use the pattern tree of Figure 1(b) and projection list {\$1,\$2,\$3}, and apply a projection to the database of Figure 1(a). Then we obtain the result shown in Figure 2(b).

A single input tree could contribute to zero, one, or more output trees in a projection. This number could be zero, if there is no witness to the specified pattern in the given input tree. It could be more than one, if some of the nodes retained from the witnesses to the specified pattern do not have any ancestor-descendant relationships. This notion of projection is strictly more general than relational projection. If we wish to ensure that projection results in no more than one output tree for each input tree, all we have to do is to add a new root node labeled \$0 to the pattern tree, with an **ad** edge to the previous root of the pattern tree, and include \$0 in the projection list PL.

Projection can also be used to return entire trees from the input collection that have an embedding of a pattern tree. To do so, all we have to do is to add a new root node labeled \$0 to the pattern tree, with an **ad** edge to the previous root of the pattern tree, and include \$0* in the projection list PL.

In relational algebra, one is dealing with "rectangular" tables, so that selection and projection are orthogonal operations: one chooses rows, the other chooses columns. With trees, we do not have the same "rectangular" structure

---

[3] Other relatives are permitted as for selection, but suppressed in our exposition.

to our data. As such selection and projection are not so obviously orthogonal. Yet, they are very different and independent operations, and are generalizations of their respective relational counterparts. Compare the projection result shown in Figure 2(b) for the pattern tree of Figure 1(b) and the database of Figure 1(a), with the selection result shown in Figure 2(a) for the same pattern tree and database.

## 5.3 Product

The product operation takes a pair of collections $C$ and $D$ as input and produces an output collection corresponding to the "juxtaposition" of every pair of trees from $C$ and $D$. More precisely, $C \times D$ produces an output collection as follows.

- for each pair of trees $T_i \in C$ and $T_j \in D$, $C \times D$ contains a tree, whose root is a new node, with a tag name of tax_prod_root, a null pedigree, and no other attributes or content; its left child is the root of $T_i$, while its right child is the root of $T_j$.
- for each node in the left and right subtrees of the new root node, all attribute values, including pedigree, are the same as in the input collections.

The choice of a null pedigree for the newly created root nodes reflects the fact that these nodes do *not* have their origins in the input collections. Since data trees are ordered, $C \times D$ and $D \times C$ are not the same. This departure from the relational world is justified since order is irrelevant for tuples but important for data trees which correspond to XML documents. As in relational algebra, join can be expressed as product followed by selection.

## 5.4 Grouping

Unlike the relational model, we separate grouping and aggregation. The rationale is that grouping has a natural direct role to play for restructuring data trees, orthogonally to aggregation. Due to lack of space, we present only grouping here.

The objective is to split a collection into subsets of (not necessarily disjoint) data trees and represent each subset as an ordered tree in some meaningful way. As a motivating example, consider a collection of book elements grouped by title. We may wish to group this collection by author, thus generating subsets of book elements authored by a given author. Multiple authorship naturally leads to overlapping subsets. We can represent each subset in any desired manner, e.g., by the alphabetical order of the titles or by the year of publication.

In relational grouping, it is easy to specify the grouping attributes. In our case, we will need to use a tree value function for this purpose. Formally, the groupby operator $\gamma$ takes a collection as input and the following parameters.

- A pattern tree $P$; this is the pattern used for grouping. Corresponding to each witness tree $T_j$ of $P$, we keep track of the source tree $I_j$ from which it was obtained.

- A *grouping tree value function* that partitions the set $\mathcal{W}$ of witness trees of $\mathcal{P}$ against the collection $\mathcal{C}$. Typically, this grouping function will be instantiated by means of a *grouping list* that lists elements (by label in $\mathcal{P}$), and/or attributes of elements, whose values are used to obtain the required partition. The default comparison of element values is "shallow", ignoring subelement structure. Element labels in a grouping list may possibly be followed by a '*', in which case not just the element but the entire sub-tree rooted at this element is matched.
- An *ordering* tree value function *orfun* that maps data trees to a totally ordered domain. This function is used to order members of a group for output, in the manner described below.

The output tree $S_i$ corresponding to each group $\mathcal{W}_i$ is formed as follows: the root of $S_i$ has tag `tax_group_root`, a null pedigree and two children; its left child $\ell$ has tag `tax_grouping_basis`, a null pedigree, and a sub-tree rooted at this node that captures the grouping basis; its right child $r$ has tag `tax_group_subroot`, a null pedigree; its children are the roots of source trees corresponding to witness trees in $\mathcal{W}_i$, arranged in increasing order w.r.t. the value $orfun(T_j)$, $I_j$ being the source tree associated with the witness tree $T_j$. Source trees having more than one witness tree will appear more than once in the output – once corresponding to each witness tree.

When a grouping operation is performed, the result should include not just a bunch of groups, but also "labels" associated with each group identifying the basis for creation of this group. In relational systems, this is the set of grouping attributes for the group. A generic grouping basis function must specify the manner in which this information is to be retained, under the `tax_grouping_basis` node of the result. In the typical case of a grouping list being used to partition, the grouping list can also be applied as a projection list parameter to obtain a projection of the source trees associated with each group, so their existing structure is preserved. These projections, by definition, must all be identical within a group, except for their pedigree. By convention, we associate the least of the pedigree values for each node, and eliminate the rest. The result is made a child of the `tax_grouping_basis` node. If the projection returns a forest, the original order is preserved among the trees in this forest.

Consider the database of Figure 2(a). Apply grouping to it based on the pattern tree of Figure 1(b), grouped by author, and ordered by year. The result is shown in Figure 3. If this grouping had been applied to an XML database consisting of one tree for each book in the example database of Figure 1(a), one of the books (published in 1970) would appear in two groups, one for each of the authors. Lastly, if we apply grouping to this same collection using a TVF that maps each book to its number of authors, then we will obtain a collection of books grouped by number of authors, with the books in a group ordered in a manner dictated by the ordering TVF.

A few words regarding the way collections of source trees are partitioned are in order. For every node label of the form $i in the grouping list, we use a shallow notion of equality: two matches of this node are equal provided their contents

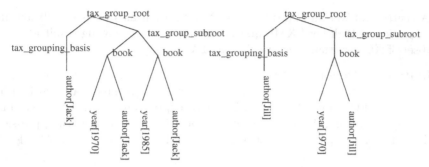

**Fig. 3.** Grouping the witness trees of Fig 2(a) by Author (grouping TVF ≡ `$3.content` in the pattern tree, shown in Figure 1(b)), and ordering each group by year (*orfun* ≡ `$2.content`)

(set of attribute-value pairs, except for pedigree) are identical. For every node label of the form `$i*` in the grouping list, we use a deep notion of equality. Under this, two matches of this node are equal provided there is an isomorphism between the subtrees rooted at these matching nodes, that preserves order and node contents (except for pedigree). Note the difference with tree equality, based on isomorphism that preserves pedigree as well.

In short, equality can be shallow or deep, and it can be by value (without pedigree) or by complete tree equality (including pedigree). The appropriate notion should be used in each circumstance.

*Duplicate Elimination by Value:* Due to the presence of the pedigree attribute, two distinct nodes in the input, even if identical in value, are not considered duplicates for purposes of set operations. However, there is often the need to eliminate duplicates by value of (specified) attributes. For example the `distinct` operator in XQuery would require it. We can show that duplicate elimination of nodes by value can be expressed in TAX.

*Other Operators:* As in the relational model, we fall back on set theory for set union, intersection and difference. One can also define operators for aggregation, for renaming, and for structural manipulation of trees (e.g., reordering). Both pattern trees and TVFs play a central role in their definitions. These are discussed in the full version of this paper.

## 6  Expressive Power of TAX

In this section, we summarize our results on the expressive power of TAX. Details are provided in the full version of the paper.

**Theorem 1. (Completeness for RA with Aggregation) :** There is an encoding scheme *Rep* that maps relational databases to data tree representations such that, for every relational database $D$, and for every expression $Q$ in relational algebra extended with aggregation, there is a corresponding expression $Q'$ in TAX such that $Q'(Rep(D)) = Rep(Q(D))$. ∎

A central motivation in designing TAX is to use it as a basis for efficient implementation of high level XML query languages. The following result identifies a subset of XQuery that is expressible in TAX.

**Definition 3 (Canonical XQuery Statement)**  A *canonical XQuery statement* is a "FLWR" expression of XQuery [7] such that: (i) the variable declaration range in each FOR and LET clause is a path expression; (ii) there are no function calls or recursion in any expression; and (iii) all regular path expressions used involve only constants, wildcards and may further use '/' and '//'. ∎

**Theorem 2. (Canonical XQuery Translation)** :    Let $Q$ be a canonical XQuery statement such that no ancestor-descendant relationships that are not present in the input collection are introduced by $Q$. Then there is an expression $E$ in TAX that is equivalent to $Q$. ∎

Similar translation theorems can be shown for Quilt and XML-QL.

## 7    Related Work

There is no shortage of algebras for data manipulation. Ever since Codd's seminal paper [8] there have been efforts to extend relational algebra in one direction or another. We mention a few relevant ones here, and relegate a detailed discussion to the full version of the paper.

Gyssens et al. [13] present a grammar-based algebra for manipulating tree-structured data, and show that it is equivalent to a calculus. The tree manipulations are all performed in the manner of production rules, and there is no clear path to efficient *set-oriented* implementation. Also, this work predates XML by quite a bit, and there is no obvious means for mapping XML into this data model.

Tree pattern matching is a well-studied problem, with notions of regular expressions, grammars, etc. being extended from strings to trees (see, e.g., [14]). These ideas have been incorporated into an object-oriented database, and an algebra developed for these in the Aqua project [20]. The focus of this algebra is the identification of pattern matches, and their rewriting, in the style of grammar production rules. Our notion of tree pattern and witness trees follows Aqua in spirit. However, Aqua has no counterpart for most TAX operators.

Algebras and query languages have also been proposed over graphs (see, e.g., [10,18,1,5]). These algebras focus on pattern matching in graphs. Since trees are a special case of graphs, our notions of pattern tree match may appear at first glance to be a special case of these works. However, there are differences in complexity of evaluation and in several details, such as the notion of order so important to XML trees. Moreover, in graphs there is no simple notion of ancestor/descendant—just a much heavier notion of reachability. A consequence is that these algebras spend considerable intellectual effort on managing recursion, an issue that we are able to side-step by explicitly including ancestor/descendant as a primitive. In short, graph algebras should indeed be considered intellectual precursors of the current work, but the specifics of XML trees are such that TAX cannot simply be a considered a specialization.

Even in the XML context, several algebras have been proposed. [3] is an influential early work that has impacted XML schema specification. However, there is no real manipulation algebra described in that paper. [12] proposes an algebra carefully tailor-made for Quilt. This algebra, like the XDuce system [15], is focused on type system issues. In [9], the authors present an algebra for XML, defined as an extension to relational algebra, that is practical and implemented. However, the main object of manipulation in this algebra, as in XML-QL, is the tuple and not the tree. A "bind" operator is used to create sets of (tuples of) bindings for specified labeled nodes. Due to the consequent loss of structure, this scheme very quickly breaks down when complex analyses are required. Similarly, [16] describes a navigational algebra for querying XML, treating individual nodes as the unit of manipulation, rather than whole trees. SAL [4] is an algebra for XML documents viewed as a graph, with ordered lists of nodes as the unit of manipulation. The major intellectual focus of this algebra are operators for manipulating ordered lists. There are other contributions, such as the notion of a "data exception" to handle missing values, a notion necessitated by the algebra's use of SQL (and hence the relational model underlying it) as the query language exemplar. Finally, [21] deals with many aspects of XML updates. In this paper, we do not consider updates.

## 8   Summary and Status

We have presented TAX, a Tree Algebra for XML, which extends relational algebra by considering collections of ordered labeled trees instead of relations as the basic unit of manipulation. In spite of the potentially complex structure of the trees involved, and the heterogeneity in a collection, TAX has only a few operators more than relational algebra. Furthermore, each of its operators uses the same basic structure for its parameters.

While we believe that the definition of TAX is a significant intellectual accomplishment, our primary purpose in defining it is to use it as the basis for query evaluation and optimization. We are currently building the TIMBER XML database system using TAX at its core for query evaluation and optimization. Work on query optimization is currently underway.

## Acknowledgements

The work of Jagadish and Thompson was supported by NSF under grant IIS-9986030, while that of Lakshmanan was supported by NSERC (Canada) and a seed grant from IIT - Bombay.

## References

1. S. Abiteboul, D. Quass, J. McHugh, J. Widom, and J. Wiener. The Lorel query language for semistructured data. *Journal on Digital Libraries*, 1(1), 1996.

2. S. Al-Khalifa, H. V. Jagadish, N. Koudas, J. M. Patel, D. Srivastava, and Y. Wu. Structural joins: Efficient matching of XML query patterns. In *Proc. ICDE*, 2002.
3. D. Beech, A. Malhotra, and M. Rys. A formal data model and algebra for XML. W3C XML Query Working Group Note, Sep. 1999.
4. C. Beeri and Y. Tzaban. SAL: An algebra for Semi-Structured Data and XML. In *Proc. SIGMOD WebDB workshop*, June 1999.
5. P. Buneman, S. Davidson, G. Hillebrand, and D. Suciu. A query language and optimization techniques for unstructured data. In *Proc. SIGMOD*, June 1996.
6. D. Chamberlin, J. Robie, and D. Florescu. Quilt: An XML query language for heterogeneous data sources. In *Proc. SIGMOD WebDB workshop*, May 2000.
7. D. Chamberlin, D. Florescu, J. Robie, J. Simeon, and M. Stefanescu. XQuery: A query language for XML. W3C Working Draft. 15 Feb. 2001.
8. E. F. Codd. A relational model of data for large shared data banks. *CACM* 13(6), pages 377–387, 1970.
9. V. Christophides, S. Cluet, and J. Simeon. On wrapping query languages and efficient XML integration. In *Proc. SIGMOD*, pages 141–152, 2000.
10. M. P. Consens and A. O. Mendelzon. Graphlog: A visual formalism for real life recursion. In *Proc. PODS*, Apr. 1990.
11. A. Deutsch, M. Fernandez, D. Florescu, A. Levy, and D. Suciu. A query language for XML. In *Proc. WWW*, 1999.
12. M. Fernandez, J. Simeon, and P. Wadler. An algebra for XML query. In *Proc. FSTTCS*, Delhi, December 2000.
13. M. Gyssens, J. Paredaens, and D. Van Gucht. A grammar-based approach towards unifying hierarchical data models. In *Proc. SIGMOD*, pages 263–272, 1989.
14. C. M. Hoffmann and M. J. O'Donnell. Pattern-matching in trees. *JACM* Vol. 29, pages 68–95, 1982.
15. H. Hosoya and B. C. Pierce. XDuce: A Typed XML Processing Language. In *Proc. SIGMOD WebDB workshop*, May 2000.
16. B. Ludascher, Y. Papakonstantinou, and P. Velikhov. Navigation-driven evaluation of virtual mediated views. In *Proc. EDBT*, pp. 150–165, 2000.
17. Y. Papakonstantinou and V. Vianu. DTD inference for views of XML data. In *Proc. PODS*, 2000.
18. J. Paradaens, J. Van den Bussche, D. Van Gucht, *et al*. An Overview of GOOD *ACM SIGMOD Record*, March 1992.
19. J. Shanmugasundaram, H. Gang, K. Tufte, C. Zhang, D. DeWitt, and J. Naughton. Relational databases for querying XML documents: Limitations and opportunities. In *Proc. VLDB*, 1999.
20. B. Subramanian, T. Leung, S. Vandenberg, S. Zdonik. The AQUA approach to querying lists and trees in object-oriented databases. In *Proc. ICDE*, 1995.
21. I. Tatarinov, Z. G. Ives, A. Y. Halevy, and D. S. Weld. Updating XML. In *Proc. SIGMOD*, 2001.
22. World Wide Web Consortium. The document object model.
    http://www.w3.org/DOM/
23. C. Zhang, J. Naughton, D. DeWitt, Q. Luo, and G. Lohman. On supporting containment queries in relational database management systems. In *Proc. SIGMOD*, May 2001.

# A Rule-Based Querying
# and Updating Language for XML

Wolfgang May

Institut für Informatik, Universität Freiburg, Germany
may@informatik.uni-freiburg.de

**Abstract.** We present XPathLog as a Datalog-style extension to XPath. The querying part extends XPath with binding variables to XML nodes that are "traversed" when evaluating an XPath expression. Data manipulation is done in a rule-based way. In contrast to other approaches, the XPath-based syntax and semantics is also used for a declarative specification how the database should be *updated*: XPath filters are interpreted as specifications of elements and properties that should be added to the database. In this paper, we focus on the theoretical aspects of XPathLog. XPathLog has been implemented in the LoPiX system [LoP01].

## 1 Introduction

XML has been designed and accepted as *the* framework for semi-structured data where it plays the same role as the relational model for classical databases. Specialized languages are available for XML querying, e.g., XML-QL [DFF+99], XQuery[1] and for transformations of XML sources, e.g., XSL(T) (also XML-QL and XQuery can be used for generating new XML documents from given ones since their output format is XML). Whereas XSLT and XML Query do not provide update constructs, a proposal for updates in XQuery has been presented in [TIHW01]; for a comparison with our approach, see [MB01]. For writing applications for creating and manipulating XML data, the dominating language is Java, with the DOM model as a data structure where applications are built on.

We describe a completely XPath-based approach for querying and manipulating XML data. Whereas XSLT, XML-QL, and XQuery use XML patterns for generating output, our language deviates from these approaches: the underlying XML database is seen as a semantical structure that (i) serves for answering XPathLog queries that are XPath reference expressions extended with variables, and that (ii) can also be updated by XPathLog expressions, using the variable bindings for a constructive semantics of rule heads. Our choice of a Datalog-like design yields a *declarative* language on a theoretically well-investigated base.

An early, informal presentation of XPathLog could be found in [May01c]. In contrast, in the present paper, we focus on the formal aspects of XPathLog as a programming language. Special considerations on updates on XML data and an appropriate extension of the data model can be found in [MB01].

---

[1] all W3C XML notions, e.g., XML, XSLT, DOM, XPath, XLink, and XQuery can be found at [W3C].

G. Grahne and G. Ghelli (Eds.): DBPL 2001, LNCS 2397, pp. 165–181, 2002.

**Structure of the Paper.** An introduction to XPathLog by examples is presented in Section 2. Section 3 introduces the underlying semantical structures. XPathLog is investigated as a rule-based XML data manipulation language in Sections 4 (Queries) and 5 (Updates). Section 6 concludes the paper. An extended version of the paper can be found at [May01a].

## 2   XPath-Logic: Adding Variable Bindings to XPath

**XPath.** XPath is the common language for addressing node sets in XML documents. It is based on navigation through the XML tree by *location paths* of the form *//step/step/...step*. Every *location step* is of the form *axis::nodetest[filter]\**, denoting that navigation goes along the given axis in the XML document. Along the chosen axis, all elements that satisfy the *nodetest* (the *nodetest* specifies the nodetype or an elementtype) are selected. From these, the ones qualify which satisfy the given *filter(s)* (applied iteratively – roughly spoken, predicates over XPath expressions which state conditions on a node). Starting with this (local) result set, the next location step is applied (for details, see [XPa99], or the formal semantics given in [Wad99]). The most frequently used axes are abbreviated as *path*/nodetest for *path*/child::nodetest, *path*//nodetest for *path*/descendant-or-self/child::nodetest, and *path*/@nodetest for *path*/attribute::nodetest.

**Example 1 (XPath)**
*Consider the following excerpt of the* MONDIAL *database [Mon] for illustrations.*

```
<!ELEMENT mondial (country+, organization+, ...)>
<!ELEMENT country (name, city+, ...)>
  <!ATTLIST country car_code ID #REQUIRED   capital IDREFS #REQUIRED>
                 memberships IDREFS #IMPLIED

<!ELEMENT name (#PCDATA)>
<!ELEMENT city (name, population*)>  <!ATTLIST city ... >
<!ELEMENT population (#PCDATA)>
  <!ATTLIST population year CDATA #IMPLIED>

<!ELEMENT organization (name, abbrev, members*)>
  <!ATTLIST organization id ID #REQUIRED   seat IDREF #IMPLIED>
<!ELEMENT abbrev (#PCDATA)>
<!ELEMENT members EMPTY>
  <!ATTLIST members type CDATA #REQUIRED
                    country IDREFS #REQUIRED>

<country car_code="CH" capital="cty-Bern" memberships="org-efta org-un ... ">
    <name>Switzerland</name>
    <city id="cty-Bern" name="Bern">
       <population year="91">134393</population> ... </city>
    :
</country>
```

```
<organization id="org-un" seat="cty-USA-NewYork">
  <name>United Nations</name>  <abbrev>UN</abbrev>
  <members type="member" country="F E A CZ D ..."/>
</organization>
```

*The XPath expression*

//country[@car_code]/city[population/text()>100000]/name/text()

*returns all names of cities s.t. the city belongs (i.e., is a subelement) to a country where a car_code attribute exists and the city's population is higher than 100000.*

XPath is only an addressing mechanism, not a full querying language like, e.g., the SQL querying construct. It provides the base for most XML querying languages, which extend it with their special constructs (e.g., functional style in XSL(T), and SQL/OQL style (e.g., joins) in XQuery). For XPathLog, the extension feature are Datalog style variable bindings, joins, and rules.

**Adding Variable Bindings to XPath.**  We extend the XPath syntax with the Datalog-style variable concept (and implicit dereferencing). Instead of a result set, for every match, a tuple of *variable bindings* is returned that can be used in the rule head. The variables are bound to the names/nodes/literals (for i.e., **CDATA** or **NMTOKENS** attributes) that result from the respective match; the formal semantics is based on that of XPath given in [Wad99].

**Definition 1 (Reference Expressions)**

– An *XPath-Logic reference expression* is an XPath *AbsoluteLocationPath* (we refer to the definition numbering in [XPa99, Chap. 2]) where the XPath syntax is extended as follows:

  • In XPath-Logic steps, $axis :: nodetest$ may be replaced by $axis :: nodetest \rightarrow V$, $axis :: V$, or $axis :: V \rightarrow W$ where $V$ and $W$ are variables:

[4] Step ::=AxisSpec NodeTest Pred* | AxisSpec NodeTest "->" Var Pred*
            | AxisSpec Var Pred* | AxisSpec Var "->" Var Pred*

– XPath-Logic *LocationPaths* may begin with constants or variables:

[2b] ConstantLocationPath ::=constant "/" RelativeLocationPath
                           | variable "/" RelativeLocationPath

XPath-Logic combines first-order logic and reference expressions, similar to F-Logic [KLW95]. XPathLog is the Horn fragment of XPath-Logic, i.e., logical rules over reference expressions and predicates over them (see Section 4). We first give some intuitive examples for XPathLog reference expressions:

**Example 2 (Reference Expressions)**

**Pure XPath Expressions:** *pure XPath expressions (i.e., without variables) are interpreted as existential queries that return* true *if the result set is non-empty:*

?- //country[name/text()="Germany"]//city/name.
true

*since the country element which has a name subelement with the text contents "Germany" contains at least one city descendant with a name subelement.*

**Output Result Set:**  *The query "?- xpath→N" for any xpath binds N to all nodes belonging to the result set of xpath. For a result set consisting of elements, logical ids are returned:*

?- //country[name/text()="Germany"]//city→C.
C/*berlin*          <!-- *berlin* and *freiburg* are references to the corresponding
C/*freiburg*          nodes of type *city* in the XML database -->
:

**Additional Variables:**  *XPathLog allows to bind all nodes which are considered by an expression (both by the access path to the result set, and in the filters): The following expression returns all tuples $(N_1, C, N_2)$ such that the city with name $N_2$ belongs to the country with name $N_1$ and car code C:*

?- //country[name/text()→N1 and @car_code→C]//city/name/text()→N2.
N2/"Berlin"    C/"D"   N1/"Germany"
N2/"Freiburg"  C/"D"   N1/"Germany"
:

**Dereferencing:**  *For all organizations, give the name of the seat city and all names and types of members. Dereferencing is done implicitly by path expressions including reference attributes, here,* **organization/@seat** *navigates to the city element whose id equals the value of the seat attribute of the organization:*

?- //organization[abbrev/text()→A and @seat/name/text()→S]
                  /members[@type→T]/@country/name/text()→N.

*One element of the answer set is e.g.,*

A/"UN"    S/"New York"    T/"member"    N/"Germany"

*Note that the original XPath syntax also allows such expressions, but their semantics is empty.*

**Variables at NodeTest Position.**  *For data restructuring and integration, the intuitiveness and declarativeness of a language gains much from variables ranging not only over data, but also over schema concepts (e.g., in F-Logic [KLW95,LHL+98]). As specified in the above syntax, variables can also occur at* NodeTest *position of navigation steps. In this case, they are bound to the element or attribute names.*

**Navigation Variables:**  *Are there elements that have a name subelement with the* PCDATA *contents "Monaco", and of which type are they?*

?- //Type→X[name/text()→ "Monaco"].
   Type/country  X/*country-monaco*
   Type/city     X/*city-monaco*

**Schema Querying:**  *The use of variables at name positions further allows schema querying, e.g., to give all names of subelements of elements of type city:*

```
?- //city/N.
N/name
N/population
:
```

*Schema querying can e.g. be used for validation wrt. a DTD or a given XML-Schema (which can be present as an XML tree in the same XPathLog database).*

# 3    XML Instances As Semantical Structures

Logic-oriented frameworks are in general based on a semantical structure. We represent XML instances by an XTreeGraph [MB01] which is represented formally by an *X-structure*. The XTreeGraph data model is a conservative extension of the DOM/XML Query Data Model, thus, all central notions such as the DOM API, XPath, XML-QL, XQuery, XML Schema etc. also apply to it. The full theory can be found in [May01a].

**Definition 2 (X-Structure)** Given an XML instance, the universe consists of
- $\mathcal{N}$, a set of names (i.e., element and attribute names),
- $\mathcal{V}$, a set of nodes, and
- $\mathcal{L}$, a set of literals.

An *X-structure* $\mathcal{X}$ over a given universe consists of an interpretation $\mathcal{I}_\mathcal{X}$ of predicates over the universe, and a (partial) mapping that associates with every $x \in \mathcal{V}$ two lists of pairs:
- $\mathcal{A}_\mathcal{X}(\text{child}, x) \in ((\mathcal{V} \cup \mathcal{L}) \times \mathcal{N})^{\mathbb{N}}$    and
- $\mathcal{A}_\mathcal{X}(\text{attribute}, x) \in ((\mathcal{V} \cup \mathcal{L}) \times \mathcal{N})^{\mathbb{N}}$ (resolving reference attributes by nodes).

E.g., $\mathcal{A}_\mathcal{X}(\text{child}, x) = ((v_1, n_1), (v_1, n_2), \ldots)$ denotes that the first child of $x$ is $v_1$ and it is of element type $n_1$ and so on.

There is a canonical mapping from the set of XML instances to the set of X-structures. An X-structure contains only the basic facts about the XML tree. For the other axes, $\mathcal{A}_\mathcal{X}(axis, x)$ is derived from $\mathcal{A}_\mathcal{X}(\text{child}, x)$ according to the XML specification.

Note that X-structures not necessarily describe a tree: the underlying data model is an *edge-labeled graph* which allows elements to have multiple parents. Thus, an X-structure can represent multiple, overlapping trees – or *tree views* on the X-structure. XPathLog rules allow for re-linking elements into tree (view)s, merging elements, and introducing synonyms for names (cf. [MB01]).

**Evaluation of XPath-Logic Formulas over X-Structures.** The semantics of XPath-Logic formulas wrt. an X-structure is defined by operators $\mathcal{S}$ and $\mathcal{Q}$ derived from the formal semantics given in [Wad99] (extended with variable bindings). Here, this *model-theoretic* semantics is not given in detail (see [May01a]); instead, Section 4.2 defines an equivalent *algebraic* semantics which is used for *evaluating* XPathLog queries. For variable-free absolute reference expressions (i.e., pure XPath expressions) without navigating along reference attributes, and splitting NMTOKENS attributes, the semantics coincides with the one given in [Wad99]: For every such XPath expression *expr*,

$$\mathcal{S}_{\mathcal{X}}(expr, \emptyset) = \mathcal{S}[[expr]](root)$$

where $\mathcal{S}[[expr]](root)$ is as defined in [Wad99] and enumerated wrt. document order. For absolute expressions containing variables,

$$\mathcal{S}_{\mathcal{X}}(expr, \emptyset) \subseteq \mathcal{S}[[expr]](root)$$

since join variables may further restrict the result set.

# 4  XPathLog: The Horn Fragment of XPath-Logic

Similar to the case of Datalog which is the quantifier-free Horn fragment of predicate logic, XPathLog is a Datalog style language based on XPath-Logic. XPathLog queries are conjunctions of XPath-Logic literals with *free* variables. Similar to Datalog, the answers to the query are given in terms of *variable bindings*. Especially, the semantics of XPathLog queries *combines* the XPath *result set semantics* with the Datalog *variable bindings semantics*.

- an *XPathLog atom* is either an XPath-Logic reference expression (cf. Def. 1) or a predicate expression over them.
- an *XPathLog atom* is *definite* if it uses only the child, sibling, and attribute axes, and it does not contain negation, disjunction, or *proximity position predicates* (these atoms are allowed in rule heads; the excluded features would cause ambiguities what update is intended).
- an *XPathLog query* is a list ?- $L_1, \ldots, L_n$ of literals.
- an *XPathLog rule* is a formula of the form $A_1, \ldots, A_n \leftarrow L_1, \ldots, L_n$ where $L_i$ are literals and $A_i$ are definite atoms. $L_1, \ldots, L_n$ is the *body* of the rule, evaluated as a conjunction. The list of atoms in the rule head is also interpreted as a conjunction.

## 4.1  Query Semantics: Data Model

The answer semantics of XPathLog reference expressions is defined wrt. an X-structure as an *annotated result list*, i.e.,

- a result list, and
- with every element of the result list, a list of variable bindings is associated.

**Definition 3 (Semantics)** Let Var denote the variables in an expression. Then,

$$\text{VarBdgs} := \bigcup_{n \in \mathbb{N}_0} 2^{((\mathcal{V} \cup \mathcal{L} \cup \mathcal{N})^n)^{(\text{Var}^n)}}$$

is the set of sets of variable assignments. We use $\beta$ for denoting an individual variable binding, and $\xi \in \text{VarBdgs}$ for denoting a set of variable bindings.

The set {*true*} is the lowest element in VarBdgs (representing the bindings for an empty set of variables); in contrast, ∅ means that there is no variable binding which satisfies a given requirement.

$$\text{AnnotRes} := ((\mathcal{V} \cup \mathcal{L}) \times \text{VarBdgs})$$

is the set of annotated results. The answer semantics of an XPath-Logic reference expression is then an *annotated result list*. For an annotated result list $\theta$,

- $\text{Res}(\theta) \in (\mathcal{V} \cup \mathcal{L})^{\mathbb{N}}$ is the projection on the first component, i.e., the pure result list of the underlying XPath expression, and
- $\text{Bdgs}(\theta, x) \in \text{VarBdgs}$ is the second component of the element of $\theta$ whose first component is $x$, i.e., the list of variable bindings obtained for the result $x$.

The semantics of a predicate is either $(true, \xi)$ for some $\xi \in \text{VarBdgs}$, or $(false, \emptyset)$ (the special case of the above where there is no result element).

As shown in the formal semantics given later in Figures 1 and 2, the first component (i.e., the result set) is used for inductively defining the (internal) semantics of *navigation* expresssions, whereas the second component yields the Datalog-style answer sets of the literals which is then used in the (external) *logical semantics* of queries.

**Example 3 (Semantics)** *Let $\mathcal{X}$ be the canonical X-structure to the XML instance given in Example 1. The first organization is the UN, assume the next one to be the EU, etc. The semantics of the expression*

//organization→O[member/@country[@car_code→C and name/text()→N]]
                    /abbrev/text()→A.

*is the annotated result list*

list(( "UN" , {(O/*un*, A/ "UN" , C/ "AL" , N/ "Albania" ),
              (O/*un*, A/ "UN" , C/ "GR" , N/ "Greece" ),
                              :                      }),
      ( "EU" , {(O/*eu*, A/ "EU" , C/ "D" , N/ "Germany" ),
               (O/*eu*, A/ "EU" , C/ "F" , N/ "France" ),
                              :                      }),
      :                                               )

*The projection to the first component, i.e., ( "UN" , "EU" ,. . . ) is the result list of the underlying XPath expression*

//organization[member/@country[@car_code and name/text()]]/abbrev/text() ,

*and the second component gives the variable bindings obtained for each result. Note that the second component* may *contain the first component as some variable binding, but this is not necessary.*

*If only the 7th element of the result set of the above query is of interest,*

//organization→O[. . . ][7]/abbrev/text()→A

*yields the abbreviation of the 7th organization, together with a set of variable bindings for O, A, C, and N. This is much different from defining a seman-*

*tics yielding simply a list of variable bindings for O, A, C, and N which would presumably yield the bindings for the 7th member of the UN.*

## 4.2   Semantics of Expressions

When evaluating XPathLog expressions, the basic (non-annotated) result lists are provided by projecting $\mathcal{A}_{\mathcal{X}}(axis, v)$ to its first component for every node $v$ in $\mathcal{X}$. Recall that for $\mathcal{A}_{\mathcal{X}}(\text{attribute}, x)$, the result set contains literals in case of non-reference attributes, and element nodes in case of reference attributes.

The semantics definition evaluates formulas and expressions wrt. a given set of variable bindings which results from evaluating the left path of an XPath expression, or from other literals of the same query. This approach allows for a more efficient evaluation of joins (*sideways information passing strategy*), and is especially needed for evaluating *negated* expressions: negation is defined similar to the relational "minus" operator, excluding some bindings from a given set of potential results. Thus, for variables occurring in the scope of a negation, the input answer set to the negation must already provide potential bindings. This leads to a notion of *safety* similar to Datalog.

**Definition 4** The semantics is defined by operators $\mathcal{SB}$ and $\mathcal{QB}$ (given in Figures 1 and 2) derived from the formal semantics given in [Wad99]:

- $\mathcal{SB}_{\mathcal{X}}$ : (RefExprs × VarBdgs) → AnnotRes$^{\text{IN}}$   % *absolute path expressions*
  (Axes × $\mathcal{V}$ × RefExprs × VarBdgs) → AnnotRes$^{\text{IN}}$   % *relative* "
  evaluates reference expressions wrt. an axis and a context node and returns a list of pairs as described above.

- $\mathcal{QB}_{\mathcal{X}}$ : (PredExprs × $\mathcal{V}$ × VarBdgs) → VarBdgs
  evaluates predicates and filters wrt. a context node and returns a set of variable bindings.

$\mathcal{SB}$ and $\mathcal{QB}$ are equivalent to the above-mentioned model-theoretic semantics $\mathcal{S}$ and $\mathcal{Q}$; they extend the semantics given in [Wad99]:

**Theorem 1 (Correctness of $\mathcal{SB}$ and $\mathcal{QB}$)** For every *absolute* (in general, containing free variables) XPathLog expression *expr*,

$$\text{Res}(\mathcal{SB}_{\mathcal{X}}(expr, \emptyset)) = \bigcup\nolimits_{\beta \in (\mathcal{V} \cup \mathcal{L} \cup \mathcal{N})^{\text{free}(expr)}} \mathcal{S}_{\mathcal{X}}(expr, \beta) \subseteq \mathcal{S}[[expr]](root)$$

where $\mathcal{S}[[expr]](x)$ is as defined in [Wad99]. More detailed, $\mathcal{SB}$ and $\mathcal{QB}$ relate to the model-theoretic semantics $\mathcal{S}$ and $\mathcal{Q}$ as follows: for all $x \in \mathcal{V} \cup \mathcal{L} \cup \mathcal{N}$,

$$(x \in \text{Res}(\mathcal{SB}_{\mathcal{X}}(expr, \emptyset)) \text{ and } \beta \in \text{Bdgs}(\mathcal{SB}_{\mathcal{X}}(expr, \emptyset), x)) \Leftrightarrow x \in \mathcal{S}_{\mathcal{X}}(expr, \beta)$$
$$\beta \in \mathcal{QB}_{\mathcal{X}}(expr, root, \emptyset) \Leftrightarrow \mathcal{Q}_{\mathcal{X}}(expr, root, \beta) .$$

The proof of the theorem uses a lemma that encapsulates the structural induction, and gives more insight into the computation of the result set.

Expressions as literals:  $\quad \mathcal{SB}_\mathcal{X}(refExpr) = \mathcal{SB}_\mathcal{X}(refExpr, \emptyset)$

Entry points: rooted paths:  $\quad \mathcal{SB}_\mathcal{X}^{any}(/p, Bdgs) = \mathcal{SB}_\mathcal{X}^{any}(p, root, Bdgs)$

Entry points: constants $x \in \mathcal{V}$: $\mathcal{SB}_\mathcal{X}^{any}(c/p, Bdgs) = \mathcal{SB}_\mathcal{X}^{any}(p, c, Bdgs)$
  (this is used e.g., when multiple documents are handled; but also in the core
  XPathLog language, names/identifiers may be associated to nodes.)

Entry points: variables $v \in \mathrm{Var}$:

$$\mathcal{SB}_\mathcal{X}^{any}(V/p, Bdgs) = concat_{(x,n) \in \mathcal{A}_\mathcal{X}(\mathrm{descendants},root)}(\mathcal{SB}_\mathcal{X}^{any}(p, x, Bdgs \bowtie \{V/x\}))$$

Location step: $\mathcal{SB}_\mathcal{X}^{any}(axis :: pattern, x, Bdgs) = \mathcal{SB}_\mathcal{X}^{axis}(pattern, x, Bdgs)$

Node test, no filter:

$\mathcal{SB}_\mathcal{X}^{a}(name, x, Bdgs) \;= list_{(v,n) \in \mathcal{A}_\mathcal{X}(a,x),\; n=name}(v, \{true\} \bowtie Bdgs)$

$\mathcal{SB}_\mathcal{X}^{a}(node(), x, Bdgs) = list_{(v,n) \in \mathcal{A}_\mathcal{X}(a,x),\; v \in \mathcal{V}}(v, \{true\} \bowtie Bdgs)$

$\mathcal{SB}_\mathcal{X}^{a}(text(), x, Bdgs) \;= list_{(v,n) \in \mathcal{A}_\mathcal{X}(a,x),\; v \in \mathcal{L}}(v, \{true\} \bowtie Bdgs)$

$\mathcal{SB}_\mathcal{X}^{a}(N, x) \qquad\qquad\;\; = list_{(v,n) \in \mathcal{A}_\mathcal{X}(a,x)}(v, \{N/v\} \bowtie Bdgs)$

Step with variable:

$\mathcal{SB}_\mathcal{X}^{a}(pattern \rightarrow V, x, Bdgs) = list_{(y,\xi) \in \mathcal{SB}_\mathcal{X}^{a}(pattern,x,Bdgs)}(y, \xi \bowtie \{V/y\})$

Filter:  $\mathcal{SB}_\mathcal{X}^{a}(pattern[filter], x, Bdgs) =$

$$list_{\substack{(y, \xi) \,\in\, \mathcal{SB}_\mathcal{X}^{a}(pattern,\, x,\, Bdgs) \\ \mathcal{QB}_\mathcal{X}(filter, y, \xi') \neq \emptyset}} (y, \; \mathcal{QB}_\mathcal{X}(filter, y, \xi') \setminus \{Pos, Size\})$$

  If the filter does not contain *proximity position predicates*, $\xi' := \xi$, otherwise
  let $L := \mathcal{SB}_\mathcal{X}^{a}(pattern, x, Bdgs)$, and then for every $(y, \xi)$ in $L$, $\xi'$ extends $\xi$
  with bindings of the pseudo variables $Size$ and $Pos$: start with $\xi' = \emptyset$. Then,
  for every $\beta \in \xi$, the list $L' = list_{(y,\xi) \in L \text{ s.t. } \beta \in \xi}(y)$ contains all nodes which are
  selected *for the variable assignment* $\beta$. Then $size := size(L')$, and for every $y$,
  let $j$ the index of $x_1$ in $L'$, $pos := j$ if $a$ is a forward axis, and $pos := size{+}1{-}j$
  if $a$ is a backward axis (cf. [Wad99]). Add $\beta_{size,pos}^{Size,Pos}$ to $\xi'$. After evaluating the
  filter, the pseudo variables $Size$ and $Pos$ are again removed from the bindings.

Path:  $\quad \mathcal{SB}_\mathcal{X}^{a}(p_1/p_2, x, Bdgs) = concat_{(y,\xi) \in \mathcal{SB}_\mathcal{X}^{a}(p_1,x,Bdgs)}(\mathcal{SB}_\mathcal{X}^{a}(p_2, y, \xi))$

Constants: $\mathcal{SB}_\mathcal{X}^{a}(value, x, Bdgs) = (value, Bdgs)$

Variables:  $\mathcal{SB}_\mathcal{X}^{a}(V, x, Bdgs) = list_{\beta \in Bdgs}(\beta(V), \{\beta' \in Bdgs \mid \beta(V) = \beta'(V)\})$

Context-related functions use the pseudo-variables $Size$ and $Pos$:

$\mathcal{SB}_\mathcal{X}^{any}(position(), x, Bdgs) = list_{\beta \in Bdgs}(\beta(Pos), \{\beta' \in Bdgs \mid \beta(Pos) = \beta'(Pos)\})$

$\mathcal{SB}_\mathcal{X}^{any}(last(), x, Bdgs) = list_{\beta \in Bdgs}(\beta(Pos), \{\beta' \in Bdgs \mid \beta(Size) = \beta'(Size)\})$

Arithmetics:

$$\mathcal{SB}_\mathcal{X}^{a}(expr_1 \; op \; expr_2, x, Bdgs) = list_{\substack{(x_1, \zeta_1) \,\in\, \mathcal{SB}_\mathcal{X}^{a}(expr_1,\, x,\, \beta), \\ (x_2, \zeta_2) \,\in\, \mathcal{SB}_\mathcal{X}^{a}(expr_2,\, x,\, \beta),}}(x_1 \; op \; x_2, \xi_1 \bowtie \xi_2)$$

$$\text{group by } x_1 \; op \; x_2$$

**Fig. 1.** Definition of $\mathcal{SB}$

**Lemma 2 (Correctness of $\mathcal{SB}$ and $\mathcal{QB}$: Structural Induction)** The correctness of the answers semantics of XPathLog expressions mirrors the generation of answer sets by the evaluation: The input set $Bdgs$ of Bindings *may*
contain bindings for the free variables of an expression. If for some variable *var*,
no binding is given, the result *extends Bdgs* with bindings of *var*. If bindings
are given for *var*, this specifies a *constraint* on the answers (join variables).

---

Reference expressions (existential semantics) in filters:
$$\mathcal{QB}_\mathcal{X}(refExpr, x, Bdgs) = \bigcup_{(y,\xi) \in \mathcal{SB}_\mathcal{X}^{any}(refExpr, x, Bdgs)} \xi$$

Predicate expressions: $\mathcal{QB}_\mathcal{X}(pred(arg_1, \ldots, arg_n), x, Bdgs) =$
$$\bigcup_{\substack{(x_1, \xi_1) \in \mathcal{SB}_\mathcal{X}^{any}(arg_1, x, Bdgs), \ldots, \\ (x_n, \xi_n) \in \mathcal{SB}_\mathcal{X}^{any}(arg_n, x, Bdgs) \\ (x_1, \ldots, x_n) \in \mathcal{I}_\mathcal{X}(pred)}} \xi_1 \bowtie \ldots \bowtie \xi_n$$

Conjunction:
$$\mathcal{QB}_\mathcal{X}(A \text{ and } B, x, Bdgs) = \mathcal{QB}_\mathcal{X}(A, x, Bdgs) \bowtie \mathcal{QB}_\mathcal{X}(B, x, \mathcal{QB}_\mathcal{X}(A, x, Bdgs))$$

Negated Expressions:

$\mathcal{QB}_\mathcal{X}(\text{not } A, x, Bdgs) =$
$Bdgs - \{\beta \in Bdgs \mid \text{ there is a } \beta' \in \mathcal{QB}_\mathcal{X}(A, x, Bdgs) \text{ s.t. } \beta \leq \beta'\}$

*Bdgs* contributes a set of bindings of *safe variables*. For two tuples $\beta_1, \beta_2$, of variable bindings, let $\beta_1 \leq \beta_2$ if $\beta_1$ is subsumed by $\beta_2$ (i.e., all variable bindings in $\beta_1$ occur also in $\beta_2$). Intuitively, in this case, if $\beta_1$ is "abandoned", $\beta_2$ should also be abandoned.

**Fig. 2.** Definition of $\mathcal{QB}$

- For every *absolute* expression *expr*, (i.e., $expr = /expr'$) and every set *Bdgs* of variable bindings,

  $x \in \text{Res}(\mathcal{SB}_\mathcal{X}(expr, Bdgs))$ and $\beta \in \text{Bdgs}(\mathcal{SB}_\mathcal{X}(expr, Bdgs), x) \Leftrightarrow$
  $x \in \mathcal{S}_\mathcal{X}(expr, \beta)$ and $\beta$ completes some $\beta' \in Bdgs$ with free(*expr*) .

- For every expression *expr*, *v*, and *Bdgs*,

  $x \in \text{Res}(\mathcal{SB}_\mathcal{X}(expr, v, Bdgs))$ and $\beta \in \text{Bdgs}(\mathcal{SB}_\mathcal{X}(expr, v, Bdgs), x) \Leftrightarrow$
  $x \in \mathcal{S}_\mathcal{X}(expr, v, \beta)$ and $\beta$ completes some $\beta' \in Bdgs$ with free(*expr*) .

- For every predicate expression *predExpr*, *v*, and *Bdgs*,

  $\beta \in \mathcal{QB}_\mathcal{X}(predExpr, v, Bdgs) \Leftrightarrow$
  $\mathcal{Q}_\mathcal{X}(predExpr, v, \beta)$ and $\beta$ completes some $\beta' \in Bdgs$ with free(*predExpr*). □

## 4.3  Queries in XPathLog

Similar to Datalog, evaluation of a query ?- $\mathsf{L}_1, \ldots, \mathsf{L}_n$ results in a set of tuples of variable bindings to elements of the universe.

**Definition 5** Given an X-Structure $\mathcal{X}$, the answer to ?- $\mathsf{L}_1, \ldots, \mathsf{L}_n$ is the set
$$\text{answers}_\mathcal{X}(L_1, \ldots, L_n) := \mathcal{QB}_\mathcal{X}(L_1 \text{ and } \ldots \text{ and } L_n, root, \emptyset)$$
of tuples of variable bindings.

The above semantics is implemented in the LoPiX system [LoP01] for evaluating queries and rule bodies. For negated subgoals (also in filters), safety is concerned with the propagation of variable bindings in *Bdgs*. The variable are then propagated to the rule head where facts are added to the model.

**Querying Distributed XML Data.** As a data format tailored to the use over the Web, XML data is not required to be self-contained on an individual server, but may include *links* to XML data on other servers. The XML linking functionality is specified in the *XML Linking Language (XLink)* by providing special tags in the xlink: namespace that tell an application that an element has XLink functionality. Such elements can be seen as embedded view definitions, given as a query against another document where suitable information can be found. Thus, this view has to be evaluated when the element is actually traversed in a query. Since these elements are "normal" XML elements, the XLink semantics can be expressed in XPathLog programs. Work on this area is part of the project. First results and proposals can be found in [May01a].

# 5 Updates: XPathLog Rules and Programs

Using *XPath expressions* and *logical rules* for specifying an update is perhaps the most important difference to approaches like XSLT, XML-QL, or XQuery where the structure to be *generated* is always specified by XML patterns (this implies that these languages do not allow for updating existing nodes – e.g., adding children or attributes –, but only for generating complete nodes). In contrast, in XPathLog, existing nodes are communicated via variables to the head, where they are *extended* when appearing at host position of atoms. Further considerations on updates on XML data can be found in [MB01].

## 5.1 Updates in XPathLog

The head of an XPathLog rule is a set of definite XPathLog atoms. When used in the head, the / operator and the [...] construct specify which properties should be added or updated (thus, [...] does not act as a filter, but as a *constructor*). Additionally, when manipulating subelements, copying (for data transformation) or linking (for data integration) can be specified.

Note that – similar to Datalog – the pure XPathLog language does *not* allow to delete or replace existing nodes. Thus, modifications are always monotonic in the sense that existing "things" remain (although, since children may be inserted between already existing children, the evaluation of proximity position predicates is non-monotonic; similar to aggregration operators in related approaches). XPathLog can be extended by deletions, in the style of Datalog⁻⁻. Together with stratification, this leads to a more procedural semantics.

## 5.2 Atomization

Below, we present an alternative semantics of atoms that provides the base for the semantics of reference expressions in *rule heads*. The semantics is equivalent to the one presented before for all *definite* atoms, i.e., atoms allowed in rule heads. It resolves reference expressions in their constituting atomic steps of the form n[$axis$::e→w]. atomize is defined by structural induction corresponding to the induction steps when defining $\mathcal{SB}_\chi$:

---

entry case: atomize($/remainder$) = atomize(root$/remainder$)

Paths are resolved into steps and filters are isolated:
atomize($path/axis :: nodetest \rightarrow var[filter] /remainder$) =
    atomize($path[axis :: nodetest \rightarrow var]$) $\cup$
    atomize($var[filter]$) $\cup$ atomize($var/remainder$) ,
atomize($path/axis :: nodetest[filter]/remainder$) =
    atomize($path[axis :: nodetest \rightarrow \_X]$) $\cup$
    atomize($var[filter]$) $\cup$ atomize($\_X/remainder$) .
    where $\_X$ is a new variable

Conjunctions in filters are separated:
atomize($var[pred_1 \wedge \ldots \wedge pred_n]$) = atomize($var[pred_1], \ldots, var[pred_n]$)

Predicates in filters (including the case $path[expr]$):
atomize($var[pred(expr_1, \ldots, expr_n)]$) = atomize($equality(var, expr_1, \_X_1)$) $\cup \ldots \cup$
                        atomize($equality(var, expr_n, \_X_n)$) $\cup \{pred(\_X_1, \ldots, \_X_n)\}$

where $equality(path, expr, X)$ is defined as follows
(if $expr_i$ is a constant, it is not replaced by a variable):
• $expr \rightarrow X$ if $expr$ is of the form $//remainder$, or
• $path/expr \rightarrow X$ if $expr$ is of the form $axis :: nodetest\ remainder$.

---

**Fig. 3.** Definition of atomize

## Definition 6 (Atomization of Formulas) The mapping

$$\text{atomize} : \text{XPathLogExprs} \rightarrow 2^{\text{XPathLogAtom}}$$

defined in Figure 3 resolves XPath-Logic reference expressions into a set of atomic expressions.

## Example 4 (Atomization)

?- //organization→O[name/text()→ON and
                        @seat = members/@country[name/text()→CN]/@capital].

*is atomized into*

?- root[descendant::organization→O], O[name→_ON], _ON[text()→ON],
    O[@seat→_S], O[members→_M], _M[@country→_C], _C[@country→_Cap],
    _S = _Cap, _C[name→_CN], _CN[text()→CN].

**Theorem 3 (Equivalence)** The above semantics is equivalent to the one presented in Def. 4 for all *definite* XPathLog atoms: For every X-structure $\mathcal{X}$,

$$\text{answers}_{\mathcal{X}}(query) = \text{answers}_{\mathcal{X}}(\text{atomize}(query)) .$$

Again, the theorem is proven by structural induction, using the following Lemma that describes the use of auxiliary variables:

**Lemma 4 (Correctness of atomize)** For every X-structure $\mathcal{X}$ and every definite XPath-Logic atom *expr*,

- for every variable assignment $\beta$ of free($expr$) s.t. $\mathcal{Q}_{\mathcal{X}}(expr, x, \beta)$, there exists an extension $\beta' \supseteq \beta$ of free(atomize($expr$)) s.t. $\mathcal{Q}_{\mathcal{X}}(\text{atomize}(expr), x, \beta')$, and
- for every variable assignment $\beta'$ of free(atomize($expr$)) such that $\mathcal{Q}_{\mathcal{X}}(\text{atomize}(expr), x, \beta')$, also $\mathcal{Q}_{\mathcal{X}}(expr, x, \beta'|_{\text{free}(expr)})$.

## 5.3  Updates

**Modification of Elements.**  When using the child or attribute axis for updates, the host of the expression gives the element to be updated or extended; when a sibling axis is used, effectively the parent of the host is extended with a new subelement.

**Attributes.**  A ground-instantiated atom of the form n[@a→v] specifies that the attribute @a of the node $n$ should be set or extended with $v$. If $v$ is not a literal value but a node, a reference to $v$ is stored.

**Example 5 (Attributes)** *We add the data code to Switzerland, and make it a member of the European Union:*
C[@datacode→"ch"], C[@memberships→O] :-
       //country→C[@car_code= "CH"],  //organization→O[abbrev/text()→ "EU"].

results in  <country datacode="ch" car_code="CH" capital="cty-bern"
                          memberships="org-efta org-un org-eu ..."> ... </country>

We discuss insertion of new subelements after showing how to create elements.

**Elements.**  Elements can be created as *free* elements by atoms of the form /name[...] (meaning "some element of type name" – this is interpreted to create an element which is not a subelement of any other element), or as subelements.

**Example 6** *We create a new (free) country element with some properties:*
/country[@car_code→ "BAV" and @capital→X and city→X and city→Y] :-
       //city→X[name/text()="Munich"],  //city→Y[name/text()="Nurnberg"].
*Note that the two city elements are* linked *as subelements. This operation has no equivalent in the "classical" XML model: these elements are now children of two country elements (cf. [MB01]).*

Already existing elements can be assigned as subelements to existing elements by using filter syntax in the rule head: A ground instantiated atom n[child::s→m] makes $m$ a subelement of type $s$ of $n$. In this case, in the X-structure, $m$ is *linked* as $n/s$ somewhere (no position specified). If the atom is of the form $n$[child($i$)::s→m] or n[following-sibling($j$)::s→m], this means that the new element to be inserted should be made the $i$th subelement of $n$ or $j$th sibling of $n$.

**Example 7** *The following two rules are equivalent to the above one:*
/country[@car_code→ "BAV"].
C[@capital→X and city→X and city→Y] :- //country→C[@car_code= "BAV"].
       //city→X[name/text()→ "Munich"],  //city→Y[name/text()→ "Nurnberg"],

*Here, the first rule creates a free element, whereas the second rule uses the variable binding of C for inserting subelements and attributes.*

**Generation of Elements by Path Expressions.**   Additionally, subelements can be created by *path expressions* in the rule head which create nested elements that satisfy the given path expression. The atomization introduces local variables which occur *only in the head* of the rule, i.e., the result is syntactically not a valid Logic Programming rule. The problem is solved by processing the resulting atoms in an ordering such that the local variables are bound to the nodes/objects which are generated.

**Example 8** *Bavaria gets a (PCDATA) subelement name:*

C/name[text()→"Bavaria"] :- //country→C[@car_code="BAV"].

*Here, the atomized version of the rule is*
C[name→_N], _N[text()→"Bavaria"] :-
    root[descendant::country→C], C[@car_code="BAV"].

*The body produces the variable binding  C/bavaria. When the head is evaluated, first, the fact bavaria[child::name→x'] is inserted, adding an (empty) name subelement x' to bavaria and binding the local variable _N to x'. Then, the second atom is evaluated, generating the text contents to x'.*

### 5.4   Formal Semantics of XPathLog Programs

In contrast to Datalog where it does not matter if a fact is "inserted" into the database several times (e.g., once in every round, conforming with the formal definition of the $T_P$ operator), here subelements must be created exactly once for each instantiation of a rule. For XPathLog, the $T_P$ operator is extended with bookkeeping about the ground instances of inserted rule heads. Additionally, the insertion of subelements adds some nonmonotonicity: adding an atom n[child(i)::e→v] (or n[sibling(i)::e→v]) adds a new subelement at the $i$th position (or as $i$th sibling), making the original $i$th child/sibling the $i+1$th etc. In case of multiple extensions to the same element, the indexes are evaluated wrt. the original structure. If several insertions effect the same position, they may be executed in arbitrary ordering.

**Definition 7** Given an X-structure $\mathcal{X}$ and a set $\mathcal{I}$ of ground atoms (to be inserted), the new X-structure $\mathcal{X}' = \mathcal{X} \prec \mathcal{I}$ is obtained from $\mathcal{X}$ as follows:
- initialize  $\mathcal{A}_{\mathcal{X}'}(\text{child}, v)) := \mathcal{A}_{\mathcal{X}}(\text{child}, v))$, and
  $\mathcal{A}_{\mathcal{X}'}(\text{attribute}, v)) := \mathcal{A}_{\mathcal{X}}(\text{attribute}, v))$, for all nodes $v \in \mathcal{V}$, and
  $\mathcal{I}_{\mathcal{X}'}(p) := \mathcal{I}_{\mathcal{X}}(p) \cup \{(x_1, \ldots, x_n) \mid p(x_1, \ldots, x_n) \in \mathcal{I}$ is a predicate atom$\}$
- for all elements of $\mathcal{A}_{\mathcal{X}}(\text{child}, x)$, $\alpha(\mathcal{A}_{\mathcal{X}}(\text{child}, x)[i]) := \mathcal{A}_{\mathcal{X}'}(\text{child}, x)[i]$.
- for all atoms p[child(i)::e→y] $\in \mathcal{I}$, insert $(y, e)$ into $\mathcal{A}_{\mathcal{X}'}(\text{child}, p)$ immediately after $\alpha(\mathcal{A}_{\mathcal{X}}(\text{child}, p)[i])$.

– for all atoms x[following-sibling(i)::e→y] $\in \mathcal{I}$ s.t. p[child(j)::e→x] $\in \mathcal{X}$, insert
  $(y, e)$ into $\mathcal{A}_{\mathcal{X}'}$(child, $p$) immediately after $\alpha(\mathcal{A}_{\mathcal{X}}$(child, $x)[j{+}i])$. Similar for
  preceding-sibling.

– for all atoms p[@a→y] $\in \mathcal{I}$, append $(y, a)$ to $\mathcal{A}_{\mathcal{X}'}$(attribute, $p$).

**Definition 8 ($\mathcal{IX}_P$-Operator)** The $\mathcal{IX}$-operator works on pairs $(\mathcal{X}, Dic)$
where $\mathcal{X}$ is an X-structure, and $Dic$ is a dictionary which associates to every
rule a set $\xi$ of bindings which have been instantiated in the current iteration.
Let
$(\mathcal{X}, Dic){+}(\{(r_1, \beta_1), \ldots, (r_n, \beta_n)\}) :=$
$(\mathcal{X} \prec \{\beta_i(\text{atomize}(head(r_i))) \mid 1 \le i \le n\}, Dic.insert(\{(r_1, \beta_1), \ldots, (r_n, \beta_n)\})))$,
and $(\mathcal{X}, Dic) \downarrow_1 := \mathcal{X}$ .
For an XPathLog program $P$ and an X-structure $\mathcal{X}$,

$$\mathcal{IX}_P(\mathcal{X}, B) \quad := (\mathcal{X}, B){+}\{(r, \beta) \mid r = (h \leftarrow b) \in P \text{ and } \mathcal{X} \models \beta(b), \text{ and } (r, \beta) \notin B\},$$
$$\mathcal{IX}_P^0(\mathcal{X}) \quad := (\mathcal{X}, \emptyset) ,$$
$$\mathcal{IX}_P^{i+1}(\mathcal{X}, B) := \mathcal{IX}_P(T\mathcal{X}_P^i(\mathcal{X})) ,$$
$$\mathcal{IX}_P^\omega(\mathcal{X}, B) := \begin{cases} \lim_{i \to \infty} \mathcal{IX}_P^i(\mathcal{X}) \text{ if the sequence } \mathcal{IX}_P^0(\mathcal{X}), \mathcal{IX}_P^1(\mathcal{X}), \ldots \text{ converges,} \\ \bot \quad \text{otherwise.} \end{cases}$$

The input to an XPathLog program is an XML document $\mathcal{D}$, respectively, the
corresponding canonical X-structure $\mathcal{X}_{\mathcal{D}}$. The application of a positive XPathLog
program $P$ wrt. a given XML document $\mathcal{D}$ is defined as $P(\mathcal{D}) = (\mathcal{IX}_P^\omega(\mathcal{D}_{\mathcal{X}}, \emptyset)) \downarrow_1$.
Note that for pure Datalog programs $P$, evaluation wrt. $\mathcal{IX}_P$ does not change
the semantics, i.e., $\mathcal{IX}_P^\omega(\emptyset) = T_P^\omega(\emptyset)$ .

**General XPathLog Programs.** An XPathLog program is a declarative specification how to create a set of XML documents from one or more input documents. Since the intention of XPathLog programs is in general to implement
a stepwise process (which is also mirrored by the bottom-up evaluation strategy), the notion of *stratification* provides a solution to the problems raised by
negation. User defined stratification is supported in the LoPiX system [LoP01].

**Expressiveness and Complexity.** The relationship between XPath, XML-
QL, XQuery, and the XML Query Algebra on one side, and and XPathLog on
the other is similar as between SQL and the relational algebra on one side, and
Datalog on the other side: The output size of XML-QL and XQuery statements
is always polynomially bounded wrt. the input size (and also the computational
complexity is polynomial), and even more both are only "relationally complete".
In contrast, XPathLog allows for recursion – similar to Datalog. Thus, problems
like e.g. the transitive closure can be expressed. Even more, the result trees can
be infinite (infinitely iterating the generation of new elements), i.e., the execution
of XPathLog programs can be nonterminating (same as Datalog with function
symbols or object creation, and as F-Logic). Note that XSLT – as a functional-
style transformation language – has the same expressive power as XPathLog.
Also XML-QL and XQuery can be used for generating new XML documents

from given ones since their output format is XML, but they can only compute polynomial transformations.

# 6   Related Work and Conclusion

Other approaches to semi-structured data, especially focusing on semi-structured data as databases (in contrast to documents) are OEM [GMPQ+97], STRUDEL [FFLS97], YATL [CDSS99], and F-Logic [KLW95,LHL+98], using "proprietary" pre-XML semi-structured data models. With these, also Datalog style languages have been used for manipulating and integrating semi-structured data(bases). The OEM-based *Lorel* language has been migrated to XML in [GMW99].

Most of the XML languages are based on XPath: XPath provides the basis for the transformation language XSLT, which is – similar to XPathLog – rule-based, but following a functional idea. XQuery is a comprehensive XPath-based XML query language which also directly produces XML output. XML-QL [DFF+99] is another querying/transformation language based on matching of XML-style patterns. Whereas XSLT and XML-QL do not provide update constructs, a proposal for updates in XQuery has been presented in [TIHW01]. A detailed investigation of updates in XML, also relating XPathLog to [TIHW01] can be found in [MB01].

XPathLog allows for view definition and updates of XML data in a declarative way. It is completely XPath-based, i.e., both the rule bodies and the rule heads use an extended XPath syntax, thereby defining an update semantics for XPath expressions. The close relationship with XPath ensures that its declarative semantics is well understood from the XML perspective. Especially the nature of rule based bottom-up programming is easily understandable for XSLT practitioners, providing even more functionality. The Logic Programming background provides a strong theoretical foundation of the language. XPathLog can be used both for querying XML documents, and for restructuring and integration of XML sources (cf. [MB01]). XPathLog has been implemented in the LoPiX system [LoP01].

# References

CDSS99.     S. Cluet, C. Delobel, J. Siméon, and K. Smaga. Your Mediators need Data Conversion. In *ACM Intl. Conf. on Management of Data (SIG-MOD)*, 1999.

DFF+99.     A. Deutsch, M. Fernandez, D. Florescu, A. Levy, and D. Suciu. XML-QL: A Query Language for XML. In *8th. WWW Conference*. W3C, 1999. W3C Technical Report, www.w3.org/TR/NOTE-xml-ql.

FFLS97.     M. Fernandez, D. Florescu, A. Levy, and D. Suciu. A Query Language for a Web-Site Management System. *SIGMOD Record*, 26(3):4–11, 1997.

GMPQ+97.    H. Garcia-Molina, Y. Papakonstantinou, D. Quass, A. Rajaraman, Y. Sagiv, J. Ullman, V. Vassalos, and J. Widom. The TSIMMIS Approach to Mediation: Data Models and Languages. *Journal of Intelligent Information Systems*, 8(2), 1997.

A Rule-Based Querying and Updating Language for XML 181

GMW99.   R. Goldman, J. McHugh, and J. Widom. From semistructured data to XML: Migrating the Lore data model and query language. In *WebDB*, 1999.

HKL⁺98.   R. Himmeröder, P.-T. Kandzia, B. Ludäscher, W. May, and G. Lausen. Search, Analysis, and Integration of Web Documents: A Case Study with FLORID. In *Proc. Intl. Workshop on Deductive Databases and Logic Programming (DDLP'98)*, 1998.

KLW95.   M. Kifer, G. Lausen, and J. Wu. Logical Foundations of Object-Oriented and Frame-Based Languages. *Journal of the ACM*, 42(4):741–843, July 1995.

LHL⁺98.   B. Ludäscher, R. Himmeröder, G. Lausen, W. May, and C. Schlepphorst. Managing Semistructured Data with FLORID: A Deductive Object-Oriented Perspective. *Information Systems*, 23(8):589–612, 1998.

LoP01.   W. May. LoPiX: A System for XML Data Integration and Manipulation. In *Intl. Conf. on Very Large Data Bases (VLDB), Demo Session*, 2001. See also http://www.informatik.uni-freiburg.de/~may/lopix

May01a.   W. May. A Logic-Based Approach for Declarative XML Data Manipulation. Available from http://www.informatik.uni-freiburg.de/~may/lopix/.

May01c.   W. May. XPathLog: A Declarative, Native XML Data Manipulation Language. In *Intl. Database Engineering and Applications Symp. (IDEAS'01)*. IEEE CS Press, 2001.

MB01.   W. May and E. Behrends. On an XML Data Model for Data Integration. In *Intl. Workshop on Foundations of Models and Languages for Data and Objects (FMLDO 2001)*, To appear with Springer LNCS, 2001.

Mon.   The MONDIAL Database. http://www.informatik.uni-freiburg.de/~may/Mondial/

TIHW01.   I. Tatarinov, Z. G. Ives, A. Halevy, and D. Weld. Updating XML. *ACM Intl. Conf. on Management of Data (SIGMOD)*, 2001.

Wad99.   P. Wadler. Two semantics for XPath. 1999. http://www.cs.bell-labs.com/who/wadler/topics/xml.html.

W3C.   W3C – The World Wide Web Consortium http://www.w3.org.

XPa99.   XML Path Language (XPath). http://www.w3.org/TR/xpath, 1999.

# Linear Approximation of Semi-algebraic Spatial Databases Using Transitive Closure Logic, in Arbitrary Dimension

Floris Geerts

University of Limburg, Belgium
`floris.geerts@luc.ac.be`

**Abstract.** We consider $n$-dimensional semi-algebraic spatial databases. We compute in first-order logic extended with a transitive closure operator, a linear spatial database which characterizes the semi-algebraic spatial database up to a homeomorphism. In this way, we generalize our earlier results to semi-algebraic spatial databases in arbitrary dimensions, our earlier results being true for only two dimensions.

Consequently, we can prove that first-order logic with a transitive closure operator extended with stop conditions, can express all Boolean topological queries on semi-algebraic spatial databases of arbitrary dimension.

## 1 Introduction

Conceptually, spatial databases are possibly infinite sets of points in the $n$-dimensional Euclidean space $\mathbf{R}^n$. The framework of constraint databases, introduced in 1990 by Kanellakis, Kuper and Revesz [14,17], provides an elegant and powerful model for spatial databases. One distinguishes between *semi-algebraic spatial databases*, which store semi-algebraic sets, and *linear spatial databases*, which store semi-linear sets.

First-order logic FO over these databases yields a query language with rather poor expressive power. Its inability to define queries relying on recursion, suggests the extension of these query languages with a recursion mechanism. In this paper we consider the extension of first-order logic with transitive closure operators. Other attempts to introduce recursion mechanisms to first-order logics can be found in [9] and [15,16]. A less traditional extension of FO which can express some recursive queries is the Path Logic [3]. This logic is able to express recursive queries like the query which ask whether a database is connected, or whether two points are path connected, but the exact expressive power of this logic is not known.

First-order logic extended with a transitive closure operator, denoted by FO+TC, shares with most programming languages the disadvantage that the evaluation of its formulas is not guaranteed to terminate. However, whenever the evaluation of a formula terminates, it evaluates to an output within the constraint model.

G. Grahne and G. Ghelli (Eds.): DBPL 2001, LNCS 2397, pp. 182–197, 2002.

It is known that FO+TC with some kind of stopping condition is computationally complete on linear spatial databases where only rational coefficients are involved [8]. Indeed, this logic, denoted by FO+TCS, can easily seen to be complete on finite databases. The completeness of this logic on all linear spatial databases, is then obtained using a finite representation of these databases given by Vandeurzen et al. [20]. Since both the encoding and decoding between a linear spatial database and this finite representation are expressible in FO+TCS, we may conclude the completeness of this logic on linear spatial databases.

The use of this finite representation to obtain expressibility results for linear spatial database is ubiquitous [4,9,15,16,21]. We show that we can construct in FO+TC, a linear spatial database (and hence also a finite representation) which is homeomorphic to a given semi-algebraic spatial database input. We call this the *linearization* of a semi-algebraic spatial database. We prove that this construction terminates on all spatial database inputs. This was only known in the plane [8], and the generalization to arbitrary dimensions is far from trivial and uses results of differential topology [12], of Shiota [19] and of Rannou [18].

A direct consequence is that FO+TCS is computationally complete for Boolean topological queries on semi-algebraic spatial database. This is rather remarkable because a transitive closure, used as a recursion mechanism, is weaker than, e.g., a while-loop.

As alternative approach for expressing all topological properties of semi-algebraic spatial databases, one could add a generalized quantifier for each of these properties to FO. The query language obtained in this way is closed, i.e., every query evaluates to an output within the constraint model [3]. However, from a programming language point of view, it is more desirable to extend FO with a single programming feature (like a transitive closure operator), then to extend FO with uncountably many new features (since there are uncountably many topological properties).

The paper is organized as follows. In Sect. 2, we introduce the definitions of spatial databases, queries, and define the transitive closure logics. Section 3 shows that first-order logic is able to extract a large amount of topological information from a spatial database. This information is then put into use in Sect. 4 where we construct the linearization of a semi-algebraic spatial database. The completeness of the transitive closure logic for Boolean topological queries, is then obtained in Sect. 5. We conclude the paper with some remarks in Sect. 6

## 2    Preliminaries

A *semi-algebraic set in* $\mathbf{R}^n$ is a set of points that can be defined as a Boolean combination (union, intersection and complement) of sets of the form

$$\{(x_1, \ldots, x_n) \mid P(x_1, \ldots, x_n) \; \sigma \; 0\},$$

where $P(x_1, \ldots, x_n)$ is a multi-variate polynomial in the variables $x_1, \ldots, x_n$ with algebraic coefficients and $\sigma \in \{>, \leq\}$. A *database schema* $\mathcal{S}$ is a finite set of relation names, each with a given arity. A *semi-algebraic spatial database* over

$S$ assigns to each $S \in \mathcal{S}$ a semi-algebraic set $S^D$ in $\mathbf{R}^k$, where $k$ is the arity of $S$. If only linear polynomials are involved, one speaks about *semi-linear sets* and *linear spatial databases*. A $k$-ary *query over* $S$ is a function mapping each database over $S$ to a semi-algebraic set in $\mathbf{R}^k$.

As query language we use *first-order logic* (FO) over the vocabulary $(+, \cdot, 0, 1, <)$ expanded with the relation names in $\mathcal{S}$. A formula $\varphi(x_1, \ldots, x_k)$ expresses a $k$-ary query defined by

$$\varphi(D) := \{(x_1, \ldots, x_k) \mid \langle \mathbf{R}, D \rangle \models \varphi(x_1, \ldots, x_k)\},$$

for any database $D$. Note that $\varphi(D)$ is always semi-algebraic because all relations in $D$ are; indeed, by Tarski's theorem, relations that are first-order definable on the real ordered field are precisely the semi-algebraic sets.

As example of a query expressed in FO is the following:

$$(\exists \varepsilon > 0)(\forall x_1') \cdots (\forall x_n')(\|\boldsymbol{x} - \boldsymbol{x}'\| < \varepsilon \rightarrow S(x_1', \ldots, x_n')),$$

where $\boldsymbol{x} = (x_1, \ldots, x_n)$, and $\boldsymbol{x}' = (x_1', \ldots, x_n')$. This query maps the set $S$ to its interior. However, not every query is first-order expressible: the query which asks whether a spatial database is connected is not expressible in FO. This result and other results related to spatial databases have recently been collected in a single volume [17, Chapters 3 and 4].

We now define two extensions of first-order logic FO, both able to compute the transitive closure of a spatial database. We already introduced these logics in the context of planar spatial databases [8], but their definition did not rely on the planarity condition. These logics are not appealing from a query language point of view, since one can easily define queries with non-semi-algebraic output, hence leaving the constraint database framework. This is why we look at these recursive extensions from a programming language point of view. As in almost every programming language, programs can be written that don't halt, but it is the programmer's task to write terminating programs.

It is for this reason that we will define our logics as subclasses of programs of FO+WHILE, which is FO extended with the standard programming features of assignment statements, sequential compositions, and while-loops [13]. More specifically, a program in FO+WHILE over a schema $\mathcal{S}$, is a sequence of *assignment statements* and *while-loops*. A sufficient supply of *relation variables* is assumed, which are interpreted as new relation names not present in the given schema $\mathcal{S}$.

An assignment statement is an expression of the form

$$X := \{\boldsymbol{x} \mid \varphi(\boldsymbol{x})\},$$

where $X$ is a relation variable of arity equal to the length of the vector $\boldsymbol{x}$ of variables, and $\varphi$ is a formula in FO extended with relation variables introduced in previously occurring assignment statements.

A while-loop is an expression of the form

$$\text{WHILE} \quad \varphi \quad \text{DO} \quad P \quad \text{OD}.$$

where $\varphi$ is as above, but *without* free variables, and $P$ is in turn an FO+WHILE program, which is called the *body* of the loop.

The semantics of the program applied to an input spatial database $D$ is the operational, step-by-step execution. The effect of an assignment statement is to evaluate the query on the right-hand side on the input spatial database $D$ augmented with the values of the previously assigned relation variables, and to assign the result of this evaluation to a relation variable on the left-hand side. The effect of a while-loop is to execute the body as long as $\varphi$ evaluates to true.

It is a consequence of the closure of the logic FO, that every program expresses a computable query in FO, which however may be only partially defined because of non-terminating loops.

We now state the definitions of the programming languages FO+TC and FO+TCS.

Let $R$ be a relation variable of even arity $2k$. The following program TC:

$$X := R; Y := \emptyset; \quad (Y \text{ has arity } 2k)$$
$$\text{WHILE} \quad Y \neq X \quad \text{DO}$$
$$Y := X;$$
$$X := X \cup \{(x_1, \ldots, x_k, y_1, \ldots, y_k) \mid \exists z_1 \ldots \exists z_k (X(x_1, \ldots, x_k, z_1, \ldots, z_k)$$
$$\wedge X(z_1, \ldots, z_k, y_1, \ldots, y_k)\}$$
$$\text{OD.}$$

computes the transitive closure of the relation $R$. We shall use the notation $\mathrm{TC}(R)$ for the relation name to which we assign the result of executing the program TC on the relation $R$ in case the while-loop halts, and let $\mathrm{TC}(R)$ be undefined otherwise.

**Definition 1.** *The transitive closure logic* FO+TC *is the class of* FO+WHILE-*programs in which only programs of the above form are allowed on relation names in the schema $\mathcal{S}$ extended with relation names introduced in previously occurring assignment statements.*

Remark that inside the transitive closure no free variables are allowed! This makes FO+TC a rather weak logic, but it is sufficient for our purposes.

As an example, let $\mathcal{S} = (S)$ and let $D$ be a linear database over $\mathcal{S}$. Define the $2n$-ary relation *Path*,

$$Path(D) = \{(r, s) \mid (\exists \lambda)(0 \leq \lambda \leq 1 \wedge (\forall t)(t = \lambda \cdot r + (1 - \lambda) \cdot s \rightarrow S^D(t))\},$$

where $s, t \in \mathbf{R}^n$. It is easy to prove that the program TC terminates on every linear database $D$. Moreover, a pair of points $p$ and $q$ is in the relation $\mathrm{TC}(Path(D))$ if and only if they belong to the same connected component of $D$. Hence the connectivity of a linear database is expressible in FO+TC.

We now introduce an extension of FO+TC which allows some general FO-formula without free variables $\sigma$ in the condition in the while-loop. More specific, consider the following program TCS:

$X := R; Y := \emptyset;$    ($Y$ has arity $2k$)
WHILE   $Y \neq X \wedge \neg\sigma(X)$   DO
  $Y := X;$
  $X := X \cup \{(x_1, \ldots, x_k, y_1, \ldots, y_k) \mid \exists z_1 \ldots \exists z_k (X(x_1, \ldots, x_k, z_1, \ldots, z_k)$
$\wedge\, X(z_1, \ldots, z_k, y_1, \ldots, y_k)\}$
OD.

The condition $\sigma$ is called the *stop condition*. This program computes either the transitive closure of the relation $R$, in case the condition $\sigma$ is never satisfied, or it computes the first $p$-stages of the transitive closure of the relation of $R$, where $p$ is the minimal number of cycles of the while-loop such that the condition $\sigma$ is satisfied. We shall denote by $\mathrm{TCS}(R)$ the relation name to which we assign the result of executing the program TCS on the relation $R$, in case the while-loop halts, and let $\mathrm{TCS}(R)$ be undefined, otherwise. The relation name $X$ is reserved for the current stage in the computation inside a while-loop.

**Definition 2.** *The transitive closure logic with stop condition* FO+TCS *is the class of* FO+WHILE-*programs in which only programs of the above form are allowed on relation names in the schema $S$ extended with relation names introduced in previously occurring assignment statements.*

Note again that no free variables are allowed inside the transitive closure. It is then also surprising that this logic is already computationally complete for Boolean topological queries. As an example, let $R := \{(x, y) \mid y = 2x\}$ whose transitive closure $\mathrm{TC}(R)$ is not a semi-algebraic set. Take as stop condition the formula $\sigma(X) := X(1, 8)$. The while-loop then terminates after three cycles, and the result is a semi-linear set consisting of three lines through the origin.

## 3   Local Topological Characterization

A well-known property of semi-algebraic sets, is that locally around each point, a semi-algebraic set is homeomorphic to a cone. Let $A$ be a semi-algebraic set in $\mathbf{R}^n$. A *cone radius of $A$ in a point $p$*, is a radius around $p$ in which this behavior shows. A first question one can ask, is whether a *cone radius query* is expressible in FO. This query must return for a semi-algebraic set $A$, a set of pairs $(r, p)$ giving for every point $p$ a cone radius $r$ of $A$ in $p$. A second question one can ask is whether there exists a *uniform cone radius* of a semi-algebraic set $A$. By a uniform cone radius, we mean a real number which is a cone radius of $A$ in every point of $A$. We will answer these questions in the following sections.

### 3.1   Expressibility of the Cone Radius in FO

Let $A \subseteq \mathbf{R}^n$ be a semi-algebraic set and $p \in \mathbf{R}^n$. We define the *cone with base $A$ and top $p$* as the union of all closed line segments between $p$ and points in $A$. We denote this set by $\mathrm{Cone}(A, p)$. For a point $p \in \mathbf{R}^n$ and $\varepsilon > 0$, denote the closed ball centered at $p$ with radius $\varepsilon$ by $B^n(p, \varepsilon)$, and denote its boundary sphere by $S^{n-1}(p, \varepsilon)$. We denote the closure of a set $A$ by $\mathrm{clo}(A)$, and the interior of $A$

by int($A$). The following theorem formalizes the property of semi-algebraic set mentioned above. The boundary of $A$, clo($A$) $- A$, will be denoted by $\partial A$.

**Theorem 1 ([1,5]).** *Let $A \subseteq \mathbf{R}^n$ be a semi-algebraic set and $p$ a point of $A$. Then there is a real number $\varepsilon > 0$ such that the intersection $A \cap B^n(p, \varepsilon)$ is homeomorphic to the set* Cone($A \cap S^{n-1}(p, \varepsilon), p$).

A naive way of checking in first-order logic whether a real number $r$ is a cone radius of $A$ in $p$, is just testing if the sets Cone($A \cap S^{n-1}(p, \varepsilon), p$) and $A \cap B^n(p, \varepsilon)$ are homeomorphic. However, it is known that the query which tests whether two semi-algebraic sets in $\mathbf{R}^n$ (with $n > 1$) are homeomorphic, is not in FO [2,10,11].

We showed rather ad hoc, that a cone radius query is first-order expressible for planar spatial databases [7]. The following result extends this to $n$-dimensional semi-algebraic spatial databases.

**Theorem 2.** *Let $A$ be a semi-algebraic set in $\mathbf{R}^n$. There exists a cone radius query*

$$\varphi_{radius} : A \mapsto \{(r, p) \mid r \text{ is a cone radius of } A \text{ in } p\},$$

*which is expressible in FO.*

*Proof (sketch).* We first sketch the prove in case $A$ is a closed semi-algebraic set which has a tangent space in every of its points, and then sketch how the general case can be treated.

**Case 1.** $A$ is closed and $A$ has a tangent space in every of its points.

Let $p \in \mathbf{R}^n$ and let $f_p : A \to \mathbf{R} : x \mapsto \|x - p\|^2$, where $\|\cdot\|$ denote the Euclidean distance. The tangent space of $A$ in $x$, denoted by $T_x A$, is the secant limits set

$$T_x A := \bigcap_{\eta > 0} \text{clo}(\{\lambda(u - v) \in \mathbf{R}^n \mid \lambda \in \mathbf{R} \wedge u, v \in A \cap B^n(x, \eta)\}),$$

and hence the query $\varphi_{\text{tangent}} : A \mapsto (x, T_x A)$ is expressible in FO (see [18] for more details). The mapping $f : A \to \mathbf{R}$ induces a linear mapping, called the *differential* between tangent spaces, $df_p : T_x A \to \mathbf{R}$ which maps (as it can be easily verified) a tangent vector $v \in T_x A$ to the scalar product $2v \cdot (x - p) \in \mathbf{R}$.

We now use Thom's First Isotopy Lemma [19, Theorem II.6.2], which says (adapted to our setting) that **if** (i) in every point of $A$ the tangent space exists (which is the case by assumption), (ii) the mapping $f_p : A \to \mathbf{R}$ is continuous and has continuous derivatives (this is the case), (iii) the set $f_p^{-1}([c, d])$ is a compact set for any closed interval $[c, d]$ of $\mathbf{R}$ (this is true since $A$ is closed), and (iv)

$$f_p|(A \cap \text{int}(B^n(p, b) - \{p\})) \longrightarrow (0, b) \subseteq \mathbf{R} \tag{1}$$

has no critical points (this will shortly be explained), **then** there exists a homeomorphism

$$h' : (A \cap S^{n-1}(p, c)) \times (0, c] \to A \cap B^n(p, c) - \{p\}, \tag{2}$$

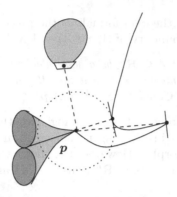

**Fig. 1.** Illustration of the cone radius query of Theorem 2.

where $c \in (0, b)$. Moreover, there exists such a homeomorphism $h'$ for any $c \in (0, b)$. Since the cylindrical set at the left in (2) is homeomorphic to the cone set $\mathrm{Cone}(A \cap S^{n-1}(p, c), p) - \{p\}$ in a straightforward way, we obtain a homeomorphism $h$ between

$$h : A \cap B^n(p, c) - \{p\} \to \mathrm{Cone}(A \cap S^{n-1}(p, c), p) - \{p\}.$$

This homeomorphism can easily be extended to $A \cap B^n(p, c)$ by defining $h(p) = p$. In this way, we have shown that any $c \in (0, b)$ is in fact a cone radius of $A$ in the point $p$. To show that there exists a cone radius query which is expressible in FO, we need to show that for each point $p$, an interval $(0, b)$ is expressible in FO, satisfying condition (1), the other conditions being trivially satisfied. The *critical points* of $f_p|A$ are defined as the points $x$ in $A$ such that the differential $df_p|A$ is not surjective. From this we can deduce that $x$ is a critical point of $f_p|A$ if and only if $2v \cdot (x - p) = 0$ for all tangent vectors $v \in T_x A$. In other words, $x$ is a critical point of $f_p|A$ if and only if $T_x A$ is orthogonal to the vector $x - p$. This can clearly be expressed in FO. Define the set of *critical values* of $f_p|A$ as the image by $f_p$ of the critical points. It is a consequence of Sard's Theorem [1, Theorem 2.5.11] that this is a finite set. We therefore, define $\varphi_{\mathrm{radius}}$ as

$$\varphi_{\mathrm{radius}} : A \mapsto \{(r', p) \mid \forall \text{ critical values } r \text{ of } f_p \Rightarrow r' < r\}.$$

This concludes the proof for the case that $A$ is closed and in all points of $A$ the tangent space exists. We have illustrated the construction in the proof in Figure 1. In this figure, we have drawn a spatial database centered around the point $p$, and also identified points $q$ whose tangent lines are orthogonal to the vector $p - q$. We have drawn dotted circles through these points. Note that the topology of the intersection of a circle with center at the point $p$, and the spatial database, is unchanged between two consecutive dotted circles, as is predicted by Thom's Isotopy Lemma.

**Case 2.** $A$ is an arbitrary semi-algebraic set in $\mathbf{R}^n$.

We then consider a Whitney stratification (decomposition into a finite number of sets, called strata) of the closure of $A$, such that $A$ is the union of connected components of these strata. The strata are semi-algebraic sets satisfying Whitney's condition and in each point of a stratum the tangent space exists [18]. We then find an interval $(0, b)$ such that condition (iv) is satisfied simultaneously for all strata. Thom's First Isotopy Lemma for sets admitting a Whitney stratification (like semi-algebraic sets), guarantees again the correctness of this procedure. To show the expressibility in FO, it is sufficient to prove that a Whitney stratification is expressible in first-order logic. This can be shown using results from Rannou [18] by not expecting the strata to be connected and not expecting the so-called frontier condition on the stratification.                                  □

## 3.2   Uniform Cone Radius Decomposition

Although every point of a semi-algebraic set has a cone radius which is strictly greater than zero (Theorem 1), we are now interested in finding a *uniform cone radius* of a semi-algebraic set. We define the uniform cone radius of semi-algebraic set $A \subseteq \mathbf{R}^n$ as a real number $\varepsilon_A > 0$ such that $\varepsilon_A$ is a cone radius of $A$ in all its points. As shall be clear from the next Section, this radius offers the right information for constructing a *linearization of $A$*, i.e., a linear set homeomorphic to $A$.

A first observation is that the uniform cone radius of a semi-algebraic set, or even a semi-linear set not always exists. Consider for example two lines in $\mathbf{R}^3$ which intersect in a point $p$. It is clear that the cone radius of points approaching the point $p$ converge to zero. We define the $\varepsilon$-neighborhood of a semi-algebraic set $A \subset \mathbf{R}^n$ as

$$A^\varepsilon := \{x \in \mathbf{R}^n \mid (\exists y)\, (y \in A \wedge \|x - y\| < \varepsilon)\}.$$

**Theorem 3.** *Let $A$ be a semi-algebraic set in $\mathbf{R}^n$. Then there exists a finite decomposition into semi-algebraic sets* $\mathrm{clo}(A) = A_d \cup A_{d-1} \cdots A_\ell$, *satisfying* $\dim(A_\ell) < \cdots < \dim(A_{d-1}) < \dim(A_d) = \dim(A)$, *and such that for any tuple* $\varepsilon = (\varepsilon_1, \ldots, \varepsilon_n)$ *of positive real numbers, the sets*

$$A_i - \bigcup_{j=\ell}^{i-1} A_j^{\varepsilon_j}, \quad \text{for } i = \ell, \ldots, d, \tag{3}$$

*all have a uniform cone radius if they are not empty.*

*Proof (sketch).* We first define a semi-algebraic mapping $\gamma : \mathrm{clo}(A) \to \mathbf{R}$ which associates to each point $p$ of $A$ a cone radius of $A$ in $p$, and to each point of $\mathrm{clo}(A) - A$ a cone radius of $\mathbf{R}^n - A$ in $p$. In view of Theorem 2, this mapping is FO+POLY-definable. Define the set

$$\Gamma(A) := \{p \in \mathrm{clo}(A) \mid \gamma|A \text{ is not continuous in } p\}.$$

It can be shown that the dimension of the semi-algebraic set $\Gamma(A)$, is strictly less than the dimension of $A$.

We shall denote the closure in $clo(A)$ of the set $\Gamma(A)$, by $\Sigma(A)$. Furthermore, let $\Sigma^d(A) := clo(A)$, $\Sigma^{d-1}(A) := \Sigma(A)$, and let $\Sigma^k(A) := \Sigma(\Sigma^{k+1}(A))$, for $k = \ell, \ell+1, \ldots, d$, where $\ell$ is minimal integer such that $\Sigma^\ell(A) \neq \emptyset$.

Define for $k = \ell, \ell+1, \ldots, d$, the semi-algebraic sets $A_k := \Sigma^{k+1}(A) - \Sigma^k(A)$. In this way we obtain a decomposition of $clo(A)$. Now, $A_\ell$ is the set for which the set $\Sigma(A_\ell)$ is empty, and $A_\ell$ is closed. Hence, $\gamma(A_\ell)$ is closed because $\gamma|A$ is continuous, and we define the uniform cone radius of $A_\ell$ as

$$\varepsilon_\ell := \min\{\gamma(\boldsymbol{p}) \mid \boldsymbol{p} \in A_\ell\}.$$

We now prove the theorem for $A_{i+1} - \bigcup_{j=\ell}^i A_j^{\varepsilon_j}$. Let $\eta = \min\{\varepsilon_\ell, \ldots, \varepsilon_i\}$, then we have,

$$\Sigma^i(A)^\eta \subseteq \bigcup_{j=\ell}^i A_j^{\varepsilon_j}.$$

Similarly as for $A_\ell$, $\Sigma^{i+1}(A) - \Sigma^i(A)^\eta$ is closed and the restriction of $\gamma$ to $(\Sigma^{i+1}(A) - \Sigma^i(A)^\eta)$ is continuous. Hence, the following minimum exists

$$\varepsilon_{i+1} := \min\{\gamma(\boldsymbol{p}) \mid \boldsymbol{p} \in A_{i+1} - \bigcup_{j=\ell}^i A_j^{\varepsilon_j}\}$$

and is a uniform cone radius of $A_{i+1} - \bigcup_{j=\ell}^i A_j^{\varepsilon_j}$.                    □

Define the queries $\varphi_{\text{uniform},k} : A \mapsto \emptyset$ if $k > \dim(A)$, and $\varphi_{\text{uniform},k} : A \mapsto A_k \cap A$ if $k \leqslant \dim(A)$. Note that for $k < \ell$, the result of the query $\varphi_{\text{uniform},k}$ will be the empty set. The next corollary follows immediately from the construction in the proof of Theorem 3 and the fact that the query $\varphi_{\dim} : A \mapsto \dim(A)$ is expressible in FO (see [18]).

**Corollary 1.** *Let $A$ be a semi-algebraic set in $\mathbf{R}^n$, then the queries $\varphi_{uniform,k}$, for $k = 1, \ldots, n$, are all expressible in FO.*

## 4    Linearization of a Semi-algebraic Set

The aim of this section is to construct a semi-linear set $\hat{A} \subset \mathbf{R}^n$ which is homeomorphic to a given semi-algebraic set $A \subset \mathbf{R}^n$. We call the set $\hat{A}$ the *linearization* of $A$. We may assume that $A$ is a bounded semi-algebraic set (if $A$ is unbounded, we first apply the homeomorphism $\boldsymbol{x} \mapsto \boldsymbol{x}/(1 + \|\boldsymbol{x}\|)$)

Let $A$ be a semi-algebraic set in $\mathbf{R}^n$, and let $\boldsymbol{p}$ be a point in $A$. Let $\varepsilon_{\boldsymbol{p}}$ be a cone radius of $A$ in $\boldsymbol{p}$. Consider an $n$-dimensional box $B$, defined as $[a_1, a_1 + \delta] \times \cdots \times [a_n, a_n + \delta] \subset \mathbf{R}^n$, such that $\boldsymbol{p}$ is in the interior of the box $B$, and such that the diagonal of $B$ (which equals $\sqrt{n}\delta$), is smaller than $\varepsilon_{\boldsymbol{p}}$. We know from Theorem 1, that with respect to the topology of $A$, inside a ball *Ball* of radius

$\varepsilon_p$ around $p$, the semi-algebraic set $A$ can be replaced with $\mathrm{Cone}(A \cap \partial Ball, p)$. We can prove an equivalent of Theorem 1, where $n$-dimensional boxes replace the $n$-dimensional balls. Due to space limitations, we omit the details. Hence, with respect to the topology of $A$, inside $B$, the semi-algebraic set $A$ can be replaced with $\mathrm{Cone}(A \cap \partial B, p)$. The whole idea of the algorithm is based on the observation that *a cone is semi-linear if its base set is semi-linear.*

Therefore, in order to linearize the set $B \cap A$, we could first try to linearize the set $\partial B \cap A$ on the boundary of the box in such a way that it remains on the boundary of the box, and then construct the cone.

This suggests the following algorithm which takes as input a semi-algebraic set $A$, and outputs a linearization $\hat{A}$ of $A$. Let $\mathcal{P}_k$ with $k = 0, \ldots, n$, denote finite relations consisting of pairs $(B, p)$, where $B$ is a $k$-dimensional box and $p \in \mathrm{int}(B)$.

LINEARIZE$(A, n)$:

- If $n = 0$, this means that $A$ is a finite set. We then add $(p, p)$ to $\mathcal{P}_0$ for each $p \in A$.
- Cover $A$ with $n$-dimensional boxes $\{B_n^{(i)} \mid i \in I_n\}$ for some finite index set $I_n$, such that for each $i \in I_n$, there exists a point $p_{B_n^{(i)}}$ in the interior of $B_n^{(i)}$, whose cone radius exceeds the diagonal of this box. For each $i \in I_n$, we add all pairs $(B_n^{(i)}, p_{B_n^{(i)}})$ to the relation $\mathcal{P}_n$.
- If $n > 0$, then apply LINEARIZE$(A \cap B', n - 1)$, where $B'$ is an $(n - 1)$-dimensional box on the boundary of some box $B_n^{(i)}$. Here, we interpret $A \cap B'$ as a semi-algebraic set in $\mathbf{R}^{n-1}$. This can easily be achieved since the $(n-1)$-dimensional boxes are parallel to one of the coordinate planes $H_i := \{x \in \mathbf{R}^n \mid x_i = 0\}$.
- Inductively, the algorithm constructed a linear set $\hat{A}_{n-1}$ on the boundaries of each $n$-dimensional box $B$ in $\mathcal{P}_n$ such that $\partial B \cap A$ is homeomorphic to $\partial B \cap \hat{A}_{n-1}$. We now construct the cone with top $p_B$ and base $\partial B \cap \hat{A}_{n-1}$ for each pair $(B, p_B) \in \mathcal{P}_n$. By definition of the points $p_B$ this gives a set homeomorphic to $A \cap B$. When the cones are constructed for all boxes in $\mathcal{P}_n$, we have obtained a linear set $\hat{A}_n$ which is homeomorphic to the input set $A$.

We now explain two steps of the algorithm LINEARIZE in more detail.

## 4.1   Construction of the Box Covering

We define the $n$-dimensional standard grid of size $\delta$ as the set of $n$-dimensional boxes of the form $[k_1\delta, (k_1 + 1)\delta] \times \cdots [k_n\delta, (k_n + 1)\delta]$, where $k_1, k_2, \ldots, k_n \in \mathbf{Z}$. We define a *box covering of size $\delta$* of a semi-algebraic set $A$, denoted by $A_\delta$, as a those boxes in the standard grid of size $\delta$, which intersect the closure of $A$. By the Dichotomy Theorem [4], it is easy to show that the query which maps a semi-algebraic set to its box covering of size $\delta$ is not expressible in FO+POLY.

**Lemma 1.** *The query $\varphi_{cover} : A \mapsto A_\delta$ which maps a spatial database to its the box covering of size $\delta$, is expressible in* FO+TC.

*Proof (sketch).* One represents boxes of size $\delta$ by means of $2n$-tuples $(a_1, a_1 + \delta, \ldots, a_n, a_n + \delta)$ of real numbers $a_i \in \mathbf{R}$. Let $\mathcal{B}$ be the set of all such tuples, and define an $4n$-ary adjacency relation $Adj$ on this set. We have that $Adj(B_1, B_2)$ for two tuples $B_1$ and $B_2$ of $\mathcal{B}$ if the intersection of the boxes they represent is the union of lower (less than $n$) dimensional pieces of these boxes. As above, we may assume that $A$ is bounded. We define the bounding box of $A$, as the set $[-M, M]^n$ such that $1/2$-neighborhood $A^{1/2}$ is strictly included in $[-M, M]^n$. The computation of the transitive closure $\text{TC}\{Adj(B_1, B_2) \mid B_i \cap [-M, M]^n \neq \emptyset\}$ then terminates, and the box covering $A_\delta$ of size $\delta$ are those boxes in this transitive closure which are in relation with the $(0, \delta, \ldots, 0, \delta)$ and intersect the closure of $A$. □

Suppose that a uniform cone radius of $A$ exists. Let $\varepsilon$ such radius, and let $A_\delta$ be the box covering of $A$ of size $\delta$, where $\delta^2 < (\varepsilon^2/n)$. We require for this covering that for each $n$-dimensional box $B \in A_\delta$ we have that $\text{int}(B) \cap A \neq \emptyset$, so we can select a point $p_B$ in this interior whose cone radius is larger than the diagonal $\delta$ of $B$.

Of course, this property is not automatically satisfied. Some of the boxes in $A_\delta$ may intersect $A$ only in its boundary. To avoid this, we bring the covering $A_\delta$ in *general position* [12]. Formally, we require that $A_\delta$ and $A$ are *transversal* in $\mathbf{R}^n$, or in symbols, that $A_\delta \pitchfork A$. The formal definition of transversality only makes sense when all points in $A_\delta$ and $A$ have a tangent spaces. So we shall consider a decomposition of $A_\delta$ and $A$ into sets such that the tangent space exists in every point of these sets. The construction of these decompositions is similar (but easier) to the decomposition in Theorem 2 and can also be performed in FO. So, let $A = \{A_0, \ldots, A_n\}$, and $A_\delta = \{A_{\delta,0}, \ldots, A_{\delta,n}\}$ the decompositions of $A$ and $A_\delta$. Then $A_\delta$ is called transversal to $A$ in $\mathbf{R}^n$, if $A_{\delta,i}$ is transversal to $A_j$ in $\mathbf{R}^n$ for any $i$ and $j$. This means that in every point $x$ in the intersection $A_\delta \cap A$, the following holds for any $i$ and $j$,

$$T_x A_{\delta,i} \oplus T_x A_j = \mathbf{R}^n. \tag{4}$$

To get an idea of what this transversality condition means, we suppose that $n = 3$, that $A_\delta$ consist of a single box $B$ and that the dimension of $A$ equals two. Moreover, we assume that the tangent space exists in every point of $A$. We decompose the box $B$ into its interior $A_{\delta,3}$, its 6 two-dimensional faces $A_{\delta,2}$, its 12 one-dimensional edges $A_{\delta,1}$, and its 8 vertices $A_{\delta,0}$. From condition 4 and the fact that $\dim(A) = 2$, it follows that $A$ cannot intersect in one of vertices in $A_{\delta,0}$. Figure 2 shows one examples of a transversal (left) and two non-transversal intersections (right) of $A$ with the edges and faces of $B$. It is easy to show that if a box $B$ intersects $A$ transversally, then $\text{int}(B) \cap A \neq \emptyset$, so the question is how to force the transversality of $A$ and boxes in $A_\delta$. Fortunately, *almost all* coverings are already fine. More specifically, we can prove the following lemma

**Lemma 2.** *Let $A$ be a semi-algebraic set in $\mathbf{R}^n$, and let $B$ a $n$-dimensional box. Let $b$ be a positive real number. Define the set of vectors*

$$T_b(B) := \{v \in \mathbf{R}^n \mid \|v\| < b \wedge B + v \pitchfork A\},$$

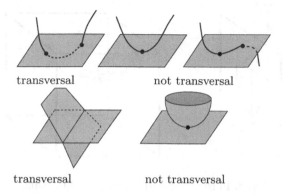

transversal                    not transversal

transversal                    not transversal

**Fig. 2.** Illustration of the notion of transversality.

where $B + v = \{x \mid x - v \in B\}$ is a translation of $B$. Then $T_b$ is dense in the set of vectors of norm smaller than $b$.

Consider the covering $A_\delta$ and let $d$ be the minimal distance from $A$ to the boundary of $A_\delta$. From the above lemma, we then can always select a translation $\tau \in T_{d/2}(B)$ such that $B + \tau \pitchfork A$, with $B \in A_\delta$. Since $A_\delta$ consists of a finite number of boxes, the set $\bigcap_i T_{d/2}(B_i)$ is also dense in the set of vectors of norm less than $d/2$. We can select a vector $v$ in this intersection in FO. Indeed, transversality and hence also the set $T_b$ for any $b > 0$ are expressible in FO. Since this translation is strictly smaller than $d$, $\mathbb{A} + \tau$ is still a covering of $A$, and we have found a covering which has the desired properties.

Suppose that $A$ has no uniform cone radius. Then we apply Theorem 3 and we get the decomposition $A = A_\ell \cup \ldots \cup A_d$. We start with a box covering $A_\delta^\ell$ of $A_\ell$, because this set has a uniform cone radius. Suppose that we already have constructed a box covering $A_\delta^{k-1}$ of the set $A_\ell \cup \ldots \cup A_{k-1}$. We then consider the set $A' = A_k - (A_\ell \cup \ldots \cup A_{k-1})^{d_{k-1}}$, where $d_{k-1}$ is a positive real number satisfying certain conditions.

This numbers ensure that after translating the covering $A_\delta^{k-1}$ with a small translation, no new pieces of $A_k$ get uncovered. So it is sufficient to cover the set $A'$. This is possible because by Theorem 3 this set has a uniform cone radius. We take the intersection $A_{\delta,\cap}$ of the coverings $(A')_\delta$ and $A_\delta^{k-1}$, and define

$$A_\delta^k = A_\delta^{k-1} \cup ((A')_\delta - A_{\delta,\cap}).$$

We then show an equivalent of Lemma 2 which takes into account the multiple sets $A_\ell, \ldots, A_d$. In this way, we obtain a covering $A_\delta$ which satisfies our requirements.

To conclude, we construct a relation $R = \{(B, p) \mid B \in A_\delta \wedge p \in A \cap \mathrm{int}(B)\}$. Note that for every box $B \in A_\delta$ there exists at least a single point $p$ in its interior. So, we can select a unique representative $p_B$ in the interior of $B$. We define the relation $\mathcal{P}_n$ containing the pairs $(B, p_B)$ for each $B \in A_\delta$. Of course, the points $p_B$ will be the tops of the cones, when linearizing the set $A$.

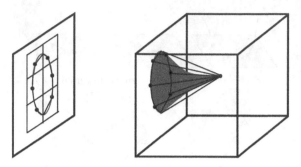

**Fig. 3.** Illustration of the algorithm LINEARIZE.

### 4.2   Inductive Application of the Algorithm

Consider for the moment a single $n$-dimensional box $B$ of the covering $A_\delta$. We regard the intersection $\partial B \cap A$ as the union of $2n$ $(n-1)$-dimensional sets parallel to one of $n$-coordinate planes $H_i$. We identify these sets with $\mathbf{R}^{n-1}$ by means of an orthogonal projection. The box covering construction can then be applied to this set in $\mathbf{R}^{n-1}$. Finally we can then bring it back, using the inverse projection, to the boundary of the box.

Let us focus on a single hyperplane $H$ which is identified with $\mathbf{R}^{n-1}$. We want to cover the intersection of $\partial B \cap A \cap H$ with $(n-1)$-dimensional boxes. In the last section, we saw that we sometimes needed to translate the covering a bit in order to satisfy our requirements. Moreover, we want the covering to be compatible with the $(n-1)$-dimensional boxes, induced by the intersection of the covering $A_\delta$ with the hyperplane $H$. In this way, we will be able to construct a homeomorphism between $A$ and the linearization $\hat{A}$ in a patchwork-like way. However, some of the boundaries of the $(n-1)$-dimensional boxes will come from this intersection, while others are from the new covering in the hyperplane $H$. While we may translate this last covering, we need to keep the intersection induced by $A_\delta$ fixed. Otherwise, we would have to construct a parameterized box covering, which is not possible in FO+TC since no free variables are allowed inside a transitive closure. Thanks to the following property, the boxes induced by this intersection are already in general position.

**Proposition 1.** *Let $A_\delta$ be an $n$-dimensional box covering which intersects a semi-algebraic set $A$ in $\mathbf{R}^n$ transversally. Let $H$ be an $(n-1)$-hyperplane in which $(n-1)$-dimensional boxes $B'_1, \dots, B'_k$ on the boundaries of boxes of $A_\delta$ lie. Then the set of boxes $B'_1, \dots, B'_k$ intersects the set $A \cap H$ transversally in $H$.*

So, we only need to bring the new box covering in general position.We then may apply the same construction to all boundaries of all boxes in $A_\delta$. In this way we obtain a relation $\mathcal{P}_{n-1}$ consisting of pairs $(B, \boldsymbol{p}_B)$ where $B$ is box in one of the $n-1$-dimensional coverings.

In Figure 3 we illustrated the idea of the algorithm on a simple three-dimensional example. The set inside the box is linearized, after linearizing the figure on the left face of the cube and then constructing the cone, as showed in the figure.

### 4.3  Expressing the Construction in Transitive Closure Logic

From Lemma 1 we know that the query $\varphi_{\text{cover}}$ is expressible in FO+TC. Corollary 1 shows that the queries $\varphi_{\text{uniform},k}$ are all expressible in FO. From the construction above, it is clear that a translation vector of Lemma 2 can be selected in FO. This shows that the basic ingredients of the algorithm LINEARIZE, are expressible in FO+TC. Since the dimension of the real space $\mathbf{R}^n$ is fixed, we only get a recursion depth of $n$ in the algorithm, and this can be written as a single FO formula. In short,

**Theorem 4.** *It is possible in* FO+TC, *to construct a semi-linear set* $\hat{A}$ *which is homeomorphic to the original semi-algebraic set* $A$.

## 5  Completeness Result

We now refine the geometric construction such that the $n+1$ relations $\mathcal{P}_n, \ldots, \mathcal{P}_0$ consists of rational values only.

**Theorem 5.** *Rational linearizations of spatial databases are expressible in the transitive closure logic* FO+TC.

*Proof.* We can obtain this result easily by modifying the proof of Theorem 4 such that boxes are used which have corner points with rational coordinates. The selection of the top of the cones in these boxes then consists of selecting the center of the box, which has rational coordinates also.    □

We now recall the definition of a complete query language. A logic $\mathcal{L}$ is called *complete* for a class of databases if for each computable query $Q$ on this class of databases, there exists a formula $\varphi_Q \in \mathcal{L}$, such that for each database $D$ in this class,

$$Q(D) := \{\boldsymbol{x} \mid \langle D, \boldsymbol{x} \rangle \models \varphi_Q(\boldsymbol{x})\}.$$

Nothing is said however on the evaluation of these formulas $\varphi_Q$. A logic $\mathcal{L}$ is said to be *computationally complete* if it is complete and if the query $Q$ is defined on a database $D$, then the evaluation of $\varphi_Q(D)$ must be finite.

For arbitrary spatial databases we show that FO+TCS is computationally complete for Boolean topological queries. A query $Q$ is said to be *topological*, if for any two spatial databases $A$ and $B$ for which there exists a homeomorphism $h$ of $\mathbf{R}^n$ such that $h(A) = B$, then $Q(A) = Q(B)$ holds.

We will need the following result

**Theorem 6 ([8]).** FO+TCS *is computationally complete on linear spatial databases involving only rational coefficients.*

A direct consequence is then:

**Theorem 7.** *All computable Boolean topological queries on spatial databases can be expressed in* FO+TCS *in an effective way.*

*Proof.* by Theorem 5, there exists an FO+TC formula $Q_{\text{approx}}$ that defines, for any given spatial database $A$, a linear spatial database $\hat{A}$ such that there exists a homeomorphism $h$ from $\mathbf{R}^n$ to $\mathbf{R}^n$ such that $h(A) = \hat{A}$.

Let $Q$ be a Boolean topological computable query. Since $Q$ is computable, it is in particular computable on linear spatial databases involving only rational coefficients, and therefore, by Theorem 6 expressible on these databases by an FO+TCS formula $\varphi_Q$. It is clear that

$$Q(A) := \text{True iff } \varphi_Q(Q_{\text{approx}}(A)) := \text{True},$$

which concludes the proof. $\qquad\qquad\qquad\qquad\qquad\qquad\qquad\qquad\qquad\qquad\square$

# 6   Concluding Remarks

We showed that it is possible in first-order logic extended with a transitive closure operator to construct from a semi-algebraic spatial database, a homeomorphic linear spatial database. The existence of a finite representation of linear spatial database, makes it possible to obtain expressiveness results. It is an interesting question whether there exists natural extensions of FO, which can compute a finite representation of semi-algebraic spatial databases, without the deviation to the linear case.

# References

1. R. Benedetti and J.J. Risler. *Real Algebraic and Semi-algebraic Sets.* Hermann, Paris, 1990.
2. M. Benedikt, G. Dong, L. Libkin, and L. Wong. Relational expressive power of constraint query languages. *Journal of the ACM*, 45(1):1–34, 1998.
3. M. Benedikt, M. Grohe, L. Libkin, and L. Segoufin. Reachability and connectivity queries in constraint databases. In *Proceedings of the 19th ACM Symposium on Principles of Database Systems*, pages 104–115. ACM Press, 2000.
4. M. Benedikt and L. Libkin. Safe constraint queries. *SIAM Journal of Computing*, 29(5):1652–1682, 2000.
5. J. Bochnak, M. Coste, and M.-F. Roy. *Real Algebraic Geometry*, volume 36 of *Ergebenisse der Mathematik und ihrer Grenzgebiete.* Springer-Verlag, 1998.
6. A. Chandra and D. Harel. Computable queries for relational data bases. *Journal of Computer and System Sciences*, 21(2):156–178, 1980.
7. F. Geerts and B. Kuijpers. Expressing topological connectivity of spatial databases. In *Research Issues in Structured and Semistructured Database Programming. Proceedings of the 8th International Workshop on Database Programming Languages*, volume 1949 of *Lecture Notes in Computer Science*, pages 224–238. Springer-Verlag, 1999.
8. F. Geerts and B. Kuijpers. Linear approximation of planar spatial databases using transitive-closure logic. In *Proceedings of the 19th ACM Symposium on Principles of Database Systems*, pages 126–135. ACM Press, 2000.

9. S. Grumbach and G. Kuper. Tractable recursion over geometric data. In G. Smolka, editor, *Proceedings of the 3rd Conference on Principles and Practice of Constraint Programming*, volume 1330 of Lecture Notes in Computer Science, pages 450–462. Springer-Verlag, 1997.

10. S. Grumbach and J. Su. Finitely representable databases. *Journal of Computer and System Sciences*, 55(2):273–298, 1997.

11. S. Grumbach and J. Su. Queries with arithmetical constraints. *Theoretical Computer Science*, 173(1):151–181, 1997.

12. V. Guillemin and A. Pollack. *Differential topology*. Prentice-Hall, 1974.

13. M. Gyssens, J. Van den Bussche, and D. Van Gucht. Complete geometrical query languages. *Journal of Computer and System Sciences*, 58(1):483–511, 1999.

14. P.C. Kanellakis, G.M. Kuper, and P.Z. Revesz. Constraint query languages. *Journal of Computer and System Science*, 51(1):26–52, 1995.

15. S. Kreutzer. Fixed-point query languages for linear constraint databases. In *Proceedings of the 19th ACM Symposium on Principles of Database Systems*, pages 116–125. ACM Press, 2000.

16. S. Kreutzer. Query languages for constraint databases: First-order logic, fixed-points, and convex hulls. In J. Van den Bussche and V. Vianu, editors, *Proceedings of the 9th International Conference on Database Theory*, volume 1973 of *Lecture Notes in Computer Science*, pages 248–262. Springer-Verlag, 2001.

17. G.M. Kuper, J. Paredaens, and L. Libkin, editors. *Constraint Databases*. Springer-Verlag, 1999.

18. E. Rannou. The complexity of stratification computation. *Discrete and Computational Geometry*, 19:47–79, 1998.

19. M. Shiota. *Geometry of Subanalytic and Semialgebraic Sets*. Birkhäuser, 1997.

20. L. Vandeurzen, M. Gyssens, and D. Van Gucht. An expressive language for linear spatial database queries. In *Proceedings of the 17th ACM Symposium on Principles of Database Systems*, pages 109–118. ACM Press, 1998.

21. L. Vandeurzen, M. Gyssens, and D. Van Gucht. On query languages for linear queries definable with polynomial constraints. In E. F. Freuder, editor, *Proceedings of the 2nd Conference on Principles and Practice of Constraint Programming*, volume 1118 of *Lecture Notes in Computer Science*, pages 468–481, Springer-Verlag, 1996.

# A Theory of Spatio-temporal Database Queries

Floris Geerts, Sofie Haesevoets, and Bart Kuijpers

University of Limburg
Department WNI, B-3590 Diepenbeek, Belgium
{floris.geerts,sofie.haesevoets,bart.kuijpers}@luc.ac.be

**Abstract.** We address a fundamental question concerning spatio-temporal database systems: "What are exactly spatio-temporal queries?" We define spatio-temporal queries to be computable mappings that are also *generic*, meaning that the result of a query may only depend to a limited extent on the actual internal representation of the spatio-temporal data. Genericity is defined as invariance under transformations that preserve certain characteristics of spatio-temporal data (e.g., collinearity, distance, velocity, acceleration, ...) that are relevant to a database user. These transformations also respect the monotone nature of time.

We investigate different genericity classes relative to the constraint database model for spatio-temporal databases and we identify sound and complete languages for the first-order, respectively the computable, queries in these genericity classes.

## 1 Introduction

Since the early 1990s, various database systems have been developed to handle spatial data [1,5,10,14,16,26] and solid theories for such systems have been proposed and studied [21,23]. Conceptually, spatial databases are possibly infinite sets of points in a real space $\mathbf{R}^n$. In more recent years, we have seen the emergence of database systems and applications that are dealing with *spatio-temporal data* [4,7,12,15,25]. Conceptually, spatio-temporal data can be modeled as infinite spatial sets that move or change in time, i.e., sets in $\mathbf{R}^n \times \mathbf{R}$.

A much acclaimed method for effectively representing infinite geometrical figures is provided by the *constraint database model*, that was introduced in 1990 by Kanellakis, Kuper and Revesz [18] (recently an overview of the area of constraint databases appeared [24]). Until recently this model has been used mainly in the area of spatial databases, but it provides an equally elegant and efficient way to model spatio-temporal data [7,8,9,13,20]. In the setting of the constraint model, a spatio-temporal database in $\mathbf{R}^n \times \mathbf{R}$ is finitely represented as a Boolean combination of polynomial equalities and inequalities. Figure 1 depicts the spatio-temporal database $\{(x, y; t) \mid x^2 + y^2 + t^2 \leq 1 \vee (x^2 + y^2 + (t - 2)^2 = 1 \wedge t \leq 5/2) \vee (x^2 + y^2 + (t - 3)^2 = 1 \wedge t > 5/2)\}$ in $\mathbf{R}^2 \times \mathbf{R}$.

A number of theoretical studies have appeared on the status of time and its relation with space in systems that model moving objects. Erwig et al. [11] give a taxonomy of applications ranging from those that rely on a step-wise

G. Grahne and G. Ghelli (Eds.): DBPL 2001, LNCS 2397, pp. 198–212, 2002.

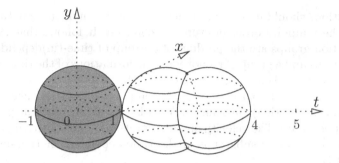

**Fig. 1.** An example of a spatio-temporal database in $\mathbf{R}^2 \times \mathbf{R}$.

constant geometry to applications which need more complete integration of space and time (like for instance a continuous description of a trajectory). MOST, an example of the latter category, relies on a strong interaction of the space and time components (since the space variables are described by linear polynomials in time) and provides a query language that is a combination of a spatial query language and a temporal logic. On the other range of the spectrum, variable independence (defined in terms of orthographic dimension) gives rise to a less expressive data model which has the advantage of a lower complexity of query evaluation [13,22].

We study spatio-temporal queries from the perspective of expressive power, and do this against the background of the full modeling and querying power of the constraint database model and the first-order and computationally complete languages it offers. We ask which expressions in these languages may be considered as *reasonable* spatio-temporal queries. In database theory it is usually required that the result of queries should only to a certain limited extent depend on the actual internal representation of databases and that queries should only ask for properties that are shared by "isomorphic" encodings of the same data. The meaning of "isomorphic" may be influenced by the actual database application and by which notions are relevant in it. In the context of the relational database model, Chandra and Harel [6] formalized this independence of the actual encoding in terms of the notion of *genericity*. Paredaens, Van den Bussche and Van Gucht [23] identified a hierarchy of genericity classes for spatial database applications. The generic queries in the different classes focus on different geometrical and topological aspects of the spatial data. On a technical level, generic queries are defined as being invariant under those transformations of the data that preserve the relevant aspects of the data. Whereas Chandra and Harel considered the group of the isomorphisms (that possibly fix some elements of the domain) in the case of relational databases, Paredaens, Van den Bussche and Van Gucht identified different geometrical and topological transformation groups (affinities, isometries, translations, homeomorphisms ...) for spatial database applications.

We investigate which notions of genericity are appropriate for spatio-temporal databases and which transformation groups express them. We observe that the transformations should first and foremost respect the monotone nature of time, i.e., leave the temporal order of events unchanged. It follows that the relevant transformation groups are the product of a group of time-(in)dependent spatial transformations and a group of monotone transformations of the time-component of the spatio-temporal data. Next, we focus on the former groups and study which of them leave different spatial and spatio-temporal properties (like collinearity, distance and orientation) unchanged. We also focus on physical properties of spatio-temporal data (like velocity and acceleration). The transformation groups that we consider are all subgroups of the time-dependent or time-independent affinities of $\mathbf{R}^n \times \mathbf{R}$.

We study the notion of spatio-temporal genericity relative to two popular query languages in the constraint model: first-order logic over the reals (FO) and an extension of this logic with a while-loop (FO + While). Queries in both languages are known to be effectively computable (given termination in the case of FO + While-programs) and FO + While is known to be a computationally complete language on spatio-temporal databases [28]. First, we show that all the genericity classes are undecidable. We show that the considered classes of generic first-order queries are recursively enumerable, however. Hereto, we define first-order point-based languages in which variables range over points in $\mathbf{R}^n \times \mathbf{R}$ and which contain certain point predicates. These point-based languages are shown to be sound and complete for the first-order queries in the considered genericity classes. We have also shown that extensions of these point-based logics with a While-loop give sound and complete languages for the computable queries in the different genericity classes. Our results are inspired by similar results that were obtained by Gyssens, Van den Bussche and Van Gucht in the context of spatial databases [17]. However, mainly our results for genericity notions described by time-dependent transformations require new proof techniques.

This paper is organized as follows. In Section 2, we define spatio-temporal databases, spatio-temporal queries, and the constraint query languages FO and FO + While. In Section 3, we define a number of genericity notions. In Section 4 and 5, we present sound and complete first-order and computationally complete query languages for the different notions of genericity. In Section 6, we end with a discussion of some open problems.

## 2   Definitions and Preliminaries

We denote the set of the real numbers by $\mathbf{R}$.

### 2.1   Spatio-temporal Databases

In the following, we will consider $n$-dimensional spatial figures that change in time ($n \geq 2$). A moving figure is described by means of an (often infinite) set of tuples $(x_1, x_2, \ldots, x_n; t)$ in $\mathbf{R}^n \times \mathbf{R}$ , where $(x_1, x_2, \ldots, x_n)$ represent the spatial coordinates of a point in the $n$-dimensional real space $\mathbf{R}^n$ and $t$ is the time coordinate in $\mathbf{R}$. We will work with spatio-temporal data that can be modeled in the constraint model.

**Definition 1.** An (*n-dimensional*) *spatio-temporal database*[1] is a set $\{(x_1, x_2, \ldots, x_n; t) \in \mathbf{R}^n \times \mathbf{R} \mid \varphi(x_1, x_2, \ldots, x_n; t)\}$, where $\varphi(x_1, x_2, \ldots, x_n; t)$ is a formula built with the logical connectives $\wedge, \vee, \neg$ from atomic formulas of the form $p(x_1, x_2, \ldots, x_n, t) > 0$, with $p(x_1, x_2, \ldots, x_n, t)$ a polynomial with integer coefficients and real variables $x_1, x_2, \ldots, x_n, t$. □

Figure 1 in the Introduction gives an illustration of a 2-dimensional spatio-temporal database. It shows at its beginning (i.e., at $t = -1$) a single point in the origin of $\mathbf{R}^2$. Then it shows a disk whose radius increases and later decreases and ends in a point at moment $t = 1$, followed by a circle whose radius increases, decreases, increases and then shrinks to a point.

## 2.2  Spatio-temporal Database Queries

Here, we give a first definition of a query. In the next section, we will impose further conditions on the nature of these mappings.

**Definition 2.** A *spatio-temporal database query* is a computable function that maps spatio-temporal databases to spatio-temporal databases. □

## 2.3  Constraint Query Languages

In this paper, we will consider two popular constraint query languages: first-order logic and an extension of this logic with a while-loop.

First-order logic over the reals (in other words, the relational calculus augmented with polynomial inequality constraints $p(x_1, x_2, ..., x_m) > 0$), FO for short, has been well-studied as a query language in the context of spatial databases [18,23]. In the setting of spatio-temporal databases it can be used similarly as a query language. For instance, the calculus formula $\mathcal{S}(x, y; t) \wedge (\exists x_0)(\exists y_0)(\exists r > 0)(\forall x)(\forall y)\big((x - x_0)^2 + (y - y_0)^2 = r^2 \leftrightarrow \mathcal{S}(x, y; t)\big)$ selects those snapshots from a spatio-temporal database $\mathcal{S}$ where it shows a circle. It is well-known that FO-formulas can be effectively evaluated on spatio-temporal databases in the constraint model and that the output can be represented in the same constraint formalism [28].

It is known that the extension of first-order logic over the reals with a while-loop, FO + While for short, yields a computationally complete language for constraint databases [28]. An FO + While-program is a finite sequence of *statements* and *while-loops*. Each statement has the form

$$R := \{(x_1, \ldots, x_k) \mid \varphi(x_1, \ldots, x_k)\},$$

---

[1] The results in this paper can be extended straightforwardly to the situation where a spatio-temporal database consists of more such sets and where these sets are accompanied by classical thematic information. However, because the complete problem that is discussed here is captured by this simplified model, we stick to it for reasons of simplicity of exposition.

with $R$ a relation variable of arity $k$ and $\varphi$ a formula in FO augmented with previously introduced relation variables. A while-loop has the form

$$\textbf{while } \varphi \textbf{ do } P \,,$$

where $P$ is a program and $\varphi$ is a sentence in FO augmented with previously introduced relation variables. Semantically, a FO + While-program expresses a spatio-temporal query in the obvious way as soon as one of its relation variables has been designated as the output variable.

# 3    Spatio-temporal Genericity

For simplicity we consider from now on only queries that take an $n$-dimensional spatio-temporal database as input and also output an $n$-dimensional spatio-temporal database (variations are possible but straightforward). As stated in the Introduction, we are interested in spatio-temporal database queries that are invariant under the elements of a certain spatio-temporal transformation group

$$\mathcal{F} = \{f \mid f = (f_1, f_2, \ldots, f_n, f_t) : \mathbf{R}^n \times \mathbf{R} \to \mathbf{R}^n \times \mathbf{R}\}.$$

In the remainder of this section, we will impose two further conditions on these transformations. The first condition is a purely temporal one (it concerns the order of events), whereas the second is a purely spatial or spatio-temporal condition that reflects the nature of the queries one is interested in.

## 3.1    Temporal Condition

An *event* is a subset of $\mathbf{R}^n \times \mathbf{R}$. The projection of an event $A$ on the time-axis is denoted by $\pi_t(A)$ and called the *time-interval* of $A$.

Let $A$ and $B$ be events. In Allen's terminology [2,3], $A$ and $B$ are called *co-temporal* if $\pi_t(A) = \pi_t(B)$ (we denote this by $A =_t B$). Allen says $A$ is *before* $B$ if $t_A < t_B$ for all $t_A \in \pi_t(A)$ and all $t_B \in \pi_t(B)$ (we denote this by $A <_t B$). Remark that $A \leq_t B := A =_t B$ or $A <_t B$ is an order on time-intervals. We say that a transformation $f : \mathbf{R}^n \times \mathbf{R} \to \mathbf{R}^n \times \mathbf{R}$ *preserves the order of events* if for all events $A$ and $B$, $A =_t B$ implies $f(A) =_t f(B)$ and $A <_t B$ implies $f(A) <_t f(B)$.

**Proposition 1.** *A transformation* $f = (f_1, f_2, \ldots, f_n, f_t) : \mathbf{R}^n \times \mathbf{R} \to \mathbf{R}^n \times \mathbf{R}$ *preserves the order of events if and only if $f_t$ is a strictly monotone function of $t$ alone.*    □

**Proof.** The only-if direction is clear. To prove the other direction, let $f = (f_1, f_2, \ldots, f_n, f_t)$ be a transformation of $\mathbf{R}^n \times \mathbf{R}$. Consider any two events $A = \{(x_1, x_2, \ldots, x_n, t)\}$ and $B = \{(x'_1, x'_2, \ldots, x'_n, t)\}$. Then $f_t(x_1, x_2, \ldots, x_n, t) = f_t(x'_1, x'_2, \ldots, x'_n, t)$. This shows that $f_t$ is a function of $t$ alone.

Consider any two events $A = \{(x_1, x_2, \ldots, x_n, t_A)\}$ and $B = \{(x_1, x_2, \ldots, x_n, t_B)\}$ with $t_A < t_B$. Then $f_t(t_A) < f_t(t_B)$. This shows that $f_t$ is a strictly monotone function of $t$.    □

Since we require that transformations preserve the order of events, we can write the transformation groups of interest as a product of groups:

$$\mathcal{F} = (\mathcal{F}_{st}, \mathcal{F}_t) = \{(f_{st}, f_t) \mid f_{st} = (f_1, f_2, \ldots, f_n) : \mathbf{R}^n \times \mathbf{R} \to \mathbf{R}^n, \; f_t : \mathbf{R} \to \mathbf{R}\}.$$

The groups $\mathcal{F}_t$ that we will consider are:
- $\mathcal{A}_t = \{t \mapsto a \cdot t + b \mid a, b \in \mathbf{R} \text{ and } a > 0\}$, i.e., the monotone affinities of the time-line;
- $\mathcal{T}_t = \{t \mapsto t + b \mid b \in \mathbf{R}\}$, i.e., the translations of the time-line; and
- $Id_t = \{\mathrm{id}\}$, i.e., the identity.

## 3.2 Spatial and Spatio-temporal Conditions

For what concerns the spatial (or spatio-temporal) part, we consider transformations of the form:

$$\begin{pmatrix} x_1 \\ x_2 \\ \vdots \\ x_n \\ t \end{pmatrix} \mapsto \begin{pmatrix} a_{11}(t) & a_{12}(t) & \cdots & a_{1n}(t) \\ a_{21}(t) & a_{22}(t) & \cdots & a_{2n}(t) \\ \vdots & \vdots & \cdots & \vdots \\ a_{n1}(t) & a_{n2}(t) & \cdots & a_{nn}(t) \end{pmatrix} \cdot \begin{pmatrix} x_1 \\ x_2 \\ \vdots \\ x_n \end{pmatrix} + \begin{pmatrix} b_1(t) \\ b_2(t) \\ \vdots \\ b_n(t) \end{pmatrix},$$

where the $a_{ij}$ and $b_i$ are functions from $\mathbf{R}$ to $\mathbf{R}$.

We will consider the following groups $\mathcal{F}_{st}$ of transformations:
- $\mathcal{A}_{st}$, the group of transformations of the above form where the $a_{ij}(t)$ and $b_i(t)$ are arbitrary functions of $t$ such that the matrix of the $a_{ij}(t)$ has an inverse for each value of $t$ (these are the time-dependent affinities);
- $\mathcal{A}_{st}^f$, the subgroup of $\mathcal{A}_{st}$ consisting of transformations for which the functions $a_{ij}(t)$ and $b_i(t)$ only take a finite number of values;
- $\mathcal{A}_{st}^c$, the subgroup of $\mathcal{A}_{st}$ consisting of transformations for which the functions $a_{ij}(t)$ are constants and $b_i(t)$ are linear functions of $t$;
- $\mathcal{S}_{st}, \mathcal{S}_{st}^f, \mathcal{S}_{st}^c$, the subgroups of the above where the matrix of the $a_{ij}(t)$ represents at each moment a similarity;
- $\mathcal{I}_{st}, \mathcal{I}_{st}^f, \mathcal{I}_{st}^c$, the subgroups of the above where the determinant of the matrix consisting of the $a_{ij}(t)$ equals 1 at each moment (i.e., the isometries);
- $\mathcal{T}_{st}, \mathcal{T}_{st}^f, \mathcal{T}_{st}^c$, the subgroups of the above where the matrix consisting of the $a_{ij}(t)$ is the identity matrix (i.e., the translations).

## 3.3 Physical Conditions

The following groups are of interest when notions such as velocity, acceleration and force are important in an application. These transformation groups can be found by solving the differential equations that express that these notions are preserved. We consider these notions for arbitrary and rigid motions, respectively.

- $\mathcal{V}_{st}$, the subgroup of $\mathcal{A}_{st}^c$ where the $b_i$ are constants. This group of transformations preserves the *velocity vector*.
- $\mathcal{V}(\mathcal{R})_{st}$, the subgroup of $\mathcal{I}_{st}^c$ where the $b_i$ are constants. This group of transformations preserves the *velocity vector* of a moving object in rigid motion.
- $\mathcal{AC}_{st}$, is the group $\mathcal{A}_{st}^c$. This group of transformations preserves the *acceleration vector* of a moving object.
- $\mathcal{AC}(\mathcal{R})_{st}$, is the group $\mathcal{I}_{st}^c$. This group of transformations preserves the *acceleration vector* of a moving object in rigid motion.

In physics it is custom to consider only translations (i.e., $\mathcal{T}_t$) for what concerns the time-dimension.

## 3.4 Spatio-temporal Genericity: Definition

Finally, we define genericity of spatio-temporal database queries.

**Definition 3.** Let $\mathcal{F}_{st}$ and $\mathcal{F}_t$ be two of the above groups. Let $Q$ be a spatio-temporal database query. We call $Q$ $(\mathcal{F}_{st}, \mathcal{F}_t)$-*generic* if and only if for all spatio-temporal databases $\mathcal{S}_1$ and $\mathcal{S}_2$ for which there exists a $f = (f_{st}, f_t) \in (\mathcal{F}_{st}, \mathcal{F}_t)$ such that $f(\mathcal{S}_1) = \mathcal{S}_2$ also $f(Q(\mathcal{S}_1)) = Q(\mathcal{S}_2)$ holds. □

# 4  Sound and Complete Languages for the Generic First-Order Spatio-temporal Queries

In this section, we study the $(\mathcal{F}_{st}, \mathcal{F}_t)$-generic queries that are expressible in FO. To start with, we give a general undecidability result. It can be proven using standard techniques from constraint databases [19].

**Theorem 1.** *For all non-trivial groups $\mathcal{F}_{st}$, $\mathcal{F}_t$ mentioned in the previous section, $(\mathcal{F}_{st}, \mathcal{F}_t)$-genericity of spatio-temporal* FO *queries is undecidable.* □

We will show that the first-order queries that are $(\mathcal{F}_{st}, \mathcal{F}_t)$-generic are recursively enumerable, however. We will show this by giving sound and complete languages for the FO queries of the different genericity classes. These languages are point-based logics of the following form.

**Point-Based Logics.** We define a number of first-order point-based languages that we shall denote by $\mathcal{P}(\{P_1, P_2, \ldots, P_m\})$, where the $P_i$ are point-predicates. The variables $p, q, r, \ldots$ in $\mathcal{P}(\{P_1, P_2, \ldots, P_m\})$ represent points in $\mathbf{R}^n \times \mathbf{R}$. The atomic formulas of $\mathcal{P}(\{P_1, P_2, \ldots, P_m\})$ are $\mathcal{S}(p)$, meaning that the point $p$ belongs to the input database $\mathcal{S}$, and $P_i(p, q, r, \ldots)$. The formulas of $\mathcal{P}(\{P_1, P_2, \ldots, P_m\})$ are built from atomic formulas using the connectives $\wedge, \vee, \neg$ and quantification of point variables $(\exists p)$, $(\forall p)$. □

In the remainder of this section, we first discuss notions of genericity determined by time-independent transformations with applications to physics and next focus on time-dependent transformations.

## 4.1    Genericity for Time-Independent Transformations

In this section, we give a general result concerning $(\mathcal{F}_{st}, \mathcal{F}_t)$-generic queries where $\mathcal{F}_{st}$ is a group of time-independent affinities of $\mathbf{R}^n \times \mathbf{R}$.

Let $(O, E_1, E_2, \ldots, E_{n+1})$ denote the standard coordinate system of $\mathbf{R}^n \times \mathbf{R}$. Let the point-predicate $\mathbf{Between}^{n+1}$ be such that $\mathbf{Between}^{n+1}(p, q, r)$ expresses that the points $p$, $q$, $r$ in $\mathbf{R}^n \times \mathbf{R}$ are collinear and that $q$ is between $p$ and $r$. Let the predicate $\mathbf{Before}$ be such that $\mathbf{Before}(p, q)$ expresses that the time coordinate of $p$ is less than or equal to the time coordinate of $q$.

The following meta-theorem can be proven using techniques introduced by Gyssens, Van den Bussche and Van Gucht [17].

**Theorem 2.** *Let $\mathcal{F}_{st}$ be a subgroup of $\mathcal{A}_{st}^c$ and let $\mathcal{F}_t$ be a subgroup of $\mathcal{A}_t$. Let $\{P_1, P_2, \ldots, P_m\}$ be a set of point-predicates that contains $\mathbf{Between}^{n+1}$ and $\mathbf{Before}$. If the predicates in $\{P_1, P_2, \ldots, P_m\}$ are FO expressible and invariant under the transformations of $(\mathcal{F}_{st}, \mathcal{F}_t)$ and if the fact "$(p_0, p_1, p_2, \ldots, p_{n+1})$ is the image of the standard coordinate system $(O, E_1, E_2, \ldots, E_{n+1})$ under some element $f$ of $(\mathcal{F}_{st}, \mathcal{F}_t)$" is expressible in $\mathcal{P}(\{P_1, P_2, \ldots, P_m\})$, then $\mathcal{P}(\{P_1, P_2, \ldots, P_m\})$ is sound and complete for the $(\mathcal{F}_{st}, \mathcal{F}_t)$-generic FO queries.* $\qquad\square$

We apply the previous theorem to some groups $(\mathcal{F}_{st}^c, \mathcal{F}_t)$. Further applications can be found in the next subsection. We need to introduce some further point predicates:

- $\mathbf{UnitTime}(p, q)$ expresses that the points $p, q \in \mathbf{R}^n \times \mathbf{R}$ have time-coordinates $p_t$ and $q_t$ such that $|p_t - q_t| = 1$;
- $+_\mathbf{t}(p, q, r)$ holds for spatio-temporal points $p, q, r$ with time-coordinates $p_t$, $q_t$ and $r_t$ if and only if $p_t + q_t = r_t$; $*_\mathbf{t}$ is defined similarly;
- the unary predicates $\mathbf{0_t}$ and $\mathbf{1_t}$ express that the time-coordinate of a point equals zero and one respectively;
- the predicates $\leq_i (p, q)$ $(1 \leq i \leq n)$ express that the $i$th spatial coordinate of $p$ is less or equal than the $i$th spatial coordinate of $q$;
- $\mathbf{EqDist}(p, q, r, s)$ is true if the distance between two co-temporal points $p$ and $q$ equals the distance between the two co-temporal points $r$ and $s$;
- $\mathbf{UnitDist}(p, q)$ expresses that $p, q$ are co-temporal and that the spatial distance between $p$ and $q$ equals one; and finally
- $\mathbf{Pos}^{n+1}(p_0, p_1, p_2, \ldots, p_{n+1})$ expresses that $(p_0, p_1, p_2, \ldots, p_{n+1})$ form a positively oriented $(n + 1)$-dimensional coordinate system.

**Corollary 1.** *Let $(\mathcal{F}_{st}, \mathcal{F}_t)$ be a group from Table 1 and let $\Pi(\mathcal{F}_{st}, \mathcal{F}_t)$ be as in Table 1. The point language $\mathcal{P}(\Pi(\mathcal{F}_{st}, \mathcal{F}_t))$ is sound and complete for the $(\mathcal{F}_{st}, \mathcal{F}_t)$-generic FO queries.* $\qquad\square$

## 4.2    Applications to Physics

Here, we focus on the transformation groups $(\mathcal{V}_{st}, \mathcal{T}_t)$, $(\mathcal{V}(\mathcal{R})_{st}, \mathcal{T}_t)$, $(\mathcal{AC}_{st}, \mathcal{T}_t)$ and $(\mathcal{AC}(\mathcal{R})_{st}, \mathcal{T}_t)$. To formulate our results we need to define one more point-predicate, namely $=_{\mathbf{space}}$. If $p = (p_1, \ldots, p_n, p_t)$, $q = (q_1, \ldots, q_n, q_t) \in \mathbf{R}^n \times \mathbf{R}$, then $=_{\mathbf{space}}(p, q)$ if and only if $p_i = q_i$ for $1 \leq i \leq n$.

The following results can be proven using Theorem 2.

**Table 1.** The different sets of point predicates for a number of spatio-temporal genericity notions. In the last three cases, we have $\mathcal{F}_t \in \{\mathcal{A}_t, \mathcal{T}_t, Id_t\}$.

| $(\mathcal{F}_{st}, \mathcal{F}_t)$ | Sets of point predicates $\Pi(\mathcal{F}_{st}, \mathcal{F}_t)$ |
|---|---|
| $(\mathcal{A}_{st}^c, \mathcal{A}_t)$ | $\{\mathbf{Between}^{n+1}, \mathbf{Before}\}$ |
| $(\mathcal{A}_{st}^c, \mathcal{T}_t)$ | $\{\mathbf{Between}^{n+1}, \mathbf{Before}, \mathbf{UnitTime}\}$ |
| $(\mathcal{A}_{st}^c, Id_t)$ | $\{\mathbf{Between}^{n+1}, \mathbf{Before}, \mathbf{UnitTime}, +_t, *_t, 0_t, 1_t\}$ |
| $(\mathcal{S}_{st}^c, \mathcal{F}_t)$ | $\Pi(\mathcal{A}_{st}^c, \mathcal{F}_t) \cup \{\mathbf{EqDist}\}$ |
| $(\mathcal{I}_{st}^c, \mathcal{F}_t)$ | $\Pi(\mathcal{A}_{st}^c, \mathcal{F}_t) \cup \{\mathbf{EqDist}, \mathbf{UnitDist}\}$ |
| $(\mathcal{T}_{st}^c, \mathcal{F}_t)$ | $\Pi(\mathcal{A}_{st}^c, \mathcal{F}_t) \cup \{\mathbf{EqDist}, \mathbf{UnitDist}, \leq_i (1 \leq i \leq n), \mathbf{Pos}^{n+1}\}$ |

**Table 2.** The different point-predicate sets for the physical genericity notions.

| $(\mathcal{F}_{st}, \mathcal{T}_t)$ | Set of point predicates $\Pi(\mathcal{F}_{st}, \mathcal{T}_t)$ |
|---|---|
| $(\mathcal{V}_{st}, \mathcal{T}_t)$ | $\{\mathbf{Between}^{n+1}, \mathbf{Before}, \mathbf{UnitTime}, =_{\mathrm{space}}\}$ |
| $(\mathcal{V}(\mathcal{R})_{st}, \mathcal{T}_t)$ | $\{\mathbf{Between}^{n+1}, \mathbf{Before}, \mathbf{UnitTime}, =_{\mathrm{space}}, \mathbf{EqDist}, \mathbf{UnitDist}\}$ |
| $(\mathcal{AC}_{st}, \mathcal{T}_t)$ | $\{\mathbf{Between}^{n+1}, \mathbf{Before}, \mathbf{UnitTime}\}$ |
| $(\mathcal{AC}(\mathcal{R})_{st}, \mathcal{T}_t)$ | $\{\mathbf{Between}^{n+1}, \mathbf{Before}, \mathbf{UnitTime}, \mathbf{EqDist}, \mathbf{UnitDist}\}$ |

**Theorem 3.** *Let $(\mathcal{F}_{st}, \mathcal{T}_t)$ be a group from Table 2 and let $\Pi(\mathcal{F}_{st}, \mathcal{T}_t)$ be as in Table 2. The point language $\mathcal{P}(\Pi(\mathcal{F}_{st}, \mathcal{T}_t))$ is sound and complete for the $(\mathcal{F}_{st}, \mathcal{T}_t)$-generic FO queries.* □

### 4.3   Genericity for Time-Dependent Transformations

Here, we focus on notions of genericity determined by time-dependent transformations. Our first result in this context shows that we can restrict our attention, without loss of generality, to piece-wise constant transformations. The proof of this proposition is postponed until the end of this section.

**Proposition 2.** *Let $Q$ be a spatio-temporal FO query and let $\mathcal{F}_{st}$ be $\mathcal{A}_{st}$, $\mathcal{S}_{st}$, $\mathcal{I}_{st}$ or $\mathcal{T}_{st}$ and $\mathcal{F}_t$ be $\mathcal{A}_t$, $\mathcal{T}_t$ or $Id_t$. Then $Q$ is $(\mathcal{F}_{st}, \mathcal{F}_t)$-generic if and only if it is $(\mathcal{F}_{st}^f, \mathcal{F}_t)$-generic.* □

We first focus on the group $(\mathcal{A}_{st}^f, \mathcal{A}_t)$. To formulate our result we need to define some additional point predicates:
- **Between**$^n(p, q, r)$ expresses that three points $p, q, r \in \mathbf{R}^n \times \mathbf{R}$ that are co-temporal are collinear and that $q$ is between $p$ and $r$;
- **EqCR**$(p, q, r, p', q', r')$ expresses that the cross ratio[2] of three co-temporal and collinear points $p$, $q$, $r$ equals the cross ratio of three co-temporal and collinear points $p'$, $q'$, $r'$;
- **EqCR**$^{\mathbf{st}}(p, q, r, p', q', r')$ expresses that the cross ratio of three co-temporal and collinear points $p$, $q$, $r$ equals the cross ratio of the time coordinates of the points $p'$, $q'$, $r'$.

---

[2] The cross ratio of three collinear points $p$, $q$, $r$ is $\frac{|pq|}{|pr|}$. It is known that the cross ratio is an affine invariant.

**Theorem 4.** *The point language* $\mathcal{P}(\{\mathbf{Between}^n, \mathbf{Before}, \mathbf{EqCR}, \mathbf{EqCR}^{\mathbf{st}}\})$ *is sound and complete for the* $(\mathcal{A}_{st}^f, \mathcal{A}_t)$-*generic FO queries.*    □

**Proof sketch.** It is easily verified that the predicates $\mathbf{Between}^n$, $\mathbf{Before}$, $\mathbf{EqCR}$ and $\mathbf{EqCR}^{\mathbf{st}}$ are expressible in the language FO and that all these predicates are invariant under transformations in the group $(\mathcal{A}_{st}^f, \mathcal{A}_t)$. We can then prove by induction on the formulas in $\mathcal{P}(\{\mathbf{Between}^n, \mathbf{Before}, \mathbf{EqCR}, \mathbf{EqCR}^{\mathbf{st}}\})$ that they are $(\mathcal{A}_{st}^f, \mathcal{A}_t)$-generic. This proves soundness.

For completeness, it suffices to show that every FO formula $\varphi$ can be simulated in $\mathcal{P}(\{\mathbf{Between}^n, \mathbf{Before}, \mathbf{EqCR}, \mathbf{EqCR}^{\mathbf{st}}\})$ by a formula $\bar{\varphi}$ in the sense that $\mathcal{T} \models \varphi$ if and only if $f(\mathcal{T}) \models \bar{\varphi}$ with $f$ some transformation from the group $(\mathcal{A}_{st}^f, \mathcal{A}_t)$. For $(\mathcal{A}_{st}^f, \mathcal{A}_t)$-generic FO formulas this implies that they can be equivalently expressed in $\mathcal{P}(\{\mathbf{Between}^n, \mathbf{Before}, \mathbf{EqCR}, \mathbf{EqCR}^{\mathbf{st}}\})$.

Let $\varphi$ be a FO formula that we assume to be in prenex normal form. We now sketch the translation of an FO formula $\varphi$ into a formula $\bar{\varphi}$ of $\mathcal{P}(\{\mathbf{Between}^n, \mathbf{Before}, \mathbf{EqCR}, \mathbf{EqCR}^{\mathbf{st}}\})$. In this translation, first the atomic formulas of $\varphi$ are translated and the connectives and quantifiers are later added in an almost natural way. First of all, in the description of $\bar{\varphi}$ two moments in time $p_{t_O}$ and $p_{t_E}$ are chosen such that $\neg\mathbf{Before}(p_{t_E}, p_{t_O})$ (time moments are represented in $\bar{\varphi}$ by spatio-temporal points). Next, in the hyperplane of points that are co-temporal with $p_{t_O}$ an affine coordinate system $(O, E_1, E_2, \ldots, E_n)$ is chosen (this can be expressed using the predicate $\mathbf{Between}^n$ only [17]). The arithmetic operations on real variables (which are translated into point variables on the line $OE_1$) will be simulated, using only $\mathbf{Between}^n$, in the *computation plane* $(O, E_1, E_2)$ (using techniques similar to those used by Tarski [27]; see also [17]).

An appearance of $\mathcal{T}(x_1, \ldots, x_n; t)$ in $\varphi$ is translated into a conjunction of three formulas. The first is $\mathcal{T}(p)$. For the second, we chose an affine coordinate system $(O^p, E_1^p, E_2^p, \ldots, E_n^p)$ in the plane of points that are co-temporal with $p$; determine in this plane the spatial coordinates $p_1, p_2, \ldots, p_n$ of $p$ with respect to the coordinate system $(O^p, E_1^p, E_2^p, \ldots, E_n^p)$; and, using the point-predicate $\mathbf{EqCR}$, communicate these coordinates to the line $OE_1$ in the computation plane. The third conjunct communicates the time coordinate of $p$ to the computation plane as $p_t$, using the expression $\mathbf{EqCR}^{\mathbf{st}}(O, E_1, p_t, p_{t_O}, p_{t_E}, p)$.

When all atomic subformulas of $\varphi$ have been translated, the logical connectives can be added almost naturally (care has to be taken that in connecting, e.g., the subformulas $\mathcal{T}(x_1, \ldots, x_n; t)$ and $\mathcal{T}(x_1', \ldots, x_n'; t')$ it is important that if $t = t'$, then the same affine coordinate system is used in their translation; hereto all possible orders of the time variables in the formula $\varphi$ are considered and the same affine coordinate system is used for co-temporal events).    □

**Proof of Proposition 2.** Note that we only consider a finite number of moments in time in the previous proof (there are only a finite number of time variables in any FO formula $\varphi$). This implies that the transformation groups $\mathcal{A}_{st}^f$ and $\mathcal{A}_{st}$ yield the same results. In between the moments of time that are considered, it is indeed not important which transformation function is used.    □

**Table 3.** The different sets of point predicate for some spatio-temporal genericity notions. In the last three cases, we have $\mathcal{F}_t \in \{\mathcal{A}_t, \mathcal{T}_t, Id_t\}$.

| $(\mathcal{F}_{st}, \mathcal{F}_t)$ | Sets of point predicates $\Pi(\mathcal{F}_{st}, \mathcal{F}_t)$ |
|---|---|
| $(\mathcal{A}_{st}^{(f)}, \mathcal{A}_t)$ | $\{\mathbf{Between}^n, \mathbf{Before}, \mathbf{EqCR}, \mathbf{EqCR^{st}}\}$ |
| $(\mathcal{A}_{st}^{(f)}, \mathcal{I}_t)$ | $\{\mathbf{Between}^n, \mathbf{Before}, \mathbf{EqCR}, \mathbf{EqCR^{st}}, \mathbf{UnitTime}\}$ |
| $(\mathcal{A}_{st}^{(f)}, Id_t)$ | $\{\mathbf{Between}^n, \mathbf{Before}, \mathbf{EqCR}, \mathbf{EqCR^{st}}, \mathbf{UnitTime}, +_t, *_t, 0_t, 1_t\}$ |
| $(\mathcal{S}_{st}^{(f)}, \mathcal{F}_t)$ | $\Pi(\mathcal{A}_{st}^{(f)}, \mathcal{F}_t) \cup \{\mathbf{EqDist^{cotemp}}\}$ |
| $(\mathcal{I}_{st}^{(f)}, \mathcal{F}_t)$ | $\Pi(\mathcal{A}_{st}^{(f)}, \mathcal{F}_t) \cup \{\mathbf{EqDist^{cotemp}}, \mathbf{UnitDist}\}$ |
| $(\mathcal{T}_{st}^{(f)}, \mathcal{F}_t)$ | $\Pi(\mathcal{A}_{st}^{(f)}, \mathcal{F}_t) \cup \{\mathbf{EqDist^{cotemp}}, \mathbf{UnitDist}, \leq_i (1 \leq i \leq n), \mathbf{Pos}^n\}$ |

Theorem 4 has a number of corollaries. We need two extra point predicates, namely $\mathbf{EqDist^{cotemp}}$ and $\mathbf{Pos}^n$:

- $\mathbf{EqDist^{cotemp}}(p, q, r, s)$ is true if and only if for four co-temporal points $p, q, r$ and $s$ the distance between $p$ and $q$ equals the distance between $r$ and $s$; and
- $\mathbf{Pos}^n(p_0, p_1, \ldots, p_n)$ expresses that for $n + 1$ co-temporal points $p_0, p_1, \ldots, p_n$, $(p_0, p_1, \ldots, p_n)$ forms a positively oriented coordinate system.

**Corollary 2.** *Let* $(\mathcal{F}_{st}, \mathcal{F}_t)$ *and* $\Pi(\mathcal{F}_{st}, \mathcal{F}_t)$ *be taken from Table 3. The language* $\mathcal{P}(\Pi(\mathcal{F}_{st}, \mathcal{F}_t))$ *is sound and complete for the* $(\mathcal{F}_{st}, \mathcal{F}_t)$*-generic FO queries.* □

## 5   Sound and Complete Languages for the Generic Computable Spatio-temporal Queries

In this section, we show that most of the languages $\mathcal{P}(\{P_1, P_2, \ldots, P_m\})$ of the previous section, when augmented with While, yield sound and computationally complete languages for the genericity classes characterized by the point-predicates $P_1, P_2, \ldots, P_m$.

**Point-Based Logics Extended with While.** Let $\{P_1, P_2, \ldots, P_m\}$ be a finite set of point predicates. Syntactically, a *program* in the language $\mathcal{P}(\{P_1, P_2, \ldots, P_m\})$ + While is then a finite sequence of *statements* and *while-loops*. Each statement has the form

$$R := \{(p_1, \ldots, p_k) \mid \varphi(p_1, \ldots, p_k)\},$$

with $R$ a relation variable of arity $k$ (the variables $p_i$ range over $\mathbf{R}^n \times \mathbf{R}$) and $\varphi$ a formula in $\mathcal{P}(\{P_1, P_2, \ldots, P_m\})$ in which relation names of input relations and of previously introduced relation variables may be used. A while-loop has the form

**while** $\varphi$ **do** $P$ ,

where $P$ is a program and $\varphi$ is a sentence in $\mathcal{P}(\{P_1, P_2, \ldots, P_m\})$ augmented with previously introduced relation variables.

Semantically, a program in the query language $\mathcal{P}(\{P_1, P_2, \ldots, P_m\})$ + While expresses a spatio-temporal query in the obvious way as soon as one of its relation variables has been designated as the output variable. □

We follow the same structure as in the previous section. We first discuss notions of genericity determined by time-independent transformations with applications to physics and then focus on time-dependent transformations.

## 5.1  Genericity for Time-Independent Transformations

In this section, we prove a general result concerning computable $(\mathcal{F}_{st}, \mathcal{F}_t)$-generic queries where $(\mathcal{F}_{st}, \mathcal{F}_t)$ is a time-independent affinity of $\mathbf{R}^n \times \mathbf{R}$.

Let $(O, E_1, E_2, \ldots, E_{n+1})$ be the standard coordinate system of $\mathbf{R}^n \times \mathbf{R}$. The following meta-theorem can then be proven, using techniques introduced by Gyssens, Van den Bussche and Van Gucht [17].

**Theorem 5.** *Let $\mathcal{F}_{st}$ be a subgroup of $\mathcal{A}_{st}^c$ and let $\mathcal{F}_t$ be a subgroup of $\mathcal{A}_t$. Let $\{P_1, P_2, \ldots, P_m\}$ be a set of point predicates that contains* **Between**$^{n+1}$ *and* **Before**. *If the predicates in $\{P_1, P_2, \ldots, P_m\}$ are FO expressible and invariant under the transformations of $(\mathcal{F}_{st}, \mathcal{F}_t)$ and if the fact "$(p_0, p_1, p_2, \ldots, p_{n+1})$ is the image of the standard coordinate system $(O, E_1, E_2, \ldots, E_{n+1})$ under some element $f$ of $(\mathcal{F}_{st}, \mathcal{F}_t)$" is expressible in $\mathcal{P}(\{P_1, P_2, \ldots, P_m\})$, then $\mathcal{P}(\{P_1, P_2, \ldots, P_m\})$+While is sound and complete for the computable $(\mathcal{F}_{st}, \mathcal{F}_t)$-generic queries.* □

We apply the previous theorem to some groups $(\mathcal{F}_{st}^c, \mathcal{F}_t)$. Further applications can be found in the next subsection.

**Corollary 3.** *Let $(\mathcal{F}_{st}, \mathcal{F}_t)$ be a group from Table 1 and let $\Pi(\mathcal{F}_{st}, \mathcal{F}_t)$ be as in Table 1. The point language $\mathcal{P}(\Pi(\mathcal{F}_{st}, \mathcal{F}_t))$ + While is sound and complete for the computable $(\mathcal{F}_{st}, \mathcal{F}_t)$-generic queries.* □

## 5.2  Applications to Physics

Here, we focus again on the transformation groups $(\mathcal{V}_{st}, \mathcal{T}_t)$, $(\mathcal{V}(\mathcal{R})_{st}, \mathcal{T}_t)$, $(\mathcal{AC}_{st}, \mathcal{T}_t)$ and $(\mathcal{AC}(\mathcal{R})_{st}, \mathcal{T}_t)$. The following results can be proven using Theorem 5.

**Theorem 6.** *Let $(\mathcal{F}_{st}, \mathcal{T}_t)$ be a group from Table 2 and let $\Pi(\mathcal{F}_{st}, \mathcal{T}_t)$ be as in Table 2. The point language $\mathcal{P}(\Pi(\mathcal{F}_{st}, \mathcal{T}_t))$ + While is sound and complete for the computable $(\mathcal{F}_{st}, \mathcal{I}_t)$-generic queries.* □

## 5.3  Genericity for Time-Dependent Transformations

Finally, we study notions of genericity determined by time-dependent transformations. Here, we only show results for the groups of arbitrary time-dependent transformations $\mathcal{F}_{st}$. For the groups $\mathcal{F}_{st}^f$ the problem of identifying sound and complete languages is open.

**Theorem 7.** *The point language $\mathcal{P}(\{$**Between**$^n$, **Before**, **EqCR**, **EqCR**$^{st}\})$ + While is sound and complete for the $(\mathcal{A}_{st}, \mathcal{A}_t)$-generic computable queries.* □

**Proof Sketch.** We show that an $(\mathcal{A}_{st}, \mathcal{A}_t)$-generic computable query $Q$ can be simulated in the language $\mathcal{P}(\{\mathbf{Between}^n, \mathbf{Before}, \mathbf{EqCR}, \mathbf{EqCR^{st}}\})$ + While. This simulation is broken up into three steps: (1) an input database $\mathcal{S}$ is encoded as a natural number $N(\mathcal{S})$; (2) $Q$ is simulated by a computable function $\bar{Q}$ on natural numbers; and (3) $\bar{Q}(N(\mathcal{S}))$ is decoded into a spatio-temporal database. Since all three steps can be expressed in $\mathcal{P}(\{\mathbf{Between}^n, \mathbf{Before}, \mathbf{EqCR}, \mathbf{EqCR^{st}}\})$ + While, as we will show, this gives us the desired result.

Steps (2) and (3) differ little from the ones described by Gyssens, Van den Bussche and Van Gucht [17], so we skip them in this sketch. The major difference is in step (1). Essentially, step (1) is a loop over the natural numbers, where for each number $N$ it is tested whether or not $N$ encodes an image of the database $\mathcal{S}$ under a transformation $f \in (\mathcal{A}_{st}, \mathcal{A}_t)$. The fact that $N$ encodes some spatio-temporal database $\mathcal{S}_N$ can be expressed in $\mathcal{P}(\{\mathbf{Between}^n, \mathbf{Before}, \mathbf{EqCR}, \mathbf{EqCR^{st}}\})$ + While by modifying the technique of Gyssens, Van den Bussche and Van Gucht [17] to the technique of the *computation plane* explained in the proof of Theorem 4. In $\mathcal{P}(\{\mathbf{Between}^n, \mathbf{Before}, \mathbf{EqCR}, \mathbf{EqCR^{st}}\})$ it can then be expressed that $\mathcal{S}_N$ can be transformed into $\mathcal{S}$ by an element of the group $(\mathcal{A}_{st}, \mathcal{A}_t)$. Indeed, in the language FO it can be expressed that for all moments in time $t$ there exists an affinity $A_t$ such that a spatial point $p$ belongs to the snapshot of $\mathcal{S}_N$ at moment $t$ if and only if $A_t(p)$ belongs to the snapshot $\mathcal{S}$ at time $f_t(t)$, where $f_t$ is an element of $\mathcal{A}_t$. Using Theorem 4, it can therefore also be expressed in $\mathcal{P}(\{\mathbf{Between}^n, \mathbf{Before}, \mathbf{EqCR}, \mathbf{EqCR^{st}}\})$. □

The previous theorem has a number of corollaries.

**Corollary 4.** *Let $(\mathcal{F}_{st}, \mathcal{F}_t)$ be one of the groups $(\mathcal{A}_{st}, \mathcal{A}_t)$, $(\mathcal{A}_{st}, \mathcal{I}_t)$, $(\mathcal{A}_{st}, Id_t)$, $(\mathcal{S}_{st}, \mathcal{G}_t)$, $(\mathcal{I}_{st}, \mathcal{G}_t)$, or $(\mathcal{T}_{st}, \mathcal{G}_t)$ with $\mathcal{G}_t \in \{\mathcal{A}_t, \mathcal{I}_t, Id_t\}$ and let $\Pi(\mathcal{F}_{st}, \mathcal{F}_t)$ be as in Table 3. The point language $\mathcal{P}(\Pi(\mathcal{F}_{st}, \mathcal{F}_t))$ + While is sound and complete for the $(\mathcal{F}_{st}, \mathcal{F}_t)$-generic computable queries.* □

# 6    Conclusion and Discussion

We have investigated different genericity classes relative to the constraint database model for spatio-temporal databases and we have identified sound and complete languages for the first-order, respectively the computable, queries in (most of) these genericity classes. Some results were obtained by techniques introduced by Gyssens, Van den Bussche and Van Gucht [17], but for time-dependent transformations we have introduced new proof techniques.

For what concerns computationally complete languages these techniques seem to be insufficient to deal with the genericity notions that are expressed by the groups $(\mathcal{A}_{st}^f, \mathcal{A}_t)$, $(\mathcal{A}_{st}^f, \mathcal{I}_t)$, $(\mathcal{A}_{st}^f, Id_t)$, $(\mathcal{S}_{st}^f, \mathcal{G}_t)$, $(\mathcal{I}_{st}^f, \mathcal{G}_t)$, and $(\mathcal{T}_{st}^f, \mathcal{G}_t)$ with $\mathcal{G}_t \in \{\mathcal{A}_t, \mathcal{I}_t, Id_t\}$. The problem in adapting the proof technique of Theorem 7 to these groups is that it is not clear how we can express in the respective point-based logics that two spatio-temporal databases can be mapped to each other by some piece-wise constant affinity. Indeed, since the number of pieces is not defined *a priori*, this might not be expressible. This would imply that yet another new proof technique would be required to deal with the remaining cases.

# References

1. D. Abel and B. C. Ooi (eds.), *Advances in spatial databases—3rd Symposium (SSD'93)*, Lecture Notes in Computer Science, vol. 692, Springer-Verlag, 1993.
2. J. F. Allen, *Maintaining knowledge about temporal intervals*, Communications of the ACM **26** (1983), no. 11, 832–843.
3. J. F. Allen and G. Ferguson, *Actions and events in interval temporal logic*, Journal of Logic and Computation **4** (1994), no. 5, 531–579.
4. M. H. Böhlen, Ch. S. Jensen, and M. Scholl (eds.), *Proceedings of the international workshop on spatio-temporal database management (STDBM'99)*, Lecture Notes in Computer Science, vol. 1678, Springer, 1999.
5. A. Buchmann (ed.), *Design and implementation of large spatial databases—1st Symposium (SSD'89)*, Lecture Notes in Computer Science, vol. 409, Springer-Verlag, 1989.
6. A. K. Chandra and D. Harel, *Computable queries for relational data bases*, Journal of Computer and System Sciences **21** (1980), no. 2, 156–178.
7. C. X. Chen and C. Zaniolo, *SQLST: A spatio-temporal data model and query language*, Conceptual Modeling (ER'00) (V. Storey, A. Laender, S. Liddle, eds.), Lecture Notes in Computer Science, vol. 1920, Springer-Verlag, 2000, pp. 96–111.
8. J. Chomicki and P. Revesz, *Constraint-based interoperability of spatio-temporal databases*, in [26], pp. 142–161.
9. J. Chomicki and P. Revesz, *A geometric framework for specifying spatiotemporal objects*, Proceedings of the 6th International Workshop on Temporal Representation and Reasoning, IEEE Computer Society, 1999, pp. 41–46.
10. M. J. Egenhofer and J. R. Herring (eds.), *Advances in spatial databases—4th Symposium (SSD'95)*, Lecture Notes in Computer Science, vol. 951, Springer-Verlag, 1995.
11. M. Erwig, R. H. Güting, M. Schneider, and M. Vazirgiannis, *Spatio-temporal data types: An approach to modeling and querying moving objects in databases*, GeoInformatica **3** (1999), no. 3, 269–296.
12. A. Frank, S. Grumbach, R. Güting, C. Jensen, M. Koubarakis, N. Lorentzos, Y. Manopoulos, E. Nardelli, B. Pernici, H.-J. Schek, M. Scholl, T. Sellis, B. Theodoulidis, and P. Widmayer, *Chorochronos: A research network for spatiotemporal database systems*, SIGMOD Record **28** (1999), 12–21.
13. S. Grumbach, P. Rigaux, and L. Segoufin, *Spatio-temporal data handling with constraints*, Proceedings of the 6th international symposium on Advances in Geographic Information Systems (ACM-GIS'98) (R. Laurini, K. Makki, and N. Pissinou, eds.), 1998, pp. 106–111.
14. O. Gunther and H.-J. Schek (eds.), *Advances in spatial databases—2nd Symposium (SSD '91)*, Lecture Notes in Computer Science, vol. 525, Springer-Verlag, 1991.
15. R. H. Güting, M. H. Bohlen, M. Erwig, C. S. Jensen, N. A. Lorentzos, M. Schneider, and M. Vazirgiannis, *A foundation for representing and querying moving objects*, ACM Transactions on Databases Systems **25** (2000), 1–42.
16. R.H. Güting (ed.), *Advances in spatial databases—6th Symposium (SSD'99)*, Lecture Notes in Computer Science, vol. 1651, Springer-Verlag, 1999.
17. M. Gyssens, J. Van den Bussche, and D. Van Gucht, *Complete geometric query languages*, Journal of Computer and System Sciences **58** (1999), no. 3, 483–511.
18. P. C. Kanellakis, G. M. Kuper, and P.Z. Revesz, *Constraint query languages*, Journal of Computer and System Sciences **51** (1995), 26–52 (also in Proceedings of the 9th ACM Symposium on Principles of Database Systems (PODS'90), ACM Press, 1990, pp. 299–313).

19. B. Kuijpers and D. Van Gucht, *Genericity in spatial databases*, Chapter 12 in [24], pp. 293–304.
20. B. Kuijpers, J. Paredaens, and D. Van Gucht, *Towards a theory of movie database queries*, Proceedings of the 7th International Workshop on Temporal Representation and Reasoning, IEEE Computer Society, 2000, pp. 95–102.
21. G. Kuper and M. Scholl, *Geographic information systems*, Constraint databases (J. Paredaens, G. Kuper, and L. Libkin, eds.), Springer-Verlag, 2000, pp. 175–198.
22. L. Libkin, *Variable independence, quantifier elimination, and constraint representation*, Automata, Languages and Programming, 27th International Colloquium (ICALP 2000) (U. Montanari, J. D. P. Rolim, and E. Welzl, eds.), Lecture Notes in Computer Science, vol. 1853, Springer-Verlag, 2000, pp. 260–271.
23. J. Paredaens, J. Van den Bussche, and D. Van Gucht, *Towards a theory of spatial database queries*, Proceedings of the 13th ACM Symposium on Principles of Database Systems (PODS'94), ACM Press, 1994, pp. 279–288.
24. J. Paredaens, G. Kuper, and L. Libkin (eds.), *Constraint databases*, Springer-Verlag, 2000.
25. D. Pfoser and N. Tryfona, *Requirements, definitions and notations for spatiotemporal application environments*, Proceedings of the 6th International Symposium on Advances in Geographic Information Systems (ACM-GIS'98) (R. Laurini, K. Makki, and N. Pissinou, eds.), 1998, pp. 124–130.
26. M. Scholl and A. Voisard (eds.), *Advances in spatial databases—5th Symposium (SSD'97)*, Lecture Notes in Computer Science, vol. 1262, Springer-Verlag, 1997.
27. W. Schwabhäuser, W. Szmielew, and A. Tarski, *Metamathematische methoden in der geometrie*, Springer-Verlag, 1983.
28. J. Van den Bussche, *Constraint databases, queries and query languages*, Chapter 2 in [24], pp. 21–54.

# An Application-Specific Database

Kathleen Fisher[1], Colin Goodall[2], Karin Högstedt[1], and Anne Rogers[1]

[1] AT&T Labs, Shannon Laboratory
180 Park Avenue, Florham Park, NJ 07932, USA
{kfisher,karin,amr}@research.att.com
[2] 200 S. Laurel Ave, Middletown, NJ 07748
cgoodall@ems.att.com

**Abstract.** *Signatures* are evolving profiles of entities extracted from streams of transactional data. For a stream of credit card transactions, for example, an entity might be a credit card number and a signature the average purchase amount. Signatures provide a high-level view of data in a transactional data warehouse and help data analysts focus their attention on interesting subsets of the data in such warehouses. Traditional databases are not designed for such applications. They impose overhead for services not necessary in such applications, such as indexing, declarative querying, and transaction support. Hancock is a C-based domain-specific programming language with an embedded domain-specific database designed for computing signatures. In this paper, we describe Hancock's database mechanism, evaluate its performance, and compare an application written in Hancock with an equivalent application written in Daytona [5], a very efficient relational database system.

## 1 Introduction

Recent advances in processing speed and disk technology have made it possible to process and store vast amounts of data, enabling new kinds of information applications. One such application involves mining daily transaction streams for information about the entities described in the transactions. Examples of such streams include AT&T's daily call-detail data, which contains one record per call, credit card transaction data, which contains one record per purchase, and TCPDUMP data, which contains one record per IP packet passing through a tap point. The entities of interest in these streams might be telephone numbers, credit card numbers, and IP addresses, respectively. If such transactional data simply flows into a data warehouse, it can be difficult to find which entities are "interesting" for a particular application because of the sheer volume of data. Where should data analysts choose to focus their attention?

One solution to this problem is to tap the transactional stream as it flows into the data warehouse and use the resulting information to build and maintain "signatures," which are small profiles of the entities in the stream [3]. Signatures evolve over time in response to additional transactions. Analysts design these signatures to capture the "essence" of the entities mentioned in the stream along

G. Grahne and G. Ghelli (Eds.): DBPL 2001, LNCS 2397, pp. 213–227, 2002.

desired dimensions. These signatures serve as a high-level summary of the contents of a transaction warehouse and allow analysts to focus their attention on entities with interesting signatures. For example, a signature in the call-detail case might associate with each telephone number the average daily number of international calls made from that telephone number. Analysts might use this information to detect fraud, *e.g.*, if the number is higher than usual. AT&T has used signatures for a number of years to significant financial advantage [2,3].

Local anecdotal evidence suggested that traditional databases were not suited to the task of building and maintaining signatures because they could not perform adequately. In particular, traditional databases had difficulty loading the daily transactions in a timely fashion[1].

Consequently, data analysts at AT&T wrote their initial signature programs using an *ad hoc* representation for their signature data that they custom designed for each program. They indexed their representation only by the identifiers associated with the entities they were tracking. To make their applications fault-tolerant, they took daily snapshots of their signature collections, providing a coarse-grained roll-back mechanism. Their implementations were well-tailored for the desired class of applications, and they met performance requirements set by the analysts and the consumers of their data.

Despite the success of the data produced by the initial signature programs, the analysts were not satisfied with the programs themselves because they were hard to write and maintain. Although the per-entity code was conceptually very simple (count the number of international calls, *etc.*), the code to manage the volume of data efficiently was not. This infrastructure code swamped the per-entity code, making programs difficult to write and maintain. Analysts had written a handful of successful applications using this technique, but the complexity of the programs dissuaded them from writing more. Maintenance was a problem because the analysts had to review the programs periodically to ensure that they complied with current federal regulations. Hence although analysts thought signatures very useful, they were at a loss as to how to compute them: traditional databases were too slow, and the *ad hoc* approaches were too complex.

In response to this problem, we designed Hancock, which is a C-based domain-specific programming language with support for a domain-specific database embedded within it. The goal of the Hancock project is to make it easy to read, write, and maintain programs that compute signatures from transactional data. All of the original signature programs have been re-written in Hancock, and the new versions have been running in production for several years now. In addition, analysts have designed new signatures using Hancock, and the maintenance problem is now much simpler.

An earlier paper [2] describes the Hancock language; in this paper, we focus on Hancock's domain-specific database mechanism and its performance. In Section 2, we discuss the performance requirements for signature applications. Section 3 presents Hancock's `map` abstraction, which is the language interface to Hancock's database mechanism. We describe the implementation of maps in Section 4 and performance results in Section 5. In Section 6, we compare the performance of a signature application written in Hancock with the performance of the same application written in Daytona[5], a relational database system tuned for high-volume applications. Finally, we conclude in Section 7.

## 2   Requirements

Maintainable signature programs are useless if their performance fails to meet the requirements of their user base. Programs written in Hancock must satisfy requirements regarding the time necessary to process a new batch of transactions, the amount of disk space necessary to store the signatures for a given application, and the time necessary to lookup the signatures associated with various collections of customers. We discuss each of these requirements in turn.

We must be able to process all the transactions in a batch before the next batch arrives so that we do not fall behind. In addition, we must have sufficient head-room to allow us to catch up if machine maintenance, data transmission errors, or disk failures cause system down-time. Signature collections must be space efficient, because given extra disk space signature researchers can *always* devise new information to compute.

The third performance constraint imposed on the Hancock system involves the time required to query data stored in signature collections. There are four different ways in which users access this data, each with its own time constraint. The first type of access arises when a person types an entity identifier into a web interface. This person expects to receive the associated signature within web time — a second or so. The second type of usage involves retrieving the data for collections of several hundred thousand identifiers. Analysts feed such lists into the system and expect to have the associated signatures within the length of time necessary to get a cup of coffee — roughly five minutes. The third access pattern occurs when an analyst wishes to examine the signatures of all the entities stored in a signature collection, perhaps to look for anomalies or to compute aggregates. For such computations, the analyst needs to be able to make several such passes over the data in one day; hence these computations can take no more than an hour (and preferably less). We call the fourth type of access to signature data *unordered* references. Unlike typical accesses, a sequence of unordered references does not exhibit good spatial locality. Such references occur during signature construction when data analysts look up the signatures of secondary identifiers appearing in the transactional data. Although unordered references are less important to our application class than the previous three access patterns, they should be supported to the degree possible without violating any of the other performance constraints.

## 3   Hancock Maps

Hancock provides an abstraction, called maps, for representing persistent collections of signatures. Unlike traditional databases, Hancock maps provide an extremely limited set of operations: associating a signature with a key, retrieving or updating the signature associated with a key, removing a key from the database, asking if a given key has an associated signature, and iterating over a range of keys with stored signatures. To avoid the associated overhead, Hancock maps do not support transactions, locking, secondary indices, or declarative querying. In the remainder of this section, we describe the functionality of maps in more detail.

## 3.1   Map Declarations

A Hancock programmer describes the structure of a map using a map type declaration, which has the following form:

```
map sig_m {
    key id_t;
    value sig_t;
    default SIG_DEFAULT;
};
```

This declaration specifies a new map type named sig_m. We describe each of the clauses in this declaration in turn.

The key clause indicates that sig_m maps will be indexed by values of type id_t. Such values typically represent some form of identification number, for example, telephone numbers, credit card numbers, or IP addresses. Programmers determine, in part, the underlying structure of a map through the map key specification. We will discuss the connection between map keys and map structure in Section 4.1 after we explain how maps are implemented.

The value clause specifies the type of data to be associated with each key. This type can be any C type of statically-known size. We refer to a key with a value in a given map as an *active* key and to an active key and its associated value as an *item*.

The default clause specifies a value to be returned when a programmer requests data for an inactive key. The default may be a constant, as is SIG_DEFAULT in this example, or a function. A constant default must be a constant expression that has the value type of the map. A function default specifies the name of a function that computes a default value for a given key.

Hancock maps provide generic compression for their values. In some cases, application programmers may have domain-specific knowledge that enables them to write custom compression functions that are significantly better than the defaults. So, in addition to the key, value, and default clauses, Hancock allows the programmer to specify optional compress and decompress clauses, which specify functions to compress and decompress values. Hancock allows compression functions to use variable-width schemes, because they often yield better compression ratios.

Variables can be declared using the usual C syntax (for example sig_m m). To connect a map on disk with a Hancock variable m, we must associate the name of the file containing the map with the variable. Hancock provides *initializing declarations* to make this connection. For example, the following statement, sig_m m = "09-Aug-2001.m";, declares that the variable m has type sig_m and can be found on disk in the file named "09-Aug-2001.m".

## 3.2    Map Operations

Hancock provides four operations for manipulating items in maps: read, write, test, and remove. Hancock's indexing operator, written <: ... :>, can be used as an r-value (for reading) or as an l-value (for writing). Hancock's test operator, written @<: .. :>, queries a map to determine whether the key is active. Finally, Hancock's map remove operator, written \<:..:>, removes an item. As an example, the following code first reads the value for the key id from map m, writes a different value newsig into map m for the key id, tests whether the key id1 is active, and if so removes that item.

```
sig_m m;
id_t id,id1;
sig_t oldsig, newsig;

oldsig = m<:id:>;       /* Read id's data */
    ⋮
newsig = ...
m<:id:> = newsig;       /* Write id's data */

if (m@<:id1:>)          /* Test id1  */
   m\<:id1:>            /* Remove id1's data */
```

Hancock also provides a mechanism for performing an operation on every active key in a map by combining Hancock's iterate statement, which allows a programmer to consume a stream of data, with an expression for creating a stream from a map. The expression m[startKeyExpr..stopKeyExpr] generates a stream of active keys from m that fall between the value of the expressions startKeyExpr and stopKeyExpr inclusive. A detailed discussion of Hancock's iterate statement can be found in the Hancock manual [4].

## 4    Implementation

Hancock's map implementation is a variant of a data structure used in AT&T's Global Fraud Management System. The original data structure, which mapped phone numbers to values, was designed to support efficient updates and efficient queries for single keys. This data structure split each key (a phone number) into two pieces: a primary key, which identified a *block* of data, and a secondary key, which identified a particular *entry* in a block. The primary key was used to index into an array that gave the location of the corresponding block in the file. The values in the blocks were of uniform size and the blocks were fully populated by using a (constant) default value for inactive keys. The design allowed the location of an entry to be computed directly from the location of the block.

This data structure worked well for references that had good locality. Analysts obtained the desired locality for transaction streams by sorting the records by the key. Given ordered records, each block in the file would need to be read/written at most once during an update. The design also worked well for

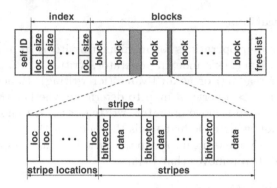

**Fig. 1.** The on-disk data representation of a Hancock map.

single-key queries because each such reference would take exactly two disk reads: one to consult the index and one to read the block. Despite its strengths, this data structure was not sufficient for our purposes because fully populating the blocks wasted space and did not support unordered references efficiently.

Our design, which is essentially a multi-level table[1], uses compression to reduce the disk space needed to store maps. The programmer chooses the unit of compression based on the characteristics of an application. It breaks the blocks into sub-blocks, which we call *stripes*, and includes a stripe index in the block. To read an entry from a block, the runtime system uses the block index to find the block in the file, reads the stripe index from the file, uses the stripe index to find the stripe, reads the stripe, decompresses it, and finally, returns the desired value.

Our design also uses caching to address the problem of unordered references. One class of applications that generates unordered references uses a second key from a transaction as a map index during an update. These references tend to show some locality, especially when a significant portion of the working set can be retained. To address the problem of unordered references, our implementation caches recently-accessed compressed stripes.

Figure 1 shows the on-disk representation used by our implementation. It includes a self-identification field, a block index, an unordered set of blocks, and a free-list for unused space. The self-identification information is used to match the file against the declared type of a map to help prevent users from inadvertently using a map with the wrong type for an application. Each block contains a stripe index followed by the stripes, in order. The in-memory representation, which is not shown, includes only the index and a cache of recently accessed stripes.

## 4.1 Defining Key Types

In Section 2, we mentioned that Hancock programmers determine, in part, the structure of a map. In particular, programmers determine the size of the primary

---

[1] Other applications, such as paging or IP address lookup for routing[6,7,8] use variants of a multi-level table to support large key spaces.

index and the stripe size for a map by specifying the type of the key, which must have the following restricted form: the key type must be a C struct type, it must have three fields, and those fields must have Hancock range types. For a value with such a type, the first field corresponds to the block number, the second to the stripe number within that block, and the third to the particular element in that stripe. The fields are required to have range types (integers in a given range) to bound the number and size of the blocks and stripes.

The main tradeoff to consider when deciding the block size is the size of the index (12 bytes per entry on disk, 20 in memory). Choosing a stripe size, on the other hand, requires weighing various considerations, including the cost of decompressing values, the size of a decompressed stripe in relation to the processor's primary and secondary cache sizes, and the expected mix of access patterns for the data.

## 5   Performance Results

In this section, we describe experimental results that show that the performance of Hancock maps meets the criteria presented in Section 2. We start by describing our experimental set-up.

The experiments were performed on one processor of an SGI Origin 2000. The processor, an R12000, has split 32KB instruction and data caches and an 8MB secondary cache. The machine has more than 6GB of main memory.

We report *real* time that was computed using the Unix time utility. Time reports the elapsed time the measured command spent running (real), the CPU time spent in execution of the command and its children (user), and the CPU time spent executing system code by the command and its children (system).

We use two Hancock maps in our experiments. The first, called *activity*, maps phone numbers to three-byte values. The sample map we use has more than 464M active keys. It uses a simple compression function that compresses three-byte values into two bytes. The second, called *features*, maps phone numbers to 124 byte values. The sample features map we use has 163M active keys. The user-specified compression function for this map generates a variable number of bytes per record.

Both maps use the key type show in Figure 2. This type uses the first six digits of a phone number, called the *exchange*, as the primary key, while the last four digits (called the *line*) are split between the secondary and tertiary keys depending on the stripe size (MAXENTRY).

In Section 2, we described a set of performance requirements for signature programs. We must be able to process all the updates for a given day in one day with enough headroom to allow for system-related problems (such as network downtime). We must use disk space efficiently. And we must be able to answer single-key queries in one second, work-list queries in five minutes, and map iteration queries in under an hour.

In this section, we discuss Hancock's performance in light of these requirements using a stripe size of 100 entries for the two maps; we selected this size because it has the best overall performance.

```
#define MAXEXCHANGE 1000000
#define MAXLINE 10000
#define MAXENTRY 100
#define MAXSTRIPE (MAXLINE/MAXENTRY)

range npanxx_r = [0 .. (MAXEXCHANGE-1)];
range stripe_r = [0 .. (MAXSTRIPE-1)];
range entry_r = [0 .. (MAXENTRY-1)];

struct key_t {
  npanxx_r primary;
  stripe_r secondary;
  entry_r tertiary;
};
```

**Fig. 2.** Key type for activity and features maps.

**Table 1.** Summary of cold query times for a stripe size of 100 entries.

| Query type | Activity | Features |
|---|---|---|
| single | 1.1s | 1.1s |
| unordered | 209.9s | 242.7s |
| ordered | 11s + 25.3s | 11s + 37.4s |
| iteration | 1023.1s | 738.4s |

To determine the cost of accessing a map during a daily update, we measured the performance of a Hancock program that performs one map read and one map write for each call in an ordered daily call stream. We chose this restricted program because different applications have widely different per call computation costs that are unrelated to the performance of Hancock maps. Using a call stream with more than 275M calls, the restricted programs took roughly 19 minutes for the activity map and 30 minutes for the features map. For comparison purposes, a program that simply consumes the stream took slightly less than eight minutes.

Hancock maps are reasonably space-efficient. Representing each item directly would take eight bytes for the activity map (five for the key and three for the value) and 129 bytes (5+124) for the features map. The activity map, which is 1.27GB in size, uses 2.7 bytes per item including the overhead from the block index, the stripe location vectors, and the bitvectors. The features map is 1.10GB in size. It uses a much more aggressive compression function (it also has more data to work with) that consumes 6.7 bytes per item including overhead.

Table 1 presents a summary of map query performance. We ran each experiment multiple times, but we report the first or *cold* times, because they were higher than all the other runs and they best approximate the experience of a user. The single-key experiment (`single`) requested the data for a single key. The work list experiments requested data for an unordered list of 156,051 keys that we obtained from a colleague (`unordered`). The performance data for the ordered case (`ordered`) include the cost of sorting the keys (11s). The map iteration experiment (`iteration`) iterated over the map reading the data for each active key in the map, but not performing computation on the extracted values.

In summary, Hancock maps have reasonable update performance, reasonable disk usage, and meet the query performance requirements from Section 2.

# 6   A Database Comparison

This section compares the performance of two different implementations of a simplified production application for analyzing calling-card records. We wrote one implementation in Hancock and another in Cymbal, the programming language provided by Daytona[5], a highly efficient database management system.

Although the obvious point of comparison for Hancock would have been an SQL implementation for some popular commercial database system such as Oracle, we did not do such an experiment because we wanted to be as fair as possible. To that end, we selected Daytona rather than a commercial database because Daytona is highly efficient both for loading large volumes of information on a daily basis[2] and for supporting fast queries on that data. Its efficiency makes it the preferred database at AT&T for production data analysis applications. We used Cymbal rather than SQL, which Daytona also supports, because Cymbal programs can be highly tuned and a quick, back-of-the-envelope experiment convinced us that an SQL implementation would be much too slow to be competitive with the Hancock implementation.

The application we use for our experiments maintains usage statistics for a subset of the calling cards seen on the AT&T network. Each day, the application uses the records that describe the day's calls to compute statistics for each card, including the number of calls, the number of zero-length calls, the number of call attempts (short calls), the total duration of all calls, and the total (approximate) charge. This application uses a ten-digit canonicalized version of the calling card number as the key. It associates seven day's worth of usage statistics with each such key. The call records, which include the card number, the date of the call, the call duration, and the standard rate (charge) for the call, are stored in a Daytona database.

## 6.1   The Hancock Implementation

The Hancock implementation cannot access the call records directly because they are stored in a Daytona database. Instead, we wrote a Daytona program to pull the calls from the database and produce a stream of C structs, one per call. The Hancock implementation reads this stream from a UNIX pipe. An alternative implementation would pull the calls from the "raw" feed before they were entered into the database. In practice, we use this approach for many

---

[2] A Daytona database currently holds more than a year's worth of call detail data. The largest table in this database contains over 100 billion rows and will continue to grow until it reaches about 200 billion records in August 2002.

```
typedef struct {
  int calls;
  int zeros;
  int attempts;
  int secs;
  int rate;
} usage_t;

typedef struct { usage_t u[7]; } vusage_t;

int statsCompress(vusage_t *block, unsigned char *to, int to_ext);
int statsUncompress(unsigned char *from, int from_size, vusage_t *to);

 map cnStats_m {
 key cnbr_t;
 value vusage_t;
 default { {0,0,0,0,0}, ... };
 compress statsCompress;
 decompress statsUncompress;
}
```

**Fig. 3.** Definition for cnStats map.

Hancock applications, but for this experiment we used data that was already stored in Daytona. For most of our experiments, we report times that include the cost of pulling the calls from the database,, but we give some results in Section 6.3 that show the performance of Hancock without the cost of pulling the calls from the database.

The usage statistics are stored in a Hancock map with the definition shown in Figure 3. The ten-digit keys are decomposed into physical keys of type cnbr_t as follows: the first five digits are used as the primary key or block number, the next two as the stripe number, and the remaining three as the entry number.

The implementation of the usage collection program is straightforward: sort the input stream by the canonicalized card number, which puts all calls charged to a given card adjacent in the stream. As each new card is seen, look up the current value for that card in the map. Use each call record to update the usage statistics as appropriate. After seeing the last record for a card number, put the the final result back into the map.

## 6.2   The Daytona Implementation

Daytona is a commercial-grade database system. It provides fully-indexed and horizontally-partitioned data tables with several levels of locking, and it supports parallel processing. Daytona's programming language, Cymbal, supports both procedural and declarative programming, including an extension of SQL. Programs written in Cymbal are translated to C and then compiled and linked to runtime libraries.

After some trial-and-error, we implemented a strategy for computing usage that is both efficient and reasonably expressible in Daytona. We store the usage statistics in a Daytona database containing one record for each card number. Each such record contains one field for the card number and 35 integer-valued HEKA-coded[3] fields for the computed statistics. The records are represented on disk in ASCII with the fields separated by pipes and the records separated by newlines. On average, these records take 51 bytes.

The computation has three steps:

1. Loop over the call records, growing and updating an associative array indexed by card numbers.
2. Loop over the entire usage database, updating in-place the entries for keys that have records in the associative array (*i.e.*, cards that had calls in the stream). Mark records in the associative array as they are incorporated into the database. Update the index.
3. Loop over the associative array, appending a new entry to the end of the database for each unmarked record. Update the index.

Looping over the database to do the updates guarantees that access to the database will be sequential.

We report results for two versions of the Daytona implementation: one sequential and one parallel. The parallel program is very similar to the sequential program. The usage database includes ten horizontal partitions. Each process in the parallel program is assigned one of ten partitions of the key space. Each process reads each call record, but only processes those records with keys in its partition. Cymbal contains constructs that make it easy to parallelize Daytona programs in this way.

## 6.3   Experimental Results

In this section, we report on the performance of the Hancock and Daytona versions of our application. We performed our experiments on a production SUN Ultra Enterprise 10000 Starfire with 64 250-MHZ processors and 30GB of memory. As a vehicle for timing experiments, this machine is less than ideal because varying contention for resources yields non-uniform timings. However, we had to use it as our experimental platform because it is where the call database is kept.

The first set of experiments computes the usage database for seven days of calls, one day at a time. Most days had two million calls, except days one and two, which had 1.1 million calls. Table 2 contains running times for updating the usage information. We ran each experiment three times (except those marked with an asterisk, which we ran twice). We report the minimum **real** time for the three runs. We also report the **user** and **system** time that corresponded to the minimum **real** time and their sum. Note that the sum of **user** and **system** time may be larger than the **real** (or elapsed) time because the application may run on multiple processors in parallel. We report the minimum because there was a high variance for the sequential Daytona implementation. The Hancock implementation showed at most a 10% difference in running time between runs,

---

[3] HEKA is a compact encoding supported as a basic type in Cymbal.

**Table 2.** Performance for computing the usage database for seven successive days. Results are reported for the minimum `real` time over three runs (except those marked with an asterisk which we ran twice).

Hancock version

|             | Day 0     | Day 1     | Day 2     | Day 3     | Day 4     | Day 5     | Day 6     |
|-------------|-----------|-----------|-----------|-----------|-----------|-----------|-----------|
| `real`      | 8m49s     | 8m3s      | 8m2s      | 10m14s    | 10m0s     | 9m54s     | 9m57s     |
| `user`      | 8m31s     | 7m28s     | 7m22s     | 9m27s     | 9m8s      | 9m9       | 9m8s      |
| `system`    | 4m15s     | 3m11s     | 3m0s      | 5m8s      | 5m15s     | 4m58s     | 4m58s     |
| `user+system` | 12m46s  | 10m39s    | 10m22s    | 14m35s    | 14m23s    | 14m7s     | 14m6s     |

|              | Day 0    | Day 1    | Day 2    | Day 3    | Day 4    | Day 5    | Day 6    |
|--------------|----------|----------|----------|----------|----------|----------|----------|
| `memory`     | 123.8MB  | 123.8MB  | 123.8MB  | 123.8MB  | 123.8MB  | 123.8MB  | 123.8MB  |
| `disk space` | 64.4MB   | 80.3MB   | 91.4MB   | 106.8MB  | 119.2MB  | 129.8MB  | 139.3MB  |

Sequential Daytona version

|              | Day 0   | Day 1   | Day 2   | Day 3   | Day 4   | Day 5*  | Day 6*  |
|--------------|---------|---------|---------|---------|---------|---------|---------|
| `real`       | 10m52s  | 15m5s   | 16m37s  | 25m52s  | 31m44s  | 37m1s   | 37m42   |
| `user`       | 9m52s   | 9m35s   | 10m4s   | 13m37s  | 14m13s  | 15m28s  | 15m11s  |
| `system`     | 0m48s   | 5m50s   | 6m23s   | 12m4s   | 17m18s  | 22m46s  | 23m43s  |
| `user+system`| 10m40s  | 15m25s  | 16m27s  | 25m41s  | 31m31s  | 38m14s  | 38m54s  |

|              | Day 0   | Day 1   | Day 2   | Day 3   | Day 4   | Day 5   | Day 6   |
|--------------|---------|---------|---------|---------|---------|---------|---------|
| `memory`     | 214.7MB | 172.5MB | 184.4MB | 273.9MB | 279.6MB | 298.4MB | 297.0MB |
| `disk space` | 51.5MB  | 61.3MB  | 74.5MB  | 105.6MB | 120.5MB | 133.3MB | 146.3MB |

Parallel Daytona version*

|              | Day 0   | Day 1   | Day 2   | Day 3   | Day 4   | Day 5   | Day 6   |
|--------------|---------|---------|---------|---------|---------|---------|---------|
| `real`       | 7m6s    | 6m22s   | 6m15s   | 7m9s    | 6m42s   | 6m36s   | 6m36s   |
| `user`       | 6m39s   | 53m28s  | 43m9s   | 50m12s  | 55m54s  | 53m58s  | 54m29s  |
| `system`     | 0m11s   | 2m18s   | 4m21s   | 5m16s   | 8m32s   | 11m54s  | 13m20s  |
| `user+system`| 6m50s   | 55m46s  | 47m30s  | 55m38s  | 64m26s  | 65m52s  | 67m49s  |

|          | Day 0   | Day 1   | Day 2   | Day 3   | Day 4   | Day 5   | Day 6   |
|----------|---------|---------|---------|---------|---------|---------|---------|
| `memory` | 175.5MB | 144.4MB | 250.2MB | 249.1MB | 441.9MB | 472.6MB | 558.6MB |

while timings for the sequential Daytona implementation differed by as much as 30%, in part because the machine's load varied more during these experiments.

Comparing the `real` times reported in Table 2, the Hancock program outperforms the sequential Daytona program, but it is slower than the parallel Daytona program for the daily computations. The sum of `user` plus `system` time accounts for this difference in resource consumption. Using this metric, the Hancock program outperforms both Daytona versions after the first day.

Table 2 also gives the maximum memory footprint corresponding to the run with the minimum `real` time for the three implementations. Hancock requires substantially less memory than the Daytona implementations; the difference becomes more pronounced later in the week. The memory usage of the Hancock programs is a function of the map key types used in the programs. As a result, it is constant across the days. The memory usage of the Daytona programs is bounded by the size of the associative array and the number of previously active card numbers that are updated during the second phase of the computation. Later in the week, more of the card numbers that appear in a given day will be in the database already and generate updates rather than appends, which explains why the memory footprint grows as the week progresses.

Table 2 also shows the disk space used to store the usage statistics database. The disk space for the index in the Daytona implementations varied slightly between runs. We report the disk space for the sequential run with the minimum **real** time. The Hancock maps are substantially larger than the Daytona databases (up to 30%) for the early days of the week, but the situation reverses towards the end of the week. Hancock's map implementation has more up-front overhead than Daytona's database implementation, but Hancock has a smaller per-item incremental cost. The table does not include the temporary disk space used by the Hancock implementation. It uses between 36 to 65MB for sorting. Plus the temporary space needed for "yesterday's" map.

**Computing Weekly Usage Database.** The daily experiments reported in the previous section reflect how these program would be used in practice, but the amount of data involved is quite small. In this section, we report performance results computing the usage data using a full week's worth of calls in one run (see Table 3). Please note that due to a mistake when collecting the data for this experiment we used a slightly different version of the Hancock program that uses less memory, but has similar performance. While still modest, this experiment does show some issues that will arise as we scale to larger applications.

As in the previous experiment, the parallel Daytona version has the best performance, but it uses substantial resources. The Hancock program outperforms the sequential Daytona program on the **real**-time metric, but not on the "sum of **user** and **system**"-time metric. The Daytona program that pulls calls from the database is a bottleneck for this computation. We measured the effect of the Daytona portion of the computation by running only the Hancock program, using a file to hold the pre-pulled calls. The column labelled "Hancock Only" in Table 3 gives the result of this experiment, showing that the Hancock program outperforms both Daytona implementations when drawing its data from disk. In our experience, this approach is how Hancock programs are used in practice: data is pulled once from a database, sorted, and then used by many Hancock applications (or Hancock receives a "raw" data feed directly).

## 6.4 Summary

Large data management applications, such as computing signatures, require good locality of reference to perform efficiently. Our Hancock and Daytona implementations for computing signatures achieve good locality in very different ways, leading to different resource usage profiles. Our Daytona implementation uses associative arrays to store intermediate results and then makes updates in database order at the cost of substantial processor and memory resources. In contrast, our Hancock implementation sorts the data to obtain good locality of reference at the cost of the sort and temporary disk space. We should note that

**Table 3.** Performance for computing usage statistics from one week's calls, starting with an empty database. Time reported is the minimum `real` time over three runs (except those marked with an asterisk, which we ran twice). Reported memory size is the maximum memory size for the minimum `real`-time run.

|              | Hancock + Pull | Hancock Only | Sequential Daytona* | Parallel Daytona* |
|--------------|---------------|--------------|---------------------|-------------------|
| `real`       | 34m4s         | 20m35s       | 46m52s              | 23m42s            |
| `user`       | 33m41s        | 8m6s         | 43m51s              | 4h4m50s           |
| `system`     | 26m7s         | 24m41s       | 4m23s               | 5m3s              |
| `user+system`| 59m48s        | 32m47s       | 48m14s              | 4h9m53s           |

|          |         |         |          |           |
|----------|---------|---------|----------|-----------|
| `memory` | 72.0MB  | 65.5MB  | 587.1MB  | 1622.4MB  |

it would be possible, if somewhat unnatural, to implement the algorithm used in the Hancock program in Daytona and vice versa. By removing the difference in algorithms, we could learn more about the implications of using Hancock maps as contrasted to a conventional database table with indices.

We omitted our experiments on query performance for this application because of space constraints, but both Daytona and Hancock had no trouble meeting the guidelines.

For our, admittedly modest, experiment, the approach used in the parallel Daytona implementation is faster than the sorting approach used in the Hancock implementation, but it requires much more memory and more processors. The question of which system would work better for computing signatures on the full volume of AT&T's daily call detail data, which is two orders of magnitude larger than our calling-card application, remains. In practice, Hancock has shown itself to work well for such applications. We do not know whether the Daytona approach will handle larger scale signature applications, but the amount of memory needed for our modest application suggests that it may not scale much further as is.

## 7    Conclusion

In this paper, we described a domain-specific database embedded within Hancock, a language for computing signatures. Hancock makes designing and maintaining programs such programs easier, while meeting a set of performance criteria for daily load, individual query, work-list query, and map iteration times.

The paper provides a modest comparison with Daytona, a high-performance database, by writing a simple application in both systems. The results of our experiment are somewhat mixed. Given unlimited computing resources and a sophisticated Cymbal programmer, Daytona is somewhat faster for the card-usage application. The Hancock implementation takes slightly longer and requires more temporary disk space; however, it requires substantially less memory, fewer processors, and less programmer expertise.

Hancock is available for non-commercial use from the Hancock website: `www.research.att.com/projects/hancock`.

# References

1. David Belanger, Kenneth Church, and Andrew Hume. Virtual data warehousing, data publishing, and call detail. In *Processings of Databases in Telecommunications 1999, International Workshop.*, 1999. Also appears in Springer Verlag LNCS 1819 (pp. 106-117).
2. Corinna Cortes, Kathleen Fisher, Daryl Pregibon, Anne Rogers, and Frederick Smith. Hancock: A language for extracting signatures from data streams. In *Proceedings of the Sixth International Conference on Knowledge Discovery and Data Mining*, pages 9–17, August 2000.
3. Corinna Cortes and Daryl Pregibon. Giga mining. In *Proceedings of the Fourth International Conference on Knowledge Discovery and Data Mining*, 1998.
4. Kathleen Fisher, Karin Högstedt, Anne Rogers, and Frederick Smith. Hancock 1.1 manual. See www.research.att.com/projects/hancock, 2001.
5. Rick Greer. Daytona and the fourth-generation language Cymbal. In Alex Delis, Christos Faloutsos, and Shahram Ghandeharizadeh, editors, *SIGMOD 1999, Proceedings ACM SIGMOD International Conference on Management of Data, June 1-3, 1999, Philadephia, Pennsylvania, USA*. ACM Press, 1999. Also available at www.research.att.com/projects/daytona.
6. P. Gupta, S. Lin, and M. McKeown. Routing lookups in hardware and memory access speeds. In *Proc. 17th Ann. Joint Conf. of the IEEE Computer and Communications Societies*, volume 3, pages 1240–7, 1998.
7. N.-F. Huang, S.-M. Zhao, J.-Y. Pan, and C.-A. Su. A fast IP routing lookup scheme for gigabit switching routers. In *Proc. 18th Ann. Joint Conf. of the IEEE Computer and Communications Societies*, volume 3, pages 1429–36, 1999.
8. B. Lampson, V. Srinivasan, and G. Varghese. IP lookups using multiway and multicolumn search. *IEEE/ACM Transactions on Networking*, 7(3):324–34, 1999.

# A Model Theory
# for Generic Schema Management

Suad Alagić* and Philip A. Bernstein

Microsoft Research
One Microsoft Way, Redmond, WA 98052-6399
alagic@cs.usm.maine.edu, philbe@microsoft.com

**Abstract.** The core of a model theory for generic schema management is developed. This theory has two distinctive features: it applies to a variety of categories of schemas, and it applies to transformations of both the schema structure and its integrity constraints. A subtle problem of schema integration is considered in its general form, not bound to any particular category of schemas. The proposed solution, as well as the overall theory, is based entirely on schema morphisms that carry both structural and semantic properties. Duality results that apply to the schema and the data levels are established. These results lead to the main contribution of this paper: a formal schema and data management framework for generic schema management. Implications of this theory are established that apply to integrity problems in schema integration. The theory is illustrated by a particular category of schemas with object-oriented features along with typical database integrity constraints.

## 1   Introduction

This paper presents the core results of a model theory for generic schema management, by which we mean schema and database transformation capabilities that are independent of a particular data model. Such transformations require major database programming tasks, such as integrating source schemas when building a data warehouse or integrating different user views into an overall database schema. In spite of nontrivial typing issues created by such transformations, database programming and other relevant paradigms have been primarily suited to dealing with structural aspects of those transformations. A major challenge is in properly addressing semantics: the integrity constraints associated with database schemas.

A second major challenge is in developing such a model theory that is applicable to a variety of data models, such as the relational, object-oriented, and XML models [25]. This is challenging because schemas and their underlying databases are very different in these three major categories of models as are languages and their underlying logics used for expressing the integrity constraints.

---

* Current address: Computer Science Department, University of Southern Maine, 96 Falmouth Street, P.O. Box 9300, Portland, ME 04104-9300

G. Grahne and G. Ghelli (Eds.): DBPL 2001, LNCS 2397, pp. 228–246, 2002.

On the pragmatic side, generic schema management operations and tools have been considered in [4], and more specific system implications in [5,22]. These papers argue that many difficult and expensive database programming problems involve the manipulation of mappings between schemas. Examples are populating a data warehouse from data sources, exposing a set of data sources as an integrated schema, generating a web site wrapper, generating an object-oriented wrapper for relational data, and mapping an XML schema to a relational schema. Despite many commonalities of these schema management problems, tools and languages are typically engineered for only one problem area. A more attractive approach would be to build generic schema management tools and languages that would apply to all of these problems, with only some customization required for the data model and problem at hand. The formal open problem is to find a suitable model theory that would be able to handle this generality.

Our proposed model theory has a categorical flavor, manifested in the use of arrows that appear at two levels. At the meta level the arrows represent schema transformations. For example, an arrow could map a data source schema to a data warehouse schema, or two arrows could map each of two data source schemas into a mediated schema. These transformations are defined as schema morphisms that map the structural properties and integrity constraints of a schema. At the data level the arrows are data transformations specified as database morphisms. Database morphisms map the actual data sets in a manner that is compatible with the operations available on those sets and that preserves the schema's integrity constraints.

There are several implications of this arrow-theoretic approach. The first is that it leads to a very general view of the schema integration problem expressed entirely in terms of arrows. The generality is accomplished by using a particular categorical construction which applies to a variety of categories of schemas [12,14,19]. The specific nature of arrows used in this construction is determined by the category of schemas that defines the kind of structural and integrity transformations that the arrows actually represent.

The second implication is in the formal results that relate properties of arrows at the meta level and the data level. These results reveal a subtle duality manifested in the reversal of the corresponding arrows between the two levels. They also provide guidance for how to define schema transformations appropriately, in particular, so that the arrows preserve integrity constraints.

The third, most important implication is a formal framework for generic schema and data management which applies to a variety of data models. This is really the main contribution of this paper. This formal framework includes and relates the two levels (schema and data transformations) and captures both structural properties and integrity constraints. A key component of this theory is a strong integrity requirement on the permissible structural schema transformations so that they preserve the integrity constraints. This model theory relies on earlier results on a general model theory for a variety of programming paradigms and of associated logic paradigms [11,12].

We apply the proposed formal theory to two situations. First, we apply it to schema integration, where we prove results that are generic across data models and include a proper treatment of the integrity constraints. Second, we use it as a pattern for defining a data model, one based on abstract data types, which includes object-oriented features and typical database integrity constraints.

The paper is organized as follows. Section 2 starts with basic definitions, followed by a running example of a particular category of object-oriented schemas. The basic categorical definitions are given in Section 3, particularly the use of morphisms to represent schema mappings. Sections 4 through 6 are the core of the paper. Section 4 shows how to express the schema integration problem using morphisms. Section 5 introduces the notion of a generic schema transformation framework, specifies the condition for such a framework to preserve database integrity and proves the implications on schema integration. Section 6 shows how the proposed model theory applies to the category of schemas of the running example. Section 7 discusses related work and concludes.

## 2   Schemas

A database schema consists of two components: a schema signature and the associated integrity constraints. A schema signature specifies structural and operational features of a database schema. Its typical components are signatures for data types and their operations and signatures for *database sets* (relations, collections, etc.), illustrated in Example 1. Note that type signatures for collections determine the signatures for operations on collections. Signatures for integrity constraints are logical expressions whose form is determined by the choice of a particular logic and syntax of the constraint language. A feature of the definitions below is that they are sufficiently general to apply to a variety of schema signatures and associated constraint languages.

**Definition 1.** *(Schemas) A database schema Sch is a pair Sch = (Sig, E) where Sig is a schema signature and E is a set of integrity constraints expressed as sentences (formulae of a chosen logic with all variables quantified).*

This paper uses examples based on a category of schemas of an object-oriented style. Schemas of this category have user-defined abstract data types specified as Java interfaces. A schema signature consists of the specification of those types and of collection objects which represent the actual database. The integrity constraints are specified in Horn clause logic. We use typical database constraints: those expressing key dependencies and referential integrity constraints.

*Example 1.* (Sample schema)
```
schema Publishers {
interface Publisher
{ String publisherId();
  String name();
  String location();
  Set<Publication> publications();
}
```

```
interface Publication
{ String publicationId();
  String title();
  int    year();
  Publisher    publisher();
  Set<String> keywords();
}
Collection<Publisher>    dbPublishers;
Collection<Publication> dbPubs;
Constraints:
Publication X,Y;   Publisher Z,W;
dbPubs.member(X) :-  dbPublishers.member(Z), Z.publications.member(X);
dbPublishers.member(Z) :-  dbPubs.member(X), X.publisher.equals(Z);
Z.equals(W) :- dbPublishers.member(Z), dbPublishers.member(W),
               Z.publisherId().equals(W.publisherId());
X.equals(Y) :- dbPubs.member(X), dbPubs.member(Y),
               X.publicationId().equals(Y.publicationId());
}
```

As Java interfaces lack general-purpose constraint specifications, such constraints are omitted from our examples. However, this omission is by no means a limitation of our approach (see [1,2]). Note that **equals** is a method of the Java root class **Object** which is intended to be overridden to provide a data type specific meaning of equality. If this is the standard notion of equality then the logic paradigm becomes Horn clause logic with equality as in [13].

A database is a model for a schema. Given a schema signature $Sig$, the collection of all databases that *conform to Sig* (*implement Sig*) is denoted by $Db(Sig)$. A database $d$ that implements $Sig$ would thus have to implement the signatures of data types in $Sig$ as sets and the operation signatures as functions. Signatures for database sets would also have to be interpreted as sets, bags etc.

If a database $d$ that conforms to a schema signature $Sig$ satisfies the integrity constraints $E$, we say that $d$ is consistent with respect to the schema $(Sig, E)$. This is expressed by the satisfaction relation, denoted $\models$, between databases and the sets of sentences (i.e., integrity constraints) that they satisfy.

**Definition 2.** *(Database consistency) A database d is consistent with respect to the schema* $(Sig, E)$ *iff d belongs to* $Db(Sig)$ *and* $d \models e$ *for all* $e \in E$.

## 3   Schema Morphisms

In this approach the schema signatures for a given data model are required to constitute a category, denoted **Sig**. The same applies to the schemas. Schema transformations within a particular category of schemas are viewed as morphisms of that category. This approach allows us to talk about schemas without specifying their data model (i.e. category).

Formally, a *category* **C** consists of the following [19]:
– A collection of objects and a collection of arrows (morphisms).
– Each arrow has its domain object and its codomain object.

- If $f : X \to Y$ and $g : Y \to Z$ are arrows of $\mathbf{C}$, then $f$ and $g$ are composed into an arrow $gf : X \to Z$.
- The composition of arrows is associative, i.e., if $f : X \to Y$, $g : Y \to Z$ and $h : Z \to W$ are arrows of $\mathbf{C}$, then $h(gf) = (hg)f$.
- Each object $X$ of $\mathbf{C}$ is equipped with the identity arrow $1_X$ with the property that for any arrow $f : X \to Y$, $1_Y f = f$ and $f 1_X = f$.

The collection of all databases $Db(Sig)$ conforming to a given schema signature $Sig$ is required to constitute a category, with database morphisms that satisfy the above categorical requirements.

Schema morphisms are defined as mappings of schema signatures that preserve the integrity constraints.

**Definition 3.** *(Schema morphisms) A morphism of schemas $Sch_1 = (Sig_1, E_1)$ and $Sch_2 = (Sig_2, E_2)$ consists of a morphism $\phi : Sig_1 \to Sig_2$ of schema signatures which extends to a mapping of constraints, such that for all databases $d$ in $Db(Sig_2)$, if $d \models e_2$ for all $e_2 \in E_2$ then $d \models \phi(e_1)$ for all $e_1 \in E_1$.*

An equivalent condition is that $\phi(e_1)$ is in the closure of $E_2$ for all $e_1 \in E_1$. A particular case is $\phi(e_1) \in E_2$.

Definition 3 implies that schemas and their morphisms constitute a category, which we denote by **Sch**. The last condition in Definition 3 differentiates this work from many others. It requires that the integrity constraints of the source schema are transformed into constraints that are consistent with those of the target. This is expressed in a model-oriented fashion: a database that satisfies the constraints of the target schema also satisfies the transformed constraints of the source schema (as they appear in the target).

In Definition 1, distinguishing the notions of schema signature and schema (i.e., a schema signature plus its integrity constraints) leads to two notions of schema equivalence. The first one is just structural, based on schema signature morphisms. The second is semantic, requiring structural equivalence plus the semantic equivalence expressed in terms of integrity constraints.

**Definition 4.** *(Schema equivalence) Let $Sch_1$ and $Sch_2$ be two schemas*

- *$Sch_1$ and $Sch_2$ are structurally equivalent if there exists a pair of schema signature morphisms $f : Sig_1 \to Sig_2$ and $g : Sig_2 \to Sig_1$ such that $fg = 1_{Sig_2}$ and $gf = 1_{Sig_1}$.*
- *$Sch_1$ and $Sch_2$ are equivalent if the above condition is satisfied for schema morphisms $f$ and $g$.*

The category of all schemas for a given data model is required to include the initial schema $Sch_0$ that contains basic features implicitly available in any other schema (for example, predefined standard types such as Boolean, integer and string, and their associated constraints). $Sch_0$ typically does not contain signatures for database sets but does contain type signatures for the required collection types. Any other schema $Sch_X$ implicitly extends $Sch_0$ by a unique schema morphism $Sch_0 \to Sch_X$. The uniqueness requirement means that there is one standard way of incorporating $Sch_0$ into $Sch_X$ which makes $Sch_0$ a sub-schema of $Sch_X$.

The notion of a subschema $Sch_1$ of $Sch_2$ may be expressed by the categorical requirement that a monic arrow (schema morphism) $m : Sch_1 \rightarrow Sch_2$ exists. This means that given schema morphisms $f : Sch_X \rightarrow Sch_1$ and $g : Sch_X \rightarrow Sch_1$, $mf = mg$ implies $f = g$ [19]. In familiar cases, monic arrows are injections.

## 4   Schema Integration

A particularly important problem in schema management is schema integration [6,23,24]. Here, we are given two (or more) schemas and are asked to produce an integrated schema that can represent the information content of the given schemas. In one version of the problem, which we treat here, the integrated schema is populated with data and the given schemas are defined as views of the integrated schema.

All published schema integration results we know of are tied to a particular data model (i.e., to a particular category of schemas). By contrast, our approach applies to different categories of schemas. Moreover, it addresses the subtle problem of merging the integrity constraints of two schemas. These two distinctive features are accomplished by expressing the idea of schema integration in terms of morphisms of schemas. This way both structural and semantic conditions are taken into account.

**Definition 5.** *(Schema integration) An integration $Sch_{12}$ of schemas $Sch_1$ and $Sch_2$ is defined by the following commutative diagram of schema morphisms:*

$$
\begin{array}{ccc}
Sch_m & \xrightarrow{\phi_1} & Sch_1 \\
\phi_2\downarrow & & p\downarrow \\
Sch_2 & \xrightarrow{q} & Sch_{12}
\end{array}
$$

Two schemas are integrated over their matching part $Sch_m$. Two schemas always have a matching part: the initial schema $Sch_0$. The matching part $Sch_m$ is typically a subschema of both $Sch_1$ and $Sch_2$. The commutativity of the above diagram asserts that the two composite schema morphisms $p\phi_1$ and $q\phi_2$ are identical. This means that $Sch_m$ appears the same in $Sch_{12}$ whichever path (via $Sch_1$ or $Sch_2$) is taken.

*Example 2.* (Schema integration) We show the integration $Sch_{12}$ of $Sch_1$ (in Example 1) with another schema, $Sch_2$, such that $Sch_1$ and $Sch_2$ can be defined as views of $Sch_{12}$. First, we define $Sch_2$ as follows:

```
schema Authors {
interface Author
{ String authorId();
  String name();
  Date   dateOfBirth();
  Collection<Book> books();
  }
```

```
interface Book
{ String publicationID();
  String title();
  int     year();
  String publisher();
  Set<String> keywords();
  float   price();
  Collection<Author> authors();
}
Collection<Author> dbAuthors;
Collection<Book>    dbBooks;
Constraints:
Author X,Y; Book Z,W;
dbBooks.member(Z)    :- dbAuthors.member(X), X.books.member(Z);
dbAuthors.member(X) :- dbBooks.member(Z),   Z.authors.member(X);
X.equals(Y) :- dbAuthors.member(X), dbAuthors.member(Y),
               X.authorId().equals(Y.authorId());
Z.equals(W) :- dbBooks.member(Z), dbBooks.member(W),
               Z.ISBN().equals(W.ISBN())
}
```

A schema $Sch_{12}$ that integrates $Sch_1$ and $Sch_2$ is given below:

```
schema Publications {
import Publishers.Publisher;
import Publishers.Publication;
import Authors.Author;
interface Book extends Publication // integrates Book and Publication
{ float price();
  Collection<Author> authors();
}
Collection<Publisher>   dbPublishers;
Collection<Publication> dbPubs;
Collection<Author> dbAuthors;
Collection<Book>    dbBooks;
Constraints:
import Publishers.Constraints;
import Authors.Constraints;
Publication X;
dbPubs.member(X) :- dbBooks.member((Book)X) // add another constraint
}
```

Among all integrations $Sch_{12}$ of schemas $S_1$ and $S_2$, the schema-join of $Sch_1$ and $Sch_2$ denoted $Sch_1*Sch_2$, if it exists, has a distinctive property: it represents the minimal integration of $Sch_1$ and $Sch_2$. This notion is specified below entirely in terms of schema morphisms by a categorical construction called a *pushout* [19].

**Definition 6.** *(Schema join) Schema-join $Sch_1 * Sch_2$ of schemas $Sch_1$ and $Sch_2$ is defined by the following commutative diagram of schema morphisms:*

$$
\begin{array}{ccc}
Sch_m & \xrightarrow{\phi_1} & Sch_1 \\
\phi_2\downarrow & & h\downarrow \\
Sch_2 & \xrightarrow{k} & Sch_1 * Sch_2
\end{array}
$$

*with the following property: Given any integration $Sch_{12}$ of schemas $Sch_1$ and $Sch_2$ as defined in Definition 5 above, there exists a unique schema morphism $\phi : Sch_1 * Sch_2 \rightarrow Sch_{12}$ such that $\phi k = q$ and $\phi h = p$.*

A specific construction of schema-join is presented in Section 6. The fact that schema integration and schema-join are expressed entirely in terms of arrows representing schema morphisms has two distinctive implications: (i) both structural and database integrity properties are integrated, and (ii) the notion of schema integration is data model independent. Specific notions of schema integration are obtained by choosing a particular category of schemas which includes its schema morphisms.

## 5   Generic Schema Transformation Framework

The categorical approach developed so far leads to a very general notion of a data model. This model has two levels. The meta level consists of database schemas and their transformations expressed as schema morphisms. This transformation-based view is quite different from the standard notions of a data model. At the instance level these transformations operate on databases that conform to schemas at the meta level.

The notion of database integrity plays a fundamental role in this formal framework. The acceptable transformations at both levels are required to satisfy the integrity constraints. This integrity requirement is expressed as a condition that involves acceptable schema signature transformations and the satisfaction relation between databases and the integrity constraints.

The framework is proposed as a formal pattern for defining data models such that schema management and the associated database transformations have well-defined formal meanings. As such, it offers interesting observations on the relationships between the two levels which are sometimes quite different from the usual views of schema and data transformations. An example is the reversal of the directions of transformations at the two levels. Schema management operations such as schema integration have particularly desirable semantic properties when the conditions for this formal framework are satisfied.

The core of this model theory requires just one more categorical notion: a morphism of categories. Given categories **C** and **B**, a *functor $F :$* **C** $\rightarrow$ **B** consists of two related functions with the following properties [19]:

– The object function which assigns to each object $X$ of **C** an object $FX$ of **B**.
– The arrow function which assigns to each arrow $h : X \rightarrow Y$ of **C** an arrow $Fh : FX \rightarrow FY$ of **B**.
– $F(1_X) = 1_{FX}$ and $F(gh) = F(g)F(h)$, the latter whenever the composite $gh$ is defined.

Two functors play a crucial role in this theory. The first one is *Sen* : **Sign** $\rightarrow$ **Set** where **Set** denotes the category of sets. If *Sig* is a schema signature, then *Sen(Sig)* is the set of all well-formed sentences (integrity constraints) over *Sig*. Many constraint languages, hence many *Sen* functors, are possible for a given data model (i.e., which implies a choice of **Sign**). *Sen* is determined by the choice of logic that specifies the syntax of sentences of the constraint language. This syntax is defined starting with the features of a schema signature. The schema signature typically determines the terms of the constraint language, and the logic determines the formulae based on those terms. This is why *Sen* maps a schema signature into a set of sentences over that signature. *Sen* also maps a schema signature morphism to a function that transforms the sets of sentences.

The second functor is $Db : \mathbf{Sign} \to \mathbf{Cat}^{op}$. For each signature $Sig$, $Db(Sig)$ is the category of $Sig$ databases, together with their morphisms. These database morphisms represent data transformations, which correspond to the schema transformations represented by arrows in **Sign**. **Cat** denotes the category of categories. Objects of **Cat** are categories and arrows of **Cat** are functors. $\mathbf{Cat}^{op}$ differs from **Cat** only to the extent that the direction of its arrows is reversed. This reversal of the direction of arrows that happens going from schemas to their databases is one of the subtle and characteristic features of this model theory.

Recall that databases in the category $Db(Sig)$ are not necessarily consistent with respect to a set of integrity constraints $E$. The notion of database integrity is captured by the satisfaction relation $\models$ between databases in $Db(Sig)$ and sets of sentences over $Sig$.

We now have the machinery to define the notion of data model described in the beginning of this section. To emphasize the transformation-based view relative to classical data models, we give it a new name.

**Definition 7.** *(Schema transformation framework) A schema transformation framework consists of:*

- *A category of schema signatures* **Sign** *equipped with the initial object. This category consists of objects representing schema signatures together with their morphisms.*
- *A functor Sen :* **Sign** $\to$ **Set***. Sen(Sig) is a set of sentences over the schema signature Sig.*
- *A functor Db :* **Sign** $\to$ $\mathbf{Cat}^{op}$*. For each signature Sig, Db(Sig) is the category of Sig databases, together with their morphisms.*
- *For each signature Sig, a relation* $\models_{Sig} \subseteq \mid Db(Sig) \mid \times Sen(Sig)$ *called the satisfaction relation.* $\mid Db(Sig) \mid$ *denotes the set of objects of the category Db(Sig).*
- *For each schema signature morphism* $\phi : Sig_A \to Sig_B$*, the following Integrity Requirement holds for each* $Sig_B$ *database* $d_B$ *and each sentence* $e \in Sen(Sig_A)$*:*

$$d_B \models_{Sig_B} Sen(\phi)(e) \text{ iff } Db(\phi)(d_B) \models_{Sig_A} e.$$

The above definition is based on [11]. Its relationships are represented by the following diagram:

$$
\begin{array}{ccc}
Db(Sig_A) & \overset{\models_{Sig_A}}{\longrightarrow} & Sen(Sig_A) \\
Db(\phi) \uparrow & & \downarrow Sen(\phi) \\
Db(Sig_B) & \overset{\models_{Sig_B}}{\longrightarrow} & Sen(Sig_B)
\end{array}
$$

Note the reversal of the direction of the arrow $Db(\phi)$ relative to $Sen(\phi)$. $Sen(\phi)$ maps each constraint in $Sen(Sig_A)$ to a constraint in $Sen(Sig_B)$. By contrast, $Db(\phi)$ maps each database in $Db(Sig_B)$ to a database in $Db(Sig_A)$. If we think of $\phi$ as a mapping from a logical database schema $Sig_A$ into a physical schema

$Sig_B$, then $Db(\phi)$ tells how to materialize a view in $Db(Sig_A)$ from a database in $Db(Sig_B)$.

To see why this reversal of arrows happens, consider an injective schema morphism $\phi : Sch_1 \to Sch_2$ which makes $Sch_1$ a subschema of $Sch_2$. $Sch_2$ just extends the signatures and the constraints of $Sch_1$ (we assume a monotonic logic such as Horn clause logic). A database that is consistent with respect to $Sch_2$ is also (by projection) consistent with $Sch_1$. The other way around does not hold.

The *Integrity Requirement* puts a very strong semantic restriction on the permissible schema signature transformations (schema morphisms). It only allows ones that preserve the validity of constraints. That is, suppose $\phi$ maps constraint $e_A$ to $e_B$ (more precisely, $e_B = (Db)(\phi)(e_A)$ for $e_A \in Sen(Sig_A)$). Then the *Integrity Requirement* says that $e_B$ is valid in a database $d_B$ iff $e_A$ is valid in the $Sig_A$ database that corresponds to $d_B$ (i.e., in $Db(\phi)(d_B)$).

The *Integrity Requirement* applies directly to the problem of schema integration in Definition 6. It ensures that each valid database of the integrated schema corresponds to valid databases of the schemas to be integrated. This point is made precise in the following theorem.

**Theorem 1.** *(Materializing subschemas) Suppose $Sch_1$ and $Sch_2$ are schemas that are integrated into $Sch_{12}$ relative to some schema transformation framework. Given a consistent database $d$ in $Db(Sch_{12})$, it is possible to construct databases $d_1$ and $d_2$ that are consistent relative to schema $Sch_1$ and schema $Sch_2$ respectively.*

*Proof.* We have schema morphisms $\phi_1 : Sch_1 \to Sch_{12}$ and $\phi_2 : Sch_2 \to Sch_{12}$ where $Sch_1 = (Sig_1, E_1)$ and $Sch_2 = (Sig_2, E_2)$. We construct database $d_1$ as $Db(\phi_1)(d)$ and database $d_2$ as $Db(\phi_2)(d)$.

Since $d$ is a consistent database and $\phi_1$ and $\phi_2$ are schema morphisms, Definition 3 implies:

- $d \models_{Sig_{12}} (Sen)(\phi_1)(e)$ for all $e \in E_1$
- $d \models_{Sig_{12}} (Sen)(\phi_2)(e)$ for all $e \in E_2$.

We can now complete the proof by applying the Integrity Requirement to the above two lines, yielding:

- $Db(\phi_1)(d) \models_{Sig_1} e$ for all $e \in E_1$
- $Db(\phi_2)(d) \models_{Sig_2} e$ for all $e \in E_2$.

In essence, databases conforming to $Sch_1$ and $Sch_2$ are materialized views of $Sch_{12}$. Thus, the above theorem relates the consistency of databases conforming to the integrated schema to those of the materialized views. This is an unusual perspective in that views typically do not have integrity constraints.

Note that in order to make this proof possible both the reversal of arrows and the Integrity Requirement are essential.

**Corollary 1.** *(Schema-joins) Let $Sch_{12}$ be an integration of schemas $Sch_1$ and $Sch_2$ relative to a schema transformation framework. Let $d$ be a consistent database in the category $Db(Sig_{12})$. If $Sch_1 * Sch_2 = (Sig_{1*2}, E_{1*2})$ exists, then there is a canonical way to construct a consistent database $d_*$ in the category $Db(Sig_{1*2})$.*

*Proof.* By Definition 6, there is a unique $\phi : Sch_1 * Sch_2 \rightarrow Sch_{12}$. $d_*$ is constructed as $Db(\phi)(d)$. Since $d$ is consistent, by Theorem 1 so is $d_*$.

Corollary 1 says that for any consistent database of an integrated schema, there exists a corresponding (minimal) consistent database of the schema-join of the two schemas that were integrated. The canonical arrow $Db(\phi)$ is a recipe for constructing that (minimal) consistent database.

# 6    An Application of Schema Transformation Frameworks

One role of the generic schema transformation framework is to serve as a formal generic pattern for defining new data models, with well defined meanings for schema and data transformations. This section gives a detailed description of how one constructs such a data model: a category of schemas and their databases for Examples 1 and 2, which we call **Objc** (OO with Constraints).

A schema of **Objc** consists of a collection of sorts (type names) some of which are predefined in the initial schema $Sch_0$ and which in particular must include the sort Boolean along with the standard axioms. The others are abstract data types defined in the schema itself; each is a set of method signatures specified as a Java interface. The is-a (inheritance) relationship thus amounts to the subset relation which agrees with the rules of the Java type system. A schema contains collection objects which are the actual database sets. To specify their type, a parametric $Collection < T >$ type is used and instantiated with the required element type selected among the abstract data types defined in the schema.

**Definition 8.** *(Objc schema signatures) A schema signature consists of:*
- *A finite set of sorts $S$, which includes Boolean.*
- *A finite set of interfaces $A$ (abstract data types) such that $A \subseteq S$.*
- *An interface $A_k$ is a set of method signatures of the form $C\ m(C_1\ x_1, C_2\ x_2,$ $\ldots, C_n\ x_n)$ where $C \in S$ and $C_i \in S$ for $i = 1, 2, \ldots, n$. (m is the method name, $C$ is the return type, and $C_i$ is the type of parameter $x_i$.)*
- *If the interface $A_k$ extends the interface $A_l$ (inheritance) then $A_l \subseteq A_k$.*
- *A finite set of collection signatures $\{Collection < A_j >: X_j\}$ where $A_j \in A$ and $Collection < A_j > \in S$.*

To specify the type of data sets of a schema, parametric collection types are required. The issue of parametric types is a major one by itself. It will be elaborated only to a limited extent here by showing that a specific collection type (i.e., for a specific element type) is obtained from a parametric type by the same pushout construction [12] that we used for schema integration.

**Definition 9.** *(Objc collection types) An instantiated collection interface Collection $< A >$ is defined by the following pushout diagram*

$$
\begin{array}{ccc}
T & \longrightarrow & Collection < T > \\
\downarrow & & h \downarrow \\
A & \xrightarrow{\ k\ } & Collection < A >
\end{array}
$$

In the above definition a parametric interface *Collection* $< T >$ is viewed as a morphism $T \to Collection < T >$. The substitution $T \to A$ and instantiation *Collection* $< T > \to$ *Collection* $< A >$ are also morphisms. The morphism $A \to Collection < A >$ is obtained from $T \to Collection < T >$ and the substitution $T \to A$.

The above construction generalizes the usual views of instantiated parametric types. If a pushout is based on schema morphisms (which apply to both structural properties and integrity constraints), not just on signature morphisms, then the notion of instantiation of parametric types becomes semantic in nature.

Constraints are sentences expressed in Horn clause logic. Terms include method invocations and thus appear in the object-oriented form. Atoms are invocations of Boolean methods. This limited logic is sufficiently expressive to capture most typical database constraints, such as key and inclusion dependencies.

**Definition 10.** *(Objc constraints) For a given schema signature Sig with sorts S:*

- *A collection object of type Collection $< A_k >$ is a term of type Collection $< A_k >$.*
- *A variable X of type $A_k$ where $A_k \in S$ is a term of type $A_k$.*
- *If a is a term of type $A_k$, $a_1, a_2, \ldots, a_n$ are terms of respective types $A_1, A_2$, $\ldots, A_n$, C $m(A_1, A_2, \ldots, A_n)$ is a method of the interface $A_k$ of Sig, then $a.m(a_1, a_2, \ldots, a_n)$ is a term of type C.*
- *With the above definitions, an atom is of the form $a.m(a_1, a_2, \ldots, a_n)$ where m's result type is Boolean.*
- *A constraint is of the form $p \leftarrow p_1, p_2, \ldots, p_n$ where $p, p_1, p_2, \ldots, p_n$ are atoms.*

Permissible schema signature transformations of **Objc** are defined below as schema signature morphisms. Their core is a mapping of sorts, extended to signatures of methods and collection objects. This mapping is the identity on the inital schema's predefined sorts, so these sorts have the same interpretation in all **Objc** schemas. Note that *Collection* $< T >$ is not intended to have methods with arguments of type *Collection* $< T >$, so that *Collection* $< A_k >$ would be a structural subtype of *Collection* $< A_l >$ if $A_k$ is a subtype of $A_l$.

**Definition 11.** *(Objc schema signature morphisms) A morphism of schema signatures $\phi : Sig_1 \to Sig_2$ consists of the following:*

- *An injective mapping of sorts $\phi : S_1 \to S_2$ such that*
  - *$\phi(s) = s$ for $s \in S_0$ where $S_0$ are the sorts of the initial schema $Sch_0$.*
  - *$\phi(Collection < A_i >) = Collection < \phi(A_i) >$*
- *$\phi$ applies to interfaces as follows:*
  *$\phi(C \ m(C_1, C_2, \ldots, C_n)) = \phi(C) \ \phi(m)(\phi(C_1), \phi(C_2), \ldots, \phi(C_n))$*
- *$\phi$ maps collection objects of $Sig_1$ into collection objects of $Sig_2$ such that*
  *$\phi(Collection < A_j >: X_j) = \phi(Collection < A_j >) : \phi(X_j)$.*

The above definition is intended to allow a mapping of an abstract data type to its extension with possible renaming and possibly enforcing structural subtyping conditions.

The notion of schema signature morphism is extended below to a schema morphism. The extension maps the integrity constraints in accordance with the mapping of the sorts in a schema signature morphism.

**Definition 12.** *(**Objc** schema morphisms) A morphism of schemas* $\phi : Sch_1 \to Sch_2$ *is a schema signature morphism* $\phi : Sig_1 \to Sig_2$ *such that* $\phi$ *extends to a function* $E_1 \to E_2$ *as follows:*

- $\phi(x_s) = x_{\phi(s)}$
- $\phi(a.m(a_1, a_2, \ldots, a_n)) = \phi(a).\phi(m)(\phi(a_1), \ldots, \phi(a_n))$, *where* $m$ *may be a Boolean method.*
- $\phi(p \leftarrow p_1, p_2, \ldots, p_n) = \phi(p) \leftarrow \phi(p_1), \phi(p_2), \ldots, \phi(p_n)$

Given Definitions 10 and 11, the definition of the *Sen* functor is immediate and so is the verification of its functorial properties.

**Definition 13.** *(**Objc** Sen functor) Define Sen :* **Sign** $\to$ **Set** *as follows:*

- *Sen(Sig) is a set of sentences of the form* $\{p \leftarrow p_1, p_2, \ldots, p_n\}$ *where* $p, p_1, p_2, \ldots, p_n$ *are atoms according to Definition 10.*
- *Given a schema signature morphism* $\phi : Sig_1 \to Sig_2$,
  $Sen(\phi)(\{p \leftarrow p_1, p_2, \ldots, p_n\}) = \{\phi(p) \leftarrow \phi(p_1), \phi(p_2), \ldots, \phi(p_n)\}$.

**Proposition 1.** *(**Objc** Sen functor) Then Sen is a functor* **Sign** $\to$ **Set**.

*Proof.* Sen obviously preserves the identity schema signature morphism, i.e. $Sen(1_{Sig}) = 1_{Sen(Sig)}$ and the composition of schema signature morphisms, i.e., $Sen(\phi_1\phi_2) = Sen(\phi_1)Sen(\phi_2)$.

A database for a given **Objc** schema includes a domain for each sort in the schema. A domain is a set equipped with functions representing the interpretation of the method signatures. A database also includes the actual data sets, one for each collection object signature in the schema. By Definition 2, a database for a given schema must be consistent.

**Definition 14.** *(**Objc** databases) A database d for a given schema Sch = (Sig, E) consists of the following:*

- *A collection of sets (domains)* $\{D_s \mid s \in S\}$ *where* $S$ *is the set of sorts of Sig. S includes Boolean, whose domain is true and false.*
- *For each method* $m$ *of an interface* $A_k$ *with signature* $C\ m(C_1\ x_1, C_2\ x_2, \ldots, C_n\ x_n)$ *a function* $f_m : D_w \to D_C$ *where* $D_w = D_{A_k} \times D_{C_1} \times \ldots \times D_{C_n}$ *with* $w = A_k C_1 \ldots C_n$.
- *For each collection variable of type Collection* $< A_k >$ *a set with elements from the domain* $D_k$.
- *If* $A_l \subseteq A_k$ *then there exists a function (projection)* $D_k \to D_l$ *and thus also a function Collection* $< D_k > \to$ *Collection* $< D_l >$.

- *Let $e$ be a constraint with variables $X$ such that $X_s \subseteq X$ is a set of variables in $X$ of sort $s$. If $\theta$ is a substitution of variables in $e$ (i.e. a family of functions $X_s \to D_s$) then $e < \theta >$ evaluates to true.*

Although collections in the above definition are interpreted as sets, in general they can be bags.

To complete the above definition, we must specify its morphisms of the category of databases: a family of functions, one per database domain, that map the actual data sets as well. These maps are required to satisfy two conditions: a standard algebraic condition that applies to operations on the original domains and their images, and a condition that applies to the integrity constraints. As we are talking here about the category of databases for a schema, not just for a schema signature, database morphisms are required to map each consistent database into another consistent database.

**Definition 15.** *(Database morphisms for* **Objc** *schemas) Let $d$ and $d'$ be databases consistent with respect to a schema $(Sig, E)$. Then a database morphism $h : D \to D'$ is a family of functions $h_s : D_s \to D'_s$ for $s \in S$ where $S$ stands for the set of sorts of $Sig$.*

- *For each method $m$ of interface $A_k$ with signature $C\ m(C_1\ x_1, C_2\ x_2, \ldots, C_n\ x_n)$ and $a \in D_w$, $h_s(f_m(a)) = f'_m(h_w(a))$ holds, where $h_w$ is a product of functions $h_{A_k} \times h_{C_1} \times \ldots \times h_{C_n}$ when $w = A_k C_1 C_2 \ldots C_n$, as in the following diagram:*

$$
\begin{array}{ccc}
D_w & \xrightarrow{f_m} & D_C \\
h_w \downarrow & & \downarrow h_C \\
D'_w & \xrightarrow{f'_m} & D'_C
\end{array}
$$

- *Suppose $e \in E$ has variables $X$. If $\theta_s : X_s \to D_s$ is a substitution of variables for $X$ and $e < \theta >$ evaluates to true, then so does $e < \theta' >$, where $\theta'$ is constructed as the composition of $\theta_s$ and $h_s$.*

**Definition 16.** *(Db functor for* **Objc** *schemas) Define Db as follows:*
  *$Db(Sig)$ is a category with objects and arrows defined in 14 and 15. Given $\phi : Sig_1 \to Sig_2$, $Db(\phi)$ is defined as:*
- *If $d_2$ is a $Sig_2$ database with domains $\{D_s \mid s \in S_2\}$ then $Db(\phi)(d_2)$ is a $Sig_1$ database with domains $\{D_s \mid s \in \phi(S_1)\}$. The same applies to the collection objects.*
- *A morphism $h : d_2 \to d'_2$ of $Sig_2$ databases (a family of functions $\{h_s \mid s \in S_2\}$) is mapped into a morphism $Db(\phi)(h)$ of $Sig_1$ databases by restricting $h$ to the family of functions $\{h_s \mid s \in \phi(S_1)\}$.*

Prop. 2 specifies how the $Db$ functor is constructed and how its functorial properties are verified. Note that $D_s$ and $h_s$ now correspond to the sort $\phi^{-1}(s) \in S_1$.

**Proposition 2.** *(Db functor for* **Objc** *schemas) Db in Definition 16 is a functor* **Sign** $\to$ **Cat**$^{op}$.

*Proof.* A schema signature morphism $\phi : Sig_1 \rightarrow Sig_2$ according to Definition 11 maps to a database morphism $Db(\phi) : Db(Sig_2) \rightarrow Db(Sig_1)$ according to the above construction and Definition 15. The family $Db(\phi)(d_2) \rightarrow Db(\phi)(d'_2)$ is a $Sig_1$ database morphism, because $h$ is a morphism of $Sig_2$ databases. Two properties are essential here: the injective mapping of sorts required in Definition 11 of schema signature morphisms and mapping of collections as specified in Definition 14.

The developments presented so far in this section lead to two theorems. The first one asserts that the paradigm satisfies the conditions of Definition 7 and thus is a schema transformation framework. It is based on the already established functors *Sen* and *Db*.

**Theorem 2.** *(A schema transformation framework)*
- *Let the category of schema signatures* **Objc** *be defined according to Definitions 8 and 11.*
- *Define the functor Sen :* **Sign** $\rightarrow$ **Set** *according to Proposition 1.*
- *Define the functor Db :* **Sign** $\rightarrow$ **Cat**$^{op}$ *according to the Proposition 2 so that the category $Db(Sig)$ is defined according to Definitions 14 and 15.*
- *The satisfaction relation is also specified in Definitions 14 and 15.*

*Under the above conditions the* Integrity Requirement *holds.*

*Proof.* We have to prove that each schema signature morphism $\phi : Sig_A \rightarrow Sig_B$ in Definition 11 satisfies the *Integrity Requirement*, that is, $d_B \models_{Sig_B} Sen(\phi)(e)$ iff $Db(\phi)(d_B) \models_{Sig_A} e$ holds for each sentence $e \in Sen(Sig_A)$.

Given $e \in Sen(Sig_A)$, $Sen(\phi)(e)$ is defined by Proposition 1. For a given object $d_B$ of the category $Db(Sig_B)$, $Db(\phi)(d_B)$ is defined in Proposition 2. The proof amounts to:

$$d_B \models_{Sig_B} (\phi(p) \leftarrow \phi(p_1), \phi(p_2), \ldots, \phi(p_n)) \text{ iff}$$

$$Db(\phi)(d_B) \models_{Sig_A} (p \leftarrow p_1, p_2, \ldots, p_n).$$

The second theorem establishes the existence of the schema-join of any two schemas of this schema transformation framework. This result provides a standard technique for integrating two **Objc** schemas. This integration is both structural and semantic (i.e. the integrity constraints are properly integrated) because it is based entirely on schema morphisms according to the pushout construction in Definition 6.

**Theorem 3.** *The schema-join of any two* **Objc** *schemas over the initial schema $Sch_0$ exists.*

*Proof.* Given schemas $Sch_1$ and $Sch_2$ the integrated schema $Sch_1 * Sch_2$ is defined as follows: (i) $S_{Sch_1*Sch_2} = S_1 \cup S_2$ (sorts), (ii) $A_{Sch_1*Sch_2} = A_{Sch_1} \sqcup A_{Sch_2}$ (interfaces), (iii) $C_{Sch_1*Sch_2} = C_{Sch_1} \sqcup C_{Sch_2}$ (collections), and (iv) $E_{Sch_1*Sch_2} = E_{Sch_1} \sqcup E_{Sch_2}$ (constraints).

With this construction $Sch_1$ and $Sch_2$ are subschemas of $Sch_1 * Sch_2$ since we have two injective schema morphisms $\phi_1 : Sch_1 \to Sch_1 * Sch_2$ and $\phi_2 : Sch_2 \to Sch_1 * Sch_2$.

Suppose that we are given $p : Sch_1 \to S_{12}$ and $q : Sch_2 \to S_{12}$. The required schema morphism $\phi : Sch_1 * Sch_2 \to Sch_{12}$ is defined on the sorts as follows: $\phi(s) = p(s)$ for $s \in S_1$ and $\phi(s) = q(s)$ for $s \in S_2$.

Note that $\phi_1(s) = s$ for $s \in S_0$ and $\phi_2(s) = s$ for $s \in S_0$. So $\phi$ is well defined for $s \in S_1 \cap S_2$.

As interfaces, collections and constraints of $Sch_1 * Sch_2$ are defined as disjoint unions of the corresponding components of $Sch_1$ and $Sch_2$, we have $\phi h = p$ and $\phi k = q$.

Note that with the choice of a different logic the above result would not necessarily hold. The union of constraints could lead to a set of sentences for which there is no database (particularly in a given category) that satisfies the constraints (represents a model for the constraints) $\phi_1(E_1)$ and $\phi_2(E_2)$ (see Definition 3).

# 7  Conclusions and Related Work

The main contribution of this paper is a model theory for generic schema management. While the ideas on generic schema management proposed so far have been mostly informal [4] and pragmatic [5], this paper shows that a formal framework for such generic tools does indeed exist.

A distinctive feature of the presented paradigm is that it applies to a variety of categories of schemas and to a variety of logic bases for expressing database integrity constraints. This level of generality is accomplished by making use of a categorical model theory called *institutions*, proposed for programming language paradigms [11]. We believe ours is the first application of this theory to database models and languages. An earlier attempt in [17] is similar in spirit, but is less general. It also does not address the logic basis and preservation of integrity constraints and lacks provable results.

The core of this model theory is a general, transformation-oriented definition of a data model. This generic schema management framework serves as a pattern for constructing data models in such a way that schema transformations as well as the associated database transformations have well-defined meaning. As a rule, most well known data models have not been constructed in such a spirit. Furthermore, this framework is intended to be applied to data models that are still not completely or formally established, such as XML. A further distinctive feature of this framework is that it has a strong database integrity requirement as its possibly most fundamental component.

This paper also shows how to address some well-known problems such as schema equivalence [15,16] and schema integration [6] at this level of generality. The results are independent of a particular category of schemas and apply to both structural properties and integrity constraints. The requirement for proper handling of the integrity constraints in those problems is one of the contributions of this paper. Furthermore, this approach is independent of a particular logic paradigm used as a basis for the constraint language.

Contrary to the published work on schema and data transformations (schema integration in particular) in which transformations at the meta and data levels have the same direction [21], this paper reveals a subtlety not considered in the relevant papers. The subtlety is manifested in the reversal of the transformation arrows at the two levels. This observation is an important component of the presented model theory, having both pragmatic and mathematical significance.

In this paper one option is that schema transformations must satisfy particular structural subtyping conditions. Such a strict discipline has its place in programming languages, but it is often not satisfied in schema transformations. Furthermore, if the abstract data types are equipped with constraints, semantic compatibility notions such as behavioral subtyping [18] become a major issue. Model theoretic implications of behavioral compatibility issues in mapping abstract data types equipped with constraints are given in [1].

In a model in which inheritance is identified with subtyping (as in Java) a single partial order of sorts is required. This introduces further subtleties in schema transformations and schema integration. Models with different types of ordering of sorts are elaborated in [1] and [3]. The relevant results on pushouts of algebraic specifications are given in [14].

The idea of organizing schemas in a particular category which is a partial order with least upper bounds and greatest lower bounds (a lattice) appeared in [8]. By contrast, the categorical approach presented here relies on pushout and pullback [19], which are much more general notions than greatest lower and least upper bound. This approach also generalizes [8] by considering the database level, not just the schema level, and by being applicable to a variety of schema categories, including such features as methods and constraints.

In this paper we do not consider the problem of mapping one schema transformation framework (for example, relational) into another (for example, object-oriented). This situation is captured by the notion of a morphism of schema transformation frameworks (following [11,17]), and is a topic of work in progress.

The formal paradigm presented in this paper applies to appropriately simplified XML schemas [25]. The reasons are: the nature of the type system of the XML Schema, the kind of the integrity constraints (keys and referential integrity constraints) expressible in XML schemas (also considered in [10]), and the existence of the initial schema (more precisely, a name space). Space limitations do not allow further elaboration of these important implications of the development presented in this paper. However, application of this model theory to the XML data model is a major topic of future research.

Constraints (mostly key and inclusion dependencies) for XML models have been investigated in some recent papers such as [7,9,10]. In [10] keys, functional dependencies and foreign keys are based on attributes and investigated in the presence of DTDs. Subtyping or type extensions are not considered. In [7] a more elaborate structure of keys is considered but irrrespective of the typing issues.

Both results are particularly relevant because of their model-theoretic nature and results related to their notion of satisfaction.

This paper is not addressing explicitly modeling of database dynamics. But this is by no means a limitation of the paradigm. Database dynamics is taken into account by choosing the *Sen* functor for a suitable temporal logic. A development of such a paradigm is given in [1,2,3].

# Acknowledgments

We are grateful for many helpful suggested improvements from Alon Halevy, Svetlana Kouznetsova, Renée Miller, and the anonymous referees.

# References

1. Alagić, S.: Semantics of temporal classes, *Information and Computation 163*, pp. 60-102, 2000.
2. Alagić, S.: Constrained matching is type safe, Proc. of the Sixth Int. Workshop on Database Programming Languages, *LNCS 1369*, Springer-Verlag, pp. 78-96, 1998.
3. Alagić, S. and M. Alagić, Order-sorted model theory for temporal executable specifications, *Theoretical Computer Science 179*, pp. 273-299, 1997.
4. Bernstein, P. A. , A. Halevy, R. A. Pottinger: A vision for management of complex models, *ACM SIGMOD Record 29(4)*, pp. 54-63, 2000.
5. Bernstein, P.A. and E. Rahm: Data warehouse scenarios for model management, ER 2000, *LNCS 1920*, Springer-Verlag, pp. 1-15.
6. Batini, C., M. Lenzerini, S. B. Navathe: A comparative analysis of methodologies for database schema integration, *ACM Comp. Surveys 18(4)*, pp. 323-364, 1986.
7. P. Buneman, S. Davidson, W. Fan, C. Hara, W-C. Tan, Reasoning about keys for XML, DBPL 2001 (Databases and Programming Languages), *Lecture Notes in Computer Science* (this volume).
8. Buneman, P., S. Davidson, and A. Kosky: Theoretical aspects of schema merging, EDBT 1992, pp. 152-167.
9. P. Buneman, W. Fan, J. Simeon and S. Weinstein, Constraints for semistructured data and XML, *ACM SIGMOD Record 30(1)*, pp. 47-54, 2001.
10. Fan, W. and L. Libkin, On XML integrity constraints in the presence of DTDs, *PODS 2001*, pp. 114-125.
11. Goguen, J. and R. Burstall, Institutions: Abstract model theory for specification and programming, *Journal of the ACM 39(1)*, pp. 92-146, 1992.
12. Goguen, J.: Types as theories, in: G. M. Reed, A. W. Roscoe and R. F. Wachter, *Topology and Category Theory in Computer Science*, Clarendon Press, Oxford, pp. 357-390, 1991.
13. Goguen, J. and J. Meseguer, Order-sorted algebra I: Equational deduction for multiple inheritance, overloading, exceptions and partial operations, *Theoretical Computer Science 105*, pp. 217-273, 1992.
14. Haxthausen, A.E. and F. Nickl: Pushouts of order-sorted algebraic specifications, in M. Wirsing and M. Nivat, eds., Algebraic Methodology and Software Tech. (AMAST 96), *LNCS 1101*, Springer-Verlag, pp. 132-147, 1996.
15. Hull, R.: Relative information capacity of simple relational database schemata, *SIAM Journal of Computing 15(3)*, pp. 856-886, 1986.

16. Hull, R.: Managing semantic heterogeneity in databases: A theoretical perspective, *PODS 1997*, 51-61.
17. Kalinichenko, L.A.: Methods and tools for equivalent data model mapping construction, *EDBT 1990, LNCS 416*, Springer-Verlag, pp. 92-119.
18. Liskov, B. and J. M. Wing: A behavioral notion of subtyping, *ACM TOPLAS 16*, pp. 1811-1841.
19. Mac Lane, S.: *Categories for a Working Mathematician*, Springer, 1998.
20. Madhavan, J., P. A. Bernstein, E. Rahm: Generic schema matching with Cupid, *VLDB 2001*, pp. 49-58.
21. Miller, R. J., Y. E. Ioannidis, R. Ramakrishnan, Schema equivalence in heterogeneous systems: Bridging theory and practice, *Information Systems 19(1)*, pp. 3-31, 1994.
22. Rahm, E. and P.A. Bernstein: On matching schemas automatically. *VLDB Journal 10(4)*, pp. 334-350, 2001.
23. Spaccapietra, S., C. Parent, Y. Dupont: Model independent assertions for integration of heterogeneous schemas, *VLDB Journal 1*, pp. 81-126, 1992.
24. Spaccapietra, S. and C. Parent: View integration: A step forward in solving structural conflicts, *IEEE TKDE 6(2)*, pp. 258 - 274, 1994.
25. W3C: XML Schema, http://www.w3c.org/XML/schema, 2001.

# View Serializable Updates
# of Concurrent Index Structures

Stavros Cosmadakis[1], Kleoni Ioannidou[2], and Stergios Stergiou[3]

[1] University of Patras
[2] University of Toronto
[3] University of Athens

**Abstract.** We present new algorithms for concurrent reading and updating of B*-trees and binary search trees. Our algorithms are based on the well-known link technique, and improve previously proposed solutions in several respects. We prove formally that our algorithms are correct. We show that they satisfy a *view serializability* criterion, which fails for previous solutions. This stronger serializability criterion is central to the proof that several subtle (but essential) optimizations incorporated in our algorithms are correct.

## 1 Introduction

Multi-user database systems have to synchronize processes that access the data, so that each process sees a consistent view [BHG87, P86, GR93]. Special-purpose synchronization techniques, designed around specific search structures, have a long history; surveys are given in [GM97, SW97]).

Among algorithms for concurrent access to B-trees (a very common index structure [BMcC72]), those designed around the *link technique* [LY81] seem to be most successful [J90]. The technique was originally proposed in [KL80] (for binary search trees). It achieves constant number of simultaneous locks per operation (search, insertion or deletion) by requiring the (small) overhead of including an extra link pointer at each node. This pointer is used to redirect searches that may have read an outdated version of the node.

The main concurrent algorithms for B-trees which use the link technique [S86, S85] assume that deletions are relatively infrequent ([LY81] does not deal with deletions). In these cases it is sensible to delegate the *rebalancing* of the tree (an operation necessary to prevent performance deterioration) to separate processes. The idea was introduced in [KL80] (for binary search trees). Since the rebalancing processes run asynchronously to the main operations, the tree may become temporarily unbalanced. Subsequent algorithms for B-trees rebalance the tree with separate processes, designed so that the tree is "approximately balanced" at all times [LF96, NSW87].

Separate processes can also be used to perform garbage collection of deleted nodes in concurrent search structures (a task that is often delicate [JL96]). Treating the maintenance (rebalancing, garbage collection) of the structure separately has been a recurrent theme in concurrent data structures [GM97, SW97]. It simplifies substan-

G. Grahne and G. Ghelli (Eds.): DBPL 2001, LNCS 2397, pp. 247–262, 2002.
© Springer-Verlag Berlin Heidelberg 2002

tially the design of concurrent algorithms, since synchronization of the main operations with the maintenance operations is left to the general-purpose mechanisms of the system. It also facilitates analysis and proof of correctness of these algorithms (often a lengthy and convoluted task [GM97]).

In this work we take a complementary view. We design concurrent algorithms for $B^*$-trees and binary search trees, where the maintenance is done by the search and update processes themselves. Thus the rebalancing and garbage collection operations are not postponed, and the structure can be searched as efficiently as possible at all times. Such fine-tuned algorithms may be of interest for applications which require efficient on-line access to data, e.g. e-commerce [ABS99]. Since each operation does its own maintenance as it is running, our algorithms ensure efficient access without any assumptions about the relative frequency of updates (which usually need maintenance afterwards) vs. searches (which usually need none).

In section 2 we present an algorithm for $B^*$-trees. Our solution requires only small additional overhead (one more link pointer per node) compared to [LY81]. Compared to the previous solution, where maintenance is done separately ([S86], see also [S85]), our algorithm has to lock one more node per update (insertion or deletion) operation. Since update processes have to search the structure, the decrease in the allowable concurrency of updates is compensated by the increase in the efficiency of searches. Also, in the solution of [S86] a search may end up in the wrong node and thus have to restart; this does not occur with our algorithm.

In section 3 we present an algorithm for binary search trees. We redesign the deletion and search algorithms in [ML84] to maintain the tree at the same time. Compared to the solution of [ML84], our algorithm uses less auxiliary space to redirect searches; and dispenses with the data structures [ML84] uses to manage the independent maintenance processes. We lock no more nodes per operation than [ML84]; we lock one node less per typical deletion operation.

Our algorithms maintain the following property of the search structure: if a non-deleted node has a pointer to a deleted node $n$, then $n$ will have no pointers to further deleted nodes. We use this property to simplify the control structure of our algorithms (see Remarks 2.3.1, 2.4.1, 3.4.1). It can also be used to simplify and speed up garbage collection techniques based on reference counting [JL96].

To prove that the above property holds, we have to consider the intermediate states of the structure. The intermediate states are not highlighted in correctness proofs for concurrent algorithms for data structures, which are usually formalized by some variant of *final state serializability* [SG88, SK80, LY81, S86, KL80, ML84], or *conflict serializability* [SG88, SK80]. As a matter of fact, correctness proofs for (concurrent algorithms for) $B^*$-trees and binary search trees are often presented as "informal" [LY81, KL80, ML84], or even omitted [SG88, S86]. This is not incidental: in our view, the obvious approach to proving correctness is by induction on time, and final-state serializability is not a strong enough hypothesis for such an argument to go through – mainly because of the subtleties of deletion algorithms. Also, it is not clear how to define a reasonable notion of conflict – again because of deletion, which in general will result in non-local updating to the structure.

We sidestep these difficulties by using *view serializability* as a correctness criterion. The notion we use is an adaptation of view serializability for databases consisting of atomic entities (defined in [BHG87, P86]). View serializability is a stronger requirement than final-state serializability, and seems the right way to formulate correctness assertions that are proved by induction on time. It implies that, at any point in time, the state of the structure will be the state that would have resulted if the search and update operations had run sequentially. Consequently, view serializability makes it possible to transfer properties of sequential algorithms to concurrent algorithms. For the particular case of our algorithm for binary search trees, view serializability implies that the tree will be balanced on the average (since this holds for the sequential algorithm [K97], which our algorithm adapts to a concurrent setting). We note that view serializability fails for the algorithm of [S86]; this is the reason a search may end up in the wrong node (and thus have to restart). We do not know if view serializability holds for the algorithm of [ML84].

# 2    B*-Trees

## 2.1    Preliminaries

The B-tree [BMcC72] is a secondary-memory index structure for files of data records. We consider the $B^*$-tree, a variant of the B-tree described in [W74].

In a $B^*$-tree data reside at the leaves, and the internal nodes are used to guide searches through the tree. Each data record has a key, and key values are taken from some totally ordered set. A node of the tree contains a sequence of pairs $(v, p)$, where $v$ is a key value and $p$ is a pointer. The pairs in a node are arranged in ascending order of the key values (from left to right). Further, all key values in the nodes of some level (at the same distance from the root) are arranged in an ascending sequence (from left to right). Every node contains at least M and at most 2M pairs, where M is fixed (M≥2); the only exception is the root, which can contain at least 2 and at most 2M pairs. A $B^*$-tree is balanced, i.e. all paths from the root to a leaf have the same length.

Let $(v_i, p_i)$, $i≥1$, be the sequence of pairs contained in a node $n$. If $n$ is a leaf, $p_i$ is a pointer to a data record with key $v_i$. If $n$ is an internal node, $p_i$ is a pointer to (the root of) a subtree containing all key values $v$ in the tree, with $v_{i-1} < v ≤ v_i$. The value $v_0$ is taken to be $-\infty$ if $n$ is the leftmost node of its level; if there is a node $m$ immediately to the left of $n$, $v_0$ is taken to be the maximum of the key values in $m$. Note that $v_i$ equals the maximum key value of the node that $p_i$ points to.

We use a modification of the $B^*$-tree described in [LY81]. In a $B^{link}$-tree each node $n$ contains an additional pair $(high\_key, link\_pointer)$. The link pointer of $n$ points to a node of the same level, immediately to the right of $n$; $high\_key$ is an upper bound for the key values in $n$. If $n$ is an internal node, the high key equals the maximum key value in $n$. Note that, if $n$ is an internal node pointed to by $p$, the father of $n$ contains a pair $(v, p)$ where $v$ is the high key of $n$.

We consider a version of the $B^{link}$-tree where each node $n$ is further expanded by a pair $(low\_key, left\_pointer)$. The left pointer of $n$ points to a node of the same level immediately to the left of $n$; $low\_key$ is smaller than any key value in $n$. This extension to the basic structure of the $B^{link}$-tree will be useful for our deletion algorithm. Note that the link pointer and the left pointer of a node $n$ are the only ones which lead sideways (to nodes of the same level as $n$); all other pointers lead down (to nodes of the next level).

A detailed description of B-trees and their variants can be found in [GR93].

We will describe algorithms for concurrent search, insertion and deletion in $B^{link}$-trees. We assume that "read" and "write" operations on nodes are atomic (this can be ensured at the hardware level, e.g. by latching). To enforce atomicity of search and update operations we use *write-locks*, as well as the link pointers and the left pointers. At any time, at most one process can hold a lock on a given node. The instruction *lock(p)* (*p* is a pointer) requests a lock on the node that *p* points to. After requesting a lock, a process pauses until the lock is granted. The instruction *unlock(p)* releases the lock, so it may be granted to another process. A process cannot modify a node unless it holds a lock on it. However, we use no read-locks, so any process can read a node at any time (this happens also in several other algorithms based on the link technique [SG88, LY81, S86, KL80, ML84]).

## 2.2    Search

Our algorithm to search through a $B^{link}$-tree for a key $v$ is based on the sequential algorithm [W74] (see also [LY81, S86]). Starting from the root, we visit nodes of the tree at successive levels until we find $v$; or determine that it does not exist in the tree. At each node $n$ we compare $v$ with the key values contained in $n$, and determine the appropriate pointer in $n$ to be followed to find the next node. Recall that locked nodes can be read.

When several processes are running concurrently the following complication has to be considered. A search process obtains a pointer to a node $n$; by the time it reads $n$, another process D has deleted it. This means that $n$ has been merged by D into the node immediately to its left.

To deal with this we extend the search algorithm as follows: each node $n$ contains an additional bit, which is set when $n$ is deleted. When a process S reads a node $n$, it first checks if it has been deleted; if so, S deduces that the only usable information in $n$ is its left pointer. After a node is deleted, it is left in the tree until all processes which have obtained a pointer to it have terminated.

The procedure *find_recent(p)* follows left pointers, starting from $p$, until it finds (and returns) a non-deleted node A. It also returns a pointer $a$ to A; $a$ is used by the update algorithms.

The procedure *scan_node(v,p,n)* compares the key value $v$ to the contents of the non-deleted node $n$, pointed to by $p$. It follows pointers as needed, until it finds a non-deleted node A of the next level. It returns A and a pointer $a$ to A ($a$ is used by the update algorithms).

The main *search* procedure starts from the root of the tree (found via a global pointer *root*) and uses the procedure *scan_node* to proceed through successive levels of the tree.

Search does not lock any nodes.

## 2.3    Insertion

Our algorithm to insert a key $v$ in a $B^{link}$-tree extends the algorithm described in [LY81] (see also [S86]). We first search through the tree until we find an appropriate leaf $n$ and lock it, or determine that $v$ already exists in the tree (procedure *search_insert*). We insert $v$ in $n$, and then we maintain the tree structure (procedure *main_insert*). If $n$ became overfull after adding $v$, we split $n$; the link pointer of $n$ is set to point to the new node created, to redirect searches that obtained a pointer to $n$

before it was split. We then insert an appropriate key and pointer in the father of *n*; this may result in splitting the father, and so on. We adapt these ideas to our extended version of B$^{link}$-trees, containing left pointers.

The procedure *search_insert* is similar to *search*. It puts into a stack the pointers to the nodes it visits. The stack is then used by the maintenance phase (procedure *main_insert*), to back up through the tree. At the level of leaves, *search_insert* uses the procedure *search_level* to locate the appropriate leaf and lock it.

The procedure *search_level(v,p)* is analogous to *scan_node*. Starting from the node pointed to by *p*, it follows link pointers and left pointers as needed, until it finds a non-deleted node *A* of the same level, where the key *v* should be inserted.

The difference from *scan_node* is that *search_level* locks the node *A* before returning it. Since other processes may change *A* while *search_level* is waiting for the lock to be granted, *search_level* checks that this has not happened; otherwise it unlocks the node and resumes searching.

The procedure *main_insert(v,t,p,n,s)* adds the *(key, pointer)* pair *(v, t)* to the locked node *n*, pointed to by *p*. It splits *n* if it has to. Then it locates the father of *n*, using the top of the stack *s* and the high key of *n*, and locks it; this is done using *search_level*, since the father of *n* may have been deleted (by another process) after it was put in the stack. The procedure *main_insert(v,t,p,n,s)* then adds to the father of *n* a *(key, pointer)* pair to guide searches to the new node created by the split. Observe that the left pointer of the right neighbor of *n* has to be updated, to point to the new node created.

In the following pseudocode we assume that the stack of pointers used to back up through the tree does not become empty. This may not be the case, e.g. if the root of the tree was split by another insertion process, and a new root was created. We also assume that the root is not reached. This may not be the case either, e.g. if the root was deleted by another process, and its descendant became the new root. The details of the omitted cases will be given in the full paper.

The function *contents(p)* reads the node pointed to by *p*. The function *write(p,B)* writes *B* into the node pointed to by *p*. The function *new_node(A)* creates a new node with contents *A*, and returns a pointer to it.

```
procedure
  main_insert(v:key,
               t:pointer,
               p:pointer,
               n:node,
               s:stack)
  N := n  with an additional pair (v,t)
  if N  has at most 2M keys
    then  write(p,N)
          unlock(p)
          exit
  if N  has more than 2M keys
    then
      d := link_pointer(n)
      lock(d)
      A  :=  the right half of N, with a left pointer set to p and a link pointer equal to d
      a  :=  new_node(A)
      B  :=  the left half of N, with a link pointer set to a and a left pointer equal to the left
             pointer of n
```

```
write(p,B)
D := contents(d)
D' := a node obtained from D  by  setting the left pointer to a
write(d,D')
unlock(d)
k := high_key(n)
[f,F] := search_level(k,top(s))
unlock(p)
F' := a node obtained from F  by adjusting the key value k  to be high_key(B)  and
       inserting the pair (k,a)
write(f,F')
main_insert(k,a,f,F',pop(s))
exit
```

### 2.3.1    Remarks on *main_insert*

Since the node *n* is non-deleted, its right neighbor is non-deleted either; this is an invariant property of the deletion algorithm. Thus the right neighbor of *n* can be found by following the link pointer of *n*; it is not necessary to invoke *find_recent*.

We do not need to lock the new node (pointed to by *a*) created by the split. It will not be deleted by another process while its left neighbor *n* is locked, or the father of *n* is locked; this is enforced by the deletion algorithm. Thus the father of *n* is updated correctly, with a new (*key, pointer*) pair that guides searches to the new node created by the split.

*Main_insert* locks both *n* and its right neighbor, say *D*, before it splits *n*. It follows that the new node will not be split by another insertion process, while *D* is kept locked (*D* is also the right neighbor of the new node). Thus the left pointer of *D* is updated correctly, to point to the new node.

The node *D* is unlocked as soon as its left pointer is updated to point to the new node. Then the father of *n* is located and locked, and *n* is unlocked. Thus insertion never holds more than 2 locks simultaneously.

## 2.4    Deletion

Our algorithm to delete a key *v* from a $B^{link}$-tree is based on the sequential algorithm [W74]. We first search through the tree until we find an appropriate leaf *n* and lock it, or determine that *v* does not exist in the tree (procedure *search_delete*). We delete *v* from *n*, and then we maintain the tree structure (procedure *main_delete*). If *n* has too few keys after deleting *v*, we either *rearrange n* by transfering a key from its left neighbor, or *merge n* into its left neighbor. Then we modify the father of *n*; this may result in deleting a key from the father (if *n* was merged), and so on. We adapt these ideas to our extended version of $B^{link}$-trees, containing left pointers.

The procedure *search_delete* is similar to *search_insert*. It returns a stack *s* of pointers to the nodes it visited; this is used by the maintenance phase (procedure *main_delete*), to back up through the tree. At the level of leaves, *search_delete* uses the procedure *search_level_2* to locate the appropriate leaf and lock it.

The procedure *search_level_2(v,p)* is similar to *search_level*. Starting from the node pointed to by *p*, it follows link pointers and left pointers as needed, until it finds a non-deleted node *A* of the same level, containing the key *v*.

The difference from *search_level* is that *search_level_2* locks a node *A* containing *v* and also its left neighbor *B*, to be used to rearrange or merge *A* after *v* is deleted. The two nodes are locked from left to right, to be consistent with the order of lockings in insertion processes; otherwise deadlock could occur. Thus, *search_level_2* first locks *B* and then locks *B*'s right neighbor, say *A'*. Since other processes may change *A* or *B* while *search_level_2* is waiting for the locks to be granted, it checks that *B* has not been deleted, and that *A'* is the same as *A*; if not, it unlocks both nodes and resumes searching.

The procedure *main_delete(q,m,p,n,s)* maintains the tree structure as necessary, after a *(key, pointer)* pair has just been deleted from node *n*. The node *m* is *n*'s left neighbor; *q, p* point to *m, n* respectively. The nodes *m, n* are both locked.

First the father of *n*, say *F*, is located, using the stack *s* and the high key of *n*; then *F* is locked, using *search_level_2*. If *m* can spare a key, the maximum key of *m* is moved to *n* (rearrange); the nodes *n, F, m* are modified appropriately (in that order). If *m* is already as small as it is allowed to be, *n* is merged into *m*, and subsequently deleted. The *(key, pointer)* pair of the father of *n* that guides searches to *n* is deleted. Observe that the left pointer of the right neighbor of *n* has to be updated, to point to *m*.

In the following pseudocode we assume that the stack of pointers used to back up through the tree does not become empty, and that the root is not reached. We also assume that the nodes *m, n* are brothers; in general, they are cousins (in the same generation). The details of the omitted cases will be given in the full paper.

```
procedure
  main_delete(q:pointer,m:node,p:pointer,n:node,s:stack)
    if n has at least M keys
      then unlock(p,q)
            exit
    k := high_key(n)
    [u,U,f,F] := search_level_2(k,top(s))
    if m has at least M+1 keys
      then
          n' := a node obtained from n by adding the maximum key of m and adjusting the
                low key of n
          write(p,n')
          F' := a node obtained from F by adjusting the key value high_key(m) to be the
                second largest key of m
          write(f,F')
          m' := a node obtained from m by deleting the maximum key of m and adjusting the
                high key of m
          write(q,m')
          unlock(p,q,f,u)
          exit

if m,n together have fewer than 2M+1 keys
  then
```

```
m′ := a node obtained by merging  n into m
write(q,m′)
n′ := a node obtained from n  by marking it as deleted
write(p,n′)
unlock(p)
d := link_pointer(n)
lock(d)
D := contents(d)
D′ := a node obtained from D  by setting the left pointer to q
write(d,D′)
F′ := a node obtained from F  by deleting the pair (high_key(n),p)  and adjusting
        the key value high_key(m) to be high_key(n)
write(f,F′)
unlock(d,q)
main_delete(u,U,f,F,pop(s))
exit
```

### 2.4.1    Remarks on *main_delete*

The deletion algorithm maintains the following invariant properties.

1. A link pointer from a non-deleted node points to a non-deleted node.

2. If a left pointer (or pointer to the next level) from a non-deleted node points to a deleted node $n$, then the left pointer of $n$ points to a non-deleted node.

These properties can be verified by inspecting the sequences of modifications of nodes in *main_delete*. They imply that the right neighbor of a non-deleted node can be found by following its link pointer (it is not necessary to invoke *find_recent*). Also, the left neighbor of a non-deleted node can be found by following at most two left pointers.

The right neighbor of $n$, say $D$, is only locked after $n$ is unlocked. Thus deletion never holds more than 4 locks simultaneously. The left neighbor of $D$ is either $m$ or $n$, depending on whether $n$ has been deleted or not; so the left neighbor of $D$ is always locked. It follows that $D$ can not be deleted by another process, so the left pointer of $D$ is updated correctly, to point to $m$.

## 2.5    Correctness

Search never locks any nodes. Insertion and deletion always lock nodes in the same order: from left to right within the same level, and from a level to a higher one (closer to the root). Thus the following is obvious.

### 2.5.1    Proposition

The B*-tree algorithms never lead to deadlock.

We now review in brief some basic notions in concurrency control theory, as applied to our algorithms; detailed expositions are found in [BHG87, P86].

The state at time $\tau$ is the tree at time $\tau$, together with the values of the variables of all procedures at time $\tau$.

A read step is a function from a state to a next one, defined by the execution of an instruction a := contents(N).

A write step is a function from a state to a next one, defined by the execution of an instruction $write$(p,N), or p := $new\_node$(N).

A step is either a read step or a write step.

A transaction is a sequence of steps resulting from the execution of a single search, insertion, or deletion.

A schedule is a sequence of steps resulting from interleaving the steps of some transactions, so that the order of the steps of each transaction is preserved.

If $\pi$ is a total order of a set of transactions $\{T_1,...,T_K\}$, we denote by $T_{\pi(i)}$ the $i$-th transaction of the set, in the sense of $\pi$.

### 2.5.2    Definition

1. Let $\sigma$ be a schedule, and let $\pi$ be a total order of $\{T_1,...,T_K\}$ (the transactions of $\sigma$). We say that $\pi$ is a view serialization for $\sigma$, if, *for each time instant* $\tau$: the tree just before time $\tau$ is the same as the tree resulting from executing (starting from the initial tree) the sequence of write steps $\sigma'_1, \sigma'_2... \sigma'_{\cdot}$, where $\sigma'_i$ stands for the write steps of $T_{\pi(i)}$ that were executed before time $\tau$, for i = 1,...,K.

2. A schedule $\sigma$ is view serializable if there exists a view serialization for $\sigma$.

Our main correctness result is the following.

### 2.5.3    Theorem

Every schedule produced by the B*-tree algorithms is view serializable.

We describe the main ideas involved in the proof of Theorem 2.5.3.

Let $\Sigma_i$ denote the set of nodes that are written by transaction $T_i$.

### 2.5.4    Lemma

If some node in $\Sigma_i \cap \Sigma_j$ was written first by $T_j$, then $T_i$ was the first one to write each node in $\Sigma_i \cap \Sigma_j$.

The proof of the above result is based on the following observations, which will be shown in detail in the full paper.

a.  Each set $\Sigma_i$ is a sequence of nodes starting with a leaf, and going from a node to its father.

b.  If $T_i$ was the first one to write a node $n$ in $\Sigma_i \cap \Sigma_j$, then $T_i$ was the first one to write the father of $n$.

Lemma 2.5.4 justifies the following definition.

### 2.5.5    Definition

The transaction $T_i$ precedes $T_j$ if, for every node $n$ in $\Sigma_i \cap \Sigma_j$, transaction $T_i$ was the first one to write $n$.

### 2.5.6    Lemma

The relation "precedes" is a partial order.

To prove Theorem 2.5.3 we show that the relation "precedes" on the transactions of a schedule $\sigma$ gives (by topological sorting) a view serialization for $\sigma$. We proceed by induction on time, using a characterization of the intermediate states resulting from sequences of write steps as in Definition 2.5.2. This characterization is based on the same observations as Lemma 2.5.4. The details will be given in the full paper.

# 3    Binary Search Trees

## 3.1    Preliminaries

The binary search tree [K97] is a main-memory index structure for files of data records. Each data record has a key, and key values are taken from some totally ordered set. A node $n$ of the tree contains a key value $key(n)$, and pointers $data(n)$, $left(n)$ and $right(n)$. $Data(n)$ points to a data record with key equal to $key(n)$. $Left(n)$ (respectively $right(n)$) points to (the root of) a left (respectively right) subtree containing all key values $v$ in the tree, with $v < key(n)$ (respectively $v > key(n)$). A binary search tree need not be balanced (pointers to subtrees may be NIL).

We use a modification of the binary search tree as in [ML84]. Each node $n$ contains an additional pointer $father(n)$, pointing to its father. It also contains an additional pair $(back\_key(n), back\_pointer(n))$. The *back pointer* of $n$ points to an ancestor of $n$ (or is NIL); it is followed when searching for a key value at least as large as the *back_key* of $n$. If $n$ has a non-NIL back pointer, the right subtree of $n$ will contain all key values $v$ in the tree, with $back\_key(n) > v > key(n)$). This extension to the basic structure of the binary search tree will be useful for our deletion algorithm.

## 3.2    Search

Our algorithm to search through a binary search tree for a key $v$ is based on the sequential algorithm [K97] (see also [ML84]). Starting from the root, we visit nodes of the tree successively until we find $v$; or determine that it does not exist in the tree. At each node $n$ we compare $v$ with the key of $n$, and determine the appropriate pointer in $n$ to be followed to find the next node. Recall that locked nodes can be read.

To deal with deleted nodes we extend the search algorithm as follows: each node $n$ contains an additional bit, which is set when $n$ is deleted. When a process S reads a node $n$, it first checks if it has been deleted; if so, S deduces that the only usable information in $n$ is its father pointer. After a node is deleted, it is left in the tree until all processes which have obtained a pointer to it have terminated.

The procedure *find_recent(p)* follows father pointers, starting from $p$, until it finds (and returns) a non-deleted node $A$. It also returns a pointer $a$ to $A$; $a$ is used by the update algorithms.

The procedure *next_node(v,p,n)* compares the key value $v$ to the contents of the non-deleted node $n$, pointed to by $p$. It follows pointers until it finds a next non-deleted node $A$. It returns $A$ and a pointer $a$ to $A$ (to be used by the update algorithms).

When *next_node(v,p,n)* follows a back pointer (or sequence of back pointers) reaching a deleted node $m$, it does not follow the father pointer of $m$. Instead it backtracks to $n$ and proceeds from there, this time ignoring the back pointer if it has not changed. This is necessary to avoid cycling forever through the tree; the reason this may happen will be clear when we describe the deletion algorithm, and the use of back pointers.

In the following pseudocode, *next_node* also updates the back pointer of *n* (thus it must lock *n* beforehand). This variant speeds up subsequent searches.

```
procedure
  next_node(v:key, p:pointer, n:node)
returns         a:pointer, A:node
  a := the pointer in ncorresponding to the key value v
  if a is a left pointer or a right pointer
    then
      [a,A] := find_recent(a)
      return a,A
    else %% a is a back pointer
    lock(p)
    A := contents(p)
    if A ≠ n
      then
        unlock(p)
        [a,A] := next_node(v,p,A)
        return a,A
        exit
    nextptr := a
    while nextptr ≠ NIL do
      back_pointer(n) := nextptr

      N := contents(nextptr)
      nextptr := the pointer in N corresponding to the key value v
      if nextptr is not a back pointer
          then nextptr := NIL
      od
    if N is a deleted node
      then
          n' := a node obtained from n by setting its back pointer to NIL
        write(p,n')
        unlock(p)
        [a,A] := next_node(v,p,n')
        return a,A
        exit
    unlock(p)
    [a,A] := next_node(v,back_pointer(n),N)
    return a,A
```

The function *contents(p)* reads the node pointed to by *p*.

The procedure *next_node* never holds more than 1 lock.

The main *search* procedure starts from the root of the tree (found via a global pointer *root*) and uses the procedure *next_node* to proceed through successive nodes of the tree.

Search never holds more than 1 lock.

## 3.3    Insertion

Our algorithm to insert a key $v$ in a binary search tree is based on the sequential algorithm [K97] (see also [ML84]). We first search through the tree until we find an appropriate node $n$ and lock it, or determine that $v$ already exists in the tree. We then insert $v$ in $n$ as its left or right child.

The procedure *search_insert(v,p)* is analogous to *search*. Starting from the node pointed to by $p$, it uses the procedure *next_node* to proceed through successive nodes of the tree, until it finds a non-deleted node $A$, where the key $v$ should be inserted.

The difference from *search* is that *search_insert* locks the node before returning it. Since other processes may change $A$ while *search_insert* is waiting for the lock to be granted, *search_insert* checks that this has not happened; otherwise it unlocks the node and resumes searching.

Insertion never holds more than 1 lock.

## 3.4    Deletion

Our algorithm to delete a key $v$ from a binary search tree is based on the sequential algorithm [K97], and the link technique of [ML84]. We first search through the tree until we find an appropriate node $n$ and lock it, or determine that $v$ does not exist in the tree.

Let $n$ be a node with key $v$. To delete $v$ from the tree, we proceed as follows.

**Case 1:** $n$ has at most one child.

Let $f$ be the father of $n$; let $c$ be the child of $n$, if any.

We lock $f$, $n$, in that order. This is accomplished by the procedure *search_delete*, which is an adaptation of *search_insert*. We use the same idea as in *search_level_2* (which locked the left neighbor of a node and the node, in that order). We first lock $f$, and then lock its child $n'$. We check that $f$ has not been deleted, and that $n'$ is the same as $n$; if either check fails we unlock both nodes and resume searching.

If $n$ has a non-NIL *back_pointer*, we copy the (*back_key*, *back_pointer*) pair of $n$ into $f$.

We set the pointer of $f$ that points to $n$, to point to $c$, the child of $n$.

We mark $n$ as deleted.

We unlock $n$.

We lock the node $c$. Since $n$ is no longer locked, we find $c$ by following the corresponding child pointer of $f$.

We set the father pointer of $c$ to point to $f$.

We unlock $c, f$.

The pseudocode for a procedure *delete1* can be written easily from the above description.

**Case 2:** $n$ has two children.

We lock $n$.

Let $m$ be the node of the left subtree of $n$ with the largest key. Let $f$ be the father of $m$.

We lock $f$, $m$, in that order. This is accomplished by a procedure *search_delete_ right*, which is a straightforward adaptation of *search_delete*; we start at the left child of $n$, and keep following *right pointers* until we reach a node with no right child. The pseudocode for *search_delete_right* can be written easily (from the pseudocode for *search_delete*).

We set the key of $n$ to $key(m)$.

We set the back pointer of $f$ to point to $n$; we set the back key of $f$ to $key(m)$.

We delete $m$. By its choice $m$ has no right child, so it is deleted as in Case 1.

The pseudocode for a procedure *delete2* can be written easily from the above description.

### 3.4.1    Remarks

Consider a search process S looking for a key between $key(m)$ and $key(n)$. Assume S sees $n$ before it is modified, but reaches $m$ when it is deleted. Then S will be redirected to the modified $n$, through the back pointer of $f$.

Now consider the case that S reaches the modified $n$ after it has been deleted. It would be wrong to follow the father pointer of $n$; this would eventually send S back to $f$, so it would fall into an infinite loop. Instead (see procedure *next_node*) S backtracks to $f$, and continues from there, this time ignoring the back pointer of $f$ if it has not changed.

The deletion algorithm maintains the following invariant properties.

1. A child pointer from a non-deleted node points to a non-deleted node.
2. If a father pointer from a non-deleted node points to a deleted node $n$, then the father pointer of $n$ points to a non-deleted node.

These properties can be verified by inspecting the sequences of modifications of nodes in the deletion algorithm. They imply that the child of a non-deleted node can be found by following its child pointer (it is not necessary to invoke *find_recent*). Also, the father of a non-deleted node can be found by following at most two father pointers.

In Case 1 the child of $n$, say $c$, is only locked after $n$ is unlocked. Thus deletion never holds more than 3 locks simultaneously (no more than 2 locks in Case 1). The child of $f$ is either $c$ or $n$, depending on whether $n$ has been deleted or not; so the father of $c$ is always locked. It follows that $c$ can not be deleted by another process, so the child pointer of $f$ is updated correctly, to point to $c$.

### 3.5    Correctness

Search and insertion only lock one node at a time. Deletion always locks nodes in the same order: from a node to its descendants. Thus the following is obvious.

### 3.5.1    Proposition

The binary search tree algorithms never lead to deadlock.

Our main correctness result is the following.

### 3.5.2    Theorem

Every schedule produced by the binary search tree algorithms is view serializable.

We describe the main ideas involved in the proof of Theorem 3.5.2.

Let $\Sigma_i$ denote the set of nodes that are written by transaction $T_i$.

### 3.5.3    Lemma

If some node in $\Sigma_i \cap \Sigma_j$ was written first by $T_i$, then $T_i$ was the first one to write each node in $\Sigma_i \cap \Sigma_j$.

The above result is shown by an exhaustive case analysis (recall that each transaction locks at most 3 nodes). The main cases are based on the following observation, which will be shown in detail in the full paper.

Suppose the deletion processes $T_1$, $T_2$ write nodes $n_1$, $f_1$, $m_1$ and nodes $n_2$, $f_2$, $m_2$ respectively (see Case 2). If $T_1$, $T_2$ both write some node, and fewer than 3 nodes are written by both processes, then exactly one node is written by both processes; moreover, $n_2 \equiv f_1$ or $n_2 \equiv m_1$, or $n_1 \equiv f_2$ or $n_1 \equiv m_2$.

Lemma 3.5.3 justifies the following definition.

### 3.5.4    Definition

The transaction $T_i$ precedes $T_j$ if, for every node $n$ in $\Sigma_i \cap \Sigma_j$, transaction $T_i$ was the first one to write $n$.

### 3.5.5    Lemma

The relation "precedes" is a partial order.

To prove Theorem 3.5.2 we show that the relation "precedes" on the transactions of a schedule $\sigma$ gives (by topological sorting) a view serialization for $\sigma$. This is done by induction on time, using a characterization of the intermediate states resulting from sequences of write steps as in Definition 2.5.2. This characterization is based on the same observation as Lemma 3.5.3. The details will be given in the full paper.

## 4    Conclusions and Open Problems

We have presented concurrent algorithms for B*-trees and binary search trees, where the maintenance of the structure is done by the search and update processes themselves. We have given formal correctness proofs for our algorithms. Our arguments highlight a view serializability criterion which we believe is necessary to fully analyze several subtleties of the algorithms (introduced mainly by deletion operations).

We speculate that our algorithms should compare favorably with previous solutions if deletions are frequent. However, we can only make qualitative comparisons at this point; further work is needed to obtain a more clear picture.

The basic link technique we are using has been influential in work dealing with distribution [JC92]; recovery [LS97]; other concurrency control techniques [RSBLSD97]; and other application domains [KB95, KMH97]. Our approach to concurrent data structure design may be of interest in these cases as well. Insisting on view serializability as a correctness criterion may lead to algorithms that are more directly amenable to well-developed tools, such as amortized analysis [K97] and fringe analysis [EZGMW82, PM85].

Finally, it remains to be seen if our approach can be applied to search trees found in commercial database systems, where tree accesses are based on search predicates (imposing the danger of phantom problems [GR93]); or where schedules are distinguishing between record-level and page-level operations [M90, M96].

# References

[ABS99] S. Abiteboul, P. Buneman, D. Suciu. Data on the Web: From Relations to Semi-structured Data and XML. Morgan Kaufmann, 1999.

[BMcC72] R. Bayer, E. McCreight. Organization and maintenance of large ordered indexes. *Acta Informatica* 1 (1972), 173-189.

[BHG87] P. Bernstein, V. Hadzilacos, N. Goodman. Concurrency Control and Recovery in Database Systems. Addison-Wesley, 1987.

[EZGMW82] B. Eisenbarth, N. Ziviani, G. H. Gonnet, K. Mehlhorn, D. Wood.The Theory of Fringe Analysis and Its Application to 2-3 Trees and B-Trees. *Information and Control* 55, 1-3 (1982), 125-174.

[GM97] J. Gabarro, X. Messeguer. A unified approach to concurrent and parallel algorithms on balanced data structures. Tech. Report LSI9733, Universitat Politecnica de Catalunya, 1997.

[GR93] J. N. Gray, A. Reuter. Transaction Processing: Concepts and Techniques. Morgan Kaufmann, 1993.

[J90] T. Johnson. The Performance of Concurrent Data Structure Algorithms. PhD thesis, NYU Dept. of Computer Science, 1990.

[JC92] T. Johnson, A. Colbrook. A Distributed Data-Balanced Dictionary Based on the B-Link Tree. *Proc. 6th International Parallel Processing Symposium*, 319-325, 1992.

[JL96] R. Jones, R. Lins. Garbage Collection: Algorithms for Automatic Dynamic Memory Management. Wiley, 1996.

[K97] D. E. Knuth. The Art of Computer Programming. Addison Wesley, 1997.

[KB95] M. Kornacker, D. Banks. High-Concurrency Locking in R-Trees. *VLDB* 1995, 134-145.

[KMH97] M. Kornacker, C. Mohan, J. M. Hellerstein. Concurrency and Recovery in Generalized Search Trees. *SIGMOD* 1997, 62-72.

[KL80] H. T. Kung, P. L. Lehman. Concurrent manipulation of binary search trees. *ACM Transactions on Database Systems* 5, 3 (1980), 354-382.

[LF96] K. Larsen, R. Fagerberg. Efficient rebalancing of B-trees with relaxed balance. *IJFCS* 7, 2 (1996), 169-186.

[LY81] P. L. Lehman, S. Bing Yao. Efficient locking for concurrent operations on B-trees. *ACM Transactions on Database Systems* 6, 4 (1981), 650-670.

[LS97] D. B. Lomet, B. Salzberg. Concurrency and Recovery for Index Trees. *VLDB Journal* 6, 3 (1997), 224-240.

[ML84] U. Manber, R. E. Ladner. Concurrency control in a dynamic search structure. *ACM Transactions on Database Systems* 9, 3 (1984), 439-455.

[M90] C. Mohan. ARIES/KVL: A Key-Value Locking Method for Concurrency Control of Multiaction Transactions Operating on B-Tree Indexes. *VLDB* 1990, 392-405.

[M96] C. Mohan. Concurrency Control and Recovery Methods for B+-Tree Indexes: ARIES/KVL and ARIES/IM. *Performance of Concurrency Control Mechanisms in Centralized Database Systems* 1996, 248-306.

[NSW87] O. Nurmi, E. Soisalon-Soininen, D. Wood. Concurrency control in database structures with relaxed balance. *ACM PODS* 1987, 170-176.

[P86] C. Papadimitriou. The Theory of Database Concurrency Control. Computer Science Press, 1986.

[PM85] P. V. Poblete, J. Ian Munro. The Analysis of a Fringe Heuristic for Binary Search Trees. *Journal of Algorithms* 6, 3 (1985), 336-350.

[RSBLSD97] R. Rastogi, S. Seshadri, P. Bohannon, D. W. Leinbaugh, A. Silberschatz, S. Sudarshan. Logical and Physical Versioning in Main Memory Databases. *VLDB* 1997, 86-95.

[S86] Y. Sagiv. Concurrent operations on B*-trees with overtaking. *Journal of Computer and System Sciences* 33, (1986), 275-296.

[S85] B. Salzberg. Restructuring the Lehman-Yao tree. Tech. Report BS-85-21, Northeastern University, 1985.

[SG88] D. Shasha, N. Goodman. Concurrent Search Structure Algorithms. *ACM Transactions on Database Systems* 13, 1 (1988), 53-90.

[SK80] A. Silberschatz, Z. Kedem. Consistency in Hierarchical Database Systems. *JACM* 27, 1 (1980), 72-80.

[SW97] E. Soisalon-Soininen, P. Widmayer. Relaxed balancing in search trees. Advances in Algorithmics, Languages and Complexity: Essays in Honor of R. V. Book (D. Du and K. Ko, Eds.), 267-283. Kluwer Academic, 1997.

[W74] H. Wedekind. On the selection of access paths in data base systems. *Data base management* (J. W. Klimbie and K. L. Koffeman, Eds.), 385-397. North-Holland, 1974.

# SQL4X: A Flexible Query Language for XML and Relational Databases

Sara Cohen, Yaron Kanza, and Yehoshua Sagiv *

The Hebrew University, Institute of Computer Science, Jerusalem 91904, Israel

**Abstract.** SQL4X, a powerful language for simultaneously querying both relational and XML databases is presented. Using SQL4X, one can create both relations and XML documents as query results. Thus, SQL4X can be thought of as an *integration language*. In order to allow easy integration of XML documents with varied structures, SQL4X uses *flexible semantics* when querying XML. SQL4X is also a powerful query language. It can express quantification, negation, aggregation, grouping and path expressions.

Datalog$_{4x}$ and Tree-Datalog$_{4x}$, extensions of Datalog, are defined as elegant abstract models for SQL4X queries. Query containment is characterized for many common classes of SQL4X queries. Specifically, for Datalog$_{4x}$ queries, a complete characterization of containment of conjunctive queries and of unions of queries is presented. Equivalence of Datalog$_{4x}$ queries under bag-set semantics is also characterized. A sufficient condition for containment of Tree-Datalog$_{4x}$ queries is presented. This condition is shown to be complete for a large class of common queries.

## 1 Introduction

The increasing popularity of XML has inspired the proposal of many XML query languages. Some of the better known languages are XQuery [CCF+01], Lorel [AQM+96,GMW99], XML-QL [DFF+98,DFF+99] and XSL [Cla99]. The language presented in this paper, called SQL4X, has several important features lacking in other languages.

The design philosophy of SQL4X is to extend SQL and relational database technology in order to support XML. The syntax of SQL4X is very similar to standard SQL syntax. In fact, SQL4X is defined to be SQL with a few additional features. This allows easy and natural implementation of SQL4X over a relational database, in a way that automatically utilizes advanced database features, such as indexing and query optimization. We have already implemented SQL4X with little effort over the Oracle Database System.

In many common scenarios, it is necessary to integrate relational and XML databases. Therefore, in SQL4X we allow simultaneous querying of both relations

---

* This work was supported in part by Grant 9481-3-00 from the Israeli Ministry of Science.

G. Grahne and G. Ghelli (Eds.): DBPL 2001, LNCS 2397, pp. 263–280, 2002.

and XML documents. Similarly, our queries can create both relations and XML documents as query results. Thus, SQL4X can be thought of as an *integration language*. In order to allow easy integration of XML documents with varied structures, SQL4X uses *flexible semantics,* as defined in [KS01], for querying XML. In order to deal gracefully with partial information, queries in SQL4X return either an empty table or an empty XML fragment when the conditions of the query cannot be satisfied.

Elegant abstract models, such as Datalog, have been defined for SQL queries. This has allowed scores of researchers to tackle problems such as containment, equivalence and view usability of classes of SQL queries. Such results have inspired many optimization techniques which, in turn, allow relational databases to be efficiently accessed [CM77,ASU79,JK83,LMSS93,CKPS95]. We show how techniques for query containment of SQL queries can be extended to containment of SQL4X queries. Thus, known results about containment of relational queries can be applied to SQL4X queries.

Since SQL4X is simply an extension of SQL and the two languages are very similar, our language is easy to learn for anyone familiar with both SQL and XML. Furthermore, we expect that SQL4X will naturally evolve as the SQL standard changes and develops. In addition to the features stated above, SQL4X is also a powerful query language. It can express negation, quantification, aggregation and grouping.

In Section 2 our data model is presented. Section 3 presents the SQL4X language, by examples. In Section 4 we present results for containment of queries that generate relations, and in Section 5 containment of queries that generate documents is discussed. Section 6 compares SQL4X to other query languages and concludes.

## 2   Data Model

Using SQL4X, one can simultaneously query data sources in two formats: tables and documents. Tables are represented as relations and are not discussed further. Documents are represented using rooted labeled ordered trees. As in the OEM data model, we assume that each node has a unique id[1]. Since we will not assume that documents have associated schemas, in this paper trees representing documents do not follow ID and IDREF links.

Let $\mathcal{L}$ be a set of labels. Formally, an *ordered rooted labeled tree* is a 4-tuple $t = (N, E, r, \prec)$ where *(1)* $N$ is a set of nodes; *(2)* $E \subseteq N \times N \times \mathcal{L}$ is a set of labeled edges that gives rise to a tree-like structure; *(3)* $r \in N$ is the root; and *(4)* $\prec$ is a partial order on $N$, which defines a complete order on sibling nodes. We say that a node $n$ is *complex* if it has at least one outgoing edge. Otherwise, $n$ is *atomic*. We denote the atomic nodes of $N$ by $N_a$.

---

[1] We do not assume that the unique id is actually present in the document. Instead, our system generates unique ids as needed. There is no relationship between system generated ids and values of ID attributes of elements. Id values can be generated, for example, using XPointer [DMD01].

**Table 1.** Functions defined on nodes which can be used in SQL4X queries.

| Function | Value |
|---|---|
| oid($n$) | object id of $n$ |
| label($n$) | label of $n$'s incoming edge, or null if $n$ is the root |
| data($n$) | the set of subtrees below $n$ |
| | (i.e., the document fragment surrounded by $n$) |
| text($n$) | the concatenation of the strings in the atomic nodes of data($n$) |
| index($n$) | (the number of siblings with the label label($n$) preceding $n$) + 1 |
| doc($n$) | the document in which $n$ appears |
| is_att($n$) | true if $n$ is an attribute, false otherwise |
| path($n$) | the labels on the path from the root to $n$, or null if $n$ is the root |
| path($n,m$) | the labels on the path between $n$ and $m$, if $n$ is above $m$; |
| | the labels on the path between $m$ and $n$, if $m$ is above $m$; |
| | otherwise, null |
| distance($n,m$) | the number of edges on the path from $n$ to $m$; |
| | the value is positive (negative) if $m$ is below (above) $n$; |
| | the value is null if $n$ and $m$ are not connected |

Let $\mathcal{A}$ be a set of strings, including the empty string $\epsilon$. A *document* is a pair $x = (t, \alpha)$ where $t = (N, E, r, \prec)$ is a tree and $\alpha \colon N_a \to \mathcal{A}$ is a function that maps the atomic nodes in $N$ to strings. A *database* is a pair $\mathcal{D} = (R, X)$, where $R$ is a set of relations and $X$ is a set of documents.

Functions defined on document nodes, and which can be used in SQL4X queries, are presented in Table 1.

*Example 1.* In Figure 1, a document fragment and corresponding tree are depicted. The following are some values of the functions in Table 1 on nodes in the tree from Figure 1: *(1)* text(10) = Victor Vianu, *(2)* label(10) = author, *(3)* data(10) = <first>Victor</first><last>Vianu</last>, *(4)* index(10) = 3, *(5)* path(10) = inproceedings.author *(6)* path(11,2) = author.first and *(7)* distance(11,2) = -2.

## 3   Language Definition

SQL4X is an extension of SQL. We assume that the reader is familiar with SQL. Thus, we only present the features that are not part of SQL. Most of our presentation will be by example. The examples are mainly inspired by [FSW99] which presents examples of queries in several XML query languages.

An SQL4X query begins with one of the following two declarations: *(1)* QUERY AS RELATION or *(2)* QUERY AS DOCUMENT. If Declaration 1 is present, the result of the query is a relation, as in a standard SQL query. We call such queries *relation-generating queries*. If, instead, Declaration 2 is present, the result is an XML document. Such queries are called *document-generating queries*. For

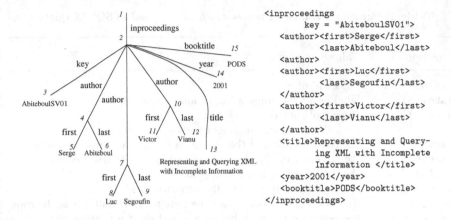

```
<inproceedings
      key = "AbiteboulSV01">
   <author><first>Serge</first>
         <last>Abiteboul</last>
   <author>
   <author><first>Luc</first>
         <last>Segoufin</last>
   </author>
   <author><first>Victor</first>
         <last>Vianu</last>
   </author>
   <title>Representing and Query-
         ing XML with Incomplete
         Information </title>
   <year>2001</year>
   <booktitle>PODS</booktitle>
</inproceedings>
```

**Fig. 1.** Labeled tree corresponding to the document fragment.

relation-generating queries, only the FROM clause is interpreted differently from a standard SQL query. In document-generating queries, the SELECT clause is also interpreted in a non-standard fashion.

### 3.1   FROM Clause Extensions

We allow the FROM clause of an SQL4X query to contain table names, possibly with aliases. As in SQL, including a relation $R(a_1, \ldots, a_n)$ in the FROM clause of a query implicitly defines *field variables* $a_1, \ldots, a_n$ that range over the values in the columns $a_1, \ldots, a_n$, respectively, in the table $R$. We allow additional constructs in the FROM clause that define *node variables* that range over nodes in an XML document tree. The construct

$$v \; l \; \text{of} \; \text{'fname-exp'}$$

defines a node variable $v$ that ranges over nodes with the incoming label $l$ in files *matching* 'fname-exp' (with matching defined by the SQL function LIKE). Similarly, the construct

$$v \; l \; \text{of} \; u$$

defines a node variable $v$ that ranges over nodes with the incoming label $l$ that are connected by a path to the node variable $u$. Note that this implies that $u$ is either an ancestor or a descendant of $v$ (or $u = v$) in a document tree. The functions in Table 1 can all be used in an SQL4X query.

*Example 2.* Suppose that the document pods01.xml contains many document fragments of the type depicted in Figure 1. Suppose also that the relation Affiliation(name, institution) is a table that contains information about the affiliation of prominent database researchers. The following query returns a list of pairs of INRIA authors and titles of their articles as described in pods01.xml.

```
QUERY AS RELATION
SELECT text(a) AS author, text(t) AS title
FROM i inproceedings of 'pods01.xml', a author of i, t title of i,
     Affiliation
WHERE name = text(a) and institution = 'INRIA'
```

Including the relation `Affiliation` in the `FROM` clause automatically defines the variables `name` and `institution`. Note that the author and title pairs will in fact be such that the author wrote an article with the corresponding title. This is ensured by requiring that there be a path between both $i$ and $a$, and $i$ and $t$.

The reader will also observe the simple fashion in which relations and documents were simultaneously queried. XML documents, such as `pods01.xml` can be downloaded from the DBLP website [Ley], and then integrated with information residing in a relational database.

*Example 3.* Consider a database containing many XML documents `pods01.xml`, `pods00.xml`, `pods99.xml`, etc., each of which contains information about articles published in the PODS conference of the corresponding year. We can find the names of the documents in which Vianu published an article, along with the titles of the articles, with the following query:

```
QUERY AS RELATION
SELECT doc(l) AS docname, text(t) AS title
FROM i inproceedings of 'pods__.xml', l last of i, t title of i
WHERE text(l) = 'Vianu'
ORDER BY text(t)
```

It is of interest to note that although elements with label `last` do not appear directly below elements with labels `inproceedings`, the query will still retrieve the required data. This is true since the query only requires the existence of a *path* between $i$ and $l$. This allows querying of documents even when the exact structure of the document is not completely known.

## 3.2   SELECT Clause Extensions

Relation-generating SQL4X queries contain `SELECT` clauses exactly as in SQL. We discuss the interpretation of the `SELECT` clause in a document-generating query. In many ways our extensions to the `SELECT` clause are not significantly different from constructs in query languages such as XML-QL [DFF+98] and XQL [RLS98]. However, our language differs in being a rather natural extension of SQL. We will also demonstrate the use of SQL constructs such as quantification and aggregation in SQL4X.

**Basic Rules.** A `SELECT` clause has the same form as an XML document fragment. Specifically, it may contain tags, attributes and SQL expressions that evaluate to values. Everything written outside of a tag or as the value of an attribute is assumed to be an expression that must be computed.

*Example 4.* Recall the query in Example 2. Suppose we are interested in the same result, but as an XML document. We will retrieve in addition the year of publication of the articles. This is almost accomplished with the query below. The query returns the desired result, but without a root document element.

```
QUERY AS DOCUMENT
SELECT <pair><author> data(a) </author>
              <title year = data(y)> data(t) </title> </pair>
FROM i inproceedings of 'pods01.xml', a author of i, t title of i,
     y year of i, Affiliation
WHERE name = text(a) and institution = 'INRIA'
```

As explained above, `data(a)` and `data(t)` are interpreted as expressions, since they are outside of a tag. Similarly, `data(y)` is interpreted as an expression since it is the value of an attribute. This query produces a string (or document) consisting of many fragments of the following form:

```
<pair> <author><first> Serge </first>
               <last> Abiteboul </last> </author>
       <title year = ''2001''> Representing and Querying XML
       with Incomplete Information. </title> </pair>
```

**Embedding Queries in a Document.** The query in Example 4 did not actually produce a legal XML document since there was no *root tag* in the document, i.e., a tag that enclosed all of the information in the document. Creating such an enclosing tag is quite simple. In an SQL4X query, standard SQL clauses can be placed between XML elements. The result of evaluating such a query is obtained by evaluating the SQL-like portion of the query and then pasting its result between the XML tags.

*Example 5.* The following query will produce a list of all the titles and authors in `pods01.xml`.

```
QUERY AS DOCUMENT
<bib> <titles> (SELECT DISTINCT <title> data(t) </title>
                FROM t title of 'pods01.xml')
      </titles>
      <authors> (SELECT DISTINCT <author> data(a) </author>
                FROM a author of 'pods01.xml')
      </authors> </bib>
```

As in a standard SQL query, the `DISTINCT` keyword will eliminate duplicate document fragments.

**Subqueries in the SELECT Clause.** Standard SQL allows subqueries in the `SELECT` clause. These subqueries must return single values. Similarly, we allow subqueries in the `SELECT` clause, and each such subquery returns a document fragment. The semantics of query evaluation with such subqueries is exactly as in SQL, i.e., nested-loop semantics.

## 3.3   Advanced Features

There are several advanced features in SQL4X that give additional expressive power beyond the constructs in SQL. This section is devoted to describing these features.

**Aggregation.** Since all SQL constructs can be used in SQL4X, standard aggregate functions from SQL can be used in SQL4X queries. It is possible to use GROUP BY and HAVING clauses in an SQL4X query. An additional aggregate function is available in SQL4X. The ALL aggregate function concatenates the set of document fragments to which it is applied. Use of the ALL aggregate function can sometimes eliminate the need for a subquery.

*Example 6.* The query below finds for each author in pods01.xml, all the articles that she has written. Note that it is possible to formulate an equivalent query which uses a subquery and does not use the ALL aggregate function.

```
QUERY AS DOCUMENT
<bib>
SELECT <inproceedings><author> data(a) </author>
                    ALL(<title> data(t) </title>)
      </inproceedings>
FROM i inproceedings of 'pods01.xml', a author of i, t title of i
GROUP BY data(a)
</bib>
```

The function ALL(DISTINCT ...) can be used to eliminate duplicates in the function arguments.

**Integrating Documents with Different Structures.** The construct for binding node variables, *v l* of *u*, only requires the existence of a path between *v* and *u*. This greatly differs from other common XML query languages which require exact matching of the structure. In other languages, a regular expression can be used to simulate this flexible matching ability. Even then, it may be difficult to formulate queries that rely heavily upon flexible matchings.

*Example 7.* Suppose that we have a database that holds documents describing courses, students taking courses and professors teaching courses. Some documents were written by students, some by professors and some were written for course needs. Yet, all these documents use the element names student, course, teacher, sname, cname and tname. However, the documents are structured in different hierarchies depending on the point of view of the creator. It is possible to get a single view of all these documents, with the course at the top of the hierarchy, using the following query.

```
QUERY AS DOCUMENT
<info>
SELECT <course>
        <name> data(nc) <name>
        <teachers> ALL(<teacher> data(nt) </teacher>) </teachers>
        <students> ALL(<student> data(ns) </student>) </students>
       </course>
FROM c course of '%.xml', nc cname of c, t teacher of c,
     nt tname of teacher, s student of c, ns sname of student
GROUP BY data(nc)
<info>
```

Note that using '%.xml' will cause the query to be applied to all documents in the database. If desired, one can restrict the structure of the documents that are used to create the results. For example, it is possible to require that the queried document has teacher hierarchically above course by adding distance(t,c) > 0 to the WHERE clause of the query. Adding distance(t,c) = 1 to the WHERE clause restricts course elements to be children of teacher elements.

**Negation and Label Variables.** SQL4X can express queries with negation. Negation in SQL4X is similar to negation in SQL and is expressed with the not exists or not in constructs preceding a subquery.

SQL4X has *labels variables*. Label variables are variables that are bound to labels. Labels variables are useful for expressing path expressions. Due to a lack of space we will not discuss negation and label variables further.

# 4    Relation-Generating Queries

Relation-generating queries are similar to standard SQL queries. The important addition is the ability to query XML documents, in addition to relations. We show that it is possible to use classical techniques from relational queries to determine containment for such queries. We start by considering important restricted classes of SQL4X queries. Results from these classes can be built upon to derive results for more general queries. To simplify the presentation, we assume in this section that at most one document is queried in the FROM clause. Thus, in this section a database is a pair $\mathcal{D} = (R, x)$ where $R$ is a set of relations and $x$ is a single document. This restriction can easily be lifted to yield results for queries with any number of documents in the FROM clause.

## 4.1    Syntax and Semantics

We use an extended Datalog syntax, called Datalog$_{4x}$, for our queries. Variables are denoted by $u$, $v$, $w$. A term, denoted $s$ or $t$, is a variable or a constant. Predicates symbols are denoted as $p$, $q$, $r$. A *relational atom* has the form $p(s_1, \ldots, s_k)$ where $s_i$ are terms and $p$ is a predicate of arity $k$. We sometimes use $p(\bar{s})$, where

$\bar{s}$ is a tuple of terms, as an alternative notation. A *label atom* has the form $\langle l \downarrow u \rangle$ where $u$ is a variable and $l$ is a constant, called the *incoming label* of $u$. A *path atom* has the form $\langle u \sim v \rangle$, where $u$ and $v$ are variables. Variables appearing in label atoms or in path atoms are called *node variables*. An *atom* is a relational atom, a label atom or a path atom.

We consider safe conjunctive Datalog$_{4x}$ queries. Such queries have the form

$$q(\bar{s}) \leftarrow p_1(\bar{s}_1) \& \ldots \& p_n(\bar{s}_n) \& \\ \langle l_1 \downarrow u_1 \rangle \& \ldots \& \langle l_k \downarrow u_k \rangle \& \langle v_1 \sim w_1 \rangle \& \ldots \& \langle v_m \sim w_m \rangle \tag{1}$$

where *(1)* all the variables in the head appear in the body, i.e., the variables in $\bar{s}$ appear among $\bar{s}_1, \ldots, \bar{s}_n, u_1, \ldots, u_k, v_1, \ldots, v_m, w_1, \ldots, w_m$; and *(2)* all the node variables have incoming labels, i.e., for all $v_i$ ($w_i$) there is a variable $u_j$ such that $v_i = u_j$ ($w_i = u_j$). The variables in $\bar{s}$ are called the *distinguished variables*. We write a query as $q(\bar{s}) \leftarrow B(\bar{t})$ when the structure of the body is not important. We sometimes denote the above query by $q(\bar{s})$, or simply by $q$.

An *assignment* $\varphi$ is a mapping of the terms in a query to constants, such that each constant is mapped to itself. Assignments are naturally extended to tuples and atoms. Satisfaction of a relational atom with respect to an assignment and a database is defined in the usual fashion. An assignment $\varphi$ satisfies a path atom $\langle u \sim v \rangle$ with respect to a database containing the document $x$ if $\varphi(v)$ is the object id of a node in $x$ connected by a (possibly empty) path to a node with object id $\varphi(u)$. The assignment $\varphi$ satisfies $\langle l \downarrow u \rangle$ with respect to a document $x$ if $\varphi(u)$ is the object id of a node in $x$ with the incoming label $l$.

A conjunctive query $q(\bar{s}) \leftarrow B(\bar{t})$ defines a relation $q^{\mathcal{D}}$ for a given database $\mathcal{D}$ as follows

$$q^{\mathcal{D}} := \{\varphi(\bar{s}) \mid \varphi \text{ satisfies } B(\bar{t}) \text{ w.r.t. } \mathcal{D}\}$$

We say that a query $q$ is *satisfiable* if it returns a non-empty result for some database $\mathcal{D}$, i.e., $q^{\mathcal{D}} \neq \emptyset$.

**Proposition 1.** *A query $q$ is satisfiable if and only if it does not contain label atoms $\langle l \downarrow u \rangle$ and $\langle l' \downarrow u \rangle$ such that $l \neq l'$.*

Satisfiability can be determined in linear time. In the sequel we only consider satisfiable queries.

*Example 8.* The following query is a Datalog$_{4x}$ version of the query in Example 2. In order to conform with Datalog syntax, we have represented the function text by a binary relation, textval. Note that in order to correctly model this function as a relation, it must be assumed that the second field of the predicate textval is functionally dependent on the first field. However, a discussion of functional dependencies is beyond the scope of this paper.

```
pairs(ta, tt) ← ⟨inproceedings ↓ i⟩ & ⟨author ↓ a⟩ & ⟨title ↓ t⟩ &
                ⟨a ∼ i⟩ & ⟨t ∼ i⟩ &
                textval(a, ta) & affiliation(ta, 'INRIA') & textval(t, tt)
```

## 4.2  Containment of Datalog$_{4x}$ Queries

It is possible to characterize containment of conjunctive Datalog$_{4x}$ queries using similar methods to those for conjunctive Datalog queries. Query containment is defined here in the usual fashion. We present necessary and sufficient characterizations for query containment.

Let $q(\bar{s})$ and $q'(\bar{s})$ be conjunctive Datalog$_{4x}$ queries. A *homomorphism* from $q'$ to $q$ is a substitution $\theta$ of the variables in $q'$ by terms in $q$ that maps each distinguished variable to itself, such that *(1)* for all relational atoms $a'$ in $q'$, $\theta(a')$ is in $q$; *(2)* for all label atoms $\langle l \downarrow u' \rangle$ in $q'$, $\langle l \downarrow \theta(u') \rangle$ is in $q$; and *(3)* for all path atoms $\langle u' \sim v' \rangle$ in $q'$, either $\langle \theta(u') \sim \theta(v') \rangle$ or $\langle \theta(v') \sim \theta(u') \rangle$ is in $q$.

A query $q$ is *contained* in a query $q'$, written $q \subseteq q'$ if for all databases $\mathcal{D}$, it holds that $q^{\mathcal{D}} \subseteq q'^{\mathcal{D}}$.

**Theorem 1.** *Let $q(\bar{s}) \leftarrow B(\bar{t})$ and $q'(\bar{s}) \leftarrow B'(\bar{t}')$ be queries. If there exists a homomorphism from $q'$ to $q$, then $q$ is contained in $q'$.*

The condition in Theorem 1 is not necessary. It is possible that there is no homomorphism from $q'$ to $q$ and yet, $q$ is contained in $q'$.

*Example 9.* Consider the queries

$$q(z) \leftarrow a(z)\ \&\ \langle l \downarrow u \rangle\ \&\ \langle l \downarrow v \rangle\ \&\ \langle l \downarrow w \rangle\ \&\ \langle l \downarrow y \rangle\ \&$$
$$\langle u \sim v \rangle\ \&\ \langle v \sim w \rangle\ \&\ \langle w \sim y \rangle\ \&\ \langle y \sim u \rangle$$
$$q'(z) \leftarrow a(z)\ \&\ \langle l \downarrow u \rangle\ \&\ \langle l \downarrow v \rangle\ \&\ \langle l \downarrow w \rangle\ \&\ \langle l \downarrow y \rangle\ \&$$
$$\langle u \sim v \rangle\ \&\ \langle v \sim w \rangle\ \&\ \langle w \sim y \rangle\ \&\ \langle y \sim u \rangle\ \&\ \langle v \sim y \rangle$$

Clearly $q' \subseteq q$. By exhaustive search one can verify that it is impossible to create a tree with nodes $u$, $v$, $w$, $y$ connected in the manner required by $q$ without either $u$ and $w$ or $v$ and $y$ being connected. Intuitively, this follows since the path atoms create a cycle. Thus, $q$ is equal to the union of the queries

$$q_1(z) \leftarrow a(z)\ \&\ \langle l \downarrow u \rangle\ \&\ \langle l \downarrow v \rangle\ \&\ \langle l \downarrow w \rangle\ \&\ \langle l \downarrow y \rangle\ \&$$
$$\langle u \sim v \rangle\ \&\ \langle v \sim w \rangle\ \&\ \langle w \sim y \rangle\ \&\ \langle y \sim u \rangle\ \&\ \langle u \sim w \rangle$$
$$q_2(z) \leftarrow a(z)\ \&\ \langle l \downarrow u \rangle\ \&\ \langle l \downarrow v \rangle\ \&\ \langle l \downarrow w \rangle\ \&\ \langle l \downarrow y \rangle\ \&$$
$$\langle u \sim v \rangle\ \&\ \langle v \sim w \rangle\ \&\ \langle w \sim y \rangle\ \&\ \langle y \sim u \rangle\ \&\ \langle v \sim y \rangle$$

Note that $q_1 \subseteq q'$ and $q_2 \subseteq q'$. Thus, $q \subseteq q'$, even though there is no homomorphism from $q'$ to $q$.

In order to present a necessary and sufficient condition for containment, we introduce some definitions. Consider a conjunction of label and path atoms $C = \langle l_1 \downarrow u_1 \rangle\ \&\ \ldots\ \&\ \langle l_k \downarrow u_k \rangle\ \&\ \langle v_1 \sim w_1 \rangle\ \&\ \ldots\ \&\ \langle v_m \sim w_m \rangle$. An assignment $\varphi$ *exactly satisfies* $C$ with respect to a document $x$ if *(1)* $\varphi$ satisfies all the atoms in $C$ with respect to $x$, *and (2)* for all $v_i$ and $w_j$, if $\langle v_i \sim w_j \rangle \notin C$ and $\langle w_j \sim v_i \rangle \notin C$, then $\varphi$ does not satisfy $\langle v_i \sim w_j \rangle$ with respect to $x$. If there is a document $x$ and an assignment $\varphi$ such that $\varphi$ exactly satisfies the conjunction of path and label atoms in $q$ with respect to $x$, then we say that $q$ is *exactly satisfiable*. Note that for $q$ to be exactly satisfiable, it must contain path nodes $\langle w \sim w \rangle$ for all node variables $w$ in $q$. We call such path atoms *self-path atoms*. Consider the query $q(\bar{s})$ in Equation 1. We say that $q'(\bar{s})$ is an *extension* of $q(\bar{s})$ if *(1)* $q'$ contains exactly the same relational atoms and label atoms as $q$; and *(2)* $q'$ contains all the path atoms in $q$ and possibly additional path atoms with the node variables from $q$.

We say that $q'$ is an *exactly satisfiable extension* of $q$ if $q'$ is an extension of $q$ and $q'$ is exactly satisfiable.

**Theorem 2.** *Consider queries $q$ and $q'$. Then $q \subseteq q'$ if and only if for all exactly satisfiable extensions $q_e$ of $q$, there is a homomorphism from $q'$ to $q_e$.*

**Corollary 1.** *Consider queries $q$ and $q'$. Suppose that $q$ is exactly satisfiable. Then $q \subseteq q'$ if and only if there is a homomorphism from $q'$ to $q$.*

Corollary 1 motivates the following question. What is the complexity of checking if a query $q$ is exactly satisfiable? Suppose that $q$ has $k$ node variables. We can show that if $q$ is exactly satisfiable, then there is an assignment $\varphi$ and a document $x$ with nodes $N$ such that $\varphi$ exactly satisfies the path and label atoms in $q$ with respect to $x$ and $|N| = k+1$. From this, follows that it suffices to check document trees with only $k+1$ nodes. However, there are an exponential number of such documents. Luckily, it turns out that this problem can be solved in polynomial time by a constructive proof mechanism. Specifically, there is an algorithm that given a query $q$ creates, in polynomial time, a document $x$ such that $q$ exactly satisfies $x$, if such a document exists.

**Theorem 3.** *Given a query $q$, it is possible to decide in polynomial time if $q$ is exactly satisfiable.*

Finally, we present an upper bound on the complexity of checking containment of $\mathsf{Datalog}_{4x}$ queries.

**Proposition 2.** *Determining containment of $\mathsf{Datalog}_{4x}$ queries is in $\Pi_2^P$.*

## 4.3   Extending Containment Results

In the previous subsection, the basic foundation for characterizing query containment has been laid. It is possible to extend these results for additional classes of queries. We give these results briefly.

**Unions of Queries.** The semantics of query evaluation is extended in the obvious fashion to unions of queries. Containment of union of queries is characterized by the following theorem.

**Theorem 4.** *Consider unions of queries $\bigcup_i q_i$ and $\bigcup_j q'_j$. Then $\bigcup_i q_i \subseteq \bigcup_j q'_j$ if and only if for all $q_i \in \bigcup_i q_i$ and for all exactly satisfiable extensions $q_{i_e}$ of $q_i$, there is a $q'_j \in \bigcup_j q'_j$ for which there is a homomorphism from $q'_j$ to $q_{i_e}$.*

Allowing unions of queries does not increase the complexity of query containment.

**Corollary 2.** *Determining containment of unions of* Datalog$_{4x}$ *queries is in* $\Pi_2^P$.

**Aggregate Queries and Bag-Set Semantics.** We consider queries with the *all* and *all distinct* aggregate functions. A formal accounting of the semantics of aggregate Datalog$_{4x}$ queries is not presented. See [NSS98,CNS99] for details about aggregate Datalog queries. We show how reasoning about queries with *all distinct* can be reduced to reasoning about non-aggregate queries (under set semantics). Similarly, reasoning about queries with the *all* function can be reduced to reasoning about non-aggregate queries under bag-set semantics. Queries are evaluated under *bag-set semantics*, if their input is a set, while their output is a bag (see [CV93]).

We consider aggregate queries with one of the following forms:

$$q(\bar{s}, all(y)) \leftarrow B(\bar{t}) \tag{2a}$$

$$q(\bar{s}, all(distinct\ y)) \leftarrow B(\bar{t}) \tag{2b}$$

where $\bar{s}$ are the *grouping variables*. The aggregate functions find for each satisfying assignment of $\bar{s}$, the set of all (distinct) satisfying assignments for $y$. Given an aggregate query $q$ as defined above, the *core* of $q$, denoted $\check{q}$, is the query $\check{q}(\bar{s}, y) \leftarrow B(\bar{t})$. We consider aggregate queries having safe conjunctive Datalog$_{4x}$ cores. We present an example and then characterize containment of aggregate queries.

*Example 10.* The following query groups authors with all the titles of their articles, as in Example 6.

allPapers($ta$, $all(distinct\ tt)$) ← $\langle$inproceedings $\downarrow i\rangle$ & $\langle$author $\downarrow a\rangle$ &
   $\langle$title $\downarrow t\rangle$ & $\langle a \sim i\rangle$ & $\langle t \sim i\rangle$ & textval($a, ta$) & textval($t, tt$)

**Proposition 3.** *Given the queries* $q(\bar{s}, all(distinct\ y))$ *and* $q'(\bar{s}, all(distinct\ y))$, *then* $q \subseteq q'$ *if and only if* $\check{q} \subseteq \check{q}'$.

**Proposition 4.** *Given the queries* $q(\bar{s}, all(y))$ *and* $q'(\bar{s}, all(y))$, *then* $q \subseteq q'$ *if and only* $\check{q}$ *is contained in* $\check{q}'$ *under bag set semantics.*

Query containment under bag-set semantics is not known to be decidable [CV93,IR95]. Equivalence of Datalog queries under bag-set semantics has been characterized [CV93,NSS98,CNS99]. We extend these characterizations to deal with bag-set equivalence among Datalog$_{4x}$ queries. We say that $q$ is *isomorphic* to $q'$ if there is a homomorphism $\theta$ from $q'$ to $q$ such that *(1)* $\theta$ is a bijection on the relational and label atoms of $q$; and *(2)* for all path atoms $\langle u \sim v\rangle$ in $q$, at least one of $\langle \theta^{-1}(u) \sim \theta^{-1}(v)\rangle$ and $\langle \theta^{-1}(v) \sim \theta^{-1}(u)\rangle$ is in $q'$.

Given sets of queries $Q = \{q_i\}_{i \in \mathcal{I}}$ and $Q' = \{q'_j\}_{j \in \mathcal{J}}$, we say that $Q$ is isomorphic to $Q'$ if there is a bijection $\gamma$ from $Q'$ to $Q$ such that for all $q'_j \in Q'$, it holds that $q'_j$ is isomorphic to $\gamma(q'_j)$.

**Theorem 5.** *Let $q$ and $q'$ be* Datalog$_{4x}$ *queries. Then $q$ is equivalent to $q'$ under bag-set semantics if and only if the set of exactly satisfiable extensions of $q$ is isomorphic to the set of exactly satisfiable extensions of $q'$.*

**Corollary 3.** *Bag-set equivalence of* Datalog$_{4x}$ *queries can be decided in polynomial space.*

**Corollary 4.** *Let $q$ and $q'$ be exactly satisfiable* Datalog$_{4x}$ *queries. Then $q$ is bag-set equivalent to $q'$ if and only if $q$ is isomorphic to $q'$.*

As for Datalog queries, it is possible to identify classes of Datalog$_{4x}$ queries for which equivalence can be decided in polynomial time. We say that a query $q$ is *linear* if, in $q$, *(1)* no two relational atoms have the same predicate; *and (2)* no two label atoms have the same label, i.e., $l \neq l'$ for all $\langle l \downarrow u \rangle$ and $\langle l' \downarrow u' \rangle$ in $q$.

**Theorem 6.** *Bag-set equivalence of linear exactly satisfiable* Datalog$_{4x}$ *queries can be decided in polynomial time.*

# 5  Document-Generating Queries

We consider document-generating queries. We present an abstract notation and discuss containment results. As in the previous section, we assume that at most one document is queried in a single query. As an additional simplification, we consider the output of a query to be unordered. Thus, documents are *unordered* rooted labeled trees, associated with a function mapping atomic nodes to values.

## 5.1  Syntax and Semantics

We use an extended Datalog syntax, called Tree-Datalog$_{4x}$. As in Datalog$_{4x}$, there are three types of atoms: relational atoms, label atoms and path atoms. A query is a rooted labeled tree, with (possibly empty) conjunctions of atoms attached to its edges and terms attached to its leaf nodes. Formally, a Tree-Datalog$_{4x}$ query is a triple $q = (t, \Psi, \tau)$ where *(1)* $t = (N, E, r)$ is a rooted labeled tree; *(2)* $\Psi$ associates each $e \in E$ with a conjunction of atoms, called the *condition* of $e$; and *(3)* $\tau$ associates each atomic node $n \in N_a$ with a term. We say that a variable $v$ is *introduced* in an edge $e$ if $v$ appears in $\Psi(e)$ *and* $v$ does not appear in $\Psi(e')$ for any $e'$ above $e$ in $t$. A query is *safe* if every variable associated with a leaf node $n$ is introduced in an edge above $n$. A query is in *normal form* if no variable $v$ is introduced in two different edges[2]. In the sequel we assume that all queries are safe and are in normal form.

Tree-Datalog$_{4x}$ queries have semantics similar to nested-loops. Variables appearing in the condition associated with an edge get their values at the place where they are introduced. Assignments to atoms are extended to trees in the natural fashion. Thus, an assignment is applied to a tree by applying the assignment to all the conditions associated with the tree's edges and all the variables that are associated with the tree's leaves.

---

[2] Any query in non-normal form has an equivalent query in normal form.

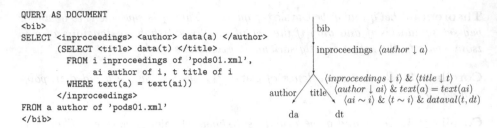

**Fig. 2.** An SQL4X query and its Tree-Datalog$_{4x}$ query.

Let $q = (t, \Psi, \tau)$ be a query. Suppose that $n$ is a node in $t$. Then $q_{|n}$ is the query defined by the subtree of $q$ rooted at $n$. Let $q = (t_q, \Psi, \tau)$ be a query and let $\mathcal{D}$ be a database. We denote the result of evaluating $q$ with respect to $\mathcal{D}$ by $q^{\mathcal{D}}$ and it is obtained in the following fashion:

- If $t_q$ consists only of single node $r_q$ then $q^{\mathcal{D}}$ is the document $x = (t_x, \alpha)$ where $t_x = (\{r_x\}, \emptyset, r_x)$ and $\alpha(r_x) = \tau(r_q)$. Note that $\tau(r_q)$ must be a constant since $q$ is safe.
- Otherwise, suppose that the outgoing edges from the root $r_q$ are $e_1, \ldots, e_k$ where $e_i = (r_q, n_i, l_i)$. Let $\Phi_i$ be the set of satisfying assignments of $\Psi(e_i)$ into $\mathcal{D}$. Suppose that at least one of the sets $\Phi_i$ is non-empty. For each $\varphi \in \Phi_i$, we apply $\varphi$ to $q$ and then evaluate its subtree rooted at $n_i$ on $\mathcal{D}$. Formally, we define $X_i$ to be

$$X_i := \{(\varphi(q)_{|n_i})^{\mathcal{D}} \mid \varphi \in \Phi_i\}.$$

Let $N(X_i)$ be the set of nodes of documents in $X_i$. Similarly, we define $E(X_i)$, $r(X_i)$ and $\alpha(X_i)$. Then $q^{\mathcal{D}}$ is the document $x = ((N_x, E_x, r_x), \alpha)$ where

- $N_x = \{r_x\} \bigcup_i N(X_i)$;
- $E_x = \bigcup_i E(X_i) \cup \{(r_x, r_i, l_i) \mid r_i \in r(X_i)\}$;
- $r_x$ is a new node, not appearing in $N(X_i)$ for any $i$;
- $\alpha = \bigcup_i \alpha(X_i)$.

- Otherwise, the conditions associated with the outgoing edges of the root are all unsatisfiable. Then $q^{\mathcal{D}}$ is the document $x = (t_x, \alpha)$ where $t_x = (\{r_x\}, \emptyset, r_x)$ and $\alpha(r_x) = \epsilon$ (the empty string).

*Example 11.* Figure 2 shows an SQL4X query that finds for each author the set of articles that she has written. The Tree-Datalog$_{4x}$ version of this query is also depicted in Figure 2, beside the query. Note that the condition associated with the edge labeled bib in the tree is an empty conjunction of atoms. Thus, there is one satisfying assignment of this edge's condition, the empty assignment.

## 5.2 Containment of Tree-Datalog$_{4x}$ Queries

In this section we consider the problem of determining containment of Tree-Datalog$_{4x}$ queries. As in Section 4.2, we use methods similar to those for standard Datalog queries.

Let $t = (N, E, r)$ and $t' = (N', E', r')$ be trees. A *tree homomorphism* from $t$ to $t'$ is a mapping $\mu$ from $N$ to $N'$, such that *(1)* the root is mapped to the root, i.e., $\mu(r) = r'$; and *(2)* edges are mapped to edges, i.e., $(n_1, n_2, l) \in E$ implies $(\mu(n_1), \mu(n_2), l) \in E'$. Let $x = (t, \alpha)$ and $x' = (t', \alpha')$ be documents. We say that $x$ is *contained* in $x'$ if there is a tree homomorphism $\mu$ from $t$ to $t'$ such that nonempty constants in the leaf nodes of $x$ are preserved, i.e., for all leaf nodes $n$ in $t$ either $\alpha(n) = \alpha'(\mu(n))$ or $\alpha(n) = \epsilon$. We say that query $q$ is *contained* in query $q'$ if for all databases $\mathcal{D}$, it holds that $q^{\mathcal{D}}$ is contained in $q'^{\mathcal{D}}$.

Given a tree $t$ we say that an edge $e$ is *above* an edge $e'$ if the path from the root of $t$ to $e'$ passes through $e$. If $e$ is above $e'$, we write $e < e'$. If $e$ is either above $e'$ or equal to $e'$, we write $e \leq e'$.

**Theorem 7.** *Let $q = (t, \Psi, \tau)$ and $q' = (t', \Psi', \tau')$ be* Tree-Datalog$_{4x}$ *queries. Then $q \subseteq q'$ if there is a tree homomorphism $\mu$ from $t$ to $t'$ and a mapping $\theta$ of the variables in $q'$ to the terms in $q$ such that*

- *values in atomic nodes are equated, i.e., for all leaf nodes $n$ in $t$*

$$\tau(n) = \theta(\tau'(\mu(n)));$$

- *for all edges $e_1$ in $t$ and atoms $a'$ in $\Psi'(\mu(e_1))$ there is an edge $e_2$ in $t$, with $e_2 \leq e_1$, such that*
  - *if $a'$ is a relational atom or a label atom, then $\theta(a') \in \Psi(e_2)$ and*
  - *if $a' = \langle u' \sim v' \rangle$ is a path atom, then either $\langle \theta(u') \sim \theta(v') \rangle \in \Psi(e_2)$ or $\langle \theta(v') \sim \theta(u') \rangle \in \Psi(e_2)$.*

For special cases it turns out that the condition in Theorem 7 is also a necessary condition. Let $q = (t, \Psi, \tau)$ be a query. Each path of edges $e_1, \ldots, e_m$ in $t$ defines a Datalog$_{4x}$ query $q_{e_1, \ldots, e_m}$ as follows $q_{e_1, \ldots, e_m}() \leftarrow \Psi(e_1) \& \ldots \& \Psi(e_m)$.

We say that a Tree-Datalog$_{4x}$ query $q = (t, \Psi, \tau)$ is *linear* if *(1)* $t$ does not contain a node $n$ with outgoing edges $(n, n_1, l_1)$ and $(n, n_2, l_2)$ such that $l_1 = l_2$; and *(2)* each path in $t$ defines a linear Datalog$_{4x}$ query. We say that $q$ is *exactly satisfiable* if every path in $q$, starting from $q$'s root, defines an exactly satisfiable Datalog$_{4x}$ query. Exactly satisfiable linear queries are rather common. For example, the query in Figure 2 would be both exactly satisfiable and linear if self-path atoms were added for all node variables.

**Theorem 8.** *The condition in Theorem 7 is a necessary condition for containment of exactly satisfiable linear* Tree-Datalog$_{4x}$ *queries.*

**Corollary 5.** *Containment of exactly satisfiable linear* Tree-Datalog$_{4x}$ *queries can be decided in polynomial time.*

# 6    Related Work and Conclusion

Path queries are essentially queries defining path expressions. Path queries have been studied in [CDLV99,CDLV00,FLS98]. In [FLS98], containment of $\text{STRUQL}_0$ queries was considered. Specifically, it was shown that testing containment of simple $\text{STRUQL}_0$ queries is NP-complete. $\text{Datalog}_{4x}$ queries without relational atoms can be written as a union of simple $\text{STRUQL}_0$ queries. However, our results do not follow directly from the results in [FLS98] since *(1)* $\text{Datalog}_{4x}$ is evaluated over a tree, while $\text{STRUQL}_0$ is evaluated over a graph and *(2)* translating $\text{Datalog}_{4x}$ queries into $\text{STRUQL}_0$ incurs an exponential blowup.

There are two classical ways to answer a query against data sources that are both relational and XML. One option is to convert the XML into relations and then perform the query using a relational language, such as SQL. This is difficult because of the very varied structure of XML documents. The second option is to convert the relations to XML, and then use an XML query language. This method was explored in the SilkRoute system [FST00] which allows the definition of XML views over a relational database. In SQL4X we presented a third option. Our query language allows simultaneous querying of relations and XML and allows the user to choose the target data model. SQL4X also uses flexible semantics, which makes integrating varied documents with the same ontology easier (see Example 7).

XQuery [CCF+01] is one of the most prominent recently proposed query languages for XML. While SQL4X is appropriate for data integration, XQuery does not have the ability to query relations or to produce relations. In addition, SQL4X can be used as a *transformation language* to translate data between the relational and XML data models. SQL4X was defined as extension of SQL, and thus, can be efficiently implemented over a relational database system. XQuery, on the other hand, is a new language designed specifically for XML and probably will not be implemented in a relational database system. However, XQuery allows general XPath path expressions, whereas SQL4X currently has rather limited path expressions. This limitation allows SQL4X queries to be translated to SQL queries, for processing. SQL4X uses a flexible semantics, allowing the user to state that nodes are connected in some direction by a path. Flexible semantics can be captured in XQuery in a straight-forward fashion if the ancestor axis of XPath is supported. Support for this axis is currently under discussion since the ancestor axis does not appear in the abbreviated XPath syntax. Otherwise, translating an SQL4X query to XQuery may require an exponential blowup of the query.

Extending our characterizations for query containment to cases where queries contain functions from Table 1 is left for future work. We also intend to extend SQL4X to allow for use of general XPath expressions. The effect of such extensions on the complexity of containment is another important open problem.

# References

AQM⁺96.  S. Abiteboul, D. Quass, J. McHugh, J. Widom, and J. Wiener. The Lorel query language for semistructured data. Technical report, The Stanford University Database Group, 1996.

ASU79.  A.V. Aho, Y. Sagiv, and J.D. Ullman. Efficient optimization of a class of relational expressions. *ACM Transactions on Database Systems*, 4(4):435–454, 1979.

CCF⁺01.  D. Chamberlin, J. Clark, D. Florescu, J. Robie, J. Siméon, and M. Stefanescu. XQuery 1.0: An XML query language, June 2001. Available at http://www.w3.org/TR/xquery.

CDLV99.  D. Calvanese, G. De Giacomo, M. Lenzerini, and M. Vardi. Rewriting of regular expressions and regular path queries. In Ch. Papadimitriou, editor, *Proc. 18th Symposium on Principles of Database Systems*, Philadelphia (Pennsylvania, USA), May 1999. ACM Press.

CDLV00.  D. Calvanese, G. De Giacomo, M. Lenzerini, and M. Vardi. Answering regular path queries using views. In *Proc. 16th International Conference on Data Engineering*, pages 389–398, San Diego (California, USA), March 2000. IEEE Computer Society.

CKPS95.  S. Chaudhuri, S. Krishnamurthy, S. Potarnianos, and K. Shim. Optimizing queries with materialized views. In P.S.Yu and A.L.P. Chen, editors, *Proc. 11th International Conference on Data Engineering*, Taipei, March 1995. IEEE Computer Society.

Cla99.  J. Clark. XSL transformations (XSLT specification), 1999. Available at http://www.w3.org/ TR/WD-xslt.

CM77.  A.K. Chandra and P.M. Merlin. Optimal implementation of conjunctive queries in relational databases. In *Proc. 9th Annual ACM Symposium on Theory of Computing*, 1977.

CNS99.  S. Cohen, W. Nutt, and A. Serebrenik. Rewriting aggregate queries using views. In Ch. Papadimitriou, editor, *Proc. 18th Symposium on Principles of Database Systems*, Philadelphia (Pennsylvania, USA), May 1999. ACM Press.

CV93.  S. Chaudhuri and M. Vardi. Optimization of real conjunctive queries. In *Proc. 12th Symposium on Principles of Database Systems*, Washington (D.C., USA), May 1993. ACM Press.

DFF⁺98.  A. Deutsch, M. Fernandez, D. Florescu, A. Levy, and D. Suciu. XML-QL: A query language for XML, 1998. Available at http://www.w3.org/TR/NOTE-xml-ql.

DFF⁺99.  A. Deutsch, M. Fernandez, D. Florescu, A. Levy, and D. Suciu. A query language for XML. In *8th Int. World Wide Web Conference (WWW8)*, Toronto (Canada), May 1999. Available at http://www8.org/fullpaper.html.

DMD01.  S. DeRose, E. Maler, and R. Daniel. XML pointer language (XPointer) 1.0, 2001. Available at http://www.w3.org/TR/xptr.

FLS98.  D. Florescu, A.Y. Levy, and D. Suciu. Query containment for conjunctive queries with regular expressions. In J. Paredaens, editor, *Proc. 17th Symposium on Principles of Database Systems*, pages 139–148, Seattle (Washington, USA), June 1998. ACM Press.

FST00.  M. Fernandez, D. Suciu, and W. Tan. Silkroute: Trading between relations and XML. In *Proc. 9th International World Wide Web Conference*, Amsterdam (Netherlands), May 2000. Available at http://www9.org/w9cdrom.

FSW99.    M. Fernandez, J. Siméon, and P. Wadler. XML query languages: Experiences and exemplars, 1999. Available at
http://www.w3.org/1999/09/ql/docs/xquery.html.

GL99.     G. Grahne and L. V. S. Lakshmanan. On the difference between navigating semistructered data and querying it. In *8th International Workshop on Database Programming Languages*, Kinloch Rannoch (Scotland), September 1999.

GMW99.    R. Goldman, J. McHugh, and J. Widom. From semistructured data to XML/: Migrating the Lore data model and query language. In S. Cluet and T. Milo, editors, *Proc. 2nd International Workshop on the Web and Databases*, Philadelphia, (Pennsylvania, USA), June 1999.

IR95.     Y.E. Ioannidis and R. Ramakrishnan. Beyond relations as sets. *ACM Transactions on Database Systems*, 20(3):288–324, 1995.

JK83.     D.S. Johnson and A. Klug. Optimizing conjunctive queries that contain untyped variables. *SIAM Journal on Computing*, 12(4):616–640, 1983.

KS01.     Y. Kanza and Y. Sagiv. Flexible queries over semistructured data. In *Proc. 20th Symposium on Principles of Database Systems*, Santa Barbara (California, USA), May 2001. ACM Press.

Ley.      M. Ley. DBLP website. Available at
http://www.informatik.uni-trier.de/~ley/db.

LMSS93.   A.Y. Levy, I. Singh Mumick, Y. Sagiv, and O. Shmueli. Equivalence, query-reachability, and satisfiability in Datalog extensions. In *Proc. 12th Symposium on Principles of Database Systems*, pages 109–122, Washington (D.C., USA), May 1993. ACM Press.

NSS98.    W. Nutt, Y. Sagiv, and S. Shurin. Deciding equivalences among aggregate queries. In J. Paredaens, editor, *Proc. 17th Symposium on Principles of Database Systems*, pages 214–223, Seattle (Washington, USA), June 1998. ACM Press. Long version as Report of Esprit LTR DWQ.

RLS98.    J. Robie, J. Lapp, and D. Schach. XML query language (XQL), 1998. Available at http://www.w3.org/TandS/QL/QL98/pp/xql.html.

# ERX-QL: Querying an Entity-Relationship DB to Obtain XML Documents

Giuseppe Psaila

Università degli Studi di Bergamo
Facoltà di Ingegneria
Viale Marconi 5 - I-24044 Dalmine (BG), Italy
psaila@unibg.it

**Abstract.** Perspective scenarios of e-commerce applications, in particular B2B applications, based on the exchange of XML documents open new research issues in the field of information systems and XML data management. In fact, information systems will have to generate XML documents, obtained by querying the underlying DBMS.

This paper informally introduces the ERX-Query Language (ERX-QL), under development as part of ERX Data Management System (developed at University of Bergamo). ERX-QL deals with the problem of formulating declarative queries to extract data from within a database and directly generate XML documents. This way, ERX-QL naturally deals with recursive and nested XML structures. Furthermore, the rich extended ER database provided by the ERX system makes ERX-QL rich and powerful, thus suitable, with minor changes, to be adopted on classical RDBMSs.

## 1 Introduction

Next generation information systems will have to support new functionality concerned with e-commerce services and Business-to-Business (B2B) applications. In such a context, an information system will have to strongly interact with third party information systems, in order to receive information and documents but also to send information and documents. An example can be represented by the case of integrated supply chains.

The emerging technology to support the exchange of data and documents is represented by XML, which has been defined to play the role of the standard format for document exchange over the Internet. XML documents are semi-structured, since they have a flexible syntactic structure based on tag (mark-up) nesting, which may contain unstructured information.

Hence, in the near future, information systems will be extended with the capability of querying the underlying database and generate XML documents. However, at the current stage the technology does not support this crucial task with solutions that allow a declarative specification of queries. Apart from SQL Server 2000, which extends SQL to represent flat tables produced by queries as XML documents, we are aware of only one attempt [5] in such directions (i.e. from a DBMS, relational but not only, to XML).

G. Grahne and G. Ghelli (Eds.): DBPL 2001, LNCS 2397, pp. 281–299, 2002.

In this paper, we report about our on-going work, the definition of the ERX Query Language (for short ERX-QL). under development at University of Bergamo as part of the ERX Data Management System[1]. This is a system designed to store and manage data coming from XML Documents. The data model supported by the ERX system is the ERX (Entity Relationship for XML) data model, a variant of the classical Entity-Relationship model developed to model and manage concepts and data reported in XML documents, directly at a conceptual level; this way, semantics (the typical task of an ER model) of XML data is put in evidence independently of the XML syntax. A description of the ERX system can be found in [11], where design choices and system architecture are discussed, and we motivate the reason why we are realizing an ER database.

ERX-QL provides query capabilities to the ERX system, with two main characteristics. First of all, a query must be able to extract data from within the ER database provided by the ERX system; this task requires suitable constructs to navigate the ER schema. Second, the result of a query must be an XML document; consequently, ERX-QL must be naturally able to deal with nested and recursive XML structures. ERX-QL is then a two face language, for which the closure property (typical of relational algebra) cannot hold, because the result of a query is not representable by means of an ERX schema.

ERX-QL deals with the rich ERX model, that is richer than the classical ER model. However, the problem is general and from a side independent of the data model provided by the DBMS. In particular, ERX is richer than relational databases, the most common DBMSs in use, then ERX-QL can be easily modified to operate on such an information source.

The paper is organized as follows. Section 2 briefly introduces the ERX Data Model and shows a case study (Section 2.3) exploited in the rest of the paper. The main contribution of the paper is the introduction to the ERX Query Language (Section 3), that is informally described, by means of examples. Finally, Section 4 draws the conclusions and briefly discusses related work.

## 2    ERX Data Model

First of all, we have to introduce the ERX Data Model, on which ERX-QL has been developed. We introduce concepts allowed in the model, then (Section 2.3) discuss a case study.

### 2.1    Inter-module Schema

An ERX Schema is described on two distinct levels: the *Inter-Module Schema* and the *Intra-Module Schema*. The former is described hereafter, the latter is introduced in Section 2.2.

An ERX Schema is a collection of *modules*. A module groups together homogeneous concepts. It has associated the so-called *intra-module schema*.

---

[1] Work supported by Pro Universitate Bergomansi, Bergamo, Italy

A module has a non-empty set of *interfaces*, each one depicted as a labeled dashed rectangle. An interface is an entry point to the intra-module schema of the module.

Module interfaces are associated by *inter-module relationships*, depicted as labeled diamonds with two lines from the diamond to the connected interfaces. These lines are labeled with a *cardinality constraint* $(l\!:\!u)$ (lower and upper bound of associated interface instances, respectively).

Thus, modules are a modularization mechanism: modules can be defined in isolation and then assembled together by means of inter-module relationships. The final result is a clear data model with two abstraction levels, the *Inter-Module* schema and the *Intra-Module* schema, this latter one discussed in the following Section.

## 2.2  Intra-module Schema

An *entity* describes a complex (structured) concept of the source XML documents. Entities are represented as solid line rectangles; the entity name is inside the rectangle. An *instance* of an entity is a particular occurrence of a concept in the source documents. Different occurrences of a concept in XML documents correspond to different *instances* of the corresponding entity.

Entities can have *attributes*: they represent elementary concepts associated to an entity. Attributes are represented as small circles, labeled with the name, and connected to the entity they belong to by a solid line. Entity attributes can be used to represent both attributes appearing in XML tags and textual content of tags.

The ERX Data Model does not consider *key attributes*. In fact, each entity instance is automatically and implicitly assigned a unique identifier by the system.

Attribute names are associated to a qualifier, which indicates specific properties of the attribute. Qualifiers (R) and (I) denotes that the attribute is *required* or *implied* (i.e. optional), respectively. Notice that ERX attributes are not typed, but are generic strings. This choice is coherent with XML, which considers only textual information for tag attributes and tag content.

A *relationship* describes correlations existing between two entities. A relationship is represented as a labeled diamond connected to the associated entities by solid lines; these lines are labeled with a *cardinality constraint* $(l\!:\!u)$ (denoting lower and upper bound of associated entity instances, respectively).

A complex form of relationship is represented by a *relationship with alternatives*. These are always binary relationship, where each side is connected to a set of entities. Denoting as $S_1$ and $S_2$ the two sets of entities connected to side 1 and 2, respectively, an instance of the relationship associates an instance of an entity $e_{1,i} \in S_1$ to an instance of an entity $e_{2,j} \in S_2$.

Orthogonally, a relationship can be a *containment relationship*. Containment relationships are represented as normal relationships, except for the fact that lines are edges oriented from the containing to the contained entity; the cardinality (1:1) on the contained side is mandatory (and omitted).

Containment relationships have an implicit numerical property, named *order*: this property denotes the actual position occupied by the tag corresponding to the contained entity instance in the content of the container tag.

Containment relationships appear in the ERX Schema when it is necessary to model the fact that a concept exists in that it is contained in another concept.

Attributes can have an additional qualifier U: *context* (unique), which means that only one instance can have a given value for the attribute in the specified *context*: this can be the same entity or another entity that contains the entity owning the attribute through a chain of containment relationships.

*Specialization hierarchies* are possible in ERX. Sub-entities are connected to the super-entity by joined branches, with an arrow entering the super-entity. ERX hierarchies are only total and exclusive: an instance of the root belongs to one and only one leaf entity.

Entities are connected to interfaces be means of *links*. A link is represented by a labeled circle with solid lines, one from the circle to the interface, one or more from the circle to the entities. Multiple entities connected to the same link are alternatives, i.e. from the interface it is possible to reach instances of several entities.

## 2.3  Case Study

At this point, we are able to illustrate an ERX Schema that will play the role of case study in the rest of the paper. The illustrated database has been designed to collect and store information concerning computer and electronic device market.

*Modules.* The ERX Schema is composed of three modules. Module *M-Provider* describes brands and providers. Module *M-Product* describes products and their technical characteristics. Module *M-PriceList* collects information from catalogues, such as prices, special offers, etc..

*Inter-module Relationships.* Inter-module relationships (Figure 2.d) show that modules are correlated in the following way.

A product is associated to one and only one brand; this is denoted by relationship *Produces* that connects interface *I-Product* of module *M-Product* to interface *I-Brand* of module *M-Provider*, with cardinality (1:1) on the *M-Product* side.

A product can appear as an item in zero or more price-lists; this is denoted by relationship *In-PriceList*, which connects interface *I-Product* of module *M-Product* to interface *I-Item* of module *M-PriceList*, with cardinality (0:N) on the *M-Product* side.

A price-list is published by one and only one provider; this is denoted by relationship *Publishes*, which connects interface *I-PriceList* of module *M-PriceList* to interface *I-Provider* of module *M-Provider*, with cardinality (1:1) on the *M-PriceList* side.

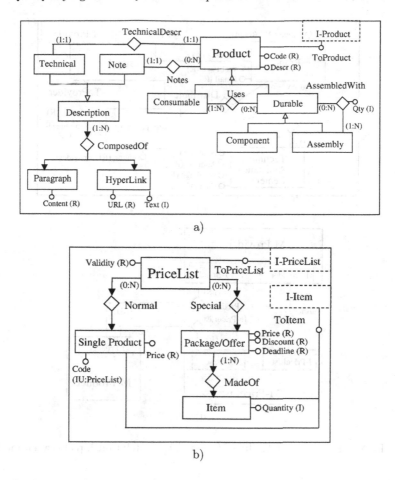

**Fig. 1.** ERX Schema for a) Module *M-Product*, b) Module *Price List*.

*Intra-module Schema* Module *M-Provider* (Figure 2.c) contains three entities. Entity *Brand* describes brands; entity *Provider* describes providers; entity *Technical Assistance Center* describes possibly existing technical assistance centers for both brands and providers.

Two relationships are in the module. Relationship *Distribute* denotes which brands are distributed by providers; obviously, this is a many-to-many relationship. In contrast, relationship named *Assists* denotes that a technical assistance center assists both brands and providers; this is a relationship with alternatives, because an instance of entity *Technical Assistance Center* is associated, alternatively, to instances of entity *Brand* or entity *Provider*.

Finally, links *ToProvider* and *ToBrand* connect interfaces *I-Provider* and *I-Brand* to entities *Provider* and *Brand*, respectively.

In module *M-Product* (Figure 1.a) we find a product hierarchy. Entity *Product* is specialized into two sub-entities, named *Consumable* and *Durable*. Notice

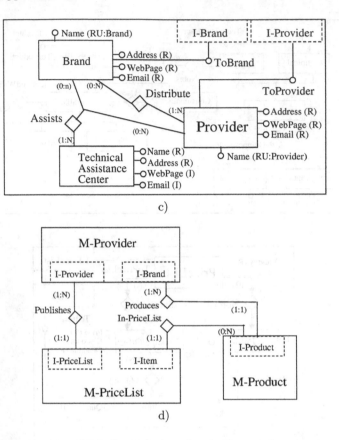

**Fig. 2.** ERX Schema for C) Module *M-Provider*, d) Relationships between modules.

the many-to-many relationship named *Uses*, which associates a durable product to the proper consumable products (e.g. a printer and its toner cartridge). Entity *Durable* is further specialized into two sub-entities, named *Component* and *Assembly*: in fact, there are products that are obtained assembling basic components (a computer is composed of mother board, hard-disk, key-board, etc.). Relationship *AssembledWith* associates an assembly to its components; notice attribute *qty*, that indicates how many components of the same type compose the assembly. Products are associated to a brand through interface *I-Product* and the Inter-Module relationship *Produces*.

Products are associated two types of textual descriptions, i.e. a mandatory technical description (entity *Technical*) and a possibly empty set of notes (entity *Notes*). They are sub-entities of a hierarchy, rooted in entity *Description*. No attributes are defined: in fact, an instance of entity *Description* allows to reach the textual descriptions, represented by instances of entities *Paragraph* and *Hyperlink*.

As far as entities *Paragraph* and *HyperLink* are concerned, notice that they are associated to entity *Description* by a containment relationship named *ComposedOf* (conceptually a description contains paragraphs and hyper-links) In particular, observe attribute *Content* of entity *Paragraph*, describing text appearing as content of XML tags.

Finally, a link named *ToProduct* connects entity *Product* to the interface *I-Product*.

Module *M-PriceList* (Figure 1.b) collects data about catalogues and price lists. An instance of entity *PricaList* corresponds to a specific catalogue. A price-list contains two kinds of information: prices for single products, and prices for packages or special offers. The former case is described by entity *SingleProduct*; the latter case is represented by entity *Package/Offer*. Both entities are associated to entity *PriceList* by means of two distinct containment relationships, named *Normal* and *Special*,respectively (a price-list is composed of, hence contains, price items).

Let us now consider entity *SingleProduct*: it has associated two attributes, *Price* and *Code*. The former is the price, while the latter is the code used in many catalogues (hence possibly missing) to identify each item.

Entity *Package/Offer* is similar, but a package is composed of several items: the price is established for the overall package (see attribute *Price* of entity *Package/Offer*), but it is necessary to know which are the products included in the package; these are described by entity *Item*.

Both entities *SingleProduct* and *Item* are connected to interface *I-Item* through the link with alternative named *ToItem*.

## 3   ERX Query Language

Let us now address the main topic of our discussion, the ERX Query Language.

An ERX Query accesses the ERX database to select data represented as entity instances and uses these data to produce a new XML document. An ERX Query is an XML document itself, based on a suitable set of tags.

*Basic Concepts.* We now define some basic concepts and terminology. The ERX Query Language selects *Entity Instances* from the ERX database, which is an *Entity Database*. Each entity instance has a set of *Entity Attributes* and a set of *Entity Properties*: the former are the string valued attributes reported in the ERX schema; the latter are numeric valued attributes that denotes unique instance identifiers (in the sequel named *OID*) and containment orders (in the sequel named *corder*) featuring instances of containment relationships.

In order to make clear the following paragraphs, we call as *i-attribute* and *i-property* an attribute and a property (resp.) of selected entity instances, we call *q-tag* and *q-attribute* a tag (or element) and an attribute (resp.) constituting the constructs of the ERX Query Language, and we call *o-tag* and *o-attribute* a tag (or element) and an attribute (resp.) generated by the query in the output XML document.

## 3.1  Basic Structure

Suppose the user wants to generate an XML document describing *providers which reside in the city "City 1"*. This is a simple ERX query that can be formulated as follows.

```
<ERXQL>
  <ERX-QUERY>
    <OUTPUT>
      <NEW-TAG Name="Providers">
      <FOR-EACH>
        <SELECT>
          <FROM Entity="Provider" InModule="M-Provider">
            <WHERE>
              <VALUE-OF Attribute="City"/> <EQ/>
              <VALUE-OF Constant="City 1" Type="String"/>
            </WHERE>
          </FROM>
        </SELECT>
        <OUTPUT>
          <NEW-EMPTY-TAG Name="PROVIDER">
            <NEW-ATTRIBUTE Name="Firm_Name" AttributeValue="Name"/>
          </NEW-EMPTY-TAG>
        </OUTPUT>
      </FOR-EACH>
      </NEW-TAG>
    </OUTPUT>
  </ERX-QUERY>
</ERXQL>
```

The core of the query is constituted by the FOR-EACH q-tag, which is composed by two parts: the *selection* part and the *output* part. The former selects entity instances from the ERX database, the latter generates the corresponding o-tags.

The SELECT q-tag denotes the selection part. It selects a set of entity instances from the ERX database, The source entity is denoted by the FROM q-tag, in which the pair of q-attributes Entity and InModule denote the entity name and the ERX module containing the entity, respectively. The optional WHERE q-tag specifies the selection condition.

For each selected instance, the OUTPUT q-tag describes how to generate the corresponding portion of output document. Generation of o-tags is specified by means of suitable q-tags.

- NEW-TAG. This q-tag generates a new o-tag whose name is specified by the q-attribute Name. The content of NEW-TAG in the query generates both the o-attributes and the content of the o-tag.

- NEW-EMPTY-TAG. This q-tag generates empty o-tags, whose name is specified by the q-attribute Name. The content of NEW-EMPTY-TAG in the query defines the o-attributes for the o-tag.
- NEW-ATTRIBUTE. This q-tag can appear only inside NEW-TAG or NEW-EMPTY-TAG; it defines an o-attribute for the o-tag, whose name is described by q-attribute Name and whose value is defined either by the q-attribute AttributeValue, which denotes an i-attribute of the selected entity instance, or by the q-attribute PropertyValue, which denotes an i-property of the selected entity instance, or by the q-attribute ConstantValue, which specifies a constant string value.
- NEW-TEXT. This q-tag generates textual content into the output document. The source of the textual content can be either an i-attribute, whose name is specified by the q-attribute AttributeValue, or an i-property, whose name is specified by the q-attribute PropertyValue, or a constant value, specified by the q-attribute ConstantValue.

The overall query is described by an ERX-QUERY q-tag, which contains the mandatory OUTPUT q-tag, whose goal is to specify the root element of the output XML document.

Let us consider in detail the sample query. The SELECT q-tag selects entity instances from the entity *Provider* in module *M-Provider* such that their i-attribute *City* has value "City 1". In particular, the selection condition is expressed as

```
<VALUE-OF Attribute="City"/> <EQ/>
<VALUE-OF Constant="City 1" Type="String"/>
```

where the first occurrence of VALUE-OF q-tag references the i-attribute *City* by means of the q-attribute Attribute, the second occurrence denotes a constant value by means of the q-attribute Constant, and the EQ q-tag denotes the comparison operator "=" (q-tags NEQ, LT, LEQ, GT, GEQ correspond to the comparison operators "$\neq$", "$<$", "$\leq$", "$>$", "$\geq$", respectively).

For each selected entity instance, the OUTPUT q-tag generates an empty o-tag named PROVIDER, with one o-attribute called Firm_Name, whose value is the value of the i-attribute *Name*.

Finally, observe that the list of PROVIDER o-tags is enclosed in a Providers o-tag.

If we suppose that two providers are selected, with name "Computer Shop" and "Computer Store", the XML document produced by the query might be the following.

```
<Providers>
  <PROVIDER Firm_Name="Computer Store"/>
  <PROVIDER Firm_Name="Computer Shop"/>
</Providers>
```

## 3.2   Managing Relationships and Links

Suppose we want to formulate the following query: *produce a list of brands located in city "City 1" and providers located in city "City 2", both assisted by technical assistance centers located in city "City 1".*

```
<ERXQL>
  <ERX-QUERY>
    <OUTPUT>
      <NEW-TAG Name="List">
      <FOR-EACH>
        <SELECT Distinct="Yes">
          <FROM Entity="TechnicalAssistanceCenter"
                InModule="M-Provider">
            <WHERE>
              <VALUE-OF Attribute="City"/> <EQ/>
                <VALUE-OF Constant="City 1" Type="String"/>
            </WHERE>
            <FOLLOW Relationship="Assists">
              <WHERE-ON-TYPE Entity="BRAND">
                <VALUE-OF Attribute="City"/> <EQ/>
                  <VALUE-OF Constant="City 1"/>
              </WHERE-ON-TYPE>
              <WHERE-ON-TYPE Entity="PROVIDER">
                <VALUE-OF ATtribute="City"/> <EQ/>
                  <VALUE-OF Constant="City 2"/>
              </WHERE-ON-TYPE>
            </FOLLOW>
          </FROM>
        </SELECT>
        <OUTPUT-ON-TYPE Entity="BRAND">
          <NEW-EMPTY-TAG Name="BRAND">
            <NEW-ATTRIBUTE Name="Brand_Name"
                           AttributeValue="Name"/>
          </NEW-EMPTY-TAG>
        </OUTPUT-ON-TYPE>
        <OUTPUT-ON-TYPE Entity="PROVIDER">
          <NEW-EMPTY-TAG Name="PROVIDER">
            <NEW-ATTRIBUTE Name="Firm_Name"
                           AttributeValue="Name"/>
          </NEW-EMPTY-TAG>
        </OUTPUT-ON-TYPE>
      </FOR-EACH>
      </NEW-TAG>
    </OUTPUT>
  </ERX-QUERY>
</ERXQL>
```

Looking at the ERX Schema in Figure 2, entities *Brand* and *Provider* are connected to the *TechnicalAssistanceCenter* by relationship *Assists*. The query addresses two problems: at first, it has to navigate the relationship; second, it obtains instances coming from two different entities.

The query selects the instances selected by theFROM and WHERE q-tags as source instances; then, moving from the selected instances of *TechnicalAssistanceCenter*, it navigates the relationship *Assists* by means of the FOLLOW q-tag (the q-attribute Relationship denotes the relationship to navigate), to reach the associated instances of entities *Brand* or *Provider*. Its result is the set of target instances reached through the relationship; source instances are completely lost by the FOLLOW operation.

Due to alternatives, the result of the navigation is a polymorphic set of instances; then it is necessary to separately select them: the first WHERE-ON-TYPE q-tag selects *Brand* instances located in city "City 1", while the second one selects *Provider* instances located in city "City 2" (q-attribute Entity of the WHERE-ON-TYPE q-tag specifies the considered entity instances).

Similarly, the output part has to deal with the same situation. In place of the OUTPUT q-tag, we find a sequence of OUTPUT-ON-TYPE q-tags, each one specific for a given target instance.

To conclude, observe the q-attribute Distinct in the q-tag SELECT: when set to "Yes" (the default is "No") it eliminates duplicated instances from the resulting instance set. In the sample query, it may happens that a brand or provider has several assistance points in the same city.

ERX-QL allows the use of a construct similar to FOLLOW to follow relationships inside selection predicates (WHERE q-tag). Furthermore, ERX-QL provides the JOIN q-tag, which performs the classical join between two sets of instances, generally connected by a relationship. For the sake of brevity we do not report these two constructs.

*Links and Inter-module Relationships.* Queries can navigate not only Intra-Module relationships, but links and Inter-Module relationships as well; this happens when it is necessary to bring together instances in different modules.

Consider the following query: *produce a document containing the list of products produced by brands located in city "City 1"*. For the sake of brevity, we report only the fragment with the SELECT q-tag.

```
<SELECT>
  <FROM Entity="Brand" InModule="M-Provider">
    <WHERE>
     <VALUE-OF Attribute="City"/> <EQ/>
      <VALUE-OF Constant="City 1" Type="String"/>
    </WHERE>
    <FOLLOW Link="ToBrand">
      <FOLLOW Relationship="Produces">
        <FOLLOW Link="ToProduct"/>
      </FOLLOW>
```

```
        </FOLLOW>
      </FROM>
    </SELECT>
```

The problem is solved by a concatenated navigation (see Figure 1 and Figure 2). The three nested FOLLOW q-tags must be interpreted as follows. The first one (<FOLLOW Link="ToBrand">) moves from instances of entity *Brand* and reaches instances of interface *I-Brand* connected to the source entity instances through link *ToBrand*. The second ,FOLLOW q-tag (<FOLLOW Relationship= "Produces">) reaches the interface *I-Product* through the Inter-Module relationship *Produces*, and obtains the interface instances linked to the desired products. Finally, the third FOLLOW q-tag (<FOLLOW Link="ToProduct"/>) reaches the desired instances of entity *Product* in module *M-Product*, navigating the *ToProduct* link.

The result is a set of instances of entity *Product* in module *M-Product*, obtained moving from instances of entity *Brand* in module *M-Provider*.

### 3.3 Nested Queries

In the above examples, we considered only one nesting level in the output document, i.e. the root o-tag and the o-tags generated by the FOR-EACH q-tag.

However, the intrinsic nested syntactic structure of XML requires query languages devoted to generate new XML documents to support nested queries. A solution similar to nested SQL queries is not adequate: nested SQL queries are exploited in selection conditions, but do not affect the schema of the result. In contrast, in our context we need nested queries able to generate parts of the output document. For this reason, ERX-QL supports nested queries inside OUTPUT and OUTPUT-ON-TYPE q-tags.

As an example, consider the following query: *generate a document listing all special offers (packages) appearing in some price.list, showing the end of validity for price-lists.*

```
<ERXQL>
  <ERX-QUERY>
    <OUTPUT>
      <NEW-TAG Name="Packages">
      <FOR-EACH>
        <SELECT>
          <FROM Entity="PriceList" InModule="M-PriceList"/>
        </SELECT>
        <OUTPUT>
          <NEW-TAG Name="PriceList">
            <NEW-TAG Name="Validity">
             <NEW-TEXT AttributeValue="Validity"/>
            </NEW-TAG>
          <FOR-EACH>
```

```
      <IMPORT Property="OID" As="pl"/>
      <SELECT>
       <FROM-INSTANCE Entity="PriceList"
               InModule="M-PriceList" ImportedValue="pl">
          <FOLLOW Relationship="Special"/>
       </FROM-INSTANCE>
       <ORDER-BY Property="pos"/>
      </SELECT>
      <OUTPUT>
        <NEW-TAG Name="PACKAGE">
          <NEW-ATTRIBUTE Name="Number"
                         PropertyValue="pos"/>
          <NEW-ATTRIBUTE Name="Price"
                         AttributeValue="Price"/>
        </NEW-TAG>
      </OUTPUT>
     </FOR-EACH>
     </NEW-TAG>
    </OUTPUT>
   </FOR-EACH>
   </NEW-TAG>
  </OUTPUT>
 </ERX-QUERY>
</ERXQL>
```

The first FOR-EACH q-tag has a simple selection part which selects all instances
from entity *PriceList* in module *M-PriceList*. At this point while generating the
output for each price-list instance (notice the generation of an o-tag PriceList
whose content is the value of the i-attribute *Validity*), it is necessary to fill-in
the content of this o-tag with data about the packages in entity Package/Offer
associated with the current *PriceList* instance.

This task is performed by a FOR-EACH q-tag nested in the OUTPUT q-tag.
Since the scope of a FOR-EACH q-tag is isolated from the context, by means of
the IMPORT q-tag we define a link with the external context, importing the OID
i-property (the identifier of the current *PriceList* instance) that is renamed as
pl. This way, the nested selection part is able to navigate the ERX schema moving from the current *PriceList* instance. Notice that the import q-tag <IMPORT
Property="OID" As="pl"/> imports the desired i-property by means of the q-
attribute Property; in alternative, the q-attribute Attribute denotes that an
i-attribute is imported.

The inner selection part does not contain a FROM q-tag. In contrast, it contains
a FROM-INSTANCE q-tag, which denotes that the selection starts from one single
instance. In particular, the tag

```
<FROM-INSTANCE Entity="PriceList"
            InModule="M-PriceList" ImportedValue="pl">
```

```
<FOLLOW Relationship="Special"/>
</FROM-INSTANCE>
```

means that only one single instance is selected from entity *PriceList* in module *M-PriceList*, the one whose identifier (OID) has the imported value p1. Then, a FOLLOW q-tag moves from this instance and selects all associated instances in entity *Package/Offer* through relationship *Special*; the result is a possibly empty set of instances, due to cardinality constraint (0:N).

The following OUTPUT q-tag simply generates an occurrence of o-tag PACKAGE for each selected package.

Notice that a third FOR-EACH q-tag might be further nested, to obtain lists of items composing each package. For the sake of brevity we do not report such an example, which is straightforward.

## 3.4   Query Libraries

The above examples put in evidence that an ERX query can become long and unreadable. This happens when the output document has a complex nested structure, and is due to the XML syntax chosen for ERX-QL.

However, there is another topic to consider: XML allows recursive structures, typically similar to tree, whose depth is not a-priori known. A query language designed to generate XML documents must provide recursive constructs.

In the previous section, we considered *instant queries*, i.e. queries that exist in the system meanwhile they are under execution and of which the system does not keep trace after their execution terminates. ERX-QL provides *named queries*: a named query is defined before it is used and has a name; it can be called by another query (both instant and named) and can be directly recursive; this way, it is possible to break a complex query in several sub-queries, to improve readability and better manage complexity; furthermore, it is possible to generate recursive structures without knowing their depth in advance.

Furthermore, named queries can be *temporary* or *persistent*. A named query is made persistent when its definition associates the query to a specific *library*. The idea is the following: the ERX database is associated a set of *query libraries*; each query library contains a set of named queries which are permanently stored in the ERX-DB (similarly to SQL views). Inside a query library we have *Intra-Module queries* and *Inter-Module* queries: the former are associated to a specific ERX module and their scope is limited to elements appearing in the module (an Intra-module query cannot traverse inter-module relationships); the latter can operate on the entire ERX schema and can navigate both inter-module and intra-module relationships.

By these concepts, it is possible to create a pool of named queries, and build complex queries incrementally, moving from simple intra-module queries to complex inter-module queries assembled with intra-module queries.

Suppose we want to formulate the following query: *generate an XML document with short descriptions of durable products.*

This is a typical query in the sample ERX DB, and can be managed by a persistent named query.

```
<ERXQL>
  <DEF-QUERY Name="GenDurable" InModule="M-Product"
             InLibrary ="SampleLibrary">
    <PARAMETER Name="DurableOID" Type="OID"/>
    <FOR-EACH>
      <SELECT>
        <FROM-INSTANCE Entity="Durable"
                       ParameterValue="DurableOID"/>
      </SELECT>
      <OUTPUT-ON-TYPE Entity="Durable/Component">
        <NEW-TAG Name="Product">
          <NEW-ATTRIBUTE Name="PID" AttributeValue="Code"/>
          <NEW-TEXT AttributeValue="Descr"/>
        </NEW-TAG>
      </OUTPUT-ON-TYPE>
      <OUTPUT-ON-TYPE Entity="Durable/Assembly">
        <NEW-TAG Name="Product">
          <NEW-ATTRIBUTE Name="PID" AttributeValue="Code"/>
          <NEW-TEXT AttributeValue="descr"/>
          <FOR-EACH>
            <IMPORT Property="OID" As="AssemblyOID"/>
            <SELECT>
              <FROM-INSTANCE Entity="Assembly"
                             InModule="M-Product"
                             ParameterValue="AssemblyOID">
                <FOLLOW Relationship="AssembledWith"/>
              </FROM-INSTANCE>
            </SELECT>
            <OUTPUT>
              <CALL-QUERY Name="GenDurable" InModule="M-Product"
                          InLibrary="SampleLibrary">
                <WITH-PARAMETER Name="DurableOID"
                                PropertyValue="OID"/>
              </CALL-QUERY>
            </OUTPUT>
          </FOR-EACH>
        </NEW-TAG>
      </OUTPUT-ON-TYPE>
    </FOR-EACH>
  </DEF-QUERY>
</ERXQL>
```

The DEF-QUERY q-tag defines a named query, whose name is GenDurable, belonging to library SampleLibrary and associated to module *M-Product*; this means that the scope of the query will be limited to elements in that module.

The q-tag defines a query parameter named DurableOID: this means that the query is parametric w.r.t. the identifier (OID) of the instance of entity *Durable* to process. As a result, in ERX-QL scope environments are composed by four sets of valued objects, i.e. i-attributes, i-properties, imported values, query parameters; consequently, the five q-attributes AttributeValue, PropertyValue, ImportedValue, ParameterValue and ConstantValue can be alternatively used in those q-tags, such as NEW-ATTRIBUTE and NEW-TEXT, that need valued objects.

The external FOR-EACH q-tag selects the *Durable* instance identified by parameter DurableOID, in order to be aware of its attribute; then, different output is necessary, depending on the sub-entity in the hierarchy in which the instance actually is (ERX hierarchies are only total and exclusive). If the instance is a *Component* (denoted by the path expression Durable/Component) the o-tag Product is filled in and no recursion is needed. Otherwise the instance is an assembly (denoted by the path expression Durable/Assembly) and it may contain other durable products, as represented in the ERX Schema by relationship *AssembledWith*.

For this latter case, it is necessary to define a sub-query (nested FOR-EACH q-tag) which moving from the current instance navigates relationship *AssembledWith* and selects a new set of *Durable* instances. For each newly selected instance, the q-tag

```
<CALL-QUERY Name="GenDurable" InModule="M-Product"
            InLibrary="SampleLibrary">
  <WITH-PARAMETER Name="DurableOID" PropertyValue="OID"/>
</CALL-QUERY>
```

recursively calls query GenDurable, passing the identifier (OID) of the current *Durable* instance as actual parameter.

Based on this named query, it is possible to formulate an instant query, that produces the complete document.

```
<ERXQL>
  <ERX-QUERY>
    <OUTPUT>
      <NEW-TAG Name="ProductList">
      <FOR-EACH>
        <SELECT>
          <FROM Entity="Durable" InModule="M-Product"/>
        </SELECT>
        <OUTPUT>
          <CALL-QUERY Name="GenDurable"
                      InModule="M-Product"
                      InLibrary="SampleLibrary">
```

```
        <WITH-PARAMETER Name="DurableOID"
                        PropertyValue="OID"/>
      </CALL-QUERY>
     </OUTPUT>
    </FOR-EACH>
   </NEW-TAG>
  </OUTPUT>
 </ERX-QUERY>
</ERXQL>
```

Only observe the q-tag CALL-QUERY inside the OUTPUT q-tag: for each selected instance of *Durable*, it calls the named query GenDurable, to actually generate the XML fragment describing each durable product.

To clarify, we report a sample XML output document, that cannot be obtained without recursion.

```
<Products>
 <PRODUCT PID="D1">
  Assembly 1
   <PRODUCT PID="D2">
    Assembly 2
    <PRODUCT PID="C1"> Component 1 </PRODUCT>
   </PRODUCT>
   <PRODUCT PID="C2"> Component 2 </PRODUCT>
  </PRODUCT>
  <PRODUCT PID="D2">
   Durable 2
   <PRODUCT PID="C1"> Component 1 </PRODUCT>
  </PRODUCT>
</Products>
```

# 4   Conclusions

In this paper, we described the current state of our work, devoted to the definition of ERX-QL. This query language is part of the ERX Data Management System, which is under development at University of Bergamo. The data model provided by the system is named ERX (Entity-Relationship for XML), since it is a variant of the classical Entity-Relationship conceptual model, devised to capture data coming from XML documents.

The aim of ERX-QL is the declarative specification of queries that extract data from within the ERX database and generate XML documents. We informally described its features, by means of a running example. In particular, we discussed ERX schema navigation facilities, nested queries constructs, query recursion and the concept of query library. We are now completing the definition of the language. In particular, we are defining the notion of *template*, i.e. a query which is generic w.r.t. the output format of selected entity instances; the same query template can be instantiated in different manners, in order to obtain different XML output formats for the same selected instances.

In conclusion, we can say that ERX-QL is effective in the formulation of complex queries and in the generation of complex XML documents. We want to notice that although ERX-QL is designed to retrieve data from an Entity-Relationship database, the approach is general and might be applied to other data models provided by DBMSs, such as Relational DBMSs, Object-Oriented DBMSs, Object-Relational DBMSs. In particular, for RDBMSs a sub-set of ERX-QL selection constructs is sufficient, while for other ones it should be sufficient to slightly extend semantics of the FOLLOW q-tags to deal with attributes defined as lists or bags.

*Related Work.* Since its introduction [6] a large amount of work has been done about the ER model, and several ER query languages where proposed. These works (in the references we report only a short list) considered several approaches, such as denotational semantics, SQL-like or OQL-like query languages, graphical query languages, and considered various properties of these languages, such as closure and completeness. The selection constructs of ERX-QL certainly inspire to them.

As far as XML query languages are concerned, in literature we can find several proposals [12,7,4]; however, these languages are meant to query directly XML documents, in order, e.g., to restructure them. Their application context is clearly different w.r.t. the one considered for ERX-QL.

The only proposal close to ERX-QL is the *Quilt* language [5], a query language defined to query different data sources and generate XML documents. It can be possibly applied to query relational DBMSs. Apart form the fact that it is not based on an XML syntax, Quilt does not provide (as far as we know) concepts like recursive queries and query libraries similar to those provided by ERX-QL.

# References

1. M. Andries and G. Engels. A hybrid query language for an extended entity-relationship model. *Journal of Visual Languages and Computing*, 7(3):321–352, 1996.
2. P. Atzeni and P. P. Chen. Completeness of query languages for the entity-relationship model. In *Proceedings of the Second International Conference on the Entity-Relationship Approach (ER'81), Washington, DC, USA, October 12-14, 1981*, pages 109–122. North Holland, 1981.
3. A. C. Bloesch and T. A. Halpin. Conceptual queries using ConQuer-II. In *ER '97, 16th International Conference on Conceptual Modeling, Los Angeles, California, USA, November 3-5, 1997, Proceedings*, volume 1331, pages 113–126. Springer, 1997.
4. S. Ceri, S. Comai, E. Damiani, P. Fraternali, and L. Tanca. Complex queries in xml-gl. In *Proc. ACM SAC 2000 Symposium on Applied Computing*, Como, Italy, 2000.

5. D. D. Chamberlin, J. Robie, and D. Florescu. Quilt: An xml query language for heterogeneous data sources. In *Proc. WebDB Workshop*, Dallas, Texas (USA), May 2000.
6. P. P. Chen. The entity-relationship model - toward a unified view of data. *TODS*, 1(1):9–36, 1976.
7. A. Deutsch, M. Fernandez, D. Florescu, , A. Levy, and D. Suciu. Xml-ql: A query language for xml. (Tech.Rep. NOTE-xml-ql-19980819), August 1998.
8. V. M. Markowitz and Y. Raz. A modified relational algebra and its use in an entity-relationship environment. In *Proceedings of the 3rd Int. Conf. on Entity-Relationship Approach (ER'83)*, pages 315–328. North Holland, 1983.
9. J. McHugh and J. Widom. Query optimization for xml. In *Proc. 25th VLDB Conference*, Edinburgh, Scotland, September 1999.
10. Christine Parent, Hélène Rolin, Kokou Yétongnon, and Stefano Spaccapietra. An er calculus for the entity-relationship complex model. In *Proceedings of the Eight International Conference on Enity-Relationship Approach, Toronto, Canada, 18-20 October, 1989*, pages 361–384. North-Holland, 1989.
11. G. Psaila and D. Brugali. The ERX data management system. In *Proceedings of IC-2001, Second International Conference on Internet Computing, Las Vegas, Nevada, USA, 26-28 June 2001*.
12. J. Robie, J. Lapp, and D. Schach. *XML Query Language (XQL)*. http://www.w3.org/TandS/QL/QL98/pp/xql.html, 1998.
13. T. R. Rogers and R. G. G. Cattell. Entity-relationship database user interfaces. In *Proceedings of the Sixth International Conference on Entity-Relationship Approach, New York, USA, November 9-11, 1987*, pages 353–365. North-Holland, 1987.
14. J. Shammugasundaram, K. Tufte, G. He, C. Zhang, D. DeWitt, and J. Naughton. Relational databases for querying xml documents: Limitations and opportunities. In *Proc. 25th VLDB Conference*, Edinburgh, Scotland, September 1999.
15. K. Subieta and M. Missala. Semantics of query languages for the entity-relationship model. In *Proceedings of the Fifth International Conference on Entity-Relationship Approach, Dijon, France, November 17-19, 1986*, pages 197–216. North-Holland, 1986.

# Optimising Active Database Rules by Partial Evaluation and Abstract Interpretation

James Bailey[1], Alexandra Poulovassilis[2], and Simon Courtenage[3]

[1] Dept. of Computer Science, University of Melbourne
jbailey@cs.mu.oz.au
[2] School of Computer Science and Information Systems, Birkbeck College,
Univ. of London
ap@dcs.bbk.ac.uk
[3] Cavendish School of Computer Science, University of Westminster
courtes@westminster.ac.uk

**Abstract.** A key issue for active databases is optimising the execution event-condition-action rules. In this paper we show how partial evaluation provides a formal and general route to optimising such rules. We produce a specialised version of the rule execution semantics for each possible sequence of actions that may execute from the current database state. This gives the opportunity to optimise rule execution for each particular sequence of actions. We obtain information about possible sequences of rule executions actions by applying abstract interpretation to the rule execution semantics. Our techniques are applicable both statically, i.e. at rule compilation time, and dynamically, during rule execution.

## 1 Introduction

Active databases provide reactive functionality by supporting event-condition-action rules of the form 'on *event* if *condition* do *actions*'. Active rules allow reactive functionality to be defined and managed centrally within the database rather than being encoded in diverse applications programs. Active rules thus have the potential to improve the robustness and maintainability of database applications. However, poor performance is one of the main reasons that application developers cite in their reluctance to deploy active rules [14]. Thus, optimising the run-time execution of active rules is a key issue for their wider acceptance and deployment. Given their data-intensive nature, previous research has aimed at either adopting existing database optimisation techniques, or developing special-purpose solutions for improving execution efficiency. In contrast, in this paper we show how the programming language framework of *partial evaluation* provides a formal and general route to optimising active database rules.

Partial evaluation [13,12] aims to improve program efficiency by producing specialised versions of the program for specific input values. In the case of sets of active rules, the 'program' being optimised is the rule execution semantics and the 'input values' are the current database state and the rule actions currently

G. Grahne and G. Ghelli (Eds.): DBPL 2001, LNCS 2397, pp. 300–317, 2002.

awaiting execution. Producing a specialised version of the rule execution semantics for each possible sequence of actions that may execute on that database state provides the opportunity to optimise rule execution for each particular sequence of actions, for example by abstraction of common sub-queries from the sequences of conditions that will need to be evaluated.

We obtain information about possible sequences of actions by applying abstract interpretation [1,6,18] to the rule execution semantics, using an abstract representation of the current database state and current action(s) awaiting execution. In [2], we presented a framework for termination analysis of active rules using abstract interpretation. Here, we use similar techniques for generating the set of input values with respect to which the rule execution semantics should be partially evaluated and optimised. Our techniques are applicable both statically, i.e. at rule compilation time, and dynamically, during rule execution.

The contributions of this work are as follows: We introduce for the first time partial evaluation and abstract interpretation as techniques for globally optimising sets of active rules. The combination of these techniques generalises a number of optimisations already found in the active database literature. A key difference between this previous work and our approach is that our optimisations are automatically derived using general principles. This places rule optimisation on a sound theoretical footing, and also provides the opportunity to discover new optimisations. In particular, we show how abstract interpretation can be used to generate information about sequences of rule actions that will be executed, and this approach produces more possibilities for rule optimisation than previous graph-based analyses.

This paper is structured as follows. Section 2 specifies the rule execution semantics that we assume for the purposes of this paper and discusses abstract interpretation of these semantics. It also shows how abstract interpretation can be integrated with rule execution in order to avoid condition evaluation by making use of cheap incremental inferencing techniques. Section 3 shows how partial evaluation can be used for optimising specialisations of the rule execution semantics for single rule actions. Section 4 extends the approach to possible sequences of rule actions, using abstract interpretation to derive such sequences. Section 5 shows how abstract interpretation can also be applied at run-time, to generate sequences of rule actions that will definitely be executed so that these can be dynamically optimised. Section 6 discusses the costs and benefits our techniques and compares our approach with related work on optimising active rules. Section 7 summarises our contributions and outlines directions for future work.

## 2 Rule Optimisation Using Abstract Interpretation

### 2.1 The Rule Execution Semantics

We specify the rule execution semantics that we are assuming for the purposes of this paper using a typed functional meta language supporting lazy evaluation [20]. The rule execution semantics are expressed as a function, *execSched*, which takes as input a *database* and a *schedule*.

The schedule consists of a list rule actions to be executed. The database consists of a set relation names and an extent associated with each one. Relations are of three kinds: user-defined relations and, for each user-defined relation $R$, two *event* relations, *insEventR* and *delEventR* and two *delta* relations $\triangle R$ and $\triangledown R$. *insEventR* (*delEventR*) is non-empty if and only if the latest action executed was an insertion into (deletion from) $R$. $\triangle R$ ($\triangledown R$) contains the tuples inserted into (deleted from) $R$ by the latest action executed[1].

Active rules take the form 'on *event* if *condition* do *actions*'. The event part may be $\triangle R$, $\triangledown R$, *insEventR* or *delEventR*, for some $R$. The condition part is a query. We define a rule's *event-condition* query to be the conjunction of its event query and its condition query. A rule is said to be *triggered* if the relation specified in its event part evaluates to non-empty. A rule *fires* if it is triggered and its condition part evaluates to non-empty i.e. if its event-condition query evaluates to non-empty.

Each rule has a list of one or more actions, each action being of the form *Ins R q* or *Del R q* for some user-defined relation $R$ and query $q$. Each rule also has a *coupling mode*, which may be either *Immediate* or *Deferred*. With Immediate coupling mode, if the rule fires then its actions are prefixed to the current schedule; with Deferred coupling mode, they are suffixed. If multiple rules with the same coupling mode fire, the actions of higher-priority rules precede those of lower-priority ones on the schedule. We assume that all rules have the same *binding mode*, whereby the delta relation names in each action's query part, $q$, are bound to the database state in which the rule's condition is evaluated and all other relation names in $q$ are bound to the database state in which the action is executed. A greater variety of coupling modes and binding modes can be handled by our rule analysis and optimisation techniques, which are generically applicable, but here we confine ourselves to this subset for ease of exposition. We refer the reader to [19] for a detailed description of the coupling and binding possibilities for active rules, and to [14] for an in-depth discussion of the practical aspects of deploying active rules in database applications.

We specify the rule execution semantics as a recursive function *execSched* which takes a database and schedule, and repeatedly executes the first action on the schedule, updating the schedule with the actions of rules that fire along the way (we use `teletype` font to specify *execSched* below in order to emphasize that it is an executable specification). If *execSched* terminates, it outputs the final database state and the final, empty, schedule. If it fails to terminate, it produces no output:

```
execSched : (DBState,Schedule) -> (DBState,Schedule)
execSched (db,[]) = (db,[])
execSched (db,a:s) =
    execSched o schedRules (exec (a,db), a:s)
```

---

[1]   Allowing both event and delta relations means that both *semantic* and *syntactic* triggering are supported.

```
schedRules : (DBState,Schedule) -> (DBState,Schedule)
schedRules (db,a:s) =
    let (db,pre,suf) = fold schedRule (db,[],[]) (triggers a)
    in  (db,pre++s++suf)

schedRule : RuleId -> (DBState,Schedule,Schedule) ->
                      (DBState,Schedule,Schedule)
schedRule i (db,pre,suf) =
    if (eval (ecq i) db) = {}
    then (db,pre,suf)
    else updateSched (actions i,mode i,db,pre,suf)

updateSched (actions,Immediate,db,pre,suf) =
    (db, pre ++ (bind actions db),suf)
updateSched (actions,Deferred, db,pre,suf) =
    (db, pre, suf ++ (bind actions db))
```

In the above specification, we assume that rules are identified by unique rule identifiers. The functions *ecq*, *actions* and *mode* take a rule identifier and return the event-condition query, the list of actions, and the mode of the rule, respectively. The function *triggers* takes a rule action, and returns the id's of rules triggered by that action, in order of their priority.

The function *exec* executes an action $a$ on a database $db$ and returns the updated database. The function *schedRules* applies the function *schedRule* to each rule triggered by $a$ (in order of the rules' priority). *schedRule* determines whether a given rule fires by invoking the *eval* function to evaluate its event-condition query w.r.t the current database state. If so, *updateSched* is called to update the schedule prefix or suffix. The function *bind* replaces the delta relation names in an action's query part by the contents of these relations in the current database state. ○ denotes function composition, [] the empty list, $(x : y)$ a list with head $x$ and tail $y$, and ++ is the list append operator. We also assume the following function which "folds" a binary function $f$ into a list:

```
fold f x []     = x
fold f x (y:ys) = fold f (f y x) ys
```

**Discussion.** The above rule execution semantics are a simplification of the framework we presented in [2]. The optimisation techniques we describe here are applicable to the full framework, but we confine ourselves to this subset for ease of exposition. The above semantics encompass most of the functionality of SQL3's statement-level triggers [15] – see [3] for a full discussion of this point. They do not encompass BEFORE triggers or UPDATE events but the optimisation techniques we describe here are easily extended to these also. The above semantics do encompass semantic triggering and Deferred rule coupling, which are not supported in SQL3. Finally, do not directly consider row-level triggers here but we outline how they too could be handled in the Conclusions section.

## 2.2   The Abstract Execution Semantics

The abstract counterpart to *execSched* is *execSched\**, given below. *execSched\**
is identical to *execSched* except that it operates on abstract databases and
abstract schedules, and that at the "leaves" of the computation the functions *eval*
and *exec* are replaced by abstract counterparts *eval\** and *exec\**; we distinguish
abstract types and functions from their concrete counterparts by suffixing their
names with a '*'.

An abstract database consists of a set of identifiers and an abstract value
associated with one. Generally, these abstract values will be drawn from different
domains for different abstractions. An abstract schedule consists of a list of abstract actions. An abstract action may contain abstract values in its query part,
arising from the binding of delta relation names to the current abstract database
state. Rules and queries are syntactic objects which are common to both the
concrete and the abstract semantics. The functions *triggers*, *ecq*, *actions* and
*updateSched* are the same in both semantics (in particular, *updateSched* and
*bind* are polymorphic over concrete and abstract database states and schedules):

```
execSched* : (DBState*,Schedule*) -> (DBState*,Schedule*)
execSched* (db*,[])    = (db*,[])
execSched* (db*,a*:s*) =
    execSched* o schedRules* (exec* (a*,db*), a*:s*)

schedRules* : (DBState*,Schedule*) -> (DBState*,Schedule*)
schedRules* (db*,a*:s*) =
    let (db*,pre*,suf*) = fold schedRule* (db*,[],[]) (triggers a*)
    in  (db*,pre* ++ s*++ suf*)

schedRule* : RuleId -> (DBState*,Schedule*,Schedule*) ->
                       (DBState*,Schedule*,Schedule*)
schedRule* i (db*,pre*,suf*) =
    if (eval* (ecq i) db* = False)
    then (db*,pre*,suf*)
    else updateSched (actions i,mode i,db*,pre*,suf*))
```

In general, there is no guarantee that *execSched\** will terminate and so we
need a criterion for halting it. If the abstract domain is finite (which it is for
the abstraction that we use for rule optimisation) a simple way is to maintain
a history of the $(db^*, head\ s^*)$ arguments passed to *execSched\** and to halt if a
repeating argument is detected – this is also the approach that we adopted for
dynamic analysis of rule termination and it is discussed in [3]. In practice, the
length of the execution history is unlikely to be large and thus such checking can
be done efficiently.

In [2], we discussed the use of abstract interpretation for rule termination
analysis and we identified three specific abstractions, two suitable for static analysis and one for dynamic analysis. In [3], we further explored the third of these
abstractions and we addressed the pragmatics of dynamic termination analysis

in active databases. Here, we briefly review this abstraction again since, as we will see later, it can also be used for rule optimisation.

With this abstraction, the abstract database consists of an identifier corresponding to each event query and each condition query in the rule set. These identifiers are assigned values from the 3-valued domain $\{True, False, Unknown\}$.

$exec^*$ uses a function $infer$ to deduce new truth values for these queries. $infer$ takes a query $q$, a truth value inferred for $q$ w.r.t. a previous abstract database state, and the sequence of actions applied to the database since that inference, and returns a new truth value for $q$. This inferencing is performed using incremental techniques that determine the effect of updates on queries [10,21]. For reasons of space, we do not repeat here the inferencing algorithms that we use, and refer the reader to [3] for their details. Since the properties being tested are undecidable in general, it is of course possible that $Unknown$ truth values will be inferred for queries.

$eval^*$ $q$ $db^*$ returns the truth value of the event-condition query $q$ in the current abstract database $db^*$. Notice that an $Unknown$ truth value for an event-condition query is treated in the same way as $True$ by the abstract execution semantics i.e. if it is not known whether a rule would fire, the abstract execution assumes that it $will$ fire. In this way, the abstract execution encompasses all possible actual executions, and perhaps also some additional ones. It thus gives a conservative test for rule termination, in that if $execSched^*$ $(db^*, s^*)$ terminates so will $execSched$ $(db, s)$ for all databases $db$ and schedules $s$ whose abstract representation is $db^*$ and $s^*$ respectively[2].

**Example 1.** Consider the following rule set. Assume that all the rules have Immediate coupling mode, rule 2 has higher priority than rule 3, and rule 4 higher priority than rule 5.

1 : on $\triangle R_9$          2 : on $\triangle R_0$          3 : on $\triangle R_0$
   if $R_1 - R_0$         if $R_2 \cup (R_3 \bowtie R_4)$        if $(R_3 \bowtie R_4) - R_5$
   do $Ins\ R_0\ R_1$       do $Del\ R_1\ (R_7 \times R_8)$    do $Ins\ R_5\ R_3 \cup (R_7 \times R_8)$

4 : on $\triangle R_5$          5 : on $\triangle R_5$
   if $R_2 \cup (R_3 \bowtie R_4)$       if $R_7 \times R_8$
   do $Del\ R_4\ (R_5 \cup R_6)$        do $Ins\ R_9\ (R_7 \times R_8)$

The triggering graph of these rules is as follows:

---

[2] We note that this is a departure from standard abstract interpretation where both branches of the conditional would be pursued and then merged. We can simplify this in our setting provided the abstraction correctly represents the effect on the abstract database state of rules scheduled in the abstract execution which would not be scheduled in some concretisation of this abstract execution. This property is indeed satisfied by the particular abstraction we are concerned with here.

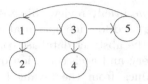

Given an initial schedule consisting of the action of rule 1, i.e. $[Ins\ R_0\ R_1]$, and an initial abstract database in which all condition queries have value *Unknown*, a trace of the abstract execution of these rules on each successive call to $execSched^*$ is as follows, where $c_i$ denotes the condition query of rule $i$ and $a_i$ the action of rule $i$:

| Iteration | $c_1$ | $c_2$ | $c_3$ | $c_4$ | $c_5$ | Schedule |
|---|---|---|---|---|---|---|
| 1 | U | U | U | U | U | $[a_1]$ |
| 2 | F | U | U | U | U | $[a_2, a_3]$ |
| 3 | F | U | U | U | U | $[a_3]$ |
| 4 | F | U | U | U | U | $[a_4, a_5]$ |
| 5 | F | U | U | U | U | $[a_5]$ |

We see that the execution of rule 1's action on iteration 1 causes its condition to become False (the details of the inferencing techniques used to deduce this can be found in [3]). Thereafter rule 1's condition remains False. At iteration 5, it is evaluated again and its falsity means that rule 1 cannot fire at this point. We can therefore conclude that if rule 1 is the first rule triggered then rule execution will definitely terminate within 5 iterations. ∎

In general, our rule termination test consts of running $execSched^*$ once for each possible initial singleton schedule, with an initial abstract database in which all queries have an *Unknown* value. If all invocations of $execSched^*$ terminate, then definite termination of the set of active rules can be concluded. Otherwise, the set of rules is deemed to be possibly non-terminating. We refer the reader to [2,3] for a more detailed discussion of abstract interpretation for rule termination analysis. In Section 2.3 below we turn to its use for rule optimisation. Before doing so, we first consider the issue of the *correctness* of the abstract semantics.

An abstract database approximates a number of real databases and an abstract schedule a number of real schedules. These possible concretisations are obtained by applying a *concretisation function* to the abstract database or schedule. Suppose the following holds for all $db^* \in DBState^*$ and $s^* \in Schedule^*$, where *conc* is the concretisation function corresponding to the chosen abstraction (see [2] for details of *conc*):

$$conc\ (execSched^*\ (db^*, s^*)) \supseteq \{execSched\ (db, s) \mid (db, s) \in conc\ (db^*, s^*)\}\ (1)$$

The LHS of this condition is the set of database/schedule pairs whose abstract representation is the output of $execSched^*\ (db^*, s^*)$. The RHS is the set of database/schedule pairs output by $execSched\ (db, s)$ for all $(db, s)$ whose abstract representation is $(db^*, s^*)$. Thus, condition (1) states that abstract execution from an initial state $(db^*, s^*)$ represents a superset of the set of real executions from all $(db, s)$ whose abstract representation is $(db^*, s^*)$.

Two rule properties for which $execSched^*$ is conservative if (1) holds are *rule termination* and *rule unreachability*: for the first, if $execSched^*$ $(db^*, s^*)$ terminates, then so must all $execSched$ $(db, s)$ such that $(db, s) \in conc$ $(db^*, s^*)$; for the second, if a rule $i$ is not scheduled during the execution of $execSched^*$ $(db^*, s^*)$ then it cannot be scheduled during the execution of any $execSched$ $(db, s)$ such that $(db, s) \in conc$ $(db^*, s^*)$. The following theorem gives sufficient conditions for (1) to hold:

**Theorem 1.** Condition (1) holds if
(i) for all abstract actions $a^*$ and abstract databases $db^*$,
$conc$ $(exec^*$ $(a^*, db^*)) \supseteq \{exec$ $(a, db) \mid (a, db) \in conc$ $(a^*, db^*)\}$, and
(ii) for all event-condition queries $q$ and abstract databases $db^*$,
$eval^*$ $q$ $db^* = False \Rightarrow (\forall db \in conc$ $db^*$ . $eval$ $q$ $db = \{\})$. ∎

An example of a rule property for which (1) is not sufficient is *rule reachability*, in that if a rule $i$ is scheduled during $execSched^*$ $(db^*, s^*)$ then it may, or may not, be scheduled during some $execSched$ $(db, s)$ such that $(db, s) \in conc$ $(db^*, s^*)$. However, suppose that in addition to (1) the converse also holds for all $db^* \in DBState^*$ and $s^* \in Schedule^*$:

$$\{execSched$ $(db, s) \mid (db, s) \in conc$ $(db^*, s^*)\} \supseteq conc$ $(execSched^*$ $(db^*, s^*)) \quad (2)$$

Then, if a rule $i$ is scheduled during $execSched^*$ $(db^*, s^*)$, it must be scheduled during all $execSched$ $(db, s)$ such that $(db, s) \in conc$ $(db^*, s^*)$.

**Theorem 2.** Condition (2) holds if
(i) for all abstract actions $a^*$ and abstract databases $db^*$,
$\{exec$ $(a, db) \mid (a, db) \in conc$ $(a^*, db^*)\} \supseteq conc$ $(exec^*$ $(a^*, db^*))$, and
(ii) for all event-condition queries $q$ and abstract databases $db^*$,
$eval^*$ $q$ $db^* \neq False \Rightarrow (\forall db \in conc$ $db^*$ . $eval$ $q$ $db \neq \{\})$. ∎

**Observation.** The abstraction described in [3] and used in Example 1 above satisfies the conditions of Theorem 1. It also satisfies the conditions of Theorem 2 provided $eval^*$ returns only True or False i.e. not if $eval^*$ returns $Unknown$. This is because $Unknown$ event-condition queries are treated as $True$ by $execSched^*$ whereas they may be $False$ in some concrete execution.

## 2.3   Mixed Execution Semantics

Our first observation regarding rule optimisation is that it is possible to use the abstract execution to optimise the concrete execution by not evaluating an event-condition query using $eval$ if its abstract value is inferred to be $True$ or $False$ by $eval^*$. Conversely, after using $eval$ to evaluate event-condition queries whose abstract value is currently $Unknown$, it is possible to upgrade this value to $True$ or $False$ in the abstract database state. This in turn will result in more precise future inferencing of abstract values, and hence in further gains in avoiding query evaluation.

These two observations lead to our *mixed* execution semantics, specified by the function $execSchedM$ below, whereby the concrete and abstract executions proceed together. The abstract database state is consulted for the presence of definite truth values, and it is updated after undertaking query evaluation when this is necessary:

```
execSchedM : (DBState,Schedule,DBState*,Schedule*) ->
              (DBState,Schedule,DBState*,Schedule*)
execSchedM (db,[],db*,[]) = (db,[],db*,[])
execSchedM (db,a:s,db*,a*:s*) =
  execSchedM o schedRulesM (exec (a,db),a:s,exec* (a*,db*),a*:s*)

schedRulesM (db,a:s,db*,a*:s*) =
  let (db,pre,suf,db*,pre*,suf*) =
      fold schedRuleM (db,[],[],db*,[],[]) (triggers a)
  in  (db,pre++s++suf,db*,pre*++s*++suf*)

schedRuleM i (db,pre,suf,db*,pre*,suf*) =
  case (eval* (ecq i) db*) of
    False  :(db,pre,suf,db*,pre*,suf*);
    True   :updateSchedM (actions i,mode i,db,pre,suf,db*,pre*,suf*);
    Unknown:let newdb* = replaceVal (ecq i) db* (eval (ecq i) db)
            in  schedRuleM i (db,pre,suf,newdb*,pre*,suf*)

updateSchedM (actions,Immediate,db,pre,suf,db*,pre*,suf*) =
  (db,pre++(bind actions db),suf,db*,pre*++(bind actions db*),suf*)
updateSchedM (actions,Deferred, db,pre,suf,db*,pre*,suf*) =
  (db,pre,suf++(bind actions db),db*,pre*,suf*++(bind actions db*))
```

Here the function *replaceVal* takes a query $q$, an abstract database $db^*$, and a concrete value, *val*, for the query, and replaces the abstract value of $q$ in $db^*$ by *True* or *False* depending on whether *val* is non-empty or empty.

To illustrate, consider again the rule set in Example 1. Suppose we have the same initial schedule and abstract database state. Suppose also that in the initial actual database state, the conditions of rules 2 and 4 would evaluate to empty and those of rules 3 and 5 to non-empty. Then a trace of the abstract database state and schedule on each successive call to *execSchedM* is shown below. We see that at iteration 1, the event-condition queries of rules 2 and 3 are evaluated, the abstract database state is updated accordingly and rule 3 fires. At iteration 2, the event-condition queries of rules 4 and 5 are evaluated, the abstract database state is updated and rule 5 fires. At iteration 3, the abstract value of condition 1 can be used to infer that rule 1 won't fire after the execution of rule 5's action – rule 1's event-condition query need not be evaluated. Notice also how the abstract database state has been "upgraded" with more definite information by this rule execution and will thus be more useful for optimising future rule executions:

| Iteration | $c_1$ | $c_2$ | $c_3$ | $c_4$ | $c_5$ | Schedule |
|-----------|-------|-------|-------|-------|-------|----------|
| 1         | $U$   | $U$   | $U$   | $U$   | $U$   | $[a_1]$  |
| 2         | $F$   | $F$   | $T$   | $U$   | $U$   | $[a_3]$  |
| 3         | $F$   | $F$   | $T$   | $F$   | $T$   | $[a_5]$  |

**Observation.** For any $(db, s, db^*, s^*)$ such that $(db, s) \in conc\ (db^*, s^*)$, let

$$(db', s', db'^*, s'^*) = schedRulesM\ (exec\ (head\ s, db), s, exec^*\ (head\ s^*, db^*), s^*)$$

Then it is possible to show that:

$$(db', s') = schedRules\ (exec\ (head\ s, db), s) \tag{3}$$

$$(db', s') \in conc\ (db'^*, s'^*) \tag{4}$$

$$conc\ (db'^*, s'^*) \subseteq schedRules^*\ (exec^*\ (head\ s^*, db^*), s^*) \tag{5}$$

In other words, the mixed execution gives at each step the same database/ schedule pair as the real execution, and an abstract database/schedule pair which is at least as precise as the one in the abstract execution would be.

## 3   Rule Optimisation Using Partial Evaluation

Partial evaluation [13,12] aims to improve program efficiency by producing specialised versions of the program for specific input values. Here we show how partial evaluation can be applied to the problem of optimising a given set of active rules. A sequence of rewriting steps is performed on the definition of $execSched$, preserving its semantics but resulting in a specialisation of it for each form of rule action. Each specialisation is then optimised *for that particular form of rule action*. The rewriting steps are as follows:

**Step 1**: Produce an equation defining $execSched$ for each possible form of action $a_1, ..., a_n$ appearing in the current rule set:

$$execSched\ (db, a_1 : s) = execSched \circ schedRules\ (exec\ (a_1, db), a_1 : s)$$
$$execSched\ (db, a_2 : s) = execSched \circ schedRules\ (exec\ (a_2, db), a_2 : s)\ ...$$

By "form of action" we mean whether the action is an insertion or deletion, and with respect to which relation. Thus, for the rule set given in Example 1, the forms of action are $Ins\ R_0\ q$, $Del\ R_1\ q$, $Ins\ R_5\ q$, $Del\ R_4\ q$ and $Ins\ R_9\ q$, and one specialisation will be produced for $execSched$ for each of these.

**Step 2**: Also produce an equation defining $schedRules(db, a : s)$ for each form of action:

$$schedRules\ (db, a_1 : s) = let\ (db, pre, suf) =$$
$$fold\ schedRule\ (db, [], [])\ (triggers\ a_1)$$
$$in\ (db, pre + +s + +suf)$$
$$schedRules\ (db, a_2 : s) = let\ (db, pre, suf) =$$
$$fold\ schedRule\ (db, [], [])\ (triggers\ a_2)$$
$$in\ (db, pre + +s + +suf)\ ...$$

**Step 3**: Replace each call to $triggers\ a_i$ above by the specific list of rule identifiers triggered by the action $a_i$, and unfold the applications of $fold$. At this point it is useful to switch to a concrete example rule set. Considering again the rule set of Example 1, the specialisations of $schedRules$ for this are:

$$schedRules \ (db, Ins \ R_0 \ q : s) = let \ (db, pre, suf) \ =$$
$$schedRule \ (schedRule \ (db, [\,], [\,]) \ 2) \ 3$$
$$in \ (db, pre ++ s ++ suf)$$
$$schedRules \ (db, Del \ R_1 \ q : s) = let \ (db, pre, suf) \ = \ (db, [\,], [\,])$$
$$in \ (db, pre ++ s ++ suf)$$
$$schedRules \ (db, Ins \ R_5 \ q : s) = let \ (db, pre, suf) \ =$$
$$schedRule \ (schedRule \ (db, [\,], [\,]) \ 4) \ 5$$
$$in \ (db, pre ++ s ++ suf)$$
$$schedRules \ (db, Del \ R_4 \ q : s) = let \ (db, pre, suf) \ = \ (db, [\,], [\,])$$
$$in \ (db, pre ++ s ++ suf)$$
$$schedRules \ (db, Ins \ R_9 \ q : s) = let \ (db, pre, suf) \ =$$
$$schedRule \ (db, [\,], [\,]) \ 1$$
$$in \ (db, pre ++ s ++ suf)$$

**Step 4**: Unfold the calls to $schedRule$ – we just develop the first equation from now on:

$$schedRules \ (db, Ins \ R_0 \ q : s) = let \ (db, pre, suf) \ =$$
$$if \ (eval \ (ecq \ 2) \ db) = \{\}$$
$$then \ if \ (eval \ (ecq \ 3) \ db) = \{\}$$
$$then \ (db, [\,], [\,])$$
$$else \ (db, [\,] ++ (bind \ (actions \ 3) \ db), [\,])$$
$$else \ if \ (eval \ (ecq \ 3) \ db) = \{\}$$
$$then \ (db, [\,] ++ (bind \ (actions \ 2) \ db), [\,])$$
$$else \ (db, [\,] ++ (bind \ (actions \ 2) \ db) ++$$
$$(bind \ (actions \ 3) \ db), [\,])$$
$$in \quad (db, pre ++ s ++ suf)$$

**Step 5**: Finally, in the RHS of the resulting equations, unfold the calls to $ecq$ and simplify applications of $++$ to the empty list:

$$let \ (db, pre, suf) =$$
$$if \ (eval \ (\Delta R_0 \times (R_2 \cup (R_3 \bowtie R_4))) \ db) = \{\}$$
$$then \ if \ (eval \ (\Delta R_0 \times ((R_3 \bowtie R_4) - R_5)) \ db) = \{\}$$
$$then \ (db, [\,], [\,])$$
$$else \ (db, (bind \ (actions \ 3) \ db), [\,])$$
$$else \ if \ (eval \ (\Delta R_0 \times ((R_3 \bowtie R_4) - R_5)) \ db) = \{\}$$

$$then \ (db, (bind \ (actions \ 2) \ db), [\,])$$
$$else \ (db, (bind \ (actions \ 2) \ db) + +$$
$$(bind \ (actions \ 3) \ db), [\,])$$
$$in \ (db, pre + +s + +suf)$$

The above transformations have brought together all of the event-condition query evaluations that will result from the execution of a specific form of rule action (it is possible to use a standard partial evaluator to implement these transformations). It is now possible to apply standard optimisation techniques to each resulting equation of *schedRules*. For example, common sub-queries can be abstracted from the event-condition queries so that they are evaluated at most once e.g. the sub-queries $\Delta R_0$ and $R_3 \bowtie R_4$ from the event-condition queries of rules 2 and 3 above. It is also possible for *eval* to use previous values of queries with respect to past database states to incrementally evaluate these queries with respect to the current database state [21,9,4,23,10].

Finally, abstract execution can be "mixed into" the partially evaluated rule execution code, and hence can further optimise it, in the same way as for the original rule execution code in Section 2.3.

## 4   Specialising for Possible Sequences of Actions

In Section 3 our specialisations of *execSched* were for single rule actions. Suppose we can determine that a *sequence* of actions $[a_1, ..., a_n]$ may appear on the schedule without any action $a_i$, $1 \le i < n$, triggering any rule, so that the values of *pre* and *suf* returned by *schedRules* are known to be empty for this sequence of actions. Then *execSched* can be specialised for such sequences of actions also. Doing this presents the opportunity to optimise such sequences of actions (note that these specialisations are additional to the single-action specialisations already generated by the treatment described in the previous section).

Such sequences of actions can be derived from the abstract execution traces obtained by running *execSched** once for each possible initial singleton schedule, in each case with an initial abstract database state in which all queries have an *Unknown* value c.f. our test for rule termination described in Section 2.2. Doing this for the rule set of Example 1, we find that the actions of rules 2 and 3 may be placed consecutively on the schedule by the execution of rule 1's action and that rule 2's action can never fire any other rule. Denoting by $a_2$ and $a_3$ the actions of rules 2 and 3 ($a_2 = Del \ R_1 \ (R_7 \times R_8)$, $a_3 = Ins \ R_5 \ (R_3 \cup (R_7 \times R_8)))$, we can therefore generate this additional specialisation for *execSched*:

$$execSched \ (db, a_2 : a_3 : s) = execSched \circ schedRules \ (exec \ (a_2, db), a_2 : a_3 : s)$$

The RHS of this equation reduces to

$$execSched \circ schedRules \ (exec \ (a_3, exec \ (a_2, db)), a_3 : s)$$

Standard update optimisation techniques can now be applied to this RHS. For example, in the query parts of actions $a_2$ and $a_3$ notice the common sub-query

$R_7 \times R_8$ whose value is independent of the effect of action $a_2$. This common sub-query can be abstracted out from the two applications of *exec* and evaluated only once. Incremental evaluation of action queries, or sub-queries thereof, using their previous values is also possible.

Note that such sequences of actions do not *definitely* have to appear on the schedule, only that there is the *possibility* that they may appear. If a sequence does not appear then this specialisation of *execSched* will simply not be invoked. For example, rules 2 and 3 have different condition queries, so it may be the case that only one fires after some execution of rule 1's action rather than both of them. In such a case the individual specialisation of *execSched* matching $a_2$ or $a_3$ would be invoked rather than the specialisation for the sequence $a_2, a_3$.

We note that with the rule set of Example 1, simple inspection of the triggering graph would also have derived $a_2, a_3$ as a possible execution sequence, since rule 2 triggers no other rule. However, our abstract interpretation approach can yield more possibilities for optimisation than simple analysis of the triggering graph. For example, consider Example 1 again, this time with the addition of an extra rule Rule 6:on $\triangledown R_1$ if $R_7 \times R_8$ do *Del* $R_9$ $R_7 \times R_8$, having immediate coupling mode. This new rule is triggered by rule 2 and does not trigger any rule. If rule 1 is the first rule triggered, then the abstract execution trace is:

| Iteration | $c_1$ | $c_2$ | $c_3$ | $c_4$ | $c_5$ | $c_6$ | Schedule |
|-----------|-------|-------|-------|-------|-------|-------|----------|
| 1 | $U$ | $U$ | $U$ | $U$ | $U$ | $U$ | $[a_1]$ |
| 2 | $F$ | $U$ | $U$ | $U$ | $U$ | $U$ | $[a_2, a_3]$ |
| 3 | $F$ | $U$ | $U$ | $U$ | $U$ | $U$ | $[a_6, a_3]$ |
| 4 | $F$ | $U$ | $U$ | $U$ | $U$ | $U$ | $[a_3]$ |
| 5 | $F$ | $U$ | $U$ | $U$ | $U$ | $U$ | $[a_4, a_5]$ |
| 6 | $F$ | $U$ | $U$ | $U$ | $U$ | $U$ | $[a_5]$ |

We see that $a_6, a_3$ is a possible sequence of actions on the schedule, and that $a_6$ can never fire any other rule. We can therefore generate this additional specialisation for *execSched*:

$$execSched\ (db, a_6 : a_3 : s) = execSched \circ schedRules\ (exec\ (a_6, db), a_6 : a_3 : s)$$

The RHS of this equation reduces to

$$execSched \circ schedRules\ (exec\ (a_3, exec\ (a_6, db)), a_3 : s)$$

and standard update optimisation techniques such as abstraction of common sub-expressions can now be applied to this RHS.

# 5   Dynamic Specialisation for Definite Sequences of Actions

So far the optimisation techniques we have described have been static ones i.e. applicable at compile-time. If we know at run-time that certain action execution sequences will *definitely* be followed from the current database state and schedule, then we can use this knowledge to dynamically perform further unfoldings of *execSched*, and thereby create further opportunities for update optimisation. This kind of definite execution information can be obtained by using a modified version of *execSched\** that halts if *eval\** returns *Unknown* (see the Observation in Section 2.2). To illustrate, consider again the set of rules in Example 1, this time with the input abstract database state shown below and with rule 1 just having been triggered. The abstract execution trace using *execSched\** is:

| Iteration | $c_1$ | $c_2$ | $c_3$ | $c_4$ | $c_5$ | Schedule |
|-----------|-------|-------|-------|-------|-------|----------|
| 1 | $T$ | $T$ | $T$ | $T$ | $U$ | $[a_1]$ |
| 2 | $F$ | $T$ | $T$ | $T$ | $U$ | $[a_2, a_3]$ |
| 3 | $F$ | $T$ | $T$ | $T$ | $U$ | $[a_3]$ |
| 4 | $F$ | $T$ | $U$ | $T$ | $U$ | $[a_4]$ or $[a_4, a_5]$ |

At iterations 1-3, *eval\** returns True or False when applied to the event-condition queries of rules 2 and 3. At iteration 4, *eval\** returns Unknown for rule 5's event-condition query and we halt the analysis. We conclude that $a_1, a_2, a_3, a_4$ is a definite execution sequence from this execution state. We can therefore dynamically generate an equation for $execSched(db, a_1 : s)$ which performs four unfoldings of *execSched*:

$execSched\ (db, a_1 : s)\ =$
$\quad execSched \circ schedRules\ (exec\ (a_4, exec\ (a_3, exec\ (a_2, exec\ (a_1, db)))), a_4 : s)$

We can then optimise the RHS of this equation.

Note that this dynamically generated code is applicable only to the given execution state. After it has been executed, this specialisation becomes invalid and the default specialisation for $a_1$ generated at compile time is the only one that can correctly be used without further dynamic analysis.

Abstract execution can again be "mixed into" the dynamically specialised code. Note that this will now just retrace the already computed abstract execution trace up to the *Unknown* event-condition query, and will therefore not need to be updated by the concrete execution until that point.

The overall rule execution cycle using dynamic specialisation is as follows:

```
repeat
    from the current concrete and abstract states (db,s), (db*,s*)
        execute execSched* till Unknown is encountered;
    generate specialised execSchedM;
    execute specialised execSchedM;
until s = []
```

We note that these dynamically generated specialisations subsume the specialisations generated statically in Sections 3 and 4. The precise trade-off between the cost of dynamically generating the specialised *execSchedM* code versus the gain of using this rather than the statically generated default specialisations needs to be determined empirically, and this is an area of ongoing work.

## 6   Discussion

We have extended the PFL active database system [22] with some of the analysis and optimisation techniques described here. In particular, we have implemented the single-action specialisation described in Section 3, and the abstract interpretation approach to dynamic termination analysis described in [3] and Section 2.2 above. We have not yet amalgamated the abstract interpretation and partial evaluation techniques to obtain the mixed semantics and the multi-action specialisations, and this is an area of ongoing work.

In our implementation of the single-action specialisations, active rules are "compiled" into one 0-ary scheduling function for each rule action. These scheduling functions correspond to the specialised equations of *schedRules** in Section 3. The scheduling functions are defined in PFL itself and so can be optimised using the same query optimiser as for other PFL queries/functions e.g. to perform common sub-expression abstraction. During rule execution, after an action has been executed its scheduling function is evaluated to determine which rules have fired, and how the schedule needs to be updated as a result. The costs incurred by our techniques are low. For undertaking the analysis/optimisation they are:

(i)  Deriving possible/definite execution sequences using abstract interpretation. Given $n$ rule actions, to statically derive all 'possible' sequences, *execSched** needs to be run at most $n$ times. To dynamically derive a definite execution sequence from some execution state, *execSched** needs to be run once. The cost of the abstract inferencing itself is negligible, being based on simple query rewriting.

(ii) Generating the specialisations. In the worst case this is $\mathcal{O}(s \times n)$ for $s$ specialisations and $n$ rules (for a 'complete' triggering graph where each action fires all the rules).

The costs incurred during rule execution are:

(iii) Matching schedule prefixes with respect to specialisations. This retrieves a scheduling function from the database using a hash index on the function name and hence has $\mathcal{O}(1)$ cost.

(iv) Performing abstract inferencing as part of the "mixed" execution. Again, the cost of this is negligible, being based on simple query rewriting.

A key question is what kinds of rule sets are likely to benefit from our partial evaluation approach? An important feature of our technique is that it presents an opportunity to abstract common sub-expressions from conditions and action queries of rules that are evaluated as part of the same execution sequence. Consequently, it will be particularly effective for rule sets where conditions and/or action queries are significantly overlapping e.g. a set of rules that incrementally maintains the contents of a collection of similar views, such as a data cube, in response to updates on the underlying base relations.

The benefit of performing mixed abstract and actual execution depends on the precision of the abstract inferencing (but as we have noted above, this is cheap to carry out and so always worth doing). The precision of the abstract inferencing depends on the complexity of the conditions and action queries. If these are relatively simple (e.g. for simple alerter triggers or for triggers performing log updates) then inferencing will more often produce definite information about the truth/falsity of conditions, and so performing mixed execution will give commensurately greater speed-ups.

## 6.1   Related Work

There has been much work on local optimisation of the condition parts of active rules: [11] proposes discrimination networks for optimising repetitive evaluations of single rules, and strategies used by other systems are reviewed in [24,19]. There has been less research, however, on global rule optimisation. The two main papers containing relevant work in this area are [16] and [7].

[16] generates alternative versions of triggers according to the different ways in which they can be invoked from a top-level transaction. Differences from our work are that: (a) The optimisations are not couched in the framework of partial evaluation and it is consequently more difficult to see the broad relationships and how they can be extended. (b) The complex behaviour of chained rule execution is not the focus for generating specialised versions of triggers. Instead, triggers are generated according to the way in which they are initially invoked from the host transaction. (c) The integration of analysis information is not made explicit and the notions of definite and possible execution sequences are not a feature.

[7] discusses optimisation of multiple rules and an optimisation is identified in the case when multiple rules are triggered by an action and none of them can trigger further rules. The main difference from our work is that the method for identifying multiple rules whose behaviour can be globally optimised is based on a simpler analysis of the triggering graph. Consequently, it does not take into account information about the current database state, and possible/definite execution sequences from it, as derived by our analysis.

A third paper, [8] looks at optimisation in the context of large numbers of triggers. However, the techniques proposed are not meant for triggers that can have arbitrary relational conditions/actions, and it is assumed that many of the triggers will be identical except for constant values. Finally, one of the few other uses of abstract interpretation in a database setting is [5], which discusses the use of abstract interpretation for queries over graph schemata.

## 7   Conclusions

We have described how abstract interpretation and partial evaluation can be used for optimising active database rules. Abstract interpretation can be "mixed into" the rule execution to avoid query evaluation by making use of cheap incremental inferencing techniques. Partial evaluation can be applied at compile-time to yield a specialised version of the rule execution semantics for each possible rule action. This brings together into one expression all of the event-condition query evaluations that will arise after the execution of that action. Standard query optimisation techniques can then be applied to this expression, for example abstraction of common sub-expressions and incremental evaluation.

Abstraction of common sub-expressions and incremental evaluation have been proposed before for active rules [16,7]. The key difference between this work and our partial evaluation approach is that our optimisations are automatically derived using general principles. This places rule optimisation on a sound theoretical footing, encompassing many previous optimisation approaches, and also providing the opportunity to discover new ones. For example, we have shown how it is possible to use the abstract execution traces to produce specialised code for possible or definite sequences of actions, and such multi-action specialisations have not been proposed before.

We are currently implementing the mixed semantics and the multi-action specialisations within our PFL prototype. The next step will be to investigate the cost/benefit of dynamic versus static specialisation. Further work involves extending our optimisation techniques to row-level triggers. Our techniques for generating single-action specialisations can be re-used for these. In [3] we discussed how our abstract semantics can be modified to analyse row-level triggers also. This was in the context of termination analysis, but we believe that the same approach can be used for optimising row-level triggers and in particular for generating definite/possible execution sequences and hence multi-action specialisations – this is an area of ongoing investigation.

One avenue of further research is to investigate more closely the relationships between the abstractions and partial evaluation methods used in this paper, and the long-standing use of these techniques in functional and logic programming [1,13,17,12]. Another promising area is to investigate the use of more sophisticated abstract domains in order to gain higher precision, and to evaluate the tradeoff between domain complexity and efficiency of the abstract semantics.

# References

1. S. Abramsky and C. Hankin, editors. *Abstract Interpretation of Declarative Languages*. Ellis Horwood, 1987.
2. J. Bailey and A. Poulovassilis. An abstract interpretation framework for termination analysis of active rules. In *Proc. 7th Int. Workshop on Database Programming Languages LNCS 1949*, pages 249–266, Scotland, 1999.
3. J. Bailey, A. Poulovassilis, and P. Newson. A dynamic approach to termination analysis for active database rules. In *Proc. 1st Int. Conf. on Computational Logic (DOOD'2000 stream), LNCS 1861*, pages 1106–1120, London, 2000.
4. E. Baralis and J. Widom. Using delta relations to optimize condition evaluation in active databases. In *Proc. 2nd Int. Workshop on Rules in Database Systems (RIDS-95), LNCS 985*, pages 292–308, Athens, 1995.
5. A. Cortesi, A. Dovier, E. Quintarelli, and L. Tanca. Operational and abstract semantics of a query language for semi-structured information. In *Proc. 6th Int. Workshop on Deductive Databases and Logic Programming (DDLP'98)*, pages 127–140 GMD Report 22, ISSN 1435–2702, 1998.

6. P. Cousot and R. Cousot. Abstract interpretation frameworks. *Journal of Logic Programming*, 13(2&3):103–179, 1992.
7. A. Dinn, N. W. Paton, and M. Howard Williams. Active rule analysis and optimisation in the Rock and Roll deductive object oriented database. *Information Systems*, 24(4):327–352, 1999.
8. Eric N. Hanson et al. Scalable trigger processing. In *Proc. 15th ICDE*, pages 266–275, Sydney, 1999.
9. F. Fabret, M. Regnier, and E. Simon. An adaptive algorit hm for increment al evaluation of production rules in databases. In *Proc. 19th VLDB*, pages 455–467, Dublin, Ireland, 1993.
10. T. Griffin, L. Libkin, and H. Trickey. A correction to Incremental recomputation of active relational expressions by Qian and Wiederhold. *IEEE Trans. on Knowledge and Data Engineering*, 9(3):508–511, 1997.
11. E. Hanson. Rule condition testing and action execution in Ariel. In *Proc. SIGMOD 1992*, pages 49–58, San Diego, 1992.
12. N Jones. An introduction to partial evaluation. *ACM Computing Surveys*, 28(3):480–503, 1996.
13. N. Jones, C. Gomard, and P. Sestoft. *Partial Evaluation and Automatic Program Generation*. Prentice Hall, 1993.
14. A. Kotz-Dittrich and E. Simon. Active database Systems: Expectations, Commerical Experience and Beyond. In Paton [19], pages 367–404.
15. K. Kulkarni, N. Mattos, and R. Cochrane. Active database features in SQL3. In Paton [19], pages 197–219.
16. F. Llirbat, F. Fabret, and E. Simon. Eliminating costly redundant computations from SQL trigger executions. In *Proc. SIGMOD 1997*, pages 428–439, 1997.
17. K. Marriott, H. Søndergaard, and N. D. Jones. Denotational abstract interpretation of logic programs. *ACM TOPLAS*, 16(3):607–648, 1994.
18. F. Nielson, H.R. Nielson, and C. Hankin. *Principles of Program Analysis*. Springer-Verlag, 1999.
19. N. Paton, editor. *Active Rules in Database Systems*. Springer-Verlag, 1999.
20. S. Peyton Jones. *The implementation of functional programming languages*. Prentice-Hall, 1987.
21. X. Qian and G. Wiederhold. Incremental recomputation of active relational expressions. *IEEE Trans. on Knowledge and Data Engineering*, 3(3):337–341, 1991.
22. S. Reddi, A. Poulovassilis, and C. Small. PFL: An active functional DBPL. In Paton [19], pages 297–308.
23. Martin Sköld and Tore Risch. Using partial differencing for efficient monitoring of deferred complex rule conditions. In Stanley Y. W. Su, editor, *Proc. 12th ICDE*, pages 392–401, 1996.
24. J. Widom and S. Ceri. *Active Database Systems*. Morgan-Kaufmann, San Mateo, California, 1995.

# Simulation of Advanced Transaction Models Using GOLOG*

Iluju Kiringa

Department of Computer Science
University of Toronto, Toronto, Canada
kiringai@cs.toronto.edu

**Abstract.** We propose a logical framework for describing, reasoning about, and simulating transaction models that relax some of the ACID (Atomicity-Consistency-Isolation-Durability) properties of classical transactions. Such extensions, usually called *advanced transaction models* (ATMs), have been proposed for dealing with new database applications involving long-lived, endless, and cooperative activities. Our approach appeals to non-Markovian theories, in which one may refer to past states other than the previous one. We specify an ATM as a suitable non-Markovian theory of the situation calculus, and its properties, including the relaxed ACID properties, as formulas of the same calculus. We use our framework to formalize classical and closed nested transactions. We first formulate each ATM and its properties as a theory of a certain kind and formulas of the situation calculus, respectively. We then define a legal database log as one whose actions are all possible and in which all the *Commit* and *Rollback* actions must occur whenever they are possible. After that, we show that the known properties of the ATM, including the (possibly relaxed) ACID constraints, are properties of legal logs and logical consequences of the theory corresponding to that ATM. Finally, we show how to use such a specification as a background theory for transaction programs written in the situation calculus based programming language GOLOG.

## 1 Introduction

Transaction systems that constitute the state of the art in database systems have a flat structure defined in terms of the so-called ACID (Atomicity-Consistency-Isolation-Durability) properties. From the system point of view, a database transaction is a sequence of operations on the database state, which exhibit the ACID properties and are bracketed by *Begin* and *Commit* or *Begin* and *Rollback* ([10]). A transaction makes the results of its operations durable when nothing goes wrong before its normal end by executing a *Commit* operation, upon which the database cannot be rolled back. Should anything go wrong before the commitment, the transaction rolls the database back to the state before beginning.

---

* An extended abstract reporting on this work appears in *Proceedings of KRDB-2001, Rome, September, 2001*. This research is supported by NSERC, IRIS, and ITRC.

G. Grahne and G. Ghelli (Eds.): DBPL 2001, LNCS 2397, pp. 318–341, 2002.

Various transaction models have been proposed to extend the classical flat transactions by relaxing some of the ACID properties (see [8],[11] for a collection of the best examples of these models). Such extensions, generally called *advanced transaction models* (ATMs), are proposed for dealing with new applications involving long-lived, endless, and cooperative activities. The ATMs aim at improving the functionality and the performance of the new applications.

The ATMs, however, have been proposed in an *ad hoc* fashion, thus lacking in generality in a way that it is not obvious to compare the different ATMs, to exactly say how they extend the traditional flat model, and to formulate their properties in a way that one clearly sees which new functionality has been added, or which one has been subtracted. To address these questions, there is a need for a general and common framework within which to specify ATMs, simulate these, specify their properties, and reason about these properties. Thus far, ACTA ([6],[5]) seems to our knowledge the only framework addressing these questions at a high level of generality. In ACTA, a first order logic-like language is used to capture the semantics of any ATM.

In this paper, we address the problem of specifying database transactions at the logical level using the situation calculus ([21]). Our approach appeals to non-Markovian theories([9]), in which one may refer to past states other than the previous one. We provide the formal semantics of an ATM by specifying it as a theory of the situation calculus called *basic relational theory*, which is a set of sentences suitable for non-Markovian control in the context of database transactions; the properties of the ATM, including the relaxed ACID properties, are expressed as formulas of the same calculus that logically follow from the basic relational theory. We illustrate our framework by formalizing classical transactions ([10]) and closed nested transactions ([23]). We first formulate each transaction model and its properties as a basic relational theory and formulas of the situation calculus, respectively. We then define a legal database log as one whose actions are all possible and in which all the *Commit* and *Rollback* actions must occur whenever they are possible. After that, we show that the known properties of the transaction model, including the relaxed ACID constraints, are properties of legal logs and logical consequences of the basic relational theory corresponding to that transaction model. Finally, we show how to use such a specification as a background theory for transaction programs written in the situation calculus based programming language GOLOG.

The main contributions of this paper can be summarized as follows:

1. We construct logical theories called basic relational theories to formalize ATMs along the tradition set by the ACTA framework ([5]); basic relational theories are non-markovian theories in which one may explicitly refer to all past states, and not only the to the previous one. They provide the formal semantics of the corresponding ATMs. They are an extension of the classical relational theories of [19] to the database transaction setting.

2. We extend the notion of *legal database logs* introduced in [20] to accomodate transactional actions such as *Begin, Commit*, etc. These logs are first class citizen of the logic and properties of the ATM are expressed as formulas of the

situation calculus that logically follow from the basic relational theory representing that ATM.

3. Our approach goes far beyond constructing logical theories, as it provides one with an implementable specification, thus allowing one to automatically check many properties of the specification using an interpreter. Our implementable specifications are written in an extension of GOLOG that includes parallelism ([7]). We specify an interpreter for running these specifications and show that this interpreter generates only legal logs.

## 2    Logical Foundations

We use a *basic relational language*, which is a fragment of the situation calculus ([21],[9]) that is suitable for modeling relational database transactions. The language is a many-sorted second order language with sorts for *actions*, *situations*, and *objects*. *Actions* are first order terms consisting of an action function symbol and its arguments, *situations* are first order terms denoting finite sequences of actions, and *objects* represent domain specific individuals other than actions and situations. In formalizing databases, actions correspond to the elementary database operations of inserting, deleting and updating relational tuples, and situations represent the database *log*. Relations and functions whose truth values vary from situation to situation are called *fluents*, and are denoted by predicate symbols and function symbols with the two last arguments being a transaction identifier and a situation term. As an example, $a\_del(accid, branchid, accbal, tellerid, t)$ represents the action of deleting tuples from the relation *accounts* which is represented by the fluent $accounts(accid, branchid, accbal, tellerid, t, s)$.

A basic relational language has an alphabet with variables and a finite number of constants for each sort, a finite number of function symbols called *action functions*, a finite number of function symbols called *situation independent functions*, a finite number of function symbols called *functional fluents*, a finite number of predicate symbols called *situation independent predicates*, and a finite number of predicate symbols called *relational fluents*. Situations are represented using a binary function symbol $do$: $do(a, s)$ denotes the sequence resulting from adding the action $a$ to the sequence $s$. There is a distinguished constant $S_0$ denoting the initial situation; $S_0$ stands for the empty action sequence. The language also includes special predicates $Poss$, and $\sqsubseteq$; $Poss(a, s)$ means that the action $a$ is possible in the situation $s$, and $s \sqsubseteq s'$ states that the situation $s'$ is reachable from $s$ by performing some sequence of actions. In database terms, $s \sqsubseteq s'$ means that $s$ is a proper sublog of the log $s'$.

For simplicity, we consider basic relational languages whose only primitive update operations correspond to insertion or deletion of tuples into relations. For each such relation $F(x, t, s)$, where $x$ is a tuple of objects, $t$ is a transaction argument, and $s$ is a situation argument, a *primitive internal action* is a parameterized primitive action of the situation calculus of the form $F\_ins(x, t)$ or $F\_del(x, t)$. Intuitively, $F\_ins(x, t)$ and $F\_del(x, t)$ denote the actions of inserting the tuple $x$ into and deleting it from the relation $F$ by the transaction $t$, respectively; for convenience, we will abbreviate long symbols when necessary (e.g., $account\_ins(x,t)$ will be abbreviated as $a\_ins(x,t)$). Below, we will use the following abbreviation:

$$writes(a, F, t) =_{df} (\exists x).a = F\_ins(x,t) \lor a = F\_del(x,t),$$

one for each fluent. We distinguish the primitive internal actions from *primitive external actions* which are $Begin(t)$, $Commit(t)$, $End(t)$, and $Rollback(t)$, whose meaning will be clear in the sequel of this paper; these are external as they do not specifically affect the content of the database. The argument $t$ is a unique transaction identifier.

A dynamic domain is axiomatized in the situation calculus with non-Markovian axioms which describe *how* and under what *conditions* the domain is changing or not changing as a result of performing actions. Such axioms are called basic action theory in [21]. They comprise the following: domain independent foundational axioms for situations; action precondition axioms, one for each action term, stating the conditions of change; successor state axioms, one for each fluent, stating how change occurs; unique names axioms for action terms; and axioms describing the initial situation. Finally, by convention in this paper, a free variable will always be implicitly bound by a prenex universal quantifier. Basic action theories of [21] are capturing Markovian control. they have been extended to non-Markovian control in [9].

## 3   The Specification Framework

In [6], five building blocks for ATMs are identified: *history*, intertransaction *dependencies*, *visibility* of operations on database objects, *conflict* between operations, and *delegation* of responsibility for objects visible to a transaction. We now show how these building blocks are represented in the situation calculus[1].

In the situation calculus, the history of [6] corresponds to the log. We extend the basic action theories of [21] to include a specification of relational database transactions, by giving action precondition axioms for external actions such as $Begin(t)$, $End(t)$, $Commit(t)$, $Rollback(t)$, $Spawn(t, t')$, etc. $Commit(t)$ and $Rollback(t)$ are coercive actions that must occur whenever they are possible. We also give successor state axioms that state how change occurs in databases in the presence of both internal and external actions. All these axioms provide the *first dimension* of the situation calculus framework for axiomatizing transactions, namely the axiomatization of the effects of transactions on fluents; they also comprise axioms indicating which transactions are conflicting with each other, and what sublogs of the current log are visible; which visible sublogs are delegated to the transactions is expressed implicitly in successor state axioms.

A useful concept that underlies most of the ATMs is that of responsibility over changes operated on data items. For example, in a nested transaction, a

---

[1] As visibility plays no further role in this paper, we will omit this aspect

parent transaction will take responsibility of changes done by any of its committed children. The only way we can keep track of those reponsibilities is to look at the transaction arguments of the actions present in the log. To that end, we introduce a fluent $responsible(t, a, s)$, which intuitively means that transaction $t$ is responsible for the action $a$ in the log s, which we characterize with an appropriate successor state axiom of the form

$$responsible(t, a', do(a, s)) \equiv \Phi_{tm}(t, a, a', s),$$

where $\Phi_{tm}(t, a, a', s)$ is a transaction model-dependent first order formula whose only free variables are among $t, a, a',$, and $s$. For example, in the flat transactions, we will have the following, simple axiom:

$$responsible(t, a, s) \equiv (\exists a', \boldsymbol{x})a = a'(\boldsymbol{x}, t);$$

i.e., each transaction is considered responsible for any action whose last argument bears its name.

To express conflicts between transactions, we need the predicate $termAct(a, t)$ and the fluents $updConflict(a, a', s)$ and $transConflict(t, t', s)$, whose intuitive meaning is that the action $a$ is a terminal action of $t$, the action $a$ is conflicting with the action $a'$ in $s$, and the transaction $t$ is conflicting with the transaction $t'$ in $s$; their characterization is as follows:

$$termAct(a, t) =_{df} a = Commit(t) \vee a = Rollback(t)$$

$$updConflict(a, a', s) =_{df} \bigvee_{F \in \mathcal{F}} (\exists \boldsymbol{x}) \neg [F(\boldsymbol{x}, t, do(a, do(a', s)))$$

$$\equiv F(\boldsymbol{x}, t, do(a', do(a, s)))];$$

here, $\mathcal{F}$ is the set of fluents of the relational language; the later definition says that two internal actions $a$ and $a'$ conflict in the log $s$ iff the value of the fluents depends on the order in which $a$ and $a'$ appear in $s$;

$$transConflict(t, t', do(a, s)) \equiv t \neq t' \wedge responsible(t', a, s) \wedge$$
$$(\exists a', s')[responsible(t, a', s) \wedge do(a', s') \sqsubset s \wedge updConflict(a', a, s)] \vee$$
$$transConflict(t, t', s) \wedge \neg termAct(a, t); \tag{1}$$

i.e., transaction $t$ conflicts with transaction $t'$ in the log $s$ iff $t'$ executes an internal action $a$ after $t$ has executed an internal action $a'$ that conflicts with $a$ in the log $s$. Notice that we define $updConfilct(a, a', s)$ in terms of performing action $a$ and action $a'$ one immediately after the other and vice-versa; in the definition of $transConflict(t, t', s)$, however, we allow action $a'$ to be executed long before action $a$. This does not mean that actions that are performed between $a'$ and $a$ are irrelevant with respect to update conflicts. Rather, (1) just means that actions $a$ and $a'$ conflicts whenever executing one immediately after the other *would* results in a discrepancy in the truth value of at leat one of the relational fluents; and (1) allows for the possibility of other update conflicts arising between $a'$ and other actions before the execution of $a$.

A further useful fluent that we provide in the framework is $readsFrom(t, t', s)$. This is used in most transaction models as a source of dependencies among transactions, and intuitively means that the transaction $t$ reads a value written by the transaction $t'$ in the log $s$. The axiomatizer must provide a successor state axiom for this fluent depending on the application.

The *second dimension* of the situation calculus framework is made of dependencies between transactions. All the dependencies expressed in ACTA ([6]) can also be expressed in the situation calculus. Some sample dependencies are:

**Commit Dependency** of $t$ on $t'$

$$do(Commit(t), s) \sqsubset s^* \supset$$
$$[do(Commit(t'), s') \sqsubseteq s^* \supset do(Commit(t'), s') \sqsubset do(Commit(t), s)];$$

i.e., If $t$ commits in a log $s^*$, then, whenever $t'$ also commits in $s^*$, $t'$ commits before $t$.

**Strong Commit Dependency** of $t$ on $t'$

$$(\exists s')do(Commit(t'), s') \sqsubset s^* \supset (\exists s)do(Commit(t), s) \sqsubseteq s^*;$$

i.e., If $t'$ commits in a log $s^*$, then $t$ must also commit in that log.

**Rollback Dependency** of $t$ on $t'$

$$(\exists s')do(Rollback(t'), s') \sqsubset s^* \supset (\exists s)do(Rollback(t), s) \sqsubseteq s^*;$$

i.e., If $t'$ rolls back in a log $s^*$, then $t$ must also roll back in that log.

**Weak Rollback Dependency** of $t$ on $t'$

$$do(Rollback(t'), s') \sqsubset s^* \supset$$
$$\{(\forall s)[s \sqsubset s^* \wedge do(Commit(t), s) \not\sqsubseteq do(Rollback(t'), s')] \supset$$
$$(\exists s'')do(Rollback(t), s'') \sqsubseteq s^*\};$$

i.e., If $t'$ rolls back in a log $s^*$, then, whenever $t$ does not commit before $t'$, $t$ must also roll back in $s^*$.

As we shall see below, all these dependencies are properties of legal database logs of various transaction models.

To control dependencies that may develop among running transactions, we use a set of predicates denoting these dependencies. So, we use $c\_dep(t, t', s)$, $sc\_dep(t, t', s)$, $r\_dep(t, t', s)$, and $wr\_dep(t, t', s)$ to denote the commit, strong commit, rollback, and weak rollback dependencies, respectively. These are fluents whose truth value is changed by the relevant transaction models by taking into account dependencies generated by the execution of its external actions (*external dependencies*) and those generated by the execution of its internal actions (*internal dependencies*). As an example, in the nested transaction model, we have the following successor state axiom for $wr\_dep(t, t', s)$:

$$wr\_dep(t, t', do(a, s)) \equiv a = Spawn(t, t') \vee$$
$$wr\_dep(t, t', s) \wedge \neg termAct(a, t) \wedge \neg termAct(a, t').$$

This says that a weak rollback dependency of $t$ on $t'$ arises in $do(a, s)$ when either $a$ is the action of $t$ spawning $t'$, or that dependency existed already in $s$ and neither $t$ nor $t'$ terminated with the action $a$.

## 4   Flat Transactions

Flat transactions exhibit ACID properties. This section introduces a characterization of flat transactions in terms of theories of the situation calculus. These
theories give axioms of flat transaction models that constrain database logs in
such a way that these logs satisfy important correctness properties of database
transaction, including the ACID properties.

A sequence of database actions is a *flat transaction* iff it is a sequence
$[a_1, \ldots, a_n]$, where the $a_1$ must be *Begin*, and $a_n$ must be either *Commit(t)*,
or *Rollback(t)*; $a_i, i = 2, \cdots, n-1$, may be any of the primitive actions, except *Begin(t)*, *Rollback(t)*, and *Commit(t)*; here, as before, the argument $t$ is a
unique identifier for the atomic transaction. Flat transactions can be sequenced
or run in parallel. Notice that we do not introduce a term of a new sort for transactions, as is the case in [3]; we treat transactions as run-time activities, whose
compile-time counterparts will be GOLOG programs introduced in Section 6.
We refer to transactions by their names that are of sort *object*.

The axiomatization of a dynamic relational database with flat transaction
properties comprises the following classes of axioms:

**Foundational Axioms.** These are constraints imposed on the structure of
database logs to characterize them as finite sequences of updates. They play
an important role in proving the theorems of this paper. Since, for space reasons, we shall omit these proofs, we also omit the foundational axioms.

**Integrity Constraints.** These are constraints imposed on the data in the
database at a given situation $s$; their set is denoted by $\mathcal{IC}_e$ for constraints that
must be enforced at each update execution, and by $\mathcal{IC}_v$ for those that must be
verified at the end of the flat transaction.

**Update Precondition Axioms.** There is one for each internal action $A(\boldsymbol{x}, t)$,
with syntactic form

$$Poss(A(\boldsymbol{x}, t), s) \equiv (\exists t')\Pi_A(\boldsymbol{x}, t', s) \wedge IC^e(do(A(\boldsymbol{x}, t), s)) \wedge running(t, s). \quad (2)$$

Here, $\Pi_A(\boldsymbol{x}, t, s)$ is a formula with free variables among $\boldsymbol{x}, t$, and $s$. These axioms
characterize the preconditions of the update $A$; $IC^e(s)$ and $running(t, s)$ are
defined as follows:

$$IC^e(s) =_{df} \bigwedge_{IC \in \mathcal{IC}_e} IC(s). \quad (3)$$

$$running(t, s) =_{df} (\exists s').do(Begin(t), s') \sqsubseteq s \wedge$$
$$(\forall a, s'')[do(Begin(t), s') \sqsubset do(a, s'') \sqsubset s \supset a \neq Rollback(t) \wedge a \neq End(t)]. \quad (4)$$

In a banking Credit/Debit example formalized below, the following states that
it is possible to insert a tuple into the *teller* relation relative to the database
log $s$ iff, as a result of performing the actions in the log, that tuple would not
already be present in the *teller* relation, the integrity constraints are satisfied,
and transaction $t$ is running.

$$Poss(t\_delete(tid, tbal, t), s) \equiv (\exists t')teller(tid, tbal, t', s) \land$$
$$IC^e(do(t\_delete(tid, tbal, t), s)) \land running(t, s). \tag{5}$$

**Successor State Axioms.** These have the syntactic form

$$F(\boldsymbol{x}, t, do(a, s)) \equiv (\exists t')\Phi_F(\boldsymbol{x}, a, \boldsymbol{t'}, s) \land \neg(\exists t'')a = Rollback(t'') \lor$$
$$(\exists t'')a = Rollback(t'') \land restoreBeginPoint(F, \boldsymbol{x}, t'', s), \tag{6}$$

where $\Phi_F(\boldsymbol{x}, a, \boldsymbol{t}, s)$ is a formula with free variables among $\boldsymbol{x}, a, \boldsymbol{t}, s$. There is one such axiom for each relational fluent $F$, and $restoreBeginPoint(F, \boldsymbol{x}, t, s)$ is defined as follows:

$$restoreBeginPoint(F, \boldsymbol{x}, t, s) =_{df}$$
$$[(\exists a^*, s', s^*, t').do(Begin(t), s') \sqsubset do(a^*, s^*) \sqsubseteq s \land$$
$$writes(a^*, F, t) \land F(\boldsymbol{x}, t', s')] \lor \tag{7}$$
$$[(\forall a^*, s^*, s').do(Begin(t), s') \sqsubset do(a^*, s^*) \sqsubseteq s \supset$$
$$\neg writes(a^*, F, t)] \land (\exists t')F(\boldsymbol{x}, t', s).$$

Intuitively, $restoreBeginPoint(F, \boldsymbol{x}, t, s)$ means that the system restores the value that the fluent $F$ with arguments $\boldsymbol{x}$ had before the execution of the $Begin$ action of the transaction $t$ in the log $s$ if the transaction $t$ has updated $F$; it keeps the value it had in $s$ otherwise. Given the actual situation $s$, the successor state axioms characterize the truth values of the fluent $F$ in the next situation $do(a, s)$ in terms of all the past situations. In the banking example, the following states that the tuple $(tid, tbal)$ will be in the $teller$ relation relative to the log $do(a, s)$ iff the last database operation $a$ in the log inserted it there, or it was already in the $teller$ relation relative to the log $s$, and $a$ didn't delete it; all this, provided that the operation $a$ is not rolling the database back. In the case the operation $a$ is rolling the database back, the $tellers$ relation will get a value according to the logic of (7).

$$tellers(tid, tbal, t, do(a, s)) \equiv ((\exists t_1)a = t\_insert(tid, tbal, t_1) \lor$$
$$(\exists t_2)tellers(tid, tbal, t_2, s) \land \neg(\exists t_3)a = t\_delete(tid, tbal, t_3)) \land$$
$$\neg(\exists t')a = Rollback(t') \lor$$
$$(\exists t').a = Rollback(t') \land restoreBeginPoint(tellers, (tid, tbal), t', s).$$

**Precondition Axioms for External Actions.** This is a set of action precondition axioms for the transaction specific actions $Begin(t)$, $End(t)$, $Commit(t)$, and $Rollback(t)$. The external actions of flat transactions have the following precondition axioms:

$$Poss(Begin(t), s) \equiv \neg(\exists s')do(Begin(t), s') \sqsubseteq s, \tag{8}$$
$$Poss(End(t), s) \equiv running(t, s), \tag{9}$$
$$Poss(Commit(t), s) \equiv (\exists s').s = do(End(t), s') \land \bigwedge_{IC \in \mathcal{IC}_v} IC(s) \land \tag{10}$$
$$(\forall t')[sc\_dep(t, t', s) \supset (\exists s'')do(Commit(t'), s'') \sqsubseteq s],$$

$$Poss(Rollback(t), s) \equiv (\exists s')[s = do(End(t), s') \wedge \neg \bigwedge_{IC \in \mathcal{IC}_v} IC(s)] \vee$$

$$(\exists t', s'')[r\_dep(t, t', s) \wedge do(Rollback(t'), s'') \sqsubseteq s]. \tag{11}$$

**Dependency Axioms.** These are transaction model-dependent axioms of the form

$$dep(t, t', do(a, s)) \equiv \mathcal{C}(t, t', a, s), \tag{12}$$

where $\mathcal{C}(t, t', a, s)$ is a condition involving the conflict relation between internal actions of any two transactions $t$ and $t'$, and $dep(t, t', s)$ is one of the dependency predicates $c\_dep(t, t', s)$, $sc\_dep(t, t', s)$, etc. These axioms are used to capture the notion of *recoverability, avoiding cascading rollbacks*, etc, of the classical concurrency control theory ([2]). For example, to achieve recoverability, avoid cascading rollbacks, the following axioms are used, respectively:

$$r\_dep(t, t', s) =_{df} transConflict(t, t', s), \tag{13}$$

$$sc\_dep(t, t', s) =_{df} readsFrom(t, t', s). \tag{14}$$

The first axiom says that a transaction conflicting with another transaction generates a rollback dependency, and the second says that a transaction reading from another transaction generates a strong commit dependency.

**Unique Names Axioms.** These state that the primitive updates and the objects of the domain are pairwise unequal.

**Initial Database.** This is a set of first order sentences specifying the initial database state. They are completion axioms of the form

$$(\forall \boldsymbol{x}, t).F(\boldsymbol{x}, t, S_0) \equiv \boldsymbol{x} = \boldsymbol{C}^{(1)} \vee \ldots \vee \boldsymbol{x} = \boldsymbol{C}^{(r)}, \tag{15}$$

one for each fluent $F$. Here, the $\boldsymbol{C}^i$ are tuples of constants. Also, $\mathcal{D}_{S_0}$ includes unique name axioms for constants of the database, and axioms stating the conflicting updates. Axioms of the form (15) say that our theories accommodate a complete initial database state, which is commonly the case in relational databases as unveiled in [19]. This requirement is made to keep the theory simple and to reflect the standard practice in databases. It has the theoretical advantage of simplifying the establishment of logical entailments in the initial database; moreover, it has the practical advantage of facilitating rapid prototyping of the ATMs using Prolog which embodies negation by failure, a notion close to the completion axioms used here.

One striking feature of our axioms is the use of the predicate $\sqsubset$ on the right hand side of action precondition axioms and successor state axioms. That is, they are capturing the notion of a situation being located in the past relative to the current situation which we express with the predicate $\sqsubset$ in the situation calculus. Thus they are capturing non-Markovian control. We call these axioms a *basic relational theory*, and define a relational database as a pair $(\mathfrak{R}, \mathcal{D})$, where $\mathfrak{R}$ is a relational language and $\mathcal{D}$ is a basic relational theory.

A fundamental property of $Rollback(t)$ and $Commit(t)$ actions is that, the database system *must* execute them in any database state in which they are possible. In this sense, they are coercive actions, and we call them *system actions*:

$$systemAct(a,t) =_{df} a = Commit(t) \vee a = Rollback(t).$$

We constrain legal logs to include these mandatory system actions, as well as the requirement that all actions in the log be possible:

$$
\begin{aligned}
legal(s) =_{df} (\forall a, s^*)&[do(a, s^*) \sqsubseteq s \supset Poss(a, s^*)] \wedge \\
(\forall a', a'', s', t)&[systemAct(a', t) \wedge responsible(t, a') \wedge \\
responsible(t, a'') &\wedge Poss(a', s') \wedge do(a'', s') \sqsubset s \supset a' = a''].
\end{aligned}
\tag{16}
$$

Simple properties such as well-formedness of atomic transactions ([16]) can be formulated and proven.

**Theorem 1. (Well-Formedness)** *Suppose $\mathcal{D}$ is a basic relational theory. Then no transaction may commit and then roll back, and conversely; i.e.,*

$$
\begin{aligned}
\mathcal{D} \models legal(s) \supset \\
(\forall s')\{[do(Commit(t), s') \sqsubset s \supset \neg(\exists s'')do(Rollback(t), s'') \sqsubset s] \wedge \\
[do(Rollback(t), s') \sqsubset s \supset \neg(\exists s'')do(Commit(t), s'') \sqsubset s]\}.
\end{aligned}
$$

These properties are similar to the fundamental axioms, applicable to all transactions, of [6]. They rule out all the ill-formed transactions such as

$$
\begin{aligned}
[Begin(t), a\_ins(A_1, B_1, -1000, T_1), \\
Commit(t), a\_del(A_1, B_1, -1000, T_1), Rollback(t)].
\end{aligned}
$$

**Theorem 2.** *Suppose $\mathcal{D}$ is a basic relational theory. Then any legal log satisfies the strong commit and rollback dependency properties; i.e.,*

$$
\begin{aligned}
\mathcal{D} \models legal(s) \supset \\
(\forall t, t')\{sc\_dep(t, t', s) \supset \\
[(\exists s')do(Commit(t'), s') \sqsubset s \supset (\exists s^*)do(Commit(t), s^*) \sqsubseteq s] \wedge \\
c\_dep(t, t', s) \supset \\
[(\exists s')do(Rollback(t'), s') \sqsubset s \supset (\exists s^*)do(Rollback(t), s^*) \sqsubset s]\}.
\end{aligned}
$$

Now we turn to the ACID properties, which are the most important properties of flat transactions.

**Theorem 3. (Atomicity)** *Suppose $\mathcal{D}$ is a relational theory. Then for every relational fluent $F$*

$$
\begin{aligned}
\mathcal{D} \models legal(s) \supset \\
(\forall t, s_1, s_2)\{do(Begin(t), s_1) \sqsubset do(a, s_2) \sqsubset s \wedge \\
(\exists a^*, s^*)[do(Begin(t), s_1) \sqsubset do(a^*, s^*) \sqsubset do(a, s_2) \wedge writes(a^*, F, t)] \supset \\
[(a = Rollback(t) \supset ((\exists t_1)F(\boldsymbol{x}, t_1, do(a, s_2)) \equiv (\exists t_2)F(\boldsymbol{x}, t_2, s_1))) \wedge \\
(a = Commit(t) \supset ((\exists t_1)F(\boldsymbol{x}, t_1, do(a, s_2)) \equiv (\exists t_2)F(\boldsymbol{x}, t_2, s_2)))]\}.
\end{aligned}
$$

This says that rolling back restores any modified fluent to the value it had just before the last $Begin(t)$ action, and committing endorses the value it had in the situation just before the $Commit(t)$ action.

**Theorem 4. (Consistency)** *Suppose $\mathcal{D}$ is a relational theory. Then All integrity constraints are satisfied at committed logs; i.e.,*

$$\mathcal{D} \models legal(s) \supset \{do(Commit(t), s') \sqsubseteq s \supset \bigwedge_{IC \in \mathcal{IC}_v \cup \mathcal{IC}_e} IC(do(Commit(t), s'))\}.$$

**Theorem 5.** *$\mathcal{D}$ is satisfiable iff $\mathcal{D}_{S_0} \cup \mathcal{D}_{una} \cup \mathcal{D}_{IC}[S_0]$ is[2]. In other words, provided the constraints are consistent with the initial database state and unique names for actions, then the entire relational theory is satisfiable, and conversely.*

Some properties of transactions need the notions of committed and rolled back updates. With the predicates $committed(t, s)$ and $rolledBack(t, s)$, we express these notions in the situation calculus using the following axioms:

$$committed(a, s) =_{df} (\exists t, s').responsible(t, a, s) \wedge do(Commit(t), s') \sqsubseteq s,$$
$$rolledBack(a, s) =_{df} (\exists t, s').responsible(t, a, s) \wedge do(Rollback(t), s') \sqsubseteq s.$$

**Theorem 6. (Durability)** *Suppose $\mathcal{D}$ is a relational theory. Then whenever an update is committed or rolled back by a transaction, another transaction can not change this fact:*

$$\mathcal{D} \models legal(s) \supset$$
$$\{do(Rollback(t), s') \sqsubseteq s \wedge \neg responsible(t, a) \supset$$
$$[Committed(a, s') \equiv Committed(a, do(Rollback(t), s'))] \wedge$$
$$[rolledBack(a, s') \equiv rolledBack(a, do(Rollback(t), s'))].$$

**Definition 1. (Serializability)**

$$transConflict^*(t, t', s) =_{df} (\forall C)[(\forall t)C(t, t, s) \wedge$$
$$(\forall s, t, t', t'')[C(t, t'', s) \wedge transConflict(t'', t', s) \supset C(t, t', s)] \supset C(t, t', s)],$$
$$serializable(s) =_{df} (\forall t).do(Commit(t), s') \sqsubset s \supset \neg transConflict^*(t, t, s).$$

**Theorem 7. (Isolation)** *Suppose $\mathcal{D}$ is a relational theory. Then*

$$\mathcal{D} \models legal(s) \supset serializable(s).$$

# 5    Closed Nested Transactions

Nested transactions ([17]) are the best known example of ATMs. A nested transaction is a set of transactions (called subtransactions) forming a tree structure, meaning that any given transaction, the parent, may spawn a subtransaction, the child, nested in it. A child commits only if its parent has committed. If

---

[2] Here, $\mathcal{D}_{IC}[S_0]$ is the set $\mathcal{D}_{IC}$ relativized to the situation $S_0$.

a parent transaction rolls back, all its children are rolled back. However, if a child rolls back, the parent may execute a recovery procedure of its own. Each subtransaction, except the root, fulfills the A, C, and I among the ACID properties. The root (level 1) of the tree structure is the only transaction to satisfy all of the ACID properties. This version of nested transactions is called closed because of this inability of subtransactions to durably commit independently of the outcome of the root transaction ([23]).

A root transaction $t$ is a sequence $[a_1, \ldots, a_n]$ of primitive actions, where $a_1$ must be $Begin(t)$, and $a_n$ must be either $Commit(t)$, or $Rollback(t)$; $a_i, i = 2, \cdots, n-1$, may be any of the primitive actions, except $Begin(t)$, $Commit(t)$, and $Rollback(t)$, but including $Spawn(t,t')$, $Rollback(t')$, and $Commit(t')$, with $t \neq t'$. A child transaction $t$ is a sequence $[a_1, \ldots, a_n]$ of primitive actions, where $a_1$ must be $Spwan(t',t)$, and $a_n$ must be either $Commit(t)$, or $Rollback(t)$; $a_i, i = 2, \cdots, n-1$, may be any of the primitive actions, except $Spawn(t,t')$, $Commit(t)$, and $Rollback(t)$, but including $Spawn(t^*,t^{**})$, $Rollback(t^{**})$, and $Commit(t^{**})$, with $t \neq t^{**}$. We capture the typical relationships that hold between transactions in the hierarchy of a nested transaction with the fluents $transOf(t,a,s)$, $parent(t,t',s)$ and $ancestor(t,t',s)$, which are introduced in the following successor state axiom and abbreviation, respectively:

$$transOf(t,a,s) \equiv (\exists a').a = a'(\boldsymbol{x},t), \tag{17}$$

$$parent(t,t',do(a,s)) \equiv a = Spawn(t,t') \vee$$
$$parent(t,t',s) \wedge \neg termAct(a,t) \wedge \neg termAct(a,t'), \tag{18}$$

$$ancestor(t,t',s) =_{df} (\forall A)[(\forall t)A(t,t,s) \wedge$$
$$(\forall s,t,t',t'')[A(t,t'',s) \wedge parent(t'',t',s) \supset A(t,t',s)] \supset A(t,t',s)]. \tag{19}$$

Responsibility over actions that are executed and conflicts between transactions are specified with the following axioms:

$$responsible(t,a',do(a,s)) \equiv transOf(t,a',s) \wedge \neg(\exists t^*)parent(t,t^*,s) \vee$$
$$(\exists t^*)[parent(t,t^*,s) \wedge a = Commit(t^*) \wedge responsible(t^*,a')] \vee \tag{20}$$
$$responsible(t,a',s) \wedge \neg termAct(a,t),$$

$$transConflictNT(t,t',do(a,s)) \equiv t \neq t' \wedge responsible(t',a,s) \wedge$$
$$(\exists a',s')[responsible(t,a',s) \wedge updConflict(a',a,s) \wedge do(a',s') \sqsubset s \wedge$$
$$\neg responsible(t,a,s) \wedge running(t',s) \wedge ((\exists t'')parent(t,t'',s) \supset \tag{21}$$
$$\neg ancestor(t,t',s)) \vee$$
$$transConflictNT(t,t',s) \wedge \neg termAct(a,t);$$

Intuitively, (21) means that transaction $t$ conflicts with transaction $t'$ in the log $s$ iff $t$ and $t'$ are not equal, internal actions they are responsible for are conflicting in $s$, $t$ is not responsible for the action of $t'$ it is conflicting with, $t'$ is running; moreover, a transaction cannot conflict with actions his ancestors are responsible for. Due to the presence of the new external action *Spawn*, we need to redefine $running(t, s)$ as follows:

$$running(t, s) =_{df} (\exists s').\{do(Begin(t), s') \sqsubseteq s \wedge$$
$$(\forall a, s'')[do(Begin(t), s') \sqsubset do(a, s'') \sqsubset s \supset a \neq Rollback(t) \wedge a \neq End(t)] \vee$$
$$(\exists t').do(Spawn(t', t), s') \sqsubseteq s \wedge \tag{22}$$
$$(\forall a, s'')[do(Spawn(t', t), s') \sqsubset do(a, s'') \sqsubset s \supset a \neq Rollback(t) \wedge a \neq End(t)]\}.$$

Now the external actions of nested transactions have the following precondition axioms:

$$Poss(Begin(t), s) \equiv \neg(\exists t')parent(t', t, s) \wedge$$
$$[s = S_0 \vee (\exists s', t').t \neq t' \wedge do(Begin(t'), s') \sqsubset s], \tag{23}$$
$$Poss(Spawn(t, t'), s) \equiv t \neq t' \wedge$$
$$(\exists s', t'')[do(Begin(t), s') \sqsubset s \vee do(Spawn(t'', t), s') \sqsubset s], \tag{24}$$
$$Poss(End(t), s) \equiv running(t, s), \tag{25}$$
$$Poss(Commit(t), s) \equiv (\exists s').s = do(End(t), s') \wedge \bigwedge_{IC \in \mathcal{IC}_v} IC(s) \wedge$$
$$(\forall t')[sc\_dep(t, t', s) \supset (\exists s'')do(Commit(t'), s'') \sqsubseteq s] \wedge \tag{26}$$
$$(\forall t')[c\_dep(t, t', s) \wedge \neg(\exists s^*)do(Rollback(t'), s^*) \sqsubseteq s \supset$$
$$(\exists s')do(Commit(t'), s') \sqsubset s)],$$
$$Poss(Rollback(t), s) \equiv (\exists s').s = do(End(t), s') \wedge \neg \bigwedge_{IC \in \mathcal{IC}_v} IC(s) \vee$$
$$(\exists t', s'').r\_dep(t, t', s) \wedge do(Rollback(t'), s'') \sqsubset s' \vee \tag{27}$$
$$(\exists t', s^*).wr\_dep(t, t', s) \wedge do(Rollback(t'), s^*) \sqsubset s \wedge$$
$$\neg(\exists s^{**})do(Commit(t), s^{**}) \sqsubset do(Rollback(t'), s^*),$$

Dependency axioms characterizing the fluents $r\_dep$, $c\_dep$, $sc\_dep$, and $wr\_dep$ are:

$$r\_dep(t, t', s) \equiv transConflictNT(t, t', s), \tag{28}$$
$$sc\_dep(t, t', s) \equiv readsFrom(t, t', s), \tag{29}$$
$$c\_dep(t, t', do(a, s)) \equiv a = Spawn(t, t') \vee$$
$$c\_dep(t, t', s) \wedge \neg termAct(a, t) \wedge \neg termAct(a, t'), \tag{30}$$
$$wr\_dep(t, t', do(a, s)) \equiv a = Spawn(t', t) \vee$$
$$wr\_dep(t, t', s) \wedge \neg termAct(a, t) \wedge \neg termAct(a, t'). \tag{31}$$

As an example of what they mean, the last axiom says that a transaction spawning another transaction generates a weak rollback dependency of the later one on the first one, and this dependency ends when either transactions execute a terminating action.

The successor state axioms for nested transactions are of the form:

$$F(\boldsymbol{x}, t, do(a, s)) \equiv (\exists \boldsymbol{t'}) \Phi_F(\boldsymbol{x}, a, \boldsymbol{t'}, s) \wedge \neg(\exists t'')a = Rollback(t'') \vee$$
$$[(\exists t'').a = Rollback(t'') \wedge \neg(\exists t^*)parent(t^*, t'', s) \wedge$$
$$restoreBeginPoint(F, \boldsymbol{x}, t'', s)] \vee \qquad (32)$$
$$[(\exists t'').a = Rollback(t'') \wedge (\exists t^*)parent(t^*, t'', s) \wedge$$
$$restoreSpawnPoint(F, \boldsymbol{x}, t'', s)],$$

one for each fluent of the relational language. Here $\Phi_F(\boldsymbol{x}, a, \boldsymbol{t}, s)$ is a formula with free variables among $\boldsymbol{x}, a, \boldsymbol{t}$, and $s$; $restoreBeginPoint(F, \boldsymbol{x}, t, s)$ is defined in (7), and $restoreSpawnPoint(F, \boldsymbol{x}, t, s)$ is an abbreviation similar to (7), where $Spawn(t, t')$ is used instead of $Begin(t)$.

A basic relational theory for nested transactions is defined as in Section 4, but where the relational language includes $Spawn(t, t')$ as a further action, and the axioms (23) – (24) replace axioms (8) – (11), the axioms (28) – (31) replace the axioms (13) – (14), and the set $\mathcal{D}_{ss}$ is a set of successor state axioms of the form (32). All the other axioms of Section 4 remain unchanged.

Now we state some of the properties of nested transactions as an illustration of how such properties are formulated in the situation calculus. Similarly to Theorem 2, we can show that a basic relational theory for nested transactions logically implies the commit and weak rollback dependency properties. Atomicity and serializability can also be shown.

The following is a typical property of closed nested transactions:

**Theorem 8. (No-Orphan-Commit: [6])** *Suppose $\mathcal{D}$ is a relational theory. Then, whenever a child's parent terminates before the parent does, the child is rolled back;i.e.,*

$$\mathcal{D} \models legal(s) \supset$$
$$\{parent(t, t', s) \wedge termAct(a, t) \wedge$$
$$do(Commit(t'), s') \not\sqsubseteq do(a, s'') \sqsubseteq s \supset (\exists s^*)do(Rollback(t'), s^*) \sqsubseteq s\}.$$

This property, combined with the atomicity of all subtransactions of the nested transaction tree, leads to the fact that, should a root transaction roll back, then so must all its subtransactions, also the committed ones. This is where the D in the ACID acronym is relaxed for subtransactions.

# 6   Simulating ATMs

GOLOG, introduced in [13] and enhanced with parallelism in [7] (ConGolog), is a situation calculus-based programming language for defining complex actions in terms of a set of primitive actions axiomatized in the situation calculus. It has the following Algol-like control structures *Sequence* ($[\alpha \,;\, \beta]$; Do action $\alpha$, followed by action $\beta$); *Test actions* ($p?$; Test the truth value of expression $p$ in the current situation); *Nondeterministic action choice* ($\alpha \mid \beta$; Do $\alpha$ or $\beta$); *Nondeterministic choice of arguments* (($\pi x)\alpha$; nondeterministically pick a value for $x$, and for that value of $x$, do action $\alpha$); *Conditionals* and *while* loops; and *Procedures*, including recursion. *nil* represent the empty program. The following are ConGolog constructs for expressing parallelism: *Concurrency* ($[\alpha \parallel \beta]$; Do $\alpha$ and $\beta$ in parallel); *Concurrent iteration* ($\alpha^{\parallel}$; Do $\alpha$ zero or more times in parallel). The purpose of this section is to show how GOLOG programs are used to capture transaction programs and how the semantics of these programs is used to simulate the ATMs. The development in this section is restricted to closed nested transactions.

## 6.1   Well-Formed GOLOG Programs

GOLOG syntax is built using consructs that suppress any reference to situations in which test are evaluated. These will be restored at run time by the GOLOG interpreter.

**Definition 2.** *The situation suppressed-terms and formulas are terms and formulas in which the situation arguments of fluents have been removed.*

Notice that the situation terms like $S_0$, $do(A, S_0)$, etc are situation-suppressed terms. Calling such situation terms "situation"-suppressed might sound counterintuitive. However, this definition just means that situation-suppressed formulas are first order and may still mention situation terms, but never as last argument of relational fluents; therefore situation-suppressed formulas quantify only over those situations that are mentioned in equalities between terms of sort *situations* and in $\sqsubset$ atoms. For example, the following is a situation-suppressed formula:

$$S_0 \sqsubset do(A, (do(B, S_0))) \wedge (\forall x, y, z, w, t)[accounts(x, y, z, w, t) \supset z \geq 0],$$

whereas the following is not:

$$S_0 \sqsubset do(A, (do(B, S_0))) \wedge (\forall x, y, z, w, t, s)[accounts(x, y, z, w, t, s) \supset z \geq 0].$$

**Definition 3. (Well Formed GOLOG Programs)** *A GOLOG program has the following syntax:*

$$\langle prog \rangle ::= \langle internal\ action \rangle \mid \langle test\ action \rangle? \mid (\langle prog \rangle; \langle prog \rangle) \mid$$
$$(\langle prog \rangle | \langle prog \rangle) \mid (\langle prog \rangle \parallel \langle prog \rangle) \mid (\pi x) \langle prog \rangle \mid$$
$$\langle prog \rangle^* \mid (Spawn(t, t'); \langle prog \rangle; End(t')) \mid \langle procedure\ call \rangle \mid$$
$$(\mathbf{proc}\ P_1(\boldsymbol{x}_1) \langle prog \rangle\ \mathbf{endProc}\ ; \cdots ;$$
$$\mathbf{proc}\ P_n(\boldsymbol{x}_n) \langle prog \rangle\ \mathbf{endProc}\ ; \langle prog \rangle)$$

*Notice that*

1. *$\langle internal\ action \rangle$ is a situation-suppressed internal action term.*
2. *$\langle test\ action \rangle$ is a situation-suppressed formula.*
3. *The variable $x$ in $(\pi x) \langle prog \rangle$ must be of sort actions or objects, never of sort situations.*

4. ⟨*procedure call*⟩ *is a predicate – a procedure name – of the form* $P(t_1, \cdots, t_n)$
   *where the* $t_i$ *are situation-suppressed terms whose sorts match those of the*
   *n arguments in the declaration of P.*

*A well formed GOLOG program is syntactically defined as follows:*

$$\langle wfprog \rangle ::= (\textbf{proc } P_1(x_1)\langle prog \rangle \textbf{ endProc}; \cdots;$$
$$\textbf{proc } P_n(x_n)\langle prog \rangle \textbf{ endProc};$$
$$Begin(t); \langle prog \rangle; End(t))$$

## 6.2   Semantics of GOLOG Programs

With the ultimate goal of handling database transactions, it is appropriate to
adopt an operational semantics of GOLOG programs based on a single-step
execution of these programs; such a semantics is introduced in ([7]). First, two
special predicates $Trans$ and $Final$ are introduced. $Trans(\delta, s, \delta', s')$ means that
program $\delta$ may perform one step in situation $s$, ending up in situation $s'$, where
program $\delta'$ remains to be executed. $Final(\delta, s)$ means that program $\delta$ may terminate in situation $s$. A single step here is either a primitive or a testing action.
Then the two predicates are characterized by appropriate axioms. These axioms
contain, for example, the following cases (See [7] for full details):

$$Trans(\delta_1; \delta_2, s, \delta, s') \equiv Final(\delta_1, s) \wedge Trans(\delta_2, s, \delta, s') \vee$$
$$(\exists \gamma).\delta = (\gamma; \delta_2) \wedge Trans(\delta_1, s, \gamma, s'),$$
$$Trans(\delta_1|\delta_2, s, \delta, s') \equiv Trans(\delta_1, s, \delta, s') \vee Trans(\delta_2, s, \delta, s')$$

to express the semantics of sequences and nondeterministic choice of actions,
respectively. Notice that equivalences like those above are translating GOLOG
constructs into formulas of the situation calculus.

Our definition of $Trans$ differs from that of [7] with respect to the handling
of primitive and test actions:

**Definition 4. (Semantics of $Trans$)**

$$Trans(a, s, a', s') =_{df} Poss(a, s) \wedge a' = nil \wedge$$
$$\{(\exists a'', s'', t)[s'' = do(a, s) \wedge systemAct(a'', t) \wedge Poss(a'', s'') \wedge s' = do(a'', s'')] \vee$$
$$s' = do(a, s) \wedge [(\forall a'', t)systemAct(a'', t) \supset \neg Poss(a'', s)]\}, \tag{33}$$
$$Trans(\phi?, s, a', s') =_{df} Holds(\phi, s, s') \wedge a' = nil. \tag{34}$$

In the definition above, we take particularities of system actions into account
when processing primitive actions. These actions must occur whenever possible,
so the interpreter must test for their possibility upon each performance of a
primitive action. The formula (33) captures this requirement; it intuitively means
that the primitive action $a$ may legally execute one step in the log $s$, ending in
log $s'$ where $a'$ remains to be executed iff $a$ is possible, the remaining action $a'$
is the empty transaction, and either any possible system action $a''$ is executed

immediately after the primitive action $a$ has been executed and the log $s'$ contains
the action $a$ followed by the system action $a''$, or no system action is possible
and the log $s'$ contains only the action $a$. The formula (34) says that the test
action $\phi$? may legally be performed one or more steps in the log $s$, ending in log
$s'$ where $a'$ remains to be executed iff $\phi$ holds in $s$, yielding a log $s'$ in a way to
be explained below, and $a'$ is an empty program.

Given situation calculus axioms of a domain theory, an execution of a program $\delta$ in situation $s$ is the task of finding some $s'$ such that there is a final
configuration $(\delta', s')$, for some remaining program $\delta'$, after performing a couple
of transitions from $\delta, s$ to $\delta', s'$. Program execution is captured by using the abbreviation $Do(\delta, s, s')$ ([21]). In the single-step semantics, $Do(\delta, s, s')$ intuitively
means that program $\delta$ is single-steped until the remainder of program $\delta$ may
terminate in situation $s'$; and $s'$ is one of the logs reached by single-stepinging
the program $\delta$, beginning in a given situation $s$. Formally, $Do(\delta, s, s')$ is defined
as follows ([7]):

$$Do(\delta, s, s') =_{df} (\exists \delta').Trans^*(\delta, s, \delta', s') \wedge Final(\delta', s'),$$

where $Trans^*$ denotes the transitive closure of $Trans$. Finally, a program execution starting in situation $S_0$ is formally the task of finding some situation $s'$
such that $\mathcal{D} \models Do(\delta, S_0, s')$, where $\mathcal{D}$ is the domain theory.

**Definition 5.** *We use the notation $\phi[s]$ to denote the situation calculus formula
obtained from a given formula $\phi$ by restoring the situation argument $s$ in all the
fluents (as their last argument) occurring in $\phi$.*

The predicate $Holds(\phi, s, s')$ captures the revised Lloyd-Topor transformations of [21]; these are transformations in the style of Lloyd-Topor([14]), but
without its auxilliary predicates. The predicate $Holds(\phi, s, s')$ takes a formula
$\phi$ and establish whether it holds in the log $s$ or not. If $\phi$ is a fluent literal, then
the next log $s'$ will be $do(\phi, s)$; if it is a nonfluent literal, then $s' = s$; otherwise
revised Lloyd-Topor transformations are performed on $\phi$ until we reach literals.
We capture this semantics as follows:

**Definition 6. (Semantics of $Holds$)**

$Holds(\phi, s, s') =_{df} \phi[s] \wedge s' = do(\phi, s),$ *when $\phi$ is a fluent literal,*

$Holds(\phi, s, s') =_{df} \phi[s] \wedge s' = s,$ *when $\phi$ is a nonfluent literal,*

$Holds((\phi_1 \wedge \phi_2), s, s') =_{df} (\exists s'').Holds(\phi_1, s, s'') \wedge Holds(\phi_2, s'', s'),$

$Holds((\phi_1 \vee \phi_2)?, s, s') =_{df} Holds(\phi_1, s, s') \vee Holds(\phi_2, s, s'),$

$Holds((\phi_1 \supset \phi_2), s, s') =_{df} Holds(\neg \phi_1 \vee \phi_2, s, s'),$

$Holds((\phi_1 \equiv \phi_2), s, s') =_{df} Holds((\phi_1 \supset \phi_2) \wedge (\phi_2 \supset \phi_1), s, s'),$

$Holds((\forall x)\phi, s, s') =_{df} Holds(\neg(\exists x)\neg\phi, s, s'),$

$Holds((\exists x)\phi, s, s') =_{df} Holds(\phi, s, s'),$

$Holds(\neg\neg\phi, s, s') =_{df} Holds(\phi, s, s'),$

$Holds(\neg(\phi_1 \wedge \phi_2), s, s') =_{df} Holds(\neg\phi_1, s, s') \vee Holds(\neg\phi_2, s, s'),$

$Holds(\neg(\phi_1 \vee \phi_2), s, s') =_{df} (\exists s'').Holds(\neg\phi_1, s, s'') \wedge Holds(\neg\phi_2, s'', s'),$

$Holds(\neg(\phi_1 \supset \phi_2), s, s') =_{df} Holds(\neg\neg(\phi_1 \vee \phi_2), s, s'),$

$Holds(\neg(\phi_1 \equiv \phi_2), s, s') =_{df} Holds(\neg[(\phi_1 \supset \phi_2) \wedge (\phi_2 \supset \phi_1)], s, s'),$

$Holds(\neg(\forall x)\phi, s, s') =_{df} Holds((\exists x)\neg\phi, s, s'),$

$Holds(\neg(\exists x)\phi, s, s') =_{df} \neg Holds(\phi, s, s').$

Definition 6 expresses a particular semantics for test actions that is appropriate for handling database transactions. It is important to notice how our test actions are different than those of [7] and why they are needed. Our test actions differ from those of ConGolog ([7]) in two ways. First of all, unlike in ConGolog, ours are genuine actions and not merely tests that may be forgotten as soon as they are executed. We record test actions in the log; i.e. performing a test changes the situation. Second, depending on the syntactic form of the formula in the test, we may end up executing more than just a "single step". More precisely, more than one single actions are added to the log whenever more than one tests of fluent literals are involved in the formula being tested. This semantics is dictated by the very nature of ATMs. Here, test actions correspond to database reading actions. A transaction has no means of remembering which transaction it had read from other than to record reading actions in the log. This cannot be done with the semantics for test action found in [7]. In other words, in the absence of test actions in the log, the semantics of [7] has no straightforward way to express such things as transaction $T_1$ reads data from transaction $T_2$.

## 6.3    Simulation

We use the GOLOG language as a transaction language for specifying and simulating ATMs at the logical level. To simulate a specific ATM, we first pick the appropriate basic relational theory $\mathcal{D}$ corresponding to that ATM. Then, we write a GOLOG program $T$ expressing the desired transactional behavior. Now simulating the program $T$ amounts to the theorem proving task of establishing the entailment $\mathcal{D} \models (\exists s') Do(prog, S_0, s')$, where $S_0$ is the initial, empty log.

A *Do*-based GOLOG interpreter for the situation calculus, written in Prolog, is described in [13]. To run our specification of transactions, we need to modify the GOLOG semantics and interpreter defined in [13] to accommodate the changes described above and also non-Markovian tests. Thus it is possible to test at the interpreter level whether a log is a sublog of another log. The interpreter provides an operator implementing the predicate $\sqsubseteq$ which, therefore, needs not be hand-coded by the programmer.

We consider a Debit/Credit example which we now describe to illustrate how to formulate a relational theory for nested transactions.

The database involves a relational language with:

**Fluents:** $accounts(aid, bid, abal, t, s)$, $branches(bid, bbal, bname, t, s)$, $tellers(tid, tbal, t, s)$, and $served(aid, s)$.

**Situation Independent Predicate**: $requested(aid, req)$.
**Action Functions**: $a\_insert(aid, bid, abal, tid, t)$, $a\_delete(aid, bid, abal, tid, t)$, $t\_insert(tid, tbal, t)$, $t\_delete(tid, tbal, t)$, $b\_insert(bid, bbal, bname, t)$, $b\_delete(bid, bbal, bname, t)$, and $report(aid)$.
**Constants**: $Ray$, $Iluju$, $Misha$, $Ho$, etc.

The meaning of the arguments of fluents are self explanatory; and the relational language also includes the external actions of nested transactions. Domain closure and unique name axioms are given in the usual way; thus we concentrate ourself on the remaining axioms. We enforce the following IC ($\in \mathcal{IC}_e$):

$$accounts(aid, bid, abal, tid, t, s) \wedge accounts(aid, bid', abal', tid', t', s) \supset$$
$$bid = bid', abal = abal', tid = tid',$$

and similar ICs for $branches$ and $tellers$; and we have to verify the IC ($\in \mathcal{IC}_v$)

$$accounts(aid, bid, abal, tid, t, s) \supset abal \geq 0$$

at transaction's end.

A sample update precondition axiom is given in (5).

The following is a successor state axiom for the fluent $accounts(aid, bid, abal, tid, t, s)$:

$$accounts(aid, bid, abal, tid, t, do(a, s))$$
$$\equiv (\exists t_1)(a = a\_insert(aid, bid, abal, tid, t_1) \vee$$
$$(\exists t_2)accounts(aid, bid, abal, tid, t_2, s) \wedge$$
$$\neg(\exists t_3)a = a\_delete(aid, bid, abal, tid)) \wedge$$
$$\neg(\exists t')a = Rollback(t') \vee$$
$$(\exists t').a = Rollback(t') \wedge \neg(\exists t'')parent(t'', t', s) \wedge$$
$$restoreBeginPoint(F, (aid, bid, abal, tid), t', s) \vee$$
$$a = Rollback(t') \wedge (\exists t'')parent(t'', t', s) \wedge$$
$$restoreSpawnPoint(accounts(aid, bid, abal, tid), t', s).$$

This states that the tuple $(aid, bid, abal, tid)$ will be in the $accounts$ relation relative to the log $do(a, s)$ iff the last database operation $a$ in the log inserted it there, or it was already in the $accounts$ relation relative to the log $s$, and $a$ didn't delete it; all this, provided that the operation $a$ is not rolling the database back. If $a$ is rolling the database back, the value of the $accounts$ relation at the beginning of the (sub)transaction will be restored.

Finally, the following successor state axiom is used for synchronization purposes:

$$served(aid, do(a, s)) \equiv report(aid) \vee served(aid, s).$$

The action $report(aid)$, whose precondition axiom is

$$Poss(report(aid), s) \equiv true,$$

is used to make the fluent by indicating that a request emitted by the owner of the account $aid$ has been granted. These requests are registered in the situation independent predicate $requested(aid, req)$.

Now we give the following GOLOG procedures which are well-formed and capture the essence of the debit/credit example:

**proc** $a\_update(t, aid, amt)$

  $(\pi \ bid, abal, abal', tid)[accounts(aid, bid, abal, tid, t)? \ ;$

    $[abal' = abal + amt]? \ ; a\_del(aid, bid, abal, tid, t) \ ; a\_ins(aid, bid, abal', tid, t)]$

**endProc**

**proc** $execDebitCredit(t, bid, tid, aid, amt)$

    $a\_update(aid, amt) \ ;$

    $(\pi \ abal) \ [accounts(aid, bid, abal, tid, t)? \ ;$

                      $t\_update(t, tid, amt) \ ; b\_update(t, bid, amt)]$

**endProc**

**proc** $processReq(t, tid, aid, amt)$

  $(\pi \ bid, abal)[accounts(aid, bid, abal, tid, t)? \ ;$

    $execDebitCredit(t, bid, tid, aid, amt)] \ ;$

**endProc**

**proc** $processTrans(t)$

    $Begin(t); \ [(\pi \ bid, aid, abal, tid, req).$

               $\{accounts(aid, bid, abal, tid, t) \wedge$

                    $requested(aid, req) \wedge \neg served(aid)\}? \ ; report(aid) \ ;$

                  $Spawn(t, aid) \ ; \ processReq(t, tid, aid, req) \ ; \ End(aid)]^{\parallel} \ ;$

            $\neg((\exists \ aid, req)requested(aid, req))? \ ; \ End(t)$

**endProc**

Procedures $t\_update(tid, amt)$ and $b\_update(bid, amt)$ similar to the first procedure can be given for updating teller and branch balances, respectively. The ACI(D) properties are enforced by the interpreter that either commits work done so far or rolls it back whenever the database general ICs are violated. Thus, well formed programs are a specification of transactions with the full scale of a programming language at the logical level. Notice that a formula $\phi$ in a test $\phi$? is in fact a situation suppressed formula whose situation argument is restored at run-time by the interpreter. Notice also the use of the concurrent iteration in the last procedure; this spawns a new child transaction for each account that emitted a request but have not yet been served. For simplicity in this example, we have assumed that each account has at most one request; this allows us to use the account identifiers $aid$ to denote spawn subtransactions.

Now we can simulate the program, say $processTrans(T)$, by performing the theorem proving task of establishing the entailment

$$\mathcal{D} \models (\exists s')\ Do(processTrans(T), S_0, s'),$$

where $S_0$ is the initial, empty log, and $\mathcal{D}$ is the basic relational theory for nested transactions that comprises the axioms above; this exactly means that we look for some log that is generated by the program $T$. We are interested in any instance of $s$ resulting from the proof obtained by establishing this entailment. Such an instance is obtained as a side-effect of this proof.

In Definition 4, we take particularities of system actions into account. These actions must occur whenever possible, so the interpreter must test for their possibility upon each performance of a primitive action. Definition 4 captures this requirement and allows us to show that $Do$ generates only legal situations:

**Theorem 9.** *Suppose $\mathcal{D}$ is a relational theory (either for flat transactions or for CNTs), and let $T$ be a well formed GOLOG program. Then,*

$$\mathcal{D} \models (\forall s).Do(T, S_0, s) \supset legal(s).$$

## 7　Related Work

The inability of the classical model for concurrency control (the serializability theory) to cope with nested transactions has been addressed in [1]. This work develops a serializability theory for nested transactions. The new serializability model is articulated around the notion of computation, a generalization of the notion of history which is central to the classical serializability theory. Like the history of the classical model, a computation involves the execution of database primitive and complex operations. Unlike the history, which is a sequence of primitive operations, a computation is a tree. The interleaving of several computations constitute a partially ordered forest. Similarly to the classical case, a forest is correct (i.e. serializable) iff it is equivalent to a serial execution of the involved trees. This criterion is used to prove the correctness of concurrency control algorithms, i.e. schedulers. Correctness is considered as a property of computations generated by a scheduler. This is in spirit similar to what our Theorem 9 conveys, if we view the GOLOG interpreter as a scheduler. However, we do not go that far in this paper to deal with the proof of correctness of given schedulers. In addition to that, we still consider a linear log. This might have an implicit tree-structure that has yet to be extracted to compare our logical approach with the tree-approach of [1].

Chrysanthis and Ramamritham ([6],[5]) present a framework called ACTA which allows to specify effects of transactions on objects and on other transactions. Our framework is similar to ACTA. In fact, we use the same building blocks for ATMs as those used in ACTA. However, the reasoning capability of the situation calculus exceeds that of ACTA for the following reasons: (1) the database log is a first class citizen of the situation calculus, and the semantics of all transaction operations – *Commit*, *Rollback*, etc. – are defined with respect to constraints on this log. Nowhere have we seen a quantification over histories in ACTA, so that there is no straitforward way of expressing closed form formulas involving histories in ACTA. (2) Our approach goes far beyond ACTA as it is an implementable specification, thus allowing one to automatically check many properties of the specification using an interpreter. To that end, the main implementation theorems needed are formulated in [21]. Finally, (3) although ACTA deals with the dynamics of database objects, it is never explicitly formulated as a logic for actions.

In [3], Bertossi *et al.* propose a situation calculus-based formalization of database transactions. They extend Reiter's specification of database updates to transactions. In fact, the idea of using transactional actions like *Begin*, *Rollback*, *End*, and *Commit* for flat transactions was first introduced in [3], as was the the axiomatization of the notion of consistency verification at the transaction end. Our approach, however, is based on a situation calculus that is explicitly non-Markovian. Moreover, our work goes beyond pure flat transactions to deal with an account of notions such as serializability and atomicity, and with ATMs which are more complex.

*Transaction Logic* ([4]) and *Statelog* ([15]) are languages for database state change that include a clean model theory. These approaches, unlike the situation calculus, do not view elementary updates as first order terms; they appeal to special purpose semantics to account for database transactions; finally, they are not general enough to be used for modeling any given transaction model or "inventing" a new one from scratch at a sufficiently high level as is the case in ACTA and the situation calculus. However, one should distinguish between the full logic and its Horn fragment. Many of the limitations mentioned above concern the Horn fragment, not the full logic.

# 8    Conclusion and Future Work

One must distinguish between our approach which is a purely logical, abstract specification in which all system properties are formulated relative to the database log, and an implementation which normally materializes the database using progression ([21]). This is the distinguishing feature of our approach. The database log is a first class citizen of the logic, and the semantics of all transaction operations – *Commit*, *Rollback*, etc. – are defined with respect to this log.

As we acknowledged it in the introduction, database transaction processing is now a mature area of research. However, one needs to know whether our formalization indeed captures any existing theory, such as ACTA, at the same level of generality. Therefore, one needs to prove the correctness of the formalization. For example, we need an effective translation of our basic relational theories into ACTA axioms for a relational database and then show that the legal logs for the situation calculus basic relational theory are precisely the correct histories for its translation into a relational ACTA system.

Thus far, we have given axioms that accommodate a complete initial database state. This, however, is not a requirement of the theory we are presenting. Therefore our account could, for example, accommodate initial databases with null values, open initial database states, initial databases accounting for object orientation, or initial semistructured databases. These are just a examples of some of the generalizations that our initial databases could admit.

Finally, it is important to notice that the only place where the second order nature of our framework is needed is in the proof of the properties of the transaction models that rely on a second order induction principle contained in the foundational axioms mentioned in Section 4. For the Markovian situation calculus, it is shown in [18] that the second order nature of this language is not at all needed in simulating basic action theories. It remains to show that this is also the case for the non-Markovian setting.

The framework described in this work is currently being implemented using a regression mechanism described in [9]. On-going work extending the framework includes: accounting for some of the recent ATMs, for example those reported in [11] and open nested transactions proposed in the context of mobile computing, implementing the specifications of significant ATMs, proving the correctness of the approach, introducing on-line, that is actual execution of transactions, as opposed to off-line or hypothetical execution. We will also consider modeling active rules and different active rule processing mechanisms within the framework of this paper in the near future ([12]). Finally, we will explore ways of making this framework part of a logic-based development methodology for ATMs. Such a methodology would exhibit the important advantage of uniformity in many of its phases by using the single language of the situation calculus.

## Acknowledgments

Ray Reiter, Alfredo Gabaldon, and Javier Pinto deserve many thanks for helpful discussions and encouragements. Special thanks to Ray Reiter who suggested the link between ATMs and non-Markovian theories, and Fahiem Bacchus who suggested reinforcing the simulation aspect of the framework. We were supported by NSERC, IRIS, and ITRC and would like to gratefully mention them.

## References

1. C. Beri, P.A. Bernstein, and N. Goodman. A model for concurrency in nested transactions systems. *Journal of the ACM*, 36(2):230–269, 1989.
2. P.A. Bernstein, V. Hadzilacos, and N. Goodman. *Concurrency control and recovery in database systems*. Addison-Wesley, Reading, MA, 1987.
3. L. Bertossi, J. Pinto, and R. Valdivia. Specifying database transactions and active rules in the situation calculus. In H. Levesque and F. Pirri, editors, *Logical Foundations of Cognitive Agents. Contributions in Honor of Ray Reiter*, pages 41–56, New-York, 1999. Springer Verlag.
4. A. Bonner and M. Kifer. A logic for programming database transactions. In J. Chomicki and Saake G., editors, *Logics for Databases and Information Systems*. Kluwer Academic Publishers, 1998. Chapter 5.
5. P. Chrysanthis and K. Ramamritham. Synthesis of extended transaction models. *ACM Transactions on Database Systems*, 19(3):450–491, 1994.

6. P.K. Chrysanthis. *ACTA, A Framework for Modeling and Reasoning about Extended Transactions*. PhD thesis, Department of Computer and Information Science, University of Massachusetts, Amherst, 1991.
7. G. De Giacomo, Y. Lespérance, and H.J. Levesque. Reasoning about concurrent execution, prioritized interrupts, and exogeneous actions in the situation calculus. In *Proceedings of the Fifteenth International Joint Conference on Artificial Intelligence*, pages 1221–1226, 1997.
8. Ahmed K. Elmagarmid. *Database transaction models for advanced applications*. Morgan Kaufmann, San Mateo, CA, 1992.
9. A. Gabaldon. Non-markovian control in the situation calculus. In G. Lakemeyer, editor, *Proceedings of the Second International Cognitive Robotics Workshop*, pages 28–33, Berlin, 2000.
10. J. Gray and Reuter A. *Transaction Processing: Concepts and Techniques*. Morgan Kaufmann Publishers, San Mateo, CA, 1995.
11. S. Jajodia and L. Kerschberg. *Advanced Transaction Models and Architectures*. Kluwer Academic Publishers, Boston, 1997.
12. I. Kiringa. *A Formal Account of Relational Active Databases in the Situation Calculus*. PhD thesis, Computer Science, University of Toronto, Toronto, forthcoming.
13. H. Levesque, R. Reiter, Y. Lespérance, Fangzhen Lin, and R.B. Scherl. Golog: A logic programming language for dynamic domains. *J. of Logic Programming, Special Issue on Actions*, 31(1-3):59–83, 1997.
14. J.W. Lloyd. *Foundations of Logic Programming, Second, Extended Edition*. Springer-Verlag, Berlin, 1988.
15. B. Ludäscher, W. May, and G. Lausen. Nested transactions in a logical language for active rules. Technical Report Jun20-1, Technical Univ. of Munich, June 1996.
16. N. Lynch, M.M. Merritt, W. Weihl, and A. Fekete. A theory of atomic transactions. In M. Gyssens, J. Parendaens, and D. Van Gucht, editors, *Proceedings of the Second International Conference on Database Theory*, pages 41–71, Berlin, 1988. Springer Verlag. LNCS 326.
17. J. Moss. *Nested Transactions: An Approach to Reliable Distributed Computing*. Information Systems Series. The MIT Press, Cambridge, MA, 1985.
18. F. Pirri and R. Reiter. Some contributions to the metatheory of the situation calculus. *Journal of the ACM*, 46(3):325–364, 1999.
19. R. Reiter. Towards a logical reconstruction of relational database theory. In M. Brodie, J. Mylopoulos, and J. Schmidt, editors, *On Conceptual Modelling*, pages 163–189, New-York, 1984. Springer Verlag.
20. R. Reiter. On specifying database updates. *J. of Logic Programming*, 25:25–91, 1995.
21. R. Reiter. *Knowledge in Action: Logical Foundations for Describing and Implementing Dynamical Systems*. MIT Press, Cambridge, 2001.
22. E. Ternovskaia. Automata theory for reasoning about automata. In *Proceedings of the Sixteenth International Joint Conference on Artificial Intelligence*, pages 153–158, 1999.
23. G. Weikum and H.J. Schek. Concepts and applications of multilevel transactions and open nested transactions. In A.K. Elmagarmid, editor, *Database Transaction Models for Advanced Applications*, pages 516–553, San Mateo, CA, 1992. Morgan Kaufmann.

# Author Index

# Lecture Notes in Computer Science

For information about Vols. 1–2371
please contact your bookseller or Springer-Verlag

Vol. 2407: A.C. Kakas, F. Sadri (Eds.), Computational Logic: Logic Programming and Beyond. Part I. XII, 678 pages. 2002. (Subseries LNAI).

Vol. 2408: A.C. Kakas, F. Sadri (Eds.), Computational Logic: Logic Programming and Beyond. Part II. XII, 628 pages. 2002. (Subseries LNAI).

Vol. 2409: D.M. Mount, C. Stein (Eds.), Algorithm Engineering and Experiments. Proceedings, 2002. VIII, 207 pages. 2002.

Vol. 2410: V.A. Carreño, C.A. Muñoz, S. Tahar (Eds.), Theorem Proving in Higher Order Logics. Proceedings, 2002. X, 349 pages. 2002.

Vol. 2412: H. Yin, N. Allinson, R. Freeman, J. Keane, S. Hubbard (Eds.), Intelligent Data Engineering and Automated Learning – IDEAL 2002. Proceedings, 2002. XV, 597 pages. 2002.

Vol. 2413: K. Kuwabara, J. Lee (Eds.), Intelligent Agents and Multi-Agent Systems. Proceedings, 2002. X, 221 pages. 2002. (Subseries LNAI).

Vol. 2414: F. Mattern, M. Naghshineh (Eds.), Pervasive Computing. Proceedings, 2002. XI, 298 pages. 2002.

Vol. 2415: J.R. Dorronsoro (Ed.), Artificial Neural Networks – ICANN 2002. Proceedings, 2002. XXVIII, 1382 pages. 2002.

Vol. 2416: S. Craw, A. Preece (Eds.), Advances in Case-Based Reasoning. Proceedings, 2002. XII, 656 pages. 2002. (Subseries LNAI).

Vol. 2417: M. Ishizuka, A. Sattar (Eds.), PRICAI 2002: Trends in Artificial Intelligence. Proceedings, 2002. XX, 623 pages. 2002. (Subseries LNAI).

Vol. 2418: D. Wells, L. Williams (Eds.), Extreme Programming and Agile Methods – XP/Agile Universe 2002. Proceedings, 2002. XII, 292 pages. 2002.

Vol. 2419: X. Meng, J. Su, Y. Wang (Eds.), Advances in Web-Age Information Management. Proceedings, 2002. XV, 446 pages. 2002.

Vol. 2420: K. Diks, W. Rytter (Eds.), Mathematical Foundations of Computer Science 2002. Proceedings, 2002. XII, 652 pages. 2002.

Vol. 2421: L. Brim, P. Jančar, M. Křetínský, A. Kučera (Eds.), CONCUR 2002 – Concurrency Theory. Proceedings, 2002. XII, 611 pages. 2002.

Vol. 2422: H. Kirchner, Ch. Ringeissen (Eds.), Algebraic Methodology and Software Technology. Proceedings, 2002. XI, 503 pages. 2002.

Vol. 2423: D. Lopresti, J. Hu, R. Kashi (Eds.), Document Analysis Systems V. Proceedings, 2002. XIII, 570 pages. 2002.

Vol. 2425: Z. Bellahsène, D. Patel, C. Rolland (Eds.), Object-Oriented Information Systems. Proceedings, 2002. XIII, 550 pages. 2002.

Vol. 2426: J.-M. Bruel, Z. Bellahsène (Eds.), Advances in Object-Oriented Information Systems.Procdings, 2002. IX, 314 pages. 2002.

Vol. 2430: T. Elomaa, H. Mannila, H. Toivonen (Eds.), Machine Learning: ECML 2002. Proceedings, 2002. XIII, 532 pages. 2002. (Subseries LNAI).

Vol. 2431: T. Elomaa, H. Mannila, H. Toivonen (Eds.), Principles of Data Mining and Knowledge Discovery. Proceedings, 2002. XIV, 514 pages. 2002. (Subseries LNAI).

Vol. 2435: Y. Manolopoulos, P. Návrat (Eds.), Advances in Databases and Information Systems. Proceedings, 2002. XIII, 415 pages. 2002.

Vol. 2436: J. Fong, C.T. Cheung, H.V. Leong, Q. Li (Eds.), Advances in Web-Based Learning. Proceedings, 2002. XIII, 434 pages. 2002.

Vol. 2438: M. Glesner, P. Zipf, M. Renovell (Eds.), Field-Programmable Logic and Applications. Proceedings, 2002. XXII, 1187 pages. 2002.

Vol. 2439: J.J. Merelo Guervós, P. Adamidis, H.-G. Beyer, J.-L. Fernández-Villacañas, H.-P. Schwefel (Eds.), Parallel Problem Solving from Nature – PPSN VII. Proceedings, 2002. XXII, 947 pages. 2002.

Vol. 2440: J.M. Haake, J.A. Pino (Eds.), Groupware: Design, Implementation and Use. Proceedings, 2002. XII, 285 pages. 2002.

Vol. 2442: M. Yung (Ed.), Advances in Cryptology – CRYPTO 2002. Proceedings, 2002. XIV, 627 pages. 2002.

Vol. 2443: D. Scott (Ed.), Artificial Intelligence: Methodology, Systems, and Applications. Proceedings, 2002. X, 279 pages. 2002. (Subseries LNAI).

Vol. 2444: A. Buchmann, F. Casati, L. Fiege, M.-C. Hsu, M.-C. Shan (Eds.), Technologies for E-Services. Proceedings, 2002. X, 171 pages. 2002.

Vol. 2445: C. Anagnostopoulou, M. Ferrand, A. Smaill (Eds.), Music and Artificial Intelligence. Proceedings, 2002. VIII, 207 pages. 2002. (Subseries LNAI).

Vol. 2446: M. Klusch, S. Ossowski, O. Shehory (Eds.), Cooperative Information Agents VI. Proceedings, 2002. XI, 321 pages. 2002. (Subseries LNAI).

Vol. 2447: D.J. Hand, N.M. Adams, R.J. Bolton (Eds.), Pattern Detection and Discovery. Proceedings, 2002. XII, 227 pages. 2002. (Subseries LNAI).

Vol. 2448: P. Sojka, I. Kopeček, K. Pala (Eds.), Text, Speech and Dialogue. Proceedings, 2002. XII, 481 pages. 2002. (Subseries LNAI).

Vol. 2451: B. Hochet, A.J. Acosta, M.J. Bellido (Eds.), Integrated Circuit Design. Proceedings, 2002. XVI, 496 pages. 2002.

Vol. 2453: A. Hameurlain, R. Cicchetti, R. Traunmüller (Eds.), Database and Expert Systems Applications. Proceedings, 2002. XVIII, 951 pages. 2002.

Vol. 2454: Y. Kambayashi, W. Winiwarter, M. Arikawa (Eds.), Data Warehousing and Knowledge Discovery. Proceedings, 2002. XIII, 339 pages. 2002.

Vol. 2455: K. Bauknecht, A M. Tjoa, G. Quirchmayr (Eds.), E-Commerce and Web Technologies. Proceedings, 2002. XIV, 414 pages. 2002.

Vol. 2456: R. Traunmüller, K. Lenk (Eds.), Electronic Government. Proceedings, 2002. XIII, 486 pages. 2002.

Vol. 2469: W. Damm, E.-R. Olderog (Eds.), Formal Techniques in Real-Time and Fault-Tolerant Systems. Proceedings, 2002. X, 455 pages. 2002.

Vol. 2470: P. Van Hentenryck (Ed.), Principles and Practice of Constraint Programming – CP 2002. Proceedings, 2002. XVI, 794 pages. 2002.

Vol. 2483: J.D.P. Rolim, S. Vadhan (Eds.), Randomization and Approximation Techniques in Computer Science. Proceedings, 2002. VIII, 275 pages. 2002.